Great Brit-Coms

Great Brit-Coms

British Television Situation Comedy

GREGORY KOSELUK

McFarland & Company, Inc., Publishers
Jefferson, North Carolina, and London

Library of Congress cataloguing data are available

Koseluk, Gregory, 1958–
Great Brit-coms: British television situation comedy / Gregory Koseluk.
p. cm.
Includes bibliographical references and index.
ISBN 0-7864-0805-7 (library binding : 50# alkaline paper) ∞
1. Television comedies — Great Britain. I. Title
PN1992.8.C66K67 2000
791.45'617 — dc21 00-58415

British Library cataloguing data are available

Manufactured in the United States of America

McFarland & Company, Inc., Publishers
Box 611, Jefferson, North Carolina 28640
www.mcfarlandpub.com

To my parents;
who endured raising Reggie Perrin
without becoming
Hyacinth Bucket and Victor Meldrew
in the process

ACKNOWLEDGMENTS

The author would like to gratefully acknowledge the help and encouragement of the many individuals without whose help this work would have indeed been more difficult. First, much thanks to the many creative personnel, actors, writers, producers, and directors who worked on the shows included in *Great Brit-Coms*. These include, in alphabetical order, Humphrey Barclay, John Barron, Colin Bean, Roy Clarke, Peter DeRosa, Diana Crystal Honey, Geoffrey Hughes, Bob Larbey, Sydney Lotterby, David Nobbs, David Ryall, and Harold Snoad, who graciously answered the author's questions regarding the various programs in which they were involved. The author would also like to thank David Croft and Jimmy Perry for their brief interviews in the midst of a hectic day at the 1998 *Dad's Army* convention. This book is in many respects a tribute to the creative work of these individuals and their colleagues.

Thanks and gratitude as well to those who have helped in the often-daunting task of trying to track down some of the more obscure episodes needed for review in this book. These include Howard Lee for his help with some of *The Good Life* episodes, Nick Randall for many *Dad's Army*, *Steptoe and Son*, and *Yes, Minister* installments, and Glenn Mitchell for *Reggie Perrin* and other shows. The support of the Dad's Army Appreciation Society and its commander in chief, Jack Wheeler, has also been invaluable. Those wishing more information about the society may write to Mr. Wheeler at 8 Sinodun Road, Wallingford, Oxon, OX 10 8AA, England. Thanks also to Dave Holmewood, president of the society's New Zealand branch.

Photographically speaking, the author is grateful to Adrian Rigelsford for his advice and sharing of photographs. In addition, many thanks to the BBC Photographic Library and especially its head librarian, Bobbie Mitchell. Ms. Mitchell's assistance and advice were invaluable to this completed volume.

On a more personal note, the author wishes to express appreciation to

Hooman Mehran for his help in acquiring radio versions of the television programs lost in the great BBC wipe of the 1970s. In addition, Mr. Mehran helped blaze the trail for me in Britain and introduced me to Glenn Mitchell. Mr. Mitchell, already singled out above for his help with acquiring tapes, is owed a great debt of thanks for his steady stream of information, opinion, and encouragement in this project. One of the great benefits of this undertaking has been getting to know him and subsequently counting him as a friend.

I would also like to thank those on the home front who have been a constant support. Special thanks to my wife, Cyndi, for her Herculean efforts in the realm of proofreading. Thank you to Katye Mantz, Elby Rogers, and David Strauss for their assistance and to Kim Peterson for her technical advice on the NTSC and PAL video formats.

Lastly, deep appreciation and love to my young son, Ian, who had to endure his Daddy taking notes on all those silly videos when I'm sure he would have preferred to be playing with me or watching *Pooh* or *Teletubbies*. Lastly, my love and gratitude to my wife, Cyndi. Some women are golf widows; my poor spouse is a book widow. Ultimately, if you enjoy this work, you must thank her for patiently supporting me in what must have seemed an unending task.

Contents

INTRODUCTION

England and America are two countries divided by a common language.

— George Bernard Shaw

While Shaw may have seen England and America as separated by a common tongue, this separation also extends to each country's sense of humor. There probably has been some strain between the English and American funny bones since 1773, when the colonists got a good chuckle over dumping some tea in Boston harbor, and the redcoats failed to get the joke. And that's about it in a nutshell, at least where the topic of television situation comedy is concerned. Americans tend to like jokes. In fact, we don't really have sit-coms — we have joke-coms. In most cases, the situation is there so the actors and actresses can crack wise about it. Often American sit-com actors just spew one-liners until they reach the final commercial break. British sit-coms are more true to their name: They are built on situations that are humorous. Many have no jokes at all and are, instead, 25 minutes of exposition and building circumstances that lead to one final big laugh.

This is not intended to be a book on all the delicate nuances of British and American humor. Rather, it is a celebration and cataloging of some points common to both sides of the pond — the places where Yank and Brit are joined at the funny bone while enjoying one of the most popular forms of entertainment in the last half of the twentieth century. In short, here is a collection of British situation comedies, or Brit-coms as they are sometimes called, that have not only earned success on their native airways but have attained a measure of popularity in the United States.

To me, it is mystifying that any British shows (especially comedies) become popular in America, and at the same time it is mystifying that these programs aren't more popular. They should be more popular simply because many of the series chronicled between these covers are among the most amusing, witty, and uproariously funny television shows ever broadcast anywhere. Yet the fact that they have been recognized Stateside at all is amazing, considering the array of elements working against their American success, including differences in senses of humor and the parochial attitude of most Americans toward their entertainment.

Americans — and I am one — too often dismiss any entertainment that originates outside of our own borders. We export vast quantities of films and television programs around the world. Yet, as an audience, we accept little from other countries. Just witness the seemingly endless string of foreign comedies (most of them French) Americanized in the last ten years (and usually with a lot lost in the translation). At least three of the Brit-coms in this book have been similarly rehashed by American television, usually with abysmal results (only *Cosby,* a weak copy of *One Foot in the Grave*, has achieved any ratings success). Why not just broadcast the original British shows on one of the major networks? The answer to that question could be a book in itself.

Since you're reading this now, you probably have some exposure to — and presumably a taste for — British humor. I've already stated what the purpose of this volume is *not*, so let's now talk about what it is. This is a book for Brit-com fans. If you are at all like me, your first exposure to British television comedy came in the mid–1970s through *Monty Python's Flying Circus.* Before *Python*, most Americans' exposure to Brit-coms was filtered through such successful adaptations as *All in the Family* (*Till Death Us Do Part*) and *Sanford and Son* (*Steptoe and Son*). The success of *Monty Python* in the United States didn't immediately open the floodgates for other British shows. It did, however, create an opening for some *Python* by-product. By the time the Pythons' circus was flying all over American television, the troupe, for all intents and purposes, had stopped performing in its original form. The group would still do films and concerts together, but there were no more of the 30-minute BBC shows that had made them famous in America. So, in 1975, with a cult following developing, American television had no new *Python* to show. Fortunately, for the BBC, PBS, and our story, they had the next best thing—*Fawlty Towers.* Pythoner John Cleese had left the group to write and star in his own situation comedy about a terribly rude innkeeper.

The first of two *Fawlty Towers* series was produced in 1975, and although it only contained six episodes, it was an immediate success when it was exported to the States. Its success opened the door for other BBC comedies for a number of reasons. First, local PBS stations reasoned that if one Brit-com had found an audience, perhaps others would also. Second, PBS stations at that time had a habit of scheduling their shows in hour-long blocks, especially in the evening hours, so it made sense for them to run two half-hour Brit-coms back to back. Thus other Brit-coms often made their entrance into the U.S. market on *Fawlty*

Towers' coattails. Finally, once American stations committed to satisfying their public's taste for Brit-coms, they had to have enough product to fill the allotted time slots. They couldn't just show the six original *Fawlty Towers* episodes indefinitely (the second series of six wasn't produced until 1979), although some came pretty close to doing that, or so it seemed at the time.

This brings me to one of the most frequently asked questions about Brit-coms: "Why don't they make more of (fill in the name of your favorite show)?" The reason why American fans have to make do with 12 *Fawlty Towers* episodes or 24 *Blackadders* or 30 *Good Neighbors* stems from the differences between American and British television. Most of us know how American television works. A show is produced and aired in hopes of becoming a ratings success. The more popular a show is with an audience, the higher the network can charge advertisers to hawk their wares during the commercial breaks. If a good show doesn't attract a big enough audience, it will find itself out of show business. A mediocre or even a poor show, in the proper time period with a big enough audience, will live on. Rare is the ratings-successful show on American TV that will voluntarily end its own run for artistic reasons, rather than waiting to milk its cash cow dry (*The Mary Tyler Moore Show* and *The Bob Newhart Show* are both notable exceptions).

The BBC, the source of the majority of Brit-coms, works quite differently. The British, or at least those with televisions, pay an annual television tax, which goes to support the BBC, which in turn produces commercial-free programming. Whereas American networks' and stations' primary concern is to have the highest-rated shows, the BBC's only concern is to have shows. NBC, CBS, and the other American broadcasting companies are in a great struggle to make sure that when you turn on your TV it will be to one of their programs. To state it somewhat simplistically: BBC's goal is that when someone turns on his or her "telly," there will be something on it.

There are benefits and pitfalls to both approaches, naturally. The BBC's approach seems to foster more control by creative personnel. One interesting way this is manifested is in British credits, where the writer/creator is given the first credit after the show's title, for example, "*Bless Me, Father* by Peter de Rosa." Most British shows are as closely linked to their authors as they are to their stars. Thus, the person who creates the show will more than likely wind up writing all the show's episodes. This system allows for a commitment to quality and fidelity to the show's original concept. As one can imagine, it also makes long series difficult. With one or two persons writing all the installments of a particular show, it is impossible to have 24-show seasons. Thus, the average Brit-com series is six shows in length. If this is well received and the writers are amenable, additional series are produced. When, as in the case of *Fawlty Towers*, the creators/writers (John Cleese and Connie Booth) decide they have done enough for whatever reason, the show's run stops.

In the United States, on the other hand, a hit show will continue as long as its producers can keep it going, regardless of whether the original creator moved on or key cast members quit or died. This usually results in hit shows — and even mediocre and poor programs — overstaying their welcome and suffering in quality.

This leads us to the shows included in this book. You will notice the title eschews the definite article. This is because this is not meant to be an exhaustive tome. If it were *The Great Brit-Coms,* I would feel obligated to include every British situation comedy that has enjoyed any popularity. Rather than do this, and make the book less complete by including more, I chose to offer a handful of programs that for various reasons are a representative sample of the best of British TV from the last 40 years.

I am certain some will disagree with my choices. There will be favorites left out. Even some of my favorites have been left out. You will not find *Porridge, Open All Hours, To the Manor Born, Absolutely Fabulous,* or *Red Dwarf* here (except briefly described in the final chapter), although a strong case could be made for each of them. If they were all included, however, this book would be far too long, far too expensive. As it is, for this volume of *Great Brit-Coms,* the criteria for covering a show included such considerations as popularity (both in England and America), concept, writing, cast, style of comedy, and when it was originally produced.

Fawlty Towers and the four *Blackadder* series are probably the most popular of the bunch in America and thus were easy choices for inclusion here. *Steptoe and Son* and *Dad's Army,* on the other hand, although two of the most popular British shows in that nation's history, are relatively unknown in America (although *Steptoe* is the template for *Sanford and Son*). Yet both are important in English television history, not only for their success, but because they influenced much of what came after. In a similar way, *The Goon Show* acted as forerunner for *Beyond the Fringe, Monty Python's Flying Circus,* and many others. *The Good Life* and *Reggie Perrin* represent the best of the BBC in the 1970s, and coincidentally or not, both struggle with the same base issue (midlife crisis) but in wildly different ways (*The Good Life* is a warm, cheery situation comedy, while *Perrin* is an eccentric, almost absurdist satire). *Bless Me, Father* is probably the least known of all the shows covered but is the best example I've ever seen on anybody's television of character-based comedy. I hope its inclusion will spur a greater appreciation among devotees of the Brit-com. *Yes, Minister* and its sequel, *Yes, Prime Minister,* contain some of the strongest political satire ever broadcast, and not surprisingly, both are textbook examples of how to write a tight, finely honed script. The four incarnations of the *Blackadder,* already cited for their popularity, are here also as the strongest mainstream representatives of the British alternative school of comedy. *Mr. Bean* is also here for its great popularity, as well as for its unique silent comedy approach to the sitcom. Both *Are You Being Served?* and *Keeping Up Appearances,* while disowned by most of Britain's critics, are still very popular—especially in the United States. As will be explained later, this is most likely due to the almost American style of both shows. Reaching into the 1990s, there is *One Foot in the Grave,* David Renwick's homage to the tribulations of retirement. Although it is the most recent of all the shows covered, *One Foot in the Grave* is an exemplary rendering of the style in which divergent plot lines and seemingly inconsequential occurrences all barrel down to meet in a comedic crescendo. Finally, there is *Chef!* Lenny Henry's usually successful updating and expansion of the *Fawlty Towers* premise.

If you have enjoyed these shows in the past, I hope these pages will bring back fond memories. If some of them are unfamiliar to you, perhaps you will be inspired to explore them for yourself. Either way, this volume has been designed as both an introduction and a reference. Each chapter begins with the background history of a particular show, followed by an episode-by-episode synopsis and critique. Each episode has been rated on a four-star system, with one star for poor and four stars for excellent. As with any such rating, this is entirely subjective. The ratings also represent the quality of the individual shows as judged against the others in the series. Thus, a four-star show of *Are You Being Served?* means that, in my opinion, it is one of the best of that series, although not on a par with a similarly rated installment from *Fawlty Towers.*

STEPTOE AND SON

BBC-TV 1962–1974

The modern history of the British situation comedy begins with the two ne'er-do-well rag-and-bone men totting under the aegis of Steptoe and Son. It is not risking hyperbole to suggest that their arrival in the first few days of 1962 did for British television what the Beatles began to do for their nation's popular music later that year. Both the Fab Four and the Totting Two helped redefine their medium, using their popularity to expand the realms of their art forms. Both displayed early on — although the Steptoes proved it from their first appearance — that they were not the typical merry mannequins that one usually found in their fields.

Steptoe and Son is a remarkable sit-com that shaped not only British television but American and global TV as well. The show's authors, Ray Galton and Alan Simpson, created a mix of humor and pathos that established new ground rules for sit-coms. Without their creation, it is arguable that *Till Death Us Do Part*, the forerunner of the American *All in the Family*, would not have seen the light of day. Of course, without *Steptoe and Son* there would never have been a *Sanford and Son*, that other Norman Lear translation that would help redefine the boundaries of television comedy in the United States. Without these shows, the shift to more realistic situations and less antiseptic comedy would not have happened when it did.

The major contribution of this program (centered around the lives of two junkmen) is not necessarily the controversy it caused; that was left more to *Till Death Us Do Part*, three years hence. Rather, it was the grim realism and generous doses of pathos that set *Steptoe* apart from its predecessors and contemporaries. Indeed, Galton and Simpson realized from the start what they had created, although they had no intention of expanding it to a series.

Steptoe and Son first saw the light of the cathode tube as the fourth installment of a Galton and Simpson series entitled *Comedy Playhouse*. This anthology series was offered to the duo by Tom Sloan, who was then the head of light entertainment at the BBC. That a pair of writers would be offered their own series, a carte blanche to create whatever their imaginations desired, and a say in the casting of their scripts is quite remarkable but certainly deserved.

Galton and Simpson had spent the last ten years writing for British comedy legend Tony Hancock. During this span, they scribed 103 radio programs, 65 television programs, a film (*The Rebel*), two stage shows, and other vehicles for the comedian. While Hancock was something of an institution in Great Britain, he was virtually unknown elsewhere. Craving the recognition that international film stardom brings, Hancock wanted his second feature film to appeal to a global audience. With this goal in mind, Galton and Simpson produced no fewer than three scripts to follow up *The Rebel*. All were rejected by the star (who eventually wrote his second film, *The Punch and Judy Man*, with Philip Oakes), leaving the writers at liberty in 1961 following their last series for Hancock.

Terming Sloan's offer as one they could not refuse, Galton and Simpson agreed to author the ten episodes of *Comedy Playhouse*. After almost a decade with Hancock, the pair looked forward to writing half-hour comedies to be performed each week by a different cast of actors, rather than comedians.

"As any comedy writer will tell you," Galton and Simpson explained in their introduction to *The Best of Steptoe and Son*, "actors are much better house-trained. They don't go through the script counting the laughs, they just learn the lines and get on with it."

Galton and Simpson's newfound liberation buoyed them through the first three scripts of *Comedy Playhouse*. The fourth installment, however, found the team struggling for an idea. According to the authors, they attempted to break their writers' block by facetiously tossing around outlandish suggestions for the next comedy. Some of the situations bandied about for their own amusement included two rat catchers in Buckingham Palace (the queen's bedroom, to be specific) and two nuns involved in a synchronized swimming drill. When Ray Galton offered the premise of two rag-and-bone men, initially his partner thought it a continuation of their game; the two men had a good laugh over the notion and promptly dropped it. Four days later, the pair resurrected the idea, for lack of producing anything better in the interim. Soon they were building a situation around their two characters: having the junkmen arguing in their yard after a day of totting. Still, the exact relationship eluded the writers. It was not until the second half of the script that Galton and Simpson realized the key idea: these two men were father and son.

The resulting script was called "The Offer," and it focused on the frustrations of the son, rapidly approaching middle age, trying to free himself from his father's influence. With the script finished, Galton and Simpson called Duncan Wood, the producer of *Comedy Playhouse*, with their choices to play the father and son. The writers wanted Wilfrid Brambell to play Albert Steptoe, the firm's senior partner, while they desired Harry H. Corbett for the role of his son, Harold Steptoe.

Although only 50 at the time, Wilfrid Brambell had made a career of playing old men. One of his earliest television roles had been in a version of George Orwell's *1984*, in which he played an octogenarian, although he was then in his early forties. From there, Brambell had played similarly aged roles in the classic sci-fi TV program *Quatermass* and the film *Flame in the Streets* (in which he played John Mills's father, despite being four years his junior). Galton and Simpson specifically recalled Brambell's work in two television plays—*Too Many Mansions* and *No Fixed Abode*—both of which found the actor portraying a destitute old-age pensioner, just the look required for their Albert Steptoe. Brambell told the *Radio Times* in 1962 that his secret to aging lay not in make-up but in not grooming. "I just stop shaving for a few days," he explained. "They dirty me down a bit, and that's it."

Brambell's technique succeeded, with the result being that when the series first started production he was mistaken for a junkman by an actual member of the trade. One day, while waiting for the cameras to roll, Brambell was standing on location in Shepherd's Bush with Hercules, the Steptoes' faithful cart horse. A genuine rag-and-bone man, watching the filming, sidled up to Brambell.

"Are they using you, mate?" the junkman asked.

Brambell confessed they were. After a few moments of scanning Brambell's pitiful visage, the real rag-and-bone man nodded.

"Oh, well," he consoled Brambell, "they'll probably give you a few bob."

Brambell's destitute appearance was further enhanced by the blackened, decayed set of false teeth he wore for the role of Albert Steptoe. In reality, Brambell was quite the fashion plate—except for the days he would don his moth-eaten rags and retrieve his gnarly teeth from the glass of gin and tonic where they resided between tapings of *Steptoe and Son*.

Galton and Simpson were especially glad to hear that Harry H. Corbett was available and willing to appear in "The Offer." According to the writers, Corbett, although relatively unknown to the general public, was one of the most highly regarded actors in England. A British combination of Orson Welles and Marlon Brando, Corbett had cofounded the Theatre Workshop in Stratford and also had started the Langham Group, an experimental company that performed the works of Shaw, Ibsen, and others on television in the 1950s.

An innovator in the field of method acting, Corbett was looked upon by his peers as highly influential. "Other actors would rush to a TV set whenever Harry was on," Galton and Simpson recalled, "and analyze the performance afterward."

In late 1961, when "The Offer" was being cast, Corbett was appearing on stage in Bristol in Shakespeare's *Henry IV*, parts 1 and 2 (according to a 1970 *Radio Times* article, Corbett was starring in *Macbeth* at the time). Hoping against hope, the authors had their teleplay sent to the actor, who agreed to leave the Bard for a week to do it. An elated Galton and Simpson later joked that going from a king of England to a rag-and-bone man in one week was the greatest comedown "since the last emperor of China."

While the role itself may have been a comedown, playing Harold Steptoe gave Corbett the broader-based fame that had eluded him in his previous work. Despite his reputation among actors, it is the part of the socially frustrated junior partner from Shepherd's Bush for which he is remembered — and justifiably so. One wonders if another actor would have brought the depth of emotion necessary to the demanding part.

Incidentally, Galton and Simpson claim that the surname "Steptoe" came from a sign over a photographic shop on a side street in Richmond, Surrey: "Steptoe and Figge." According to author Glenn Mitchell, however, there was a shop in Mitcham familiar to both writers called "Steptowe and Sons, Shoe Repairs." After the success of the television rag-and-bone men, that firm changed its name to "Five Star Shoe Repairs."

With "The Offer" over and done with, Galton and Simpson went back to working on the remaining episodes of *Comedy Playhouse*. In the meantime, on January 5, 1962, "The Offer" aired to instant success. Sensing the potential for a series, Tom Sloan approached Galton and Simpson, who promptly turned down the offer on the grounds that they didn't want to get tied to another property so soon after being liberated from Tony Hancock. In addition, the writers didn't think another five shows (the necessary number to complete a six-episode block) could be milked from the situation. Fortunately for the sake of television viewers, not to mention television history, the duo eventually relented and agreed to five more entries, which aired, along with the repeat of "The Offer," in June and July 1962. The public response was so enthusiastic that the shows were rebroadcast in August and September of the same year. *Steptoe and Son* was here to stay.

Unlike other programs, which take some time to find their creative stride and their audience, *Steptoe and Son* hit both squarely from the outset. As Alan Simpson told Gerard Kemp of the *Radio Times* in 1970, Albert and Harold Steptoe seemed to leap onto the screen fully formed. "They seemed to click into place in the first show," Simpson recalled, "and they stayed like that."

Indeed, one gets the feeling, especially in the early offerings of the show, that these are two real-life individuals upon whom the camera is eavesdropping. This quality makes some of the hard-edged humor of the series completely palatable, where it would have been rejected on less well written shows. The first series entry (not counting "The Offer," which was conceived as a one-off), "The Bird," proves this point. In that episode, Albert does what seems to be a horribly cruel and selfish thing to ruin his son's chance at happiness. Taken as a single act, it is cruel, but in the context of these characters' ongoing struggle, in which the caliber of writing demands we believe even in this seminal episode, it is entirely understandable.

The dark edge to the series can be likened to the classic bit in W. C. Fields' *The Old Fashioned Way*, in which the comedian kicks toddler Baby LeRoy right in the seat of his pants. Viewed out of context, the act is dastardly. Viewed in light of the infant torture to which Fields has been subject in the buildup to the act, it is not only justifiable but also elicits cheers from audiences. The Steptoes' frequent bouts of cruelty toward each other are equally justifiable when we accept the premise that this, which the viewing public has only been privy to since 1962, has really been going on in private since around 1925 (the year Harold Steptoe was born, according to the dating of the earlier episodes).

Ironically, another result of the two subjects of the program emerging so fully formed is that there is little exposition. Most other shows develop their characters as they go along and thus allow the audience to learn about them as the other characters (and, presumably, the writers) do. This is not the case with *Steptoe and Son* since there really aren't any other characters aside from Harold and Albert, and they already know more than they care to about each other (although Harold does discover interesting tidbits from his father's past in several episodes). Remarkably, in the entire run of the series, there is only one character aside from father and son who appears more than once (the Vicar), and he only appears twice! The end result of this closed setup is that there is little revealed about the characters because there are few outsiders to whom to reveal it. Much of the expository material about Albert and Harold appears in the later episodes and then presumably only as a means to support a particular plot (such as "Cuckoo in the Nest" from the sixth season). To illustrate the unimportance of this material, Galton and Simpson often get the facts wrong about their own creations. In "Live Now, P.A.Y.E. Later" from season seven, Albert and the Inland Revenue Department both refer to his late wife as Gladys, while in the next season's "Séance in a Wet Rag-and-Bone Yard," Albert's dearly departed is named Emily.

What is learned about Albert and Harold Steptoe is done so gradually over the years as necessitated by the individual plots. At first glance, Albert Edward Ladysmith Steptoe is the least sophisticated of the pair. A veteran of the First World War, Albert presumably inherited the family business from his father, who founded it (a fact first revealed in "The Offer," which goes unchallenged until the final episode when Harold discovers Albert is illegitimate). Albert's birthdate is given in various episodes; each time the date conflicts with another. The date given in the final episode, from his birth certificate, is

September 26, 1899. After having packed quite a lot of life into his younger years (including the fathering of at least two illegitimate offspring), Albert presumably settled down in the late teens or early twenties of the century to devote himself full time to the rag-and-bone profession. Having sown his wild oats, the elder Steptoe is the more cautious of the pair, a fact reflected in his staunchly Conservative voting record. Despite often presenting a moral posture to his son, it is clear from his past indiscretions and present practices that Albert doesn't live up to the standards he preaches to his son. Having cut a dapper figure in his youth, Albert is content to live out his old age in a relatively high but apparently comfortable (to him) level of personal filth.

Harold Albert Kitchener Steptoe, on the other hand, fancies himself a man of the world, although he has had little real-life experience outside his totting rounds in the London neighborhoods surrounding Shepherd's Bush. From the first episode, Harold is portrayed as a victim of lifelong frustration over the fact that he cannot escape from Albert. Neither is he granted the solace of a soulmate to relieve his burden, since from the second episode ("The Bird"), any attempt at romance is quickly sabotaged by his father. By the end of the first season, with the airing of "The Holiday," we learn that Harold is not even given the pleasure of brief vacations apart from Albert (ironically, the few vacations taken alone are enjoyed by Albert, who apparently has few qualms about going away by himself). The other driving force in Harold's life is his ambition to better himself and succeed, which is displayed most acutely in early episodes like "The Economist" and "The Diploma." This capitalistic drive is tempered in later entries as Harold's left-of-center, Labour party politics come increasingly to the fore.

Together, these two rag and bone men forge one of entertainment's most intense love-hate relationships, with the predominant display being the latter. Although both men claim to be morally superior to the other at times, this does not prevent them from rushing to exploit any chance for quick financial gain ("Wallah, Wallah, Catsmeat"). Of the two, Harold is more desperate for a large windfall ("The Three Feathers," "Crossed Swords"), apparently so that he might flee Albert. One of the most repeated reasons for Harold's angst is his complete inability to best his father at anything. Whatever Harold puts his hand to, Albert is more adept at—from electronics ("The Diploma") to cards ("Full House") to dancing ("Come Dancing") to acting ("A Star Is Born"). Harold is especially envious of Albert's wisdom in life, which he usually ignores at his own peril ("Is That Your Horse Outside?").

The success of the first series of *Steptoe and Son* resulted in a second series that began in January 1963. By the end of this series, encrusted with such comedic gems as "The Bath" and "A Musical Evening," approximately 22 million viewers were enjoying the pair in Britain alone. Their popularity reached across all social strata and included fans at Buckingham Palace. In November

1963, Brambell and Corbett performed a Galton and Simpson skit at the *Royal Variety* performance. A recording of the routine became a big seller, along with their performance at the *Night of 100 Stars* charity event. In addition to aristocratic fans, the show attracted the admiration of the new kings of pop music from Liverpool, the Beatles. The Fab Four included Wilfrid Brambell in their first film, *A Hard Day's Night,* playing the part of Paul McCartney's "very clean" grandfather (a repeated joke reference to Brambell's "dirty old man" alter ego, Albert Steptoe). Brambell's drawing power at the time is reflected in his fifth billing (after John, Paul, George, and Ringo) and inclusion on the film's posters. Corbett also found himself between series of *Steptoe* with several film projects of his own.

Third and fourth seasons followed in 1964 and 1965, giving the viewing public more classics, including "Homes Fit for Heroes" (in which Harold tries to abandon his father to the old folks' home), "Steptoe a La Cart," and "Pilgrim's Progress" (both using Albert's military service as a springboard to laughs). With the airing of "Pilgrim's Progress" on November 15, 1965, Galton and Simpson put the series to rest, preferring to end the Steptoes' saga while it was still at the top of its form. *Steptoe* fans would have to content themselves with the reruns of the original 27 shows and a 22-show series of radio adaptations, which began in 1966.

Galton and Simpson moved on to write *The Frankie Howerd Show.* In addition, the pair ventured to Hollywood in a failed attempt to adapt *Steptoe and Son* to American television. Apparently, while grubby lower class worked well on British television, Americans were still too optimistic in the mid-sixties to embrace such characters. According to the *Radio Times,* Mickey Rooney and Jack Benny were among those considered for the parts of Harold and Albert.

"We found that the big stumbling block to mounting the series for American TV was that *Steptoe and Son* was about unsuccessful people," Alan Simpson recalled in 1970. "Sponsors in America like TV series to be about affluent people living in nice homes."

By the early 1970s American TV had evolved enough to allow Norman Lear to successfully adapt *Steptoe* into *Sanford and Son,* starring Redd Foxx and Demond Wilson. While a ratings hit and often hilarious, *Sanford and Son* became a vehicle for its stars' charming brand of clowning and failed to retain the hard edge of the original.

In February 1969, Tom Sloan once again convinced Galton and Simpson to give a *Steptoe*-hungry public more of their favorite junkmen. Despite thinking they had fully exploited the idea back in 1965 (they also had thought they had fully exploited it in 1962 after "The Offer"), Galton and Simpson signed on for another seven shows with an option for another season after that. The writers' main reason for deciding to bring back Albert and Harold was that they were continually being asked when the Steptoes were returning. The fifth season of seven shows, which started airing in March 1970, now in color, took the better part of a year to write instead of the usual three months for the earlier seasons.

The new bunch of *Steptoes* did not disappoint, with Galton and Simpson exploring topics that perhaps had been outside of the realms of situation comedy five years earlier. The return was marked by the death of one of the main characters: Hercules, the Steptoes' faithful cart horse in the touching "A Death in the Family." In addition, the fifth season studied homosexuality, with Harold being lured into a same sex tryst ("Any Old Iron"), and illegitimacy ("Steptoe and Son — and Son!"). Unfortunately, these first color shows exist only in poor quality black-and-white versions; the originals were the victims of an ill-conceived housecleaning at the BBC in the late 1970s. Still these, along with most of the sixth season, which suffered the same fate, are well worth the eyestrain induced by viewing them.

Encouraged by the success of other British television shows that been adapted into feature-length films (*Dad's Army*, *Up Pompeii*, *On the Buses*), in 1972 Galton and Simpson penned *Steptoe and Son*, the film. In the film, Harold finally gets married (to a stripper), only to have his marriage ruined almost immediately by Albert. While the film has some fine moments, most of these are dramatic in nature. Many of the better comic moments are directly traceable to some of the television episodes ("A Musical Evening" and "And Afterwards At..." most notably). Also of note are the cameo appearance of Galton and Simpson in the film as two of the guests sitting in the church at Harold's wedding. A warning to American audiences: the video of the film *Steptoe and Son* is more readily available in the States than the television shows, and while it is enjoyable as a supplement to the TV shows, it is a poor introduction to the concept as a whole. The film scored well enough with audiences to warrant a sequel, *Steptoe and Son Ride Again*, in 1974. The second time around, the focus was definitely on lighter material as Albert and Harold tried their hand at training and racing a greyhound.

The production of the film delayed the series return of *Steptoe and Son* until February 1972, when the seventh season premiered. It is in the seventh set of shows that many believe the adventures of the pride of Shepherd's Bush reached their zenith. There certainly is much to be said for this wonderful grouping, which contains such episodes as "A Star Is Born," "Oh, What a Beautiful Mourning," "Divided We Stand," and "The Desperate Hours." Again, there was almost another two-year hiatus before the next dose of *Steptoe* would be released. This time, rather than a series, the public had to content itself with a 1973 Christmas special.

The last great wave of *Steptoe and Son* was in 1974; when the public was treated to the eighth and final season, a theatrical film, and the final episode in the guise of another Christmas special. Unfortunately, by this final go-round, the inspiration had flagged somewhat, leaving the last shows below the standard set by their predecessors but still better than the average sitcom fare.

The characters didn't die with the final episode, however. The last group of radio adaptations kept Brambell and Corbett busy, as did a 1977 tour of Australia in an act written by Galton and Simpson. More recently, with the advent of home video and subsequent airings of the classic 57 episodes, *Steptoe and Son* has enjoyed a popular resurgence. Sadly, neither Wilfrid Brambell nor Harry H. Corbett lived to see the continuance of the popularity of their work. Corbett died in 1982 from a heart attack (ironically, the malady his partner's character always faked). Brambell died three years later, in 1985.

Fortunately, their legacy of comedy lives on. Whenever the irresistibly catchy strains of Ron Grainer's signature tune ("Old Ned") are heard, fans of comedy can be assured of another claustrophobic, contentious, often uncomfortable, but almost always hilarious visit with the two most successful, unsuccessful rag-and-bone men of television history.

THE EPISODES

By Ray Galton and Alan Simpson. Produced by Duncan Wood, John Howard Davies, Graeme Muir, and Douglas Argent

Series One 1962

EPISODE 1: "THE OFFER" ★★★★

Air date on *Comedy Playhouse*: January 5, 1962. Air date as first show of series: June 7, 1962. Cast: Albert Steptoe (Wilfrid Brambell); Harold Steptoe (Harry H. Corbett)

Weary of the rag-and-bone trade, 37-year-old Harold Steptoe informs his father, Albert, that he has received a tempting offer for another job and may be leaving home.

In one tightly written, beautifully executed script, we are introduced to *Steptoe and Son*. Originally written as a one-time play for the *Comedy Playhouse* series, the strength of these 30 minutes of comedy and not a little drama launched more than 50 episodes and helped changed the face of British television. It is hard to believe while watching this bit of television that neither the authors nor the actors had any idea that they were creating a formula that they would successfully repeat for almost 12 years.

It is little wonder that the powers that be at the BBC immediately recognized the potential of *Steptoe and Son* as a series, since all the basic elements and conflicts are so well developed in "The Offer."

Britain's favorite "dirty old man," Alfred Steptoe (Wilfrid Brambell, left) confers with son Harold (Harry H. Corbett) in this still from the '70's incarnation of the long-running series. Copyright © BBC.

Perhaps the best comedy bits in the episode center around Harold and Albert's restocking of the liquor. As Harold calls out the names of the bottles collected that day, Albert scrambles to find a matching bottle among the dozens on the sidebar. After finding the right bottle, Albert gives it to his son, who pours the precious remains of liquor into the appropriate collecting bottle. Harold is chagrined to discover that one of the wine bottles collected had been used to store paraffin, thus ruining the master bottle he poured it into. Albert doesn't mind, however, and starts enjoying the slightly tainted vintage, much to his son's revulsion.

Episode 2: "The Bird" ★★★

Air Date: June 14, 1962. Cast: Albert Steptoe (Wilfrid Brambell); Harold Steptoe (Harry H. Corbett); Roxanne (Valerie Bell)

When Harold shaves twice in the same week, Albert suspects that something unusual is going on in his son's life. Harold confirms his suspicions by admitting he is meeting "a bird." Albert urges his son to stay home with his poor old father. Sympathy having failed, Albert suggests that Harold invite his girl, Roxanne, over for dinner some night. Harold agrees.

The night of the dinner, Roxanne is more than an hour late. Albert fuels Harold's irritation by suggesting that Roxanne is out with someone else. Finally, Roxanne arrives. Humiliated, Harold tells her through the door not to come back. Albert congratulates his son on standing up to the woman. After Harold goes to bed, Albert turns the clock back one hour.

The first entry aired as part of the regular series of *Steptoe and Son*, "The Bird" is a testimony to the depth of characterization that Galton and Simpson put into the series. At first, the tactics that Albert employs to keep Harold single seem to be the height of cruelty — and, indeed, they are desperate acts. Put into perspective, however, one realizes that this is just another tactic in a war that has been going on between these two men for years. Unlike those in most television series, these characters have not been born moments before the opening credits. Albert and Harold Steptoe have been in Shepherd's Bush for what (to them) must seem slightly less than an eternity. We, the audience, have just walked in on it.

One bit that has nothing to do with the plot involves a junkman's debate on antiques. Albert chides his son for picking the stuffing out of a genuine Queen Anne chair. Harold doubts its genuineness, especially since the chair is stuffed with foam rubber. He reminds his father of the time Albert took an "Elizabethan cocktail cabinet" to the British Museum for appraisal and the time he purchased a genuine Georgian record player.

EPISODE 3: "THE PIANO" ****

Air Date: June 21, 1962. Cast: Harold Steptoe (Harry H. Corbett); Albert Steptoe (Wilfrid Brambell); Piano Owner (Brian Oulton); Policeman (Roger Avon)

Harold and Albert attempt to move a grand piano from a penthouse apartment.

A meticulous examination and execution of a single situation, "The Piano" is, at times, almost Laurel-and-Hardy–like in its construction. Indeed, the situation at first seems to be developing as an homage to that pair's Academy Award–winning short, *The Music Box,* including the prospect of a piano and a flight of stairs. The Steptoes, however, establish that they have even less luck than Stan and Ollie, when they fail to get their piano past its first obstacles.

Both Corbett and Brambell are wonderfully in character as they tramp about the lavishly furnished penthouse. Harold admires the trappings and aspires to have something similar someday, while Albert wants to swipe objets d'art and look through the owner's checkbook.

Upon first arriving at the penthouse, Harold must remove his boots and put on slippers so as not to damage the antique Persian carpet. The penthouse owner keeps a cabinet filled with various sized slippers by the front door for such eventualities. Later, when Harold returns with Albert, the man excuses himself, leaving Harold to fit his father with the slippers. After one look at the collection of slippers, Albert concludes their owner must be "kinky." He then relates the story of an officer in the army, who he deemed similarly deviant because he wore football shorts under his uniform. Harold tells him that football shorts are preferable to whatever Albert must wear under his clothes, adding that his surface garments are bad enough.

When it comes to actually moving the piano, Harold suggests they take up the rug to make the instrument easier to roll. Albert starts to do so and discovers some old newspapers, which have been placed under the rug to keep it from slipping. "'Ere," he suddenly remarks to Harold with a shocked expression, "Ghandi's dead!"

EPISODE 4: "THE ECONOMIST" ***

Air Date: June 28, 1962. Cast: Albert Steptoe (Wilfrid Brambell); Harold Steptoe (Harry H. Corbett); Technician (Frank Thornton)

After reading *Economic Planning in a Capitalist Society*, Harold informs his father that the secret to financial success is bulk buying. His first volume deal: 4,000 sets of dentures.

A good script, funny situations, and typically fine performances result in a solid series entry for "The Economist." We learn quite a lot about the characters in this episode, especially Harold's intense yearning to better himself juxtaposed against Albert's desire to keep the status quo. Albert credits both conditions to the fact that he's never read a book, which, he insists, turns people into Communists. Later in the episode, it is also disclosed that one of the reasons for Albert's contentment is a coffee can full of five-pound notes, which he keeps hidden under the stairs.

One of the episode's funnier moments comes when Harold explains that he's going to get rid of the horse and cart and replace it with a ten-ton truck. Albert sentimentally insists they can't get rid of the faithful Hercules. Harold is adamant and says that in business it is strictly a matter of adapting or perishing. Calling his son a "great puddin'" Albert asks how he expects the horse to adapt itself into a ten-ton truck.

Fans of *Are You Being Served?* should recognize a younger, clean-shaven Frank Thornton as the man from the dental lab, ten years before he began his role of Captain Peacock.

EPISODE 5: "THE DIPLOMA" ***

Air Date: July 5, 1962. Cast: Albert Steptoe (Wilfrid Brambell); Harold Steptoe (Harry H. Corbett)

With business getting scarcer, Harold notifies Albert that he plans to become a television repairman.

Similar in theme to the previous episode, "The Diploma" further investigates Harold's attempts to better himself through knowledge. Here, however, instead of using his knowledge to succeed in the rag and bone business, Harold attempts a new career. This episode also examines the staple theme that whatever Harold fervently attempts and fails at, Albert succeeds at without trying.

There is a humorous topical discussion of the Common Market (which, at the time, Britain had not yet entered), which Harold contends is part of the cause of their junkyard's economic woes. Harold tells Albert that the problem will only become worse when the proposed Channel tunnel is completed. According to Harold, the tunnel will result in a flood of European rag and bone men pouring into England to strip the nation of its junk. When Albert points out that they can retaliate by going to the Continent to collect European junk, Harold reminds him that their horse can hardly make it out of the yard.

These desperate straits leave Harold little alternative but to hand in his notice. Albert protests he can't quit since he is on the two-man firm's board of directors.

EPISODE 6: "THE HOLIDAY" ★★½

Air Date: July 12, 1962. Cast: Albert Steptoe (Wilfrid Brambell); Harold Steptoe (Harry H. Corbett); Doctor (Colin Gordon)

Albert fakes a heart attack to keep Harold from going on a Mediterranean holiday without him.

More effective as a drama than as a comedy, "The Holiday" reexplores the theme from "The Offer" (and essentially the premise for the whole series). Instead of wanting to leave Albert for good, however, Harold only wants to spend his vacation away from his father. Again, the outcome is the same with Harold realizing that he is trapped in his current situation and probably will be for life. This pill is made all the more bitter since here an outsider (the Doctor) confirms it. What makes this latest realization even more tragic, however, is the sad fact that his sentence hasn't even the briefest periods of parole. Harold cannot even enjoy a two-week holiday without Albert. Albert's manipulations in "The Holiday" are almost entirely cruel, until one realizes that (in his thinking, at least) even a brief vacation for Harold may lead to a permanent separation.

Ultimately, Albert fakes a heart attack to get his way. The Doctor visits and tells Harold that, physically, Albert is fine. He cautions, however, that if Harold leaves him even for a fortnight Albert's psychological state could trigger an actual life-threatening malady. Following the doctor's advice, Harold takes Albert to Bognor.

This episode was one of the personal favorites of Wilfrid Brambell.

Series Two — 1963

Episode 1: "The Bath" ★★★½

Air date: January 3, 1963. Cast: Albert Steptoe (Wilfrid Brambell); Harold Steptoe (Harry H. Corbett); Delia (Yootha Joyce); Girl (Marjie Lawrence)

Harold decides to convert Albert's bedroom into a bathroom after his plans of a romantic evening are dashed by Albert taking a bath in the middle of the living room.

A humor-filled launch to the second series of *Steptoe and Son*, "The Bath" successfully incorporates a number of already familiar themes, including Harold's yearning to improve his lot, Albert's satisfaction with the status quo, and Albert's determination to sabotage any serious relationship Harold might forge with the opposite sex. The working of this second device is more palatable here than in "The Bird," since it is less aggressive. Here, rather than precipitate his son's romantic downfall, Albert is content to exploit circumstances — ironically set in motion by Harold — to do the job.

The sight of Albert Steptoe, sitting in a tiny washtub with his hat on, warbling "These Foolish Things" and eating his supper, sets the tone for the entire episode. Harold, naturally, is shocked that his father would choose this evening to take his quarterly bath, but Albert doesn't see why this should cause a problem, even given the imminent arrival of company. Harold explains that the tub brings down the tone of the room, as if their junk-filled living room had any tone to begin with.

Harold urges his father to vacate the tub before his date arrives since just the act of shaking her hand would be rude — either sitting down or standing up. Albert will not be rushed, however, and insists on finishing his dinner. When he drops half a jar of pickled onions in the bathwater, Albert calmly fishes out the vegetables and returns them to their container. Harold is only mildly disgusted, until he realizes that had he not witnessed the incident, his father had never told him that half the onions had been pickled in bathwater.

Albert's accommodations under the stairway also provide a good share of laughs. While Harold paints a comfortable picture of the cupboard-cum-bedroom, Albert asks what he's supposed to do with the end that slopes down to the floor. Harold logically explains that that end is for his father's feet. Similarly, Harold reasons that the abundance of spiders in the closet can be remedied by importing a few frogs. The only drawback Harold can see to this bucolic little den is that Albert will have to arise early on Thursday mornings so the gasman can read the meter.

Although unfamiliar to American audiences, Yootha Joyce, appearing as Delia, went on to become a staple of Brit-coms. She gained her greatest notoriety as Mrs. Roper in *Man About the House*, the series that would become

Americanized as *Three's Company*, as well as in its long-running spinoff, *George and Mildred.*

Episode 2: "Wallah, Wallah, Catsmeat" ★★★½

Air date: January 10, 1963. Cast: Albert Steptoe (Wilfrid Brambell); Harold Steptoe (Harry H. Corbett); Veterinarian (John Laurie); Lionel Sturgis (Leslie Dwyer); Rag-and-Bone Men (George Tovey, George Betton).

The Steptoe empire is faced with financial chaos when Hercules, their horse, becomes sick. Potential disaster is averted, however, when other rag-and-bone men offer to share their junk with Albert and Harold.Their gratitude quickly turns to opportunism, however, when they realize that they can turn a healthy profit while enjoying a two-week vacation at their colleagues' expense.

"Wallah, Wallah, Catsmeat" finds both Steptoes at the height of their incorrigibility. It also is one of the few episodes to buck the unwritten law of stasis in Brit-coms, which itself was firmly established by *Steptoe and Son*. That Harold and Albert actually come out ahead in this episode is surprising. That they do so by flagrant lying, conspiracy, and taking advantage of their neighbors' kindness is flabbergasting, especially in an early 1960s sitcom. None of this is said to denigrate the installment, which is packed with wonderful dialogueue. Still, one is left with the impression that had the episode run another five or ten minutes, it would have shown the Steptoes' scheme crashing down about them. Such an ending would have been more satisfying.

When Harold teases Albert about his abysmal luck at the football pools, Albert insists that when he does strike it rich he won't share his good fortune with his son, only with the horse. Albert dreams of retiring with Hercules to a country estate where the horse will be free to roam and frolic as he pleases.

"Hercules unchained," Harold shouts in mock triumph.

Harold then informs his father that the horse hasn't been able to gambol in years and that only the shafts of the cart have held up the animal.

There are also two funny unrelated bits, both centered on tea. In the first, Harold is visibly upset that his father adheres to the lower-class habit of pouring the milk in his cup before the tea. He asserts that he could never take Albert to the Claridge since they'd immediately spot him as a lower-class mif. When Albert asks what a "mif" is, Harold coolly explains it stands for "milk in first."

Later, while they await the vet's report, Albert tries to calm Harold's anxiety by offering him a cup of tea. Harold launches into a wonderful soliloquy about the absurdity of tea being the Englishman's panacea. He claims that his countrymen have offered the drink as the best response for everything from the Blitz to coronations to traffic accidents and even the piles.

Dad's Army fans will immediately recognize John Laurie, who turns in his usual quality performance as the unscrupulous veterinarian.

Episode 3: "The Stepmother" ★★

Air date: January 17, 1963. Cast: Albert Steptoe (Wilfrid Brambell); Harold Steptoe (Harry H. Corbett); Emma (Joan Newell)

Albert reveals to Harold that he has been dating a widow named Emma Martin and that he is engaged to her. The engagement comes to a rapid end when Emma comes to visit and becomes embroiled in a typical Steptoe argument.

A reexamination of the situation explored in "The Bird," only with the roles reversed. While "The Stepmother" suffers in comparison to the previous episode primarily because it is less humorous, this it still installment gives some interesting insights into previously unseen portions of both Steptoes' psyches. Harold, despite his constant struggles to be free, actually fears losing the security of the status quo. He is like the revolutionary who rails against the system but has no viable alternative to offer. Also, while Harold is not as active in his machinations against Albert's romances as his father is toward his, when the chips are down and the opportunity presents itself, Harold proves to be as incorrigible. We also see for the first time Harold's deep-seated reverence for his late mother.

Albert, on the other hand, bares his romantic soul in this episode. One had assumed that he had a Byronic side, but it is interesting to see it. Indeed, the opening scene, in which his date sees Albert home, is a touching revelation.

For her part, Emma kindly tries to referee a typical Steptoe argument but quickly finds herself in the middle of the battle and in over her head. When she comforts Harold over the loss of his mother, Albert takes the opportunity to insult his ex-wife. Harold lobs slurs back at Albert in retaliation, forcing Emma to defend her fiancé by reminding Harold that Albert is his father after all. Albert sneers that that is an assertion that has never been proven, precipitating a new tangent over which to fight.

After Albert has apologized to Emma, Harold restarts the quarrel by reminding Albert that he referred to Emma as "mutton done up as lamb." He does so under the reasoning that as long as the pair are forgiving each other they might as well know what they are forgiving each other for. Once Emma has left for good, Albert sadly tries to recall when he made that last fatal insult. Of course, he never did: Harold made it up.

Episode 4: "Sixty-Five Today" ★★★

Air date: January 24, 1963. Cast: Albert Steptoe (Wilfrid Brambell); Harold Steptoe (Harry H. Corbett); Bartender (Frank Thornton); Restaurant Patron (Richard Caldicot); Bar Patron (Michael Bird); Restaurant Staff (Anthony Chinn, Peter Ching, Myo Toon, Aman Tokyo)

Harold takes Albert out for a night on the town to celebrate his 65th birthday including tickets to a West End show and dinner.

"Sixty-Five Today" is a bittersweet episode, which clearly illustrates the love-hate relationship between Harold and Albert. Harold's love for his father is especially evident through his elaborate plans for Albert's birthday. Yet, at the same time, he relishes teasing his father by withholding disclosure of the plans until the last minute, making Albert think his birthday has been forgotten. Albert's softer side is much in evidence as we learn that he cherishes a sentimental birthday card from his son over any other gift.

Each stop on the birthday tour illustrates the difference in tastes between Harold and Albert. First, the pair stops at a cocktail lounge for a drink. Albert is disappointed to discover that he can't get a pint of bitter and loudly protests that the brew is a staple of the Skinners Arms. Harold tries to ignore Albert's antics and gives the bartender a detailed order for a vodka martini. His attempt at being debonair is shattered when Albert accuses him of imitating James Bond in *Dr. No*.

At the theater, Albert learns that instead of seeing a show with lots of pretty girls, Harold has brought him to see *Richard III* with Michael Redgrave. Albert proclaims the drama to be a "load of old rubbish" after the first act, adding that the acting isn't as good as that on *Z-Cars* (a popular police action program). Harold points out that Shakespeare represents Britain's history, but Albert is more interested in American cowboy stories. He recites Richard's opening speech, then observes that there is a conspicuous lack of similar prose in an episode of *Bonanza*.

EPISODE 5: "A MUSICAL EVENING" ★★★★

Air date: January 31, 1963. Cast: Albert Steptoe (Wilfrid Brambell); Harold Steptoe (Harry H. Corbett)

Harold's plans for listening to an evening of Stravinsky conflict with Albert's penchant for cheerier twist records. The musical disagreement soon escalates into a battle royal.

A marvelous execution of what *Steptoe and Son* does best: thoroughly explore a single frustrating situation with only the two main characters. There is more than a little Stan Laurel in Wilfrid Brambell's antics in this episode, as his Albert repeatedly is diverted from the more serious concerns to play with random items in the junkyard.

As usual, when Harold returns with a full cart of junk, Albert claims many of the items for himself. His latest treasures include three pictures illustrating "Charity, Virtue, and Motherhood" (which Albert likes for the "big beefy birds" displayed in them) and a bag full of shoes (he already has 60 pairs, including three sets of riding boots). Harold has found his own gold in the load:a box of old 78 records from which he hopes to add to his collection of classical music, which sets the plot in motion.

When Harold first puts on his classical music, Albert counters by starting to noisily mend shoes. The conflict between Harold's Stravinsky and Albert's cobbling is a fast and furious affair. (This too is reminiscent of the Laurel and Hardy reciprocal destruction device as used in such films as *Big Business* and *Tit for Tat.*) Realizing that he is losing, Harold puts on Wagner and brings the speaker over to where Albert is hammering. Still behind in the battle, Harold takes Albert's cobbling stand and throws it through the window. Albert retaliates by smashing Wagner on the turntable with the hammer. Soon the pair are racing around the room in a frantic attempt to destroy the other's prized possessions. The battle ends when Albert throws the keys to the record cabinet, along with all the other house, stable, and yard keys, into the junkyard.

Later, Harold tries to find the keys by scientifically reconstructing the exact trajectory of Albert's throw. They recreate the incident with a stone but only manage to lose that also. The pair experience some hope when they find the skin broken on the top of an open five-gallon can of paint Harold plunges his hand into the paint, but only manages to retrieve the stone Albert threw.

Episode 6: "Full House" ★★★

Air date: February 7, 1963. Cast: Harold Steptoe (Harry H. Corbett); Albert Steptoe (Wilfrid Brambell); Card Players (Dudley Foster, Jack Rodney, Anthony Sagar)

After ignoring his father's warnings against gambling, Harold invites some dubious friends over for poker. When they fleece Harold of his cash, Albert turns the tables on the trio of card sharks with the help of a marked deck.

Somewhat predictable but totally satisfying thanks to the strength of the execution, "Full House" is the first of two consecutive episodes that spotlight Albert's attempts at wielding his wisdom to protect his son. The results are more gratifying here than in "Is That Your Horse Outside?" since the ending is happier. While these episodes do not represent the zenith of the series, they are still enjoyable entries for the depth they expose in the main characters, particularly Albert.

When Harold first returns home, he finds Albert apparently in the middle of cleaning the house. Harold suggests that Albert hasn't been cleaning but sleeping, since his chair is still warm. Albert explains that the neighbor's cat, which often comes over to keep him company, warmed the chair. Pointing out that the entire chair is warm, Harold suggests they use the five-foot-tall feline to pull the cart. Next, when he discovers two brandy bottles drained, Harold sarcastically assumes the same giant cat drank the spirits.

Before Harold's guests arrive, Albert scrambles around the special refreshments begging for a sample like an eight-year-old before his parents' dinner party. After Albert incessantly whines for a piece of cheese, Harold relents and offers his father some Camembert, knowing that Albert hates the runny cheese. Albert refuses the cheese, but Harold insists on trying to force the cheese down his father's throat. After a titanic struggle, Harold retreats.

"Don't say I didn't offer it to you," he remarks casually.

EPISODE 7: "IS THAT YOUR HORSE OUTSIDE?" ★★½

Air date: February 14, 1963. Cast: Albert Steptoe (Wilfrid Brambell); Harold Steptoe (Harry H. Corbett); Dorthea (Patricia Haines); Next Lover (Richard Shaw); Waitress (Jo Rowbottom)

When Harold is up early and eager to get to the day's work, Albert is suspicious, especially since Harold has put on his best suit and shaved, ostensibly to collect junk. After Harold leaves, Albert follows him on bicycle and witnesses Harold, entering a rich woman's townhouse. That evening, Albert confronts Harold who eventually admits to the affair, but then tells his father to mind his own business. He insists that the woman wants him for himself and his mind, but Albert contends she is only bored and wanting a "bit of rough" in the guise of a rag-and-bone man. The next morning, Harold returns to the townhouse to discover that another working man has taken his place as the rough of the day.

Another attempt by Albert Steptoe to provide his son with the benefit of his years of experience, "Is That Your Horse Outside?" provides further glimpses into the wisdom of this sage of Oil Drum Lane. Like the previous episode, Albert tries to kindly warn Harold of his impending doom, to no avail. Unlike "Full House," however, the ending is less than sanguine due to the nature and depth of the injury to Harold. It is perhaps more comic but less kind that Harold rewards his father's concern by chasing him down the street, throwing books at him, as the final credits roll.

The episode's funniest moments come as Albert tries desperately to save Harold from a broken heart, but the firm's junior partner can hardly keep a straight face. Albert announces he is going to give Harold some serious advice, but Harold can barely hide his amusement.

"Son," Albert begins sincerely, "I'm older than you are ..."

Harold interrupts with mock astonishment and a wish that Albert would have made this revelation while he was growing up, since it would have made a profound difference in his life.

Series Three 1964

EPISODE 1: "HOMES FIT FOR HEROES" ★★★½

Air date: January 7, 1964. Cast: Albert Steptoe (Wilfrid Brambell); Harold Steptoe (Harry H. Corbett); Matron (Peggy Thorpe-Bates); Miss Lotterby (Marie Makino)

Harold explains he has to put Albert in the old folks' home since he is going away for two years on a round-the-world sloop voyage. When Albert finds out that the crew is comprised of five men and five women, he accuses Harold of merely going for the "birds." The day comes for Albert to check into the old folks' home. Harold tries to cheer up his father, but Albert refuses to even shake his son's hand. Harold is home packing when he receives a letter from the captain of the sloop returning his check and explaining that the crew has voted Harold out since, at 37, he is too much older than the rest of them. Harold glumly picks up Albert, who laughs himself silly reading the letter.

The third series begins with a marvelously bittersweet episode in which Harold finally gets rid of Albert. Unlike other similarly dramatic installments ("The Holiday," "Sixty-Five Today"), however, "Homes Fit for Heroes" has the distinction of presenting its pathos in the middle of the show and ending on a comical note. The final moments contain not only some wonderful irony but also a fitting commentary on the subject of aging.

Most of the broad comedy goes to Wilfrid Brambell's character. Harold tries to justify putting Albert in the home by claiming he has to take this chance for adventure while he's still young. Albert bitterly concludes that he is being tossed aside so his son can cruise the world with "five bits of crumpet."

Once he is brought to the home, Albert tells the Matron that he is there under protest. He warns the woman that he is a troublemaker who likes to ring bells in bed. With a devilish grin on his face, Albert adds that the Matron would be well advised to lock up the old ladies away from his lecherous grasp.

There is something chillingly prophetic about Harold's remark that he doesn't want to grow as old as Albert. He hopes he lives another 20 years, then turns in. Harry H. Corbett died 18 years later, while still in his fifties.

EPISODE 2: "THE WOODEN OVERCOATS" ★★

Air date: January 14, 1964. Cast: Albert Steptoe (Wilfrid Brambell); Harold Steptoe (Harry H. Corbett)

Harold brings home a load of coffins, much to Albert's terror. It seems the elder Steptoe considers coffins an omen of death and is loath to have them in the yard. Harold explains that he wouldn't dream of leaving them in the yard to warp and brings the boxes into the house. Rather than sleep under the same roof with the coffins, Albert leaves to sleep in the stable with the horse. Alone in the house with the "wooden overcoats," Harold's imagination starts running away with him. A storm arises and the lights go out, forcing the frightened Harold to seek refuge in the stable.

Although hampered by a slim story line, "The Wooden Overcoats" still manages to be an enjoyable, if somewhat slight, installment in the series. Much of the episode is about superstition and fear, the former believed in by Albert, while Harold exhibits the latter. Norman Percival's incidental music adds quite a bit of mood to the scary scenes.

There is a good opening sequence in which Harold returns home to find Albert sitting under a sunlamp. Stripped to his shorts and wearing dark goggles, the scrawny senior partner cuts quite a figure (Harold describes him as an "advertisement for famine relief"). The entire exercise proves futile when Harold discovers Albert is only using a regular 60-watt bulb in the lamp.

Later, Albert argues with his son over introducing the coffins to their home, warning that the boxes will only enter the house over his dead body. Harold cheerfully notes, as he carries one box inside, that under that condition he'll have at least one sale. Albert persists, ruefully intoning that the coffins will turn their home into a "house of mourning." Harold grimly reminds his father that it hasn't really been a "fun palace" in the past.

EPISODE 3: "THE LEAD MAN COMETH" ★★½

Air date: January 21, 1964. Cast: Albert Steptoe (Wilfrid Brambell); Harold Steptoe (Harry H. Corbett); Lead Man (Leonard Rossiter); Policeman (Billy Maxam)

With business slow, Harold leaps at the chance to buy a ton of scrap lead from a rather "dodgy" individual. Soon after receiving the merchandise, Albert's worst fears are confirmed when a policeman circulates a report on a ring selling stolen lead. Rather than keeping the evidence that they have received stolen goods, Harold and Albert take the lead and drop it in the river. They return home in the pouring rain to discover that their upstairs is flooded and rainwater is pouring through their ceiling. Closer inspection reveals that the stolen lead came from their own roof.

Essentially a one-gag episode, "The Lead Man Cometh" is strongest in its final payoff. The journey to the final joke is rather routine by *Steptoe and Son* standards except for the appearance of a young Leonard Rossiter, who is marvelously scurrilous in the title role.

When the Lead Man makes his offer, Harold is eager to buy the metal, no questions asked. Albert reminds him that for 85 years the firm has never engaged in any shady business. Harold takes a look around the yard and notes that honesty hasn't profited them much. When the full load is delivered, Albert is unsettled, complaining that the transaction makes him feel unclean. Harold offers ersatz sympathy before noting that Albert is long past unclean and now resides in the "filthy" range.

EPISODE 4: "STEPTOE A LA CART" ★★★★

Air date: January 28, 1964. Cast: Albert Steptoe (Wilfrid Brambell); Harold Steptoe (Harry H. Corbett); Monique (Gwendolyn Watts); Butler (Frank Thornton); Woman at Door (Lala Lloyd)

Harold has found true love at last in the form of Monique, a French au pair girl. When Harold brings Monique home to meet Albert, he is surprised to learn that his father speaks fluent French. While describing his experience in France during the war, Albert discovers that he was once billeted in Monique's hometown. The plot thickens when Monique recognizes a picture of her grandmother in Albert's photo album. The pair begin speaking excitedly, much to Harold's consternation. When he asks for an explanation, Albert informs his son that he is Monique's grandfather — her mother being the issue of his wartime romance. Realizing he has lost the girl he loves, Harold asks Monique if they can still be friends. Monique replies that they can be more than friends, since Harold is now her uncle, a fact that goes down hard with Harold.

Marvelous from start to finish, in "Steptoe a La Cart," Galton and Simpson blend a witty script, a great situation, a hysterical closing gag, and new revelations about established characters into one of the best episodes in the entire series. Added to this are topnotch performances by Brambell and Corbett, making "Steptoe a La Cart" a worthy comedy entrée. The familiar theme of Albert ruining Harold's chances for a lasting relationship with a woman is revisted. To the authors' great credit, each time this situation is explored, a new trail to ruin is blazed.

Harold's initial meeting with Monique is quite charming as the two try to communicate through broken English and French and hand motions. Harold tries to establish Monique's duties in the apartment in which she is staying. He asks if she dusts and scrubs the floors, miming the activities.

Monique recognizes the latter and admits cheerily, "Me scrubber."

Harold vehemently denies her assertion, since "scrubber" is contemptuous English slang for a girl who sleeps around.

When Albert is introduced to Monique, he gallantly kisses her hand and welcomes her in perfect French. Monique, unaware of her faux pas, remarks it is a pleasure to meet "Old Misery-Guts," as Harold evidently refers to his father.

The best moments are reserved for the revelation that Albert is Monique's grandfather. Albert, of course, is delighted, while Harold must summon every ounce of strength not to explode over the news. Monique excuses herself for a moment, leaving the two alone. In her absence, Albert happily notes Monique's physical resemblance to him, especially the fact that she has his nose and eyes. Seething, Harold agrees through clenched teeth, adding that when Monique leaves, Albert will get Harold's "bleedin' fist."

Frank Thornton is back in an amusing short turn, playing his usual stuffy, officious role but with a Cockney undertone to add a fresh twist.

Episode 5: "Sunday for Seven Days" ★★★

Air date: February 4, 1964. Cast: Albert Steptoe (Wilfrid Brambell); Harold Steptoe (Harry H. Corbett). Featuring: Michael Brennan; Michael Stainton;

Mark Singleton; Damaris Hayman; George Betton. With Alec Bregonzi; Billy Maxam; Betty Cardno; Kathleen Heath; Katie Cashfield

Harold takes Albert to see Fellini's *8½*, although Albert would prefer to see *Nudes of 1964* at the theater next door.

Many laughs fill this idiosyncratic little episode, most of which derive from the usual clash of Albert's childishness juxtaposed against his son's affected intellectual airs. Indeed, taking Albert Steptoe to see a Fellini film is as difficult, if not worse, than taking a nine-year-old child. Compromise is averted early in the episode while the pair are still at home trying to decide which movie to see. All the choices that would have been acceptable (such as *Monster from the Black Bog*) are vetoed since Albert has already seen them at mid-week matinees (much to Harold's consternation since the old man should have been working).

With their film-going options pared considerably, the pair are left with only two: the foreign film or the nudie flick. There's some amusing byplay as Albert is already confused by the title *8½*, wanting to know "8½ what?" He logically reasons that the film might as well have been called 7¾, since it probably refers to Fellini's hat size.

The actual scene in the cinema is quite good, although somewhat predictable. Albert insists on talking during the film much to the annoyance of the other patrons and his embarrassed son. When he's not conversing in a stage whisper, Albert is going back and forth to the concession stand, eating ice cream, and slurping soft drinks. The best moments, however, result when the Steptoes manage to incite a near brawl among the other audience members, while momentarily retreating to the fringes of the imbroglio. Ultimately, of course, they are ejected from the theater, although for infractions committed by Harold, not his father. After giving his father the usual lecture on his lack of culture, Harold sends Albert off to see *Nudes of 1964*— only to surreptitiously follow him moments later in a good closing gag.

The title of the episode refers to a common phrase used for advertising films in Great Britain. Films usually change on the first day of the week and run until the following Saturday, hence the title.

EPISODE 6: "THE BONDS THAT BIND US" ★★½

Air date: February 11, 1964. Cast: Albert Steptoe (Wilfrid Brambell); Harold Steptoe (Harry H. Corbett); Madge (June Whitfield)

After winning £1,000 in the monthly bond sweepstakes, Albert decides to enjoy his windfall in a "bit of a spend up"— without Harold. After five days of high living, Albert returns with a 27-year-old gold digger to whom he is engaged. Harold must convince the girl that Albert is crazy to extricate his father from the affair.

Somewhat of a Cinderella story in Steptoe mode, "The Bonds That Bind Us" provides evidence toward the long-running debate as to whether breeding or environment ultimately shapes behavior. In this case, Galton and Simpson weigh in on the side of clothes making the man as Albert is transformed into a rather dapper and dignified gentleman, much to Harold's consternation and envy. The episode's strength lies primarily in the novelty of the situation and Brambell's performance than in any particular gags. Harold's frustration at Albert's behavior is laced with threats of revenge. These, however, melt into heartfelt sympathy when he realizes his father is in danger of being hurt.

An interesting montage sequence shows Albert's metamorphosis as he journeys to the fashionable West End and indulges himself in such luxuries as a hand-tailored suit, new false teeth, and a complete beauty makeover. That evening, he returns to the junkyard complete with derby and walking stick. At first, even Harold fails to recognize his transformed father, calling the dapper gentleman "sir."

Episode 7: "The Lodger" ★★★

Air date: February 18, 1964. Cast: Harold Steptoe (Harry H. Corbett); Albert Steptoe (Wilfrid Brambell)

In the throes of yet another slump in business, Albert decides they must take in a lodger. The move would necessitate Harold giving up his room and sleeping with Albert, so naturally he is adamantly opposed to it. Backing himself in a corner, Harold announces that if a lodger comes, he will move out. Albert calls Harold's bluff, causing the younger Steptoe to strike out on his own. Eventually, the pair are reluctantly reunited when they both discover they need each other.

Another two-man show, "The Lodger" explores the subject of Harold's pride or, rather, his loss of it. At least three times in this entertaining installment, Albert strips Harold of his dignity — twice when he is ready to surrender it on his own.

The mentions early in the episode to 1926 are references to the general strike called that year in England by the union leaders in an attempt to push through more liberal policies. While staunchly socialist, Harold faults his father for failing to help the revolt; Albert, always the confirmed capitalist, responds he was too busy making a fortune off the event to care.

There is also an amusing bit when Albert earnestly tries to devise a plan to lift them out of their financial woes; Harold can only mock his father's efforts. While Albert sits in a pose akin to Rodin's *Thinker*, Harold sarcastically announces this will be the birth of the Steptoe Empire and hails his father as the noblest "ragman of them all" on the verge of ushering in the "golden age of totting."

After Albert decides they need to hire out Harold's room with the father and son sharing Albert's bed, Harold protests that he needs his privacy. Albert asks why and wants to know what Harold is doing to warrant his solitude. Harold cautiously remarks he isn't doing anything, to which Albert responds that he has no need to be "on his own." Harold says he likes being alone, unless he has a girl over. His father asks if he has had girls up to his room. Harold admits he hasn't but always is hopeful. He adds that under the new arrangement any amorous aspirations would be futile as he would know that Albert was waiting in the bed, picking his toenails.

Series Four 1965

EPISODE 1: "AND AFTERWARDS AT ..." ★★★½

Air date: October 4, 1965. Cast: Harold Steptoe (Harry H. Corbett); Albert Steptoe (Wilfrid Brambell). With George A. Cooper; Rose Hill; Joan Newell; Mollie Sugden; Robert Webber; Karol Hagar; Rita Webb; Gretchen Franklin; Fred Hugh; Leslie Sarony; George Tovey; George Hirste; Betty Cardno; Margaret Flint; Gerald Rowland; James Bulloch; Tony Lambden

Harold's wedding to the young Melanie is interrupted when the bride refuses to say "I do," and a fight erupts at the altar. Later, back home, Harold tries to fathom why he was jilted, when his relatives descend en masse to drink, bicker, and try to reclaim their gifts. Ultimately, Harold and Albert get rid of their relations by throwing the wedding presents out the window.

After a hiatus of almost a year and a half, what was intended to be the final series of *Steptoe and Son* begins with an episode packed with laughs and, as usual, some pathos. Despite his usual machinations, Albert's plans to derail another of his son's romances has been thwarted, although he tries up until the last moment—whispering incitements to Harold to jilt his intended as they sit waiting in the church. At one point, Albert nods over to the mother of the bride (well played by a pre–Mrs. Slocombe Molly Sugden from *Are You Being Served?*) and remarks that that's what Harold's wife-to-be will look like in another 20 years. This having failed, Albert tries to paint a tumultuous picture of marriage, which he concludes with the observation that the scheduled hymn ("Fight the Good Fight") is particularly fitting. As humorous as these preliminaries are they escalate into a full-blown imbroglio when the bride refuses to wed the groom, resulting in Albert offering to fight the bride's overbearing mother. As Harold and Albert ride away from the church, Albert takes the opportunity to pelt the bride's family with celebratory rice turned into ammunition.

Corbett turns in another fine performance as the shocked Harold, who would merely like a few moments alone with himself to figure out why his life has come crashing down as it has. Of course, he doesn't get that opportunity with Albert's steady and often hilarious commentary on his views of marriage preventing Harold's attempts at contemplation.

This episode also marks the first appearance of the large rabble known as the Steptoe relatives. Usually descending as a throng, they move like a swarm of locusts — only not quite as welcome. Aside from this abortive nuptial appearance, they are most often at their best at funerals as attested to in "Oh, What a Beautiful Mourning."

EPISODE 2: "CROSSED SWORDS" ★★½

Air date: October 11, 1965. Cast: Harold Steptoe (Harry H. Corbett); Albert Steptoe (Wilfrid Brambell). With Derek Nimmo; Basil Dignam; Mark Singleton; Ralph Nossek; Tim Buckland; Philip Howard; William Raynor; Frank Littlewood; Peter Thompson

Harold is ecstatic when he brings home a valuable 200-year-old porcelain figurine. Despite Albert's protestations, Harold rejects the offer of £250 from a West End antique dealer. Taking the piece to auction, Harold and Albert try to shill the price up, only to wind up with it themselves when their plan backfires. Back at home, Albert accidentally breaks the figurine while cleaning it.

"Crossed Swords" (the title refers to a quality mark on the porcelain) is a rather predictable examination of greed and the ultimate misery caused by the vice. Harold senses his find of such an exquisite figurine is a once-in-a-lifetime occurrence and is determined to make an exorbitant profit. Although it is evident from the start that somehow this rare objet d'art is destined to be smashed by the hapless Steptoes, the path to this conclusion manages to remain amusing.

There is a good opening sequence in which Albert accidentally gets trapped in the outside karsi (toilet) when a load of junk falls down and blocks the door. With nothing else to do, Albert tries to while away the hours by reading the squares of newspaper that serve as lavatory paper. Unfortunately, most of the more interesting stories are continued outside of the 3" by 3" sheets only adding to his frustration.

The visit to the antique shop is also quite funny, with Harold trying to affect a dignified air, while Albert greedily eyes the merchandise. Before the proprietor arrives, Harold advises his father not to get "tarry fingered," adding Albert is getting a reputation as "Steptoe the Klepto." Albert insists on his innocence but then tries to steal the shop's counter bell.

EPISODE 3: "THOSE MAGNIFICENT MEN AND THEIR HEATING MACHINES" ★★½

Air date: October 18, 1965. Cast: Albert Steptoe (Wilfrid Brambell); Harold Steptoe (Harry H. Corbett)

Disregarding Albert's protestations that he is not up to the task, Harold attempts to install central heating in the Steptoe home.

A return to ground explored in "The Bath," "Those Magnificent Men and Their Heating Machines" is an enjoyable if somewhat predicable installment of Steptoe lore. Its main weakness is its reliance on some mechanical apparatus (Harold's Rube Goldberg–esque interpretation of a steam heating system) to provide the main thrust of the comic climax.

Much better are the show's opening moments in which Harold mistakenly believes that Albert has killed himself by putting his head in the oven (he was only cleaning it, but he knocked himself out with a bump to the head). Guilt ridden, Harold feverishly attempts to revive his father. First, he considers giving Albert the "kiss of life" via mouth-to-mouth resuscitation. After a moment spent pondering Albert's scruffy mouth, Harold thinks better of the notion, flips the old man over, and revives him by straddling Albert's back and pumping air into him. Once Albert is brought to and the truth is revealed, Harold jumps from relief to anger and then back to his usual pattern of abuse.

There is some amusement to be had of Harold's heating system. Since the Steptoe villa is built on a concrete slab, Harold is forced to run the hot water pipes above floor level. Soon tubes and pipes are crisscrossing the house, blocking doorways and creating an overall eyesore. The best of this occurs when Harold decides to forgo the use of a radiator in Albert's room, deciding instead to use his father's hollow brass bed frame as the conduit for the hot water.

EPISODE 4: "THE SIEGE OF STEPTOE STREET" ★★★½

Air date: October 25, 1965. Cast: Harold Steptoe (Harry H. Corbett); Albert Steptoe (Wilfrid Brambell). With Robert Dorning; Lane Meddick; Edwin Brown; Bill Maxam; Charles Bird; Stan Simmons

A financial crisis in the Steptoe household forces Albert and Harold to barricade themselves in their home rather than be served summonses by an army of creditors.

A wonderfully funny offering and one that sheds more than a little light on the secret lives of Albert and Harold. As they sort out their mountain of past due bills (carefully separating them into two categories: "legal proceedings" and "final demands"), the pair accuse each other of being too extravagant, a claim that seems odd in view of their apparent lifestyle. Albert strikes the first blow, claiming that Harold has spent a small fortune on fragrances and body lotions to make himself attractive to the opposite sex. Rather than accomplishing the desired effect, Albert calls his son a "great Jessie" and remarks that the concoctions leave him smelling like an "Algerian brothel."

Harold tries to defend himself, until he notices that his father has been charging grouse, salmon, and steak on a regular basis, all the while feeding

Harold sausages and pigs' trotters. In addition, Harold discovers the old man is hiding an application to the Bunny Club in his wallet.

From this strong start, the comedy escalates to new heights when the creditors arrive en masse. Locking themselves inside the house, the Steptoes soon discover that their only provisions are a can of snails and another containing asparagus tips. Rather than give up, the pair defiantly dig in, as Harold lobs insults through the door, accusing the creditors of taking advantage of his father's insanity. To prove his contention, Harold puts a Napoleon hat on Albert and shoves him outside to sing the French national anthem.

In typical Steptoe fashion, Albert manages to turn their liabilities into profits by the end of the episode via a rather incorrigible ploy. At first, Harold deplores the ruse, but he soon warms to it, since it means a first-class nosh at a nearby Chinese restaurant.

A few inconsistencies crop up in "The Siege of Steptoe Street" but nothing that actually spoils the fun. The first is Harold's distaste at lying to his creditors. Apparently, he has developed some scruples since similarly fleecing his friends in "Wallah, Wallah, Catsmeat." In addition, Albert happily suggests they celebrate their outcome at the Chinese restaurant — after disdainfully rejecting similar cuisine in "Sixty-Five Today."

Episode 5: "A Box in Town" ★★½

Air date: November 1, 1965. Cast: Harold Steptoe (Harry H. Corbett); Albert Steptoe (Wilfrid Brambell). Featuring: Yootha Joyce; Marjorie Rhodes; Freda Bamford; Annie Leake; Hilda Barry.

After Albert intrudes once too often on his love life, Harold decides to rent a one-room flat.

Harold Steptoe finally breaks loose from his father. While threatening it from the first episode ("The Offer") and almost getting free in "Homes Fit for Heroes," Harold finally achieves his quest. Fortunately, and of course predictably, Harold's taste of freedom is not as sweet as he imagines and is therefore short-lived. The events leading up to Harold's departure (his attempt at wooing a girl in the yard at midnight and his confrontation with Albert) are somewhat forced and thus not very satisfying.

The real fun begins when Harold moves into his tiny, top story, walk-up flat. Ignoring the imposing view of the gasworks, Harold dubs his aerie a "penthouse" and immediately makes plans to get a date to take advantage of his new privacy. This soon proves to be harder than his lifelong attempt to free himself from his father. Albert, on the other hand, soon has more women than he can handle. In an amusing montage, he widely divergent plights of father and son are illustrated as Harold pines away in his flat, while Albert has no fewer than three women fighting for his affections. In the ending, which is surprisingly sweet for a *Steptoe* entry, both men are longing for the former status quo.

Yootha Joyce returns as Harold's date, Avis, after previously appearing as Delia in "The Bath." Apparently, Joyce is Harold's type of "bird" since both encounters with her have driven him to extreme efforts to get alone with her.

One note of trivia: while the Steptoes' home on Oil Drum Lane in Shepherd's Bush is a fictitious address, Harold's flat is not. He gives his address as 19 St. George's. Fans who might want to track that address down have a rather long search, however, since there are more than 50 streets, ways, and lanes honoring the dragon slayer in the London area.

Episode 6: "My Old Man's a Tory" ★★★

Air date: November 8, 1965. Cast: Harold Steptoe (Harry H. Corbett); Albert Steptoe (Wilfrid Brambell). Featuring: Dudley Foster. With Damaris Hayman; Howard Douglas; Evelyn Lund; Peter Thompson

Partisan politics splits the Steptoe household when Labourite Harold holds a party ward meeting at home despite Tory Albert's protests.

Often mentioned in other episodes, the political ideologies of Steptoe and son take center stage in this enjoyable series entry. The first half of the episode is primarily a political debate between Albert's Conservative (or Tory) party stance and Harold's Labour party affiliation.

One doesn't need to be an expert on British politics to understand most of the jokes since the basic conservative/liberal polarity now familiar in the United States was even more clearly defined in 1960s England. Indeed, the same arguments being used today (for example, excessive taxes versus compassionate social programs) are hurled back and forth by Albert and Harold. At one point, Harold says that his only regret in Labour's record is that its health care initiatives were probably what had kept Albert alive all these years. Aside from this complaint, Harold affirms that his political stance was formed after years of deep contemplation and careful research, while he swears Albert is only a Tory to fulfill a "basic desire to get right up my shonker."

The second half of the episode features Harold's ward meeting at which he hopes to become the official Labour candidate for the local council seat. Albert is against the meeting, primarily on financial reasons since holding a Labour meeting will alienate their Tory customers, who, he reasons, have a better grade of junk. Harold's dreams of political power (not to mention his aspiration that their home will evolve into something of a political and intellectual powerhouse) come quickly crashing down when the agent from party headquarters announces that they have decided to endorse another candidate. Ironically, given Harold's working-class motivation, the "comrades" have chosen a prominent physician to attract more middle-class voters.

Episode 7: "Pilgrim's Progress" ★★★★

Air date: November 15, 1965. Cast: Harold Steptoe (Harry H. Corbett); Albert Steptoe (Wilfrid Brambell). Featuring: Alan Gifford; Frank Thornton. With Sidonie Bond; Frederick Schiller; Catharina Ferraz; Tim Buckland

Harold takes Albert back to France to tour First World War battlefields and ends up waging new warfare against old allies on the plane to Paris.

When it first aired in November 1965, "Pilgrim's Progress" was slated to be the final entry in the Steptoe saga. As such, this riotous episode serves its predecessors well, providing good solid laughter from start to end.

Harold is taking the old man back to Flanders so that Albert may relive the one great adventure of his youth. He is appalled, however, to find that Albert is waiting to leave dressed in his old uniform complete with rifle and fixed bayonet. In a brief but poignant moment, Harold dissuades his father from wearing the outfit, reasoning that people will laugh at him. Instead, Albert decides to just wear his medals, even though Harold had thought he had returned them in protest when the Beatles were awarded the M.B.E. (Member of the British Empire) earlier in the year (as many decorated veterans had done).

The fun escalates when they board the plane for Paris and Albert confesses he is afraid to fly. Harold delights in taunting the novice flyer with horror stories about the perils of being sucked out of airplane windows due to the cabin being pressurized. Albert gets back some of his own by threatening to put spiders and earwigs in his son's bed upon their return to England, a thought that drives Harold to skittish distraction.

Finally, Albert winds up getting into a debate with an American and a French veteran of WWI on their lack of real support to the war effort. In a hilarious exchange, the elder Steptoe accuses the Americans of always getting to wars too late and the French of always giving up too early. The heated discussion turns physical when Albert accuses the mademoiselles of France as being too easy. Ultimately, father and son return home after spending a night in a French jail and being deported after Albert called the magistrate "an old French poof."

Frank Thornton provides his usual strong support as the French veteran who challenges Albert to a duel on the way to Paris.

Series Five 1970

Episode 1: "A Death in the Family" ★★★★

Air date: March 6, 1970. Cast: Albert Steptoe (Wilfrid Brambell); Harold Steptoe (Harry H. Corbett)

After their cart horse, Hercules, dies, the Steptoes must cope with the loss.

Back after an absence of almost five years, *Steptoe and Son* returns to the harness as strong as it departed with this excellent installment. Aside from the addition of color (unfortunately, none of the fifth season exists in color thanks to the great BBC wipe of its old tapes in the late 1970s), Galton, Simpson, Brambell, and Corbett all return as if they had been away only a week or two. (Indeed, Harold Steptoe is still not 39, even though he was 37 years old in 1962.) Alas, the only nod to the passing of the years is the faithful Hercules, who succumbs to a heart attack on the streets of London after 39 years of loyal service. Still, Hercules' passing makes excellent fodder for the *Steptoe* blend of comedy and drama.

The episode begins with Hercules' death, leaving Harold openly weeping on the street as they cart the horse away to the abattoir (incongruously, some in the studio audience saw fit to laugh at this). Once Harold breaks the tragic news to Albert, however, his mourning is over while his father's is just beginning. Harold is interested in buying a replacement horse, while Albert considers the notion of this near sacrilege. He chooses instead to make the house and indeed the business a sort of shrine to his departed beast. Although always intimated (especially in such episodes as "Wallah, Wallah, Catsmeat"), Albert's devotion to Hercules is fully explained here. It seems that Albert brought the horse into the world (born the same day as Princess Margaret) and counted the animal as his best and only friend. Harold especially takes umbrage at his father's contention that Hercules was more "like a son than a horse." Albert is also stunned that Harold had the animal "knackered" since he had a plot reserved for Hercules in the animal cemetery. Instead, the old man points out, he is fated to be served up on a plate in a Belgian restaurant — or worse, in tins of catsmeat (later, Harold is hilariously haunted by a cat food commercial).

Ultimately, the entire affair lands Albert in bed, refusing nourishment in order to join his departed pal. Only a medical emergency with the new horse, Samson (soon changed to Delilah when the nature of the animal's condition comes to light), renews the elder Steptoe's interest in life.

Amidst the poignancy, there are more than enough laughs to sustain the proceedings. Especially humorous are Albert's boasts that Hercules always paid his own way (the sale of his manure paid for his oats) and the taunt that Harold Wilson (the Labour prime minister) "don't do that, do he?" Another standout is Albert asks if Harold tried mouth-to-mouth resuscitation to revive Hercules, to which his son replies that even Mick Jagger's mouth is not big enough for that task.

EPISODE 2: "A WINTER'S TALE" ★★★

Air date: March 13, 1970. Cast: Albert Steptoe (Wilfrid Brambell); Harold Steptoe (Harry H. Corbett)

Harold books an alpine skiing holiday in Obergurgl — without Albert. Hampered by a fairly routine first half, "A Winter's Tale" finishes strongly with a delightful finale full of good physical comedy and clever dialogue. Harold reveals to his father that he has used a grant from the local council (given to provide them with an indoor toilet) to go for a winter holiday in Austria. What ensues is the usual Steptoe exchange concerning Harold's need for independence, however brief, versus Albert's need for his son's constant companionship. There is little in this argument that hasn't been visited before — most in season one's "The Holiday." Still, Galton and Simpson do add a few new twists (most notably a routine featuring Albert's habit of following Harold from room to room). There is also some humor to be had when Harold justifies his trip by saying it may actually cause him to be pleased to see Albert upon his return — then adds that this effect could last for at least a few days.

The fun begins in earnest when Albert resigns himself to the fact that Harold is leaving for his ski trip. This allows the old man to shift from his victim mode to his sarcastic commentator role. Harold enthusiastically builds a practice ski ramp from the top of the stable across the junkyard. Outfitted with his collection of ski gear obtained piecemeal on his rounds (including two skis of differing lengths), Harold struggles to move around the yard. Albert is left to read — not instructions on how to ski — corny travel brochure copy on "a day in the life of a ski bird." Harold fairly drools at his prospects — not for winter sports but for "crumpet."

All this comes to a marvelous crescendo as Harold scales the ladder — at first with his skis on — to make his trial run down Mount Steptoe. He pauses to note that Obergurgl has a ski lift, to which Albert retorts that he didn't imagine they had a giant ladder propped up the side of the slope. Quite predictably, but still wonderfully comic, Harold's only trip down his ramp leaves him with a broken leg and Albert with an all-expenses-paid trip to Austria.

EPISODE 3: "ANY OLD IRON" ★★★★

Air date: March 20, 1970. Cast: Albert Steptoe (Wilfrid Brambell); Harold Steptoe (Harry H. Corbett). Featuring: Richard Hurndall; Valerie Bell; Roger Avon

When a posh antique dealer starts visiting on a regular basis, Albert insists the man is a homosexual after Harold, while Harold contends their relationship is purely aesthetic and platonic.

Quite a daring excursion into a topic that would have been taboo in the first four seasons of *Steptoe and Son* in the early sixties, "Any Old Iron" explores its subject with little of the delicacy or sympathy afforded it in more recent decades, reflecting the attitudes of the day. Still, the situation is basically a vehicle for one of the standard Steptoe plots: Albert's experience in the ways of the world versus Harold's naïve blindness to an obvious situation. That the antique dealer, Timothy Stanhope (ably played by Richard Hurndall), is interested in

Harold is clear to everyone but the intended date. The process is similar to "Full House" from the second series, in which Harold foolishly ignores the old man's warning about the band of card sharks.

The first scenes in which Timothy courts Harold are laced with some funny innuendo, made all the more amusing by Harold's staunch refusal to believe his father's interpretation of the visitor's true intentions. There are also some good moments as Harold futilely tries to keep up his end of a conversation with Timothy on antiques. At one point he tries to urbanely agree with Timothy's assessment of the state of furniture by noting that after Chippendale "they turned out a lot of old crap!" Of course, his embarrassing faux pas on the subject are glossed over, since Timothy's main interest is not in Harold's mind.

The biggest laughs in the episode are reserved for Harold's preparations for his date with Timothy. For the occasion. Harold has unwittingly transformed himself into the early seventies version of the stereotypical gay man, complete with shoulder bag and floppy hat. Against Albert's pleas, Harold insists they are just friends. Before Harold leaves, however, Albert insists on giving his son a club to put in his "handbag" and advises him as one would a daughter going on a risky date.

Albert, for his part, although right in his assessment of the situation, is his usual coarse self, liberally using such pejoratives as "poof" and "iron hoof," the Cockney rhyming slang for the same term (hence the episode's title). Indeed, Harold accuses his father of having "poof-mania," evidently the precursor to homophobia.

In the end, Harold realizes Timothy's intentions and runs wildly through the streets to the flat of Dolly Miller, in a frantic dash to reassert his heterosexuality. Valerie Bell, who appears as the amorous Dolly Miller played the title character, Roxanne, in the first season's "The Bird."

EPISODE 4: "STEPTOE AND SON—AND SON!" ★★★★

Air date: March 27, 1970. Cast: Albert Steptoe (Wilfrid Brambell); Harold Steptoe (Harry H. Corbett). Featuring: Ann Beach; Glynn Edwards

A pregnant girl arrives on the Steptoes' doorstep and announces that Harold is the father of her baby. Harold makes preparations to marry her, despite the fact that she is a total stranger.

Simultaneously poignant and hilarious, "Steptoe and Son — And Son!" is about another subject (like the previous episode) that might not have been explored in the earlier run of the series. By the early seventies however, the social stigma attached to out-of-wedlock pregnancies was quickly evaporating, thus clearing the way for the topic to be used in a situation comedy format (although *Steptoe and Son* did touch upon the subject in series three's excellent "Steptoe a La Cart").

Here, Harold is visited by Daphne Tomlin, an almost total stranger he encountered at a party eight months previously. Despite Albert's attempts to get rid of Daphne and her forthcoming child, Harold nobly decides to own up to his responsibilities and marry the girl, even though he doesn't recall actually having sex with her. Corbett's performance is quite moving: Harold confesses he had given up hope of marrying and having a family, and now he joyously embraces it in spite of its unexpected arrival. Even Albert warms to the notion after the sweet Daphne offers to name the child after him if it is a boy. By the following day, both generations of Steptoes are happily cooing over baby clothes, although Harold refuses to let his grimy father actually touch the garments. In typical Steptoe fashion, this anticipation of felicity is quickly pulled out of their reach when the real father is revealed. Uncharacteristically, the episode ends with both leads choking back their tears and leaving to get drunk. The pain and disappointment is deep, and any closing laugh would have been terribly out of place.

The ending aside, there is plenty of amusement in the installment. Most of the laughs come in the first half, with Albert getting most of the punch lines. When Harold arrives home, Daphne is already waiting in the living room unbeknownst to him. Albert rushes out to the hallway to try and waylay his son. Before Albert can inform him of his visitor, Harold happily announces he's had a good day on the rounds and has a cartload out in the yard. Albert soberly tells him that he's got "a pramload in there," motioning to the living room. Later, when Harold discovers that his father has been reading his private diary, a Steptoe feud erupts. In mid-scream Harold stops, looks to the expectant Daphne, and politely begs her pardon momentarily, before resuming his tirade. The best comedy comes when Albert disapproves of Harold's agreement to marry Daphne. With the bride-to-be looking on, Harold chokes the old man in order to wrest a "look of joy" and a heartfelt congratulation out of him.

EPISODE 5: "THE COLOUR PROBLEM" ★★½

Air date: April 3, 1970. Cast: Albert Steptoe (Wilfrid Brambell); Harold Steptoe (Harry H. Corbett). Featuring: Anthony Sharp; Geoffrey Adams; Carmel Cryan

Albert fakes amnesia in order to wrangle a new color television set out of Harold.

Predictable in its plotting, "The Colour Problem" fails to exploit a theme, which is touched upon, central to the show's basic concept; it is quickly ignored in favor of a rather standard sitcom outline. The tension in the episode is between Harold's desire to buy a used sports car with his hard-earned money and Albert's longing for a color television set. Harold refuses, leaving Albert no alternative but to leave home. The following day, the police come to inform Harold that the old man is in the hospital suffering from amnesia. Failing to see through his father's rather transparent ploy, Harold sells the car at a loss and buys the set. Only after he has secured the set does Albert slip, letting Harold realize the illness was a ruse.

Before the device of Albert's amnesia is introduced, there are some good moments as Albert cajoles his son for the color set. The old man is tired of watching their 1937 TV (yes, the BBC did have a fledgling television service back then) through an oversized magnifying glass. Albert insists, almost as a child does, that if he had his new set he would never ask for another thing in all his life. The main obstacle to Albert's dream is Harold's own desire for a car. He, like his father concerning the TV, believes a sports car is the only missing piece to happiness and satisfaction. When Albert points out the impracticality of the auto, Harold reveals that the machine would only be bait for sex. This leads to an interesting remembrance by Albert of his own experiences in his youth with a sports car and romantic weekend trips to Brighton. Harold delights in his father's tales, clearly envisioning his own similar chances of success, while it is obvious that, as in their other father-son competitions, Harold is doomed to failure in his father's wake.

From this point, the plot slips into the usual (though still played better than average) sitcom standard. One wishes that perhaps Harold might have gotten away for his weekend, only to find that he could not follow in Albert's footsteps. It is somewhat interesting to learn that, in the throes of his self-inflicted disease, Albert's only fond recollections are for the recently departed Hercules. It is also noteworthy that, upon being brought home, the usually status quo Albert's first reaction to their home through his amnesia-clouded eyes is "Gor blimey, what a dump!"

It is ironic that while this episode is centered on a color television and was recorded in color, today it only exists in monochrome. Still, in Britain of 1970, most viewers would have watched this episode on black-and-white sets, since color sets were a novelty.

EPISODE 6: "T.B., OR NOT T.B.?" ★★★

Air date: April 10, 1970. Cast: Albert Steptoe (Wilfrid Brambell); Harold Steptoe (Harry H. Corbett). Featuring: Sidonie Bond; Lala Lloyd

When the Steptoes go for chest X-rays, Harold convinces himself that he is dying of tuberculosis.

"T.B., or Not T.B.?" features strong performances, particularly by Corbett, which help to elevate the proceedings into a better-than-average episode. The entry is somewhat schizophrenic, featuring a much livelier, joke-laden first half followed by a more introspective, although humorous finale.

The opening spotlights Harold's insistence that his father go for a free chest X-ray. Apparently, although it has never been prominently featured previously, Albert is a chain-smoker (Harold figures that the old man has smoked the equivalent of a 42-mile-long cigarette since he took up the habit at the age of eight and a half). Albert is loath to participate in the screening and is forced by his son down to the van the following morning.

After a lively exchange with the clinic's nurses, the Steptoes return home to await the results. At first, Albert is terrified that he is dying until he realizes they have sent Harold's results in his envelope. Harold has been notified to return for another test due to a technical error. Picking up on his father's paranoia, Harold is convinced this is just a gentle way to tell him he is dying. What follows is a wonderfully melodramatic bit as Harold goes into Camille mode (complete with silk robe and flowing chiffon hankie) while he awaits his return to the hospital. Albert contributes to the farce by carefully marking all the plates and utensils that Harold uses so as not to be accidentally contaminated by them. After a tearful farewell, Harold trudges off to hospital convinced he will never again see Shepherd's Bush. When Harold returns home to announce his tests were clear, he finds Albert reading the will he left behind. To make matters worse, in his brief absence, his father has already burned his bed and his clothes.

Albert's general fear of everything connected with modern health care makes for some amusing bits. He especially is worried that excessive X-rays will turn him into a monster, to which Harold counters, "Wwhat do you mean 'turn'?" Albert is also bothered by Harold's insistence that he put on clean underwear for the tests. Harold explains this is only to give the machine a fair chance of getting through the garments. Still, Albert manages to go beyond his paranoia long enough to embarrass Harold in front of the clinic's pretty nurse. Harold is especially humiliated by Albert's confession that his son has had a previous X-ray necessitated a few years earlier when the horse kicked him in his "gentiles."

Episode 7: "Men of Property" — Not available for viewing

Air date: April 17, 1970.

The Steptoes are in jeopardy of losing their Oil Drum Lane abode when they learn that the property is actually under a 99-year lease, which is about to expire.

While "Men of Property," long thought lost in the great BBC wipe of the 1970s has been rumored to be found, the episode is still not available to the public as of this writing. Fortunately, like most of the second series of *Dad's Army*, the installment was adapted for the radio.

Series Six 1970

Episode 1: "Robbery with Violence" ★★½

Air date: November 2, 1970. Cast: Albert Steptoe (Wilfrid Brambell); Harold Steptoe (Harry H. Corbett). Featuring: Dudley Foster; Edward Evans; Graham Ashley; Michael Stainton; James McManus

Albert fakes a robbery at home to conceal the fact that he has accidentally broken Harold's collection of porcelain figurines.

A lesser entry in the Steptoe saga, "Robbery with Violence" gets off to a slow start before gaining some momentum toward its close. The opening scenes, in which Albert knocks over Harold's curio cabinet and concocts his scheme to blame it on burglars fall somewhat flat. Unfortunately, like the previous season's "T.B., or Not T.B.?" the best interaction is not between the title characters but between Albert and an outsider. In this case, familiar *Steptoe* alumnus Dudley Foster ("Full House" and "My Old Man's a Tory") in the role of the police inspector serves well as the old man's foil.

Realizing that Harold will not believe that the breaking of his objets d'art was accidental, Albert ransacks his own home before knocking himself out with a fireplace poker. When Harold revives his father, Albert spins a tale wherein he battles six hulking burglars in stocking masks. Of course, the fanciful yarn begins to fray a bit under scrutiny by the police but not enough to keep Albert from becoming a local hero and celebrity for his valor. It is only in the conclusion that Harold uncovers the broken porcelain and the truth.

The funniest moments come during the police questioning. The inspector asks Albert if the criminals said anything while they were wrestling with him. After a moment's reflection Albert recalls that one yelled, "Oooh! He's kicked me in the ghoulies!" The policeman clarifies his inquiry, asking if any of the perpetrators mentioned the others by name. Unfortunately, the only names Albert can come up with are Tom, Dick, and Harry. Later, Albert recalls that five of the men were skinheads with the final one being a Pakistani. Aside from the well-known loathing of skinheads for foreigners, the inspector wonders how Albert could tell through a stocking mask that one was from Pakistan. Albert thinks a moment then remembers that the Pakistani wore a turban atop his stocking.

For some reason, the set of "Robbery with Violence" is much less cluttered than the usual view of the Steptoe parlor. It is so clear of the usual junk that it almost looks like the set for a series in its seminal pilot stage. This may have been done to focus attention on the damaged antiques, which might have otherwise been lost in the usual piles of junk around the Steptoe home.

Episode 2: "Come Dancing" ★★★★

Air date: November 9, 1970. Cast: Albert Steptoe (Wilfrid Brambell); Harold Steptoe (Harry H. Corbett). Featuring: Tony Melody

Albert teaches Harold to dance in order to help him win a girl.

Simply marvelous, "Come Dancing" is the earliest episode that survives intact in its original color format (the previous color episodes only exist in black-and-white versions). The installment builds steadily to a wonderful surprise punch line with many good routines along the way.

The opening quarter features a monologue by Corbett on the boredom of the average Sunday afternoon. While Albert snores away on the sofa, Harold wonders if Sundays were similarly dull for Henry VIII at Hampton Court. From here, his restlessness strays to a variety of subjects, including strangling Albert in his sleep and trying to silence the cuckoo clock. While Harold is nailing the clock door shut, Albert finally awaken and adds to the proceedings.

Sensing his son is troubled, Albert guesses a variety of causes, from tired blood to irregularity. He urges Harold to visit some pubs (especially the Ship and Shovel, where reportedly Harold is a regular contestant in the talent contest with his impression of Tom Jones) but to no avail. Finally, Albert realizes Harold's mood is due to girl trouble. Embarrassed, Harold confesses that he has fallen in love with a girl who loves to dance in competition, but he can't dance. Albert, not surprisingly (since he excels at everything his son struggles with), is an excellent dancer, and offers to teach Harold.

The dance instruction scenes are very funny thanks to the incongruous sight of the two Steptoes waltzing around the room. The next morning, the pair are still at it in the throes of a sensuous tango, when they are surprised by the arrival of the milkman. This, along with Albert's interpretation of the Cha-cha-cha, is priceless.

After eight days of intensive study, Harold is ready for the dance competition. He leaves home, complete with white tie and tails, to win the woman of his dreams. Before going, however, he gives his heartfelt gratitude to Albert for helping him. Albert too is gladdened by the fact that he is finally able to help his son. One senses a whole new kinship is forming between the former adversaries. Of course, in best Steptoe fashion, any hope of a better relationship is only presented to be dashed. Harold returns from the contest in shame after dancing backwards away from his partner since Albert only taught him the woman's role. The son bemoans the fact that after more than a week of lessons the only person he can dance with is his father.

Episode 3: "Two's Company" ★★★½

Air date: November 16, 1970. Cast: Albert Steptoe (Wilfrid Brambell); Harold Steptoe (Harry H. Corbett). Featuring: Jean Kent

Albert brings home his fiancée to meet Harold, but Harold and his would-be stepmother have apparently already met.

The Steptoe love-hate relationship usually resides primarily in the second half of that equation. Every so often, however, proof is provided that there is indeed a tender side to the father and son duo. "Two's Company" provides ample evidence in an episode that is simultaneously humorous, touching, and quite revealing.

The episode seems to start off by treading previously explored territory (even Harold admits as much), with Albert telling his son that he plans to get married again. In fact, the first ten minutes seem like a replay of season two's "The Stepmother," and one quickly wonders if Galton and Simpson aren't perhaps slipping. Not to worry, for if there is any stumbling to be done here, it is we over such preconceived judgments. The argument over Albert getting married quickly dissolves as Harold admits he is just being selfish and defers to his father's grasp for happiness.

In true Steptoe fashion, on the rare occasion when the two men are not conspiring against one an other, circumstances will step in to do it for them. The next evening, Albert brings his intended home to meet Harold, and immediately it is evident that something is amiss. From the moment the woman, Mrs. Goodlace, enters the room neither she nor Harold can take their eyes off the other. At first, the guess is that Harold is attracted to the widow, surprised as we all are by the fact that she is closer to his age than to the old man's. The truth finally comes out when Albert, almost beside himself with joy that the two seem to be getting along, goes out to call for a cab. It seems that Harold and Mrs. Goodlace were passionately in love with each other 20 years earlier but were separated when he was sent to Malaysia with the army.

The couple debate whether or not to tell Albert of their past. Mrs. Goodlace, although she admits that she doesn't love Albert, does not want to see him hurt. She reasons that the shock would kill him. "He ain't got long to go anyway," Harold reasons.

In the end, Harold explains the situation to his father. While both men gingerly step around each other's feelings, Mrs. Goodlace silently retreats. She leaves a note explaining that she couldn't marry either man since they are already wed. Neither Harold nor Albert understand the meaning of the note, but they perfectly illustrate their deep commitment to each other by acting like a long-time married couple as they exit.

"Two's Company" is so rich in plot that its premise launched its own series 20 years later. I doubt whether writer Bob Larbey consciously based his warm and funny *As Time Goes By* on this Steptoe gem, but all the elements are there.

Episode 4: "Tea for Two" ★½

Air date: November 23, 1970. Cast: Albert Steptoe (Wilfrid Brambell); Harold Steptoe (Harry H. Corbett). Featuring: Geoffrey Chater; Robert Raglan

Political tempers flare between Albert and Harold when Prime Minister Heath schedules a campaign visit to the Steptoe household.

A return to the theme of partisan politics Steptoe style as previous explored in "My Old Man's a Tory" from the fourth season, "Tea for Two" is for all intents and purposes a mirror image of that earlier episode. Here, instead of Harold entertaining his political soulmates, Albert has the honor—which, indeed, is an honor as he has been selected to host the prime minister for tea. In this installment, Harold, as his father previously, feels his political sensibilities are being violated by the visit and plans disruptive retaliation. The only difference is the form of the retaliation. Whereas Albert preferred to lob verbal shells at the Labour party gathering, Harold plans to entertain the Tory visitors stark naked.

As in "My Old Man's a Tory," the first ten minutes is primarily another Steptoe philosophical argument, which, although it is as sharp as ever, does suffer from having been presented before. Our interest is piqued a bit when the Tory politicos (one, played by Robert Raglan, should be familiar as the Colonel from *Dad's Army*) stop by to ask Albert to take part in their photo opportunity. Albert is delighted and immediately begins his preparations. There are some good moments here as the old man asks the politicians what sort of biscuits (cookies) the P.M. prefers or whether he'd rather have a fried egg sandwich with his tea.

By the time Harold returns to hear the news, Albert has redecorated their outdoor toilet facility, including wallpaper, carpeting (cut from the rug in Harold's room), and even toilet paper (a luxury never experienced before in their home). Harold is so impressed he considers moving into the toilet since it's nicer than any room in the house.

Unfortunately, this is the high point, since the episode ends with one of the Conservative party operatives stopping by to say Heath is behind schedule and is not coming. After the buildup, this ending provides an anticlimactic payoff.

EPISODE 5: "WITHOUT PREJUDICE" ★★★

Air date: November 30, 1970. Cast: Albert Steptoe (Wilfrid Brambell); Harold Steptoe (Harry H. Corbett). Featuring: Gerald Flood; Norman Bird. With Ernest Arnley; Tim Buckland; Philip Howard; Victor Harrington

The Steptoes' plan to move to a more affluent suburb is met with resistance from their would-be neighbors.

A simple, tidy little plot, well executed, makes "Without Prejudice" pleasant viewing. As focused as this series is on the intense interaction of its main characters, it is always a treat to see Harold and Albert venture forth from their immediate surroundings. This episode is no exception, giving Harold good opportunity to attempt to rise above his station and Albert ample chance to thwart these attempts. It is especially humorous to watch Harold carefully choose and recite his words while trying to impress his audience (in this case, an estate agent) then have his speeches fall like a house of cards when he stumbles and throws in a bit of lower-class slang.

The Steptoes' tour of their prospective home is filled with many funny touches, with Harold wanting to buy the property almost sight unseen and Albert trying to slash the asking price in half. At first, it seems as if the estate agent is loath to sell the house to such a pair of scruffs, but he soon warms to the idea as something of a practical joke on the snooty neighbors. It is an especially delicious notion when he (and we) learn that father and son plan to use their new home as the future location of their rag-and-bone business. Albert worries that the horse will ruin the oak parquet floors, while Harold plans on filling the back garden with their stock of junk (save for a small patch reserved for a genteel arrangement of cement ducklings he promised to Albert).

The neighbors get the full measure of the Steptoes when the horse is found munching on the hedge, and Albert is seen screaming from the bathroom for Harold to get him out after he has locked himself in the "karsi." On the way out, Albert manages to shock a rather dignified matron with intimations of a future affair. Not surprisingly, the next day the residents, association visits the Steptoes and offers to buy them off. Albert quickly negotiates a price, but Harold is outraged and ashamed. His mortification, however, only lasts as long as it takes for him to realize, with Albert's help, that they can repeat the money-making ruse throughout posh streets all over London.

Any fans of the series who would like clues to where exactly in Shepherd's Bush the Steptoe yard was located would get a few from this episode. First, it would have to be adjacent to an elevated highway, as shown in the show's opening shot (the vibrations from the highway were also the primary cause of the roof's leaking). This would almost certainly be the West Cross Route, the M41. Second, Oil Drum Lane (a fictitious address) is said to be approximately a half mile down the road from the BBC Television Centre at White City (Harold hopes a producer from the BBC will want to buy their house once it goes on the market).

EPISODE 6: "POT BLACK" ★★★★

Air date: December 7, 1970. Cast: Albert Steptoe (Wilfrid Brambell); Harold Steptoe (Harry H. Corbett). With George Tovey

When Harold buys a billiard table, an epic tournament evolves to determine the Steptoe snooker champion.

A grand exploration of one of the basic *Steptoe* themes: Harold's quest to do something better than his father. Fancying himself as something of an expert at billiards, Harold purchases a used table. He first envisions the table as a means to bring gentility to their home, as he dreams of evenings including snooker, port, and urbane conversation. With this in mind, Harold awaits delivery of the table dressed in formal billiards attire complete with silk vest and bow tie.

The first major delight of the episode comes with the delivery of the full-size table, which fills the Steptoes' lounge with only a tiny pathway around it. Soon Harold is forced to admit that his father was right and that the room is too small for a regulation-sized table. He outlines an elaborate plan to expand the house, but Albert suggests they merely need to drill holes along the walls to accommodate the backswings of the cue sticks.

As ludicrous as these scenes are, they are only the appetizer for the main course. Despite the crammed playing venue, Harold begins to boast about his billiards prowess. This naturally leads to the assertion that at last the son has found something at which he can best his father. This in turn leads to a game, which leads to a battle royal of billiards.

Despite the fact that Albert hasn't played in more than 40 years, he still manages to beat his son thanks to some truly horrible shots by Harold. Soon, complaining of the cramped confines of their parlor, Harold has the table moved into the yard, and the tournament continues into the wee hours. Finally, Albert lets Harold win, but only after it begins to storm. Harold is exultant but fails to see the hollowness of his victory.

The performances of the principals in "Pot Black" are excellent as many deep-seated psychological aspects of this relationship come to the fore cloaked in comic guise. The construction of the episode is very good as well, particularly the montage used to display the mammoth billiards contest. The billiards games were played by Sydney Lee and are by themselves enjoyable and sometimes amazing to watch.

EPISODE 7: "THE THREE FEATHERS" ★½

Air date: December 14, 1970. Cast: Albert Steptoe (Wilfrid Brambell); Harold Steptoe (Harry H. Corbett). Featuring: John Arnatt; John Bailey

Harold is convinced he has made a windfall when he finds a nineteenth-century Regency commode once owned by the prince regent. Unfortunately, the piece is only a modern reproduction set out as bait by a team of con men.

A fairly transparent scam comedy, "The Three Feather," is another example of Harold's greed getting the best of him as in series four's "Crossed Swords." As in that episode, Harold's avarice is contrasted with Albert's supposed honesty, although this virtue on the part of the old man rings hollow given his track record. Still, Albert does have a degree of wisdom that usually gives him the knack to know when to be honest, even if his display of probity appears disingenuous.

The actual confidence theme takes up a little more than half of the episode. The rest of the running time is filled with a rather protracted gag concerning Albert getting stuck in the lotus position while practicing yoga. The best comedy occurs as Harold proudly exhibits the commode to his father. Albert is impressed by the seeming quality of the cabinet but fails to understand what the piece of furniture's purpose is. Harold triumphantly slides out the drawer to reveal the pot.

"There's a po in it!" Albert cries in a mixture of shock and disgust. Upon further explanation by Harold on the function of commodes, Albert is surprised to discover the absence of a chain on the item. When Harold gives a history of the item, including the use of commodes by royalty behind screens at formal dinners, Albert can merely conclude they were all "dirty devils" back then.

EPISODE 8: "CUCKOO IN THE NEST" ★★

Air date: December 20, 1970. Cast: Albert Steptoe (Wilfrid Brambell); Harold Steptoe (Harry H. Corbett). Featuring: Kenneth J. Warren; with Edwin Brown

Arthur Steptoe, Albert's long-lost son from Australia, returns to claim his place in the family.

"Cuckoo in the Nest" is more drama than comedy, even more so than most of this often seriocomic series. In many respects, this is a retelling of the prodigal son, with the great exception that, after the prodigal has been given the ring, the robe, and the fatted calf, he turns out to be a totally unrepentant lout. The lout in question, convincingly portrayed by Kenneth J. Warren, is Arthur, Albert's illegitimate son from a premarital affair. In one of the funnier lines of the episode, Albert explains that he had been engaged to Arthur's mother for six years, then one night couldn't control himself any longer.

The revelation of his half brother comes as a total shock to Harold, who quickly resents Albert's total acceptance of this stranger from over 40 years past. There are some good dramatic exchanges between Harold and Albert over the latter's insistence that Arthur be made a full partner in the firm. This is the last straw for Harold, who promptly walks out, leaving his new found brother to make the rounds. With some real work to do, Arthur quickly reveals his true nature. On his first time out with the horse and cart, he sells both and runs off with the money.

The remainder of the entry is steeped in pathos as Harold is reduced to totting from a pushcart and living, a grimy little walk-up apartment (even worse than the family homestead back on Oil Drum Lane). Albert witnesses his son's plight but allows Harold to preserve his pride in order to coax him back home (unlike the similar circumstance in "The Lodger"). In a face-saving ploy, the two desperate rag-and-bone men negotiate a merger of their worthless firms (although both brag about having thriving concerns) in order to survive.

Series Seven 1972

Episode 1: "Men of Letters" ★★★½

Air date: February 21, 1972. Cast: Albert Steptoe (Wilfrid Brambell); Harold Steptoe (Harry H. Corbett). Featuring: Anthony Sharp

Harold dreams of a literary career when he is asked to contribute a history of the rag-and-bone trade to the local parish magazine.

An excellent start to what some consider the finest season of *Steptoe and Son*, "Men of Letters" provides a well-integrated script that steadily builds momentum to a strong climax. As is often the case, the tension of the plot is provided by Harold's constant attempts to outperform his father. Here, this is illustrated by a simple contest of Scrabble, a game that Harold considers educational but at which Albert handily bests him by coming up with lewd words exclusively. As his son seethes, Albert manages to justify such British vulgarisms as *sod* and *bum* by retreating to their more innocent uses.

Just when it appears that Harold will never win, his salvation arrives in a visit by the Vicar. With the church's centenary approaching, the Vicar wants an article on the history of totting in Shepherd's Bush for its magazine. Harold leaps at the chance to write it and pleads that he is a better writer. Albert, however is more knowledgeable on the subject. The dispute is settled by the toss of a coin, which Harold wins, although Albert is urged to contribute too. Immediately, Harold imagines a new career and dives into the assignment with determination. Albert, for his part, finishes his piece early.

Ultimately, Harold spends eight days on his masterpiece, the merits of which are not available for public review. It seems that all the issues of the magazine are impounded and destroyed after it is disclosed that Albert's contribution was a crossword puzzle much akin to his Scrabble games.

There is a good scene as the Steptoes entertain the Vicar, although the studio audience doesn't seem to fully appreciate some of the jokes for some reason. When the Vicar complains of sore knees due to praying, Albert casually recommends affixing the cups of a padded bra to them. Harold also takes the occasion to restate his views of Christianity, which he believes are quite intellectually formed. The Vicar reminds him, however, that his opinion of the faith is summarized in his boast that Calvin and Pascal were "berks."

Later, there is a good routine in which Harold tries to interview Albert for his article. While he tries to maintain a professional reporter's demeanor, Harold is continually sidetracked, much to Albert's delight.

Anthony Sharp, as the Vicar, previously appeared as a doctor in "The Colour Problem" from series five.

Episode 2: "A Star Is Born" ★★★★

Air date: February 28, 1972. Cast: Albert Steptoe (Wilfrid Brambell); Harold

Steptoe (Harry H. Corbett). Featuring: Trevor Bannister. With Margaret Nolan; Betty Huntley-Wright; John Quayle; Cy Town; John Anderson

Harold's attempt at starring in an amateur dramatic production is overshadowed when Albert is asked to join the cast.

Almost identical in theme to the preceding episode, "A Star Is Born" still manages to be an excellent series entry. This episode distinguishes itself from "Men of Letters" in a number of ways. First, Harold's dreams, this time of becoming a world-renowned actor, are frustrated by his father's success, rather than by a disaster. In addition, the ending is far more dramatic, as Harold's failure is not only evident to himself but is confirmed by an audience of strangers. There is one moment in particular when Harold exits the theater after the performance; a small boy stops him and asks if he's one of the actors. Harold pauses momentarily and confesses sadly that he is only a rag-and-bone man, adding, after the boy leaves, that that is all he will ever be.

Prior to this sobering ending there is as much good comedy as ever filled a *Steptoe* episode. Initially, Albert scoffs at Harold's participation in the local theater company, telling his son he's been down on the group since he saw their production of "Richard the Hundred and Eleventh" (*Richard III*). His scorn turns to mockery when he learns that Harold has been chosen to play the lead in the upcoming drama about soldiering on the Indian frontier. (Albert gleefully guesses the play to be titled) *Up Yer Khyber*, Cockney rhyming slang for *ass*— Khyber Pass: ass.) To prove his acting prowess, Harold treats the old man to his audition and then proceeds to give a marvelously ghastly imitation of Marlon Brando from *On the Waterfront*. Albert sneers that all actors are "poofs" who are forever calling each other "darling."

Soon the cast arrives at the Steptoe home for a rehearsal, and they quickly prove Albert's stereotyping of them accurate. His assessment changes when he is pressed into service to play the key part of an upper-class envoy: Lord Carrothers. Upon hearing Albert's voice, the director joyously announces that Albert is Carrothers. "That's my dad," Harold corrects, "and he's an ignorant git!" Despite Harold's protests, Albert goes on to become the hit of the performance and the darling of the cast and audience alike.

"A Star Is Born" also marks a return in style to the harder-edged relationship of earlier seasons. As recently as the sixth season, Albert was inclined to show some sympathy while besting his son ("Pot Black"). Here, however, as in the original four series, he seems to take pleasure in bursting Harold's bubble.

Trevor Bannister — still months away from his duties as Mr. Lucas in *Are You Being Served?*— is quite effective as the highly strung director of the amateur company.

Episode 3: "Oh, What a Beautiful Mourning" ★★★½

Air date: March 6, 1972. Cast: Albert Steptoe (Wilfrid Brambell); Harold Steptoe (Harry H. Corbett). Featuring: George A. Cooper. With Mollie Sugden; Rita Webb; Yvonne Antrobus; Bartlett Mullins; Tommy Godfrey; Queenie Watts; Stella Moray; Margaret Flint; Simon Cord; Gilly Flower

Harold and Albert must contend with the greater Steptoe clan as they attend the funeral of Albert's brother George.

For a show that concentrates so exclusively on the relationship of two characters, any foray into ensemble pieces is a rare and lavish treat. "Oh, What a Beautiful Mourning" is just such an episode. The first glimpse at a large Steptoe gathering since series four's "And Afterwards At ..." this episode succeeds as well as that earlier gem. Whereas the premise for that installment was Harold's abortive wedding, here the clan convenes for another Steptoe send-off. Although this is the first we as viewers are allowed to witness, apparently these family funerals run according to a rather set pattern. In addition, the affairs are quite frequent. According to Harold's summation, Albert's family "drops like flies" while "breeding like rabbits."

As in "And Afterwards At ..." the behavior of the other Steptoes make Albert and Harold look positively sophisticated by comparison. While the relatives are slightly better turned out and a little more prosperous, one would still rather spend an evening with the contentious father and son rag and bone men than their kin. As such, plenty of good jokes on the individual idiosyncrasies of the relatives are voiced by Harold and Albert. Most of these pack a double wallop, since they are first told in the opening scene at home before the funeral, then are actually illustrated by the offending party at the wake — all with no lessening of the impact.

Also like the wedding episode, the primary motivation of the assembled Steptoes seems to be greed. Although Albert and Harold are the only professional junk dealers, their relatives are high-ranking amateurs when it comes to picking over the effects of the dearly departed. Unfortunately, there is only one item, an eighteenth-century figurine, that is of any real value. According to the rules of the game, nothing can be taken from the house until after the funeral. This prompts a wildly funny race back from the gravesite in a phalanx of rented limousines. While the mourners are greatly disappointed by the surprise ending, Albert, Harold, and the viewers, especially, are not.

Viewers may remember George A. Cooper, seen here as Albert's brother Arthur, from "And Afterwards At ..." in which he played an unnamed Steptoe relative. Also seen here from that 1965 episode are Mollie Sugden and Rita Webb. In the earlier entry, Sugden played the mother of the bride, while Webb played Harold's aunt Frieda, from his mother's side of the family. Here, both women have made the dubious move into the Steptoe clan.

Episode 4: "Live Now, P.A.Y.E. Later" ★★★

Air date: March 13, 1972. Cast: Albert Steptoe (Wilfrid Brambell); Harold Steptoe (Harry H. Corbett). Featuring: Colin Gordon. With Edwin Apps; Peter Madden; Carole Roberts.

Albert must go to extreme measures to avoid being caught for income tax evasion.

Unusually broad farce for Steptoe and Son, "Live Now, P.A.Y.E. Later" features the outlandish sight of both Brambell and Corbett in drag. These impersonations are made necessary when the Inland Revenue makes inquiries regarding Albert's claiming his wife on his tax return. Rather than own up to the 30-year fraud and face two years in prison, Albert compounds the lie by dressing up as his own wife, Gladys. Oddly, the scruffy Albert makes a rather convincing little old lady, much to the shock and revulsion of his son, who must not only witness the escalation of his father's offense but wonder if the old man isn't going a little "funny" in the process.

Not only does Albert manage to convince the tax man that Mrs. Steptoe is alive and well, but he actually has his case referred to the Ministry of Health and Social Security in order to collect Gladys her back old-age pension. This windfall necessitates Albert doing his drag act on a weekly basis in order to collect the money at the post office. On his first trip out, Albert attracts the amorous attention of a retired vice-squad cop. There is a particularly funny montage, which shows Gladys at the movies and out dancing with the ex-policeman. This premise is repeated in the finale as Harold is compelled to make an appearance as his own sister, Muriel, to cover yet another lie perpetrated by Albert. Unlike his costar, Corbett makes a repulsive female; despite this fact, the Inland Revenue man apparently finds Muriel quite attractive.

There is one confusing reference in the installment. Albert tells the revenue agent that he was married in 1918. This would appear doubtful since, as he related in "Cuckoo in the Nest," he had a six-year engagement to the mother of his other son, Arthur.

Colin Gordon, very good in the role of Mr. Greenwood, the Inland Revenue agent who gets drunk at the Steptoes' hand, previously appeared all the way back in series one as the doctor in "The Holiday." The episode's title acronym stands for "pay as you earn," the British system of having taxes deducted from income at their source.

Episode 5: "Loathe Story" ★★

Air date: March 20, 1972. Cast: Albert Steptoe (Wilfrid Brambell); Harold Steptoe (Harry H. Corbett). Featuring: Raymond Huntley. With Georgina Cookson; Joanna Lumley

Harold visits a psychiatrist after he tries to kill Albert while sleepwalking.

Once there, he relates another story of how Albert ruined his chances to get married.

Many good moments highlight "Loathe Story," but unfortunately the sum of these is greater than the whole of the episode. One gets the impression that the writers had several snippets of inspiration, none of which was capable of sustaining an entire episode. What results is a nice patchwork of themes, but it is less cohesive than most series installments. Although all the material is new, there is the feel that many of the sequences are highlights pasted together from earlier shows.

The episode begins with promise as Harold and Albert attempt to play badminton in the manure-pocked yard. Of course, Harold is resplendently arrayed in tennis whites and treats each set as if he were on center court at Wimbledon (he even has a water tank and paper cups ready beside the net). As usual, Albert wins. That night, Harold has nightmares that his father is beating him at a series of games. With his subconscious unable to take any more, Harold, still asleep, rises and goes after the old man with a meat cleaver.

The scene shifts to a psychiatrist's office where Harold is pouring out his angst to the rather disinterested analyst. While the doctor keeps trying to titillate his own fixation regarding breasts; Harold tells a variety of stories about life with Albert. There are a few interesting glimpses of Harold's experiences as a young boy, including the sad story of him having to sit outside the pub every night with a lemonade and an arrowroot biscuit, as Albert enjoyed himself inside. The climax of these flashbacks is another incident in which Albert destroys yet another relationship in his son's life. This, while funny in spots, pulls all its laughs from the juxtaposition of Albert's uncouth act against the upper-class graces of Harold's prospective mother-in-law.

One of the better gags in the psychiatrist sequence involves Harold describing his two years of military service in Malaya. He valiantly explains how he was wounded twice, a victim of a variety of jungle conditions, and a constant slave to dysentery. In comparison to all his years with his father, however, Harold wistfully concludes that those were the happiest two years of his life. Harold also gives a clue to the reason for his ever-fluctuating age, when he begins to tell the doctor he is 40-something, then quickly amends that to 39.

Future star Joanna Lumley makes an appearance as Harold's brewery heiress fiancée.

Episode 6: "Divided We Stand" ★★★★

Air date: March 27, 1972. Cast: Harold Steptoe (Harry H. Corbett); Albert Steptoe (Wilfrid Brambell)

Unable to stand Albert's company any longer, Harold compartmentalizes the family home.

A marvelous *Steptoe* tour de force, which illustrates why this series is a cut above the average sitcom. Using a fairly routine situation — the dividing of a living or working space by two warring parties — Galton and Simpson exploit it to the fullest, wringing every last laugh out of it. While most standard sitcoms would stage a similar feud by painting a white line down the center of a house or office, the Steptoes build actual walls to dramatize the desperate nature of their plight. This is also the first episode since series five's "A Winter's Tale," to allow Brambell and Corbett free rein; there is no supporting cast (although a few extras appear in the closing scene as hospital personnel, they have no lines and are essentially there as props).

The episode opens with a well-written verbal match between the principals, as Harold and Albert quarrel over plans to redecorate the house. Status quo Albert opts for no refurbishment at all or, if pressed, some dark green and chocolate-colored paint to hide the dirt. He bristles at his son's bold designs borrowed from contemporary decorating magazines, likening them to the inside of a Peruvian brothel. Harold tries in vain to convince the old man that the house needs some cleaning and sprucing up but not even the discovery of a set of Albert's false teeth (lost since an air raid in 1941) convinces him. Albert is extremely grateful that his favorite set of choppers has been relocated and promptly pops them in his mouth to discover his gums have since shrunk.

As good as this opening exchange is, it is only the appetizer for some wonderful comedy. Not being able to decorate as he pleases and unable to afford a place of his own, Harold builds partitions to divide each of the rooms in half. The parlor is segmented with the wall running down the middle of a common dining table and halfway across the television screen. The kitchen is similarly partitioned with the stove and sink being equally divided for both father and son. Even the front door is replaced by two half doors. The hub of the entire series of passageways is a coin-operated turnstile in the front hall which allows each of them access to necessary portions of the house. The subsequent jokes verge on the Keatonesque, recalling to mind similar mechanical gags in such silent short subjects as *The Scarecrow* and *The Electric House*. In a telling comment on modern life, the arrangement seems to work reasonably well until it totally disintegrates over what to watch on television. Ultimately, the design for living results in disaster with Albert and Harold landing in the hospital in adjoining beds when the house catches fire and the fire brigade is hindered by the turnstiles.

EPISODE 7: "THE DESPERATE HOURS" ★★★★

Air date: April 3, 1972. Cast: Albert Steptoe (Wilfrid Brambell); Harold Steptoe (Harry H. Corbett). Guest star: Leonard Rossiter. And J. G. Devlin; Corbet Woodall; Tommy Vance

The Steptoes are held hostage in their own home, but soon both Albert and Harold find they hold much in common with their captors.

Arguably the strongest series of *Steptoe and Son* ends with another classic episode. Borrowing its title and plot directly from the 1955 Humphrey Bogart classic film, "The Desperate Hours" still manages to adapt this stock situation to the series and make it uniquely its own. For the first time in this long-running series both Albert and Harold are given the opportunity to commiserate with two individuals who truly sympathize with their daily plight. The fact that these soulmates are escaped convicts reemphasizes their own imprisonment in their Shepherd's Bush junkyard.

The action opens with father and son suffering another lean winter (much like the situation in "The Siege of Steptoe Street"). Affairs are so severe that the Steptoes are reduced to scrounging for the proper sized foreign coins to keep the electricity meter supplying power. Into this den of misery come John and Frank, two escapees from the nearby prison. At first the convicts are menacing, as they demand money, food, and transport. Upon learning, however, that they've picked the only house in the area with none of their necessities, they start sympathizing with their hostages. John, it turns out, is approximately Harold's age, while Frank is Albert's counterpart.

What follows essentially is a restatement of both Harold and Albert's basic complaints of the past ten years but from a different perspective, as they discover their captors are in the same situation. John decries the fact that he could have been a career banker had not Frank led him astray. He adds that he wouldn't even mind being incarcerated were it not for the fact that he is locked up with Frank. For his part, Frank recites the difficulties of growing old and pleads for his younger partner not to leave him. In the end, the message is that even convicts are better off than the Steptoes (Harold is even reduced to bumming cigarettes and spare change from John).

John is excellently played by Leonard Rossiter. Although still at least two years away from success in *Rising Damp* and *The Fall and Rise of Reginald Perrin*, Rossiter's reputation was such that he is afforded "guest star" status in the credits. Frank is sympathetically portrayed by J. G. Devlin, who played Regan, the IRA suspect in the "Absent Friends" episode of *Dad's Army*.

Finally, Harold casually mentions their address in this episode as 24 Oil Drum Lane. Either the house has moved, or the street has been renumbered since 1965, because in that year's "My Old Man's a Tory," the Steptoe house number is given as 32 Oil Drum Lane.

Christmas Special 1973

CHRISTMAS SPECIAL—UNTITLED ★★★

Air date: December 24, 1973. Cast: Albert Steptoe (Wilfrid Brambell); Harold Steptoe (Harry H. Corbett). With Frank Thornton; Arnold Diamond; Mary

Barclay; Peter Hughes; Valerie Bell; Jenny Cox; Peter Thornton; Sue Walker; Shirley Hafey

Harold scraps his plans for a Christmas holiday in Spain to throw a three-day party at home.

After a hiatus of over a year and a half. Steptoe and Son returned with its first holiday special. With a running time of approximately 45 minutes, the show seems more like an average episode, testimony to the quick pace of the script. Again, the old theme (actually the oldest) of the series is revisited: Harold's desire to get away from his father. This time, he is trying to spend a mere ten days away from Albert by enjoying a Christmas vacation in Majorca. As usual, Albert trots out his vast repertoire of guilt trips, with the added punch of it being Christmas, to convince Harold to stay. Harold reluctantly agrees to cash in his ticket but only to spend the money on a Christmas party to end all Christmas parties.

There are deep insights into the memories of Christmasespast, including Albert's long-dead tree, which he stores under the stairs, bringing it out each year and decorating it with a few sparse strands of tinsel garland. While Albert, the more sentimental of the pair, looks back fondly on their annual holiday rituals, Harold finds them depressing. According to Harold, their Christmas activities boil down to Albert watching television for three days, smoking, and consuming mountains of nuts and tangerines. The gift exchange always ends with Albert giving his son three handkerchiefs and a pair of Y-fronts. Little wonder Harold is desperate to escape the yearly festivities.

The opening sequence in the travel agency is good, especially with the help of Steptoe standby Frank Thornton as a snooty travel agent. Albert's first scene also is memorable as he decorates the outhouse, including gift-wrapping paper replacing the usual cut-up newspaper for toilet tissue. Unfortunately, he forgets to hang the holly wreath, leaving it instead on the toilet seat where it soon perforates the bottom of an unsuspecting Harold. As good as these small touches are, they pale in comparison to the show's finale, which concludes the festivities with a nice *Steptoe* twist as the elaborate party is cancelled at the last minute when the Steptoes contract measles.

Harold's age is once again adjusted to keep him hovering around the 40-year-old mark. When the show first premiered in 1962, Harold's age was given as 37, placing his birth in 1925. In this episode, Albert remarks to the doll ornament that he places atop their tree that she is the same age as Harold, both having arrived in 1932.

Series Eight 1974

EPISODE 1: "BACK IN FASHION" ★★★

Air date: September 4, 1974. Cast: Albert Steptoe (Wilfrid Brambell); Harold Steptoe (Harry H. Corbett); Carol (Madeline Smith); Photographer (Roy

Holder); Agent (Peter Birrel). With Michael Earl; Ava Cadell; Christine Donna; Sally Farmilor; Claire Russell; Hazel Wilson

A fashion photographer rents the junkyard for a photo shoot.

The final series of *Steptoe and Son* begins with this amusing entry, which features many of the stock situations explored in the previous seven seasons. The primary theme, although it is not evident from the outset (indeed it is not clear until the final moments of the installment) is the ongoing struggle for Harold to best the old man. There is also another lengthy discussion of British politics early in the episode, a *Steptoe* state-of-the-nation, if you will, delivered after an almost two-and-a-half-year absence. Harold, for the first time, is pessimistic in this political sequence, predicting revolution as usual but now in the guise of a right-wing coup. This reflected the attitude of many viewers, who worried over a political/industrial crisis that had occurred in Britain the previous winter. As such, the going is rather slow at the outset but picks up nicely once the plot is introduced.

Harold's spirits are lifted when a photographer and his agent scout the yard for a high fashion photo session. Delighted at the prospect of having a half dozen beautiful models around, Harold readily agrees to the shoot, although the far cagier Albert holds out for a rental fee of £60.

The next morning, Albert puts on clean clothes for the visitors, while his son attempts style by wearing a smoking jacket and dark glasses and carrying a cane. Instead of being seen as a trendsetter, Harold's appearance gets him mistaken for a blind person by the models. This provides the funniest sequence of the episode as one model in particular takes Harold under her wing, leading him around the room and showing him tender care. Unaware of the false impression he has made, Harold enjoys the attention and is surprised when the girls start to disrobe with him seated in their midst. Finally, realizing they believe him to be blind, Harold quickly excuses himself. He exits only to find Albert leering at the keyhole. Harold orders his father away and tries to plug up the keyhole but winds up falling through the door into the models' changing room. He tries to blame Albert, explaining that his absent father is the pervert, not him, but the models fail to believe him. While arguing his case, Harold notices Albert is drilling through the ceiling to get another glimpse of the girls. He rushes upstairs to catch Albert but only manages to put his foot through the floor, further implicating himself with the models.

The episode has a humorous, though predictable ending. When the photographer runs out of inspiration, Harold suggests a male model, then offers his services. Instead, Albert is chosen since, as the title states, his old clothes are back in fashion, while Harold's attempts at being trendy are woefully outdated.

One of the biggest surprises of the episode is the physical appearance of Harry H. Corbett. After two and a half years' hiatus, the actor appears bloated, looks exhausted, and seems to have aged ten years in the interval. He is no longer convincing playing a man in his early forties (he was 49 at the time).

EPISODE 2: "PORN YESTERDAY" ★★

Air date: September 11, 1974. Cast: Albert Steptoe (Wilfrid Brambell); Harold Steptoe (Harry H. Corbett). With Anthony Sharp; Dorothy Frere. And Joyce Windsor; Harry Fielder

Harold's purchase of an old Mutoscope uncovers a secret from Albert's past.

A brilliant plot idea that unfortunately never reaches its potential, "Porn Yesterday" would have worked better as a 15-minute skit during a *Royal Variety* performance special. The primary difficulty is that between the introduction of the episode's theme and the concluding joke, there is little dramatic tension or complications to sustain interest.

When Harold returns from the rounds with a "What the Butler Saw" machine — a hand-cranked, coin-operated purveyor of silent titillation — both he and Albert can't wait to view the ancient soft-core porn. As Harold watches a French selection, "Fifi and the Photographer," suddenly the picture changes to an English title from the twenties about a woman taking a bath and a randy milkman. Rather than clamoring to see, Albert quickly becomes very quiet. Soon it is clear why: Albert is the milkman.

Wilfrid Brambell turns in one of his better performances of the series; for the first time, he portrays Albert as truly victimized, at least initially. In a sympathetic piece, he explains to Harold that times were hard when he made the film, and the £5 he earned was a lot of money.

"Everything we had was in pawn," the old man explains, justifying his action.

"So was you!" Harold cries, completing the pun.

Perhaps the best joke comes as Harold tries to console himself by hoping that his mother never knew about the film. Albert quickly dashes this wish by remarking that his wife certainly was aware of it, since her sister Rose played the woman in the bathtub.

From this high point, the episode winds down as it waits for the ending when the machine is used by the Vicar for a church fete. Despite the fact that Harold has destroyed the offending short subject, another one is found, again featuring Albert. Albert becomes the star of the day as fairgoers clamber for his autograph.

Anthony Sharp returns as the Vicar ("Men of Letters"), making his the only character aside from Albert, Harold, and the two horses to make a second appearance in the series. Dorothy Frere appears as the Vicar's Wife. She would perform similar spousal duties in *The Fall and Rise of Reginald Perrin* in which she played Mrs. C. J.

Episode 3: "And So to Bed" ★★★½

Air date: September 18, 1974. Cast: Harold Steptoe (Harry H. Corbett); Albert Steptoe (Wilfrid Brambell); Marcia (Lynn Farleigh); Salesman (Angus MacKay)

After a disastrously disappointing date, Harold decides to purchase a waterbed.

The strongest episode of the final season of *Steptoe and Son*, "And So to Bed" is a skillful blending of Harold's endless struggle for success in his love life along with some good slapstick situations. In the case of the first, Harold yet again has his dreams of romance (or at least sex) thwarted when Albert and bedbugs unwittingly conspire against him in the show's opening third. As Harold waits downstairs on the couch with the eager Marcia for Albert to go to bed, the old man sits up in bed, cobbling on six pairs of old boots and sipping a drink from the same glass in which his dentures are soaking. After Albert finally goes to sleep, the pair sneak upstairs only to find Harold's bed infested with bugs. In the ensuing rumpus, caused when Marcia screams at the vermin, awakening Albert, the bed totally collapses. Tired of sleeping on somebody else's mattress, which he has picked up on the rounds, Harold is determined to buy a new bed.

There is a nice verbal exchange between Harold and Albert as the son explains the need to have a new bed of his own. Harold dreams of something unique and exotic, such as a round bed, which Albert deems unsuitable since there is no set place to rest one's feet. Albert does brighten, however, when Harold describes outfitting his new bed with black sheets. Harold thinks them erotic, while Albert appreciates the fact that they wouldn't need to be washed. The discussion leads into a diatribe by Albert on the coddled nature of modern youth juxtaposed against how tough his generation had it. He reminds Harold that as a boy his family was forced to sleep eight to a bed (Albert wistfully comments that all his former bedmates are now dead, to which his son replies that that is only natural since they didn't have gas masks back then). This line evolves into a discussion of malnutrition with Albert proclaiming he didn't reach his full adult height — puny as it is — until he was 43! The banter ends with Albert's description of his former practice of making love out in the junkyard inside a dozen old auto tires.

The comedy style for the remainder of the episode broadens as father and son visit the Bayswater Bed-O-Rama. As usual, Albert is a frightful embarrassment to Harold as he tries to establish an air of dignity for the posh salesman. Albert is particularly frustrated that modern beds go all the way to the floor, not leaving room to store the "Edgar Allen" (po, or chamber pot). After settling on a waterbed, Harold gleefully makes plans for a return visit by Marcia. The date is made but not consummated; the couple's amorous evening is ruined by Albert's accidentally stabbing the new bed, leaving a giant gash.

EPISODE 4: "THE SEVEN STEPTOERAI" ★

Air date: September 25, 1974. Cast: Harold Steptoe (Harry H. Corbett); Albert Steptoe (Wilfrid Brambell); Frankie Barrow (Henry Woolf). And Bill Weston; Stuart Fell; Paddy Ryan; Tony Smart; Billy Horrigan; Dougie Robinson; Marc Boyle; Tim Condron; Vic Armstrong; Aubrey Danvers-Walker; Ernest Jennings; David J. Graham

When a local gangster strong-arms the Steptoes for protection money, Albert organizes his senior-citizen friends into a kung-fu vigilante unit.

A nice premise that doesn't deliver, "The Seven Steptoerai" is mechanical without the usual verbal or situational cleverness one expects of Galton and Simpson. As such, the episode is one of the most routine offerings and could have been produced by any other writers on any other sitcom. Too much time is spent establishing the threat to Harold and Albert, and not enough time is afforded the resolution of the problem. While Henry Woolf, as gangster Frankie Barrow provides a colorful portrayal, his main scene goes on too long without many laughs, and there are almost none for the show's two stars. (Woolf reprised his role in *Steptoe and Son Ride Again*, the second Steptoe feature film.) In this scene, Harold and Albert are given the thankless chore of first appearing angry, then frightened.

Interest picks up considerably as Harold and Albert study their alternatives to paying Frankie £15 a week for protection. Harold suggests that the other merchants in the area band together to resist Barrow's tactics, but Albert points out this is futile given their response during WWII when only two volunteers could be recruited for the Shepherd's Bush Home Guard unit. The best moments of the offering come as Harold recalls the classic Akira Kurosawa film, *The Seven Samurai*, in which poor Japanese villagers hire mercenaries to protect them from marauding bandits. At first, Harold can't recall the title of the film past the "Seven Something." Albert guesses a number of films with seven in the title, including *The Seventh Veil, The Seven-Year Itch*, and *Snow White and the Seven Dwarfs*. While Harold only dreams of hiring samurai, Albert uses the idea to organize a band of his elderly pals, all of whom have been enjoying kung-fu films of late.

Unfortunately, this all comes too late in the episode to really develop what could have been some amusing business. Instead of seeing Albert organize the feeble fighting force, his seven pals appear in the next scene fully trained and handily put five young muscular thugs to flight in a filmed sequence that borrows its technique from cheap martial arts movies. Never is it explained how the old men accomplish their task (it would have been much more satisfying if they had used the wisdom of their years to outsmart the thugs as was done in Harold Lloyd's silent feature *Speedy*).

EPISODE 5: "UPSTAIRS, DOWNSTAIRS, UPSTAIRS, DOWNSTAIRS" ★★½

Air date: October 2, 1974. Cast: Albert Steptoe (Wilfrid Brambell); Harold Steptoe (Harry H. Corbett). Featuring: Robert James

Harold wears himself ragged playing nurse to a bedridden Albert.

It is a testimony to the depth of Galton and Simpson's craftsmanship that in this, the second to last regular episode of *Steptoe and Son*, they are still delving into the psychological make-up of their two main characters. While many of the episodes of this final season avoid such nuances, in "Upstairs, Downstairs, Upstairs, Downstairs" the practice is alive and vigorously explored. While the overall effect is not totally captivating, it is still worth the effort.

Interestingly, this is really the only two-man show in the eighth season (there is a doctor, who is used primarily to set up the situation and provide a sounding board for Harold's feelings), and both characters are allowed ample opportunity to express themselves. Albert, here of ailing back, is confined to bed for more than two weeks, and while he truly is in agony (at first this appears doubtful), he is also truly enjoying his pain for the attention it affords. His motivation is that of the sick child who, while ill enough to miss school, is well enough to enjoy the holiday. Harold, as always, is torn between his filial duty to Albert and the almost irresistible desire to wring the old man's neck when his father's constant demands mount.

The highlights include a good scene after the doctor first leaves. Harold is loath to admit that Albert is actually in pain, but after he does, he cannot resist teasing the old man before beginning his nursing chores in earnest. It is as if Harold is getting a bit of his own back — by telling Albert that he only has three days to live — as sort of a reserve against what he is sure is the coming ordeal. Once Harold assures his father he is only joking, there is a brief touching moment in which Albert expresses his appreciation to his son. He hopes he will not be a burden, but this sentiment is hardly past his lips when he begins his list of needs, which would keep a well-staffed hotel busy.

When Albert's trick back suddenly returns to health, he starts to call for Harold to share the happy news. Quickly, however, that inimitable wicked Albert Steptoe grin spreads across his face as he decides to milk his luxury a bit longer. Of course, Harold will eventually find out and reap his revenge.

EPISODE 6: "SÉANCE IN A WET RAG-AND-BONE YARD" ★½

Air date: October 10, 1974. Cast: Albert Steptoe (Wilfrid Brambell); Harold Steptoe (Harry H. Corbett); Madame Fontana (Patricia Routledge); Dorothy (Gwen Nelson). With Gilly Flower; David J. Graham

When Albert gets a new girlfriend, who's a spiritualist, he allows a séance to be held at the Steptoe home.

The last regular series installment of *Steptoe and Son* is an ineffective affair, despite an interesting appearance by Patricia Routledge as Madame Fontana, a phony medium. The construction of the episode is also interesting since it goes somewhat against type, with Albert being taken in by the claims of the psychic and Harold playing the skeptic (one could easily expect the opposite to take place given Harold's more gullible nature and willingness to explore the unconventional). Still, despite these promising signs, the episode remains on the whole uninspired and rather dull. The jokes are mainly reserved to skeptical wisecracking by Harold.

What few laughs there are come as Harold learns of his father's latest interest in the supernatural, piqued, it seems, by a relationship with a widow named Dorothy. The son listens incredulously as Albert earnestly recounts conversations had through the medium with such famous departed mortals as Columbus and Ghandi (Columbus, it turns out, spoke with an American accent, while Ghandi reassured Albert that Harold would turn out to be a fine son). While the experience excited his father, it leaves Harold with little hope for the afterlife if the most interesting thing to do there is try and contact Albert.

The next night, Madame Fontana conducts a séance in the Steptoe home. This sequence is highlighted by some rather good broad work by Routledge and some fine acting by Corbett. Harold at first enjoys ridiculing the proceedings, but he becomes genuinely shaken when the medium purports to contact his deceased mother. Soon the whole racket is exposed as merely a scheme to fob off the spiritualist's mother, Dorothy, in marriage to Albert. In the episode's final moments, however, Harold does seem to have a genuine otherworld visit from his departed mother.

As in other Steptoe episodes, there are some inconsistencies, especially in regard to Harold's current age and his age when his mother died (here that figure is given as five). Also, Albert's deceased wife is called Emily, while in "Live Now, P.A.Y.E. Later," her name is given as Gladys.

Christmas Special 1974

Christmas Special ★★★★

Air date: December 26, 1974. Cast: Harold Steptoe (Harry H. Corbett); Albert Steptoe (Wilfrid Brambell); Immigration Officer (Leon Eagles)

Despairing of another Christmas in Shepherd's Bush, Harold will do anything to get away for the holiday — even if it means taking Albert along.

A marvelous send off for one of the finest series ever to grace the airwaves, this special manages to break new ground for the characters while throwing in some rather sentimental moments as well. The earthshaking news is that, after 12 years, 8 series, and 56 episodes, Harold Steptoe finally successfully breaks free from his father. True, the escape is only a four-day hiatus, but even this minor respite is a major accomplishment, as long-time viewers will attest.

The special starts rather sedately as Harold announces that he is so desperate to spend Christmas away from home that he consents to bring Albert with him. He produces the "swear box"—a collection box for the RSPCA in the shape of three dogs—as the source of their money (Albert protests, noting that the £80 inside is a result of his cursing, but Harold declares it community property since he had to listen to the swears). True to form, Albert wants to go back to Mrs. Boxwood's boardinghouse in Bognor ("The Holiday"), but Harold insists on a vacation outside of Britain. There is some good byplay as Harold offers a variety of holiday destinations, all of which Albert rejects for various reasons. We also learn of two spots in Europe to which Albert is loath to return, since he is considered persona non grata. The first is the Soviet Union, since Albert, as part of the 1919 British Expeditionary Force, allied himself with the White Russian army against the Bolsheviks. The second is Brussels, since a wartime gag at that city's famous *Manneken-Pis* statue led to Albert's insulting the lord mayor.

Finally, after settling on Switzerland for a Christmas holiday, an extensive search is made for Albert's birth certificate, needed to obtain a passport. This segment contains several poignant moments as long-forgotten treasures are extracted from the closet as the birth certificate is sought. Harold is especially moved by finding his school cap and his favorite toy, a Number 9 London bus. Upon closer examination of the cap, Harold recites the school's Latin motto, which translates as "Know Thy Place and Be Grateful,"—which, in many ways, is a fitting coda to the series.

When Albert's birth record is finally found, it reveals a few surprises. The first is that Albert was born September 26, 1899, making him older than Harold previously thought (although about right according to series two's "Sixty-Five Today" episode). More revealing is that Albert's father is listed as unknown. The Steptoe dynasty, it seems, was founded by Albert, not his father, and the ancestral home in Shepherd's Bush was bought by his mother for £80 (ironically, the same amount they've saved to get away from it). Given his grandmother's occupation as a domestic servant to a lord, Harold briefly speculates that Albert might be illegitimately related to royalty. Albert ultimately dispels the notion, recalling his mother's fondness for the local muffin man.

The final scene reveals the brilliance of Harold's hidden agenda to get away on his own. Upon arriving at customs, Albert sails through, but Harold is denied exit from the country due to his passport having expired. Not wanting to waste a paid vacation, Albert bids his son farewell, while Harold mournfully waves from the platform. With the train gone, Harold forlornly plods away, until he suddenly breaks into a victor's trot and rushes to meet a girl waiting outside in a sports car. "It worked!" he exults as the pair drive off for four days—in Bognor!

The Steptoes confusion regarding their home address continues to the end as Albert's birth certificate places the house's location at 23 Oil Drum

Lane (see "The Desperate Hours"). In addition, Albert tells the customs official at Victoria Station that he hadn't left the country since going off to fight in the First World War. Apparently, he forgot the abortive trip to France in series four's "Pilgrim's Progress" and his jaunt to Obergurgl in series five's "A Winter's Tale."

Dad's Army

BBC-TV 1968–1977

Imagine Laurel and Hardy in ensemble cast, and there you have *Dad's Army*. The main characters of the amazingly successful situation comedy—often referred to by its legion of fans as "the Magnificent Seven"—capture the spirit and the tone of those two immortal clowns. Like Stan and Ollie before them, the men of the Walmington-on-Sea Home Guard platoon blend physical slapstick, verbal silliness, and urgent delivery into a mix that engenders nothing but the greatest warmth and affection from admirers of their work.

Dad's Army is the most British of the Brit-coms featured in this book and consequently is not fully understood or appreciated in the United States. Its lack of success in the States, however, is not due to the fact that it is too British but rather that it deals with a period in history to which most Americans simply cannot relate: the Blitz of World War II. During this finest hour of Britain's history, the island nation stood resolutely alone against the Nazi might, and against overwhelming odds it persevered to victory. At a time when Britain was facing its greatest peril, everyone pitched in for the common good. This included the Home Guard, a sort of National Guard made of local men either too old, too young, or otherwise unfit for the regular army. That a comedy should be based on such a deadly serious event in a country's past, less than 30 years after it occurred, is somewhat surprising. Indeed, some at the BBC questioned whether or not it was even appropriate inspiration for a comedy. But there lies the genius of Jimmy Perry and David Croft, the show's creators.

"*Dad's Army* is funny only because the Home Guard was in deadly earnest," noted Stanley Reynolds in *The Times* (London) in 1974. "What makes *Dad's Army* funny is the simple fact that Hitler was so very, very serious."

Alan Coren, writing the previous year in the same publication, noted that the series points out that Britain during its darkest hour was relying on every resource for its defense, including armies of men past retirement age. "There is a wider lunacy beyond the script," points out Coren, "in the fact that Clive Dunn [playing Corporal Jones, the oldest member of the platoon] might well, in theory at least, have been the only thing standing between us and Dachau."

The inspiration for a comedy about the exploits of a Home Guard unit first struck Jimmy Perry during the summer of 1967. Perry, himself an actor, was walking through St. James's Park near Buckingham Palace. "In the distance I could hear the bands playing for the changing of the guard," recalled Perry. "The red tunics of the soldiers made a brave sight—what a difference from the drab khaki battle dress of the war years, when the Home Guard had a spell of duty at the Palace."

Perry's mind raced back to when he had been a 16-year-old volunteer in the Home Guard in southwest London. Later that evening, while on a train to an acting assignment, Perry realized he had the perfect subject for a 30-minute situation comedy. Unsure where to begin, Perry got the basic construction for the show from a Sunday afternoon airing of *Oh! Mr. Porter*, the 1937 Will Hay comedy. "One of the movie's strengths," Perry told Richard Webber in *Dad's Army: A Celebration*, "was the wonderful balance of characters: a pompous man, a boy and an old man."

This combination would form the nucleus for Perry's Home Guard opus. Three days later he had completed a pilot script.

Having no previous experience as a television comedy writer, Perry took the idea to BBC producer, director, and writer David Croft, with whom he had previously worked. In addition, Croft's wife was Perry's agent. Approaching Croft in the parking garage at the BBC a few weeks later, Perry offered the script to the producer. Croft immediately loved the idea. The first-time author asked if Croft would like to write it with him. The partnership was sealed with a handshake, thus beginning one of the most successful teamings in British television history.

Together, Croft and Perry completed a second script, which, along with the first, Croft showed to Michael Mills, who was the BBC's Head of Light Entertainment at the time. Mills also liked the concept at once but felt that Perry's original title, *The Fighting Tigers*, wasn't right. Instead, Mills suggested the title *Dad's Army*, and the rest is television history.

Although it had the enthusiasm of the BBC's head of light entertainment, as well as one of its top comedy producers behind it, *Dad's Army* almost never saw the light of the cathode ray tube. The show's original concept called for the opening and closing sequences to include actual war footage, illustrating the bleak horror of the war. This grim juxtaposition, along with the fear that the show might be "taking the mickey out of" (British slang for ridiculing) the nation's great war effort, almost ended the project. "There was a lot of opposition," Croft told Tim Devlin in 1973. "We were sending up Britain's finest hour. Paul Fox, then Controller of Programmes, thought it would be a psychological mistake."

After some debate, a compromise was struck. A new opening sequence was devised that showed the characters in the present day (1968), looking back on their wartime experiences. The powers that be at the BBC felt this put the show in the proper perspective. "It meant the first episode appeared to start three times," remarked David Croft in *Dad's Army: A Celebration*. "First you had the prologue, then the familiar swastika and Union Jack credits and also the newsreel-style clippings before the show finally started. It was like a dog's dinner in my view, but that was the compromise that got the show on the air."

With the more sensitive aspects of the format ironed out, the BBC commissioned the first series of six programs, and Croft and Perry set about honing their scripts and characters. One can assume that Perry's original pompous man turned out to be Captain George Mainwaring, the local bank manager in the small fictitious seaside town of Walmington-on-Sea, where the show was set. The boy, of course was Private Pike, a mama's boy who was also a clerk in Mainwaring's bank. The old man probably was Lance Corporal Jack Jones, a gung-ho retired career soldier who was now the town's butcher. To these characters, Perry added Sergeant Arthur Wilson, Mainwaring's second in command, both in the platoon and at the bank. Wilson's character was really the defining addition to the series, giving it the dramatic tension needed to make it work. "The central conflict in the show is that of a lower middle–class bank manager [Mainwaring] who finds himself commanding a man from the upper classes [Wilson]," noted the authors of *The Guinness Book of Classic British TV*.

Mainwaring's often ill-conceived enthusiasm and energy played perfectly off of Wilson's more well-thought-out caution and provided many comedic as well as dramatic highlights throughout the run of the series.

Others characters included Frazer, a dour Scot, who was the first to express apprehension in a situation, although he invariably asserted his underlying confidence when things worked out well. Private Joe Walker was the "spiv," a stock type in British society, especially during the war. The spiv was the local character who ran his various shady enterprises just on the other side of the law, usually including such activities as black marketeering and gambling. The final character was Private Charles Godfrey, a gentle old soul who suffered from bouts of incontinence.

One would think that with such a strong core of seven characters the cast of *Dad's Army* would be set. To these men, however, Perry and Croft continued to add funny, easily identifiable types in secondary supporting roles. These included the local vicar, a rather effeminate clergyman, and his constant support, the more belligerent verger. As an added and more evident threat to

Mainwaring's authority, the writers created the character of the chief air raid warden, Hodges. Whereas Wilson caused friction with Mainwaring from above, Hodges provided it from below, being a rather coarse low-class fellow. Rounding out the main supporting cast was the character of Mrs. Pike, the molly-coddling mother of Private Pike and the semi-secret love of Sergeant Wilson. (It was long intimated, though never definitively stated, that young Pike was actually Wilson's illegitimate son.)

The important chore of actually filling these roles was quite a daunting challenge and one that turned out quite differently than it began. Originally, Jimmy Perry saw Robert Dorning (who can be seen as the bank inspector in the "Something Nasty in the Vault" episode) as Mainwaring, with Arthur Lowe as Wilson, and comedian Jack Haig as Jones. Haig would also be called upon to play Jones's twin brother, a character subsequently dropped from the series. But Haig had just been offered the lead role in a children's program and declined the offer, although he would appear in small parts in two episodes of the series and finally would play Jones for part of the tour of the *Dad's Army* stage show.

Michael Mills suggested John Le Mesurier for the part of Mainwaring. In a bit of casting that helped make the series, the writers noted that Le Mesurier would be more inspiring as the vague, upper-class Wilson rather than as the pompous middle-class Mainwaring. Jimmy Perry was still keen on having Arthur Lowe, now wanted for the lead role, but the BBC was reluctant to offer him the part. The main difficulty in casting Lowe was the fact that he was quite a recognizable TV personality but not with the BBC. Lowe had made a hit as the character of Mr. Swindley in *Coronation Street* and its sequel, *Pardon the Expression*, a major success on the rival commercial television network.

Mainwaring's part was offered instead to Thorley Walters, who declined it. Next, Jon Pertwee (*Dr. Who*) was considered. Throughout this process, Jimmy Perry kept plugging for Arthur Lowe. "Jimmy didn't have any say in those early days," recalls Lowe's son, Stephen, in his biography of his father, "but he just kept reiterating the words 'Arthur Lowe' and eventually David Croft went with him to see Arthur in *Baked Beans and Caviar* at Windsor."

Perry's persistence paid off, and eventually Arthur Lowe got the lead role.

With Jack Haig out of the picture for the part of Jones, David Croft offered the role to Clive Dunn. Although only 38 at the time, Dunn had made a career of playing comical old men, most notably on *Bootsie and Snudge*, a popular ITV series, which itself was spun off from another hit show, *The Army Game*. Dunn was interested but hesitant to take the part. "I was worried that the sergeant would be played by some actor who thought he knew how sergeants behaved," wrote Dunn in his 1986 autobiography. "The brilliant idea for John Le Mesurier to play it was still awaiting John's decision."

Dunn had worked with Le Mesurier before, and the two were friends. Thinking that Le Mesurier would give the show a needed "touch of class," Dunn held off accepting his part until Le Mesurier finally agreed to play Sergeant Wilson.

Filling out the Magnificent Seven were veteran Shakespearean actor John Laurie as Frazer, actor and playwright Arnold Ridley as Godfrey, newcomer Ian Lavender as Pike, and James Beck as Walker. Originally, Jimmy Perry had written the part of Walker for himself, but Croft and Michael Mills convinced him that he was more needed on the other side of the production.

"The *Dad's Army* team was made up of character actors with whom one could act without worrying if they would behave badly, try to upstage you, or steal the limelight by overplaying," remembered Clive Dunn. "All of them behaved well in front of the camera."

In early 1968, production on *Dad's Army* began in earnest. Working under producer Croft was production manager Harold Snoad. It was Snoad's responsibility to find the outdoor locations that would serve as the town and surrounding areas of the fictitious Walmington-on-Sea. Aside from seeking a locale that would allow the cast and crew to work with a minimum of outside interference, the area also had to fit the period of the show. Ingeniously, Snoad hit upon the idea of finding an area under the control of the Ministry of Defence. This ultimately led the production manager to the Stamford Practical Training Area, located near Thetford in Norfolk, northeast of London.

For nine seasons, the cast and crew packed up and headed for Thetford to shoot the exterior scenes for the upcoming series. Working as they were with a large ensemble cast, these maneuvers themselves were akin to running a small army. "It was always a joyous occasion to make the journey to Thetford where we were based for the exterior work," recalled Bill Pertwee, who played Hodges, in his memoirs, *Dad's Army: The Making of a Television Legend.* "In nine years of filming in Norfolk we only had three or four days of bad weather, which included one day of snow [the first day of shooting in April 1968]. So the sunny days and weeks became known as 'Croft's weather.'"

After usually two weeks of exterior shooting, the production would head back to the BBC's studios at Wood Lane in London. There, on Monday, April 15, 1968, the Walmington-on-Sea platoon made their debut for a live studio audience. By late May, the first series was finished and in the can, waiting for its summer airing (not particularly a good time to debut a series, either in Britain or America). With no indication that a British television institution had been spawned, *Dad's Army* premiered July 31, 1968.

The reviews were mixed. Michael Billington, writing in *The Times* (London), noted that the show "seemed ... to blend sentiment and humour rather uneasily as if afraid of making too much fun of a hallowed wartime institution."

Other reviews complained that the gags were "wearing on the ear" (*Daily Mail*) and the script was "feeble" (*Sunday Telegraph*). One astute observer in the *Daily Express* seemed to be in possession of a crystal ball when he wrote: "I cannot say I cracked a rib, split my sides or even raised a good hearty belly-laugh — but some instinct is still telling me that the BBC is about to come up with a classic comedy series."

Aside from the critics, a test audience convened by the BBC did little to reassure the producers of the viability of the new series. The focus group of 100 savaged the first episode, most noting that the war was over and the writers were living in the past. In addition, they didn't care for the character of Mainwaring at all. The most positive comment from the test group was a weak "quite like it." Wisely, David Croft managed to keep the results of the test audience from the powers that be at the BBC or else the history of *Dad's Army* might have ended with the first six shows. Thankfully, there was a second season, which followed in March 1969. The quality of this second grouping of six continued to build on the strong foundation of the first series. The result was not only higher ratings but also an award for Croft and Perry from the Writers' Guild for the best British TV comedy scripting for 1969 (the duo would be similarly recognized the following year).

In addition to the higher ratings received from the general public, *Dad's Army* soon became reputed to be the favorite television show of Her Majesty, Queen Elizabeth II. "And Prince Philip did a very good P.R. job for us," wrote Jimmy Perry in the 1972 *Dad's Army Official Souvenir Magazine*, "by declaring loudly in front of BBC-TV director Huw Weldon, 'You'll undoubtedly go on for ever and ever with *Dad's Army*.'"

Despite the backing of Buckingham Palace, the writers and performers were never quite certain about the renewal of the series from one season to the next. Still, the increasing popularity of the show was evident from the fact that the third series, aired in late 1969, was composed of 14 episodes, more than double the number contained in the average BBC series. The third series was also produced in color, as were all subsequent series. Series four and series five, produced in 1970 and 1972, each contained 13 episodes.

Although a new series was not created in 1971, the *Dad's Army* team was kept quite busy none-the-less. That year, an hour-long Christmas special, "The Battle of the Giants," was produced, along with a full-length feature film for Columbia Pictures. Essentially a retelling of the origins of the Walmington-on-Sea platoon, the feature film is an interesting exercise, although not as satisfying as the television episodes. One of the most unsettling aspects of the film is that the platoon is called upon to thwart a band of German commandos, who are holding hostages in the church hall.

"There was one major mistake: we saw the Germans," opined Ian Lavender to Richard Webber. "It would have been better if we'd never actually seen the reality of what Mainwaring and his platoon were up against. Although we occasionally saw glimpses of them in the TV series, it wasn't anything like what we saw in the film."

Unfortunately, while the film did afford a larger budget, thus resulting in a richer feel to the production, the larger infusion of cash meant more meddling by Columbia. "There were many arguments because Columbia didn't want what we'd conceived, and, in my view, the whole set-up was wrong — it couldn't capture the atmosphere of the TV series," explained Jimmy Perry in *Dad's Army: A Celebration.*

Although the film was a mixed undertaking, the series continued to achieve even greater success, ultimately attracting more than 18 million viewers per episode at a time when the British population was less than 60 million. The first major crisis the show faced since its faltering beginnings came in 1973 with the death of a cast member. While one would naturally suppose this to be a risk when working with such a veteran cast (both John Laurie and Arnold Ridley were in their seventies during most of the production on the nine series), surprisingly it was one of the younger stars who threw the company into turmoil. Jimmy Beck, who played the inimitable Private Joe Walker, died in August 1973 during the final work on the show's sixth season. Beck and his wife had been attending a charity event, when the actor suddenly complained of abdominal pain and was rushed to the hospital. His condition fluctuated for approximately three weeks, during which Beck was operated on for a suspected ulcer. During the procedure, the actor's pancreas burst. Beck was 44.

"In those days there was nothing that could be done," noted Beck's widow, Kay.

While Beck did appear in most of the seven episodes of the sixth season, he was conspicuously absent from the final entry of that series, "The Recruit." The studio footage for "The Recruit" was filmed before Beck's death but after his hospitalization. Croft and Perry did a quick rewrite on the script, explaining Private Walker's absence with a brief note from the character that he had gone "to the Smoke," Cockney slang for London. "At that stage," noted David Croft in *Dad's Army: A Celebration*, "we hoped that Jimmy would return in time for the next series but he died about three weeks later."

The death of Jimmy Beck left the writers with some hard questions. Did they cast another actor in the part of Walker, or replace the character with a new platoon member, or even end the series altogether? Croft and Perry quickly realized that another actor would not be accepted in the role that Beck had so much made his own. The series was too popular to end, as well, so *Dad's Army* continued without its beloved spiv. At first, for the seventh season in 1974, the writers elevated the Mr. Cheeseman character, who had appeared in the previous season's "My British Buddy." A colorful Welshman, Cheeseman was well played by actor Talfryn Thomas, but his inclusion in the front ranks of the platoon seemed obtrusive among the already well established cast. After his inclusion in the seventh season, Private Cheeseman was absent from the series' final two seasons.

Before the untimely death of James Beck, the popularity of *Dad's Army* led to its adaptation for BBC radio. Although the radio version first aired in early 1974, it was recorded in the summer of 1973. As such, Beck reprised his role of Walker for the first eight radio shows. After his death, the voice of Walker was supplied by Graham Stark and then by Larry Martyn (Mr. Mash from *Are You Being Served?*). The programs were based on Croft and Perry's TV episodes and adapted by Harold Snoad and Michael Knowles. The radio writers were well acquainted with the property, since Snoad served as production manager for the TV series and later directed a number of the shows. Knowles appeared in five of the television episodes, as well as the film. For the most part, the radio versions are faithful to their TV counterparts, but some entries varied enough from their inspiration to earn new titles. For example, TV's "Everybody's Trucking" was embellished with a circus elephant and became radio's "A Jumbo-Sized Problem." In all, 67 radio installments were recorded; they ran into 1976.

In 1975, the popular television vehicle was also adapted for another venue. Bernard Delfont approached the writers and cast with the idea of doing a stage musical of *Dad's Army*. Croft and Perry strung together some of the more popular routines from the television show along with some of the more popular songs of the period to create what the show's ads proclaimed to be "a nostalgic music and laughter show of Britain's finest hour." All of the principal cast signed on to do the stage version, except John Laurie, who thought the nightly performances in London and subsequent tour would be too exhausting. Hamish Roughead was given the part of Frazer on the stage, while actor John Bardon was hired to play Walker. The show played for six months at London's Shaftesbury Theatre before touring the country for another six months into 1976.

Also around this time, Perry and Croft were contracted to help adapt their success to American television. The result was *Rear Guard*, a series of similar concept set on Long Island, New York, during World War II. Veteran comic actor Lou Jacobi starred in the adaptation of the Mainwaring role. The pilot episode was a reworking of "The Deadly Attachment," which was probably quite appropriate considering that spies from a U-boat were captured on Long Island during the war. ABC aired the pilot in August 1976 as part of a summer comedy anthology series, but *Rear Guard* failed to generate enough interest for a full U.S. series.

Dad's Army completed its run in 1977 with "Never Too Old," the final episode of the ninth season and the 80th episode overall. Not included in that number are several *Dad's Army* sketches done over the years as part of the BBC's *Christmas Night with the Stars* programs and one musical entry from the stage show, which was aired as part of the *Royal Variety* showroom in 1975. The final episode brought the show to a conclusion of sorts, with Corporal Jones getting married to Mrs. Fox, his longtime inamorata. According to Bill Pertwee, there was brief talk of moving *Dad's Army* over to ITV, but all concerned agreed that there was little new to do with the characters.

With the series over, the actors went their separate ways; Arnold Ridley and John Laurie went back into retirement. Arthur Lowe remained most active, starring in a number of series, most notably *Potter* and *Bless Me, Father*. Lowe, John Le Mesurier, Ian Lavender, and Bill Pertwee reprised their characters in 1982 for a radio sequel to *Dad's Army*. *It Sticks Out Half a Mile* involved Mainwaring, Wilson, Pike, and Hodges in the years after the war with the former captain now running an amusement pier. Although a pilot episode was produced from a script by Harold Snoad and Michael Knowles, Arthur Lowe died in 1982 before a full series could be made. The vehicle was rewritten without Lowe's character, and 13 episodes were recorded in 1983 and aired in 1983 and 1984.

Any further possibilities of *Dad's Army*–inspired works faded throughout the years as members of the veteran cast passed away. John Laurie died in 1980, John Le Mesurier followed in 1983, and Arnold Ridley in 1988. But as the years go by, *Dad's Army* continues to attract new fans while being cherished by those who saw it during its original run. There is a growing Dad's Army Appreciation Society with a worldwide membership. The society publishes a newsletter, runs a lending library, and convenes annual conventions that feature the surviving talent from this remarkable series, which seems to have generated as much love as it has laughs.

"If you want the real reason for *Dad's Army*'s success," noted Jimmy Perry in a 1973 newspaper interview, "it is because it is based on real situations, with real people who are reacting the way we know they are going to react. The laughs are not really at what somebody says, but on how the other person reacts to it. The first is predictable. The second isn't, and it is the combination which is funny."

The show's legions of fans are indeed fortunate that such an inspired formula had such talented writers and performers to execute it over the span of 80 episodes. Perhaps John Le Mesurier, the mannerly Sergeant Wilson, said it best in his last words: "It's been rather lovely, hasn't it!"

THE EPISODES

By Jimmy Perry and David Croft (based on an idea by Jimmy Perry). Directed by David Croft, Harold Snoad, and Bob Spiers. Produced by David Croft

Series One 1968

EPISODE 1: "THE MAN AND THE HOUR" ★★★½

Air date: July 31, 1968. Cast: Capt. Mainwaring (Arthur Lowe); Sgt. Wilson (John Le Mesurier); Cpl. Jones (Clive Dunn); Pvt. Frazer (John Laurie); Pvt. Walker (James Beck); Pvt. Godfrey (Arnold Ridley); Pvt. Pike (Ian Lavender); Mrs. Pike (Janet Davies); Janet King (Caroline Dowdeswell); Bracewell (John Ringham); ARP Warden (Bill Pertwee); Soldier (Neville Hughes)

It is May 14, 1940. Hitler's forces have swept over France, and Britain stands alone against the Nazi hordes. In the Channel-side town of Walmington-on-Sea, middle-aged George Mainwaring, the local manager of Swallow's Bank, receives authorization to form a unit of a new civilian army to be known as the Local Defence Volunteers (LDV). Mainwaring immediately makes himself captain and commanding officer, while assigning his chief clerk, Arthur Wilson, to be sergeant and second in command.

"The Man and the Hour" does an excellent job of introducing the entire cast, while not sacrificing any of the humor. Perry and Croft are to be congratulated, especially in view of the size of the cast, for delivering all seven principal so fully developed. Little time is wasted in exposition that does not have a good laugh attached.

From this premiere episode, it is as if these men have been living these lives for years, and someone has suddenly decided to record them on film. Mainwaring is easily recognizable as the puffed up but essentially earnest bank manager who has long dreamt of glory only to have his opportunity finally presented in middle age. Wilson is long suffering from the gate. Jones is the dithering old fire horse who still responds to the bell but has perhaps forgotten what it means. Frazer subtly expresses his doubts of Mainwaring's abilities; Walker searches for every angle; Godfrey exudes his gentle lower middle-class politeness; Pike proves he is still a mama's boy.

This is not to imply at all that the characters do not continue to grow and develop (as in *Are You Being Served?*). They do, but the information added over the next nine years only serves to provide details and nuances. This series is a masterpiece of television from the outset.

John Ringham's character, the upper-class Bracewell, was originally slated to be a regular member of the platoon. On the first day of rehearsal, however, coauthor and producer David Croft decided there was one regular character too many, and Bracewell was out.

The series starts well with a brief pre-title sequence set in 1968 in which Alderman George Mainwaring is the guest speaker at the kickoff banquet for the I'm Backing Britain drive. The camera pans down the dais, giving a glimpse of most of the principal cast members (the glaring exception is Jones, who presumably has died) 28 years past their Home Guard days. Walker and Pike are now prosperously middle aged while Godfrey and Frazer are positively ancient. In his brief speech, Mainwaring remarks that he has always backed Britain and harks back to what was his nation's and, presumably, his finest hour. While not particularly humorous, the scene provides a touching reference point for the beginning of the series.

The scene in Mainwaring's office starts the show off in earnest as he, Wilson, and Pike sandbag the window as the first step in constructing a makeshift pillbox. Mainwaring scans the High Street and tells Wilson that any German paratroopers who light there will be as "dead as mutton from Stead and Simpson's to Timothy White's."

"We'd get a clear run down to the pier pavilion," Mainwaring adds curtly, "if that blasted woman would get out of the telephone box."

The blasted woman becomes a moot point, however, when Wilson reminds him that they haven't a machine gun.

EPISODE 2: "MUSEUM PIECE" ★★★½

Air date: August 7, 1968. Cast: Capt. Mainwaring (Arthur Lowe); Sgt. Wilson (John Le Mesurier); Cpl. Jones (Clive Dunn); Pvt. Frazer (John Laurie); Pvt. Walker (James Beck); Pvt. Godfrey (Arnold Ridley); Pvt. Pike (Ian Lavender); Mrs. Pike (Janet Davies); Janet King (Caroline Dowdeswell); Milkman (Leon Cortez); Museum Caretaker (Eric Woodburn); Boy Scout (Michael Osborne)

With his platoon armed with only one shotgun, 15 carving knives, and Corporal Jones's assegai, Captain Mainwaring attempts to commandeer rifles from the nearby Peabody Museum of Historical Army Weapons.

An excellent milking of a single situation, "Museum Piece" explores the problem of getting into the fortresslike arms museum. The only weakness in the episode is its anticlimactic ending. After finally gaining entrance to the museum, the platoon discovers that the prized carbine rifles are not there, having been requisitioned by an earlier group. This would have provided a wonderfully ironic closing had there not been seven minutes left in the episode. The device of bringing back the Chinese rocket gun is not nearly as amusing a finish and comes off a bit contrived and mechanical.

Most of the laughs, and there are plenty in "Museum Piece," are visual in nature, with the best centered on the attempt to take the museum by force. First, Captain Mainwaring decides to climb on the roof using a scaling ladder that Walker found. The ladder quickly collapses as soon as he applies his ample

The mangificent seven charge with their fearsome, albeit makeshift, weapons in this still from the feature film. *Left to right:* Lance Corporal Jones (Clive Dunn); Private Walker (James Beck); Sergeant Wilson (John Le Mesurier); Captain Mainwaring (Arthur Lowe); Private Frazer (John Laurie); Private Pike (Ian Lavender); and Private Godfrey (Arnold Ridley). Note: Arthur Lowe is not wearing his round period glasses, but his own contemporary frames. Also note the deadly manner in which Private Godfrey is brandishing his broom.

weight to it, leaving Walker to confess that the instrument is 300 years old. Godfrey, in the first of his mildly demented suggestions, offers that they can use one of the catapults on display to launch a volunteer to the roof. Fortunately, the idea is rejected in favor of trying one of the battering rams. In a quick montage, the platoon makes three runs at the door. The first fails when the ram crumbles to pieces on impact. The second goes awry when the pole goes through the trap door and disappears. The third is set for success until the elderly Jones opens both the front and back doors, leaving the invaders outside again. A final attempt to scale to the roof on a modern ladder is thwarted when the caretaker uses a 14th-century anti-siege boiling oil cauldron to dump water on the group.

EPISODE 3: "COMMAND DECISION" ★★★

Air date: August 14, 1968. Cast: Capt. Mainwaring (Arthur Lowe); Sgt. Wilson (John Le Mesurier); Cpl. Jones (Clive Dunn); Pvt. Frazer (John Laurie);

Pvt. Walker (James Beck); Pvt. Godfrey (Arnold Ridley); Pvt. Pike (Ian Lavender); Janet King (Caroline Dowdeswell); Colonel Square (Geoffrey Lumsden); Butler (Charles Hill); Soldier (Gordon Peters)

In an effort to boost sagging morale, Captain Mainwaring promises that he will get his troops rifles by the end of the week. Mainwaring is offered 20 rifles by the blustering Colonel Square, a retired veteran of the First World War, but must agree to give Square command of the platoon in return.

A solid episode up to the standards of the series, "Command Decision" offers the first real glimpse into the depth of Captain Mainwaring's character. Although he is often full of himself, when the chips are down, Mainwaring will always come through. As seen in the first episode (and throughout the series), Mainwaring's life has been building up to commanding this tiny platoon, yet here he relinquishes his life's prize for the greater good.

Geoffrey Lumsden's Colonel Blimp–like Square provides good support, as he does in his seven subsequent appearances in the role. Gordon Peters makes his first of four appearances in a variety of roles, the most notable being the lighthouse keeper in "Put That Light Out."

Colonel Square's introductory episode has some good laughs, not just for Lumsden's performance but for some simple business with a currant. Just before Square makes his entrance, Mainwaring and Wilson are enjoying a tea break. Mainwaring opens his teacake to note that wartime rationing has eliminated any fruit. Wilson's cake, on the other hand, has an abundance of currants. Mainwaring demands one, but Wilson drops it amidst the paperwork on the desk. The search for the bit of fruit is interrupted by Square's entrance. Later, however, Square spots the missing currant and swats it for a fly. Mainwaring picks up the wayward currant and pops it in his mouth. Square is stunned that a bank manager would be eating flies off his desk, while Mainwaring matter-of-factly explains that they are hard to find in wartime.

Episode 4: "The Enemy within the Gates" ★

Air date: August 21, 1968. Cast: Capt. Mainwaring (Arthur Lowe); Sgt. Wilson (John Le Mesurier); Cpl. Jones (Clive Dunn); Pvt. Frazer (John Laurie); Pvt. Walker (James Beck); Pvt. Godfrey (Arnold Ridley); Pvt. Pike (Ian Lavender); Janet King (Caroline Dowdeswell); Captain Winogrodzki (Carl Jaffe); German Pilots (Denys Peek, Nigel Rideout); ARP Warden (Bill Pertwee); Military Police Sgt. (David Davenport)

Captain Winogrodzki of the Polish army attached to GHQ informs the platoon that there is a £10 bounty for each enemy airman brought in safely. Later on patrol, Walker, Jones, and Pike are confronted by Winogrodzki, who threatens to report them for their lax patrol techniques. After he leaves, the trio capture a pair of German parachutists. They bring the pair back to the church hall, only to have them escape when Godfrey excuses them to use the bathroom.

Soon, however, the escaped Germans return, recaptured by Winogrodzki. He threatens to report Mainwaring for his sloppy security. Mainwaring storms off while Winogrodzki interrogates the prisoners. The military police arrive and mistake the thick-accented Winogrodzki for one of the prisoners, a mistake that Walker does not try to correct, especially since he receives another £10 bounty for the extra prisoner.

Slight and generally devoid of laughs, "The Enemy within the Gates" is easily the low point of the *Dad's Army* premiere season. Much of the problem stems from the ineptitude displayed by the platoon members in carrying out their duties. While it is meant to be comical, the Walmington-on-Sea Home Guard is not as funny when bungling in a real war situation. In other confrontations with the enemy (most notably "The Deadly Attachment"), they make mistakes but then eventually set them right themselves. Here, the constant sniping by the Polish captain causes our heroes to lose face, making them seem clownish rather than merely comical.

"The Enemy within the Gates" does have some amusing moments. The brief scene where Mainwaring and Wilson try their new uniform trousers (only to discover they are ladies' slacks) is fun. Godfrey's explanation of how the prisoners escaped when he took them to use the bathroom is also quite good. Unfortunately, episodes are not carried on snippets such as these.

Episode 5: "The Showing Up of Corporal Jones" ★★★

Air date: August 28, 1968. Cast: Capt. Mainwaring (Arthur Lowe); Sgt. Wilson (John Le Mesurier); Cpl. Jones (Clive Dunn); Pvt. Frazer (John Laurie); Pvt. Walker (James Beck); Pvt. Godfrey (Arnold Ridley); Pvt. Pike (Ian Lavender); Mrs. Pike (Janet Davies); Major Regan (Martin Wyldeck); Brigadier (Patrick Waddington); Caretaker (Edward Sinclair); Girl at the Window (Therese McMurray)

Major Regan from GHQ finds Corporal Jones to be dangerously inept for his duties and recommends that he be forced to resign. To be fair, Jones will be allowed to stay if he can complete the standard assault course in less than 15 minutes. Jones manages to pass the test but not without some subterfuge from his comrades.

"The Showing Up of Corporal Jones" is a vast improvement over "The Enemy within the Gates," yet has one of its same flaws. To add conflict, Perry and Croft have again introduced a regular army officer to antagonize the platoon. Instead of Captain Winogrodzki, here the culprit is the smug Major Regan. Although he would be used again in the next episode — to similar effect — thankfully Major Regan's character would not survive into subsequent series. As the series developed, the antagonist's role would be supplied by Bill Pertwee's ARP Warden character. Evidently, the writers determined that reproach from outside was funnier than from the platoon's actual superiors.

This episode also marks the first appearance of Edward Sinclair as the Verger (although he would not be called that until the third season). Therese McMurray makes her first of two appearances in the nonspeaking role (usually these aren't credited) of the Girl at the Window. Finally, this installment introduces a defining character trait for one of the principal characters: Private Godfrey's weak bladder. It is doubtful that so much pleasure was ever received from one man's incontinence.

As well done as the assault course scenes are, the best moments in "The Showing Up of Corporal Jones" have nothing to do with the plot. When the platoon's uniform tops finally arrive, they are without buttons. Mainwaring sends the men home to sew on their own buttons. Later, when they reassemble, most of the men have suitable fasteners except Frazer and Godfrey. Frazer, it seems, has used the wooden pegs off his old navy coat, while Godfrey employed the large garish rhinestone studs from his dress shirt.

A few minutes later in Mainwaring's office, Mrs. Pike enters with her son, who is wearing a pink bunny rabbit cowl. She explains that the item, left over from a pantomime show called "Bunny Babes," will make an excellent balaklava. Before they can protest, she places similar sets of ears on Wilson and Mainwaring. She then instructs the trio to stoop over so she can cut the ears off their cowls. The sight of three men in army uniforms hunched over like bunnies is made even more hilarious when Major Regan enters to meet Captain Mainwaring for the first time.

EPISODE 6: "SHOOTING PAINS" ★★★

Air date: September 4, 1968. Cast: Capt. Mainwaring (Arthur Lowe); Sgt. Wilson (John Le Mesurier); Cpl. Jones (Clive Dunn); Pvt. Frazer (John Laurie); Pvt. Walker (James Beck); Pvt. Godfrey (Arnold Ridley); Pvt. Pike (Ian Lavender); Laura la Plaz (Barbara Windsor); Mrs. Pike (Janet Davies); Janet King (Caroline Dowdeswell); Major Regan (Martin Wyldeck); Charlie Cheeseman (Jimmy Perry); Girl at the Window (Therese McMurray)

Major Regan strips the platoon of an assignment to act as the prime minister's honor guard as a punishment for poor scores at the rifle range. The platoon members are given a chance to redeem themselves if they can beat the Eastgate platoon in a shooting contest.

The day of the contest, Walker brings trick-shooting artist Laura la Plaz to the church hall and proceeds to disguise her as a soldier so that she can shoot for the platoon in the contest. After one bull's eye, la Plaz misses every remaining shot. It seems that she cannot shoot accurately without going through the positions used in her routine (one normal shot followed by shots upside down, through the legs, and backwards in a mirror). Ultimately, the platoon wins the contest, along with the honor guard selection, when Frazer turns out to be a perfect marksman.

At first, it seems the at "Shooting Pains" is a carbon copy of the preceding episode. Again the platoon must battle the disdainful Major Regan by using a scheme of Private Walker's. Here, however, they do not overcome the threat with trickery but ultimately triumph through their own skill. Thankfully, this is the last seen of the humorless major. One cannot help thinking that had he remained a main character, *Dad's Army* would have been in danger of devolving into a British version of *McHale's Navy* with Regan as its incarnation of Captain Binghamton.

Series creator and coauthor Jimmy Perry ably portrays music hall comedian Charlie Cheeseman. It is humorous to note that while Perry delivers his jokes on stage, the entire audience roars with laughter — except for the two main characters, Mainwaring and Wilson, who sit in stony silence.

"Shooting Pains" also features a rare historical gaffe. At the firing range, Pike wets the end of his rifle sight before shooting. When questioned on the practice, he replies that he saw Gary Cooper do it in a movie. Gary Cooper did it in *Sergeant York,* the classic 1941 film. Unfortunately, this episode purportedly takes place in 1940.

Frazer's own championship shooting is unorthodox at best. Frazer explains that he learned to shoot while in the navy in the First World War. In order to hit his mark, however, the Scotsman must rock his rifle up and down in an approximation of the motion of the sea.

One last note: this episode marks the first use by Lance Corporal Jones of his immortal line: "Don't panic!" This line, which quickly became a catch phrase, was of course always uttered in a frenzied state of total hysteria.

*Series Two 1969**

EPISODE 1: "OPERATION KILT" LOST EPISODE

Air date: March 1, 1969. Cast: Capt. Mainwaring (Arthur Lowe); Sgt. Wilson (John Le Mesurier); Cpl. Jones (Clive Dunn); Pvt. Frazer (John Laurie); Pvt. Walker (James Beck); Pvt. Godfrey (Arnold Ridley); Pvt. Pike (Ian Lavender); Mrs. Pike (Janet Davies); Captain Ogilvy (James Copeland)

The platoon takes part in an exercise against Captain Ogilvy's Highland Regiment. Ogilvy and his men are charged with capturing Mainwaring's headquarters. After spying on the Highlanders, the platoon sets traps to successfully capture their adversaries and win the day.

Series coauthor Perry recalled that "Operation Kilt" was a "marvelous episode," the highlight of which involved Corporal Jones's attempts at spying while disguised as a cow.

**One of the great casualties of the BBC's extremely foolish seventies decision to erase its tape backlog is the second series of* Dad's Army. *David Croft has sought existing copies of these six programs around the world, but as of this writing only "Sgt. Wilson's Little Secret" has been recovered. Fortunately for die-hard fans of* Dad's Army, *these five missing shows can be enjoyed in their radio adaptations.*

Episode 2: "The Battle of Godfrey's Cottage" Lost episode

Air date: March 8, 1969. Cast: Capt. Mainwaring (Arthur Lowe); Sgt. Wilson (John Le Mesurier); Cpl. Jones (Clive Dunn); Pvt. Frazer (John Laurie); Pvt. Walker (James Beck); Pvt. Godfrey (Arnold Ridley); Pvt. Pike (Ian Lavender); Mrs. Pike (Janet Davies); Dolly (Amy Dalby); Nan Braunton (Cissy); ARP Warden (Bill Pertwee); Private Sponge (Colin Bean)

When the invasion alarm is accidentally sounded, divergent sections of the platoon find themselves fighting each other for Godfrey's home. The brief skirmish ends when one of Godfrey's sisters inadvertently waves a surrender flag (she is actually shaking her tea cloth out the window while cleaning the kitchen). The belligerents quickly discover they are on the same side, and the ARP Warden arrives to inform them that the bell was a false alarm.

One of many unfortunate results of this episode being lost is losing the only appearance of Amy Dalby as the often-referred-to sister of Private Godfrey, Dolly. While Nan Braunton's Cissy can be seen in three other episodes, "The Battle of Godfrey's Cottage" was Dalby's only *Dad's Army* assignment.

Episode 3: "The Loneliness of the Long Distance Walker" Lost episode

Air date: March 15, 1969. Cast: Capt. Mainwaring (Arthur Lowe); Sgt. Wilson (John Le Mesurier); Cpl. Jones (Clive Dunn); Pvt. Frazer (John Laurie); Pvt. Walker (James Beck); Pvt. Godfrey (Arnold Ridley); Pvt. Pike (Ian Lavender); Brigadier—War Office (Anthony Sharp); Chairwoman (Diana King); Brigadier (Patrick Waddington); Mr. Reed (Edward Evans); Captain Cutts (Michael Knowles); Blonde (Gilda Perry); Soldier (Larry Martyn); Medical Officer (Robert Lankesheer)

Private Walker, supplier of such essential black-market goods as alcohol, cigarettes, and Godfrey's sister's fudge, is called up to military service. The platoon's various attempts at securing Walker's release from the regular army fails, and the spiv reports for service. After a few days, Walker is discharged when it is discovered that he is allergic to corned beef.

"The Loneliness of the Long Distance Walker" features Michael Knowles in his first of five guest spots on *Dad's Army.* Aside from these appearances, Knowles made numerous appearances on *Are You Being Served?* As a writer, Knowles also contributed to a number of that series' scripts and helped create the radio adaptation of *Dad's Army. Are You Being Servers* Larry Martyn (Mr. Mash) and Diana King (Mrs. Peacock) also make guest appearances here.

Episode 4: "Sgt. Wilson's Little Secret" ★★★★

Air date: March 22, 1969. Cast: Capt. Mainwaring (Arthur Lowe); Sgt. Wilson (John Le Mesurier); Cpl. Jones (Clive Dunn); Pvt. Frazer (John Laurie); Pvt. Walker (James Beck); Pvt. Godfrey (Arnold Ridley); Pvt. Pike (Ian Lavender); Mrs. Pike (Janet Davies); Little Arthur (Graham Harboard)

While Mrs. Pike is expecting a child evacuee from wartorn London, Wilson mistakenly thinks she is pregnant. When Mainwaring learns of Mrs. Pike's supposed condition, he all but orders Wilson to marry Mrs. Pike. The platoon is practicing its honor guard duties for the planned Saturday nuptials when Mrs. Pike enters to announce that the child has arrived. She introduces the young evacuee (whose name is also Arthur) to a much-relieved Wilson. (According to the next episode's script, Wilson leaves Mrs. Pike standing at the altar.)

If the caliber of the five lost episodes from the second season of *Dad's Army* are at all comparable to "Sgt. Wilson's Little Secret," then their loss is all the more acute. Every scene of this episode is a topnotch, laugh getter, evidence that by this time the series had reached its full stride. The humor is well balanced between dialogue and physical comedy, often incorporating both within the same scene. The characters are firmly established, allowing the fine ensemble cast to carry the plot with ease.

"Sgt. Wilson's Little Secret," being largely about relationships, gives us not only concrete evidence of the depth of Wilson's relationship with Mavis Pike but also our first indication of Mainwaring's association with his wife, Elizabeth. There is a wonderful scene in which Mainwaring has just told Wilson that the only way to handle women is with a firm hand. The phone rings, and it is Elizabeth, ordering her husband home. After explaining that he won't be leaving for another half hour, he hangs up the receiver and dutifully excuses himself.

While the thrust of the plot is obviously Wilson's misunderstanding concerning Mrs. Pike's condition, much of the humor is derived from two excellent platoon scenes.

The first involves Mainwaring's attempts to teach the platoon the art of camouflage. Standing on the church hall's stage, Mainwaring appears covered in foliage and tries, with Jones's help, to show how undetectable he is in front of a woodland backdrop. Unfortunately, with Jones raising and lowering the drops (and finally flying up into the rafters with one of them), the point is difficult to make.

Mainwaring then dismisses the troops, telling them to go out, devise their own camouflages, and return in an hour. Walker returns as a small haystack, which triggers Pike's allergies. Godfrey adopts a beekeeper's netting in combination with a Hawaiian lei with no real explanation for the odd combination. When the captain points out that his netting is full of holes, Godfrey gently explains that his bees are "quite friendly," as they would be with him as their owner. Frazer comes disguised as a snowman, while Jones comes dressed as a butcher. When Mainwaring points out that he is a butcher, Jones logically observes that the Germans won't know that and thus he will be able to lull them into a false sense of security.

Episode 5: "A Stripe for Frazer" Lost episode

Air date: March 29, 1969. Cast: Capt. Mainwaring (Arthur Lowe); Sgt. Wilson (John Le Mesurier); Cpl. Jones (Clive Dunn); Pvt. Frazer (John Laurie); Pvt. Walker (James Beck); Pvt. Godfrey (Arnold Ridley); Pvt. Pike (Ian Lavender); Corporal-Colonel Square (Geoffrey Lumsden); Captain Bailey (John Ringham); Policeman (Gordon Peters); Caretaker (Edward Sinclair)

Captain Bailey informs Mainwaring that he may promote a man to corporal to go along with Jones's lance corporal. Against Wilson's advice, Mainwaring decides to make Frazer another lance corporal, then let him and Jones compete for full corporal. Frazer soon alienates the platoon by bringing charges against Pike (for desertion) and Walker (for mutiny), both of which are court-martial offenses punishable by death. Corporal-Colonel Square arrives and puts Frazer on similarly trivial charges. Frazer forfeits his stripe and any chance at promotion when he attacks Square with a boat hook.

John Ringham, who played platoon member Bracewell, returns as Captain Bailey. Geoffrey Lumsden also returns as Corporal-Colonel Square (he is a retired colonel but as of yet has only been able to land a corporal's commission).

Episode 6: "Under Fire" Lost episode

Air date: April 5, 1969. Cast: Capt. Mainwaring (Arthur Lowe); Sgt. Wilson (John Le Mesurier); Cpl. Jones (Clive Dunn); Pvt. Frazer (John Laurie); Pvt. Walker (James Beck); Pvt. Godfrey (Arnold Ridley); Pvt. Pike (Ian Lavender); Mrs. Pike (Janet Davies); Corporal-Colonel Square (Geoffrey Lumsden); Captain Bailey (John Ringham); Sigmund Murphy (Ernest Ulman); ARP Warden (Bill Pertwee); Mrs. Keane (Queenie Watts); Mrs. Keen (June Petersen); Mrs. Witt (Gladys Dawson)

With the Germans using incendiary bombs, the platoon is on special alert for fires. An incendiary bomb hits the church hall, and the platoon labors to bring the resulting fire under control. Ultimately, Mrs. Pike puts the fire out by using sand from a sandbag.

Geoffrey Lumsden makes his final appearance in the rank of Corporal-Colonel Square. After this brief attachment to the Walmington-on-Sea platoon, the pompous Square is recalled to headquarters. He will next be seen, as a captain, in season four's "Don't Forget the Diver."

Series Three 1969

Episode 1: "The Armoured Might of Lance Corporal Jones" ★★½

Air date: September 11, 1969. Cast: Capt. Mainwaring (Arthur Lowe); Sgt. Wilson (John Le Mesurier); Cpl. Jones (Clive Dunn); Pvt. Frazer (John Laurie); Pvt. Walker (James Beck); Pvt. Godfrey (Arnold Ridley); Pvt. Pike (Ian

Lavender); Mrs. Pike (Janet Davies); the ARP Warden (Bill Pertwee); Vicar (Frank Williams); Mrs. Peters (Queenie Watts); Mrs. Fox (Pamela Cundell); Miss Meadows (Jean St. Clair); Mrs. Casson (Olive Mercer); Angry Man (Nigel Hawthorne); Old Man (Harold Bennett); Raymond (Dick Haydon)

Walker approaches Jones with the proposition that he offer his unused delivery van to the platoon as a transport so he can use it for his own black-market activities.

"The Armoured Might of Lance Corporal Jones" is an episode of firsts. Apart from obviously being the first show of the third season, it is the first episode filmed in color, the first to feature Jones's familiar butcher's van, and the first in which the Warden is named and given a profession (Hodges, the greengrocer). In addition, it is the premiere episode for many characters, including the Vicar and Mrs. Fox. It is also the first appearance of Harold Bennett as Mr. Blewitt (although here he is only described as the Old Man) and of Olive Mercer (who is Mrs. Casson here, but one day will be a semiregular as Mrs. Yeatman, the Verger's wife). This episode also features the only appearance, but not the only mention, of Raymond, Jones's shop assistant. Finally, a young Nigel Hawthorne shows up in a small part. Hawthorne, of course, would later go on to greater fame as Sir Humphrey in the *Yes, Minister/Prime Minister* series.

It is not surprising that with all these firsts, the episode is somewhat disjointed. It has many amusing moments, but unfortunately these are not hung on a cohesive plot. The opening scene, for example, features a lecture by Captain Mainwaring to the platoon on the dangers of poison gas. Only after he completes his talk does he realize that no one understood a word of it due to the fact that he delivered the lecture through his gas mask.

Probably the best scene in the episode is the demonstration of the converted butcher van. The van has been bulletproofed with sandbags and land mine–proofed with marble slabs on the floor from Jones's shop counters. The slabs are dispensed with, however, when Godfrey announces that his doctor has advised him against sitting on anything cold. The biggest change, however, is the inclusion of rifle holes, which are demonstrated in a hilarious drill.

Episode 2: "Battle School" ★★★

Air date: September 18, 1969. Cast: Capt. Mainwaring (Arthur Lowe); Sgt. Wilson (John Le Mesurier); Cpl. Jones (Clive Dunn); Pvt. Frazer (John Laurie); Pvt. Walker (James Beck); Pvt. Godfrey (Arnold Ridley); Pvt. Pike (Ian Lavender); Captain Rodrigues (Alan Tilvern); Major Smith (Alan Haines); Private Sponge (Colin Bean)

The platoon spends a weekend at a Home Guard battle school camp, where they battle the grizzled Captain Rodrigues, a former guerrilla fighter in the Spanish Civil War.

A strong plot line and some character study help make "Battle School" a solid episode. Through a series of blunders, Captain Mainwaring loses the confidence of his men, only to regain it again via another more opportune mishap.

There is a humorous gaffe in "Battle School" that runs against the adage that "you can't be in two places at once." Walker sneaks away from the platoon to forage for food on a nearby farm, while the others maneuver through a series of battlefield obstacles. Unfortunately, as the scenes shift back and forth, Walker can be seen in both locales! Perhaps this rare talent helped him keep one step ahead of the law in his black-market activities.

There are some good moments on the train on the way to battle school. Godfrey, as is his wont, must use the facilities. Unfortunately, there are none on the train. He tries to take his mind off his need by reciting "The Owl and the Pussycat," but the poem's references to the sea and a pea-green boat provide scant diversion. When the vehicle makes a brief signal stop, Godfrey climbs off the train but must scramble back on when it suddenly starts again. He starts reciting again, indicating he is still unrelieved.

"Battle School" features some good physical humor as Mainwaring valiantly tries to lead his men over various obstacles. With the cry of "Follow me, men," he dives into a variety of mishaps, including two plunges into deep water and one fall from a high wire into a field of mud.

EPISODE 3: "THE LION HAS PHONES" ★★★★

Air date: September 25, 1969. Cast: Capt. Mainwaring (Arthur Lowe); Sgt. Wilson (John Le Mesurier); Cpl. Jones (Clive Dunn); Pvt. Frazer (John Laurie); Pvt. Walker (James Beck); Pvt. Godfrey (Arnold Ridley); Pvt. Pike (Ian Lavender); Mrs. Pike (Janet Davies); ARP Warden (Bill Pertwee); Telephone Operator (Avril Angers); Lt. Hope Bruce (Timothy Carlton); Sgt. Walker (Stanley McGeagh); Ladies in the Queue (Pamela Cundell, Olive Mercer, Bernadette Milnes); Doreen (Gilda Perry); Betty (Linda James); Mr. Cheesewright (Richard Jacques); Boys (Colin Daniel, Carson Green)

When a German plane goes down in the town's reservoir, the platoon's communications abilities are tested.

Every scene is a winner; every line of dialogue hits its mark in this priceless entry from a classic series. The title is a parody on the title of the morale-boosting 1939 film about the RAF, *The Lion Has Wings*. That film was codirected by Michael Powell, as was the classic 1942 film mentioned in the episode, *One of Our Aircraft Is Missing*.

In the opening sequence, Captain Mainwaring leads the platoon in a series of camouflage exercises. In these brief vignettes, we see the platoon disguised as haystacks, trashcans, and gravestones. Finally, we see a line of milkcans standing in front of a barn, but instead of being camouflaged as the cans, the men are actually the wall of the barn, which it turns out, is actually an open-sided shed.

During a lecture on communications, Captain Mainwaring is forced to give lessons on how to use a phone, since Pike has been forbidden by his over-protective mother to use telephone boxes. Pike explains that, according to his mum, public phones are unhygienic because you can get "mastiffs" in your ear. Walker manages to turn a profit on the exercise, however, when he explains to a group of ladies that the platoon is lined up in front of the phone because calls are going to be rationed. He then sells the women spaces in the line so they can make their calls.

Later, when the plane comes down, Mainwaring decides they need reinforcements and dispatches Jones to call GHQ. Unfortunately, Jones gets the number inverted and calls the Plaza Cinema instead. What ensues is a hilariously confused conversation in which the cinema employee describes their current film, *One of Our Aircraft Is Missing,* while Jones believes she is talking about the downed airplane.

"It went up five minutes ago," she tells Jones, referring to the film's starting time.

Jones informs her that it certainly has come down now.

"Eric Portman and Googie Whithers are in it," she says, commenting on the film's cast.

"Are they?" Jones asks, totally confused. "Then why are they shooting at us?"

Jimmy Perry's wife, Gilda, appears as Doreen, one of the women who staffs the ticket booth at Walmington-on-Sea's Plaza Cinema. Sharp-eyed viewers may recognize a similarity between the theater manager and a regular member of the platoon's back ranks. Actor Richard Jacques played both characters.

EPISODE 4: "THE BULLET IS NOT FOR FIRING" ★

Air date: October 2, 1969. Cast: Capt. Mainwaring (Arthur Lowe); Sgt. Wilson (John Le Mesurier); Cpl. Jones (Clive Dunn); Pvt. Frazer (John Laurie); Pvt. Walker (James Beck); Pvt. Godfrey (Arnold Ridley); Pvt. Pike (Ian Lavender); Mrs. Pike (Janet Davies); Vicar (Frank Williams); Captain Pringle (Tim Barrett); Captain Cutts (Michael Knowles); Verger (Edward Sinclair); Mr. Blewitt (Harold Bennett); Mrs. Dowding (May Warden); Choir (Fred Tomlinson, Kate Forge, Eilidh McNab, Andrew Daye, Arthur Lewis)

Mainwaring insists on an unnecessary board of inquiry when the platoon uses its ammunition to shoot at a low-flying Nazi plane.

Not without some good moments, "The Bullet Is Not for Firing" eventually bogs down into a tedious and labored exercise. One of the episode's main weaknesses is in making Mainwaring the primary antagonist. While he is often revealed to have feet of clay in other episodes, that portrayal is always balanced against his strong traits. Here the captain is shown in an entirely poor light and as such is not very likable.

One of the brighter moments features the board of inquiry, which is continually being interrupted by a stream of senior citizens making their way to the Vicar's office for choir practice. Later, Jones is interrupted in the middle of his testimony by the sweet, angelic strains of the choir practicing the *Jubilate Deo*. He freezes in midsentence and gets a faraway gaze in his eyes. When Mainwaring asks what's wrong, Corporal Jones replies that he thinks he is dying and being summoned by the heavenly choir.

EPISODE 5: "SOMETHING NASTY IN THE VAULT" ★★★

Air date: October 9, 1969. Cast: Capt. Mainwaring (Arthur Lowe); Sgt. Wilson (John Le Mesurier); Cpl. Jones (Clive Dunn); Pvt. Frazer (John Laurie); Pvt. Walker (James Beck); Pvt. Godfrey (Arnold Ridley); Pvt. Pike (Ian Lavender); Mrs. Pike (Janet Davies); ARP Warden (Bill Pertwee); Captain Rogers (Norman Mitchell). Special Guest: Robert Dorning as Bank Inspector

A visit from a bank inspector is interrupted by an air raid during which an unexploded bomb is dropped into the bank's basement vault. The platoon rallies 'round, as Mainwaring and Wilson gingerly hold the bomb.

A fine tribute to the character of each of the principals, "Something Nasty in the Vault" shows most of the Magnificent Seven in unequivocally shining light. The exception is Joe Walker, who is the only one who even suggests evacuating the bank and abandoning Mainwaring and Wilson. The rest of the men acquit themselves valiantly but with plenty of space for the unique character comedy each one brings to his role.

According to his wife, Joan, John Le Mesurier was particularly fond of this episode for the situation it afforded him to work closely with Arthur Lowe. Indeed, these two masters of the craft have many wonderful moments throughout the series, but none better than when they are captive nursemaids to the bomb in the basement. There is a wonderful bit when Wilson's nose begins to itch, and Mainwaring gingerly shifts his share of the load to scratch the offending nostril. Later, in an effort to soothe his sergeant/chief clerk's fears, the staid Mainwaring even goes so far as to tell a joke. The device displays more than a hint of the storytelling Father Duddleswell, who Lowe would portray almost a decade later in *Bless Me, Father*.

Other highlights include some good physical comedy from Clive Dunn's Jones as he repeatedly falls in the hole left in the floor by the bomb, Frazer's attempts to extract the keys to the vault from Mainwaring by using a fishing pole, and Walker's vain struggle to remain honest while standing in a vault full of cash. Even Godfrey's serving of coffee to the two men is charmingly amusing.

Episode 6: "Room at the Bottom" ★★★★

Air date: October 16, 1969. Cast: Capt. Mainwaring (Arthur Lowe); Sgt. Wilson (John Le Mesurier); Cpl. Jones (Clive Dunn); Pvt. Frazer (John Laurie); Pvt. Walker (James Beck); Pvt. Godfrey (Arnold Ridley); Pvt. Pike (Ian Lavender); Drill Sgt. Gregory (Anthony Sagar); Captain Bailey (John Ringham); Verger (Edward Sinclair); Private Sponge (Colin Bean)

Mainwaring's commission as captain is ruled invalid, and he is forced to become a lieutenant, then a private.

"Room at the Bottom" has a little of each of the qualities that make *Dad's Army* one of the finest television programs of all time. In the realm of comedy, the episode provides verbal banter, broad slapstick, and subtle farce. As a drama, it contains heroism, tragedy, and some revealing character study. All of this is packed neatly into one 30-minute episode that seems at least half again as long by virtue of its wealth of entertainment. There is not an extraneous line or wasted gesture. It is a calamity that this episode was almost lost, existing as it does in only a black-and-white version.

This episode also provides a rare look into Wilson's true attitude toward Mainwaring. While Mainwaring's feelings of jealousy toward his sergeant/chief clerk often surface, Wilson usually remains stoic during these outbursts. In "Room at the Bottom," however, we learn of Wilson's corresponding envy of Mainwaring and his joyous amusement at seeing him demoted. Still, although Wilson's cooler head often saves Mainwaring from his own foolish plans, here we see that each is dependent on the other when Wilson fails miserably at trying to lead the platoon.

John Le Mesurier provides some wonderful timed turns as Sergeant Wilson reacts to the news of Mainwaring's demotion. While trying to maintain his usual impassive expression, he cannot help but break into an ironic grin, which slips into some hearty chuckles.

Arthur Lowe is marvelous in his reactions to Mainwaring's several demotions and equally brilliant in his eventual brave resignation to each step downward. He surprises everyone by showing up to take his place as a private, rather than resigning from the platoon outright. In a touching speech, he tells the men that the defense of the town comes before his personal feelings and that while he was proud to lead them as Captain Mainwaring, he will be equally proud to march with them as Private Mainwaring. The men fight back tears as Jones invites his former captain to "a little rank" in line next to him.

From pathos, the mood quickly shifts to fast-paced verbal comedy as a regular army drill sergeant arrives, by Mainwaring's arrangement, to give the men some real drilling. The drill sergeant berates each of the platoon members in turn. Finally, Mainwaring sticks up for his former subordinates, drawing the wrath of the sergeant on himself.

When the platoon participates in a mock battle, Corporal Jones volunteers to act as advance scout. He advances to a small hill then pops his head up and down over the rise to see if it is clear to advance. Unfortunately, he has stationed himself atop an anthill. When the ants start biting his leg, Jones goes into fits, ultimately removing his trousers and waving them around in an attempt to rid himself of the insects. The platoon takes this as a new and rather overt signal to advance.

EPISODE 7: "BIG GUNS" ★★★

Air date: October 23, 1969. Cast: Capt. Mainwaring (Arthur Lowe); Sgt. Wilson (John Le Mesurier); Cpl. Jones (Clive Dunn); Pvt. Frazer (John Laurie); Pvt. Walker (James Beck); Pvt. Godfrey (Arnold Ridley); Pvt. Pike (Ian Lavender); Mr. Rees (Edward Evans); Verger (Edward Sinclair); Man from Pickfords (Don Estelle); Mr. Bennett (Roy Denton)

Mainwaring and his men have their hands full when a 30-pound naval artillery gun is delivered to the platoon.

Essentially an episode composed of three sketches, each of which could stand on its own but all of which revolve around a 30-pound artillery piece, "Big Guns" is an excellent example of what a brilliant cast can do with even slight material. Although there is really little inspiration in this situation, the Magnificent Seven manage to present a highly amusing half hour on the strength of their performances and characterizations.

In this episode, we learn that former navy Chief Petty Officer Frazer served as a cook. When the others learn this, they question his boast that he fought in the great naval battle of Jutland. Frazer corrects that he was *at* Jutland, below decks, making lunch. He then informs them that it takes a real man to stay below and make shepherd's pie when the battle is raging above.

When the naval gun arrives, Mainwaring sends for ex–CPO Frazer to show the platoon how it works. One look informs the audience that Frazer has never seen the weapon, but the proud Scot tries to bluff his way through. After considerable thought, Frazer points to the barrel and concludes that the shells go in the back and come out the front. Walker accuses him of blinding them with science. The initial exercise is a success of sorts until Mainwaring guides the crew in a setting of the weapon's range and elevation. He orders the piece to be fired, not cognizant of the fact that he has maneuvered it directly at his own back.

The "toot" (a military exercise carried out with scale models) scene also has some good moments as the platoon ultimately degenerates into a roomful of little boys playing with toy soldiers and cars complete with self-produced sound effects.

EPISODE 8: "THE DAY THE BALLOON WENT UP" ★★★½

Air date: October 30, 1969. Cast: Capt. Mainwaring (Arthur Lowe); Sgt. Wilson (John Le Mesurier); Cpl. Jones (Clive Dunn); Pvt. Frazer (John Laurie);

Pvt. Walker (James Beck); Pvt. Godfrey (Arnold Ridley); Pvt. Pike (Ian Lavender); ARP Warden (Bill Pertwee); Vicar (Frank Williams); Verger (Edward Sinclair); Miss Godfrey (Nan Braunton); WAAF Sgt. (Jennifer Browne); Operations Room Officer (Andrew Carr); Girl in the Haystack (Therese McMurray); RAF Officer (Kenneth Watson); Girl on the Tandem (Vicki Lane); Mr. Blewitt (Harold Bennett); Gardener (Jack Haig)

The platoon tries to secure a wayward barrage balloon but only succeeds in sending Mainwaring aloft with the blimp when it gets away from them.

An implausible situation, a gigantic prop, and some good old slapstick make "The Day the Balloon Went Up" a classic of physical comedy on television. Although it is clear that many of the stunts were done in the studio with the use of rear screen projection, this doesn't take away from the fun. There are enough location long shots of someone dangling from the balloon (most of them not Arthur Lowe) to make the situation real. The few actual shots that Lowe performed prove he is certainly capable of the broadest physical business.

The platoon's evening parade is interrupted when the Vicar accuses Mainwaring's men of writing a vulgar word in grease pencil on the back of his spare harmonium. Eager to clear his men of the charges, Mainwaring orders his men to the top of the church tower, where the instrument is stored. Starting with Jones, Mainwaring points to the unseen vulgarity and asks the corporal if he did it. Jones, misunderstanding the question, asks if the captain means recently. Next, to the Vicar's consternation, Mainwaring makes each one duplicate the word next to the original in hopes of comparing the signatures and clearing his men.

Later, there are some imaginative sight gags with the runaway balloon and the havoc it wreaks with Captain Mainwaring dangling from it. First, Mainwaring is swung through a haystack, which of course, has the obligatory pair of lovers hiding in it. Next, a gardener is carefully shaping a piece of topiary. He finishes the task, then turns to put down his shears. In that split second, Mainwaring swings through, lopping off and removing all signs of the bush. The gardener turns around in utter confusion. Finally, as the captain swings through a backyard, he manages to snap up and get tangled in a line of wash.

Incidentally, the episode's title is a euphemism for the start of the invasion.

EPISODE 9: "WAR DANCE" ★★½

Air date: November 6, 1969. Cast: Capt. Mainwaring (Arthur Lowe); Sgt. Wilson (John Le Mesurier); Cpl. Jones (Clive Dunn); Pvt. Frazer (John Laurie); Pvt. Walker (James Beck); Pvt. Godfrey (Arnold Ridley); Pvt. Pike (Ian Lavender); Vicar (Frank Williams); Verger (Edward Sinclair); Mrs. Pike (Janet Davies); Miss Godfrey (Nan Braunton); Blodwen (Sally Douglas); Doris and Dora (Graham twins); Mrs. Yeatman (Olive Mercer); Pianist (Hugh Hastings)

Pike plans to use the occasion of a platoon dance to announce his engagement to Violet Gibbons, an ATS (Auxiliary Territorial Service) girl who previously worked in the fish-and-chip shop.

An interesting episode, "War Dance" is most successful as a study of the characters and their relationships. For the first time, it is openly suggested that Wilson is actually Pike's father. The underlying tension between Mainwaring and Wilson comes to the surface over Wilson's reluctance to take a firm hand in Pike's problem. Also, evidence of Mainwaring's less-than-idyllic relationship with his wife surfaces. What laughs there are come from the fringes of the plot, rather than from the prime situation.

Jones introduces the Verger as "Mr. Henry Yeatman" at the dance, although later episodes will establish his first name as Maurice. This episode also is the first to feature Olive Mercer as the Verger's wife, although she has appeared under other names already.

It is a treat seeing the platoon members and their dates interact in a social setting. Frazer shows up for the affair resplendent in his kilt, then cheerfully threatens anyone who might dare make fun of his native costume. Godfrey arrives in an opera cape and hat, accompanied by his sister. Mainwaring shows up by himself, with a black eye, supposedly from walking into a door. More than likely, however, the shiner came compliments of Mrs. Mainwaring after he scolded her for burning the sausage rolls.

EPISODE 10: "MENACE FROM THE DEEP" ★★★

Air date: November 13, 1969. Cast: Capt. Mainwaring (Arthur Lowe); Sgt. Wilson (John Le Mesurier); Cpl. Jones (Clive Dunn); Pvt. Frazer (John Laurie); Pvt. Walker (James Beck); Pvt. Godfrey (Arnold Ridley); Pvt. Pike (Ian Lavender); ARP Warden (Bill Pertwee); 2nd ARP Warden (Stuart Sherwin); 1st Sailor (Bill Treacher); 2nd Sailor (Larry Martyn)

The platoon must man the machine gun nest at the end of the amusement pier for a few nights before the regular sentries arrive. Unfortunately, their food drifts away when Pike fails to tie the boat securely to the pier, leaving them marooned. By the next morning, their woes are compounded when they discover a loose mine floating under the pier.

A good solid episode, the humor in "Menace from the Deep" is almost exclusively drawn from characterization. There are several good exchanges that highlight the tension under the surface between Mainwaring and Wilson; Pike's "stupid boy" portrayal has reached full flower; and Frazer gives the first of numerous doom-laden soliloquies. It is doubtful that an episode of this nature would have been successful had it come earlier in the series since most of the enjoyment comes from being comfortably familiar with this wonderful group of characters.

Arthur Lowe supplies some good slapstick as the pompous Captain Mainwaring has to take the simple task of getting into a rowboat and turn it into a lecture for his men. After carefully describing the proper method for boarding, he of course fumbles through the execution of the task and almost falls in the water. Next, he insists on rowing the boat, a feat that makes his boarding look professional.

Upon arriving at the pier, Frazer hears the wind whistling through the pilings. With his eyes bulging in terror, the mournful Scot delivers an ominous monologue likening the wind to the "cry of the ancient mariners lost in the deep." After he has thoroughly chilled his companions, Frazer nonchalantly drops his rueful demeanor to explain that he gave the same speech at a performance of the drama society.

Later, when the hungry men spot an arcade claw machine full of chocolate, Wilson immediately raises his rifle butt to break the glass. Mainwaring stops him, however, noting that such actions are ones to which their Nazi foes might resort—but not British soldiers. He insists they win the chocolate by fair means even though the attempts take all of Frazer's pennies. Ultimately, Walker comes in from his watch and breaks into the machine in seconds flat.

EPISODE 11: "BRANDED" ★★★½

Air date: November 20, 1969. Cast: Capt. Mainwaring (Arthur Lowe); Sgt. Wilson (John Le Mesurier); Cpl. Jones (Clive Dunn); Pvt. Frazer (John Laurie); Pvt. Walker (James Beck); Pvt. Godfrey (Arnold Ridley); Pvt. Pike (Ian Lavender); Chief Warden (Bill Pertwee); Miss Godfrey (Nan Braunton); 2nd ARP Warden (Stuart Sherwin); Doctor (Roger Avon)

The other members of the platoon shun Godfrey when they discover that he had been a conscientious objector in the First World War. This latter fact infuriates the martial Mainwaring. Godfrey redeems himself when he saves Mainwaring's life during a civil defense exercise gone awry.

A superb episode, "Branded" succeeds more for its dramatic impact than for its comedic merits. Like "Mum's Army" and "A. Wilson (Manager)?" from the fourth season, this entry presents a more poignant personal tale of one of the platoon members. This sort of approach works particularly well in "Branded" since its subject is dear old Private Godfrey. Fans of *Dad's Army* often cite the gentle, sweet, and slightly incontinent Godfrey as their favorite character despite the fact that he almost never delivers a joke or wisecrack (at least not intentionally). This is his episode to shine.

Unlike his character, Arnold Ridley served in the British army in the First World War before being discharged in 1917 for severe injuries. He also served briefly in the Second World War until he suffered shell shock while in service in France.

Like Charles Godfrey, most of the best moments in this episode are gentle and understated. When Godfrey arrives at a patrol rest hut to make tea for his comrades, Walker, Jones, and Pike follow Frazer's urgings to shun him.

Next, Godfrey offers them some upside-down cakes his sister made; all refuse, except Pike, who has his piece slapped out of his hand by Frazer. The men leave the hut to Godfrey, who sadly takes a bite of the cake as the scene fades out.

Later, the platoon discovers that in the previous war Godfrey had won a medal for his heroism in the medical corps. Mainwaring quickly agrees to the suggestion that Godfrey become the platoon's medical orderly.

There is one moment of raucous hilarity during the rescue drill. Jones is crawling backward out of the smoking hut when he realizes that he has forgotten the straw dummy he was supposed to have been rescuing. He starts the crawl back into the building when Hodges reaches through his legs and grabs him from behind. Jones quickly jumps up in reaction.

"'Ere! What's your game?" he asks the warden.

The execution of this simple line is so perfect that even veteran actor Bill Pertwee (Hodges) can be seen struggling to keep a straight face.

Episode 12: "Man Hunt" ★★

Air date: November 27, 1969. Cast: Capt. Mainwaring (Arthur Lowe); Sgt. Wilson (John Le Mesurier); Cpl. Jones (Clive Dunn); Pvt. Frazer (John Laurie); Pvt. Walker (James Beck); Pvt. Godfrey (Arnold Ridley); Pvt. Pike (Ian Lavender); Chief Warden (Bill Pertwee); Mrs. Pike (Janet Davies); Suspect (Patrick Tull); Large Man (Robert Moore); Small Man (Leon Cortez); Fierce Lady (Olive Mercer); Sexy Lady (Miranda Hampton); Bran (Himself). Uncredited: German Pilot (Robert Aldous)

The platoon chases a mysterious man with a foreign accent after he is seen parachuting into the woods near town.

GHQ reports that the Germans are starting to drop empty parachutes to confuse the English. In light of this, Captain Mainwaring tells the platoon that all parachutes found must be reported to determine their origin. Later, after finding an empty parachute hanging from a tree, the platoon tracks a suspicious man with a German accent. Eventually, they capture the man, who turns out to be a Viennese ornithologist who was in the woods looking for a rare bird's egg. Just then, a German pilot enters and asks Mainwaring why they have been running away, since he has been chasing them, trying to surrender.

Robert Aldous appears uncredited as the German Pilot in the final moments of this rather routine episode. Jimmy Perry added the character at the last moment to provide a stronger ending. Aldous was already playing a similar role in a *Dad's Army* skit for the *Christmas Night with the Stars* special, which was taped in tandem with "Man Hunt." Perry kept Aldous's appearance in this episode a secret until the technical rehearsal. When Aldous suddenly appeared to deliver his line, he recalls that the rest of the cast looked at him "as if I was stark raving bonkers."

One of the better bits occurs early in the episode. After hearing the order on reporting parachutes, Walker tells Captain Mainwaring that he had found a 'chute two weeks earlier and had the silk made into ladies' knickers (panties). Mainwaring asks what color the silk was in an attempt to determine the origin of the parachute (British silk is white, while German silk is cream colored). Walker cannot remember and, unfortunately, has sold all eight dozen pairs of the underwear.

In an attempt to determine what kind of parachute was found, Mainwaring, Wilson, and Walker go door to door, asking to see ladies' knickers. The results are less than satisfactory as Mainwaring gets slapped, and Walker gets a door slammed on his foot. Only Wilson's courtly manner elicits an invitation inside from a sexy young woman. When he emerges moments later, Wilson announces that the woman showed him her knickers, but they were blue.

The mystery is solved the next day when Mrs. Pike is knocked down by the tracking dog in full view of the platoon to reveal her new pair of pure white knickers.

Episode 13: "No Spring for Frazer" ★★½

Air date: December 4, 1969. Cast: Capt. Mainwaring (Arthur Lowe); Sgt. Wilson (John Le Mesurier); Cpl. Jones (Clive Dunn); Pvt. Frazer (John Laurie); Pvt. Walker (James Beck); Pvt. Godfrey (Arnold Ridley); Pvt. Pike (Ian Lavender); Vicar (Frank Williams); Verger (Edward Sinclair); Mr. Blewitt (Harold Bennett); Miss Baker (Joan Cooper); Mr. Drury (Ronnie Brandon)

When Private Frazer misplaces the butterfly spring to the Lewis gun in a coffin, the platoon is forced to follow a series of desperate measures in their attempt to retrieve it.

An enjoyable but somewhat contrived entry, "No Spring for Frazer" provides the cast with ample opportunities to go through a series of futile exercises to reach a single objective. In this respect, the episode resembles the first series' "Museum Piece," although it is not nearly as successful as that. Three years later, the same basic plot would be resurrected again for season five's "When Did You Last See Your Money?" In fact, not just the plot was revived for that entry but almost the identical situation. Unfortunately, in none of these episodes do the platoon members achieve their goals, primarily because their objectives are not where they are seeking them. In "No Spring for Frazer," for example, the vital piece of the Lewis gun is found in the Scot's pocket at the end of the show.

This episode also marks the first allusion to Frazer's career as an undertaker. Prior to this, he has been primarily thought of as an ex-sailor and fisherman who also ran the town's philately shop. Here the platoon is surprised to learn that he also makes coffins for Mr. Drury, the local undertaker. This should have been widely known, especially since Frazer helps to assist in a funeral later in the episode decked out in his undertaker's hat and suit. According to the script, Frazer picked up this vocation — along with dentistry — as a youth in the Hebrides.

Although the most memorable scenes involve the abortive attempts to retrieve the spring by breaking into the Blewitt home (where the coffin is lying in remembrance) and robbing the grave, there is a wonderful moment early in the episode at the funeral director's parlor. Mainwaring, Wilson, and Frazer enter Drury's shop to announce that they have come on urgent business. The receptionist takes this to mean that they have come to arrange the funeral of Corporal Jones. Immediately, Jones enters to vehemently protest this summons to an untimely grave, which he punctuates with repeated declarations that he will come when he's called and not a moment before.

This episode marks the first appearance of Joan Cooper (Mrs. Arthur Lowe) in *Dad's Army*. Here she portrays Miss Baker, the receptionist to Drury. She next appears as Miss Fortescue in "Time on My Hands," until settling into the role of Dolly Godfrey in the show's final years.

EPISODE 14: "SONS OF THE SEA" ★★★★

Air date: December 11, 1969. Cast: Capt. Mainwaring (Arthur Lowe); Sgt. Wilson (John Le Mesurier); Cpl. Jones (Clive Dunn); Pvt. Frazer (John Laurie); Pvt. Walker (James Beck); Pvt. Godfrey (Arnold Ridley); Pvt. Pike (Ian Lavender); Mr. Maxwell (Michael Bilton); Man on Station (Ralph Ball); 1st Soldier (John Leeson); 2nd Soldier (Jonathan Holt)

After obtaining a large rowboat, Mainwaring decides to expand the platoon's duties to include river patrol. During their first time on the water, however, they get lost in the fog and soon find themselves out on the English Channel at night. Drifting back to land, they hear French voices singing and assume they have landed in occupied France.

A masterpiece of situation comedy, "Sons of the Sea" is quintessential *Dad's Army*. The best elements are here in spades: Mainwaring's earnest but ill-conceived plans, Wilson's fatalistic warnings, Frazer's pessimism, Godfrey's most inopportune incontinence, and all the rest. What makes the laughs all the more delicious is watching our heroes be brave in what they believe to be a most dire situation, while actually they are completely safe. While they think they have landed across the channel in France, the Frenchmen they hear are actually only a group of French Canadian pilots having a party.

After hiding their boat, the men take refuge in a nearby freight car but are chagrined when the train starts moving, taking them farther inland. When the trains finally stops at a station, they are relieved to learn that they are not in France but in Eastbourne, a town near Walmington.

Once Mainwaring realizes that the freight car they have been hiding in is now taking them away from the coast, he orders the men to hop off the train and work their way back to the boat. To do this without being caught, however, the men must take off their tunics and hide them under their shirts. Rather than render them inconspicuous, the ploy only makes them ridiculous, as most of them — Jones especially — are bloated to the proportions of a highly expectant mother.

When the train makes its first stop, Mainwaring rolls open the freight car door to find a commuter staring at him from the platform. Rather than give himself away, he asks, in high school French, where they are.

The reply, "Oh ... *la gare* ... Eastbourne, actually," is priceless, as is the episode.

Series Four 1970

EPISODE 1: "THE BIG PARADE" ★★½

Air date: September 25, 1970. Cast: Capt. Mainwaring (Arthur Lowe); Sgt. Wilson (John Le Mesurier); Cpl. Jones (Clive Dunn); Pvt. Frazer (John Laurie); Pvt. Walker (James Beck); Pvt. Godfrey (Arnold Ridley); Pvt. Pike (Ian Lavender); ARP Warden (Bill Pertwee); Mrs. Pike (Janet Davies); Verger (Edward Sinclair); Private Sponge (Colin Bean); Mrs. Fox (Pamela Cundell)

When Mainwaring sees a newsreel that features an army unit sporting a ram as a mascot, he decides the platoon needs a similar beast for its appearance in an upcoming local parade. The parade itself quickly turns into a foot race when the platoon tries to outdistance the ARP wardens for the honor of leading the procession.

An oddly paced episode filled with many entertaining scenes that, although they are logically connected, never seem to gel into a cohesive whole. The first scene, in the cinema, is rather amusing as Mainwaring tries in vain to concentrate on the film while most of the other patrons seem intent on necking with each other. Outraged by the lowering of public morality, Mainwaring is especially bothered by the amorous couple seated directly in front of him. Only after the captain taps the pair on the shoulder do we see that the randy young lovers are Corporal Jones and the recently widowed Mrs. Fox.

Later, there is good physical comedy when, with much trepidation, the platoon goes out to catch a ram. Not only do they fail, but Pike winds up trapped in a bog (quicksand), necessitating an arduous and embarrassing rescue. Years later, Ian Lavender recalled this scene being particularly uncomfortable as he had to spend an entire day standing in a hole filled with water. "It was deemed a waste of time to get out for tea breaks," Lavender recalled, "so drinks — deliberately laced with liquor for warmth — were handed out on a tray nailed to a long piece of wood."

Finally, there is an odd scene in which Walker tries to masquerade a tiny young goat as a full-grown animal by sticking larger horns on it. What is particularly odd is that, upon Mainwaring's entrance, the bit seems to fall to pieces. The studio audience seems to be laughing much more heartily than the business calls for, and a number of the actors, James Beck and John Laurie in particular, appear to be fumbling or ad-libbing their lines. What with the unpredictability of animals, one can only guess that the goat was improvising a bit of business himself.

EPISODE 2: "DON'T FORGET THE DIVER" ★★★★

Air date: October 2, 1970. Cast: Capt. Mainwaring (Arthur Lowe); Sgt. Wilson (John Le Mesurier); Cpl. Jones (Clive Dunn); Pvt. Frazer (John Laurie); Pvt. Walker (James Beck); Pvt. Godfrey (Arnold Ridley); Pvt. Pike (Ian Lavender); ARP Warden (Bill Pertwee); Verger (Edward Sinclair); Vicar (Frank Williams); Capt. Square (Geoffrey Lumsden); H.G. Sergeant (Robert Raglan); Private Sponge (Colin Bean); 2nd ARP Warden (Don Estelle); Landlord (Verne Morgan)

Armed only with Frazer's diving suit, a pantomime tree trunk, and an alarm clock, the platoon is charged with capturing a windmill in a training exercise against Captain Square's Eastgate platoon.

This marvelous display of comedy is quintessential *Dad's Army* and follows a successful formula first employed in "The Lion Has Phones" episode the previous season. Simply put, this recipe for comedy contains three basic elements:

1) The platoon is faced with a challenge and formulates its plan in a brainstorming session. This meeting is invariably led by Captain Mainwaring with plenty of opportunity for verbal comedy as various members (usually Jones and Pike) provide several harebrained schemes. More often than not, a blackboard is used as the main prop.
2) Having decided on a course of action, the platoon rehearses its plan in a dry run, usually in the church hall.
3) Finally, having perfected their technique — they suppose — the men put their plan into action in a finale that provides the bulk of the episode's slapstick.

This pattern provides excellent comedy also in series five's "Brains versus Brawn."

One would think that such a repetitive blueprint would garner rather stale results, but therein lies the genius of the authors and performers of *Dad's Army*. Like comedy greats Laurel and Hardy, this ensemble is so accomplished at its craft that the actors are able to telegraph their actions and offer open inspection of their technique without spoiling the end product.

"Don't Forget the Diver" provides numerous highlights, including some fine physical comedy from Clive Dunn as Jones. The intrepid corporal is hilarious as he tries to sneak up on the isolated windmill dressed in a papier-mâché log. After managing to fall into the river, Jones is next accosted by a farsighted dog in need (probably the only one who is fooled by the tree costume) and finally winds up spinning on the blades of the windmill.

Also providing much mirth are the diversionary tactics that allow Jones to succeed in his mission. These include such ploys as four men marching with rifles on racks behind a wall to simulate a full platoon and the deliciously ridiculous idea of putting helmets on sheep to make Square think the men are disguised as the animals.

Not to be overlooked are standout turns by Geoffrey Lumsden as Square (especially in his opening bit in which he describes how he was saved from dying in the desert thanks to his pocket watch) and John Laurie as Frazer. Frazer provides another of his absorbing soliloquies; this one concerns how he managed to battle a giant squid in the South Seas and obtain his diving suit in the process.

Robert Raglan makes his first *Dad's Army* appearance in this episode, playing the level-headed sergeant to Captain Square's pompous blusterer, a Wilson to his Mainwaring. Before the end of this fourth season after two subsequent appearances by Capt. Pitchard, Raglan would settle into his more familiar role as the Colonel, which he wound up portraying for 14 episodes.

This episode is also noteworthy since it marks the first time the Verger is shown to be actually in opposition to the Walmington-on-Sea Home Guard. Prior to this, Mr. Yeatman has had his squabbles (primarily with Corporal Jones), but here his belligerency has actually pushed him to the point of spying for Captain Square against his hometown militia. Henceforth, the Verger will do this quite frequently.

EPISODE 3: "BOOTS, BOOTS, BOOTS" ★★★

Air date: October 9, 1970. Cast: Capt. Mainwaring (Arthur Lowe); Sgt. Wilson (John Le Mesurier); Cpl. Jones (Clive Dunn); Pvt. Frazer (John Laurie); Pvt. Walker (James Beck); Pvt. Godfrey (Arnold Ridley); Pvt. Pike (Ian Lavender); ARP Warden (Bill Pertwee); Mrs. Pike (Janet Davies); Mr. Sedgewick (Erik Chitty)

Captain Mainwaring institutes a series of route marches and similar exercises in an effort to toughen up the platoon members' feet.

An enjoyable entry, but one that is just shy of the highest standards set by the series. The primary flaw, if you could even term it such, is that the incidental comedy pieces outshine the double comic climax toward which the episode builds.

Mainwaring's mania about making his men's feet battle ready is best illustrated in a humorous montage sequence in which the platoon is subjected to such agonizing exercises as playing soccer barefoot (with scrawny-legged Godfrey in goal) and having shoeless foot races over broken seashells. Following this, two separate contingents of the platoon hatch a plot to dissuade Mainwaring from an upcoming 20-mile march. Unbeknownst to the other, each decides to replace Mainwaring's boots with ones a half size smaller. In consecutive scenes, both groups visit the local shoe store and go to great lengths to buy the boots, then surreptitiously swap them for the smaller size.

There's a wonderful line in the beginning of the episode when Mainwaring first describes the nature of a healthy foot. Using official army charts, the captain describes the big toe as the first metatarsal. Immediately, a confused Corporal Jones interrupts to announce that he is "not formed like other men!" The corporal clarifies his intriguing declaration by noting that instead of metatarsals, he has been given toes.

"Boots, Boots, Boots" also supplies more clues to the private life of Sergeant Wilson. When Mrs. Pike informs her clandestine Casanova that the excessive drilling is giving Frank nightmares, resulting in him screaming in the middle of the night, Wilson casually remarks that he didn't hear it. Mrs. Pike is understandably horrified at his casual slip, while naïve Frank fails to understand how his "Uncle Arthur" could hear him, since he supposedly lives miles away. Later, when Wilson and Pike attempt to buy a pair of boots, the shopkeeper assumes that the duo are father and son. While Wilson vehemently denies the allegation, he and Pike support the supposition by going through an identical series of nervous mannerisms in unison.

EPISODE 4: "SGT.—SAVE MY BOY!" ★★

Air date: October 16, 1970. Cast: Capt. Mainwaring (Arthur Lowe); Sgt. Wilson (John Le Mesurier); Cpl. Jones (Clive Dunn); Pvt. Frazer (John Laurie); Pvt. Walker (James Beck); Pvt. Godfrey (Arnold Ridley); Pvt. Pike (Ian Lavender); ARP Warden (Bill Pertwee); Mrs. Pike (Janet Davies); Engineer Officer (Michael Knowles)

The platoon is forced to find its way through a seaside minefield in the dark to rescue Private Pike, who is snagged on a barbed-wire fence.

This is a disappointing episode from a comedy standpoint, although "Sgt.— Save My Boy!" does provide some diverting drama. Unfortunately, neither the laughs nor the tension manage to take over, leaving on whole an unbalanced affair.

The best moments of comedy occur in the opening sequence in which Mainwaring gives the men a lecture on the progress of the war. After wrapping up the big picture (including the Soviet Union's entry into the conflict, placing this episode sometime during the summer of 1941), the captain applies the latest battlefront news to Walmington-on-Sea. To confuse Hitler,

Mainwaring announces that they are moving their forward command post to the Harris Orphans Holiday Home Hut on the beach. This lecture, as ridiculous as it is, is made all the more so by the seemingly endless tangential topics suggested by the men.

The actual sequence in which Mainwaring gingerly leads the men across the minefield to save Pike has moments of drama that are diffused by lighter spots, such as Godfrey making his way to the trapped Pike by another route to deliver him some tea. Michael Knowles makes a brief appearance as the Engineer, who arrives in the final moments to confidently assert that all the mines are located farther down the beach. His swagger is diminished considerably when Mainwaring hands him a mine that was buried just in front of his feet.

EPISODE 5: "DON'T FENCE ME IN" ★★★

Air date: October 23, 1970. Cast: Capt. Mainwaring (Arthur Lowe); Sgt. Wilson (John Le Mesurier); Cpl. Jones (Clive Dunn); Pvt. Frazer (John Laurie); Pvt. Walker (James Beck); Pvt. Godfrey (Arnold Ridley); Pvt. Pike (Ian Lavender); General Monteverdi (Edward Evans); Capt. Bailey (John Ringham); Italian POW (Larry Martyn)

When the platoon must guard an Italian POW camp for the weekend, Mainwaring finds the security in the facility wanting. He is even more shocked to discover that Walker is helping the prisoners escape.

A good, albeit minor entry in the series, "Don't Fence Me In" supplies its share of laughs in a less cohesive framework than usual. The best moments are incidental bits derived from the personalities of the main players. These character gags include such things as Pike's concern on their arrival that the prison camp is too quiet (reminding him of a similar occurrence in *Beau Geste*) and Godfrey being called upon to parlay with one of the prisoners since he is the only one who claims to know any Italian (unfortunately, his Italian consists of totally unacceptable phrases from operas).

The primary thrust of the episode is Mainwaring's attempts to impose his own strict code of discipline on the camp, despite the prisoners' genuine compliant geniality. He ultimately is forced to aid Walker's sneaky scheme to take the prisoners out at night to do essential war work, although Mainwaring is the one ultimately caught covering up the operation.

There is also a funny moment when the rotund Mainwaring gets stuck in one of the prisoners' escape tunnels. As various platoon members pull and push on their corpulent captain, Sgt. Wilson cannot help but recall a similar incident, which happened to Winnie the Pooh after he consumed too much honey.

Edward Evans landed his role as General Monteverdi after Jimmy Perry recalled an irate Italian waiter Evan had played almost 20 years before in repertory theater. Larry Martyn, Mr. Mash from *Are You Being Served?*, appears to good effect as the Italian POW with whom Godfrey attempts to communicate.

Episode 6: "Absent Friends" ★★★½

Air date: October 30, 1970. Cast: Capt. Mainwaring (Arthur Lowe); Sgt. Wilson (John Le Mesurier); Cpl. Jones (Clive Dunn); Pvt. Frazer (John Laurie); Pvt. Walker (James Beck); Pvt. Godfrey (Arnold Ridley); Pvt. Pike (Ian Lavender); ARP Warden (Bill Pertwee); Mrs. Pike (Janet Davies); Verger (Edward Sinclair); Regan (J. G. Devlin); Policeman (Arthur English); Shamus (Patrick Connor); Landlord (Verne Morgan); 2nd ARP Warden (Michael Lomax)

The platoon takes advantage of Mainwaring's planned absence to go off to the pub to play darts against the wardens. When the captain returns unexpectedly, however, they refuse to leave their game to come back on parade.

Good dialogue, strong situations, and above all interesting character conflicts make "Absent Friends" a standout episode in the fourth season's lineup. Aside from the obvious refusal of the men (led by Frazer, who is of course the first to deny it later) to report for duty, the underlying tension is between Mainwaring and his wife, Elizabeth, and Wilson and Mrs. Pike. For his part, Mainwaring must not only handle a disobedient platoon but a wife who adamantly insists on using her husband's influence to get some rare oxtail. Wilson, on the other hand, is faced with the prospect of losing Mrs. Pike's affections to the unsuitably coarse Warden Hodges.

In predictable but riveting fashion, both men work out their situations in entirely opposite manners. Mainwaring is tough with the men and timid toward his wife (Lowe's tentative delivery of his telephone greeting, "Hello? ... Elizabeth?" speaks volumes) and masters neither. Wilson, on the other hand, is so disconcerted by the thought of the crude Hodges with his Mavis that he has little time to think of anything else. In the final moments, while manhandling a gang of IRA hooligans (after four men have failed), Wilson puts his house in order with decisive action. That the usually courtly Wilson is adept at fisticuffs is an interesting revelation but certainly not one inconsistent with his character. While Wilson is ready in a moment to fight in the line of duty, one simply does not resort to violence for personal gain.

Clive Dunn gives his usual sterling support, especially in a brief bit filled with double entendres in which Mainwaring asks for some oxtail for his wife (Jones takes the request to mean that Mrs. Mainwaring is pregnant). Bill Pertwee also shines as the bullying Hodges, who only displays the full height of his bravado after being assured that Wilson will not fight for his woman. Arthur English, Mr. Harman of *Are You Being Served?* fame, makes his only *Dad's Army* appearance as a policeman.

Episode 7: "Put That Light Out" ★★½

Air date: November 6, 1970. Cast: Capt. Mainwaring (Arthur Lowe); Sgt. Wilson (John Le Mesurier); Cpl. Jones (Clive Dunn); Pvt. Frazer (John Laurie); Pvt. Walker (James Beck); Pvt. Godfrey (Arnold Ridley); Pvt. Pike (Ian Lavender);

ARP Warden (Bill Pertwee); 2nd ARP Warden (Stuart Sherwin); Lighthouse Keeper (Gordon Peters); Telephone Operator (Avril Angers)

Mainwaring sends Jones, Godfrey, Frazer, and Pike to set up an observation post in the lighthouse. While there, the quartet accidentally turns on the beacon, bathing the town in light as scores of German bombers approach.

"Put That Light Out" was based on an idea by Harold Snoad to include the platoon in a story involving a lighthouse. While certainly entertaining, the episode fails to shine quite as brightly as others in the series. The primary weakness lies in the fact that the cast is split, with Jones's section in the lighthouse cut off from the mainland (while the tide is in) and Mainwaring, Wilson, and Walker on shore. While this is certainly integral to the story and the situation that develops, it does blunt the usual interaction of the characters.

There are naturally some fine comic turns, most of them physical in nature. The sight of the four men in the lighthouse trying to block its beacon by attaching a blanket to two rifles and marching in step (or actually out of step) with the light is quite amusing. Mainwaring's nonchalant attempts at disabling a power transformer are also welcome.

Oddly, however, some of the better moments in the episode are given to cast members outside the Magnificent Seven. Avril Angers returns as the dizzy Telephone Operator (previously seen in "The Lion Has Phones") and delivers the same comic effect. Gordon Peters does a good turn as the Lighthouse Keeper who cannot stand the salt air. Not surprisingly (since the episode's title is something of his catch phrase), Bill Pertwee has a field day as the ARP Warden who usually gets frantic over a single flashlight showing, now going positively apoplectic over the biggest bare lightbulb of his career.

Within the starring lineup, John Laurie has another marvelous opportunity to tell one of his tales of horror (this one about a "slithery thing" that attacks a lighthouse). Arnold Ridley has an amusing but perilous moment when he uses the beacon to make giant shadow puppets over the town, unaware that he is directly in the line of fire as Mainwaring prepares to shoot out the light.

EPISODE 8: "THE TWO AND A HALF FEATHERS" ★★★

Air date: November 13, 1970. Cast: Capt. Mainwaring (Arthur Lowe); Sgt. Wilson (John Le Mesurier); Cpl. Jones (Clive Dunn); Pvt. Frazer (John Laurie); Pvt. Walker (James Beck); Pvt. Godfrey (Arnold Ridley); Pvt. Pike (Ian Lavender); ARP Warden (Bill Pertwee); Pvt. Clarke (John Cater); Edith (Wendy Richard); Edna (Queenie Watts); Doreen (Gilda Perry); Betty (Linda James); Elizabeth (Parnell McGarry); Raymond (John Ash)

Corporal Jones is sent two and a half white feathers after a regimental comrade from his past surfaces and accuses him of cowardice.

A rather elaborate affair containing more than a glimpse into the military career of Corporal Jones along with a spoof of such films as *The Four Feathers* (which, of course, the title parodies) and *Drums*. One of the highlights, at least from the point of view of novelty, is the lengthy flashback sequence, which shows Jonesy 42 years earlier in active service in the Sudan. The bit features the entire cast as either soldiers of the period or dervishes, including Arnold Ridley as a fakir. (Clive Dunn's narration of this segment gets especially big laughs thanks to his repeated risqué pronunciation of fakir.) As fun as it is to see the cast cavort in these costumes, the sequence is not entirely successful due to the nature of the parody, which relies heavily on many of the characters making references to their own particular catch phrases. There is also a tiresome gag, which is used frequently to lessening effect, involving Arthur Lowe's sergeant character, who must have his salty speech overdubbed with flatulent sounds.

Much more enjoyable is the episode's opening scene in the Walmington-on-Sea restaurant during an average lunchtime. Although not particularly rife with hilarity, the sequence provides what *Dad's Army* does best: it allows its characters to interact at a natural pace and display their own individual quirks. The scene allows Mainwaring to officiously pull rank even in a cafeteria line, Walker to nonchalantly flaunt his spiv status by enjoying an illicit piece of steak, and Wilson to become supremely flustered and embarrassed when the cafeteria's boisterous manager accuses him of never busing his own table. The bit is capped off by Jones's arrival, which leads to his graphic recounting of the bloody battle of Omdurman while Mainwaring and Wilson are trying to consume some rather nasty-looking toad-in-the-hole. Unfortunately, John Laurie and Arnold Ridley's absence from this scene prevent it from being a full cast tour de force.

There is also a marvelous little bit in the episode's finale as the platoon realizes that Clarke, having been exposed, has fled. Godfrey pauses and philosophically intones: "The moving finger writes, and having writ, moves on." The men ponder this seemingly deep thought for a moment, until Mainwaring speaks up to ask what the phrase has to do with anything that has previously gone on. Dropping off his sage's pinnacle, Godfrey must confess he hasn't the slightest idea.

John Cater is good in the guest role of Private Clarke, the man who returns from Jones's past to accuse him of being a coward. It is also interesting to see Clive Dunn sans his old-man make-up in this scene, and for American fans it is often the first clue that the actor was not as old as he appeared to be in the series. For particularly pedantic fans, the battle of Omdurman took place on September 2, 1898, placing this episode as occurring in the late summer of 1940.

EPISODE 9: "MUM'S ARMY" ★★★½

Air date: November 20, 1970. Cast: Capt. Mainwaring (Arthur Lowe); Sgt. Wilson (John Le Mesurier); Cpl. Jones (Clive Dunn); Pvt. Frazer (John Laurie); Pvt. Walker (James Beck); Pvt. Godfrey (Arnold Ridley); Pvt. Pike (Ian Lavender);

Mrs. Gray (Carmen Silvera); Mrs. Pike (Janet Davies); Edith Parish (Wendy Richard); Mrs. Fox (Pamela Cundell); Miss Ironside (Julian Burberry); Ivy Samways (Rosemary Faith); Waitress (Melita Manger); Serviceman (David Gilchrist); Mrs. Prosser (Eleanor Smale); Buffet Attendant (Deirdre Costello); Porter (Jack Le White)

When local women are recruited for the ladies' auxiliary unit, Captain Mainwaring winds up having a brief affair with one of the volunteers.

The favorite episode of series coauthor David Croft, "Mum's Army" is an interesting and poignant study into the heart of George Mainwaring. For one brief glimpse, not to be repeated, Mainwaring drops his blustering, all-for-England façade when he entertains a short tryst with the widow Fiona Gray (Carmen Silvera in a role specifically written for her).

Despite his assertions to the contrary (most recently in "Absent Friends"), Mainwaring's marriage to the unseen Elizabeth is clearly unsatisfying. Clues throughout the series attest to the fact that Mrs. Mainwaring is reclusive (he points out here that she hasn't left the house since the Munich Pact was signed in 1938), antisocial (she hasn't been to the movies since *The Jazz Singer* gave her a headache in 1927), and overly cautious (she insists on sleeping in the garden bomb shelter even when there isn't a raid). Her physical appearance can only be imagined as huge and lumbering as future episodes hint at ("The King Was in His Counting House" and "The Godiva Affair"). Mainwaring manages to fill his days and nights with his duties at the bank and the Home Guard.

Into this unhappy love life steps Fiona Gray, a recent evacuee from London. She is instantly recognizable as the type of woman Mainwaring values: traditional, graceful, and full of British pluck. A relationship quickly blossoms, recalling similar wartime romances such as the one in the film *Brief Encounter* (to which "Mum's Army" is invariably compared), although there is never any suggestion of a physical consummation of their affection. In the end, to preserve the reputation of the man she is falling in love with, Mrs. Gray returns to London, leaving Mainwaring on the verge of tears on the station platform. The scene makes this one of the few episodes of *Dad's Army* that doesn't close on a humorous note.

Even with the dramatic focus of the episode, "Mum's Army" features a good share of comedy, most of which stems from the insertion of women into the previously all-male platoon. It is amusing to note the type of woman each man brings as his candidate for the ladies' auxiliary unit, each being something of a female version of her sponsor. Walker brings his brassy girlfriend, Edith (Wendy Richards from *Are You Being Serve?*), Jones brings the meaty Mrs. Fox, and Pike brings the even shyer Ivy Samways, who, not surprisingly, he met in the candy store. For his contribution, Frazer brings Miss Ironside the lass who works at the "gas, light and coke," evidently prized by the Scot for her "sauncy" demeanor and her strong thighs.

It is a testimony to Arthur Lowe's range and versatility that, in an episode where he is the dramatic focus, he also supplies some of the strongest comedy. While interviewing the prospective lady candidates, Mainwaring chides Wilson for his overly courtly manner (likening him to suave British film star Jack Buchanan). When Mrs. Gray enters, however, Mainwaring catches himself repeating many of Wilson's flirtatious remarks. Later, when Mrs. Gray suggests that Mainwaring displays more warmth without his glasses, he attempts to go without his spectacles to hilarious results.

EPISODE 10: "THE TEST" ★★★½

Air date: November 27, 1970. Cast: Capt. Mainwaring (Arthur Lowe); Sgt. Wilson (John Le Mesurier); Cpl. Jones (Clive Dunn); Pvt. Frazer (John Laurie); Pvt. Walker (James Beck); Pvt. Godfrey (Arnold Ridley); Pvt. Pike (Ian Lavender); ARP Warden (Bill Pertwee); Vicar (Frank Williams); Verger (Edward Sinclair); Gerald (Don Estelle); Mr. Blewitt (Harold Bennett). Special Appearance as E. C. Egan: Freddie Trueman

The platoon accepts a challenge from the wardens to play in a cricket match, not knowing that Hodges has signed up a professional bowler.

An enjoyable entry, although one suspects that British audiences appreciate "The Test" more than American viewers because of its central theme of a cricket game. British fans also undoubtedly get a kick out of seeing actual cricket star Freddie Trueman guest starring as another cricket pro from an earlier time, Ernie Egan. While you don't have to be knowledgeable about the sport to enjoy "The Test," a smattering of the rules of the game will add to one's overall grasp of the proceedings.

Despite any unfamiliarity of cricket to American audiences, the core message of "The Test" rings through loud and clear. It embodies the quintessential theme of *Dad's Army* and takes it one step further. After all, the series is about a band of youthful spirits compelled to carry out their duties from inside aged bodies. Mainwaring's continual reference to the platoon as frontline fighters attests to this. Still, these ancient warriors struggle against the greatest obstacle of all, the unrelenting advance of time, to serve their country in what should be a chore for much younger men. Here, they are not only engaging in the work of younger men but also vigorously participating in the play of those half their age and less. And, like their Home Guard responsibilities, the platoon faces and overcomes the various "googlies" (akin to baseball's curveball) thrown at them by the calendar and the schemes of their human opponents.

There are some typically funny bits as the men practice in advance of their game, with Mainwaring naturally grasping the captaincy of the team much as he did the leadership of the platoon. As is his wont, Mainwaring assumes that leadership implies expertise and thus gives detailed and inadequate coaching on cricket. Wilson displays his usual wariness, while at the same time providing the team's greatest offensive showing. Jones is hilarious as he becomes the platoon's horrible, yet zealous wicket keeper.

It is especially gratifying that the day is won when the feeblest player, Godfrey, hits a six (the cricket equivalent of a home run) to cinch the victory.

The rest of the cast also shines with Walker supplying the scarce cricket balls at a black-market "discount," Frazer showing up dressed in his undertaker's suit, and Hodges scheming to show up Mainwaring by hook or by crook (his plot fails when Egan pulls out his shoulder on the first pitch). The Vicar and the Verger supply the umpiring duties, with Edward Sinclair's character providing many laughs as his newfound authority goes to his head. If there are any disappointments in the proceedings, they come from Ian Lavender, who was heartbroken that he would not be allowed to bat against his boyhood hero, Freddie Trueman.

EPISODE 11: "A. WILSON (MANAGER)?" ★★★½

Air date: December 4, 1970. Cast: Capt. Mainwaring (Arthur Lowe); Sgt. Wilson (John Le Mesurier); Cpl. Jones (Clive Dunn); Pvt. Frazer (John Laurie); Pvt. Walker (James Beck); Pvt. Godfrey (Arnold Ridley); Pvt. Pike (Ian Lavender); Vicar (Frank Williams); Verger (Edward Sinclair); Mrs. Pike (Janet Davies); Mr. West (Blake Butler); Capt. Pritchard (Robert Raglan); Mr. Boyle (Arthur Brough); Pvt. Sponge (Colin Bean); Pvt. Hastings (Hugh Hastings)

After years in Mainwaring's shadow, Wilson is given his own branch of Swallow's Bank and a commission to Second lieutenant in the Eastgate platoon of the Home Guard.

If "Mum's Army" was Arthur Lowe's chance to stretch his character into more dramatic realms, then certainly "A. Wilson (Manager)?" is the same for John Le Mesurier. Like his series costar in that fine episode of just two weeks earlier, Le Mesurier makes the most of his opportunity, delivering a marvelous study of the difficulties inherent in the life of Chief Clerk and Sergeant Arthur Wilson. Although the tension between Mainwaring and Wilson usually seethes just below the surface in all their interactions, here, with Wilson's double promotions, it all comes boiling to the top. If this installment is any indication, then most of the animosity resides in the senior-ranked Mainwaring. Upon finding out (after everyone else) of Wilson's good fortune, Mainwaring brands his long-suffering assistant as a Judas and launches into a diatribe on Wilson's easy life thanks to his public school upbringing. Wilson for his part attempts to remain nonconfrontational, although he does see fit to finally respond to some of Mainwaring's vitriol.

Despite the dramatics, there are some funny moments in "A. Wilson (Manager)?" Most of these are provided by the platoon ranks. In a rash move to show up the departing Wilson, Mainwaring promotes Pike to chief clerk (temporarily) and Jones to platoon sergeant. This latter promotion is misunderstood when orders are distributed advancing the entire platoon (except for Pike) to the higher rank. That evening, the men all show up sporting their extra stripes. One by one, Jones, Frazer, and Walker enter the empty hall to rehearse of their first speech as sergeant to a nonexistent gathering. Jones pantomimes his drill, indicating that the hallmark of his tenure will be plenty of fixed bayonets up the enemy's rear. For his part, Walker promises to be a compassionate leader, as long as you are a good customer of his black-market services. Frazer supplies the funniest turn as he harangues the imaginary gathering with a vow to be as hard as nails (he punctuates his speech by reminding the men that his name is "Frazer — spelled B–a–s–t–a–r–d!").

After this interval, the mood shifts back to the dramatic as Wilson assumes his new duties in the Eastgate branch. His gentle and congenial opening remarks to his new staff (which incidentally is bigger than Mainwaring's) is cut short by an air raid, during which a bomb destroys the bank. With nothing left of his branch but his nameplate on the door, Wilson is forced back to his old position and former rank in Walmington-on-Sea.

Arthur Brough, Mr. Grainger of *Are You Being Served?* fame, appears briefly as Wilson's chief clerk in Eastgate. "A. Wilson (Manager)?" was replayed by the BBC in a special broadcast on November 23, 1983, as a fitting tribute to John Le Mesurier, who had died 12 days earlier.

EPISODE 12: "UNINVITED GUESTS" ★★

Air date: December 11, 1970. Cast: Capt. Mainwaring (Arthur Lowe); Sgt. Wilson (John Le Mesurier); Cpl. Jones (Clive Dunn); Pvt. Frazer (John Laurie); Pvt. Walker (James Beck); Pvt. Godfrey (Arnold Ridley); Pvt. Pike (Ian Lavender); ARP Warden (Bill Pertwee); Vicar (Frank Williams); Verger (Edward Sinclair); Mrs. Cole (Rose Hill); Gerald (Don Estelle)

Tempers flare and the church hall chimney catches fire when the Home Guard and the ARP wardens are forced to share quarters for a week.

A good idea, hamstrung by a weak opening and partially redeemed by a slapstick finale, "Uninvited Guests" is one of the weaker entries in an otherwise strong fourth series of *Dad's Army*. The first ten minutes are hampered by a rather uninspired routine in which the platoon practices its communications skills by using tin cans connected with strings. When the actual situation gets going there is some fun, but even this quickly grinds down as Warden Hodges and Mainwaring bicker over the sharing of the one tiny desk in the office. It is never clearly explained exactly what the wardens have been using as their headquarters prior to this, as earlier episodes in the series indicated that both groups already shared the church hall.

The episode improves by its ending, when the cast has to put out the fire in the chimney. Bill Pertwee and Clive Dunn provide the largest share of the hijinks as they scramble atop the hall roof to reach the fire. At one point, Dunn as Corporal Jones is almost knocked off the roof by a stream of water only to be saved by Hodges. Dunn's heartfelt expression of thanks catches Pertwee off guard, resulting in the second time he managed to break up his fellow actor on camera (the first was in "Branded"). Dunn also has a funny bit in which he slides down the roof in order to reach the chimney pipe but then gets caught astride the hot metal pipe.

EPISODE 13: "FALLEN IDOL" ★★★½

Air date: December 18, 1970. Cast: Capt. Mainwaring (Arthur Lowe); Sgt. Wilson (John Le Mesurier); Cpl. Jones (Clive Dunn); Pvt. Frazer (John Laurie); Pvt. Walker (James Beck); Pvt. Godfrey (Arnold Ridley); Pvt. Pike (Ian Lavender); Capt. Square (Geoffrey Lumsden); Capt. Ashley-Jones (Rex Garner); Capt. Reed (Michael Knowles); Sergeant Major (Anthony Sagar); Mess Orderly (Tom Mennard); Capt. Pritchard (Robert Raglan)

The platoon becomes disenchanted with Captain Mainwaring when he appears to be segregating himself from them due to his rank.

Set apart by a tour de force performance by Arthur Lowe, "Fallen Idol" finishes the fourth series in strong fashion. While the rest of the cast turn in their usual fine support, Lowe's outdoes himself with a number of fine scenes that not only further define the character of the pompous little captain but also are hilarious in the process.

The platoon is off on a training weekend to drill in the use of explosives; and from the outset Mainwaring is vocal that they will all eat, sleep, and fight together. Soon after arriving, however, the blustering Captain Square impresses on Mainwaring the importance of keeping separate from the men. Following his advice, Mainwaring sets up separate sleeping arrangements. Next, Mainwaring adds insult to injury by leaving the men to have drinks in the officers' mess.

This last offense sets up the episode's main set piece, with Lowe performing his comical drunken routine, including some very good ad libs. Mainwaring, not used to anything stronger than sherry, naively volunteers for an elaborate drinking ceremony (being made a "cardinal") and soon is plastered on whiskey. Lowe's initial facial reactions to the hard stuff are marvelous. Indeed, his whole demeanor in the scene — shy and somewhat ill at ease in the presence of his peers, then silly under the influence — speaks volumes about the character and psyche of Mainwaring.

Juxtaposed against the scenes in the officers' mess is a correspondingly sullen gathering in the men's canteen as the platoon commiserates over its wayward leader. Pike is especially good as the child at the gathering, who doesn't realize the mood of the "adults" and persists in telling schoolboy riddles while those around him wish he would just be quiet. Godfrey finally gently silences him with a well-timed reply, which also gets a tremendous laugh. Pike also has some good moments in the opening scene as he frantically searches for his teddy bear (one "Mr. Snuggly"), which somehow has wound up packed by his mother in "Uncle Arthur's" bedroll.

Despite his feet of clay, Mainwaring manages to more than redeem himself in the end by a show of great courage that, like the rest of the episode, manages to be very funny while making its point.

Christmas Special 1971

"Battle of the Giants!" ★★★½

Air date: December 27, 1971. Cast: Capt. Mainwaring (Arthur Lowe); Sgt. Wilson (John Le Mesurier); Cpl. Jones (Clive Dunn); Pvt. Frazer (John Laurie); Pvt. Walker (James Beck); Pvt. Godfrey (Arnold Ridley); Pvt. Pike (Ian Lavender); ARP Warden (Bill Pertwee); Vicar (Frank Williams); Verger (Edward Sinclair); Capt. Square (Geoffrey Lumsden); Colonel (Robert Raglan); Sergeant (Charles Hill); Private Sponge (Colin Bean); Barmaid (Rosemary Faith)

The Walmington-on-Sea platoon battles the Eastgate platoon in a series of skill and initiative tests.

Essentially two separate but related plots tied together to make one hour-long special, "Battle of the Giants!" succeeds admirably at the longer length, only flagging slightly toward the end. The first half concerns Mainwaring's lack of military decoration, a deficiency that he had tried to hide but is forced to admit thanks to the prodding of his Eastgate rival, Captain Square. This revived animosity, thawed when last they met ("Fallen Idol"), sets the stage for the special's second half, in which the score is settled via an interplatoon contest.

There are several routines that stand easily among some of the best bits of *Dad's Army* ever produced. The opening features a good segment in which Jones is allowed to conduct a bayonet practice, the end result of which is Mainwaring's new hat at the end of Pike's spear. This is followed by an inspection of what the platoon members plan to wear for a ceremonial church parade (the reason the subject of medals comes up at all). While most of the men have actual campaign medals, Mainwaring, only a member of the occupational force following the First World War, does not. This sequence is filled with colorful verbal recollections of the veterans' experiences, intermingled with such light touches as Pike wearing his scout badges and Walker wearing a foreign medal given him by a sheik, who he had helped get a date.

After the studio-bound (and dialogue driven) first half, the action switches to film and location work for the remainder of the show (except for the finale, which uses a studio set made to look like the outdoor locale). These sequences feature some good physical comedy and some clever use of vehicles for comic effect. As both platoons race around the countryside in vans, trying to beat the other to the next test location, they become lost. Soon they spot each other and assume the other knows the right way to go. This results in each trying to follow the other until finally both platoons are driving around each other in a tight circle around a field.

The Walmington-on-Sea patrol is further hampered in their mission due to the fact that Warden Hodges, the Verger, and the Vicar are the contest's umpires. Bill Pertwee appears to be having the time of his life as he delivers his most blatantly adversarial performance of the series. For his trouble, he also receives the lion's share of the pratfalls, including two falls into water and being blown up by his own smoke bombs.

Of course, in the end, our heroes win the day (thanks largely to Walker's cunning) but not until a drunken Jones almost falls off a tower.

As first shown, "Battle of the Giants!" clocked in at 60 minutes. Subsequent airings have been of a version trimmed down to 55 minutes.

Series Five 1972

Episode 1: "Asleep in the Deep" ★★★½

Air date: October 6, 1972. Cast: Capt. Mainwaring (Arthur Lowe); Sgt. Wilson (John Le Mesurier); Cpl. Jones (Clive Dunn); Pvt. Frazer (John Laurie); Pvt. Walker (James Beck); Pvt. Godfrey (Arnold Ridley); Pvt. Pike (Ian Lavender); ARP Warden (Bill Pertwee); Pvt. Sponge (Colin Bean)

The platoon gets trapped while trying to rescue Walker and Godfrey from a bombed pumping station.

A meticulous exploitation of a single situation, "Asleep in the Deep" signaled a strong return of *Dad's Army* after almost two years since the last regular series episode. In the meantime, fans were treated to an hour-long special and a feature film, but the 30-minute format is where the men of the Walmington-on-Sea platoon really shine. And shine they do in this episode, which contains only the Magnificent Seven themselves, along with semi regulars Bill Pertwee and Colin Bean. In this respect, "Asleep in the Deep" is similar to some of the better pure Laurel and Hardy short subjects. In such films as *Towed in a Hole* and *Helpmates*, Stan and Ollie concentrate on a single theme with only minimal outside interference. Each member of the platoon, along with Warden Hodges, is allowed to do what he does best, and the result is delightfully funny.

The plot begins when Hodges arrives at the platoon's field post to announce that the pumping station has been bombed. Since Godfrey and Walker had been on duty there, Mainwaring and the men rush to the site. They find their comrades trapped inside an inner room with debris blocking the doorway. They manage to reach the inner room, only to be trapped themselves when Jones carelessly causes more wreckage to reblock the exit. Matters go from bad to worse when water starts gushing from the pipes, threatening to flood the underground room.

Some of the best moments in the episode concern the ongoing tension between Mainwaring and Wilson, with the former criticizing his subordinate for not displaying the proper spirit toward the general war work. At one point, after they have been entombed in the pump house, Mainwaring orders the lackadaisical sergeant to lead the men in a morale-building rendition of "Underneath the Spreading Chestnut Tree" complete with "cheerful actions." Frazer sums up the situation neatly by opining that if Sergeant Wilson is going to lead the cheerful actions, he would just as soon remain miserable.

Since much of the episode takes place in the flooded room, the set had to be constructed inside a special tank, which was then filled as the situation warranted.

Episode 2: "Keep Young and Beautiful" ★★★

Air date: October 13, 1972. Cast: Capt. Mainwaring (Arthur Lowe); Sgt. Wilson (John Le Mesurier); Cpl. Jones (Clive Dunn); Pvt. Frazer (John Laurie); Pvt. Walker (James Beck); Pvt. Godfrey (Arnold Ridley); Pvt. Pike (Ian Lavender); ARP Warden (Bill Pertwee); Minister (Derek Bond); Colonel (Robert Raglan); 1st MP (James Ottaway); 2nd MP (Charles Morgan)

The platoon members try to look more youthful after a parliamentary order threatens to shift older men from the Home Guard to the ARP.

As stated previously (see "The Test"), *Dad's Army* is in large part about a pack of old men struggling to do the job of younger men. In "Keep Young and Beautiful," the aging warriors are compelled to make their outward appearances come more closely in line with their ever-youthful spirits. The episode is logically constructed and carefully established; the situation provides ample dividends in the installment's second half.

After a disastrous training exercise, Mainwaring decides to divide the platoon by separating the younger, fitter men from the feebler ones. Wilson informs him that he has already tried to do so, resulting in a lopsided distribution of 2–21 (presumably Pike and Walker were the two fit men, although they were at the core of the training debacle). Mainwaring's criticism is blunted when he learns that some of his men may have to transfer to Hodges' ARP due to age and condition.

What follows is a series of delightfully humorous vignettes as various platoon members try to appear more vital and vigorous than they usually appear. Mainwaring attempts to reverse the ravages of time with a rather mousy-looking toupee. Wilson's attempt is built on the foundation of a foundation or, more specifically, a "gentleman's abdominal support." Mainwaring derides his subordinate for wearing "corsets" but then softens to admit he too had taken steps to be more virile. "It's not monkey glands, is it?" Wilson asks, his voice filled with distress.

The oldest members of the platoon take more drastic measures. Sensing their plight is more desperate, Jones and Godfrey pay a late night visit to Frazer's funeral parlor. In a scene steeped in ghoulish atmosphere, the undertaker beckons his friends to go lie on his slab so that he can ply his art on their aged features. The next day, as the inspection comes, the three old men have been transformed thanks to hair dye, make-up, and embalming fluid. Godfrey in particular is a frightening sight, looking, in Mainwaring's opinion, like a refugee from a bad production of *Madama Butterfly*. For his part, Frazer can only mumble since his sunken cheeks have been filled out with cotton. The best line of the proceedings comes when Mainwaring inquires how long the effects of the embalming fluid will last. The reply: Frazer isn't sure since he never dug up any of his customers to find out.

"Keep Young and Beautiful" contains a visual anomaly, which sharp-eyed viewers may notice. In the opening training sequence, Jones, Walker, and Pike fall into a stream while trying to cross it by walking over a telephone pole, while Frazer, the next in line, watches from the edge. When they arrive at the church hall, however, all four march in wearing their long underwear and carrying their wet uniforms.

EPISODE 3: "A SOLDIER'S FAREWELL" ★★★★

Air date: October 20, 1972. Cast: Capt. Mainwaring (Arthur Lowe); Sgt. Wilson (John Le Mesurier); Cpl. Jones (Clive Dunn); Pvt. Frazer (John Laurie); Pvt. Walker (James Beck); Pvt. Godfrey (Arnold Ridley); Pvt. Pike (Ian Lavender); ARP Warden (Bill Pertwee); Vicar (Frank Williams); Charles Boyer (Robert Gillespie); Greta Garbo (Joan Savage); Clippie (Joy Allen); Pvt. Sponge (Colin Bean)

After consuming a late night toasted cheese supper, Mainwaring dreams he is Napoleon at Waterloo.

Consistently funny, "A Soldier's Farewell" is a tightly written entry that manages to set up its gags — especially the ones occurring in the dream sequence — without calling attention to the construction. This fantasy sequence works much better than a similar period flashback in "The Two and a Half Feathers" since, ironically, this material is more believable in a dream setting. Whereas the earlier episode asks us to believe that all the people from Jones's past had identical traits to those he knows in the present, here the same request seems not only plausible but expected.

After a toasted cheese supper (or welsh rarebit), Mainwaring dreams he is Napoleon at Waterloo. In his dream, he carefully casts those he considers his loyal followers (Godfrey, Pike, Walker, Jones, and Sponge) as his own French troops versus others (Wilson, Frazer, and Hodges) about whom he has more than a passing doubt. Throughout the sequence, which incidentally is lavishly costumed and beautifully executed, the characters manage to weave their particular catch phrases and idiosyncrasies into the proceeding to hilarious effect. Walker and Jones especially have some good bits as they report to their emperor in fractured French. Mainwaring himself is the only character who manages to remain true to his historical counterpart — slipping only once to chide a Pike for being "stupid drummer boy!"

A brief encounter earlier in the episode with a charming Clippie (a woman bus conductor) is recalled in the dream, as Mainwaring envisions her as his perfect Josephine, another hint at the captain's unhappy marriage. Even this scene is punctuated with a strong laugh as Napoleon gives his love a picture to remember him by. Taking the picture, Josephine pulls her bus ticket validation device out of her coat, validates the picture, and then hands it back. Mainwaring/Napoleon stares at the perforated picture for a moment before deadpanning: "You've punched me on the nose."

Devoted *Dad's Army* fans may wonder about a phrase that is used throughout the series and again here in "A Soldier's Farewell": "Very tasty, very sweet." Always employed as if it were a contemporary catch phrase, the line was first used by Nan Kenway and Douglas Young on *Howdy Folks*, a BBC radio review. Later, Kenway and Young brought the phrase along to their own show, *Very Tasty, Very Sweet.*

There is one minor historical flaw, unusual in a series that is mostly accurate in this regard. As punishment for leaving the cinema before the national anthem was finished, the following night Mainwaring makes the men stand at attention while "God Save the King" is played on a phonograph. The tune is played — from a long-playing disc, which were not introduced until the late 1940s.

Episode 4: "Getting the Bird" ★★½

Air date: October 27, 1972. Cast: Capt. Mainwaring (Arthur Lowe); Sgt. Wilson (John Le Mesurier); Cpl. Jones (Clive Dunn); Pvt. Frazer (John Laurie); Pvt. Walker (James Beck); Pvt. Godfrey (Arnold Ridley); Pvt. Pike (Ian Lavender); ARP Warden (Bill Pertwee); Vicar (Frank Williams); Verger (Edward Sinclair); Mrs. Fox (Pamela Cundell); Mrs. Yeatman (Olive Mercer); Wren (Seretta Wilson); Newsreader (Alvar Lidell)

Walker helps Jones find some off-the-ration meat for his butcher shop. Unfortunately, he must empty Trafalgar Square of some of its main inhabitants to do so. Meanwhile, Wilson is causing quite a bit of gossip around town: he is being seen with a pretty young woman.

A very entertaining entry, "Getting the Bird" suffers from the problem of having too much material for its half-hour running time. While what is presumably the primary plot (since it is the one referred to in the title) is brimming with some hilarious situations, it consistently overwhelms an interesting secondary story line. One would like to see how each would have been handled if it were afforded its own episode, rather than having to double up.

The comic story involves Walker pilfering the pigeon population of one of London's busiest squares to provide Jones with some unrationed stock. Once he obtains the live birds (by doping them), Walker hides the birds in the boiler room next to Mainwaring's office in the church hall. When the pigeons awaken and start finding their way into the office, they must quickly be killed and transferred to Jones's cold storage locker. Even in this freezer, however, they become too hot a commodity. When Mainwaring learns over the radio news about the sudden drop in Trafalar's pigeon count, he orders the contraband birds disposed of immediately. Walker thinks he has found a safe hiding place for the replacement fowl until a hilarious finale proves him wrong.

As good as the comic line is, its humor only makes the overpowering of the delicate subplot that much more frustrating. Apparently, something upsetting is going on in the private life of Arthur Wilson. The mystery has caused the usually reliable sergeant to be thrown out of Mrs. Pike's home and has resulted in him going on an alcohol-assisted bender. John Le Mesurier turns in a fine performance, as does John Laurie as the gossipy Frazer, who later penitently vows to keep silent when he is the only one who discovers Wilson's secret. When finally revealed, the root causes of Wilson's odd behavior are interesting enough that one wishes they had been given more attention. If this secondary plot had been explored more deeply, the product could have been something of the caliber of such excellent episodes as "Branded" or "A. Wilson (Manager)?"

Episode 5: "The Desperate Drive of Corporal Jones" ★★

Air date: November 3, 1972. Cast: Capt. Mainwaring (Arthur Lowe); Sgt. Wilson (John Le Mesurier); Cpl. Jones (Clive Dunn); Pvt. Frazer (John Laurie); Pvt. Walker (James Beck); Pvt. Godfrey (Arnold Ridley); Pvt. Pike (Ian Lavender); ARP Warden (Bill Pertwee); Vicar (Frank Williams); Verger (Edward Sinclair); Signals Private (Larry Martyn); Artillery Officer (James Taylor)

After his comrades are mistakenly sent to the wrong location during a field exercise, Corporal Jones must take quick action to keep them from being blown up.

A fairly routine entry, "The Desperate Drive of Corporal Jones' is buoyed by some recurring gags and a comical finish. The repeated business centers on Mainwaring's new, specially made officer's coat. Double-breasted with shiny brass buttons, the garment first provokes some amusing asides by Walker and Frazer, who compare the captain to operetta film star Nelson Eddy and call him "the Chocolate Soldier." Proud of his new coat, Mainwaring insists on wearing it on the platoon's maneuvers, where it is subsequently destroyed when Pike uses it to make smoke signals. As if this ignoble fate were not enough, Wilson keeps reminding Mainwaring of the coat through various situations.

The slapstick finish is necessitated when Jones and Godfrey combine to give the platoon the wrong map directions, placing their comrades directly on the target for artillery drill. Unable to call off the practice barrage, thanks to Godfrey inadvertently cutting the phone lines in their field post, the pair must rush two miles to get the men out of harm's way. Faced with having to take two cars (in order to move the platoon) and only having one capable driver (Godfrey can't drive), Jones must improvise a solution. At first he tows the second car with Godfrey at the wheel. This quickly proves unsatisfactory when Godfrey's car gets tied around a tree (with the help of some rough stop-motion photography). Finally, in a clever bit of business, Jones manages to drive the two cars to the platoon in shifts.

There is a charming moment that nicely sums up the spirit of the series and its characters. While assuming their field post, Jones leads Godfrey into the tiny hut, severely barking orders in the most rigid military manner. But once he has the elderly private in position, Jones kindly invites him to sit down, rest, and have a cup of tea.

EPISODE 6: "IF THE CAP FITS..." ★★★½

Air date: November 10, 1972. Cast: Capt. Mainwaring (Arthur Lowe); Sgt. Wilson (John Le Mesurier); Cpl. Jones (Clive Dunn); Pvt. Frazer (John Laurie); Pvt. Walker (James Beck); Pvt. Godfrey (Arnold Ridley); Pvt. Pike (Ian Lavender); ARP Warden (Bill Pertwee); Major General Menzies (Campbell Singer); Colonel (Robert Raglan); Verger (Edward Sinclair); Sergeant (Alex McAvoy); 2nd Lieutenant (Dennis Blanch)

Mainwaring temporarily gives Frazer command of the platoon in an attempt to silence his constant complaining.

Plenty of laughs, all emanating from the well-drawn characters, grace this fine episode. The best moments go to John Laurie and Arthur Lowe, but each of the Magnificent Seven is given a good opportunity to perform. If the entry has any flaw, it is that the plot is not introduced until more than ten minutes into the episode, although the groundwork for the premise (Frazer's incessant instigating) is incorporated into the first scene. Once the notion of Frazer assuming temporary command is hatched, it does not play out as one might expect — with the platoon being in a shambles — but rather with a totally surprising outcome that reaffirms Mainwaring's ego, if not his competency as the platoon's captain.

The opening is excellent, as Mainwaring gives a lecture, complete with slides, on how to identify the enemy. As the various sketches of German soldiers appear on the screen, however, Mainwaring takes the opportunity to point out not the unique uniform markings but such things as beady eyes and red bull necks. When Pike innocently asks if there are any nice-looking Germans, Mainwaring ethnocentrically answers in the negative. This latest lecture drives Frazer to confront Mainwaring on his penchant for pointless speeches (including a three-hour oratory on why the Nazis don't play cricket).

Once in command, Frazer manages to bust both Wilson and Jones back into the ranks, promoting Walker and Pike in their places. John Le Mesurier gives an especially flustered reading as his character's genteel sensibilities are ruffled by the rude Scot. Later, while still in charge, Frazer is invited to lead the platoon in a ceremony to pipe in the haggis by a general who mistakes him for Mainwaring. This sets up the final scene, which finds a deflated Frazer once again retracting his bluster to replace it with vows of undying loyalty. It also gives us yet another hint into the marital life of Mainwaring, whose marriage, by the information given here regarding his honeymoon, was doomed from the start.

Episode 7: "The King Was in His Counting House" ★★★

Air date: November 17, 1972. Cast: Capt. Mainwaring (Arthur Lowe); Sgt. Wilson (John Le Mesurier); Cpl. Jones (Clive Dunn); Pvt. Frazer (John Laurie); Pvt. Walker (James Beck); Pvt. Godfrey (Arnold Ridley); Pvt. Pike (Ian Lavender); ARP Warden (Bill Pertwee); Vicar (Frank Williams); Verger (Edward Sinclair); Shirley (Wendy Richards); Pvt. Sponge (Colin Bean)

Mainwaring's party for the platoon is interrupted when a bomb scores a direct hit on his bank vault.

Highlighted by splendid opening sequences and a strong finale, "The King Was in His Counting House" provides good, although not spectacular, entertainment. The best moments come in the first few scenes. Mainwaring is hosting a party for number one section of the platoon, the first time any of the men have been over to his house. Although he tries as best as he knows how, Mainwaring is simply incapable of hosting a convivial evening. All his efforts to provide a relaxed social atmosphere prove to make the gathering that much more uncomfortable. At the captain's insistence, everyone is forced to address each other by his first name. After years of only referring to each other by last names, the ensuing attempts at forced familiarity are funny indeed. Frazer especially shines in the sequence as he continually mutters about the "load of rubbish" that Mainwaring calls his front room furnishings. Later, when Walker arrives with a date (Wendy Richards of *Are You Being Served?* fame), it is Frazer who comments, "Trust Joe to turn up with a tart." Also during this scene, the cast and indeed the audience are teased with the prospect of finally seeing the reclusive Mrs. Mainwaring, who can be heard clomping heavily around on the second floor. When the captain's "good lady" finally does start descending the stairs, the air raid siren sounds, causing her to beat a hasty retreat to the outdoor shelter before anyone gets a glimpse of her.

The middle section lags somewhat, as the partygoers are pressed into service retrieving then counting the contents of the bombed vault. There are some good moments, including Frazer suggesting that they transport the money in one of his coffins — but he will need some help emptying one of the boxes. The comedy revives for a lively ending in which the money is scattered all over the countryside as Mainwaring attempts to transport it to safety on the back of a horse cart, while Wilson, Pike, Walker, and Jones chase behind on bicycles.

EPISODE 8: "ALL IS SAFELY GATHERED IN" ★★★★

Air date: November 24, 1972. Cast: Capt. Mainwaring (Arthur Lowe); Sgt. Wilson (John Le Mesurier); Cpl. Jones (Clive Dunn); Pvt. Frazer (John Laurie); Pvt. Walker (James Beck); Pvt. Godfrey (Arnold Ridley); Pvt. Pike (Ian Lavender); ARP Warden (Bill Pertwee); Mrs. Prentice (Brenda Cowling); Vicar (Frank Williams); Verger (Edward Sinclair); Pvt. Sponge (Colin Bean); Judy (April Walker); Olive (Tina Cornioli)

The platoon helps a farmer's widow get in the wheat harvest.

Packed with a wonderful blend of verbal and physical business, "All Is Safely Gathered In" manages to endear itself with a sense of charm as well. Most of this quality is provided, as it must be, subtly through the relationship of Godfrey to Mrs. Prentice, the farmer's widow. Almost 50 years earlier, the platoon's most gentle soul once courted Mrs. Prentice, and his fondness for her is displayed through such meek touches as bringing her a small nosegay and tenderly holding her hand. Lest one think Godfrey is never a man of action, however, there is a brief reference to an incident that happened "that night" long ago under the influence of some potent potato wine.

Other platoon members contribute their unique talents to the harvest of laughs. Pike has some good "stupid boy" moments throughout the installment, as he is absolutely gleeful over the arrival of the platoon's new Tommy gun. Like the overgrown child he is, Pike cannot resist pretending to fire the weapon, punctuating his actions with loud "ack-ack-ack" sounds each time he gets his hand on it. Walker also provides some laughs as he keeps turning up in the haystacks with one of the three girls working on the farm. Clive Dunn gives a funny turn as he explains — with sound effects and some vaguely obscene body language — the workings of a threshing machine.

Bill Pertwee stands out as his character, the usually abrasive Hodges, turns into the soul of cooperation after having a near-death experience. The ARP Warden narrowly misses being hit by a dud bomb. He fervently seeks spiritual advice from the Vicar on his close call, wondering why his life has been spared. "I can't think" is the ineffectual clergyman's only response. Hodges' new attitude, in which he sees his primary mission in life to assist Mainwaring, is viewed skeptically by the captain, who suspects Hodges has succumbed to the temptation of strong drink.

Almost the entire cast does fall under the influence of alcohol after enjoying too much of the aforementioned potato wine at a post-harvest celebration.

The genial mood quickly devolves into a hilarious shoving match, which is reminiscent of similar group melees in such Laurel and Hardy films as *You're Darn Tootin'* and *Berth Mark*.

Brenda Cowling, delightful as Mrs. Prentice, was auditioned for the role of Mrs. Pike when the series was first being cast but lost out to Janet Davies.

EPISODE 9: "WHEN DID YOU LAST SEE YOUR MONEY?" ★★★½

Air date: December 1, 1972. Cast: Capt. Mainwaring (Arthur Lowe); Sgt. Wilson (John Le Mesurier); Cpl. Jones (Clive Dunn); Pvt. Frazer (John Laurie); Pvt. Walker (James Beck); Pvt. Godfrey (Arnold Ridley); Pvt. Pike (Ian Lavender); ARP Warden (Bill Pertwee); Vicar (Frank Williams); Verger (Edward Sinclair); Mr. Blewitt (Harold Bennett); Mr. Billings (Tony Hughes)

Corporal Jones is beside himself when he misplaces £500, which was collected by area merchants for a servicemen's canteen.

Often while analyzing the shows that make up this book, I have been surprised to discover that episodes that I previously held in high esteem crumbled under closer scrutiny. Conversely, ones I had dismissed as poor rose in my estimation when dissected. "When Did You Last See Your Money?" falls into the latter category. There is an awful lot of good comedy here. Led by the marvelous performance of Clive Dunn (who amazingly manages to double his character's usual output of wooly-mindedness), the entire cast manages to milk every laugh out of the script. This is an especially remarkable feat given the fact that the entire situation was done two seasons earlier in "No Spring for Frazer." Fortunately, unlike some other shows, which often repeated situations, Perry and Croft only did so when they had stronger material the second time around.

There is some wonderful byplay in the opening scene in the now bombed-out bank as Mainwaring chides Pike for keeping a sloppy teller cage while standing in the midst of debris. This type of gag continues in Mainwaring's office, as he insists that Wilson and Pike enter through the horribly jammed door, although the bomb damage has left a gaping entranceway through the wall to the side of it. Finally, there is a tarpaulin bulging with rainwater suspended over the manager's desk, which of course begins to drip uncontrollably when Wilson begins to play with it. Arthur Lowe punctuates these incidents with his usual slow-burning exasperation.

Once the plot is introduced — Jones's loss of the £500 — the action shifts to the terribly disconcerted butcher. There are a number of good bits — all of them earning thundering ovations from the studio audience — as the other members of the platoon attempt to help Jonesy remember where he last saw the money. Finally, a solution is extracted from Jones's subconscious when Frazer hypnotizes him into recalling that he inadvertently sent the funds to Mr. Blewitt in a chicken.

As in "No Spring for Frazer," a late night visit is paid to the Blewitt household, although this time the platoon knocks on the door. In an often-hilarious exchange, Mainwaring demands to examine the octogenarian's chicken in the name of the king. As in the earlier episode, the money is not found there but turns up unexpectedly at the last moment.

EPISODE 10: "BRAINS VERSUS BRAWN" ★★★

Air date: December 8, 1972. Cast: Capt. Mainwaring (Arthur Lowe); Sgt. Wilson (John Le Mesurier); Cpl. Jones (Clive Dunn); Pvt. Frazer (John Laurie); Pvt. Walker (James Beck); Pvt. Godfrey (Arnold Ridley); Pvt. Pike (Ian Lavender); ARP Warden (Bill Pertwee); Colonel (Robert Raglan); Verger (Edward Sinclair); Mr. Fairbrother (Anthony Roye); Waitress (Maggie Don); Bridge Corporal (Geoffrey Hughes); Dump Corporal (David Rose)

The platoon members disguise themselves as firemen in order to prove their mettle in a commando exercise.

Another nice blending of subtle character comedy with broad slapstick, "Brains versus Brawn" provides an entertaining display of both. Unfortunately, the episode's finale, while perfectly logical, fails to keep pace with some of the brighter bits that lead up to it.

The opening scene provides another interesting glimpse into life in Walmington-on-Sea outside the rigors of its Home Guard platoon. The venue this time is the Rotarian dinner, which Mainwaring attends with Wilson as his guest. This piece provides more of the gentle humor that is the true sparkle of *Dad's Army* and its star, Arthur Lowe. Providing a telling rationale for Mainwaring's Napoleon complex, the rotund bank manager attempts to present an important social front but only manages to be ignored by the other guests. Wilson, only a guest, on the other hand, effortlessly attracts the attention his superior so desperately curries, even managing a precious extra sherry from the affair's waitress. The sequence also sets up the plot, as the Colonel agrees to let the platoon prove the superiority of wit over force in an upcoming commando drill.

There's a lively strategy session scene as the platoon schemes on how to meet the objective: placing a bomb in the middle of a highly guarded petrol dump. As usual, most of the humor in this sequence comes from the outlandish ideas rejected and the silly tangents discovered (mostly by Corporal Jones). The episode's highlight comes as the plan — to attack the petrol dump disguised as a fire brigade — is finally hatched. Using one of the best props in the series — an old fire engine that Walker bought for £10 — the cast has a field day milking humor out of their equipment and uniforms. Ted Sinclair also turns in one of his more memorable bits as the Verger. Unable to find a more suitable agent, the Verger is pressed into a key role in the platoon's scheme and quickly manages to bungle it.

Fans of *Keeping Up Appearances* who may have always wondered what Daisy ever saw in Onslow in his youth will have their curiosity satisfied in this episode. A young Geoffrey Hughes plays a guard who interrogates the platoon on the way to its objective.

EPISODE 11: "A BRUSH WITH THE LAW" ★★½

Air date: December 15, 1972. Cast: Capt. Mainwaring (Arthur Lowe); Sgt. Wilson (John Le Mesurier); Cpl. Jones (Clive Dunn); Pvt. Frazer (John Laurie); Pvt. Walker (James Beck); Pvt. Godfrey (Arnold Ridley); Pvt. Pike (Ian Lavender); ARP Warden (Bill Pertwee); Vicar (Frank Williams); Verger (Edward Sinclair); Capt. Square (Geoffrey Lumsden); Mr. Wintergreen (Jeffrey Gardiner); Junior Warden (Stuart Sherwin); Lady Magistrate (Marjorie Wilde); Clerk of the Court (Chris Gannon); Usher (Toby Perkins)

Mainwaring is summoned to court on charges of violating the blackout laws by leaving a light shining from his office in the church hall.

Not one of the best installments in the series, "A Brush with the Law" manages nevertheless to be consistently amusing. With almost 20 minutes of the episode taken up by the courtroom scene, there is little time for any extra plot diversions. The one exception is a scene in which Mainwaring and Wilson inspect the men's rifles. John Le Mesurier stands out in this sequence by giving a wonderfully lackadaisical performance as his character approaches the mundane task with tongue firmly in cheek — much to Mainwaring's annoyance.

This strongly plotted episode begins as Chief Warden Hodges discovers that Mainwaring's office was showing a light for an hour. Beside himself with glee at finally getting the goods on the pompous captain, Hodges has a summons issued. Later, when the Verger confesses to Hodges that it was he who was using the office (to write his memoirs, à la Noel Coward, no less), Hodges does his best to suppress the facts.

Mainwaring's plight is made even more dire when he gets involved in a verbal battle with Captain Square, only to discover that Square will be the magistrate hearing the case. Geoffrey Lumsden turns in one of the more memorable of his consistently amusing performances as the blustering Square as he delights in prejudging and harassing Mainwaring from the bench.

"A Brush with the Law" also features a standout bit by John Laurie. Delighted at the prospect of Mainwaring having to stand trial, Frazer cheerfully opines that the captain is definitely "for the clink." When the other members of the platoon arrive to testify on their leader's behalf and offer their support, Frazer only ruefully promises he is there "to tell the truth."

Mainwaring manages to win his case but only thanks to the clever machinations of everyone's favorite spiv, Joe Walker. Despite the nature of his victory, Mainwaring proudly asserts that this is what the platoon has been fighting for all along: the integrity of British justice!

Episode 12: "Round and Round Went the Great Big Wheel" ★★★

Air date: December 22, 1972. Cast: Capt. Mainwaring (Arthur Lowe); Sgt. Wilson (John Le Mesurier); Cpl. Jones (Clive Dunn); Pvt. Frazer (John Laurie); Pvt. Walker (James Beck); Pvt. Godfrey (Arnold Ridley); Pvt. Pike (Ian Lavender); ARP Warden (Bill Pertwee); Colonel Pierce (Geoffrey Chater); Major General Sir Charles Holland (Edward Underdown); Capt. Stewart (Michael Knowles); Minister (Jeffrey Segal); Wireless Operator (John Clegg)

The platoon goes from kitchen duty to heroes when the testing of a secret weapon goes wrong.

Strong on physical humor, "Round and Round Went the Great Big Wheel" is another episode in the mold of "The Day the Balloon Went Up" and "Brains versus Brawn," deriving its impetus from a great inanimate object as a prop. Here the object is the great big wheel mentioned in the title: a radio-controlled secret weapon filled with high explosives. Although given the code name Head Poof in the opening scene, the fanciful contraption is firmly based in historic fact. First tested in 1943 (not 1941 as mentioned in the episode), an almost identical weapon, named the Great Panjandrum, was designed to roll in and blast open the Germans' coastal defenses. Rocket powered, as is the wheel in the episode, the Panjandrum proved similarly unwieldy in real life and was never used in combat, despite eight field tests.

David Croft wrote in *Dad's Army: A Celebration* that his version of the Panjandrum encountered similar problems. At first the prop was designed to be pedaled from the inside of the hub. When this solution proved unworkable, the wheel was simply pushed each time it had to be filmed. Needless to say, this made the filming slow as it would only go about 20 feet per push. This accounts for some of the relatively slow chase scenes involving the wheel and Jones's van.

Aside from the chase scenes, which are entertaining and occupy approximately half of the episode, the rest of the proceedings all build up to the secret weapon test. There are some amusing moments as the high command tries to butter up Mainwaring's ego in light of the fact that his platoon will be asked to do kitchen and latrine duty. Michael Knowles, back playing his third captain of a different name, visits Mainwaring's office to gingerly broach the nature of the assignment. He thanks the puffed-up Mainwaring for his time, noting how important a man he must be. "I wouldn't say I was all that important," Mainwaring says with feigned humility, before turning to his sergeant. "Would you, Wilson?"

At this point there is a wonderfully timed pause, as the long-suffering Wilson must decide how to answer this can't-win question. Finally, after carefully pondering the query he agrees, much to Mainwaring's consternation.

There is also a clever sequence in which the platoon squeezes into an underground crypt in order to discuss the highly secret nature of its as-yet-unknown assignment. Unfortunately, the crypt is a bit too small for the number of men crammed into it, a fact that becomes painfully evident as the platoon tries to respond to a number of simple commands in the tight quarters.

EPISODE 13: "TIME ON MY HANDS" ★★★½

Air date: December 29, 1972. Cast: Capt. Mainwaring (Arthur Lowe); Sgt. Wilson (John Le Mesurier); Cpl. Jones (Clive Dunn); Pvt. Frazer (John Laurie); Pvt. Walker (James Beck); Pvt. Godfrey (Arnold Ridley); Pvt. Pike (Ian Lavender); ARP Warden (Bill Pertwee); Vicar (Frank Williams); Verger (Edward Sinclair), Mr. Blewitt (Harold Bennett); Pvt. Sponge (Colin Bean); Miss Fortescue (Joan Cooper); Mr. Gordon (Eric Longworth); the German Pilot (Christopher Sandford)

The platoon rescues a German parachutist from the top of the town hall's tower, only to become stranded there themselves.

Yet another episode in which elaborate props are employed to excellent effect. In the case of "Time on My Hands," however, it is more of an interesting location filled with many workable props that carries the day. With a German parachutist "dangling" (one of the series' more favorite comic words) from the town hall tower, the platoon rushes into action. Unfortunately, a recent fire caused by an enemy bomb has gutted the stair to the tower, and the men must clamber up a network of rickety ladders. True to form, the only means of escape from the tower is destroyed when Jones inadvertently causes the ladder rigging to come crashing down.

There are many good mechanical gags as the platoon wrestles with the fairy tale figures that come out every quarter hour to parade around the clock. Most of these provide a field day for Clive Dunn as he gets to ride a statue of a steed, be chased by a sword-wielding knight (who manages to give it to Jonesy "right up 'im" much to the audience's delight), and finally be chased by a reaper. This last encounter leaves Jones particularly flustered as he tearfully exclaims he's been "reaped!" The tower's giant bell also presents some dodgy problems for the platoon, which are rectified at the expense of the headgear of Mainwaring, Frazer, and Jones.

If the clockwork figures of the knight and the reaper seem something less than mechanical, it is because they are in fact midgets inside costumes. Producer and co-author David Croft hit upon using the little people instead of constructing plaster or wood models.

There are a number of minor inconsistencies in the script to "Time on My Hands," which occur almost simultaneously. In the opening scene, Mainwaring and Wilson are enjoying morning coffee at Ann's Pantry (also visited in "Mum's Army") when Walker skulks in to deliver some black-market supplies. The spiv asks Mainwaring to serve as a lookout while he sneaks his illicit goods inside the café. At first, in another display of Arthur Lowe's impeccable timing, Mainwaring agrees, then he realizes what's going on and expresses his outrage at the request. He reminds Walker that he is a manager of Martin's Bank. Unfortunately, Mainwaring is the manager of the local Swallow's Bank. The writers had first toyed with using the name of Martin's Bank when they created the show, but since that firm was still in business they changed it to Swallow's. By the time the feature film was done, Martin's had gone under, so in the movie Mainwaring is indeed a manager in a Martin's branch. Second, reacting to Mainwaring's outrage at being asked to participate in black-market activities, Walker obliges by canceling Mainwaring's order for whiskey. A flustered Mainwaring explains to Wilson that it is only for medicinal purposes, but according to "Fallen Idol," Mainwaring doesn't imbibe past the occasional sherry or pint of beer. Either the authors forgot this fact, or the liquor is for Mrs. Mainwaring.

"Time on My Hands" marks the first appearance of Eric Longworth in the role of Mr. Gordon (as credited here), the town clerk (as the part is subsequently credited). Longworth's distinct style fits in nicely with the rest of the cast in what would become a semiregular role. Joan Cooper (Mrs. Arthur Lowe) makes another appearance, here as Miss Fortescue. Previously, Cooper appeared as Miss Baker in "No Spring for Frazer." After this, she would settle into appearing as Godfrey's sister, Dolly, in three installments of the series.

Series Six 1973

EPISODE 1: "THE DEADLY ATTACHMENT" ★★★★

Air date: October 31, 1973. Cast: Capt. Mainwaring (Arthur Lowe); Sgt. Wilson (John Le Mesurier); Cpl. Jones (Clive Dunn); Pvt. Frazer (John Laurie); Pvt. Walker (James Beck); Pvt. Godfrey (Arnold Ridley); Pvt. Pike (Ian Lavender); U-boat Captain (Philip Madoc); Chief Warden Hodges (Bill Pertwee); Verger (Edward Sinclair); Colonel (Robert Raglan); Private Sponge (Colin Bean)

The platoon's assignment to guard the crew of a U-boat turns dangerous when the Germans get ahold of Mainwaring's pistol.

"The Deadly Attachment," which is the favorite episode of series creator Jimmy Perry, is also one of the most linear and focused installments in the series. Aside from a brief and often hilarious discussion on how to distinguish between parachuting Nazis and parachuting nuns, the entire running time is reserved for the main situation. This also is one of the few times in the television run of *Dad's Army* in which the platoon encounters the enemy face to face (they do so in the film version, in "The Lion Has Phones," and in "Come In, Your Time Is Up"). This opportunity affords a heightened sense of drama and also comedy, thanks mostly to the performance of featured guest Philip Madoc as the U-boat Captain. Madoc is simultaneously menacing and comic in the part and adds greatly to the episode's success.

When the platoon is ordered to watch the U-boat prisoners overnight, the situation quickly devolves into a clash of wills between Mainwaring and the ship's captain. In a microcosm of the entire war, the pair engages in stereotypical verbal exchanges. Mainwaring is at his blimpish best as he asserts the moral superiority of Britain's struggle, while the Nazi affirms the purity of his race and keeps a detailed listing of all those who get in his way. The "list" is being kept so that after the German victory all old scores may be settled by the new masters. This device leads to one of the biggest laughs of the episode and probably the single line most recalled by fans of the series. When Private Pike childishly taunts the disdainful Aryan with a silly rhyme ("Hitler is a twerp..." to the tune of "Whistle While You Work"), the U-boat skipper immediately asks for his name so that he may add it to the growing list. In an attempt to keep the youngster's name off the list, Mainwaring yells out: "Don't tell him, Pike!"

Almost 30 years later (as of this writing), Ian Lavender reports that strangers will yell the line to him from across busy streets. The endearing fame of this line makes this one of Lavender's favorite episodes as well, although he confesses that during it his character can be caught giggling. Lavender pleaded with David Croft to edit out the unintentional snickers, but the producer left them in as they were in keeping with Pike's boyish character.

Other highlights of the episode include Walker taking orders for fish and chips from the U-boat crew (including Madoc's insistence that he will accept no "nasty, soggy chips") and the hilarious finale. In that sequence, the Germans have succeeded in taking the platoon captive and are marching them back to the harbor where they will all board a boat for France. As they march, their weapons unloaded, the platoon is kept in line by the fact that the U-boat Captain has a grenade down Jones's pants, and he is holding a string attached to the pin. This sets up a hysterical ending, in which disaster is averted once again by Sergeant Wilson's cool thinking and forethought.

From this episode, the beginning of the sixth series, Bill Pertwee's character is credited as Chief Warden Hodges, rather than the previously nondescript ARP Warden.

Episode 2: "My British Buddy" ★★

Air date: November 7, 1973. Cast: Capt. Mainwaring (Arthur Lowe); Sgt. Wilson (John Le Mesurier); Cpl. Jones (Clive Dunn); Pvt. Frazer (John Laurie); Pvt. Walker (James Beck); Pvt. Godfrey (Arnold Ridley); Pvt. Pike (Ian Lavender); Chief Warden Hodges (Bill Pertwee); U.S. Colonel (Alan Tilvern); Vicar (Frank Williams); Verger (Edward Sinclair); Mrs. Pike (Janet Davies); Shirley (Wendy Richard); Mrs. Fox (Pamela Cundell); Landlord (Verne Morgan); Mr. Cheeseman (Talfryn Thomas); Ivy (Suzanne Kerchiss); Colonel (Robert Raglan); U.S. Sergeant (Blain Fairman)

The platoon's welcome to a contingent of American allies degenerates into a brawl.

As in the previous episode, a strong situation drives "My British Buddy." Unfortunately, the results are not nearly as satisfying. The primary weakness lies in the fact that the situation never fully reaches its comic potential. Some of the blame for this must fall at the feet of the "guest foreigner." While in the previous episode, the Nazi U-boat Captain was both menacing and comic, here the visiting Americans are just rude and annoying. One would almost prefer the Germans back. This is not to say that the situation doesn't ring true or that the wartime behavior of the Yanks isn't accurately drawn, it just doesn't make for particularly funny interactions. One of the most distracting elements of the installment is Alan Tilvern in the role of the U.S. Colonel. Previously seen as Captain Rodrigues in "Battle School," the London-born Tilvern's accent, while probably quite convincing to British ears, is just off enough to be distracting to Americans.

While the plot itself disappoints, there are some good moments to be culled from "My British Buddy." The best scene comes the day after the brawl in the pub with the Americans. Animosity builds when the Americans start monopolizing the attention of the girlfriends of the platoon members (although why a 20-year-old American would be interested in the likes of Mrs. Pike and Mrs. Fox is somewhat mysterious). A full-fledged fight erupts when Hodges taunts the U.S. Colonel about his country coming late for yet another war (seemingly a common British complaint; see *Steptoe and Son's* "Pilgrim's Progress"). When the Colonel takes a swing at Hodges, he hits Mainwaring instead. While the fight itself is not seen, it is colorfully recounted the next day as Mainwaring compiles a report on the incident. According to the humorous accounts of the men, they held their own against the younger visitors. The funniest account involved Pike finally "being a man" when one of the Americans flirted with his girlfriend, Ivy. Unable to stand any more, Pike gave the interloper a double nose thumbing. This was quickly followed by the same soldier receiving a chair over his head from Godfrey for treading on one of his sister Dolly's upside-down cakes.

There is also a good joke when we discover that Frazer is the president of the local Caledonian Society. Unfortunately, he is the only member since Frazer threw the other Scot in town out of the society when he refused to pay a five-shilling increase in membership fees.

Janet Davies returns to the role of Mrs. Pike after an absence of three years and 18 episodes (she was last seen in "A. Wilson (Manager)?"). Here the part of Pike's girlfriend, Ivy, is played by Suzanne Kerchiss although Rosemary Faith in "Mum's Army" originally played the role. Finally, this marks the first appearance of Talfryn Thomas in the part of Cheeseman, who would briefly become a regular in the next season.

EPISODE 3: "THE ROYAL TRAIN" ★★★

Air date: November 14, 1973. Cast: Capt. Mainwaring (Arthur Lowe); Sgt. Wilson (John Le Mesurier); Cpl. Jones (Clive Dunn); Pvt. Frazer (John Laurie); Pvt. Walker (James Beck); Pvt. Godfrey (Arnold Ridley); Pvt. Pike (Ian Lavender); Chief Warden Hodges (Bill Pertwee); Vicar (Frank Williams); Verger (Edward Sinclair); Station Master (William Moore); Henry (Freddie Earlle); Bob (Ronnie Brody); Mayor (Fred McNaughton); Ticket Collector (Sue Bishop); City Gent (Bob Hornery)

The platoon assembles at the train station to serve as an honor guard when a train carrying King George VI passes through.

A good chase scene, physical comedy, and some danger help make "The Royal Train" a memorable entry in the series. The only flaw, if it can be labeled as such, is that the setup for the rousing finale is telegraphed quite obviously from the first scene. In the opening, Mainwaring enters with sleeping pills for his wife. Soon the bottle containing the pills is broken, and the tablets must be placed in a saccharine bottle, making their accidental ingestion a certainty. Fortunately, the pills are swallowed by the crew of the train preceding the royal train, making it necessary for the platoon to climb aboard and try to move the engine.

Prior to the actual train sequences, there are some good moments as Mainwaring marches the men to the station and, with maximum precaution, opens the sealed secret orders detailing their mission. After he emphasizes the need for absolute secrecy, the captain is annoyed by a steady stream of people, from ticket takers to the Verger, who not only know the secret but apparently knew before Mainwaring did. Next, there are some gently silly moments as the platoon secretly practices its drilling inside the station. Pike and Godfrey provide some amusement as they complain that since they are not carrying regular rifles they will look foolish when the rest of their comrades are presenting arms. Godfrey suggests he just wave at the king, a solution that is readily dismissed.

Once the train crew is knocked out from the sleeping pills in their tea, the fun begins in earnest. With Pike at the throttle, the platoon attempts to move the train off the main track before the king's train arrives. While Pike succeeds ably (having acquired locomotive driving skills on a school trip), they soon discover that the engineer has removed the brake wheel, and they cannot stop. In some inspired comedy, Hodges, the Verger, the Vicar, and the Mayor are soon in pursuit of the runaway train, pumping away on a handcar. Once they have successfully delivered the brake wheel, the foursome is rewarded for its trouble by having to quickly retreat when Pike throws the engine in reverse. The location shooting in this sequence is very good and adds to the excitement.

This, coupled with some good period production values (primarily in regard to the trains) help make "The Royal Train" a pleasure to watch.

EPISODE 4: "WE KNOW OUR ONIONS" ★★★½

Air date: November 21, 1973. Cast: Capt. Mainwaring (Arthur Lowe); Sgt. Wilson (John Le Mesurier); Cpl. Jones (Clive Dunn); Pvt. Frazer (John Laurie); Pvt. Walker (James Beck); Pvt. Godfrey (Arnold Ridley); Pvt. Pike (Ian Lavender); Capt. Ramsey (Fulton Mackay); Chief Warden Hodges (Bill Pertwee); Verger (Edward Sinclair); Sergeant (Alex McAvoy); NAAFI Girl (Pamela Manson); Mess Steward (Cy Town)

The platoon encounters a tough taskmaster when it goes to compete in an efficiency test.

An excellent offering highlighted by some good verbal comedy in the first half and some fine physical business imaginatively presented in the finale. The verbal humor is especially out of the ordinary for *Dad's Army*, due to its fast pace. The rapid-fire style is thanks in large part to guest star Fulton Mackay as Captain Ramsey, the hard-edged proctor for the platoon's efficiency test. Mackay, who would later turn up in another role in "The Miser's Hoard," is best remembered for his work with Ronnie Barker in *Porridge*. "We Know Our Onions" is also out of the ordinary due to the fact that it is the only episode of the series shot entirely on film and not at least partially taped before a live audience.

The platoon's objective in its test is to earn a perfect score of 12 stars. The men are trebly hampered in their quest. First, they must contend with interference from Hodges and the Verger, who have followed them to their test installation in an effort to retrieve a half ton of precious onions, which Walker has stored in Jones's van. The next impediment to their achieving their goals is the aforementioned Ramsey. Finally, their greatest obstacle is their own ineptitude and poor luck.

Upon their arrival, the Magnificent Seven are ushered into a room for a series of mental exercises. Warned that anything can happen in this verbal drill, Jones quickly responds to Ramsey's hypothetical supposition that he is a Gestapo interrogator by trying to garrote the instructor. Next, in the same interrogator's pose, Ramsey starts barking questions at a bored Wilson, asking him what he is doing in France. When Ramsey clarifies that he is in France for the purposes of the drill, Wilson politely smiles and offers the grisly captain a lackadaisical "bonjour." Frustrated by the platoon's responses, Ramsey exits and sends in the tea girl with some refreshment. Unfortunately, they have gotten the mistaken idea that this break is a trick and that the girl is actually part of the test and trying to plant a bomb. As she enters the room, they wrestle her to the ground and throw her tea urn out the window.

Next, the men are charged with scaling a mildly electrified fence in 30 minutes. In this hilarious display, the men fail miserably but ask for a time extension to tackle the problem, to which Ramsey assents. In some clever staging, the scene shifts to Ramsey enjoying his evening libation in the installation's bar. As he sips his drink, the calm of the moment is interrupted by the electrical zapping sound of Jones once again hitting the wire followed by a siren signaling the latest failed attempt. The situation is repeated twice even as midnight comes and goes, without the men succeeding.

Oddly enough, the weakest moment comes in the finale, as the platoon finally manages to prove itself a top-ranked unit through a display of initiative that impresses even Ramsey. This scene isn't particularly unfunny; it only pales in comparison to the high quality of comedy that preceded it.

Episode 5: "The Honourable Man" ★★★

Air date: November 28, 1973. Cast: Capt. Mainwaring (Arthur Lowe); Sgt. Wilson (John Le Mesurier); Cpl. Jones (Clive Dunn); Pvt. Frazer (John Laurie); Pvt. Walker (James Beck); Pvt. Godfrey (Arnold Ridley); Pvt. Pike (Ian Lavender); Chief Warden Hodges (Bill Pertwee); Vicar (Frank Williams); Verger (Edward Sinclair); Town Clerk (Eric Longworth); Mrs. Pike (Janet Davies); Russian (Gabor Vernon); Interpreter (Hana-Maria Pravda); Colonel (Robert Raglan); Mrs. Fox (Pamela Cundell); Mayor (Fred McNaughton)

Mainwaring's nose is more than a little out of joint when Wilson falls heir to a title, which makes him one of the aristocracy.

"The Honourable Man" is another closer examination of one of the series' underlying themes: the animosity between Mainwaring and Wilson. Not since "A. Wilson (Manager?)" has this deep-seated tension been given so thorough an airing, although that earlier episode is slightly more successful in doing so. One advantage of the earlier offering is the preservation of the status quo in the relationship. In "A. Wilson (Manager?)," Wilson receives his deserved promotions in both fields in which Mainwaring has been holding him back. By the story's end, however, fate intervenes to tragically return affairs to their starting place. Here, however, when Wilson's uncle dies, moving him into the lower ranks of the aristocracy, there is no change at the episode's end. While there is much ado in this episode about Wilson's new title, including some funny verbal confusion over what to call the sergeant (the best being Pike's reference to "Uncle Sergeant, the Honorable Arthur"), this quickly fades away in future episodes.

As in "A. Wilson (Manager?)," the real show here is the conflict between the top two stars, who behave ostensibly the same as in that earlier episode. Mainwaring is even more angered at Wilson's new title, since it crystallizes even further his own humble beginning, which he has had to struggle against all his life. He is especially outraged that Wilson has immediately been asked to join the golf club, an establishment that Mainwaring has been trying to get into for years (Wilson adds insult to the injury by reminding his superior that the club *is* "awfully particular"). Wilson, for his part, tries to soft-pedal his new nobility and is even slightly embarrassed by it. Still, in a wonderfully subtle playing, John Le Mesurier manages to convey this discomfort with a mixture of pleasure as well — particularly when his title chafes against Mainwaring.

The episode isn't entirely confined to the two principals, of course, with plenty of reaction coming from the other members of the cast. While most people fawn over Wilson's "honorability," Frazer is convinced that Wilson will be the same fool he has always been, with or without his title. Godfrey gently recalls waiting on many honorable persons when he worked in the retail trade and announces they were just like the commoners — except they rarely paid their bills.

Perry and Croft deftly wrap the conflict inside the confines of a plot regarding the visit of a Russian factory worker. This allows more than a little humor and a surprise ending, which manages to tie in neatly with the story line regarding Wilson.

Episode 6: "Things That Go Bump in the Night" ★½

Air date: December 5, 1973. Cast: Capt. Mainwaring (Arthur Lowe); Sgt. Wilson (John Le Mesurier); Cpl. Jones (Clive Dunn); Pvt. Frazer (John Laurie); Pvt. Walker (James Beck); Pvt. Godfrey (Arnold Ridley); Pvt. Pike (Ian Lavender); Captain Cadbury (Jonathan Cecil); Pvt. Sponge (Colin Bean)

Stranded in a storm, the platoon takes refuge in a mysterious mansion.

"Things That Go Bump in the Night" is a disappointing attempt at suspense-fright comedy, which fails to provide much of either. While the situation is fairly well presented, it runs out of steam approximately halfway through. From this point, the mystery of the estate in which the platoon has taken refuge is simply explained, and an entirely different plot is introduced, making the entire affair anticlimactic and schizophrenic.

The opening scenes are rather good, providing an ominous atmosphere for the comedy. Unfortunately, the best vehicle to exploit this mood would be via the character of Frazer. The gloomy Scot's contribution, however, is limited to his usual warnings of impending doom. What is also lacking is one of John Laurie's marvelously spooky yarns, such as the ones that enhanced "Menace from the Deep" and "Put That Light Out." There are some good moments, most of which come from Pike's repeated aquatic mishaps. Godfrey also has some nice turns, the most memorable being his recounting of an unsavory experience with his sister's small Pekingese.

The disappointing quality of the entry is all the more regrettable when one realizes it is the last appearance of James Beck's beloved roguish Joe Walker. Although not present in the earlier scenes that were shot in the studio, Beck does appear in the second half, which was filmed on location earlier. One wishes that the spiv's final appearance had been in a show that was more representative of the overall quality of the series as a whole and of Beck's talents in particular.

Episode 7: "The Recruit ★★½

Air date: December 12, 1973. Cast: Capt. Mainwaring (Arthur Lowe); Sgt. Wilson (John Le Mesurier); Cpl. Jones (Clive Dunn); Pvt. Frazer (John Laurie); Pvt. Walker (James Beck); Pvt. Godfrey (Arnold Ridley); Pvt. Pike (Ian Lavender); Chief Warden Hodges (Bill Pertwee); Vicar (Frank Williams); Verger (Edward Sinclair); Nurse (Susan Majolier); Small Boy (Lindsey Dunn)

While Captain Mainwaring is in the hospital recuperating from ingrown toenails, Sergeant Wilson allows the Vicar and the Verger to join the platoon.

A leisurely paced entry, "The Recruit" manages to remain enjoyable despite not having any particularly strong scenes or comic set pieces. The opening sequences, in Mainwaring's hospital room, are interesting by virtue of the uniqueness of the situation, but they suffer from a certain aimlessness. There are some amusing turns, however, when the platoon makes Mainwaring a present of some precious grapes, which, to the captain's revulsion, turn out to be shaved gooseberries.

The main focus of the episode, of course, is the addition to the ranks of the Vicar and the Verger. This allows Frank Williams one of his more extended periods in the limelight, and he makes the best of it. It is quite humorous to watch the ineffective, slightly effeminate Vicar attempting to take his place in the ranks. Try as he may to do his duty, the clergyman is less than effective, especially when he responds to orders with such effete phrases, earnestly delivered, as "goody, goody." Later on sentry duty, the Vicar finds it hard to bark warnings, and his order to "advance friend, and be recognized" is too full of Christian charity to be of any use. Ultimately, a funny run-in with an impertinent youth convinces the Vicar his calling lies elsewhere.

This is the first episode without the services of James Beck, although his absence is explained via a slang-filled note left on the floor in his place in line. In the letter, Walker explains he has gone up to "the Smoke" (London) for a few days to do a deal. This is the last reference to the character in the television series, although the part would be filled by another actor for the stage musical of *Dad's Army*. Despite the fact that he does not appear, Beck is given his usual closing credit.

"The Recruit" gives further evidence of the fact that although Frank Pike may be a huge fan of the movies, he would not make a very accurate film historian. Twice in this episode, he makes glaring gaffes in his knowledge of contemporary films. The first involves the recounting of the final scene of *Angels with Dirty Faces*, in which, according to Pike, Spencer Tracy plays the part of the priest (actually it was Pat O'Brien). Later, Pike justifies carrying the platoon's Tommy gun in a violin case by citing that Edward G. Robinson did likewise in *Scarface* (Robinson was not in that picture, which starred Paul Muni).

Series Seven 1974

Episode 1: "Everybody's Trucking" ★★★½

Air date: November 15, 1974. Cast: Capt. Mainwaring (Arthur Lowe); Sgt. Wilson (John Le Mesurier); Cpl. Jones (Clive Dunn); Pvt. Frazer (John Laurie); Pvt. Godfrey (Arnold Ridley); Pvt. Pike (Ian Lavender); Chief Warden Hodges (Bill Pertwee); Vicar (Frank Williams); Verger (Edward Sinclair); Mrs. Fox (Pamela Cundell); Mr. Bluett (Harold Bennett); Mrs. Yeatman (Olive Mercer); Driver (Felix Bowness); Pvt. Sponge (Colin Bean)

The platoon van gets stuck in the mud while on an important assignment.

A splendid milking of a single situation, "Everybody's Trucking" begins with a simple predicament and builds on it, resulting in a crescendo of comedy. The episode does have a rather weak opening, however, involving some rather mechanical gags centered on Jones's van. This sequence is more than a little labored, with Mainwaring repeatedly defacing the butcher's vehicle seemingly for no other reason than Jones has just finished detailing it and the script tells him to.

The meat of the episode is something worthy of a Laurel and Hardy short. While placing signposts on the road for an important exercise, the platoon encounters a stalled steamroller in the middle of the road with a calliope attached. Trying to go around the machine only leaves their van stuck in a muddy field. From here the situation escalates as first Hodges comes by in his van, then the old-age pensioners on a bus, then finally the Verger and Mrs. Fox on a motorcycle. Soon it seems that a good portion of the town is stuck in the quagmire.

The last addition, the Verger and Mrs. Fox, is especially funny, as the arrival opens more than one can of worms regarding the secret lives of Walmington residents. First, Hodges is angry since the Verger is using his motorcycle. Next, Jones is upset since Mrs. Fox is out with another man. Then, Mrs. Yeatman, the Verger's wife, who is on the bus with the senior citizens, is jealous to see her husband out with another woman. Finally, Mrs. Yeatman retaliates by proclaiming her love for the 80-plus Mr. Bluett.

Matters seems to be settling down when Wilson wisely suggests they fuel up the steamroller and use it to pull the other vehicles out of the mud. Once they get it started, Pike uses the opportunity to start the calliope. With the air filled with gay music, the senior citizens spontaneously break into a dance that serves to complete the increasingly surreal atmosphere of the day. In true *Dad's Army* fashion, the steamroller soon becomes another part of the problem rather than the solution as the episode comes to a close.

Episode 2: "A Man of Action" ★★½

Air date: November 22, 1974. Cast: Capt. Mainwaring (Arthur Lowe); Sgt. Wilson (John Le Mesurier); Cpl. Jones (Clive Dunn); Pvt. Frazer (John Laurie); Pvt.

Godfrey (Arnold Ridley); Pvt. Pike (Ian Lavender); Chief Warden Hodges (Bill Pertwee); Mr. Cheeseman (Talfryn Thomas); the Vicar (Frank Williams); Verger (Edward Sinclair); Town Clerk (Eric Longworth); Mr. Bluett (Harold Bennett); Fire Officer Dale (Arnold Peters); Inspector Baker (Jay Denyer); Capt. Swan (Robert Mill); Private Sponge (Colin Bean)

When a mine disrupts gas, water, and telephone service, Mainwaring declares martial law.

Filled with interesting and creative situations, "A Man of Action" ultimately disappoints as none of the premises manage to gel. This is a pity, since all of them provide promise, not only for the episode at hand but, for one in particular, the remainder of the series. This last one is the introduction of Talfryn Thomas's character, Cheeseman, as a replacement for the late James Beck. Rather than attempt to cast another actor in the role of Walker, Perry and Croft wisely tried to bring a new member into the platoon.

Cheeseman, a little Welsh reporter for the *Eastbourne Gazette*, was previously seen in "My British Buddy." Here, against the advice of Wilson and the warnings of Frazer, Mainwaring allows Cheeseman to join the platoon while the latter writes a series of articles on the Home Guard. This provisional arrangement allowed the authors an easy out if the character failed to meld with the established members of the platoon, which ultimately he did. Although Cheeseman's character is well drawn and has some funny moments, it is too daunting an assignment to replace Walker and to blend successfully with such an established ensemble.

The main focus of the plot, Mainwaring's declaration of martial law, is introduced too late in the episode to be fully explored. There are some good moments, however, as the captain discovers much to his surprise that Wilson heartily agrees with his decision to take charge of the town in light of the present emergency. He is even more stunned when, faced with the dire nature of the situation, Wilson actually starts barking out orders in an authoritative, military fashion. Wilson's explanation is that when the actual need arises, he is fully prepared to be a soldier, rather than just play at it. Of course, soon Mainwaring's dictatorship begins to wear thin on all concerned, leading to the abrupt ending.

The final situation, although it is actually introduced first, involves Pike getting his head stuck between the bars of a park gate. This business provides the wealth of the laughs in the episode, although it too is never resolved, leaving Mainwaring's favorite "stupid boy" trapped throughout the episode.

"A Man of Action" received a special showing in tribute to Arthur Lowe following the actor's death in 1982.

Episode 3: "Gorilla Warfare" ★★★

Air date: November 29, 1974. Cast: Capt. Mainwaring (Arthur Lowe); Sgt. Wilson (John Le Mesurier); Cpl. Jones (Clive Dunn); Pvt. Frazer (John Laurie); Pvt.

Godfrey (Arnold Ridley); Pvt. Pike (Ian Lavender); Chief Warden Hodges (Bill Pertwee); Pvt. Cheeseman (Talfryn Thomas); Verger (Edward Sinclair); Colonel (Robert Raglan); Mr. Clerk (Erik Chitty); Mother Superior (Rachel Thomas); Lieutenant (Michael Sharvell-Martin); Farmer (Verne Morgan); Lady with the Pram (Joy Allen)

The platoon must deliver a "highly important secret agent" to GHQ as part of a weekend training exercise. Unfortunately, the efforts are hampered by Hodges, the Verger, and a man in a gorilla suit.

"Gorilla Warfare" is filled with good physical comedy that moves along at a breezy clip, making this a consistently enjoyable entry. Establishing a strong premise from the start, the script never veers from it as the writers fully explore and make the most of every opportunity for laughs.

Setting out on special maneuvers, the men must deliver one of their number — designated as the secret agent — across the countryside in a two-day exercise. Not surprisingly, Mainwaring vainly appoints himself the "highly important secret agent" one moment, while deriding his rival, Captain Square, for doing the same thing the previous week. Unwilling to let Mainwaring succeed where he has failed, Square hires Hodges and the Verger to shadow the platoon in an attempt to trip them up. As always, Hodges' schemes only wind up backfiring on him in hilarious fashion.

The platoon must also face obstacles in the form of counteragents, who have been dispatched to try and capture the secret agent. Mainwaring is overcautious about these other enemies to the point that he suspects everyone they encounter — from nuns having car trouble to a mother with her baby — as being a counteragent. The real counteragent appears (disguised in a gorilla suit) but only manages to frighten Hodges and the Verger. There is also a rousing finale, involving the gorilla, motorcycle, and a hypodermic needle.

There is a good respite from the main plot, as the platoon beds down for the night in a barn. This scene provides several good bits, including Pike's request that Sergeant Wilson tell him a bedtime story before he goes to sleep and what appears to be another wild-eyed yarn by Frazer. The Scot's turn is especially humorous as he builds up a potential story about the "old empty barn," then concludes the affair with a one-liner instead, much to his comrades' and the audience's surprise.

Joy Allen, appearing briefly as a woman pushing a pram (baby carriage), appeared previously as the ticket taker and Mainwaring's dream girl in "A Soldier's Farewell."

EPISODE 4: "THE GODIVA AFFAIR" ★★★½

Air date: December 6, 1974. Cast: Capt. Mainwaring (Arthur Lowe); Sgt. Wilson (John Le Mesurier); Cpl. Jones (Clive Dunn); Pvt. Frazer (John Laurie); Pvt. Godfrey (Arnold Ridley); Pvt. Pike (Ian Lavender); Chief Warden Hodges (Bill Pertwee); Pvt. Cheeseman (Talfryn Thomas); Vicar (Frank

Williams); Verger (Edward Sinclair); Mrs. Pike (Janet Davies); Mrs. Fox (Pamela Cundell); Town Clerk (Eric Longworth); Private Day (Peter Honri); Waitress (Rosemary Faith); Pvt. Sponge (Colin Bean); Pvt. Hancock (George Hancock)

Jones's love life and the selection of a woman to play Lady Godiva in a town procession disrupt the normal activities of the platoon.

"The Godiva Affair" is like a bright string of Christmas lights, a procession of wonderful scenes all joined by a connecting thread. From a very humorous Morris dancing routine to the hysterical conclusion, each bit manages to hit its intended target.

The opening scene features the aforementioned Morris dance, the traditional English folk fertility display. The platoon members are marvelous decked out in their Morris regalia, especially Sergeant Wilson, who is surrounded by a papier-mâché horse. The dance is part of the Walmington-on-Sea drive to raise money for the purchase of a Spitfire, and Wilson's role is to canter through the audience collecting money while his comrades dance. Of course this is something of a stretch for the lackadaisical sergeant, who is ordered to gallop about and spout jocular sayings while soliciting the funds.

The other major focus of the plot is Jones's distraction over the fact that the love of his life, Mrs. Fox, has lately been entertaining Mr. Gordon, the town clerk. Clive Dunn turns in a wonderfully agitated performance throughout the episode, as do the other sides of the triangle: Pamela Cundell as the flirtatious widow and Eric Longworth as the rival. Unable to settle it himself, Jones implores Mainwaring to speak to Mrs. Fox regarding his love life. This results in a very good scene in the Marigold Tea Room, where Mainwaring tries to subtly sort out the affair but only manages to make Mrs. Fox think he is another of her admirers. Punctuating this incident is the fact that most of the platoon has been tipped off to the rumors of Mainwaring and Mrs. Fox and are intently watching from nearby tables. John Laurie has some especially funny turns rumor mongering and taking almost erotic delight at the prospect of the captain's moral downfall.

Both of these elements are joined when Mrs. Fox is selected to play Lady Godiva in the upcoming town fete. This causes a storm of controversy among the other town women, particularly Mrs. Pike and Mrs. Mainwaring, since they were bypassed in the process. One of the highlights of this sequence is the repeated use of the term "fleshings," the skin-toned body stocking to be worn by Lady Godiva. Pike especially takes delight in slowly enunciating this word, almost as if it were the first naughty word he was allowed to use. All is ultimately well, at least for Mrs. Fox and Jones, as a surprise performer assumes the role of Lady Godiva for the terrific final gag.

Rosemary Faith appears as the Waitress and one of the prospective Godivas. She previously appeared in "Mum's Army" as Pike's girlfriend, Ivy

Samways, although that role was filled by another actress in the intervening episode "My British Buddy."

Understandably, "The Godiva Affair" is the favorite episode of Eric Longworth, who appears as the Town Clerk.

EPISODE 5: "THE CAPTAIN'S CAR" ★★★½

Air date: December 13, 1974. Cast: Capt. Mainwaring (Arthur Lowe); Sgt. Wilson (John Le Mesurier); Cpl. Jones (Clive Dunn); Pvt. Frazer (John Laurie); Pvt. Godfrey (Arnold Ridley); Pvt. Pike (Ian Lavender); Chief Warden Hodges (Bill Pertwee); Pvt. Cheeseman (Talfryn Thomas); Vicar (Frank Williams); Verger (Edward Sinclair); Colonel (Robert Raglan); Town Clerk (Eric Longworth); Mayor (Fred McNaughton); Lady Maltby (Mavis Pugh); French General (John Hart Dyke); Glossip (Donald Morley)

The visit of a French General coincides with Mainwaring receiving a Rolls Royce as his personal staff car.

Another clever mixture of subtle verbal wit with gentle physical comedy helps to make "The Captain's Car" one of the better offerings of the seventh season. Ironically, the opening sequences, which comprise the more verbal parts of the show, are particularly fast-paced. Taking place in Mainwaring's office during the visit of Lady Maltby, who has stopped by to offer the platoon the use of her Rolls for the duration, this scene is a constant stream of frustration and embarrassment to Arthur Lowe's pompous little captain. First, he must once again suffer the indignity of being shown up by his sergeant/chief clerk, Wilson, who, it turns out, is a close personal friend of Lady Maltby. Having forged ahead from this point of contention, Mainwaring is attempting to vouch for the high character of his platoon members versus that of the wardens. At this point, he is interrupted, first by an insubordinate Frazer (who barks "Hey, you!" at Mainwaring), then by Pike, who enters with a bucket full of fresh horse manure for the captain's flowers. The overall effect is hilarious and demonstrates the veteran cast running on all comic cylinders.

The second half blends the camouflaging of the Rolls Royce and the visit of the French General. Mainwaring is particularly loath to act as honor guard for the dignitary, since he considers the French only adequate soldiers who cannot fight effectively after lunch. He especially dislikes their predilections for women, garlic, and sloppy kissing. Despite these prejudices, Mainwaring is miffed when he discovers that Wilson has been chosen to deliver the speech to the General, since he is the only one who is fluent in French. Matters become increasingly entangled when the platoon mistakenly camouflages two Rolls Royces, the second belonging to the Mayor. All the elements combine for a wonderful finale centered on the tiny town's welcoming ceremony for the Frenchman. The exit gag, concerning the General's insistence on kissing everyone, is particularly good, with Bill Pertwee's Hodges once again winding up the butt of the joke.

During this bit, there is also an interesting and hilarious shot as the Vicar, seeing others being kissed on the cheeks by the General, prepares for his by closing his eyes and puckering up. The somewhat effeminate and unmarried clergyman is left unsmooched by the visitor.

Mavis Pugh, who appears as Lady Maltby, made her television debut in "The Captain's Car." A veteran actress who had appeared in repertory theatre with Jimmy Perry, Pugh went on to appear in *Fawlty Towers* and two other Croft-Perry sitcoms, *It Ain't Half Hot, Mum* and *You Rang, M'Lord?*

EPISODE 6: "TURKEY DINNER" ★★

Air date: December 23, 1974. Cast: Capt. Mainwaring (Arthur Lowe); Sgt. Wilson (John Le Mesurier); Cpl. Jones (Clive Dunn); Pvt. Frazer (John Laurie); Pvt. Godfrey (Arnold Ridley); Pvt. Pike (Ian Lavender); Chief Warden Hodges (Bill Pertwee); Pvt. Cheeseman (Talfryn Thomas); Vicar (Frank Williams); Verger (Edward Sinclair); Mr. Bluett (Harold Bennett); Mrs. Fox (Pamela Cundell); Mrs. Pike (Janet Davies); Mrs. Yeatman (Olive Mercer); Farmhand (Dave Butler)

The platoon serves the old-age pensioners a turkey dinner after Jones accidentally shoots a bird on patrol.

The last episode of the seventh series, "Turkey Dinner" was delayed in its airing, probably to coincide with the Christmas holidays. It is a fitting dish for the holidays but unfortunately. like many of those fowl, this "Turkey Dinner" is a little too dry to be fully enjoyable. This is not to say that there aren't some fine moments, but the episode as a whole tends to drag, particularly in the middle during the committee meeting scene. That sequence seems to be a reworking of a similar bit in "The Honourable Man," where it is done to better effect. As in even the weakest *Dad's Army* entries, there is plenty of incidental character dialogue to make worthwhile watching.

Not surprisingly, the best moments are character based and are only incidental to the story. The first of these occurs as Mainwaring, taking a tip from a book on leadership, decides to start off the nightly parade with a joke. After telling an especially woeful joke at which no one laughs, the captain nods in approval to Wilson and asserts that his tactic has succeeded in cheering the men. Wilson, of course, then adds an offhanded aside to the proceedings, which elicits a hearty chuckle from the men, much to Mainwaring's consternation.

The scene immediately following, in which Jones describes how he came to accidentally shoot a turkey, is also good. Arthur Lowe has yet another opportunity to slowly burn through another lengthy tale, as his character must listen to a sordid description of how the platoon visited no fewer than four pubs while on patrol, getting progressively more drunk in the process. It is quite amusing to learn that the usual reserved, genteel Godfrey became particularly raucous during the evening, resulting in his bellowing out a ribald song about a monk.

The final scene has its moments, but unfortunately nothing hilarious enough to send the episode off in the grand style of some of the other entries. Instead we must be satisfied with the complications caused when Pike spills gravy on Mainwaring's formal suit just prior to the Rotary Club dinner. Had there been a little more time, one would expect this incident to escalate further than it does.

"Turkey Dinner" is the final appearance of Talfryn Thomas as Cheeseman. Ironically, it also contains some of the better moments for that character.

Series Eight 1975

Episode 1: "Ring Dem Bells" ★★★½

Air date: September 5, 1975. Cast: Capt. Mainwaring (Arthur Lowe); Sgt. Wilson (John Le Mesurier); Cpl. Jones (Clive Dunn); Pvt. Frazer (John Laurie); Pvt. Godfrey (Arnold Ridley); Pvt. Pike (Ian Lavender); Chief Warden Hodges (Bill Pertwee); Vicar (Frank Williams); Verger (Edward Sinclair); Landlord (Jack Haig); Colonel (Robert Raglan); Special Constable (Felix Bowness); Harold Forster (John Bardon); Queenie Beal (Hilda Fenemore); Barmaid (Janet Mahoney); Lady with Umbrella (Adele Strong)

The platoon members play Nazi soldiers in a training film and get mistaken for the real enemy.

A splendid entry, "Ring Dem Bells" begins the eighth season in grand style with a plausible premise that quickly escalates into a silly situation. Despite the overall high quality of the script and performances, the standout in this episode is Ian Lavender's Private Pike. After years of playing the soppy stupid boy, Lavender's character is given a chance to be an officer — albeit a Nazi one. While Pike is pretending to be an archetypal ruthless Nazi officer — no doubt like the ones he's seen in the movies — the beauty of the setup is that others outside the platoon do not know he is playing, and they find his portrayal quite convincing with hilarious consequences.

The basic plot involves the platoon taking part in a training film to be shown to other Home Guard units. There are some good moments in the opening scene as Pike excitedly chatters about being in a film, while in his office, Mainwaring is no less excited as he tries to determine his best side for the camera. The platoon is surprised to learn that they will all be playing Nazis in the epic, a fact that only bothers Mainwaring after he learns that he will not be able to play the officer (since the uniform won't fit his rotund form). Consequently, the captain refuses to take part in the film.

From this launching point, the comedy blossoms as the platoon is outfitted in the regalia of the enemy. While veterans such as Jones and Frazer bristle at wearing the German uniforms, Pike has a field day strutting, swaggering, and practicing his outrageous accent at every opportunity (including some rather impertinent lines leveled at Mainwaring). When the filming is postponed, Mainwaring tries to return the platoon to the town without its being seen and causing any undue panic (not an easy task, especially with Pike sticking out of the top of the van making Hitler salutes as he rides along). The men escape, however, for a quick pint in a pub when the captain stops to make a telephone call. There is a comic gem when the stunned landlord sees 16 Germans enter his pub led by an officer (Pike) who calmly orders "sixteen shandies mit der ginger beer!" The sighting quickly leads to panic and a red alert for the entire coast.

"Ring Dem Bells" is cited by Ian Lavender as being "quite categorically" his favorite *Dad's Army* episode. Although the alter ego of Private Pike cites the comfortable, tailored German uniforms (after seven seasons of ill-fitting, uncomfortable Home Guard uniforms) as the main reason for his preference, one would guess that his wonderfully funny performance also has something to do with the choice.

Fans of *Are You Being Served?* may recognize Hilda Fenemore, one of the cleaning ladies at Grace Brothers', who is briefly seen here in the part of Queenie Beal. This episode also marks the promotion of Colin Bean's Private Sponge to the front ranks.

Episode 2: "When You've Got to Go" ★★

Air date: September 12, 1975. Cast: Capt. Mainwaring (Arthur Lowe); Sgt. Wilson (John Le Mesurier); Cpl. Jones (Clive Dunn); Pvt. Frazer (John Laurie); Pvt. Godfrey (Arnold Ridley); Pvt. Pike (Ian Lavender); Chief Warden Hodges (Bill Pertwee); Vicar (Frank Williams); Verger (Edward Sinclair); Mrs. Pike (Janet Davies); Town Clerk (Eric Longworth); Italian Sergeant (Freddie Earlle); Doctor (Tim Barrett); Pvt. Sponge (Colin Bean); Fishfryer (Frankie Holmes)

Private Pike passes his physical exam and seems destined for service in the RAF until he takes part in the local blood drive.

The second consecutive episode to spotlight Private Frank Pike, "When You've Got to Go" concentrates even more on the "stupid boy" than the previous entry but to less effect. While consistently entertaining, the offering fails to hit any comic high points, content instead to hum along for 30 minutes at a steady pace.

The main focus of the story, Pike's impending enlistment, is interrupted to introduce a subplot involving a town blood drive. This provides some fun, as Mainwaring boasts that the platoon will bring in 100 donors to Hodges' 50. Unfortunately, it turns out that most of the platoon members are too old to donate blood, and greengrocer Hodges is offering free onions to donors who give under his sponsorship. This segment is nicely resolved when Jonesy brings in a contingent of Italian POWs accompanied by a group of nuns. With this outside help, the platoon easily makes its quota and receives a certificate of merit (although Hodges acidly suggests that the award actually be sent to Mussolini and the pope).

The blood drive also helps to resolve the main plot, by revealing that Pike has such a rare blood type that the RAF refuses to let him enlist. This isn't disclosed by Pike, however, until after he has been feted by his comrades with a special fish-and-chips dinner (because Frank has never had a dinner in his honor, and he likes fish and chips).

Janet Davies makes the most of her opportunities here as the mollycoddling Mrs. Pike, frantic over the prospect of her "baby" going into active service. Arthur Lowe also has some good turns during the fish-and-chips dinner scene as his character disdainfully dines on the common grub.

"When You've Got to Go" has one mysterious element, which seems as if it will be central to the plot but goes unexplained. Throughout the episode, Pike persists in making this odd involuntary facial expression. Although it is explained as being normal for a boy his age, it obviously is not, and one suspects the explanation of the tic will be the key to keeping Pike out of the military and in the Home Guard. Unfortunately, the mannerism, although responsible for some good laughs — especially when copied by Mainwaring — is never explained and never mentioned again. It is hinted that the expression is due to nerves, but even this is not satisfying.

EPISODE 3: "IS THERE HONEY STILL FOR TEA?" ★★★

Air date: September 19, 1975. Cast: Capt. Mainwaring (Arthur Lowe); Sgt. Wilson (John Le Mesurier); Cpl. Jones (Clive Dunn); Pvt. Frazer (John Laurie); Pvt. Godfrey (Arnold Ridley); Pvt. Pike (Ian Lavender); Chief Warden Hodges (Bill Pertwee); Man with the Door (Gordon Peters); Colonel (Robert Raglan); Sir Charles McAllister (Campbell Singer); Dolly (Joan Cooper); Cissy (Kathleen Sainsbury)

Godfrey and his sisters must vacate their beloved cottage, which is slated for destruction to make room for a new aerodrome.

A gentle and warmly amusing entry, "Is There Honey Still for Tea?" reflects the style and pacing of its main subject: the lovable Charles Godfrey. Except for some mild knockabout in the opening scene and a physical gag in the closing moments, most of the humor here is of the verbal variety.

Most of the running time is occupied with the various platoon members trying to break the news to Godfrey that his home, Cherry Tree Cottage, is going to be demolished. Mainwaring, Wilson, Jones, and Frazer pass the unpleasant assignment back and forth like a hot potato, fearing the shock will do irreparable harm to their gentle comrade. After Jones finally breaks the bad news, they discover that Godfrey already knew and didn't tell any of them so as not to upset his friends. It is the hard and crusty Frazer, however, who saves the day — and the cottage — by applying some well-timed blackmail to the government minister in charge of the aerodrome project. (It seems the social-climbing Sir Charles had a humorously disreputable past on Frazer's home Isle of Barra in the Hebrides.)

The opening scene contains some humorous moments as Mainwaring receives a new door for his bank office to replace the one that was lost in an air raid. To his utter consternation, the officious little bank manager discovers that the new door is only made of paper. This leads to some amusing gags in which the door soon becomes ripped and ultimately set ablaze.

In an interesting observation on the time sequencing of the episodes, Mainwaring mentions that it has been three months since the bank was bombed. Fans will recall the bank was actually hit twice. The first time occurred back in series three ("Something Nasty in the Vault") but caused minimal damage. The second time, which caused extensive damage and presumably the incident to which Mainwaring refers, happened in series five's "The King Was in His Counting House," three years previous. Of course in a series that ran for ten years but covered a war that only lasted six, one expects time to be elastic (much as was done in the American TV series *M*A*S*H*).

In another interesting exchange, Frank Pike remarks on his "Uncle" Arthur's sleeping arrangements. The naïve boy notes how his uncle never leaves his house until after he, Frank, has gone to bed, yet always manages to return before he gets up in the morning. From this, Pike deduces that Wilson must not get much sleep and vows to personally usher him out that evening before he retires for the night. Unfortunately, this potentially amusing possibility was never filmed; it could have provided the basis for an episode of its own.

Aside from the lost "The Battle of Godfrey's Cottage," this is the only sighting of both Godfrey sisters in a single episode. In that episode, six seasons earlier, the duo was played by a different pair of actresses.

EPISODE 4: "COME IN, YOUR TIME IS UP" ★½

Air date: September 26, 1975. Cast: Capt. Mainwaring (Arthur Lowe); Sgt. Wilson (John Le Mesurier); Cpl. Jones (Clive Dunn); Pvt. Frazer (John Laurie); Pvt. Godfrey (Arnold Ridley); Pvt. Pike (Ian Lavender); Chief Warden Hodges (Bill Pertwee); Vicar (Frank Williams); Verger (Edward Sinclair); Mr. Bluett (Harold Bennett); Pvt. Sponge (Colin Bean)

While on weekend bivouac, the platoon discovers a trio of Nazi pilots on a life raft in the middle of a lake and must bring them to shore.

A slow-paced minor entry in the series, "Come In, Your Time Is Up" suffers from the fact that the plot is not introduced until the final ten minutes. The rest of the running time is filled with some mildly amusing yet aimless business divided between two sequences.

The first sequence (and the stronger of the two) is studio recorded and involves Mainwaring conducting a lecture on outdoor skills in the Vicar's garden. He is interrupted in his lessons by Mr. Bluett, who apparently tends the ecclesiastical enclave. Such simple tasks as putting up a tent and building a fire are handled but to only mixed comic effect. There are some good verbal moments, instigated by Jones, as he examines the two-man tents and announces they are only big enough for one large man and one "tiny man." After noting that most of the individual members of the platoon are larger, Jones concludes there aren't enough tiny men to go around. The best business of this scene, however, involves Mainwaring's lesson on how to cook a hedgehog, which he illustrates with the use of a hairbrush.

A filmed location sequence comprises the second half of the program, as the platoon practices what the captain has preached in the first half. There are some comic possibilities introduced when Hodges, the Vicar, and Verger, with their Sea Scouts, arrive to camp alongside, but this doesn't live up to its promise.

The final bit, involving the Germans found adrift on the lake, never fully gels and is somewhat confusing. For example, the three airmen primarily ignore the platoon and their orders to come in to shore, except one time when they start shooting at them. What are the Germans trying to do? If they are trying to wound their would-be captors, they're not taking good advantage of their opportunities, since they earlier had a much closer-range shot. If they are trying to escape, they could merely row to the other side of the lake and easily outrun most of the members of the platoon. As it stands, it seems their only intention is to tease the enemy, which I doubt is the first duty of a downed Nazi flight crew.

EPISODE 5: "HIGH FINANCE" ★★

Air date: October 3, 1975. Cast: Capt. Mainwaring (Arthur Lowe); Sgt. Wilson (John Le Mesurier); Cpl. Jones (Clive Dunn); Pvt. Frazer (John Laurie); Pvt. Godfrey (Arnold Ridley); Pvt. Pike (Ian Lavender); Chief Warden Hodges (Bill Pertwee); Vicar (Frank Williams); Verger (Edward Sinclair); Mrs. Pike (Janet Davies); Mr. Swann (Ronnie Brody); Pvt. Sponge (Colin Bean); Miss Twelvetrees (Natalie Kent)

Acting as Jones's banker, captain, and friend, Mainwaring tries to sort out the butcher's woeful financial state.

More clever than funny, "High Finance" is one of the more strongly plot-driven episodes in the series. In fact, aside from some fun with various props, there is almost no physical humor in the offering. The plot is introduced from the first moments and is pursued single-mindedly until the final seconds. The script itself is good, although the situation, which evolves into the standard routine of everyone owing someone else the same amount, has been seen before in other venues. There is a nice twist in the last moments of the entry, however, which lands Mainwaring as the odd man out.

Aside from the apparent insolvency of Jones's business, "High Finance" also features a revisiting of Hodges' interest in the affections of Mavis Pike. First shown in series four's "Absent Friends," Hodges again woos the widow, although this time the interest is not mutual. This latest round of flirtations actually borders more on villainy in light of the proceedings, and for the first time Bill Pertwee's character comes across as more loathsome than comic. The matter, once revealed, is quickly rectified with a well-placed punch to the greengrocer's jaw by Sergeant Wilson.

Episode 6: "The Face on the Poster" ★★★½

Air date: October 10, 1975. Cast: Capt. Mainwaring (Arthur Lowe); Sgt. Wilson (John Le Mesurier); Cpl. Jones (Clive Dunn); Pvt. Frazer (John Laurie); Pvt. Godfrey (Arnold Ridley); Pvt. Pike (Ian Lavender); Chief Warden Hodges (Bill Pertwee); Vicar (Frank Williams); Verger (Edward Sinclair); Mr. Bugden (Peter Butterworth); Mr. Bluett (Harold Bennett); Polish Officer (Gabor Vernon); Pvt. Sponge (Colin Bean); Fred (Bill Tasker); Police Sergeant (Michael Bevis)

Mainwaring's plan to expand the size of the platoon via the use of recruitment posters lands the men in a prisoner-of-war camp instead.

The generally disappointing eighth season finishes on a strong note with "The Face on the Poster." The basic situation of the episode is borrowed directly from Buster Keaton's classic 1921 short, *The Goat*, in which the Great Stoneface inadvertently winds up with his face on a wanted poster for a desperado named Dead Shot Dan. Here, it is Corporal Jones who has his mug printed on a poster advertising an escaped prisoner of war. While the method in which the mistake is made is different (Keaton looks through a window while mugshots are being taken, while Jones's dilemma is purely a printer's error), the results of both are quite hilarious. Not surprisingly, Corporal Jones's plight does not inspire the same level of physical comedy, although there is a good scene in which the Polish Officer engages in a short chase with the old campaigner.

The entire affair is begun as yet another of Mainwaring's misbegotten plans. This time, he is hoping to become a major by tripling the size of the platoon. There is also some fine give and take between Mainwaring and Wilson over the former's report on his sergeant. Underappreciated as always, Wilson receives low grades from his commander on a variety of points, including appearance and alertness. Wilson only frustrates the captain further by finding the entire exercise laughable and comparing it to a school report card. There is a good running gag involving Wilson's habit of putting his hand on his hip, a trait that Mainwaring warns is close to the stance of a "Nancy boy."

Gabor Vernon makes his second appearance of the series here as the Polish Officer. Previously, he played the Russian factory worker visiting the town in season six's "The Honourable Man."

Christmas Special 1975

"My Brother and I" ★★★½

Air date: December 26, 1975. Cast: Capt. Mainwaring (Arthur Lowe); Sgt. Wilson (John Le Mesurier); Cpl. Jones (Clive Dunn); Pvt. Frazer (John Laurie); Pvt. Godfrey (Arnold Ridley); Pvt. Pike (Ian Lavender); ARP Warden (Bill Pertwee); Vicar (Frank Williams); Verger (Edward Sinclair); Chambermaid (Penny Irving); Major General (Arnold Diamond); Pvt. Sponge (Colin Bean)

Captain Mainwaring's sherry party for local dignitaries is interrupted by a visit from his black-sheep brother, Barry.

Up to the usual high standards of the series, "My Brother and I" really shines on the strength of Arthur Lowe's double duty as both Mainwaring brothers. Although it is obvious that Lowe is playing both parts, his skill at fleshing out the character of Barry is so complete that one soon forgets the fact. Using only a toupee, a checkered suit, and a slightly different accent, Lowe brings the tippling, jovial brother to full life.

The reintroduction of Barry into George Mainwaring's life is particularly ill timed for the pompous bank manager. It seems that Mainwaring is hosting a reception for town dignitaries and regional army officers when his brother comes breezing back into the area after a 15-year absence. The plot is particularly well established, and we are reminded of Mainwaring's straight-laced morals — especially in regard to the use of alcohol — before Barry arrives. The first scene with the prodigal brother is quite good, as Barry, a traveling joke-and-novelty salesman, meets Frazer on the train to Walmington-on-Sea. Barry manages quickly to insult, then ingratiate himself to the dour undertaker. Soon, the identity of the salesman is revealed, along with his mission to retrieve a pocket watch, claimed by George on their father's death. Of course, Frazer is delighted to hear of the bad blood between the brothers and anticipates a lively time of trouble.

Aside from his duty as the lively Barry, Lowe manages to provide new depth to the long-established character of George Mainwaring. In a moving scene, Mainwaring confesses he felt inferior to a brother who was always more popular, despite the fact that George's more reserved path has led him to a position of respect and trustworthiness.

The one scene shared by the brothers — seamlessly executed from a technical standpoint — provides the dramatic climax to the special. Barry is especially humorous as he insists on taunting his brother (it is never revealed which one is older) by calling him "po-face" (British slang for someone who is particularly morose, "po" being slang for a chamber pot). Barry manages to get the watch back from George by threatening to ruin his sherry party.

The comic highlight of the installment comes when Barry breaks his word and shows up at the reception anyway. The platoon works overtime (particularly Pike, who displays extraordinary concern and initiative over the affair), attempting to get Barry out of the way before he causes the captain any more embarrassment. There is a rather touching coda to the proceedings, as Wilson manages to retrieve Mainwaring's watch, only to have the more sober brother return it to Barry out of sympathy and pity for him.

Penny Irving, recognizable as Miss Bakewell, one of Mr. Grace's secretaries on *Are You Being Served?* appears briefly as a chambermaid accosted by the wayward Mainwaring brother.

Christmas Special 1976

"The Love of Three Oranges" ★★★

Air date: December 26, 1976. Cast: Capt. Mainwaring (Arthur Lowe); Sgt. Wilson (John Le Mesurier); Cpl. Jones (Clive Dunn); Pvt. Frazer (John Laurie); Pvt. Godfrey (Arnold Ridley); Pvt. Pike (Ian Lavender); ARP Warden (Bill Pertwee); Vicar (Frank Williams); Verger (Edward Sinclair); Mrs. Fox (Pamela Cundell); Mrs. Pike (Janet Davies); Dolly (Joan Cooper); Town Clerk (Eric Longworth); Mrs. Yeatman (Olive Mercer); Pvt. Sponge (Colin Bean)

Mainwaring is intent on securing an orange in a church raffle.

Another Boxing Day offering, "The Love of Three Oranges" must have seemed a special Christmas present to the viewing public since, for the first time in five years, there has been no regular season of *Dad's Army* to enjoy. The special, which is the normal 30 minutes in length, is an entertaining combination of situations, most of which revolve around a church bazaar. Most of the bits score direct hits, but there is yet another repeat of the scene in which Mainwaring appoints himself to chair a town committee. This sequence, complete with the usual complaining by Hodges, bickering between Wilson and Mrs. Pike, and interruptions by the Verger, is the least successful routine.

The special begins strongly, as the platoon members assemble to display their individual attempts at creating snow camouflage suits. This is a variation on a similar exercise from "Sgt. Wilson's Little Secret" seven years earlier, although it remains fresh and not repetitive. Of course, each of the principal platoon members shows up with some odd wrinkle to his snow disguise. Jones has covered his eyeglasses with white paper to hide his vibrant eyes, with the comic result that he looks like he is staring with pinpoints for pupils. Frazer, for lack of anything better, turns up in his mother's wedding dress. The best (or worst) attempt is displayed by Godfrey, who wears his Pierrot costume, complete with large pom-poms, left over from his stint as one of the "Gay Gondoliers."

The bazaar sequence is also amusing, with the laughs gathered from a series of vignettes scattered throughout the scene. Jones's contribution to the proceedings, a "monster brawn" (a giant jellied concoction of boiled boar), is a standout. Frazer also provides some amusement as he creates silhouettes of patrons. His cutout of Mainwaring's profile is particularly funny, as it comes out looking like a series of "round lumps." When an insulted Mainwaring points this out, the gloomy Scot defends his work by citing that the captain is indeed nothing more than a series of round lumps.

The climax of the proceedings is the raffle of the oranges donated by Hodges. With Mainwaring intent on securing one of the rare pieces of fruit as a peace offering to his wife, Hodges is determined to keep him from getting any. There is a well-executed, albeit predictable, gag in which Pike, attempting to help Mainwaring, bids against him and succeeds in inflating the price of the orange tenfold.

Series Nine 1977

EPISODE 1: "WAKE UP WALMINGTON" ★★★½

Air date: October 2, 1977. Cast: Capt. Mainwaring (Arthur Lowe); Sgt. Wilson (John Le Mesurier); Cpl. Jones (Clive Dunn); Pvt. Frazer (John Laurie); Pvt. Godfrey (Arnold Ridley); Pvt. Pike (Ian Lavender); Chief Warden Hodges (Bill Pertwee); Vicar (Frank Williams); Verger (Edward Sinclair); Captain Square (Geoffrey Lumsden); Yokel (Sam Kydd); Mr. Bluett (Harold Bennett); Colonel (Robert Raglan); Soldier (Jeffrey Holland); Van Driver (Barry Linehan); Pvt. Sponge (Colin Bean)

The platoon members disguise themselves as cutthroats and saboteurs in an attempt to shock Walmington out of a state of complacency.

The first regular series entry in two years and the first of the final season for this much-loved comedy does not disappoint. "Wake Up Walmington" features another attempt by Mainwaring to increase his importance to the war effort by launching another initiative doomed to hilarious complications. When the captain feels that the town is no longer taking the Nazi threat seriously, he leads the men to pose as fifth columnists (saboteurs) for an exercise. Disguised as desperate-looking types, or their personal interpretations of such types, the platoon takes to wandering the countryside in an effort to create a panic. The idea recalls the situation in "Ring Dem Bells" from the previous season (in fact, that incident is alluded to here), although there is enough fresh material to warrant its repetition.

As in all other episodes in which the men are called upon to exercise their initiative in regard to costumes, "Wake Up Walmington" affords plenty of opportunities for silly dress. The most ridiculous getup is Jones's nun habit, followed closely by Pike's imitation of Edward G. Robinson (in *Scarface*, he mistakenly relates). Mainwaring's disguise as a sea captain, complete with eyepatch, is actually quite good, until they encounter a real sea captain similarly dressed, and a fight ensues.

The episode ends with the platoon being spotted (again at a pub, as in "Ring Dem Bells"), and Captain Square is dispatched to round them up. Unfortunately, the writers couldn't come up with a neat closing gag, and the episode just fades out as Mainwaring and Square bicker over which one prevailed in the charade.

Fans will probably be surprised by the gaunt appearance of John Le Mesurier in this final series. Although not an alcoholic, Le Mesurier was a regular drinker who, prior to this series, was advised by his doctor to give up alcohol. This, in combination with a low-fat diet of fruits and vegetables, caused the weight to drop off the actor, resulting in his markedly different appearance.

Episode 2: "The Making of Private Pike" ★★½

Air date: October 9, 1977. Cast: Capt. Mainwaring (Arthur Lowe); Sgt. Wilson (John Le Mesurier); Cpl. Jones (Clive Dunn); Pvt. Frazer (John Laurie); Pvt. Godfrey (Arnold Ridley); Pvt. Pike (Ian Lavender); Chief Warden Hodges (Bill Pertwee); Vicar (Frank Williams); Verger (Edward Sinclair); Sylvia (Jean Gilpin); Colonel (Anthony Sharp); Brigadier (Jeffrey Segal); Mrs. Fox (Pamela Cundell); Mrs. Pike (Janet Davies); Nora (Melita Manger)

Minor scandal ensues when Frank Pike stays out all night with the niece of Warden Hodges.

A seriocomic entry focusing on the character of Pike, "The Making of Private Pike" is good in the comic bits but unfortunately does not portray its title subject in a favorable light. Pike has always been the quintessential mama's boy, but never has it been so harshly spotlighted as in this episode, where he has a date. The rendezvous is with Sylvia, the visiting niece of Hodges, and as one might expect the girl is as common as her greengrocer uncle. Interested in only necking and then sex, the girl turns cruel on poor Pikey when he continually rebuffs her hints and advances by a giggling admonition to "clear off." Sylvia dubs Pike a "soppy boy" and finally calls him retarded when the pair run out of gas, and Pike fails to take advantage of her and the situation. Instead, Pike pushes the car nine miles back to Walmington, where an angry reception awaits him.

One of the better moments of the episode comes at the end as Wilson takes a moment to have a brief man-to-man talk with Pike. The subtlety of the chat is lost on Pike, who doesn't realize that his "Uncle Arthur" is commiserating with him because he, Wilson, actually believes Pike slept with the girl, behavior that Wilson has been ostracized for in his own past.

On the comic side, the best moments come as Mainwaring is allotted a staff car (the car Pike "borrows" for his date). The pompous little captain takes great pains (some of them physical) trying to sort out the seating protocol in the tiny car in such a way as to make himself look optimally important.

For the second episode running, allusion is made to a previous season's entry (this time it's "When You've Got to Go"), perhaps an indication that the writers were beginning to run thin on ideas.

EPISODE 3: "KNIGHTS OF MADNESS" ★★★½

Air date: October 16, 1977. Cast: Capt. Mainwaring (Arthur Lowe); Sgt. Wilson (John Le Mesurier); Cpl. Jones (Clive Dunn); Pvt. Frazer (John Laurie); Pvt. Godfrey (Arnold Ridley); Pvt. Pike (Ian Lavender); Chief Warden Hodges (Bill Pertwee); Vicar (Frank Williams); Verger (Edward Sinclair); Pvt. Sponge (Colin Bean); Mrs. Pike (Janet Davies); Mrs. Yeatman (Olive Mercer); Town Clerk (Eric Longworth); Mayor (Fred McNaughton)

Mainwaring plays St. George and the platoon dresses as the dragon for a Wings for Victory celebration in Walmington. The only problem is that Hodges and his wardens plan the same display, resulting in conflict between the two rivals.

"Knights of Madness" recalls earlier episodes in the series when the comedy was a little more physical and knockabout. In fact, except for the absence of Jimmy Beck, one would guess the installment had been a lost episode from the third or fourth seasons. The episode follows the familiar template of the platoon planning an operation, practicing the operation, then executing it with complications. In this case, the operation is a reenactment of St. George slaying the dragon. Of course, the egotistical Mainwaring must play the knight, complete with a full set of armor. There's an amusing location scene in which the platoon tries to hoist the tinned captain onto his horse with definitely mixed results. This leads to St. George being outfitted with a suit of armor knitted by Godfrey's sister, Dolly.

The climax of the whole affair reads somewhat better than it actually plays on the small screen. When the rival wardens learn that the Home Guard is doing the same skit as they had planned, they rush onto the field while the first group is still performing. This results in the comical concept of the two dragons fighting each other for the field while the two St. Georges (Hodges, naturally, is the other) do similar battle. Given the unwieldy nature of the costumes, the conflict is rather awkwardly staged and thus loses some of its comic punch.

EPISODE 4: "THE MISER'S HOARD" ★★★

Air date: October 23, 1977. Cast: Capt. Mainwaring (Arthur Lowe); Sgt. Wilson (John Le Mesurier); Cpl. Jones (Clive Dunn); Pvt. Frazer (John Laurie); Pvt. Godfrey (Arnold Ridley); Pvt. Pike (Ian Lavender); Chief Warden Hodges (Bill Pertwee); Vicar (Frank Williams); Verger (Edward Sinclair); Pvt. Sponge (Colin Bean). Special Guest Appearance: Fulton Mackay as Dr. McCeavedy

When he learns that Frazer is sitting on a fortune in gold sovereigns, Mainwaring desperately tries to convince the Scot that the money belongs in the bank.

After a long distinguished career playing some of Shakespeare's best roles, it is gratifying to know that John Laurie was afforded one final episode in the last season of *Dad's Army* to be in the spotlight. "The Miser's Hoard" is an over-the-top opportunity for the Scottish actor, and he makes the most of it—with relish. The always wild-eyed Frazer is all that and more in this installment, in which it is discovered that he has thousands of pounds worth of gold saved over a lifetime of scrimping. Frazer's miserable condition has driven him close to insanity, giving Laurie even more license for his delightfully broad portrayal.

It's nice to observe that, even at this late stage in the series, the writers are still fleshing out the already well-drawn characters. The first scene in which Frazer counts his gold is both amusing and revealing. The character was always seen as being tight with money, but here the audience learns just how deep his thrift goes. After amassing thousands and continually adding to it (his profit for the week is a then very handsome £18), Frazer sits back and announces that due to his lifetime of hard work he deserves a treat. After thinking for a moment, he decides he will buy himself a small herring for supper.

Arthur Lowe is fine as always as he schemes, first subtly then overtly, for ways to get Frazer's gold cashed in for a more secure annuity. Of course, this would be purchased from his bank, with Mainwaring receiving the generous commission. Wilson is quite good as well, not only as he cautions his boss against prying into Frazer's business but later in a funny turn at playing drunk. Still, the episode really belongs to John Laurie and deservedly so.

Back for a second time as a guest star is Fulton Mackay, previously seen in series six's "We Know Our Onions" as the crusty Captain Ramsey. Here, the character actor plays a much more sedate part as the local doctor who first learns of Frazer's fortune.

EPISODE 5: "NUMBER ENGAGED" ★★★

Air date: November 6, 1977. Cast: Capt. Mainwaring (Arthur Lowe); Sgt. Wilson (John Le Mesurier); Cpl. Jones (Clive Dunn); Pvt. Frazer (John Laurie); Pvt. Godfrey (Arnold Ridley); Pvt. Pike (Ian Lavender); Chief Warden Hodges (Bill Pertwee); Vicar (Frank Williams); Verger (Edward Sinclair); GPO Man (Ronnie Brody); Army Captain (Robert Mill); Army Sergeant (Kenneth MacDonald); Van Driver (Felix Bowness); Pvt. Sponge (Colin Bean); Scottish Sergeant (Stuart McGugan); ATS Girl (Bernice Adams)

While guarding vital telephone lines, the platoon must contend with an unexploded German bomb that drops in among the wires.

A pure gag comedy, "Number Engaged" employs a nice array of knockabouts around its thin plot. The platoon is dispatched to relieve a regular army unit for the weekend with the task of guarding lines of communications. Aside from a brief opening sequence in the church office and some insert scenes inside their field tent, most of the action takes place out of doors. At first the jokes and situations are rather mild: Mainwaring orders Jones to drive over a road barrier, which results in the captain getting a face full of hot tea. The laughs build quickly, however, when during a Sunday morning field worship service, Mainwaring discovers an unexploded bomb resting on the telephone pole. At first Mainwaring valiantly, but foolishly, tries to retrieve the bomb himself with the use of a phone worker's leg spikes. After some clumsy and amusing attempts, another approach is tried. The situation reaches its peak when the men use the furniture from a passing van to build a tower in an attempt to reach the bomb. A reluctant Pike is dispatched up the wobbly column, only to have it come crashing down once he reaches the top. Finally, through Sergeant Wilson's cool logic, the device is safely brought down.

There is an interesting night scene during which Jones and Pike stand guard by the wires and imagine the important information that is being carried through the lines. Inset shots reveal the actual communications to be a soldier and his girlfriend deciding which movie to go to on their next date. This scene is better in concept than in execution and seems out of place among the slapstick of the rest of the episode.

In Richard Webber's *Dad's Army: A Celebration*, Ian Lavender recalled that he begged producer David Croft to let him do the actual stunt of climbing the furniture tower. Croft refused. Consequently, the stunt man who did the trick wound up in the hospital, following the fall from the tower. "Fancy doing it now?" Croft asked Lavender afterwards

EPISODE 6: "NEVER TOO OLD" ★★★★

Air date: November 13, 1977. Cast: Capt. Mainwaring (Arthur Lowe); Sgt. Wilson (John Le Mesurier); Cpl. Jones (Clive Dunn); Pvt. Frazer (John Laurie); Pvt. Godfrey (Arnold Ridley); Pvt. Pike (Ian Lavender); Chief Warden Hodges (Bill Pertwee); Vicar (Frank Williams); Verger (Edward Sinclair); Mrs. Fox (Pamela Cundell); Mrs. Pike (Janet Davies); Pvt. Sponge (Colin Bean); Dolly (Joan Cooper); Colonel (Robert Raglan)

The wedding celebration for Corporal Jones and Mrs. Fox is interrupted by an invasion alert.

It is typical of this remarkable television series that the authors and cast say farewell with an episode that is both humorous and touching, sentimental and respectful of its subject. The show indeed has a special feel about it, without drawing attention to itself as such. Only in the final moments does the cast step ever so slightly out of character and face the camera in a toast to the real veterans of Britain's Home Guard. This tribute comes after it has been learned that the invasion alert was a false alarm. Warden Hodges derisively tells the Magnificent Seven (absent Jimmy Beck's Joe Walker, of course) that they would be no use against real troops and exits laughing.

Pike asks Mainwaring if Hodges' assessment is true. Mainwaring affirms that it isn't, to which all the men respond that they would fight fiercely against any foe that threatened Great Britain. At this point, Wilson suggests they pay tribute to the "men who will stand together when their country needs them." The cast members then lift their cups in salute to the Home Guard.

What goes before this touching coda is topnotch material as well. Each of the principals are given something to do, and even in this final installment new facets are revealed in many of the characters. For example, in one last soliloquy, Frazer tells the sad tale of a girl he loved and lost. Presumably, his inamorata was lost to the sea, but in a typical anticlimax to the dramatic rendering, the Scot reveals that she turned up alive, years later in the Far East. Frazer's love remained stranded there, however, since he refused to send the £40 passage home. Mainwaring also reflects on his own marriage, and while he once more states the union to be a happy one, his expression says otherwise. The captain discloses as well that he married above his station and that his wife's family never approved of him. Godfrey, it is learned, also almost married, to the farmer's wife from "All Is Safely Gathered In." Only the "stupid boy," Pike, has no tales of tragic love to relate, although he does manage to enliven the others' stories with his naïveté. The biggest surprise of the episode comes as Wilson arrives for Jones's wedding in his World War I uniform, revealing to the town (and especially to an annoyed Mainwaring) that he was a decorated captain in the previous conflict.

Clive Dunn, as the rest of his comrades, sends his character out in style by expertly delivering some of the best befuddled dialogue Messieurs Perry and Croft ever wrote for the elderly lance corporal.

In keeping with the family atmosphere that had developed among the cast over the previous nine years, the wedding guests were primarily composed of family members (at least those with equity cards) of the principals. The most notable is Joan Cooper (Mrs. Arthur Lowe) appearing once again as Dolly Godfrey, Private Godfrey's sister.

All in all, "Never Too Old" is a classic finale to a classic piece of television history.

Are You Being Served?

BBC-TV 1972–1985

Are You Being Served? is an amazing phenomenon in the annals of British television. It not only ran for 69 episodes, a prodigious number for a Brit-com, but it paved the way for a wave of renewed popularity for the genre in America. It would be safe to venture that, *Fawlty Towers* aside, it is the most popular comedy import to American screens. What makes this all the more remarkable is that the show isn't nearly up to the standards of the John Cleese/Connie Booth masterpiece or at least a dozen other British comedies exported to the States. Still, *Are You Being Served?* (*AYBS?*) has been running almost uninterrupted in many U.S. markets since first appearing on these shores in the early 1990s. (The local PBS outlet in Philadelphia ran the program five nights a week as its prime time lead-in for close to five years) *AYBS?* is also one of the few Brit-coms to have an entire book devoted to its history published in the United States. There are American fan clubs as well. (Such Brit-com paragons as *Steptoe and Son* and *Dad's Army* have their appreciation societies, but these are restricted for the most part to the mother country and its commonwealth.)

Why is this show, which is generally dismissed by critics, so loved by audiences—particularly in America? It is something of the McDonald's of Brit-coms. For anyone who has done any traveling, the amazing proliferation of the Golden Arches is astounding. Even more astounding is the fact that no matter what McDonald's restaurant you step into, whether in Los Angeles, London, or Moscow, the meal will taste remarkably the same. Granted, you can find better meals, and worse meals, but McDonald's has demonstrated a great consistency when it comes to turning out hamburgers and fries.

You always know what you're going to get. True, an individual restaurant may be more attractive, or may be better run, but the food will be essentially the same.

The same can be said of the Jeremy Lloyd/David Croft concoction that was marketed to hungry comedy fans under the banner *Are You Being Served?* There are funnier, wittier programs, and, of course, some that are not as amusing. But on any given evening, the long-running show is remarkably consistent. Viewers can take comfort that there will be no jokes or situations that are unfamiliar. Shows essentially "taste" the same, and that is comforting to American audiences, who like their comedy unchallenging and predictable. In this sense, *AYBS?* is the most American of the British shows. American audiences can enjoy it for its distinct brand of British bawdiness, without straying too far from the familiar. Just like a visit to the local Mickey D's, *AYBS?* fills a need painlessly, if predictably. (None of this is meant as a slight to the restaurant or the comedy. I for one enjoy them both and admire their successes. I just wouldn't want a steady diet of either.)

That *AYBS?* is so American in style is not surprising when one considers that one of its cocreators, the one who had the original notion for the show, had worked in American television comedy. In 1971, Jeremy Lloyd was fresh off a stint writing and performing in America's highly successful *Rowan and Martin's Laugh-In* program. Having had a taste of a variety of show business genres, Lloyd thought he would next like to try his hand at writing a situation comedy. Like Jimmy Perry, the cocreator of *Dad's Army,* before him, Lloyd decided to base his show on an experience from his youth. Whereas Perry had been in Britain's Home Guard, Lloyd had experienced a similarly regimented hierarchy as a suit salesman at Simpson's, a department store in London's Piccadilly. Also like Perry, Lloyd brought his concept for a series to BBC producer David Croft.

In 1971, a new group of *Comedy Playhouse* episodes was being planned. Although it had started in 1962 as purely an outlet for the talents of writers Ray Galton and Alan Simpson, *Comedy Playhouse* had evolved into a proving ground for pilots and potential BBC comedy series. Aside from *Steptoe and Son,* which developed unintentionally from *Playhouse*'s anthology format, other hits that sprang from the series included *Till Death Us Do Part, The Liver Birds,* and *Last of the Summer Wine.* Croft decided that Lloyd's idea for a comedy set in a department store seemed solid and commissioned him to write the pilot. The pilot ran on BBC 1 on Friday, September 8, 1972, at 9:30, and it subsequently was picked up for a series beginning the following spring.

Lloyd and Croft created their series, set in the fictional Grace Brothers' store in the center of London, around a core group of characters representing the men's and ladies' departments. Jeremy Lloyd likens the cast to something of a household.

"The Grace Brothers' staff is a family," Lloyd told the authors of the *Are You Being Served?* book, "with Captain Peacock as the head of the family, Mr. Grainger as the grandfather, and Young Mr. Grace as the family patriarch."

Carrying the analogy further, one can surmise that Mrs. Slocombe is something of the mother figure, Mr. Lucas and Miss Brahms the children, and Mr. Humphries the odd uncle. This core of characters was fleshed out with another authority figure in the guise of Mr. Rumbold and with Mr. Mash (later Mr. Harman) as another voice of rebellion. Although the personnel would vary over the course of ten seasons (particularly the older men's salesman), essentially the types presented in the pilot would remain unchanged for 69 shows.

When first presented, the show featured Trevor Bannister and Mollie Sugden as its titular stars. This arrangement is borne out by the fact that for the first five seasons either Bannister or Sugden is given top billing in the credits, with Frank Thornton always in the third spot. As the show went into seasons six and seven, however, the growing popularity of the increasingly flamboyant character of Mr. Humphries moved John Inman into the starring rotation with Sugden. Interestingly, according to the authors, Bannister's character was originally conceived as the voice of sanity in the lineup, rather than as the cheeky wisecracker into which he quickly evolved.

Bannister was chosen for the prime part of Mr. Lucas (first name given on separate occasions as Dick and James) following his success in ITV's highly rated comedy *The Dustbinmen*. Although not the star of that show, which centered on the adventures of a crew of trash collectors, Bannister gave solid comedy support in the part of a character named Heavy Breathing (so-called because he thought he had a way with the women). After a three-series stint as a garbage man, Bannister bumped into David Croft in a club, and the producer offered him the pilot script for *AYBS?* At the time, Bannister recalls thinking that Lucas seemed like the main character. Indeed, many of the early plots either turn around the junior salesman or spotlight his comic ability prominently in support.

Mollie Sugden was no stranger either to television comedy or to the ranks of actors and actresses who made up producer Croft's unofficial stock company. The two first worked together in the long-running BBC comedy *Hugh and I*. In this program, Sugden played a supporting role as Mrs. Crispin, the snobbish neighbor to the show's main characters. Following this, Sugden also played the fearsome Mrs. Hutchinson on another popular show, *The Liver Birds*. When *AYBS?* was in development, Croft recalled Sugden's work and fashioned the comically blustering Mrs. Slocombe with the actress in mind.

The role of the officious floorwalker, Captain Peacock, fell to veteran character actor Frank Thornton. Thornton was already familiar to British audiences thanks to his fine supporting work in such shows as *Hancock's Half-Hour, It's a Square World*, and *Steptoe and Son*. Thanks to his height (6'2") and his ability to portray outraged authority figures, Thornton was a ready-made foil for comedians. His part in the cast of *AYBS?* is key, providing as it does the irritating but comically essential role of the middle manager. As such, the Peacock character is usually found trying to assert his authority over the sales staff, although he can also subvert the rule of his superiors and cast his lot with the peons when it suits his purpose.

Although listed fifth in the cast for the pilot offering, no individual became more closely identified with the series than John Inman. Inman came to the career role of the mincing Mr. Humphries directly from retail. It was Christmas time, and Inman was appearing in a holiday show in London while selling toys at Selfridge's department store to supplement his income. According to the character actor, a friend walked into the store and told him that David Croft was looking to cast him in the show. "I walked out of Selfridge's and never went back," recalled Inman.

Aside from selling toys, Inman had also worked in the menswear department of Austin Reed on London's fashionable Regent Street. Later, Inman credited a coworker from that store as the direct inspiration for Mr. Humphries' effeminate bounce.

While no character in the show has generated as much of a following as Mr. Humphries, neither has one created as much controversy. Inman has always contended that Mr. Humphries is not necessarily a homosexual but rather is sexually ambiguous. When the show first aired in England, however, the swishy, limp-wristed eccentric was immediately attacked by gay rights activists as the very image they were trying to combat. Protests were launched with some even demanding that the part of Mr. Humphries be written out of ensuing shows. Oddly, in these earlier episodes the character is seen at his least flamboyant. Eventually, due to his popularity with the audience at large, Inman rode out the storm and went on to eventually become the show's main character. Today, the camp Mr. Humphries, rather than being rejected by the homosexual community, is often embraced as an icon. Any controversy still generated comes usually in response to Inman's ongoing insistence that the prissy Mr. H was not gay.

Although she was only 25 when she first appeared in the *AYBS?* pilot episode, Wendy Richard was no newcomer to television. After breaking into show business ten years earlier with a bit part in "Come Outside," a novelty song that hit number one, Richard worked in a variety of roles, including BBC soap operas, *Carry On* films, action programs, and situation comedies. The most notable of the latter were appearances in Frankie Howerd's *Up Pompeii*, Patrick

McGoohan's *Danger Man*, and the perennial police favorite, *Z-Cars*. Like Mollie Sugden, Wendy Richard came to the cast of *AYBS?* via other David Croft shows. Richard's main part before that of assistant to Mrs. Slocombe was as Shirley, the girlfriend of spiv (a shady character) Private Joe Walker in *Dad's Army*. Like Inman, Richard also had practical retail experience, worked at both Selfridge's and Fortnum and Mason.

Unlike Wendy Richard, Arthur Brough, who played the show's curmudgeonly Mr. Grainger, had little on-air experience before joining the cast of *AYBS?* Although he had more than 50 years' experience in repertory theater, Brough's first television role was a tiny bit part in the "A. Wilson (Manager?)" episode of *Dad's Army*, in which he appeared as a timid bank clerk. The veteran actor's next TV part was that of Grainger, senior salesclerk of the men's department. Ironically, all this fame came 13 years after Brough had officially retired. While a TV novice, Brough's wealth of acting experience was clearly evident, as his Grainger was consistently one of the performing highlights of the first five seasons. The stage veteran was also quite beloved by those with whom he worked. Mollie Sugden recalls that Brough was always pulling "mischievous pranks," while director Bob Spiers remembers the actor often ducking out of rehearsals for brief "refreshers" in the pub next door. Bannister had especially fond memories of Brough since Brough had given the younger actor his first professional job on stage back in the late 1950's.

The final key member of the original cast was Nicholas Smith in the role of department manager Cuthbert Rumbold. Smith came to *AYBS?* after a career that included drama, comedy, and music. In fact, it was in musicals that Smith received his first professional experience. His skill at both singing and playing musical instruments is evident in a number of episodes — usually for comic effect. Smith's skill at playing the dull, often pedantic, uninspired middle manager displays his true talent. As in the case of Arthur Brough, Nicholas Smith's characterization of Rumbold provides solid comic relief especially when juxtaposed against the more flamboyant roles of John Inman and Mollie Sugden. Most of us have encountered firsthand a manager like Cuthbert Rumbold, and while this can be trying when encountered in real life, it is usually quite enjoyable in *AYBS?*

The other characters who graced the halls of Grace Brothers' department store over the years were in a seemingly constant state of flux, especially after the first five seasons. When the show first began, Mr. Mash of the maintenance department represented the lower echelon of the store's pecking order. Portrayed by Cockney actor Larry Martyn, Mash was often the voice of Labour (politically speaking) in the series, which proved to be a regular irritant to Captain Peacock. Martyn was replaced after three seasons when the fourth season of *AYBS?* conflicted with the production of the third season of *Spring and Autumn*, an ITV comedy in which the actor had a larger, though still supporting, role.

Larry Martyn's replacement was veteran comic stage actor Arthur English. While still as pro-union as the character of Mash had been, English's Mr. Harman is much less belligerent in his portrayal and thus more endearing to the audiences. English's specialty in his comic days was playing the spiv, which in many ways defines his angle-seeking role in *AYBS?*

Aside from the change in the maintenance staff, the first major change in the cast came after the fifth season, when Arthur Brough quit the series following the death of his wife, Elizabeth. After having worked alongside his wife on the stage for almost 50 years of marriage, Brough felt that he couldn't continue in the profession without her support. As is often the case with widowers, Brough passed away a few months after his wife. To replace Grainger, the producers of the show wrote in the character of Mr. Tebbs, who was played by actor James Hayter. Hayter's main claim to fame at the time was playing Mr. Kipling, the advertising spokesman for Mr. Kipling's Cakes. While fine in the role, Hayter was hampered by the fact that his character was hardly distinguishable from that of his predecessor. Watching the sixth season, one can imagine Grainger doing just about everything that had been scripted for Tebbs. Whether or not Mr. Tebbs would evolve into more of his own man, rather than a copy of Mr. Grainger, became a moot point. After the six shows of the sixth season, Mr. Kipling's Cakes approached Hayter with the concern that his appearances on *AYBS?* were reducing the effectiveness of his cake advertisements. Not surprisingly, given the less-than-meatiness of his role as Tebbs, Hayter opted to continue as Mr. Kipling.

The seventh season saw a new senior assistant introduced in the guise of Mr. Goldberg, brought to the small screen by comic actor Alfie Bass. Bass was no stranger to British television viewers, having appeared in a number of series, the most notable being the long-running *The Army Game* and its spinoff, *Bootsie and Snudge* (with Bass in the first title role). In addition, Bass had provided comic support in many films, including the classic *The Lavender Hill Mob* and the Beatles' *Help!* While the addition of Mr. Goldberg certainly helped breathe some fresh air into the series at a point when it was admittedly starting to repeat itself, unfortunately, the move proved to be ill fated. The primary difficulty lay in the fact that a cast member of Alfie Bass's expertise would be wasted unless he were given plenty to do. In an established ensemble cast already filled with eccentric comic talent, however, the writers were hard pressed to give Bass the amount of exposure Bass thought he needed to make the part worth his while. "He [Bass] thought he needed a bigger part," recalled Jeremy Lloyd to the authors of *Are You Being Served? The Inside Story*. "We couldn't make the part bigger, so he moved on."

It was a shame that an amicable compromise couldn't be reached since the eight shows that include Bass are some of the best of the series. For the eighth season, a pair of actors, Milo Sperber and Benny Lee, were brought in to play Mr. Grossman and Mr. Klein, respectively. Neither character distinguished himself, nor is it likely that either was called upon to do so. Wisely, for the final two seasons, the authors decided that the part of a senior assistant in men's wear was unnecessary, and the show went on no worse for the omission.

Of course, the greatest single upheaval in the cast of *Are You Being Served?* occurred when Trevor Bannister announced that he was leaving the show, citing that seven seasons of series comedy was enough. "I am not a great believer in getting involved too long," Bannister recalled years later to *British Television* magazine's Dan Abramson. Aside from the fear of becoming typecast as the perennial junior assistant into his middle age, Bannister also admitted that the authors were beginning to run out of fresh ideas.

Bannister's departure did not catch the show's writers unprepared, however, thanks to the expanding role afforded John Inman over the previous seasons. Still, especially with the exit of Alfie Bass, Inman needed someone with whom to interact behind the men's counter—figuratively speaking, of course. A suitable replacement was found in pop star–turned-actor Mike Berry in the part of Bert Spooner. Berry, looking younger than his approximate age of 40, joined the show in 1981 and served well for the show's final three seasons, eventually making the part his own rather than an imitation of Bannister. Berry began his show business career in the early sixties as the head of a group called Mike Berry and the Outlaws. Berry was a contemporary of the Beatles and enjoyed a fairly prosperous pop career for most of the decade. Around the beginning of the 1970s, Berry went into a variety of nonmusical ventures before branching into modeling and acting. His first big acting break was the regular role of a handyman on the children's program *Worzel Gummidge*. In 1980, Berry returned to singing with a trio of songs that hit the charts and that helped attract the attention of the producers of *Are You Being Served?*

The last role that saw change over the years was that of the store owner. This function was at first seen as a minor part when the series began (appearing only sporadically during the first season) but grew thanks to the wonderful performance of Harold Bennett as Young Mr. Grace. Bennett was another recruit from David Croft's *Dad's Army*, in which he played Mr. Blewitt, one of Walmington-on-Sea's elder residents. His inclusion as "Young" Mr. Grace was of course a built-in joke, thanks to Bennett's perilously frail appearance. Despite being physically feeble, Bennett possessed a sharp mind and a charming delivery, which turned his character's often outright lechery into benign humor. Bennett's skill at playing lust with a unique sense of innocence was all the more apparent when he retired from the part in 1981 due to advancing age. Kenneth Waller, almost 30 years younger, was brought in to play Old Mr. Grace, the elder brother to Bennett's character. Although he had regularly played older men, Waller was definitely not in the same state of ancientness as Bennett. Consequently, when called upon to essentially play the same naughtiness (apparently a strong Grace family trait) as Bennett, Waller, through little fault of his own, hadn't the same disarming quality. Sensing this, the writers dropped the character from the final two seasons of the show. A final tribute to Bennett's success at making a lasting impression rests in the fact that when the sequel was being planned, it used the demise of Young Mr. Grace, rather than his brother, as the downfall of the Grace empire.

Like many British television programs, *Are You Being Served?* took a few seasons to find its audience. Thankfully for all those concerned, the BBC remained committed to the program until it became a Top 20 hit. The rest, they say, is history. The program ran for ten seasons and could have run for more. The BBC wanted the writers to sign on for another series, but Croft and Lloyd begged off, citing that they had simply run out of ideas. "It had come logically to a conclusion," recalled Jeremy Lloyd in the *Are You Being Served?* book, "so it just ended there. But I regret that we never got round to the staff outing. We had always thought that at the end of the show, the last show should be the staff outing."

Instead, Lloyd's logical conclusion involved relative newcomer Bert Spooner, played by Mike Berry, becoming a pop music star and leaving the employ of Grace Brothers'. The departure of Trevor Bannister years earlier would have been a much more logical coda to the series, but the timing was not right.

Before the end of the regular run of the show, however, Grace Brothers' department store spawned several spinoff properties. The first of these was a stage play that ran from June to October 1976 at the Winter Gardens pavilion in the northern city of Blackpool. Scripted by Croft and Lloyd and no doubt inspired by the success of a *Dad's Army* stage show the previous year, the play starred most of the main cast except Trevor Bannister and Arthur Brough (other actors played the parts of Lucas and Grainger). The story was close in concept to the next project, a feature-length film shot the following year.

In the movie of *Are You Being Served?* the entire cast — this time including Bannister and Brough — take a group holiday to a seedy resort and get mixed up in a variety of rather predictable situations. Like many Brit-coms of the period, the film incarnation of the show failed to capture the charm that had first attracted fans to the small screen version.

In 1979, Croft and Lloyd traveled to the United States to help television producer Garry Marshall adapt *AYBS?* for American TV. A pilot, *Beanes of Boston*, was produced but never was sold. The pilot featured Jeremy Lloyd's former *Laugh-In* costar Alan Sues in the part of Mr. Humphries, veteran actor John Hillerman (a few years from playing second fiddle on *Magnum P.I.*) in the role of Mr. Peacock, and character actress Charlotte Rae (*The Facts of Life*) as

Mrs. Slocombe. In an interesting sidebar, one of the actors who auditioned for *Beanes of Boston* was Robin Williams. Although the comic gave a strong tryout, his manic style just didn't fit into the show's format. Garry Marshall, however, was impressed enough to showcase Williams in an upcoming episode of his *Happy Days* series, which, in short order, led to the series *Mork and Mindy*.

The next incarnation of the show was a version produced for Australian television in 1980 and 1981. These 15 programs, spanning two seasons, starred John Inman in his role of Mr. Humphries, transplanted to Bone Brothers' department store in the land down under. The other names were changed, although the types were kept exactly the same. Captain Peacock became Captain Wagstaff, Mrs. Slocombe became Mrs. Crawford, and so on. Even the scripts for the Aussie version were adapted directly from the British originals by Jeremy Lloyd. This may seem odd, especially since the British version had played on Australian television, but apparently it was a common practice in that country at the time.

The last appearance to date of the cast of *Are You Being Served?* was a follow-up series produced in 1992 and 1993. Entitled *Grace and Favour* (but called *Are You Being Served? Again!* in the United States), these 12 episodes spanned two seasons and reunited Inman, Sugden, Thornton, Richard, and Smith from the original cast. The premise of the show was that Young Mr. Grace had died after investing the staff's pension fund in a ramshackle country manor. The surviving staff members decide to run Millstone Manor as a resort. Despite the addition of new blood in the guise of the caretaker and his daughter (who has amorous designs on Mr. Humphries!), the show, while resurrecting the humor of the original, failed to click with audiences.

While the formula has been attempted in other venues and with other casts, the 69 original 30-minute episodes will be recalled as the lasting legacy of *Are You Being Served?* There are more sophisticated shows and certainly more subtle ones, but there are few British television comedy imports that have captured and retained as ardent a following on countless PBS stations across the United States.

THE EPISODES

By Jeremy Lloyd and David Croft (with Michael Knowles and John Chapman). Directed by Ray Butt, Bob Spiers, John Kilby, Gordon Elsbury, and Martin Shardlow. Produced by David Croft, Martin Shardlow, Bob Spiers, and Harold Snoad

Pilot episode (untitled) ★★½

Air date: September 8, 1972. Cast: Mr. Lucas (Trevor Bannister); Mrs. Slocombe (Mollie Sugden); Capt. Peacock (Frank Thornton); Mr. Granger (Arthur Brough); Mr. Humphries (John Inman); Miss Brahms (Wendy

The first, most enduring, and arguably best cast of the long-running comedy. *Left to right:* Captain Peacock (Frank Thornton); Miss Brahms (Wendy Richard); Mrs. Slocombe (Mollie Sugden); Mr. Rumbold (Nicholas Smith); Mr. Grainger (Arthur Brough); Mr. Humphries (John Inman); and Mr. Lucas (Trevor Bannister) Copyright © BBC.

Richards); Mr. Rumbold (Nicholas Smith); Mr. Mash (Larry Martyn); Customer (Michael Knowles); Young Mr. Grace (Harold Bennett); Secretary (Stephanie Gathercole)

After 25 years with a floor to itself, the men's wear department of Grace Brothers' department store is forced to share its space with the ladies' department. After some initial feigned politeness, a dispute arises over which department will be allowed to use the floor's center display piece. After appealing the matter to management, Mr. Granger's men's department wins the display. Magnanimously, Mr. Granger offers a part of the space to Mrs. Slocombe, who uses it to advertise a particularly garish bra display.

Although it would go on to great success (especially in the United States), run for almost 13 years and almost 70 episodes, *Are You Being Served?* never really develops much beyond its pilot episode. This assessment can serve either as a tribute to the strength of the show's concept or as a condemnation of the shallowness of its writing. The basic premise is already firmly in place; indeed even a good deal of the show's catch phrases and routines are in the pilot in their final form. In all fairness, some of the same observations can be made concerning the venerable *Dad's Army*. However, in the case of *AYBS?* the proof comes in the repetition exercised during the run of the series. The pilot episode delivers a great number of *AYBS?*'s stock phrases fully intact. They include:

"Glass of water for Mr. Granger." Used when the senior clerk of men's wear is shocked by events on the floor.

"Are you free?" Spoken as a mere formality when a staff member wishes to speak to another staff member even when the second is obviously not with a customer.

"It will ride up with wear." Employed, usually by the staff of the men's department, to sell coats or trousers with sleeves or legs too long.

"You've all done very well." Spoken sincerely, but with little knowledge to support the observation, by Young Mr. Grace to the staff whenever he is leaving the floor.

"Weak as water." Railed by Mrs. Slocombe whenever the men on staff display less courage than herself.

Also present in the pilot are *AYBS?*'s plethora of double entendres and innuendo, the first outlandish display (a Beauty Belle bra that lights up in the cups), and the first confused conference in Rumbold's office.

Although the final credits note that the episode is a "BBC Colour" presentation, the pilot show exists only in a black-and-white form.

Series One 1973

Episode 1: Dear Sexy Knickers ★★★

Air date: March 21, 1973. Cast: Mrs. Slocombe (Mollie Sugden); Mr. Lucas (Trevor Bannister); Capt. Peacock (Frank Thornton); Mr. Humphries (John Inman); Miss Brahms (Wendy Richard); Mr. Granger (Arthur Brough); Mr. Rumbold (Nicholas Smith); 40" Waist (Robert Raglan); 28" Inside Leg (Derek Smith)

Mr. Lucas is trying to ask out Miss Brahms under the disapproving gaze of Captain Peacock. Lucas writes her a note addressed to "Sexy Knickers" and attempts to deliver it by shooting it across the floor with a rubber band. Peacock finds the note and hands it to Mrs. Slocombe, who reads it and believes it is meant for her from Peacock.

The first series episode of *AYBS?* offers some promise upon which the rest of the installments of the long-running show do not capitalize. "Dear Sexy Knickers" offers an examination of the show's basic premise: what happens when men's and ladies' departments are forced to share space. The results are somewhat predictable but fairly well explored. The younger members (Lucas and Brahms) eye each other as prospective partners, while the older members

(Granger and Slocombe) battle for supremacy like a warring married couple. Peacock exists as an authority figure to the younger pair while acting as a somewhat biased referee for the older couple. Humphries is an impartial (sexually, at least) Greek chorus.

Although he is out of uniform, *Dad's Army* viewers may recognize the man with the 40-inch waist as Robert Raglan, the Colonel (most of the time) and Captain Pritchard (twice) from that series.

The best moments in "Dear Sexy Knickers" have little to do with the plot. They involve Mr. Humphries teaching Mr. Lucas how to "knee" a coat — loosen a tight sleeve by stretching an armhole with one's knee. When Lucas tries the same ploy with a pair of trousers, he rips them and is sent to Rumbold's office. In a marvelous little bit of confusion, Rumbold interrogates Peacock, Granger, Humphries, and Lucas in an attempt to get to the truth of the incident. Unfortunately, he only manages to become more muddled over the entire affair. This inquisition routine would become a standard in the series and often resulted in the highlight of the show in which it appeared thanks to Nicholas Smith's portrayal of Rumbold.

EPISODE 2: "OUR FIGURES ARE SLIPPING" ★★½

Air date: March 28, 1973. Cast: Mr. Lucas (Trevor Bannister); Mrs. Slocombe (Mollie Sugden); Capt. Peacock (Frank Thornton); Mr. Humphries (John Inman); Miss Brahms (Wendy Richard); Mr. Grainger (Arthur Brough); Mr. Rumbold (Nicholas Smith); Young Mr. Grace (Harold Bennett); Secretary (Stephanie Gathercole); Returned Glen Check (Peter Needham)

After four weeks of lackluster sales figures, Mr. Rumbold convenes the staff for an after-hours conference on salesmanship. Mr. Lucas is recognized as a weak member of the sales team until he redeems himself by selling Young Mr. Grace an expensive vicuna coat. After Mr. Grace departs, Rumbold commends Lucas on his salesmanship until it is revealed that the store doesn't carry vicuna coats, and Lucas has sold Mr. Grace's own garment back to him.

Rather a routine episode on a topic that will be repeated in future series of the show, "Our Figures Are Slipping" is notable for the first mention of Mrs. Slocombe's "Pussy," an animal whom the mention of will become a fixture of most of the remaining installments.

Again, the best moments are reserved for Mr. Rumbold's tiny office. When Lucas is called in to review his disappointing sales figures, Rumbold compassionately asks if his poor performance is a reflection of an unhappy home life. Lucas seizes at the excuse and relates a tale of woe about living in a one-room flat with his crippled mother, an Asian border, and an asthmatic cat. "There are days when life seems to have lost its magic," Lucas concludes as Rumbold begins to shed tears. True to form, Rumbold tries to write the story into Mr. Lucas's file and gets the details hopelessly confused.

EPISODE 3: "CAMPING IN" ★★★

Air date: April 4, 1973. Cast: Mr. Lucas (Trevor Bannister); Mrs. Slocombe (Mollie Sugden); Capt. Peacock (Frank Thornton); Mr. Humphries (John Inman); Miss Brahms (Wendy Richard); Mr. Granger (Arthur Brough); Mr. Rumbold (Nicholas Smith); Mr. Mash (Larry Martyn); Scotsman (James Copeland); 38C Cup (Anita Richardson); Large Brim with Fruit (Pamela Manson); Secretary (Stephanie Gathercole); Man with the Large Bra (David Rowlands); Leatherette Gloves (Colin Bean)

A transit strike forces the men's and ladies' departments to camp out in the department, using equipment from the sports department.

The first of many episodes in which the Grace Brothers' staff is forced to stay overnight in the store.

Colin Bean, a semiregular member of the Walmington-on-Sea Home Guard platoon in *Dad's Army*, has a small part here in the first scene, buying a pair of gloves.

Although "Camping In" is thin on plot, it manages to be an enjoyable episode for the glimpses it offers into some of the characters' pasts. There is a pleasant scene during which the cast members sit around a camp stove in their pajamas to sing songs and swap reminiscences of the war. We discover that Captain Peacock served in North Africa, Rumbold was in the Catering Corps, and Mr. Granger entertained the troops doing impersonations under the name Whimsical Willie.

Another amusing bit involves Lucas having to take the inside leg measurement of a Scotsman wearing a kilt. While Trevor Bannister manages to emote a good deal of skittishness at the prospect, the best line comes when he asks to borrow a tape measure from Granger. Looking the Scot over carefully — no doubt wondering what he does wear under that kilt — Granger finally replies dolefully that he'd rather that Lucas borrow Mr. Humphries' tape.

EPISODE 4: "HIS AND HERS" ★½

Air date: April 11, 1973. Cast: Mrs. Slocombe (Mollie Sugden); Mr. Lucas (Trevor Bannister); Capt. Peacock (Frank Thornton); Mr. Humphries (John Inman); Miss Brahms (Wendy Richard); Mr. Granger (Arthur Brough); Mr. Rumbold (Nicholas Smith); Sales Representative (Joanna Lumley); Mr. Mash (Larry Martyn); Customers (Margaret Flint, Evan Ross)

Mr. Granger's beloved center display (the one battled over in the pilot) is removed in order to make room for a point-of-purchase promotion for His and Hers perfume. While Captain Peacock is captivated with the perfume's Sales Representative, the rest of the staff rebels. Mr. Lucas rigs a microphone to ruin the sales rep's presentation, and she subsequently leaves. Only then does the staff discover that the perfume company is a subsidiary of Grace Brothers'. To atone, both departments join in to sell the fragrance.

"His and Hers" introduces yet another plot that will be repeated during the run of *AYBS?*. Here, although given the assistance of a young, pre–*Ab Fab* Joanna Lumley, the story falls flat and fizzles to a weak ending.

"His and Hers" is notable for its insight into the amorous tastes of Captain Peacock. With his wife away, Peacock tries to arrange a supper rendezvous with Mrs. Slocombe. From future episodes, we would guess that if he were to favor either of the ladies, it would be the much younger and more attractive Miss Brahms. His offer is not based on the likelihood of acceptance, however, since he quickly withdraws his invitation to Mrs. Slocombe when the perfume saleslady arrives.

Episode 5: "Diamonds Are a Man's Best Friend" ★★★½

Air date: April 18, 1973. Cast: Mrs. Slocombe (Mollie Sugden); Mr. Lucas (Trevor Bannister); Capt. Peacock (Frank Thornton); Mr. Humphries (John Inman); Miss Brahms (Wendy Richard); Mr. Granger (Arthur Brough); Mr. Rumbold (Nicholas Smith); Mr. Mash (Larry Martyn); Young Mr. Grace (Harold Bennett); Sweater Shopper (Elizabeth Larmer); Diamond Owner (Hilary Pritchard); Secretary (Stephanie Gathercole); Outsize Dress (Janet Davies); Mr. Humphries' Friend (Vicki Woolf)

A customer loses a three-carat diamond in the department and offers a £100 reward. Although the staff agrees to split the reward, one by one each of them thinks he or she has found the missing gem and hides the discovery. Finally, in Rumbold's office, it is learned that all the jewels save one are imitations that have fallen off a fancy gown. Young Mr. Grace enters with the diamond's owner and offers to double the reward, which, he informs them will go into the fund for the Grace Brother's Staff Home.

Episode five of the premiere season is far and away the best, thanks to the inclusion of a plot in the proceedings. While not necessarily a captivating plot, "Diamonds Are a Man's Best Friend" manages to be original with enough confusion to keep things interesting.

Janet Davies, *Dad's Army*'s Mrs. Pike, appears as the 38-short woman who is sold a 44-long dress with major alterations. Somewhat surprisingly, she is harder to spot without her 1940s civilian clothes than Robert Raglan and Colin Bean were to find in previous episodes sans their uniforms.

Much information can be culled from "Diamonds Are a Man's Best Friend" beyond its plot. We learn the salary range at Grace Brothers' from the lowest (Lucas makes a little over £11 per week after deductions) to the highest (unionized Mr. Mash takes home more than £60 thanks to overtime). Also revealed is the fact that the employees have regular deductions for their annual staff outing and their retirement at the company's staff home.

Within the plot itself, there is a humorous bit of pantomime when Lucas spots a gem directly between Captain Peacock's legs. Slipping up from behind, the junior clerk plants his foot over the diamond directly parallel to Peacock's feet. Peacock looks down with understated consternation then taps first one foot, then another, with Lucas finally tapping his own in an attempt to complete the charade. This neat little gag is unnecessarily repeated later by Peacock similarly trying to retrieve another stone from beneath Mrs. Slocombe. There is another twice-repeated bit, although this one fails miserably, involving Peacock, then Lucas making calls from Rumbold's office with Nicholas Smith's voice dubbed in to make the audience believe that both are expert impersonators. Why?

Series Two 1974

Episode 1: "The Clock" ★★★½

Air date: March 14, 1974. Cast: Mrs. Slocombe (Mollie Sugden); Mr. Lucas (Trevor Bannister); Capt. Peacock (Frank Thornton); Mr. Humphries (John Inman); Miss Brahms (Wendy Richard); Mr. Grainger (Arthur Brough); Mr. Rumbold (Nicholas Smith); Mr. Mash (Larry Martyn); Young Mr. Grace (Harold Bennett); Check Jacket (John Ringham); Bridal Veil (Dorothy Wayne); Mrs. Grainger (Pearl Hackney); Elsie (Hilda Fenemore); Trixie Trio (Avril Fane, Barbara Loynes, Dorothy Loynes)

A cloud of uncertainty hangs over Mr. Grainger's 65th birthday party since it is not clear whether he will be presented with a cuckoo clock, the store's symbol of forced retirement. After dinner, Rumbold is about to give Grainger the dreaded cuckoo when Young Mr. Grace arrives and mistakenly accepts the clock himself. Mr. Grace then assures a relieved Grainger that he will probably get a clock of his own in another five years.

A solid plot with good execution makes the premiere episode of the second season one of the stronger installments of *AYBS?*. Although the premise (forced retirement) would be repeated over the run of the show, the fact that this is its first use coupled with Arthur Brough's trepidation at the prospect of retirement make the show effective.

Aside from learning Mr. Grainger's complete history at Grace Brothers', we also learn the first names of Mr. Lucas (James, although this would be contradicted in season five's "The Old Order Changes") and Mr. Humphries (Wilberforce Clayborne). Mrs. Grainger is also introduced and appears to be a charming lady, despite jokes made at her expense to the contrary in other episodes.

Aside from Arthur Brough's skittish portrayal of the fretful Mr. Grainger (not only is he worried about getting the clock but also about the unchewable steak pie for dinner), the most comical moments are supplied by Mollie Sugden. Sugden delivers a convincing drunk as Mrs. Slocombe arrives at the banquet after having already consumed four vodka martinis. Frank Thornton also supplies an amusing turn while making the toast to Grainger, a bit that should make anyone who has ever suffered through an amateur speaker uncomfortable. These performances spotlight the strength of the cast in delivering top comedy when given a good story and fresh lines.

EPISODE 2: "COLD COMFORT" ★★

Air date: March 21, 1974. Cast: Mr. Lucas (Trevor Bannister); Mrs. Slocombe (Mollie Sugden); Capt. Peacock (Frank Thornton); Mr. Humphries (John Inman); Miss Brahms (Wendy Richard); Mr. Grainger (Arthur Brough); Mr. Rumbold (Nicholas Smith); Mr. Mash (Larry Martyn); Young Mr. Grace (Harold Bennett); Elsie (Hilda Fenemore); Gladys (Helen Lambert); Customers (Robert Mill, Carolyn Hudson, John Baker)

The first energy crisis forces Grace Brothers to turn off the heat on the coldest day of the year. Despite the chill, management expects the staff to work without any overcoats or gloves. The staff improvises ways to keep warm, including hair dryers, electric irons, potholders warmed in pop-up toasters, and brandy hidden in perfume atomizers.

"Cold Comfort" presents not much in the way of a plot but rather the milking of a single situation with mixed results. This episode is noteworthy as one with which Jeremy Lloyd and David Croft had assistance in writing the script from Michael Knowles. Knowles appeared as a customer in the pilot episode.

EPISODE 3: "THE THINK TANK" ★★★½

Air date: March 28, 1974. Cast: Mrs. Slocombe (Mollie Sugden); Mr. Lucas (Trevor Bannister); Capt. Peacock (Frank Thornton); Mr. Humphries (John Inman); Miss Brahms (Wendy Richard); Mr. Grainger (Arthur Brough); Mr. Rumbold (Nicholas Smith); Mr. Mash (Larry Martyn); Young Mr. Grace (Harold Bennett)

At Captain Peacock's suggestion, Mr. Rumbold convenes a staff think tank in an attempt to find a solution to falling sales. Peacock suggests they have a fashion show to draw attention to the merchandise but Rumbold refuses the idea, then restates it as his own. The staff does a demonstration of the fashion show for Young Mr. Grace, who rejects it after Rumbold has taken credit for it.

Three episodes into its second series, *AYBS?* introduced one of its most oft-repeated and most successful plot ploys: the staff performance. Although done in various ways throughout the run of the program, some of the best shows are those in which the men's and ladies' departments must put on some sort of presentation, whether it be for entertainment or exhibition purposes. That it was hit upon relatively early (only the ninth episode of 69) spotlights the limitations of keeping the series within the bounds of its original premise.

Although the rationale for the staff putting on a trial fashion show is plausible in "The Think Tank," future episodes would stretch the concept beyond believability.

This episode is also notable in that it is the first in which no customers are seen or waited upon.

"The Think Tank" brings to the fore the strained relationship between Peacock and Rumbold. Throughout the run of *AYBS?* Peacock, though a philanderer, is usually presented as more capable of management than Rumbold. In the episode's opening bit, Rumbold exercises his authority over his floorwalker by ordering Peacock to start wearing a homburg hat, since bowlers are reserved for department heads such as himself. At the think tank session, Peacock has the ideas, but Rumbold rejects them, modifies them slightly, then takes the credit. In the episode's final moments, Mr. Grace rejects Rumbold's Male and Female Modes on the Move fashion show and suggests that Peacock start wearing a bowler.

There are some good lines distributed throughout the episode. At one point Mr. Lucas opines that Grace Brothers needs trendier clothes such as those worn by pop stars.

The hopelessly out-of-date Mr. Granger inquires if this means he will have to dress like Bing Crosby.

Later, at the fashion show, Rumbold explains the concept to Young Mr. Grace, pointing out that it is targeted at the "woman in the street." "You mean tarts?" Young Mr. Grace replies with surprise.

Finally, there's a good running bit concerning how and where Mr. Mash should wash down the female mannequins. After a number of methods are barred to him, Mash is told to do it someplace discreet. During the finale of the fashion show, a nattily attired Peacock pushes the elevator button only to have the doors open to reveal Mash sponging down a curvaceous dummy.

EPISODE 4: "BIG BROTHER" ★★½

Air date: April 4, 1974. Cast: Mrs. Slocombe (Mollie Sugden); Mr. Lucas (Trevor Bannister); Capt. Peacock (Frank Thornton); Mr. Humphries (John Inman); Miss Brahms (Wendy Richard); Mr. Grainger (Arthur Brough); Mr. Rumbold (Nicholas Smith); Mr. Mash (Larry Martyn); Mr. Clegg (Donald Morley); Dr. Wainwright (Robert Raglan); Secretary (Stephanie Reeve); Underwear Customer (Joyce Cummings); Scarf Customer (Stella Kemball)

Rumbold hires a security consultant and installs surveillance cameras in an attempt to reduce shoplifting losses. The system disrupts the staff members who, when they are not playing to the cameras, feel the cameras invade their privacy. The staff ultimately rids itself of the devices by playing on Rumbold's hypochondria and making him think they should be removed under doctor's orders.

"Big Brother" features a good concept that fails to deliver due to a contrived ending. Robert Raglan returns as the doctor after playing a customer in "Dear Sexy Knickers." Michael Knowles contributed to the script.

The installation of cameras gives not only Rumbold but also the viewers a glimpse into the staff's favorite ways of goldbricking. Captain Peacock is observed pinching Miss Brahms, Miss Brahms is caught stuffing cotton into her bra, Mrs. Slocombe takes excessive trips to the ladies' room, Mr. Grainger eats pork pies on the floor, while Lucas smokes behind the cabinets.

Lucas is the first one called on the carpet. When Rumbold informs him that he doesn't want to see him smoking on the floor anymore, Lucas is quick to comply.

After promising that Rumbold will not catch him smoking again, the junior salesman asks which part of the floor *can't* be seen by the cameras.

EPISODE 5: "HOORAH FOR THE HOLIDAYS" ★½

Air date: April 11, 1974. Cast: Mr. Lucas (Trevor Bannister); Mrs. Slocombe (Mollie Sugden); Capt. Peacock (Frank Thornton); Mr. Humphries (John Inman); Miss Brahms (Wendy Richard); Mr. Grainger (Arthur Brough); Mr. Rumbold (Nicholas Smith); Mr. Mash (Larry Martyn); Young Mr. Grace (Harold Bennett); Ready-Made Suit (John Clegg); Dressing Gown (Stuart Sherwin); Irish Lady (Helen Dorward)

Mr. Rumbold announces that the store is going to close for remodeling during the first two weeks of August. The employees are urged to take their vacations at that time with a £5 bonus offered as an incentive to comply. When the staff holds out for a better offer, management counters with a paid package vacation to one of Mr. Grace's five resort locations. A slide presentation of their options reveals that none is tenable.

Unremarkable but entertaining, "Hoorah for the Holidays" closes out the show's successful second series. This episode continues the second season's reliance on fairly strong and original plots. Unfortunately, beyond this point *AYBS?* would increasingly suffer from its own success and begin to rely more and more on reworked situations and stock phrases.

This episode features the first visit to the boardroom and a glimpse at Mr. Grace's original wheelbarrow from which he used to peddle fish. Aside from a slight but amusing bit in which Humphries and Lucas try to sell a man a dressing gown, what humor there is in "Hoorah for the Holidays" is derived from the situation.

Series Three 1975

EPISODE 1: "THE HAND OF FATE" ★★★

Air date: February 27, 1975. Cast: Mrs. Slocombe (Mollie Sugden); Mr. Lucas (Trevor Bannister); Capt. Peacock (Frank Thornton); Mr. Humphries (John

Inman); Miss Brahms (Wendy Richard); Mr. Grainger (Arthur Brough); Mr. Rumbold (Nicholas Smith); Mr. Mash (Larry Martyn); Young Mr. Grace (Harold Bennett); Miss Ainesworth (Nina Francis); Japanese Customer (Eric Young); Beret Customer (Therese McMurray)

Rumbold is awaiting a decision on a promotion for himself. He explains to Captain Peacock that if he is promoted then Peacock will most likely take his place. Mr. Humphries reveals that he has a gift for reading palms and does a reading for Peacock. Humphries sees what appear to be great things for Peacock. By the end of the episode, Humphries' predictions come true but in a less than desirable form.

"The Hand of Fate" introduces a number of situations that would become staples of the remaining run of *AYBS?*. First is the patronizingly chauvinistic culture and class gags in which a foreign customer has difficulty completing a transaction. Arguably, this was used back in "Camping In" with the Scotsman who needed his first pair of trousers but not in its full-blown form. Here, a Japanese man tries to buy a raincoat as the staff speaks to him in embarrassing pidgin English.

Second, the cafeteria is introduced as a location. Although a seemingly minor innovation, few future episodes will avoid a trip to the cafeteria. Apparently, Croft and Lloyd had begun to feel the confinement of the sales floor and introduced a more informal location in which the characters could interact at a different level. It is a welcome addition.

There are a few good laughs in the cafeteria scene in which Mr. Humphries' palm-reading talent is discussed along with his ability to leave his body at will. When Mrs. Slocombe expresses a desire to leave her body, Lucas suggests that with a body like hers, perhaps her spirit wouldn't come back. Captain Peacock is skeptical until Mr. Humphries reads his palm.

Humphries observes that Captain Peacock has a particularly long lifeline that runs all the way up his sleeve. Lucas interprets this to mean that Peacock will die of old age in a railroad tunnel.

EPISODE 2: "COFFEE MORNING" ★

Air date: March 6, 1975. Cast: Mr. Lucas (Trevor Bannister); Mrs. Slocombe (Mollie Sugden); Capt. Peacock (Frank Thornton); Mr. Humphries (John Inman); Miss Brahms (Wendy Richard); Mr. Grainger (Arthur Brough); Mr. Rumbold (Nicholas Smith); Mr. Mash (Larry Martyn); Young Mr. Grace (Harold Bennett); Miss Ainesworth (Nina Francis)

When Mr. Grainger returns late from his coffee break (he was in the men's room), Rumbold orders that all staff must sign in and out before leaving the floor. The staff unanimously decides not to sign the book, but when only Mr. Grainger is singled out, they distance themselves from him. Mr. Mash, as union shop steward, organizes the staff's response, including a strike threat.

While most situation comedies thrive on good situations and strong plots, apparently that is not the case with *AYBS?*. "Coffee Morning" is all story, with few jokes hung on the framework of the plot. To borrow from Mrs. Slocombe, this "coffee" is "weak as water." Aside from allowing Arthur Brough a chance to play his pitiful sacrificial lamb bit, "Coffee Morning" has little to offer in the way of laughs.

Episode 3: "Up Captain Peacock" ★★½

Air date: March 13, 1975. Cast: Mr. Lucas (Trevor Bannister); Mrs. Slocombe (Mollie Sugden); Capt. Peacock (Frank Thornton); Mr. Humphries (John Inman); Miss Brahms (Wendy Richard); Mr. Grainger (Arthur Brough); Mr. Rumbold (Nicholas Smith); Mr. Mash (Larry Martyn); Young Mr. Grace (Harold Bennett); Bow Tie Customer (Jeffrey Segal); Man Buying the Dress (Donald Hewlett); Suit Customer (Michael Knowles); Lady Customer (Maureen Lane)

On the occasion of his 20th anniversary with Grace Brothers', Captain Peacock is given a key to the executive washroom and permission to dine in the executive dining room, although his new privileges are short lived.

Special privileges and food are the primary themes of "Up Captain Peacock," and although both crop up again throughout the series, they provide little inspiration in this episode. Indeed, the ploy of elevating one member of the staff above his or her station is used quite often in *AYBS?*, as soon as two episodes hence, where Mrs. Slocombe is the recipient. Food, or rather the lack of it, is also in the forefront when the staff is made to delay its lunchtime. As was the case in "Cold Comfort," the staff members work hard to surreptitiously provide for their creature needs.

For anyone has either worked in a clothing store or worn bow ties, there's some fun to be had when a customer enters to buy a clip-on bow tie. The prospect of selling the ersatz version of the tie is so distasteful to Grainger and Humphries that the sale is pushed along to Lucas.

Episode 4: "Cold Store" ★★★

Air date: March 20, 1975. Cast: Mrs. Slocombe (Mollie Sugden); Mr. Lucas (Trevor Bannister); Capt. Peacock (Frank Thornton); Mr. Humphries (John Inman); Miss Brahms (Wendy Richard); Mr. Grainger (Arthur Brough); Mr. Rumbold (Nicholas Smith); Mr. Mash (Larry Martyn); Young Mr. Grace (Harold Bennett); Elsie (Hilda Fenemore); Customer (Bill Martin); Woman Buying Blue Dress (Ann Sidney); Sister (Joy Allen); Woman with Alteration (Pamela Cundell); Man with Inside Leg (Gordon Peters)

Mr. Lucas attempts to feign a cold in order to keep an afternoon date, but Captain Peacock refuses to let him go home. Mrs. Slocombe actually has a cold, which she treats by drinking on the job. Miss Brahms has just had a flu shot and is under doctor's orders to keep away from anyone with a cold.

To solve the problem, Peacock has Lucas and Brahms trade places. Finally, Lucas tries to go home by faking a sprained ankle. Instead, he gets a ride to the hospital in Mr. Grace's Rolls Royce.

The faithful standby device of putting familiar characters in unfamiliar situations helps make "Cold Store" one of the better episodes of *AYBS?*'s third season. Aside from the obvious business that Bannister and Richard have as the principal focus in this installment, Sugden gets another chance to do her convincing drunk routine, and Brough has a good running joke (pardon the pun) from a bout with diarrhea.

Pamela Cundell, Corporal Jones's Mrs. Fox from *Dad's Army*, guests as the giggly woman who Mr. Lucas tries to assist with an alteration.

Lucas and Brahms swapping duties provides some good, albeit predictable jokes in "Cold Store." They are especially anticipated since both are called upon to provide services to the opposite sex. Mr. Lucas is called upon to mark for alteration a skirt on a plump and ticklish woman. Fortunately, the pat situation of having the woman outraged by a man handling her is avoided. Instead, Cundell's character thoroughly enjoys the treatment.

For her part, Miss Brahms is asked to take a man's inside leg measurement but refuses, explaining it isn't ladylike. "Well, I do it," Humphries reasons in his effeminate way.

Mr. Humphries would do the deed but is incapacitated with a stiff back. Instead, Humphries sticks an umbrella up from behind to the customer's crotch as Miss Brahms measures from the umbrella's tip to the floor at a safe distance.

EPISODE 5: "WEDDING BELLS" ★★★

Air date: March 27, 1975. Cast: Mrs. Slocombe (Mollie Sugden); Mr. Lucas (Trevor Bannister); Capt. Peacock (Frank Thornton); Mr. Humphries (John Inman); Miss Brahms (Wendy Richard); Mr. Grainger (Arthur Brough); Mr. Rumbold (Nicholas Smith); Mr. Mash (Larry Martyn); Young Mr. Grace (Harold Bennett); Man with Toupee (John Clegg); Miss Robinson (Sandra Clark); Trousers (Jay Denyer)

Mr. Grace announces he is getting married, and everyone mistakenly believes his intended will be Mrs. Slocombe.

I have criticized *Are You Being Served?* for its lack of growth by its principal characters. I must apologize, although only partially. "Wedding Bells" shows perhaps the first hint of the development of Young Mr. Grace into the renowned womanizer he would later become. Up until now, Mr. Grace has only been seen in the company of his chauffeur and is here thinking of getting married (although he has his rambunctious side, having gone to see *Last Tango in Paris* in the "Think Tank" episode). After his little talk with Mrs. Slocombe in this episode, he throws caution to the wind and continues his progress toward elderly delinquency.

During her tea with Young Mr. Grace, Mrs. Slocombe manages to present a dizzying realm of possibilities to the old gent. Mr. Grace reiterates his intention to get married. Mrs. Slocombe agrees that it is a wise and noble decision. She continues by stating that in his position he could easily cruise his yacht down to the "Caribbeano" and have bevies of young girls swarming all over him.

"Would I?" Grace asks anxiously.

Mrs. Slocombe confirms it, then goes on to explain that these girls are after only one thing.

"Are they?" he asks hopefully, obviously thinking of something entirely different.

Upon quick reflection, Mr. Grace informs Mrs. Slocombe that he isn't getting married after all. He excuses Mrs. Slocombe but not before asking her to have a yachting magazine sent up to his office.

EPISODE 6: "GERMAN WEEK" ★★★

Air date: April 3, 1975. Cast: Mr. Lucas (Trevor Bannister); Mrs. Slocombe (Mollie Sugden); Capt. Peacock (Frank Thornton); Mr. Humphries (John Inman); Miss Brahms (Wendy Richard); Mr. Grainger (Arthur Brough); Mr. Rumbold (Nicholas Smith); Mr. Mash (Larry Martyn); Young Mr. Grace (Harold Bennett); Miss Thorpe (Moira Foot); German Man (Ernst Ulman); German Woman (Joanna Lumley); Woman Customer (Anita Richardson)

At Rumbold's suggestion, Mr. Grace holds German Week, seven days set aside to sell only German goods. The staff members are outfitted in Bavarian garb and put on a demonstration of folk dancing for Mr. Grace. After viewing the exhibition, Mr. Grace decides to drop the idea of German Week.

"German Week" is essentially a three-part episode. In the first part, the jokes are based upon the funny-sounding and sometimes suggestive German words for the garments. The second part is another of the typical staff meeting scenes with most of the gags coming from Lucas insulting Slocombe and Slocombe reacting. The final segment is another "let's put on a show" bit with the staff members all appearing in lederhosen. While these routines have been used before, they are well executed and make for entertaining, if somewhat forgettable, diversion.

This episode also marks the first appearance of actress Moira Foot as Rumbold's secretary. The writers apparently had determined that a sexy secretary is funnier than one that is merely attractive. This also marks the second appearance of Joanna Lumley in what is little more than a walk-on. Lumley was just on the verge of her success as Purdey in *The New Avengers* when she appeared here.

The final segment, in which the staff dresses up in costumes and dances, is easily the highlight of "German Week." At first Captain Peacock bristles at the notion of donning lederhosen, insisting that any costume he wears must have more authority. Lucas suggests that he dress up as Hitler.

Next, there are many laughs generated when the staff members emerge one by one in their costumes. All, except for Miss Thorpe, are wearing lederhosen, suspenders, and Tyrolean hats. Mr. Humphries, as usual, gets the biggest reaction from the audience when he enters with lederhosen that are so small and tight they qualify as hot pants. Soon the demonstration degenerates, aided by a blotto Mrs. Slocombe (German wines were part of the display), into a wild face-slapping melee.

EPISODE 7: "SHOULDER TO SHOULDER" ★½

Air date: April 10, 1975. Cast: Mr. Lucas (Trevor Bannister); Mrs. Slocombe (Mollie Sugden); Capt. Peacock (Frank Thornton); Mr. Humphries (John Inman); Miss Brahms (Wendy Richard); Mr. Grainger (Arthur Brough); Mr. Rumbold (Nicholas Smith); Mr. Mash (Larry Martyn); Young Mr. Grace (Harold Bennett); Miss Thorpe (Moira Foot); Honeymoon Couple (Jonathan Cecil, Hilary Pritchard); Wig Customer (Kate Brown)

While the ladies' department is being renovated, Mrs. Slocombe and Miss Brahms are forced to share space with the men. The close quarters results in friction and fighting. When the redecorating is completed, the staff learns that it must repeat the exercise when the men's department is refurbished.

"Shoulder to Shoulder" is a return to the themes and gags of the pilot episode with a new twist added by making the shared quarters even closer. Whatever humor there is comes from routines separate from the plot. Those related to the situation are somewhat tiresome and quickly bog down into mere bickering.

A fresh idea is breathed into "Shoulder to Shoulder" when a customer calls to order a suit over the phone. The caller doesn't know his size but has a tape measure, so Mr. Humphries attempts to have the man take his own measurements. The results are less than successful but humorous. Finally, Mr. Grainger steps forward, takes the phone away, and simply asks the man his height and weight. With an air of superiority, Grainger hangs up and orders Humphries and Lucas to send out the proper size and to credit himself with the sale. Grainger's haughtiness melts to consternation, however, when Lucas reminds him that he has neglected to find out the customer's name or address.

EPISODE 8: "NEW LOOK" ½

Air date: April 17, 1975. Cast: Mr. Lucas (Trevor Bannister); Mrs. Slocombe (Mollie Sugden); Capt. Peacock (Frank Thornton); Mr. Humphries (John Inman); Miss Brahms (Wendy Richard); Mr. Grainger (Arthur Brough); Mr. Rumbold (Nicholas Smith); Mr. Mash (Larry Martyn); Young Mr. Grace (Harold Bennett); Miss Thorpe (Moira Foot); Customer (Felix Bowness)

The staff meets to review ideas submitted in the suggestion box. Mrs. Slocombe suggests that they redecorate the department in the Great Gatsby style.

She also suggests that they play 1920s music over the public address system in addition to having an announcer interrupt with news of sales. The staff makes audition tapes to see who will win the announcer's job. Ultimately, Young Mr. Grace arrives to tell them he will be the announcer. He plays the staff a tape of his audition, complete with 1920s music. Mr. Humphries breaks into a dance with the elevator girl and an unnamed salesgirl to end the show.

By "New Look," the last show of the third season, the formula writing that would increasingly mark *AYBS?* is really starting to show. All the familiar elements are here, but unfortunately, they are not scripted or executed as well as in other episodes. The show begins with some repetitive jokes centered on a new fountain display, which apparently gives all who see it an urge to run to the bathroom. From there, it is on to another staff meeting, which results in a novel idea that the staff must display to Young Mr. Grace. Finally, there is a performance bit (a dance routine with 1920s music that supposedly pays homage to 1930s musicals) to close the show. Unfortunately, although a choreographer staged the dance, it looks as impromptu and unrehearsed as apparently the script was trying to make it seem. Why the episode is even titled "New Look" is something of a mystery since there are no new decorations or styles as suggested in the script, only some old music. It would have been more aptly titled "Old Sound" or perhaps even "Old Situations."

This episode, although the final one aired in the third season, was probably scripted and filmed earlier, since Rumbold introduces Captain Peacock to Miss Thorpe, his "new secretary," although she has already appeared in the previous two shows.

Unless you'd like to hear Grainger, Humphries, and Lucas sing a brief rendition of "I Can Mend Your Umbrella," you might as well go read a book.

Michael Knowles receives script credit with Croft and Lloyd.

Christmas Special 1975

"Christmas Crackers" ★★★

Air date: December 24, 1975. Cast: Mrs. Slocombe (Mollie Sugden); Mr. Lucas (Trevor Bannister); Capt. Peacock (Frank Thornton); Mr. Humphries (John Inman); Miss Brahms (Wendy Richard); Mr. Grainger (Arthur Brough); Mr. Rumbold (Nicholas Smith); Mr. Mash (Larry Martyn); Young Mr. Grace (Harold Bennett); Canteen Waitress (Doremy Vernon)

"Christmas Crackers" is more of a series of three vignettes than a linear story. In the first, the staff assembles early to brainstorm the department's strategy to boost holiday sales. Next, they assemble for their yearly Christmas lunch. And finally, they dress up in novelty costumes to help give the store a festive atmosphere.

It is altogether fitting that *AYBS?* should have so many episodes that take place at Christmas, since it is the focal point of the retail year. Indeed, there were three such episodes made during the series' nine-season run. Incidentally, a *cracker* in Britain is a rolled-up paper party favor that contains a silly gag gift and a joke.

The opening sequence is mostly a nonstarter filled with the usual personnel banter. What really helps this episode along, as with many of *AYBS?*'s better offerings, is seeing the staff interact in a different setting. As with the fireside scene in "Camping In," the Christmas luncheon affords a more relaxed and personal glimpse of the cast. The sumptuous luncheon turns out to be a turkey so tiny that Mrs. Slocombe labels it an "emaciated budgie" and a pudding that is incinerated when Mr. Mash ignites it with wood alcohol. The final scene, in which the cast sings "Christmas Time Is Here" in novelty costumes is also pleasant. The best costumes are Captain Peacock's snowman and Grainger's Humpty Dumpty. When Mr. Humphries swans in wearing a fop costume, Mr. Lucas comments, "I see you're not bothering to dress up."

Series Four 1976

Episode 1: "No Sale" ★★★★

Air date: April 8, 1976. Cast: Mrs. Slocombe (Mollie Sugden); Mr. Lucas (Trevor Bannister); Capt. Peacock (Frank Thornton); Mr. Humphries (John Inman); Miss Brahms (Wendy Richard); Mr. Grainger (Arthur Brough); Mr. Rumbold (Nicholas Smith); Young Mr. Grace (Harold Bennett); Accounts Manager (Gordon Peter); His Wife (Anne Cunningham); Overcoat Customer (Reg Dixon); Ivy (Hilda Fennemore); Wedding Hat (Hilary Pritchard); Large Gloves (Stuart Sherwin); Check Suit (John Bardon)

Grace Brothers opens a half hour early on a trial basis. Although the staff bristles at the extra time, the scheme seems to be paying off with higher sales. In order to make sure that the time change does not become permanent, the staff agrees to work hard not to sell merchandise. The plan succeeds, and the experiment is ended.

After the extremely poor final offering of the third season, Croft and Lloyd acquit themselves well with the premiere installment of *AYBS?*'s fourth season. "No Sale" benefits from a good basic plot concept, which is introduced early and followed through until the end. There is little reliance on stock routines and catch phrases, making the entire episode seem like a breath of fresh air compared to the average output of the series.

This is the first episode without the services of Larry Martyn as Mr. Mash. It also marks the first use of Mr. Humphries' telephone routine with his mother. Comedians from Georgie Jessel to Bob Newhart have gotten great mileage out of such one-sided conversations, and John Inman certainly makes the most of his opportunities. Finally, actress Hilda Fennemore's cleaning lady character has inexplicably had her name changed from Elsie to Ivy.

As should be expected, the staff's dire attempts to kill sales elicit the biggest laughs in "No Sale." First, Mrs. Slocombe dissuades a woman from buying a £95 evening gown by convincing her husband that it will send the wrong message at his company's dinner dance. Peacock tries valiantly to counter her antisales pitch but only winds up bickering with Slocombe. Ultimately, the argument is transferred back to the couple, effectively killing the sale.

The best moment in nonsalesmanship comes at the hand of Mr. Grainger. When an affable portly gentleman comes in to buy an overcoat, Humphries and Lucas do their best to discourage the transaction. They point out that the price, quality, and color are all wrong. Still, the gentleman insists on buying the garment, saying he is impressed with the salesmen's honesty. Suddenly Mr. Grainger steps into the fray, telling the man he possesses a "fat face, piggy eyes, and a pimple" on his nose, effectively killing the sale.

"You young salesmen just don't know how *not* to sell clothes," Grainger proudly explains to his staff.

EPISODE 2: "TOP HAT AND TAILS" ★★★

Air date: April 15, 1976. Cast: Mr. Lucas (Trevor Bannister); Mrs. Slocombe (Mollie Sugden); Capt. Peacock (Frank Thornton); Mr. Humphries (John Inman); Miss Brahms (Wendy Richard); Mr. Grainger (Arthur Brough); Mr. Rumbold (Nicholas Smith); Mr. Harman (Arthur English); Young Mr. Grace (Harold Bennett);) Mr. Ludlow (Peter Greene)

Mr. Grace wants his staff to compete in the annual Golden Shoes contest, a ballroom dancing competition among area department stores. Mr. Humphries is chosen to coach the team since he was once an instructor at the Twinkle-Toes dance studios in addition to being a Sunshine Babe, at the age of eight. After rehearsing themselves to a point of some proficiency, they do a dress rehearsal for Young Mr. Grace. Mr. Grace declares the recital a shambles, except for the performance of the two animated dummies from the store's formal wear display.

"Top Hat and Tails" may seem unfamiliar to many American fans of *AYBS?* due to the fact that until 1997 it was not shown in the regular syndication run of the series in most markets (Some PBS stations tried to hype this as a "lost episode" during pledge drives, although it had been available on video in England for years.) This is unfortunate since the episode features some good physical comedy. It does this by employing the plot device of making the staff perform (this time as ballroom dancers). Unlike other uses of this ploy, however, the situation is believable, thus adding to the proceedings.

This also marks the first appearance by Arthur English in the role of the genial Mr. Harman, the maintenance man. While Larry Martyn's Mr. Mash was well played in the three seasons he appeared, English's Harman is as pro–working class without the abrasive behavior that Mash often displayed.

Although there are some rather elaborate mechanical gags, including the use of a new display, the best moments in "Top Hat and Tails" are provided by the humans. The practice session is worth watching if just for the graceful footwork of Humphries dancing with Captain Peacock as they demonstrate the quick-step. Later, when Grainger attempts to copy the moves with Miss Brahms, he appears to be doing a march through a vat full of grapes, rather than any step known in the annals of terpsichorean art. The topper, however, is Lucas's tries at dancing with Mrs. Slocombe. When she complains that he is holding her too close, Lucas counters that her back is far enough away, but it is her front that is the problem. Finally, he solves the dilemma by using the arm of a display dummy to extend his own reach.

Episode 3: "Forward Mr. Grainger" ★★★½

Air date: April 22, 1976. Cast: Mrs. Slocombe (Mollie Sugden); Mr. Lucas (Trevor Bannister); Capt. Peacock (Frank Thornton); Mr. Humphries (John Inman); Miss Brahms (Wendy Richard); Mr. Grainger (Arthur Brough); Mr. Rumbold (Nicholas Smith); Mr. Harman (Arthur English); Young Mr. Grace (Harold Bennett); Secretary (Isabella Rye)

Mr. Rumbold calls Captain Peacock into his office to explain that, while he is away at a management seminar for a month, Mr. Grainger will take his place. Usually Peacock would fill in, but the board has decided to elevate Grainger temporarily to qualify him for a higher pension grade. The promotion goes immediately to Grainger's head as he busies himself enjoying executive perks, asking for raises, and ruling the department with an iron hand. In less than a day, Grainger manages to fire Mrs. Slocombe and put Peacock on report.

"Forward Mr. Grainger" is an atypical, yet enjoyable episode; its plot is not heavily joke-laden. There are, of course, the obligatory routines, which take up the first five to ten minutes (a call from Humphries' mother, a conversation between Humphries and Lucas, Mrs. Slocombe telling Miss Brahms of her latest pub exploits), but then the plot takes up the remaining time. The episode is also fun since it gives Arthur Brough a chance to flex his acting abilities as his character goes from the sleepy senior clerk to tyrannical taskmaster to contrite penitent.

Although he is always listed last in the credits of the top six stars of *AYBS?* Brough invariably turns in delightfully entertaining performances when given the spotlight, as in "The Clock." "Forward Mr. Grainger" is just such an opportunity for the veteran actor. His portrayal of the executive model of Ernest Grainger — complete with drink in hand, oversized cigar, and ordering his secretary to have her skirt shortened — paints a comic picture to equal the best in this long-running series.

Episode 4: "Fire Practice" ★★★★

Air date: April 29, 1976. Cast: Mr. Lucas (Trevor Bannister); Mrs. Slocombe (Mollie Sugden); Capt. Peacock (Frank Thornton); Mr. Humphries (John Inman); Miss Brahms (Wendy Richard); Mr. Grainger (Arthur Brough); Mr. Rumbold (Nicholas Smith); Mr. Harman (Arthur English); Young Mr. Grace (Harold Bennett); Emir's Spokesman (Ahmed Khalil); Emir (Ahmed Osman); the Head Wife (Melody Urquhart); Fireman (Hamish Roughead Chief Fireman (Ken Barker)

Mr. Grace informs Rumbold that the store will conduct a surprise fire drill. He refuses to disclose the time to Rumbold, who immediately starts yelling "fire" every time he hears a bell the rest of the morning. An Arab Emir visits the store to outfit his 72 wives (only four of whom are present) with men's trousers. At the end of the transaction, the fire drill takes place amid much confusion. After the store is closed, the staff must stay behind to review the fire drill procedures. During the drill, a real fire forces them to evacuate.

A delight from start to finish, "Fire Practice" is one of the few episodes of *AYBS?* to make it from titles to credits without any of the extraneous filler that often slows down most installments of the series. The script contains clever dialogue without resorting to the easy double entendre, and there's also some good physical humor. The only predictable and mechanical joke comes with the use of a female CPR model.

The Emir's visit is probably one of the most consistently funny extended routines ever done on *AYBS?*. First the entire staff must sit on the floor — including a very inflexible Mr. Grainger — to transact the business as if they were in a tent in the desert. After discovering that the Emir wants to outfit his wives with trousers, the main difficulty comes when the sizes must be determined. At first, Mrs. Slocombe tries to take the measurements but she is quickly stopped when she is informed that in the Emir's country it is forbidden for women to touch women.

Peacock asks if a man may touch a woman. The Spokesman affirms that this is allowed. Lucas happily begins approaching one of the curvaceous wives with his measuring tape but stops when the Spokesman adds that a man may touch a woman, but then he must be killed. "Hardly worth the commission, is it?" Lucas remarks, as he reverses course.

After eyeing the staff, the Emir's representative allows Humphries to take the measurements, but on the condition that he doesn't touch the women. In a clever bit, Humphries directs the first wife to stand between the elevator doors and bend over. He then closes the door around her, measures the opening, and doubles it to determine her hip measurement. For the inside leg, he instructs the wife to complete a leg split on the floor; he then measures the distance from ankle to ankle and halves it for the measurement.

Finally, the Arabs want to barter for the trousers. First they offer a goat, then a rug, then one of the wives for Grainger's use.

The final scene also provides plenty of laughs but of the more physical nature. First Mr. Harman demonstrates the proper way to do a fireman's carry. He easily lifts Mr. Humphries on his back and pats him on the rump to punctuate the effortlessness of the move. "You wait 'til you're asked," Mr. Humphries responds.

Next, Lucas is ordered to demonstrate the carry by using the hefty Mrs. Slocombe. The results are hilarious as Lucas manages to hoist Slocombe on his back but then is unable to control himself under her weight. He weaves back and forth wildly, looking as if he is about to collapse as she cries out for help and the rest of the staff looks on helplessly.

Hamish Roughead, who plays the fireman in this installment, also appeared in the stage version of *Dad's Army*, filling in for John Laurie in the role of Frazer.

EPISODE 5: "FIFTY YEARS ON" ★★★

Air date: May 5, 1976. Cast: Mr. Lucas (Trevor Bannister); Mrs. Slocombe (Mollie Sugden); Capt. Peacock (Frank Thornton); Mr. Humphries (John Inman); Miss Brahms (Wendy Richard); Mr. Grainger (Arthur Brough); Mr. Rumbold (Nicholas Smith); Mr. Harman (Arthur English); Young Mr. Grace (Harold Bennett); Claude (Tony Sympson); Mrs. Claude (Mavis Pugh); Mr. Grace's Secretary (Penny Irving); Six Pound Fox (Diana Lambert)

Mrs. Slocombe's birthday is approaching, and she is dropping copious hints about wanting a present. The staff agrees to chip in for a present and a specially designed cake after they reckon that this will be her 50th birthday. When the day arrives, Mrs. Slocombe is delighted with her present but outraged when the cake — in the shape of a fat woman's bottom wearing bloomers — is emblazoned with "50." She announces she is only 46 as she storms out of the store.

It is a testimony to the strength of the fourth season that one of the weaker entries in this group would be one of the stronger in any other. "Fifty Years On" is a rather typical entry, yet one that is carried out well, with a fairly cohesive plot and good performances all around. This episode also marks the introduction of Penny Irving as Mr. Grace's secretary.

"50 Years On" has many amusing moments. The first comes as the staff tries to figure out Mrs. Slocombe's age. Initially, they try to determine it by relating to the age of her cat. Then they attempt to reason it out via a calendar of obscure world events that took place the year they think she was born.

Next, the staff tries to settle on a present. Mr. Grainger votes that they give her a cyanide tablet. He later changes this to two tablets. Mr. Rumbold suggests that they get her a certificate to a spa for a facial. Lucas is against the idea, noting that for £6 they'd hardly be able to buy enough cement to fill the wrinkles in her face.

When the gift is finally presented at the episode's conclusion, everyone takes turns peering into the box, making cryptic comments on the gift. "We're not going to tell you what it is. It's a secret," Mr. Humphries says to the camera, in a rare breaking down of the imaginary fourth wall.

Perhaps the funniest moments in the episode comes when Rumbold convenes a rehearsal to practice the singing of "Happy Birthday." Aside from being assigned difficult parts, the staff realizes that none of them know Mrs. Slocombe's first name. Rumbold suggests they practice using "uh-uh" at the appropriate section, until they discover her name. A rather lengthy debate ensues over the possibility of anywhere from one to four syllables in Slocombe's name. Soon the proceedings are reduced to a delightfully silly affair interspersed with more than a few "uh-uh-uh-uhs."

EPISODE 6: "OH WHAT A TANGLED WEB" ★★★

Air date: May 12, 1976. Cast: Mr. Lucas (Trevor Bannister); Mrs. Slocombe (Mollie Sugden); Capt. Peacock (Frank Thornton); Mr. Humphries (John Inman); Miss Brahms (Wendy Richard); Mr. Grainger (Arthur Brough); Mr. Rumbold (Nicholas Smith); Mr. Harman (Arthur English); Young Mr. Grace (Harold Bennett); Mrs. Peacock (Diana King); Miss Hazelwood (Melita Manger); Mr. Grace's Secretary (Penny Irving); Mr. Hazelwood (Michael Stainton)

Rumors about an affair between Captain Peacock and Rumbold's secretary, Miss Hazelwood, seem to be confirmed when both individuals show up late to work one morning. Soon, Mrs. Peacock arrives at the store to confront her wayward husband, followed in short order by Miss Hazelwood's irate father.

In the mold of "Forward Mr. Grainger," "Oh What a Tangled Web" presents its story line immediately and continues with hardly any filler material. Unlike the former episode, however, the situation is slightly more contrived, and the promise of it is not fully exploited. Perhaps the basic problem is one of motivation. In "Forward Mr. Grainger," we have no difficulty believing that a long-time clerk would become a tyrant when finally given a chance to manage. Here, we are asked to believe not only that Captain Peacock would have an affair but that Rumbold's secretary would have one with him. Although Peacock has a history of leering and lechery in the series, it is done in the bawdy music hall tradition. One tends to think of him as a dog that chases cars: he wouldn't know what to do if he caught one. All this aside, there are many good, previously unexplored situations here, if not all presented to perfection.

This episode gives us our first look at Mrs. Peacock, played here by Diana King. Sharp eyes will recognize her as Mrs. Lloyd from "The Wedding Party" installment of *Fawlty Towers.*

The best moments in "Oh What a Tangled Web" do not come from Peacock but rather from Mrs. Slocombe and Mr. Grainger. Slocombe is waiting in Rumbold's office for a woman from the personnel department, who is coming to interview her for another job at the store. When Mrs. Peacock enters, she takes Slocombe to be the secretary who is breaking up her marriage, while Slocombe naturally assumes her to be from personnel. What follows is a clever exchange of mismatched questions and answers during which Mrs. Peacock levels shameful accusations, which Slocombe takes to be compliments on her past work performance in the lingerie department. When Slocombe makes a vague reference to having posted for other jobs in the past, Mrs. Peacock is taken aback, thinking that Slocombe is referring to affairs. Mrs. Slocombe cheerfully confesses to doing whatever she can to get out of underwear. When Mrs. Peacock threatens to expose Slocombe's behavior to the public, the saleslady thinks she is going to be recognized for her accomplishments in retail. "Fame at last," she remarks happily.

Grainger has a similar, albeit briefer encounter with Mr. Hazelwood, which results in him having a wedding cake smashed over his head. Later, at the hearing in the boardroom, Grainger complains of being temporarily deaf due to having currants lodged in both ears.

Christmas Special 1976

"THE FATHER CHRISTMAS AFFAIR" ★★★

Air date: December 24, 1976. Cast: Mr. Lucas (Trevor Bannister); Mrs. Slocombe (Mollie Sugden); Capt. Peacock (Frank Thornton); Mr. Humphries (John Inman); Miss Brahms (Wendy Richard); Mr. Grainger (Arthur Brough); Mr. Rumbold (Nicholas Smith); Mr. Harman (Arthur English); Young Mr. Grace (Harold Bennett); Umbrella Customer (Jeanne Mockford); Cook (Doremy Vernon); Miss Bakewell (Penny Irving); Boy (Donald Waugh)

Mr. Grace offers £50 in cash to any employee wishing to be Grace Brothers' official Father Christmas.

A good Christmas Eve entry, albeit with more cheer than genuine holiday spirit.

There is the obligatory musical routine, although it has little to do with the season. A strong closing sequence helps carry the episode and makes it all worthwhile.

Doremy Vernon is home again for the holidays after making her first series appearance in the previous Christmas episode. While in "Christmas Crackers" she played a waitress, here she plays a cook. It would be three more years until she reappeared as the manager of the canteen. Also, Mr. Grace's secretary is finally given a name (for Christmas?) in this holiday episode.

When the staff gathers for its Father Christmas audition, only Rumbold and Peacock look the part, while Mrs. Slocombe seems more like a troll in her oversized red hood and white beard. Lucas *is* a troll, as he is forced to go around on his knees in a costume left over from a production of *Snow White*. Mr. Humphries tops them all when he appears in drag in a costume he borrowed from a friend, who used it in a strip show.

Series Five 1977

Episode 1: "Mrs. Slocombe Expects" ★★★

Air date: February 25, 1977. Cast: Mr. Lucas (Trevor Bannister); Mrs. Slocombe (Mollie Sugden); Capt. Peacock (Frank Thornton); Mr. Humphries (John Inman); Miss Brahms (Wendy Richard); Mr. Grainger (Arthur Brough); Mr. Rumbold (Nicholas Smith); Mr. Harman (Arthur English); Young Mr. Grace (Harold Bennett); Cleaning Woman (Hilda Fenemore); Customers (Geoffrey Adams, Jennifer Lonsdale, Elizabeth Morgan, Jeffrey Gardiner, Raymond Bowers)

Mrs. Slocombe smuggles her pregnant Pussy into the store when the arrival of the kittens is imminent.

A very entertaining episode, but oddly the best moments are not those connected with the plot. While Mrs. Slocombe's efforts to care for her cat in its moment of need are amusing — there is a cute mechanical gag that employs a tea urn with a cat's tail sticking out of the spigot — they are somewhat routine. The best moments surrounding the plot involve the men on the staff mistakenly believing that Mrs. Slocombe, rather than her cat, is expecting. In a well-played scene, Lucas, Peacock, and Humphries sit in stunned silence as they overhear the account of how the conception occurred.

Much better is the secondary story line in which the staff members impersonate customers in an attempt to stimulate business. Acting on an idea of Mr. Grace's, Miss Brahms, Mr. Humphries, and Mr. Grainger take turns pretending to be shoppers. The notion is to encourage the actual customers to buy by lavishly complimenting the quality and value of Grace Brothers' merchandise. All three attempts to implement the scheme go hilariously awry. First, Miss Brahms tries to pass herself off as a lady, complete with a fur and jewels. Unfortunately, her common Cockney accent serves to destroy the charade and drive to a pair of women away from a purchase.

Mr. Humphries' attempt goes too well when a wealthy customer insists on buying everything Humphries has admired — as a gift to Humphries! The funniest encounter is left for last as Mr. Grainger battles a gentleman for the last pair of gloves which they both have been admiring. Grainger's absorption in his role results in another lost sale despite Mr. Lucas's desperate struggle to wrest the gloves away.

Episode 2: "A Change Is as Good as a Rest" ★★★½

Air date: March 4, 1977. Cast: Mr. Lucas (Trevor Bannister); Mrs. Slocombe (Mollie Sugden); Capt. Peacock (Frank Thornton); Mr. Humphries (John

Inman); Miss Brahms (Wendy Richard); Mr. Grainger (Arthur Brough); Mr. Rumbold (Nicholas Smith); Mr. Harman (Arthur English); Young Mr. Grace (Harold Bennett); Father of the Indian Brave (Terry Duggan); Woman Buying the Bridal Doll (Jacquie Cook); Miss Bakewell (Penny Irving)

Mr. Grace orders the entire staff to change departments for a week to broaden its experience. The staff members of men's and women's clothing are sent to run the toy department.

As the title avows, a change is indeed as good as a rest, and this charming episode certainly proves the point. It is quite a treat to see the regulars in a new environment, especially since they rarely leave the familiar confines of their usual set. Apparently, the move agreed with the cast members, as they cavort through their new assignments with great delight. There is little of the usual formula, which can often serve to make so many of the other entries in the series somewhat indistinguishable.

The episode opens with a strong scene in the company's boardroom. The staff members have assembled to hear their new assignments, but mistakenly believe they are there to be fired. Grainger is elected to defiantly lead the retaliatory mass resignation. Unfortunately, only he actually resigns before they are informed of the actual plan. Arthur Brough makes the most of the opportunity to do his martyr portrayal, as he is allowed to come back on staff but only as the junior to Humphries and Lucas.

The episode shifts into high gear as the team arrives for its first day in the toy department. After being given a thorough and often hilarious briefing on the merchandise, handled in stiff military fashion by Peacock, they are set loose. Soon Mr. Humphries is enjoying giving the Funtime Freddy doll a shower, Lucas is filling Mrs. Slocombe's wetting dolls with fizzy lemonade, and Peacock is compelled to wear a propeller contraption (touted as a "whimsical novelty") on his head for demonstration purposes. Best of all, Grainger, despite his loathing of children, becomes the most successful salesperson as he plays with the model railroad. The romp ends happily as they fail to leave on time, due to the fact they are so enchanted with their playthings.

Coauthor Jeremy Lloyd picks "A Change Is as Good as a Rest" as his favorite of all *Are You Being Served?* episodes. Quite probably, he had a similarly good time researching the script in Hamley's, London's (and perhaps the world's) premier toy store.

Episode 3: "Founder's Day" ★★★

Air date: March 11, 1977. Cast: Mr. Lucas (Trevor Bannister); Mrs. Slocombe (Mollie Sugden); Capt. Peacock (Frank Thornton); Mr. Humphries (John Inman); Miss Brahms (Wendy Richard); Mr. Grainger (Arthur Brough); Mr. Rumbold (Nicholas Smith); Mr. Harman (Arthur English); Young Mr. Grace

(Harold Bennett); Fur Coat Customer (Tim Barrett); Handkerchief Customer (Bill Martin); Underwear Customer (Carole Rousseau); Miss Bakewell (Penny Irving); Decoy Secretary (Jenny Kenna)

The staff holds a tribute along the lines of "This Is Your Life" for Young Mr. Grace on his 80th birthday.

Buoyed up by a strong ending, "Founder's Day" presents some good opportunities in the limelight for Harold Bennett as Young Mr. Grace. The title, however, is something of a misnomer as the episode reveals that Mr. Grace did not found Grace Brothers' but rather inherited it from a rich uncle. In honor of the octogenarian's birthday, the department assembles to offer remembrances of him along with some amusing doctored photos and film clips.

Often the funniest moments stem from Bennett's charming delivery of one-liners offered in response to the proceedings. Mr. Grace is lured to the boardroom on the pretext of interviewing a new secretary. Once he is alone with the pretty candidate, Mr. Lucas emerges to announce that he has been brought there for one reason only. "Blackmail?" his employer deadpans.

Also quite good are the staff members' recollections of their most memorable moments — all of which seem to show Mr. Grace in the worst light but are delivered earnestly enough to be taken as tributes.

"Founder's Day" is also noteworthy as the first time John Inman appears as Mr. Humphries' mother (in a film clip). The episode also discloses Mrs. Slocombe's real name — Rachel Yiddle — although this contradicts information given in "50 Years On." The episode also contains one continuity mistake, which occurs when Mr. Rumbold is chiding the staff for writing joke names in the sign-in book. Rumbold remarks on entries made "yesterday," then later in the scene announces that "today" is Monday, meaning that the staff worked on Sunday, a practice that would not begin in London department stores until almost 20 years later and then only sporadically.

EPISODE 4: "THE OLD ORDER CHANGES" ★★

Air date: March 18, 1977. Cast: Mrs. Slocombe (Mollie Sugden); Mr. Lucas (Trevor Bannister); Capt. Peacock (Frank Thornton); Mr. Humphries (John Inman); Miss Brahms (Wendy Richard); Mr. Grainger (Arthur Brough); Mr. Rumbold (Nicholas Smith); Mr. Harman (Arthur English); Young Mr. Grace (Harold Bennett); Pants Customer (Jeffrey Holland); Cynthia (Bernice Adams)

After returning from a trip to the United States, Young Mr. Grace implements American sales techniques.

Based on an interesting premise, "The Old Order Changes" fails to live up to its promising concept. Instead, it spends half of its running time setting up the motivation for the situation then, once finally introduced, it fails to deliver with enough comic punch to justify the buildup.

The first 15 minutes are a detailed exploration of the rigid hierarchy of Grace Brothers', complete with the short tempers such a system produces. While not without its moments, this presents nothing new and quickly becomes rather tiresome with the only highlight being another of Rumbold's enjoyable confusion bits.

With the return of Mr. Grace from America, the staff is told that informality is to be the new policy of the store. Toward this end, first names are exchanged, dress is to be relaxed and suited to one's personality, and forced camaraderie is fostered. While the meeting in which this is discussed is fairly entertaining, the actual execution of the policy is rather confusing. Instead of a relaxed atmosphere, the staff quickly is steered into trying to dress in more trendy style and speaking in a sort of late sixties slang. Only Humphries, appearing in a style reminiscent of Elton John at the peak of his glitter phase, dresses in a way that expresses his own personality. Peacock is compelled to wear a floor-length African-style robe complete with frizzy wig. This all is especially forced, considering that Mr. Grace announces the new scheme while dressed in cowboy gear — about as far as one could get from the costumes thrust upon the staff. It all comes off as a rather weak excuse to dress the cast in silly costumes.

There is some fun to be had when Lucas is forced to reveal his name. He rather uncomfortably confesses it to be Dick, and is kidded for it the rest of the episode. Fans of the series may recall, however, that previously Lucas was called James in "The Clock" from series two.

Jeffrey Holland appears briefly as the Afro-sporting customer. After this appearance and a similarly small role in *Dad's Army* ("Wake Up Walmington"), Holland would become a regular on two future David Croft (with Jimmy Perry) series: *Hi-de-Hi!* and *You Rang, M'Lord?*

EPISODE 5: "TAKEOVER" ★★½

Air date: March 25, 1977. Cast: Mr. Lucas (Trevor Bannister); Mrs. Slocombe (Mollie Sugden); Capt. Peacock (Frank Thornton); Mr. Humphries (John Inman); Miss Brahms (Wendy Richard); Mr. Grainger (Arthur Brough); Mr. Rumbold (Nicholas Smith); Mr. Harman (Arthur English); Young Mr. Grace (Harold Bennett); Lady Weeble Ablesmith (Mavis Pugh); Henry Grant Hopkins (Donald Bisset); Miss Bakewell (Penny Irving)

The staff members must impersonate absent shareholders in order to avert a hostile takeover bid by a competitor.

Rather slow in starting, "Takeover" manages to build momentum for a rather farcical yet raucous ending. With the store in jeopardy of being taken over, the men's and ladies' departments are summoned to the boardroom to hear Mr. Grace's contingency plan to ward off the competition. Unfortunately, most of Mr. Grace's ideas were culled from the plots of popular crime dramas and involve such tactics as arson, extortion, and blackmail. Mr. Harman comes to the rescue with an idea for the shareholder charade. This is where the fun really begins as Harman is enlisted to play a self-made Cockney millionaire, with Slocombe and Brahms completing his family. Brahms is especially good as she is called upon to don buckteeth and a rather transparent upper-class accent. Best of all is Arthur Brough's Grainger, who impersonates an Eaton-educated Somerset landowner. Complete with a mousy toupee, Grainger's repartee is confined to saying "Oh, aye," with a silly grin on his face.

Lucas, Humphries, and Peacock are pressed into service as the meeting's kitchen staff to round out the silliness. The best moments come not from Humphries' hysterical turn as the frantic chef, as good as it is, but from Lucas and Peacock as the waiters. Since the headwaiter's uniform fits Lucas, he assumes the lead role while Peacock bristles at taking orders from the staff's junior member. At first, he refuses to be ordered about on a first-name basis by Lucas. The junior assures Peacock that he won't use familiar address, then clarifies that he will merely snap his fingers to attract the floorwalker's attention. Frank Thornton's if-looks-could-kill reactions are priceless.

EPISODE 6: "GOODBYE MR. GRAINGER" ★★★

Air date: April 1, 1977. Cast: Mrs. Slocombe (Mollie Sugden); Mr. Lucas (Trevor Bannister); Capt. Peacock (Frank Thornton); Mr. Humphries (John Inman); Miss Brahms (Wendy Richard); Mr. Grainger (Arthur Brough); Mr. Rumbold (Nicholas Smith); Mr. Harman (Arthur English); Young Mr. Grace (Harold Bennett); Corset Customer (Peggy Ashby)

Grainger is slated for forced retirement until Rumbold discovers he has won a half million pounds in the betting pools.

"Goodbye Mr. Grainger" is a refreshing change from most of the episodes of the previous few seasons. There is a marked absence of outlandish mechanical gags or implausible situations that give the staff an excuse to dress up in costumes. Instead, there is just a straightforward, believable plot, professionally executed.

As with most episodes that feature the men's department's senior clerk prominently, "Goodbye Mr. Grainger" is highlighted with a delightful performance by Arthur Brough. Brough plays his crotchety and sympathetic routines to the hilt, generating many laughs in the process. There is an especially effective scene as Grainger sits down in a darkened store to write his letter of resignation. The retirement is being forced by Grainger's recent string of ill-tempered behavior, which the staff attributes to his advancing age. The following Monday, however, Grainger is miraculously transformed to a sweet, kindly old gent. Mrs. Slocombe mistaken believes that Grainger has had a religious experience, but in actuality he has won the national football pools. While Grainger goes to buy gifts for the entire staff, management schemes to keep him on the job to avert any negative publicity that will be generated when the full story of the incident comes out to the press.

The episode, particularly the title, is sadly prophetic in light of the fact that this was Arthur Brough's second-to-last show in the series. The following Easter. his wife of almost 50 years died, prompting Brough to quit the cast due to the shock. Within two months of her death, Brough himself passed away, leaving a void in the *Are You Being Served?* company that would never successfully be filled.

EPISODE 7: "IT PAYS TO ADVERTISE" ★★★½

Air date: April 8, 1977. Cast: Mr. Lucas (Trevor Bannister); Mrs. Slocombe (Mollie Sugden); Capt. Peacock (Frank Thornton); Mr. Humphries (John Inman); Miss Brahms (Wendy Richard); Mr. Grainger (Arthur Brough); Mr. Rumbold (Nicholas Smith); Mr. Harman (Arthur English); Young Mr. Grace (Harold Bennett); Perfume Customer (Ferdy Mayne); Mr. Crawford (Raymond Bowers); Miss Bakewell (Penny Irving); Porter (Freddie Wiles)

Young Mr. Grace decides to produce a commercial for the store using talent from the men's and ladies' departments.

One of the best of the fifth season, "It Pays to Advertise" returns to the let's-put-on-a-show genre that pops up with increasing regularity. As implausible as these forays usually are, they do provide some fresh air inside the otherwise restrictive confines of Grace Brothers.

The episode begins with the unveiling of some new mannequins that Mr. Grace has had made. Working on the premise that using normal people as models will appeal to the customers, Grace has had his dummies fashioned after two of the least normal staff members: Mrs. Slocombe and Mr. Humphries. There is some rather predictable byplay as Slocombe displays outrage as Harman and Lucas manhandle her double, but some truly funny moments occur as Humphries is compelled to play statue when his likeness is removed for repair. The situation escalates when Rumbold, unaware of the switch, orders the dummies to be stripped as they are slated for advertising underwear.

The real meat of the episode comes in its final two-thirds as the staff attempts to produce a film ad for use in a cinema campaign. With Humphries as the film's high-strung director (referred to as "Mr. Peckinpoof" by Mr. Harman) and Lucas as the crew, the project is doomed to amusing failure. Best yet are Peacock and Slocombe, who are cast as a pair of strangers who meet in a lounge dressed in their fashions from Grace Brothers. Mollie Sugden is especially good as her character is compelled to play the femme fatale complete with an ill-fitting sequined dress and some rather obstreperous false eyelashes. Arthur Brough and Nicholas Smith add to the fringes of the farce with their turns as a genial bartender and gypsy accordionist, respectively.

Series Six 1978

Episode 1: "By Appointment" ★★½

Air date: November 15, 1978. Cast: Mrs. Slocombe (Mollie Sugden); Mr. Humphries (John Inman); Mr. Lucas (Trevor Bannister); Capt. Peacock (Frank Thornton); Miss Brahms (Wendy Richard); Mr. Tebbs (James Hayter); Mr. Rumbold (Nicholas Smith); Mr. Harman (Arthur English); Young Mr. Grace (Harold Bennett); Miss Bakewell (Penny Irving); Nurse (Vivienne Johnson); Ivy (Hilda Fenemore); Customer (Joy Harrington); Radio Voice (Colin Ward-Lewis)

The staff is excited over the prospect of a visit to Grace Brothers by the queen during an upcoming royal tour of the area.

Filling as it does only half of the running time, the plot for "By Appointment" is good, albeit slim, entertainment. It is a pity that so much time is taken up with repetitive and mechanical gags concerning the return of the staff from its holidays. One would much rather that the writers had explored further the many possibilities presented by the primary situation. After all, we have seen the kind of jokes presented in the opening scene before in the series, but how often would the staff get a chance to meet royalty?

Once the plot is introduced, there is a good scene in which the departments practice greeting the Queen and Prince Philip. Standing in for the royal couple are Mrs. Slocombe and Captain Peacock, both regally turned out for the exercise. Unfortunately for Peacock, but most fortuitous for the audience, the pretend prince gets his scabbard stuck in the lift door, then later loses his trousers while coming down the stairs. This rehearsal, complete with the fastidious Mr. Humphries' high-strung reactions to each new disaster, provides the bulk of the laughs. The ending is also quite good, with the staff resplendently dressed, watching the royal procession coming up the street from Rumbold's office window. The royal couple seems intent upon entering the store — until Mrs. Slocombe accidentally knocks a flower pot in front of the procession, scaring the entire entourage back to Buckingham Palace.

This episode marks the first appearance of James Hayter as Mr. Tebbs, the replacement for the late Arthur Brough's Mr. Grainger. Although not the equal of the versatile Grainger, the Tebbs character is serviceable for the situations presented him, although Hayter would not have a chance to really grow in the role. The sixth season would be the only one for Hayter, who would resign from the cast in favor of a lucrative commercial contract he held as the spokesman for Mr. Kipling's Cakes.

The sixth season also introduces a shift in the credits. For the first five seasons, the star of the show (or at least the first one mentioned in the end titles) was always either Mollie Sugden or Trevor Bannister, with Frank Thornton always third. From here on, Sugden and John Inman would share the top spot, reflecting Inman's emergence as the show's star, with Thornton and Bannister alternating in the third and fourth spots.

Episode 2: "The Club" ★★

Air date: November 22, 1978. Cast: Mr. Humphries (John Inman); Mrs. Slocombe (Mollie Sugden); Capt. Peacock (Frank Thornton); Mr. Lucas (Trevor Bannister); Miss Brahms (Wendy Richard); Mr. Tebbs (James Hayter); Mr. Rumbold (Nicholas Smith); Mr. Harman (Arthur English); Young Mr. Grace (Harold Bennett); Miss Bakewell (Penny Irving); Nurse (Vivienne Johnson); Man with Dog (Raymond Bowers); Woman with Dog (Mavis Pugh); Flexibra Customer (Dominique Don); Man with Rotating Buns (Tony Brothers)

Mr. Grace allows the staff to open its own private social club in the basement, providing they refurbish the room.

Another disjointed mishmash of double entendres, mechanical gags, and labored slapstick, "The Club" manages a few laughs along the way. The worst of the gags features yet another gimmicky mannequin, this one with rotating breasts to advertise the Flexibra. When Peacock stops a woman customer to inquire as to the display's effectiveness, the woman explains she already owns the garment — and produces her own revolving bust as proof. Even Harold Bennett, who is usually allowed some good verbal bits, is compelled into the mechanized jokes when he is fitted with a pacemaker that sounds a siren when his heart is taxed. Of course, this ensures plenty of opportunities for both his nurse and secretary to show off their knickers.

The high point of the episode is the knockabout in the basement as the crew works to hang wallpaper in its "club." This scene shows some promise, and many of the gags are good. The only drawback, however, is that physical comedy of this nature requires split-second timing to be plausible. Unfortunately, working on a weekly TV production schedule, there was not enough time for the meticulous preparation that can make such routines as seamless as they need to be. This is truly a pity, since the cast certainly does try its best.

Episode 3: "Do You Take This Man?" ★★½

Air date: November 29, 1978. Cast: Mrs. Slocombe (Mollie Sugden); Mr. Humphries (John Inman); Mr. Lucas (Trevor Bannister); Capt. Peacock (Frank Thornton); Miss Brahms (Wendy Richard); Mr. Tebbs (James Hayter); Mr. Rumbold (Nicholas Smith); Mr. Harman (Arthur English); Young Mr. Grace (Harold Bennett); Miss Bakewell (Penny Irving); Nurse (Vivienne Johnson); Wendel P. Clark (Norman Mitchell); Mr. Tomiades (Gorden Kaye); Underwear Customer (Felix Bowness); Bandleader (Stellios Chiotis)

Mrs. Slocombe is left at the altar by a Greek bouzouki player.

Not without its moments, "Do You Take This Man?" suffers from difficulties quite the reverse of most episodes. Rather than meandering along for the first ten minutes or so before finding its plot, then racing to a big finish, this episode establishes itself quickly, then falters in its punch line.

After a few throwaway gags, Mrs. Slocombe's impending marriage to the Greek musician is revealed. Throughout the middle section of the show, wedding preparations, including the fact that Mrs. Slocombe has little money with which to hold a reception, add to the momentum and anticipation. Next, it is revealed that Mrs. Slocombe has a rich American uncle who is coming from Texas to see his "little Betty" get married. Uncle promises to give the couple "a thousand" for a wedding gift, causing the bride to spend a little more freely. On the day of the wedding, the groom bolts back to Greece on the advice of a family member—his wife.

Up to this point, everything works rather well, but unfortunately, matters start to disintegrate. In order to pay for the reception and not embarrass Mrs. Slocombe in front of her guests, the staff conspires to present a sham wedding, with Mr. Humphries as the groom. This ruse gives the excuse for John Inman to wear the traditional Greek man's skirt costume (which seems the main motivation for the authors' going ahead with it). The whole charade is rather a cruel one to perpetrate on the uncle, the guests (who would surely recognize that the groom has been changed), and the distraught Mrs. Slocombe.

Next, Mollie Sugden gets an opportunity to do her drunken routine, but she sobers up immediately to participate in the closing traditional Greek dance. This dance is an audience pleaser, as most of the cast's performance bits are, but it leaves the plot unresolved. I kept waiting for the masquerade to fall apart or for Uncle Wendel to reveal what that "thousand" for a wedding present was (a thousand chickens, perhaps, from his ranch?). Instead, the whole purpose of the buildup is defeated by that blasted dance.

There are some good performances, including James Hayter's impersonation of a Greek Orthodox priest, complete with curtains for cassocks and pidgin Greek. As outrageous as Tebbs's Greek impersonation is, it doesn't hold a candle to the performance of Norman Mitchell as Uncle Wendel—another bad American accent from a British performer.

Gorden Kaye appears briefly as Mr. Tomiades. Some viewers may also recognize him from his starring role in Lloyd and Croft's *'Allo, 'Allo*.

Episode 4: "Shedding the Load" ★★½

Air date: December 6, 1978. Cast: Mr. Lucas (Trevor Bannister); Mrs. Slocombe (Mollie Sugden); Capt. Peacock (Frank Thornton); Mr. Humphries (John Inman); Miss Brahms (Wendy Richard); Mr. Tebbs (James Hayter); Mr. Rumbold (Nicholas Smith); Mr. Harman (Arthur English); Young Mr. Grace (Harold Bennett); Miss Bakewell (Penny Irving); Nurse (Vivienne Johnson)

With sales figures down, Mr. Grace orders that the staff be trimmed, then leaves it up to them to decide who goes.

The only episode to feature just the regular cast, "Shedding the Load" is a rather routine entry in the series. It is notable, however, for the revelations of how each staff member feels about the others, which come to the surface as they debate who must be fired. Each employee has a different opinion on who the unlucky colleague should be. Mr. Tebbs believes Mrs. Slocombe should go, on the basis that he thinks her a crabby old cow, while Slocombe opts for Tebbs, on similar grounds. Peacock thinks Brahms should get the axe for being uncooperative to his advances at the Christmas party; while Brahms picks Lucas on a seniority basis. Peacock is selected by Lucas for being disrespectful to Rumbold. Only Mr. Humphries neither names anyone nor is fingered by anyone else, although in a moment of temper Mrs. Slocombe does accuse him of being a "fairy cake."

The better moments of the episode occur during a special session with Mr. Grace, during which each staff member pleads his or her case. What enlivens this scene is the spirited performance of Arthur English as Mr. Harman. In his inimitable Cockney style, Harman manages to turn the somber hearing into something more akin to a horse-handicapping session, complete with running odds on each contestant. Ultimately, Mr. Tebbs offers to resign after Peacock reads his 40-plus-year service record (Tebbs makes the offer while saying that he feels he's had a rich full career, but Grace regards it merely as a boring life). Happily for all concerned, the order to trim the staff is rescinded.

EPISODE 5: "A BLISS GIRL" ★★★

Air date: December 13, 1978. Cast: Mrs. Slocombe (Mollie Sugden); Mr. Humphries (John Inman); Mr. Lucas (Trevor Bannister); Capt. Peacock (Frank Thornton); Miss Brahms (Wendy Richard); Mr. Tebbs (James Hayter); Mr. Rumbold (Nicholas Smith); Mr. Harman (Arthur English); Young Mr. Grace (Harold Bennett); Miss Bakewell (Penny Irving); Nurse (Vivienne Johnson); Customer (Jan Holden); Typist (Bernice Adams)

Mr. Humphries must staff a promotional counter for Bliss perfumes when the regular salesgirl for the company can't make it.

The strongest episode in a generally weak season, "A Bliss Girl" has a fairly cohesive plot assisted by a number of familiar yet well-executed routines. The most familiar of these is actually worked twice in the episode and involves Rumbold's habit of muddling the facts during inquiries into staff disputes. This shtick was used more frequently in the early programs and apparently fell into disuse as the seasons progressed. Despite this, it is a welcome addition to "A Bliss Girl," thanks in large part to Nicholas Smith's earnestly thick delivery and the visible exasperation it inspires in his underlings.

Aside from John Inman, who does a creditable job as the principal comedian of the installment, Frank Thornton is given good opportunity to display seething outrage in the role of Peacock. With Humphries loaned out to the Bliss counter to sell perfume, Rumbold orders Peacock to temporarily take

Humphries' place behind the men's counter under Mr. Tebbs. This insult is only compounded when Lucas insists on ribbing Peacock (whom he now refers to as Steve) and instructing him on the proper way to fold a sweater.

The climax of the episode comes as Humphries battles Mrs. Slocombe for a large commission on a fur coat. Humphries, compelled to help ladies' department customers when Slocombe and Brahms are busy, goes to extreme lengths to make the sale. Upon her return, Mrs. Slocombe attempts to ruin his sale by switching the customer to another item. Undaunted, Humphries dons the coat, a wig, heels, and a fur hat to demonstrate the overall look of the prospective ensemble. He not only succeeds in earning his commission but also manages to get asked out for dinner by a confused Mr. Grace.

Episode 6: "Happy Returns" ★★½

Air date: December 26, 1978. Cast: Mr. Lucas (Trevor Bannister); Mrs. Slocombe (Mollie Sugden); Capt. Peacock (Frank Thornton); Mr. Humphries (John Inman); Miss Brahms (Wendy Richard); Mr. Tebbs (James Hayter); Mr. Rumbold (Nicholas Smith); Mr. Harman (Arthur English); Young Mr. Grace (Harold Bennett); Miss Bakewell (Penny Irving); Nurse (Vivienne Johnson); Dancer (Michael Halsey); Waitress (Doremy Vernon)

The staff must put on a cabaret act in honor of Young Mr. Grace's birthday.

Another let's-put-on-a-show episode, "Happy Returns" does have the excuse that it aired on Boxing Day (the day after Christmas) when the British public expects a bit of broad pantomime. Still, the habit of repeating plots does wear a little thin in this exercise, especially since the authors also used Mr. Grace's birthday as a plot line in the previous season ("Founder's Day"). Ironically, the many functions presented here as birthday traditions are absent in that installment of one year prior.

There are a number of passably entertaining scenes, the best one being the birthday luncheon. At this fete, Mr. Grace serves gruel to the junior member of the staff (Lucas), treats his employees to cheese left over from the 1964 Christmas party, and gives out a pittance of a birthday bonus. Finally, the bit is punctuated by Mr. Grace attempting to open the birthday champagne. As in previous years, he fails to get the bottle uncorked, sending it back for another try next year. This gag goes somewhat awry when Peacock slams the bottle down on the table, which causes the bubbly to open with a pop. By Harold Bennett's reaction, one can guess that the wine was supposed to come gushing forth. Unfortunately, while he pleads with someone to fill the glasses before it all is gone, the champagne is nowhere to be seen, apparently sitting inertly in the bottle.

The climax of the episode is the rehearsal of the ballet of the toys. The main attraction here is another opportunity to see the cast in silly costumes, but this bit too is wearing thin. When the evening's professional entertainers arrive, wearing the same costumes, Humphries sprinkles his prop fairy dust to segue into a full-cast chorus line rendition of "Steppin' Out with My Baby." Unfortunately, this transition is done hurriedly, and any flow to the proceedings is lost. Thankfully, after a tired sixth season, new blood and inspiration would help enliven the next round of shows.

Series Seven 1979

EPISODE 1: "THE JUNIOR" ★★★★

Air date: October 19, 1979. Cast: Mr. Humphries (John Inman); Mrs. Slocombe (Mollie Sugden); Mr. Lucas (Trevor Bannister); Capt. Peacock (Frank Thornton); Mr. Goldberg (Alfie Bass); Miss Brahms (Wendy Richard); Mr. Rumbold (Nicholas Smith); Mr. Harman (Arthur English); Young Mr. Grace (Harold Bennett); Miss Bakewell (Penny Irving); Nurse (Vivienne Johnson); Mr. Webster (Tony Sympson); Mr. Bakewell (Jeffrey Gardner); Ivy (Hilda Fenemore); Customers (Harold Berens, Morris Barry, Bernard Stone); Warwick (Jimmy Mac)

When Mr. Humphries and Mr. Lucas are promoted, Mr. Goldberg is hired to be the new junior for the men's department. Soon, however, Goldberg's salesmanship proves that he deserves the top spot.

One of the strongest episodes in all the series in terms of writing, "The Junior" successfully introduces the character of Mr. Goldberg in a manner that not only gives the new part depth and interest but also sets up good conflict. This comic tension — between Mr. Goldberg and Captain Peacock — is introduced when Goldberg enters the interview and immediately recognizes his old army mate: Corporal Peacock. Of course, Peacock bristles at the insinuation that he is less than advertised, creating an amusing adversarial relationship between the two characters. Although Peacock has the advantage of authority, Goldberg has much more charm and natural guile, which help give him the upper hand. Veteran comic actor Alfie Bass is a delightful addition to the cast and breathes some much-needed fresh air into the series. It is a shame he only stayed for one season.

Prior to the introduction of Mr. Goldberg, there are some good scenes as Mr. Humphries is elevated to the position of senior sales assistant — and cries each time it is mentioned. There is also a good routine in which the staff conducts interviews for a new junior. One candidate in particular seems well suited for the job but is summarily rejected by Humphries as an undesirable type, although he instantly recognizable to the audience as a Humphries clone.

There seems to be a little behind-the-scenes confusion regarding the story of Mr. Webster, the old man who interviews for the job. In an interview for the *Are You Being Served?* book, Jeremy Lloyd remarks of constant turnover in the part of the senior salesman. He relates a story concerning an old man with a bushy white beard who interviewed for the role, then gave his address as a cardboard box. Out of pity, Lloyd says, the man got the part, but the old gent died before he could start work. Lloyd places this incident as occurring midway through the eighth season, but the story is identical to the scripted interview that takes place in this episode! Either Lloyd is confusing real life with his script, or the old man saw this episode and imitated it for his audition.

EPISODE 2: "STRONG STUFF THIS INSURANCE" ★★★★

Air date: October 26, 1979. Cast: Mr. Humphries (John Inman); Mrs. Slocombe (Mollie Sugden); Mr. Lucas (Trevor Bannister); Capt. Peacock (Frank Thornton); Mr. Goldberg (Alfie Bass); Miss Brahms (Wendy Richard); Mr. Rumbold (Nicholas Smith); Mr. Harman (Arthur English); Young Mr. Grace (Harold Bennett); Miss Bakewell (Penny Irving); Nurse (Vivienne Johnson); Ballet Instructor (Amanda Barrie); Exam Nurse (Joy Allen); Doctor (Imogen Bickford Smith); Dressing Gown Customer (Geraldine Gardner); Slocombe's Customer (Jennifer Guy)

The staff members must take medical exams as part of Grace Brothers' new pension bonus scheme.

Fresh situations delivered without excess padding help make "Strong Stuff This Insurance" another excellent entry. Following closely on the heels of "The Junior," this episode takes a different approach but still manages to score big on laughs. While most installments of *Are You Being Served?* divide into three main set pieces, here the action is segmented into five bits, helping to keep the pace up and interest high.

After a rather routine opening (the weakest of the five segments), the show shifts into high gear with each bit managing to top the previous one. The second scene features the staff members in the canteen, discussing how they plan to pass their physicals, and it is punctuated by some excellent verbal sparring between Lucas and Slocombe. Next, in an attempt to tone up, the staff goes through a comic ballet class. Here, admittedly, some of the jokes are a bit hackneyed, but they are delivered well enough to excuse their age.

The fourth routine features the embarrassing situation of the four men having to disrobe behind a waist-high screen and wait for the arrival of the doctor. This bit has the subtle (for *AYBS?*) gag of Lucas standing self-consciously naked next to Captain Peacock. After a brief glance down toward his senior's nethers, however, Lucas relaxes and even adopts somewhat of a cocky attitude upon realizing that Peacock isn't his superior in every category.

The best is saved for last, as the staff eavesdrops on the reading of the medical bulletins. Unfortunately, what is being reviewed in Mr. Grace's office is a report on the condition of his furniture. Naturally, they take the "oldest" to be Goldberg, the "pretty little piece" to be Brahms, and the "poof" (an ottoman) to be Humphries. Harman's suggestion that this last piece be stuffed causes the effeminate Mr. H to faint away for the show's finale.

In a side note, the relative ages of the staff are revealed as each is told the amount of pension bonus he or she will receive. Presumably, Brahms and Lucas are the same age since they are both in line to get £3,000 upon retirement. Humphries is next at £2,100. Peacock stands to receive £1,700, while Slocombe will go to pasture with only £700. Goldberg, at age 63, is only slated to be awarded £21.52.

Dad's Army fans may recognize Joy Allen, the Clippie from "A Soldier's Farewell," in this episode as the Exam Nurse.

Episode 3: "The Apartment" ★★★

Air date: November 2, 1979. Cast: Mr. Humphries (John Inman); Mrs. Slocombe (Mollie Sugden); Mr. Lucas (Trevor Bannister); Capt. Peacock (Frank Thornton); Mr. Goldberg (Alfie Bass); Miss Brahms (Wendy Richard); Mr. Rumbold (Nicholas Smith); Mr. Harman (Arthur English); Young Mr. Grace (Harold Bennett); Miss Bakewell (Penny Irving); Nurse (Vivienne Johnson); Customer (Jeffrey Holland)

Mrs. Slocombe sets up housekeeping on the store's fifth floor after squatters inhabit her new apartment. Soon the entire staff drops in for the night when a transit strike leaves them stranded.

An entertaining entry, "The Apartment" is the second incarnation of a plot that would be used three times in the series. Aside from the novelty (or relative novelty, seeing as how it happens two other times) of the staff having to "muck in" together for the night, the most interesting thing about this episode is the change in relationship between Mrs. Slocombe and Mr. Humphries. Although their interaction has been strained at times — recall in the fifth season's "Shedding the Load," she calls Humphries "fairy cake" — here and in the next episode they forge a firmer alliance. Perhaps this was a conscious effort on the part of the writers, reflecting John Inman's new status as the titular star of the show. Previously, Mollie Sugden's strongest counterpart was Trevor Bannister, a fact mirrored in the well-established battles between their characters. It is somewhat odd, although still absorbing, to see Mrs. Slocombe here showing a romantic interest in Humphries. Her attempt at creating romance has the hilarious effect of almost driving Humphries to tears.

There is little for the rest of the cast to do in "The Apartment." Peacock and Lucas have a few laughs when they are forced to share a bed. Regrettably, Alfie Bass's Mr. Goldberg is almost completely wasted here.

There are some good gags that derive from the situation. As Mrs. Slocombe sets up her belongings in the unused fifth floor, Mr. Harman helps create the illusion of a real home by providing a display front door. Once in place, the ten-foot-wide prop wall is honored by all who visit as an actual egress —

even when the door proves difficult to unlock. At one point, Humphries comes around the wall to instruct Slocombe on how to open the door, then retreats around front again so he can enter it properly. One strange note: Mrs. Slocombe's belongings include a full bathroom set, complete with toilet, basin, and tub — one wonders how the new tenants in her former apartment will get along without them.

Episode 4: "Mrs. Slocombe—Senior Person" ★½

Air date: November 9, 1979. Cast: Mrs. Slocombe (Mollie Sugden); Mr. Humphries (John Inman); Mr. Lucas (Trevor Bannister); Capt. Peacock (Frank Thornton); Mr. Goldberg (Alfie Bass); Miss Brahms (Wendy Richard); Mr. Rumbold (Nicholas Smith); Mr. Harman (Arthur English); Young Mr. Grace (Harold Bennett); Miss Bakewell (Penny Irving); Nurse (Vivienne Johnson); Miss Comlozi (Avril Angers); Candid Cameron (Gorden Kaye); Customer (Derrie Powell)

When Mr. Rumbold succumbs to food poisoning, Mrs. Slocombe is tagged to become temporary department head.

Another plot retreat, this one a rehash of "Forward Mr. Grainger," makes "Mrs. Slocombe — Senior Person" the low spot of the sixth season. Not only are there no new wrinkles provided — the person promoted alienates former coworkers, then repents when they are missed — but Arthur Brough seemed to have a better time in the role. In the previous incarnation of this story line, Grainger fully relished his brief stay at the top, while Slocombe merely acts bored. Unfortunately, her boredom, while clearly intended to be comic is just, well, boring.

As stated in the review for "The Apartment," Humphries is Slocombe's only friend when she assumes her higher position. Even this, however, rings hollow, as Humphries freely admits to his coworkers that he is cultivating friends on the basis of their more powerful ranking. Humphries and Lucas have a good scene as they measure Mrs. Slocombe for a new executive suit (rather extravagant, seeing as Rumbold is only scheduled to be out two weeks). Since their measuring tape only runs to 42 inches (itself an oddity), the pair stretch the tape to its limit, then bridge the gap with an office item. Thus, Slocombe's measurements turn out to be bust, 42 and a pencil; waist, 42 and a rubber band; and hips, 42 and a calendar page. Slocombe, for her part, does a marvelous slow burn as they proceed.

The best bit in the episode has absolutely nothing to do with the plot. Gorden Kaye, of *'Allo, 'Allo* fame, has a good turn as a Scotsman buying a raincoat. At first, it appears he is testing the coat for "flashing" purposes, but it turns out that he is a paparazzi photographer who must be able to conceal his camera until the last minute. One of the better lines in the sequence — the Scot describes himself as Candid Cameron — was ad-libbed by Kaye and helped pave the way for more work in Croft-Lloyd shows. Avril Angers, *Dad's Army*'s dizzy telephone operator, has a small but good role as Miss Comlozi of the cosmetics department.

EPISODE 5: "THE HERO" ★★★

Air date: November 16, 1979. Cast: Mrs. Slocombe (Mollie Sugden); Mr. Humphries (John Inman); Mr. Lucas (Trevor Bannister); Capt. Peacock (Frank Thornton); Mr. Goldberg (Alfie Bass); Miss Brahms (Wendy Richard); Mr. Rumbold (Nicholas Smith); Mr. Harman (Arthur English); Young Mr. Grace (Harold Bennett); Miss Bakewell (Penny Irving); Nurse (Vivienne Johnson); Mr. Franco (Jackie "Mr. TV" Pallo); Sock Customer (Raymond Bowers)

After challenging a coworker to a boxing match to satisfy his sense of honor, Captain Peacock gets a case of cold feet.

"The Hero" presents a lively situation without too much extraneous material. As in one of the better shows of the sixth series, "The Junior," here the jokes are character-based with most centering on the pompous ego of Captain Peacock. The deflation of the floorwalker's ego always makes for some entertaining moments, upon which Frank Thornton always manages to capitalize.

The plot turns on an embarrassing boil on Peacock's posterior, which Mr. Franco of sporting goods discovers while fitting the captain for a pair of jogging shorts. Rather than observe the honor code of his profession, Franco indiscreetly spreads word of the painful blemish until Peacock is the laughingstock of Grace Brothers. There are some amusing moments of schoolyard humor when the staff assembles for lunch and goes into hysterics any time the merest suggestion of Peacock's plight is mentioned.

Realizing he is being ridiculed storewide, Peacock protests to Rumbold and demands that Franco apologize. Rather than extract an apology, Rumbold winds up organizing a boxing match between the two men. Peacock is especially amusing as he struts around like his namesake while enjoying the attention of the store's women, who think him a hero for his stance. His bravado quickly melts, however, after he discovers that much of the admiration stems from the fact that he is a severe underdog.

The actual boxing match, which is switched to a wrestling contest, is the comic highlight of the piece. After Peacock arrives with a doctor's note excusing him from the challenge, all the other men in the department follow suit for similar reasons. Finally, Humphries is carried kicking and screaming into the ring to uphold the department's honor. Mollie Sugden is particularly good in this sequence, proving her character to be a great wrestling fan (she immediately recognizes such obscure moves as the Patagonian Nose Hold and the Brazilian Elbow Jab) and providing the climax to the proceedings.

Franco is played by a former wrestler–turned-actor, Jackie ("Mr. TV") Pallo, explaining the round of applause given upon his entrance.

Episode 6: "Anything You Can Do" ★★★

Air date: November 16, 1979. Cast: Mrs. Slocombe (Mollie Sugden); Mr. Humphries (John Inman); Mr. Lucas (Trevor Bannister); Capt. Peacock (Frank Thornton); Mr. Goldberg (Alfie Bass); Miss Brahms (Wendy Richard); Mr. Rumbold (Nicholas Smith); Mr. Harman (Arthur English); Young Mr. Grace (Harold Bennett); Miss Bakewell (Penny Irving); Nurse (Vivienne Johnson); Canteen Manageress (Doremy Vernon); Signor Balli (Ronnie Brody); Warwick (Jimmy Mac); Mohammad (Mohammad Shamsi); Elevator Girls (Sue Bishop, Belinda Lee)

While complaining of the poor quality in the store canteen, the staff members boast that they could run it better themselves. They then are given the opportunity to do so.

One of the more linear, focused plots in the series, "Anything You Can Do" establishes its premise in the opening moments and never strays from its mission. While it may not have any of the truly outrageous bits to which fans of the show are accustomed, it remains entertaining throughout.

Almost all of the gags in "Anything You Can Do" stem from the situation. Similar in concept to the delightful "A Change is as Good as a Rest," the humor arises from watching the staff attempt different jobs. In the end, the staff succeeds and wins rave reviews for its efforts, which it turns out, were largely accomplished by calling take-out restaurants. Having proven their point, they compose a joint letter of apology to the regular kitchen crew.

There are a few continuity problems in the script. First, Mr. Grace and the rest of upper management are seen enjoying their lunch in the executive dining room. Unfortunately, that room had been previously absorbed into the canteen dining room by order of an inspector in "Up Captain Peacock" (third season). Next, Mr. Humphries relates an anecdote regarding his father's behavior at home. According to the next season's "Heir Apparent," Humphries never knew his father. Finally, one cannot help but wonder who is running the men's and ladies' departments while their staffs are toiling away in the kitchen.

Episode 7: "The Agent" ★★½

Air date: November 23, 1979. Cast: Mr. Humphries (John Inman); Mrs. Slocombe (Mollie Sugden); Mr. Lucas (Trevor Bannister); Capt. Peacock (Frank Thornton); Mr. Goldberg (Alfie Bass); Miss Brahms (Wendy Richard); Mr. Rumbold (Nicholas Smith); Mr. Harman (Arthur English); Young Mr. Grace (Harold Bennett); Miss Bakewell (Penny Irving); Nurse (Vivienne Johnson); Mr. Patel (Renu Setna); Sweater Customer (Jeffrey Segal); Mrs. Maxwell (Peggy Ann Clifford); Amanda (Marella Oppenheim)

Mrs. Slocombe and Mr. Humphries have hopes of higher-paying jobs after they engage Mr. Goldberg to be their agent.

A good premise but poorly played out. While "The Agent" presents a strong plot, it is sabotaged by the fact that the story isn't introduced until almost ten minutes into the half-hour play. This rushes the conclusion along and makes the two stars of the show seem petty and unlikable. For that matter, Alfie Bass's Mr. Goldberg comes off in this entry as a rather unsavory type as well. The main difficulty in these character matters comes as Goldberg lets it be known that he is an employment agent, specializing in the retail trade. Both Slocombe and Humphries hire Goldberg, with the understanding that his fee will be their first week's wages on their new higher-paying jobs. When Goldberg's negotiations ultimately win both generous raises at Grace Brothers, both clients refuse to pay and tear up their contracts. For some reason, this elicits applause from the audience. Perhaps the audience never warmed to the Shylockish Mr. Goldberg, but one finds it difficult to like any of the principals in this greed-motivated installment.

EPISODE 8: "THE PUNCH AND JUDY AFFAIR" ★★★½

Air date: December 26, 1979. Cast: Mr. Humphries (John Inman); Mrs. Slocombe (Mollie Sugden); Mr. Lucas (Trevor Bannister); Capt. Peacock (Frank Thornton); Mr. Goldberg (Alfie Bass); Miss Brahms (Wendy Richard); Mr. Rumbold (Nicholas Smith); Mr. Harman (Arthur English); Young Mr. Grace (Harold Bennett); Miss Bakewell (Penny Irving); Nurse (Vivienne Johnson); Canteen Manageress (Doremy Vernon); Ivy (Hilda Fenemore)

To make amends for crossing a picket line during a strike, the staff agrees to put on a Punch and Judy show for the strikers' children.

Ostensibly part of the seventh series but held back a month to be shown at Christmas time, "The Punch and Judy Affair" is filled with some amusing pieces and lively comedy. The episode is only marred by a bizarre ending in which another hasty musical production number ("Kids" from *Bye, Bye, Birdie*) is slapped on the show's ending without much rhyme or reason. A similar ending was stuck on for "Happy Returns," and while both numbers are well received, their abrupt insertion leaves one with the impression that there had been some bridging sequence that was edited out due to time constraints. "The Punch and Judy Affair" would have been better concluded with an ending that remained in the established flow of the episode.

The best moments of the installment come as the staff tries to determine how to entertain the workers' children in the upcoming party. Miss Brahms suggests acting out a fairy story, but as they review the classic children's tales they quickly realize that most are heavily laden with violence and perversity. When Captain Peacock recounts the plot of "Little Red Riding Hood," Lucas listens intently, then remarks that it's just the thing for the tykes, including as it does "cannibalism, transvestitism, and meals-on-wheels."

Once they decide to do a life-sized Punch and Judy show, with the staff appearing as giant puppets, the laughter flows generously. Trevor Bannister is especially good in the role of Punch, and John Inman's Humphries, who is charged with directing the fiasco, turns in his usual amusing display of highly strung frustration. Nicholas Smith is again given the opportunity to display his versatility behind the keyboard, as he provides incidental music — much to his director's consternation.

Sadly, "The Punch and Judy Affair" marks the final appearance of Trevor Bannister and Alfie Bass in the series. Both provided professional performances and more than a few laughs. The men's counter would not be the same without them.

Series Eight 1981

EPISODE 1: "IS IT CATCHING?" ★

Air date: April 9, 1981. Cast: Mr. Humphries (John Inman); Mrs. Slocombe (Mollie Sugden); Capt. Peacock (Frank Thornton); Miss Brahms (Wendy Richard); Mr. Rumbold (Nicholas Smith); Mr. Harman (Arthur English); Young Mr. Grace (Harold Bennett); Mr. Spooner (Mike Berry); Mr. Grossman (Milo Sperber); Old Mr. Grace (Kenneth Waller); Nurse (Vivienne Johnson); Secretary (Debbie Linden); Canteen Manageress (Doremy Vernon); Doctor (John D. Collins)

The entire staff is compelled to be quarantined in the store after Mr. Humphries contracts a rare disease.

A disappointing transitional entry, which marks a turning point in the history of *Are You Being Served?* No fewer than four new characters are introduced in this episode. Unfortunately, none (save the rather nondescript role of Grace's secretary) live up to the standards set by the ones they were replacing. The major change involved Mike Berry's Mr. Spooner taking over for Trevor Bannister's Mr. Lucas. Unfortunately, while Berry, previously a pop singer, does provide some good moments in his tenure, he is hampered by the fact that his character is cast from the mold of his predecessor. This is especially evident as Spooner hurls an overly familiar insult at Mrs. Slocombe on his first day on the job. From the outset, the rest of the staff treats Spooner with the same disdain formerly reserved for Lucas. It is almost as if the authors continued to write for Lucas then merely crossed out that name and penciled in "Spooner."

The second addition, albeit for a brief five-episode tenure, is Milo Sperber in the role of Mr. Grossman, yet another senior person for the men's department. Sperber is adequate in a thankless position that continues to fade away. Kenneth Waller is brought in to take the reigns from Harold Bennett (who appears here in his last regularly scheduled episode to facilitate the transition) as the resident Mr. Grace. Waller is hampered by the fact that he is obviously far younger (53) than the part he is playing, ultimately making him a hollow replacement for the charmingly feeble Bennett. One of the difficulties is that when Bennett talked "randy," it was cute due to his obvious age. When Waller does it (his character hasn't been given its own personality either), it isn't, since one gets the sense he can still actually make good on his threats.

As for the plot, which turns up more than halfway through the proceedings, it is yet another lame excuse to make the staff sleep together in the store ("Camping In," "The Apartment"). This time, the excuse is that Humphries' is coming down with the rare, highly contagious but nonthreatening "Marines' Disease." While other members of the staff are inexplicably allowed to be quarantined in the store in comfort, the six members of the floor staff are locked in a cold cell dressed in something akin to penguin suits with nothing but a giant waterbed on which to sleep. The entire affair is rather contrived in conception and labored in delivery.

EPISODE 2: "A PERSONAL PROBLEM" ★★½

Air date: April 16, 1981. Cast: Mrs. Slocombe (Mollie Sugden); Mr. Humphries (John Inman); Capt. Peacock (Frank Thornton); Miss Brahms (Wendy Richard); Mr. Rumbold (Nicholas Smith); Mr. Harman (Arthur English); Mr. Spooner (Mike Berry); Mr. Grossman (Milo Sperber); Old Mr. Grace (Kenneth Waller); Nurse (Vivienne Johnson); Secretary (Debbie Linden); Mrs. Peacock (Diana King); Tramp (Jack Haig); Warwick (Jimmy Mac); Mohair Jumper (Pat Keen); Silk Handkerchief (Andrew Davis)

In order to make her husband jealous, Mrs. Peacock gets a job as Rumbold's secretary.

An improvement over "Is It Catching?" "A Personal Problem" returns to a more linear plot, with situations and gags that derive directly from the story. While a welcome sign, unfortunately not all the jokes are inspired. This, coupled with the fact that the basic premise is yet another retread, serves to make the episode fairly routine.

Again the Peacocks are having marital difficulties (see "Oh What a Tangled Web," series Four) due to Captain Peacock's roving eye. This time, however, the floorwalker is falsely accused by his wife of putting his hand down a young lady's blouse at a Christmas party. To teach Peacock a lesson, Mrs. Peacock not only becomes Rumbold's secretary but also makes her husband believe she is having an affair with the jug-eared department head. Either in a dash of irony, or just because of uninspired writing, in "Oh What a Tangled Web" Peacock was accused of having a Christmas party liaison with Miss Hazelwood, Rumbold's secretary at the time.

This premise leads to a string of scenes of varying comic effectiveness. The first, which is only mildly amusing, involves Peacock attempting to secure lodging for the night with acquaintances. The next finds Humphries acquiring a pen with a radio transmitter hidden in it for the purpose of bugging Rumbold's office and listening in on him and Mrs. Peacock. This bit has more promise, especially when the pen winds up in the hands of Mr. Harman in the packing department. The episode's finale has a green-eyed Peacock driven to the window ledge outside of Rumbold's office in an attempt to take a picture of his boss and wife in the throes of passion. Unfortunately, while this routine also offers some promise, it ultimately runs out of steam and requires more physical comedy than can be supplied by Frank Thornton.

Episode 3: "Front Page Story" ★★

Air date: April 23, 1981. Cast: Mr. Humphries (John Inman); Mrs. Slocombe (Mollie Sugden); Capt. Peacock (Frank Thornton); Miss Brahms (Wendy Richard); Mr. Rumbold (Nicholas Smith); Mr. Harman (Arthur English); Mr. Spooner (Mike Berry); Mr. Grossman (Milo Sperber); Old Mr. Grace (Kenneth Waller); Nurse (Vivienne Johnson); Secretary (Debbie Linden); Wig Customer (Michael Sharvell-Martin); Miss Hurst (Jennifer Guy); Miss Hepburn (Dawn Perllman); Miss Coleman (Denise Distel)

Mr. Humphries becomes editor of the store magazine and uses the position to help the department get a bonus.

A flawed entry, "Front Page Story" establishes some good situations but then fails to capitalize on them by going off into unrelated realms. The basic premise, that Humphries would be made editor of the store's newsletter, is good, but unfortunately, an issue is never produced. Instead, the episode ends with a rather convoluted beauty contest, which gives John Inman another opportunity to appear in drag. One can imagine several possibilities that would have been fresher and closer to the introduced plot. This is not to say that the beauty contest does not supply its share of laughs, which it does, but only that they have little to do with what has preceded them.

There is a good scene as the staff learns that Humphries is planning to fill his magazine with gossip — much of it about them. Unfortunately, this is all introduced too early and removes the possibility of this material being used for a logical ending. The beauty contest, which does provide the finale, is introduced as a way to obtain a long-promised bonus, which had never materialized. Rather than receiving their bonus, purported to be £600, the staff hopes to split the prize money from the beauty contest. This is farfetched, that a store that was too cheap to pay a £600 bonus to its employees and is too cheap to pay the editor of its newsletter would suddenly agree to a huge prize for a contest. The credibility strains further as the staff thinks that Miss Brahms is a shoe-in for the prize (nothing against the lovely Wendy Richards, but she is no competition for the models from the other departments). Surprisingly, the high point of all this is not John Inman's last-minute appearance in drag as "Miss Do-It-Yourself," but Mollie Sugden's entry in the contest dressed in a corset.

Episode 4: "Sit Out" ★★★

Air date: April 30, 1981. Cast: Mrs. Slocombe (Mollie Sugden); Mr.

Humphries (John Inman); Capt. Peacock (Frank Thornton); Miss Brahms (Wendy Richard); Mr. Rumbold (Nicholas Smith); Mr. Harman (Arthur English); Mr. Spooner (Mike Berry); Mr. Grossman (Milo Sperber); Old Mr. Grace (Kenneth Waller); Nurse (Vivienne Johnson); Secretary (Debbie Linden); Virginia Edwards (Louise Burton); Fireman (Martin Cochrane)

The staff barricades itself on the store roof when Mr. Grace threatens a 10 percent wage cut and a move to the bargain basement.

A better-than-average script coupled with a fairly cohesive plot help to make "Sit Out" one of the better offerings of the eighth season. While filled with many one-liners, the script has the advantage of keeping the gags, most of them snappy comebacks, from straying too far from the story line. This also helps to avoid the proceedings spinning off into any wild and farfetched tangents or veering off into unforeseen or implausible resolutions. While there are some outlandish ploys — Mr. Humphries dangling outside Mr. Grace's office window from the end of a rope, for instance — they remain within the realm of farcical possibility.

The story of "Sit Out" centers on the department's lack of sales due to a dearth of customers. Clients are so scarce that the staff is left to stand around doing the crossword puzzles. In response to this, Rumbold tries to instruct his veteran corps of clerks in sales techniques by playing a customer. In an amusing turn, Peacock provides his own demonstration by portraying a particularly obstreperous buyer. Mr. Grace interrupts the exercise to announce his own measures: the pay cut and demotion to a lower floor. After mulling it over, Peacock leads a revolt to the rooftop the following morning.

The rooftop sequence provides its share of amusing gags, most of them physical in nature. The best of these involve the staff's attempts to attract the attention of the crowds below to its grievances. There are also some good appearances by Harman (up a ventilator shaft) and Rumbold (atop the elevator). Eventually, the strikers win their case, but only because the bargain basement catches fire, an incident that necessitates their evacuation from the roof by the fire brigade (not surprisingly, Mr. Humphries is a long-lost friend of the fireman, who carries him down first).

EPISODE 5: "HEIR APPARENT" ★★½

Air date: May 7, 1981. Cast: Mrs. Slocombe (Mollie Sugden); Mr. Humphries (John Inman); Capt. Peacock (Frank Thornton); Miss Brahms (Wendy Richard); Mr. Rumbold (Nicholas Smith); Mr. Harman (Arthur English); Mr. Spooner (Mike Berry); Mr. Grossman (Milo Sperber); Old Mr. Grace (Kenneth Waller); Nurse (Vivienne Johnson); Secretary (Debbie Linden); and a guest appearance by John Inman

Mr. Humphries is groomed for success when Old Mr. Grace thinks he is his illegitimate father.

A good premise with an inconsistent delivery marks "Heir Apparent." The episode is yet another offering in the familiar mold established by

"Forward Mr. Grainger" and "Mrs. Slocombe — Senior Person," wherein a member of the floor staff suddenly finds him- or herself in a position above former colleagues. Although at least here the ploy is presented with an original twist, there are some weaknesses. The main problem is that, as in those earlier entries, the comrades left behind bristle at the sudden elevation of one of their own. Whereas Mr. Grainger and Mrs. Slocombe gave the others reason for animosity by their churlish behavior, Mr. Humphries does not in "Heir Apparent," making the staff's reaction more than a little puzzling. Also, Mr. Grace freely confesses that he is Humphries' father, then later expresses great relief when his revelation proves unwarranted.

The entire affair begins when Mr. Grace recognizes a woman in a photograph of chorus girls belonging to Mr. Humphries. He admits that he got one of the girls, named Annie, into the family way, then abandoned her, and he assumes that Mr. Humphries is the product of that liaison. This is a rather shaky beginning, given that Mr. Humphries is supposed to be carrying around a picture of a group of chorines without even knowing which one is his mother (one of the other girls was Grace's mistress).

The best moments in the program come as Mr. Humphries' mother arrives to help sort out the matter. With John Inman playing his own mother, the laughs flow a little more freely. There are especially good exchanges between Mrs. Humphries and Peacock (after a few moments of talking with the floorwalker, she happily concludes he really isn't a "toffee-nosed git") and later between Mrs. Humphries and Mr. Grace. As for the possibility that the store owner is her son's father, Mrs. Humphries dispels this categorically by establishing that he was never a milkman who got kicked by his horse, a stray parachutist, or a man who grabbed a quickie in a tunnel-of-love blackout!

EPISODE 6: "CLOSED CIRCUIT" ★★★½

Air date: May 14, 1981. Cast: Mrs. Slocombe (Mollie Sugden); Mr. Humphries (John Inman); Capt. Peacock (Frank Thornton); Miss Brahms (Wendy Richard); Mr. Rumbold (Nicholas Smith); Mr. Harman (Arthur English); Mr. Spooner (Mike Berry); Mr. Klein (Benny Lee); Old Mr. Grace (Kenneth Waller); Nurse (Vivienne Johnson); Secretary (Debbie Linden); Mr. Fortescue (Gordon Kaye); Headwaiter (Nicholas McArdle); 2nd Waiter (John D. Collins); Lord Hirly (John Oxley); Rabbi (Marty Swift); Lady Customer (Margaret Clifton)

When Miss Brahms appears in a promotional video for the store, she attracts the attentions of a handsome lord.

One of the better shows from the later series, "Closed Circuit" begins by looking like yet another retread of previously explored situations but then surprises by charting new territory. The staff is again called upon to create an advertisement ("It Pays to Advertise"); this time, however, there are a number of new twists. After having seen Mr. Humphries' frustrated director routine on several occasions, here the bit is freshened up by the inclusion of Gorden Kaye (*'Allo, 'Allo*) as his friend and professional video producer, Mr. Fortescue. Fortescue is even more highly strung than Mr. Humphries and forces his friend to act as a go-between when unkind criticism must be delivered to the staff. This routine manages to add some amusement to familiar ground. Mrs. Slocombe also supplies some laughs as she is forced to use a skin-tightening fluid in order to make her look younger on the video. Perhaps cowriter David Croft was thinking of a similar bit in his *Dad's Army* episode "Keep Young and Beautiful," in which members of the platoon act similarly.

The unsuitability of Mrs. Slocombe's performance in the video opens the door for Miss Brahms to be in the advertisement. Unfortunately, her common, squeaky voice makes it necessary for Mr. Grace's nurse to provide the audio from behind the counter while Miss Brahms mouths the words. The video is a success, especially Miss Brahms's contribution, which captivates Lord Hirly. Hirly arranges a date at an expensive restaurant with Miss Brahms, her parents, and an influential friend. In order to support the façade that Miss Brahms is not common, Peacock and Slocombe agree to play her upper-class parents, while Humphries arrives masquerading as the influential family friend — a bishop, no less.

The restaurant scene is quite a lot of fun and novel, since after eight seasons of shows the staff finally manages to get outside the store (not counting the film version).

This scene contains more than a few corny gibes, most based on the premise of commoners trying to play above their stations, but they are delivered with enough enthusiasm to rise above the groan. At one point, the waiter asks Mrs. Slocombe if she would like a drink, then congenially adds, "a nice aperitif..." Mrs. Slocombe flashes her incisors and adds, "And they're my own, too!"

The episode marks, but not overtly, the arrival of Benny Lee as Mr. Klein, substituting for Milo Sperber's Mr. Grossman, who left midseason to pursue other opportunities. No explanation is given nor is one really needed for this character, who is becoming more and more superfluous.

Episode 7: "The Erotic Dreams of Mrs. Slocombe" ★½

Air date: May 21, 1981. Cast: Mr. Humphries (John Inman); Mrs. Slocombe (Mollie Sugden); Capt. Peacock (Frank Thornton); Miss Brahms (Wendy Richard); Mr. Rumbold (Nicholas Smith); Mr. Harman (Arthur English); Mr. Spooner (Mike Berry); Mr. Klein (Benny Lee); Old Mr. Grace (Kenneth Waller); Young Mr. Grace (Harold Bennett); Nurse (Vivienne Johnson); Secretary (Louise Burton); Woman Customer (Brenda Cowling); Old Man (Jack Haig)

Mrs. Slocombe's unrequited love for Mr. Humphries drives her to the brink of alcoholism.

A very disappointing entry, "The Erotic Dreams of Mrs. Slocombe" suffers from a nasty case of schizophrenia. The show's first 20 minutes examine a rather serious subject — quite a rarity for this series — while the final third of the program brushes the entire premise aside without any resolution. The viewer is left wondering if the writers didn't paint themselves into a corner by building up a situation that they could not neatly resolve in the half-hour allotted to their opus.

The episode's basic idea — that Mrs. Slocombe is being driven half-mad by erotic dreams about Mr. Humphries — is believable in the broad comic parameters of the series. After all, Mrs. Slocombe has in the past displayed more than a passing romantic interest in the delicate men's wear clerk. The problem arises when the script calls for Mrs. Slocombe to turn to the heavy consumption of alcohol when her advances are not reciprocated. This element of the plot is escalated to near-crisis proportions with the store management getting involved and at least one coworker (Mr. Klein) fretting over the health of Mrs. Slocombe. The suggestion is advanced that Mr. Humphries needs to become the pursuer in order to cool Slocombe's ardor, and a staff visit to the ballet is seen as the perfect venue for the deed. Instead of delivering some semblance of an ending to resolve the story, however, the ballet sequence is a shambles. Poor Mollie Sugden's character is given little to do aside from passing out drunk from candy cordials, leaving John Inman's Humphries to uncharacteristically end the proceedings by physically molesting Miss Brahms! Ultimately nothing is settled as the final scene fizzles out in hurried confusion.

Sharp-eyed fans of *Dad's Army* may recognize the woman customer in this episode as Brenda Cowling, who played Mrs. Prentice in that series' "All Is Safely Gathered In."

EPISODE 8: "ROOTS?" ★★★½

Air date: December 24, 1981. Cast: Mr. Humphries (John Inman); Mrs. Slocombe (Mollie Sugden); Capt. Peacock (Frank Thornton); Miss Brahms (Wendy Richard); Mr. Rumbold (Nicholas Smith); Mr. Harman (Arthur English); Mr. Spooner (Mike Berry); Mr. Klein (Benny Lee); Old Mr. Grace (Kenneth Waller); Young Mr. Grace (Harold Bennett); Nurse (Vivienne Johnson); Secretary (Louise Burton)

The staff tries to find out Mr. Grace's lineage in order to properly salute him on the occasion of his ninetieth birthday.

As with the previous series, the eighth season of *Are You Being Served?* ends with another holiday episode filmed earlier in the year but broadcast around Christmas. Like "The Punch and Judy Affair," "Roots?" has nothing to do with the Yuletide but affords the cast extra opportunities to provide some light entertainment. Here, with a logical reason for doing so firmly grounded in the plot, the musical numbers supply a special charm without having to battle upstream against the story. As such, this is one of the better entries of the series that contain musical numbers. As with "The Punch and Judy Affair," however, one is left with the suspicion that American audiences are not treated to the same version of "Roots?" as was originally broadcast by the BBC. This is more evident in that earlier offering, with its jarring ending. Although "Roots?" ends rather smoothly, *Are You Being Served? The Inside Story* reports that the episode ends with a minstrel number, not the Somerset song that signals the finale of the American broadcast version. This would not be surprising since Christmas episodes of BBC programs often extended past the usual 30-minute running time.

Essentially, "Roots?" (or at least the American version) is composed of three musical numbers, each reflecting the staff's current information concerning Mr. Grace's ancestry. The first two are only done in rehearsal, while the final one is performed for the birthday boy at his fete. Originally, the prevailing belief was that the Graces come from Wales, which led the staff to rehearse "We'll Keep a Welcome in the Hillside" while dressed as coal miners. This amusing routine, again punctuated by Nicholas Smith's work on the keyboards, is climaxed as Mr. Humphries hits a frantic high note, encouraged by Mr. Spooner accidentally putting his pick in his coworker's groin.

After discovering that that Graces go back further — to Scotland — the crew next practices a colorful Scottish dance in full Highland regalia. Once again, John Inman provides the comic highlight as he dances barefoot around a pair of crossed swords, in routines of increasing difficulty. The climax comes as he is about to perform a split over the swords but is caught in midair at the last moment by Peacock and Rumbold. The final number involves the cast dressed as country yokels, complete with red curly beards and straw hats, singing "I Was Born in Somerset."

Harold Bennett is back briefly in the final scene as Young Mr. Grace, marking his final appearance in the series. Nicholas Smith also appears as his own brother, with a full head of bright red hair. This Rumbold sibling is the genealogist whose research into the Grace lineage makes it necessary to keep changing the tribute number. Apparently, competency in one's work is not a hallmark of any of the Rumbold family.

Series Nine 1983

Episode 1: "The Sweet Smell of Success" ★★½

Air date: April 22, 1983. Cast: Mr. Humphries (John Inman); Mrs. Slocombe (Mollie Sugden); Capt. Peacock (Frank Thornton); Miss Brahms (Wendy Richard); Mr. Rumbold (Nicholas Smith); Mr. Harman (Arthur English); Mr. Spooner (Mike Berry); Miss Belfridge (Candy Davis); Canteen Manageress (Doremy Vernon); Mrs. Peacock (Diana King); Perfume Customer (Michael Sharvell Martin); Tie Customer (Rex Robinson)

Mrs. Slocombe concocts a perfume purported to attract the opposite sex.

The show's ninth season begins with this entry, which although it holds out great promise in parts, fails to fully deliver on many potentially funny situations. Perhaps the problem lies in the fact that there are just too many bits for the constraints of the time period, and rather than cut any, Jeremy Lloyd (scripting this episode alone) decided to sacrifice continuity rather than possible laughs.

The most glaring example of this comes during a scene in which Peacock is about to be discovered by his wife alone in Rumbold's office with the comely Miss Belfridge. The pair had been bottling Mrs. Slocombe's new perfume when the scent accidentally got spilled over them. Rather than try and logically explain the situation — what self-respecting sitcom comedian would? — frantic action ensues in an attempt to cover up the innocent tryst. With the help of Humphries and Spooner, Miss Belfridge is secreted away in the closet, with Peacock relegated to hiding out the window on a window cleaner's scaffold sans trousers. Very funny and well played to this point, it fails to deliver in the final result, with Peacock emerging later with a black eye delivered by his spouse off-screen.

In addition, the premise regarding Mrs. Slocombe's odoriferous concoction is amusing, but one, unfortunately, that is not introduced until one-third of the way into the episode. The first third features some rather mechanical gags with Mr. Harman, which fail to score, drifting along as they are without an introduced plot to give them substance. The notion of perfume, of course, is nothing new to *Are You Being Served?*

Stories centered on scents were featured in series one ("His and Hers") and six ("A Bliss Girl"). Ironically, while the staff is trying to come up with a name for Mrs. Slocombe's brew, Miss Brahms suggests His and Hers, apparently no one (including the author) can recall the earlier use of the name.

This episode also marks the first appearance of Candy Davis as Miss Belfridge, Rumbold's new secretary. Miss Davis, like Penny Irving before her, was a former Page Three Girl, one of the beauties regularly featured on the third page of Britain's tabloids. Several references are made to this in the script, including one that shows Miss Belfridge performing a similar function in Grace Brothers' own executive newsletter.

EPISODE 2: "CONDUCT UNBECOMING" ★★★

Air date: April 29, 1983. Cast: Mrs. Slocombe (Mollie Sugden); Mr. Humphries (John Inman); Capt. Peacock (Frank Thornton); Miss Brahms (Wendy Richard); Mr. Rumbold (Nicholas Smith); Mr. Harman (Arthur English); Mr. Spooner (Mike Berry); Miss Belfridge (Candy Davis); Tights Customer (Frances Bennett); Woman with Pram (Gilda Perry); Mr. Wagstaff (Tony Sympson)

Mr. Humphries is forced to resign when he is accused of stealing from the till.

Long on plot, with an absence of the more outlandish situations and gimmicks that often hamper the series, "Conduct Unbecoming" is an enjoyable series entry. The episode gives John Inman a chance to play some new situations, with which he does an admirable job within his comic range.

"Conduct Unbecoming" features a rather intricate story line (especially for *Are You Being Served?*), containing more than a few twists and turns. Not only have Croft and Lloyd created an interesting set of circumstances involving some missing money, but also they carefully lay the groundwork for the episode by providing the staff with a number of adversarial situations. The episode opens with both Peacock and Humphries being late. Later, this comes into play when Humphries is summoned before a review board in connection with the missing cash.

The only glaring weakness of the episode is the mock trial scene. Although it has its amusing moments, this scene quickly lapses into realms of nonsense incompatible with the more realistic situations that have preceded it.

Tony Sympson, seen here as Mr. Wagstaff, previously appeared as Claude in "50 Years On" and Mr. Webster in "The Junior." The Woman with the Pram, who delivers Paddington Bear to Mr. Humphries, is played by Gilda Perry, the wife of producer David Croft's *Dad's Army* collaborator, Jimmy Perry.

EPISODE 3: "MEMORIES ARE MADE OF THIS" ★★

Air date: May 6, 1983. Cast: Mrs. Slocombe (Mollie Sugden); Mr. Humphries (John Inman); Capt. Peacock (Frank Thornton); Miss Brahms (Wendy Richard); Mr. Rumbold (Nicholas Smith); Mr. Harman (Arthur English); Mr. Spooner (Mike Berry); Miss Belfridge (Candy Davis); Canteen Manageress (Doremy Vernon); Mr. Walpole (Jess Conrad); Fisherman (Ballard Berkeley)

Mrs. Slocombe reverts to childhood after being struck in the head with a golf ball.

Better suspend all last vestiges of disbelief to fully enjoy this implausible entry. "Memories Are Made of This," scripted by Jeremy Lloyd without David Croft, gives Mollie Sugden ample opportunities to romp around like a little girl, and while this spectacle is often good for a few laughs, they are often of the frightening kind.

Mrs. Slocombe's reversion to childhood occurs when she is accidentally hit by a golf ball launched from a sporting goods display. That sporting goods has been moved, due to staff shortages, to share space with the clothing departments is in itself rather farfetched. Wouldn't it have been easier to move employees rather than entire departments? It just seems a rather circuitous route to knock Sugden on the noggin — almost as if the original destination of the plot had been elsewhere. Perhaps another episode in the vein of "A Change Is as Good as a Rest" had been envisioned.

Prior to the second childhood theme, the episode is taken up with Peacock's bluster over having to share the floor with Mr. Walpole, the handsome golf pro. The rest of the episode is turned over to Sugden's cavorting, with little opportunity (save for John Inman as the only one to whom Slocombe responds) for the rest of the cast to provide much in the way of comedy.

Ballard Berkeley, the Major from *Fawlty Towers*, makes a brief appearance as a sports fisherman buying some flies from Mr. Humphries.

Episode 4: "Calling All Customers" ★★

Air date: May 13, 1983. Cast: Mrs. Slocombe (Mollie Sugden); Mr. Humphries (John Inman); Capt. Peacock (Frank Thornton); Miss Brahms (Wendy Richard); Mr. Rumbold (Nicholas Smith); Mr. Harman (Arthur English); Mr. Spooner (Mike Berry); Miss Belfridge (Candy Davis); Lorry Drivers (Nosher Powell, Ron Tarr); C. B. Voices (Vicki Michelle, Robbie Coltrane)

The staff airs a drama over the citizens' band radio in order to advertise the store.

One day the men's and ladies' departments of Grace Brothers is going to demand that Mr. Grace hire an advertising agency and stop relying on them for ad campaigns. Unfortunately, that day did not come soon enough and so, in "Calling All Customers," we are once again subjected to this well-worn ploy of the writer (Jeremy Lloyd scripted this episode without the help of David Croft), which is probably only second in use to the notion that the staff spend the night in the store. This is not to say that "Calling All Customers" does not have its share of laughs or that the author hasn't given the story a few new wrinkles; it's just that it's all been done before.

Once again, the staff meets for a think tank session to devise a way to conjure up business. Once again, the store management offers to pay for the production of a commercial (this time in a C. B. radio serial). Once again, Mr. Humphries gets to play his high-strung director bit as the rest of the staff drives him to frustration by its unprofessional demeanor. Hasn't this been done enough? (Apparently not. We'll see this premise for one final curtain call in the tenth season's "The Night Club.")

There are a few bright spots. Mike Berry continues to grow nicely into the part of Bert Spooner, providing his share of the comedy in an ensemble cast that is increasingly spotlighting Mollie Sugden and John Inman. In addition, the scene in which each member of the staff presents a suggestion for a radio serial is quite good. Spooner's idea for a sci-fi drama in which the government is controlled by a giant jelly is intriguing, while Captain Peacock's "Peacock of Arabia," taken almost verbatim from T. E. Lawrence, also provides some amusement. The scene in which the staff plays on the CB radio is also humorous as Spooner almost gets himself arrested while chatting up a policewoman, while Slocombe causes a lorry driver to have an accident by relating tales of her prize-winning cat. The male voice heard over the radio is none other than Robbie Coltrane, who became well known in such vehicles as the television show *Cracker* and the film *Nuns on the Run*.

Episode 5: "Monkey Business" ★★★½

Air date: May 20, 1983. Cast: Mr. Humphries (John Inman); Mrs. Slocombe (Mollie Sugden); Capt. Peacock (Frank Thornton); Miss Brahms (Wendy Richard); Mr. Rumbold (Nicholas Smith); Mr. Harman (Arthur English); Mr. Spooner (Mike Berry); Miss Belfridge (Candy Davis); Mr. Kagato (Eifa Kusuhara); Prime Minister's Secretary (John D. Collins); Fur Coat Customer (John Biggersby); His Secretary (Lisa Anselmi); Mr. Yamoto (Kristopher Kum); Monkey (Rusty Goffe); Voice of Mrs. Thatcher (Jan Ravens)

The staff drops its protest over wages to help save Grace Brothers from a takeover bid by the Japanese.

The second consecutive episode scripted solely by Jeremy Lloyd, "Monkey Business" is easily the best entry in the show's ninth season. Although part of this multiplotted offering repeats premises of an earlier show (season five's "Takeover"), none of the details are repeated. In addition, most of the situations are entirely fresh, helping to give "Monkey Business" a feel more akin to the earlier seasons.

There are at least three plots vying for attention in the episode's 30-minute running time. The first involves the staff's disappointment at not receiving a promised pay raise and the uprising that results. This plot, while good for a few laughs, is quickly jettisoned when it is learned that the store is about to be taken over by a Japanese concern. These story lines are bridged by the third situation: an escaped monkey loose in the store.

In a refreshing twist, the staff attempts to avert the takeover by appealing directly to the prime minister (then Margaret Thatcher). Dressed in their finest, the contingent makes the visit to Downing Street, where they are ushered into the cabinet room. This scene offers a nice blend of gags, including Captain Peacock's long-winded musing about the historical importance of the room juxtaposed against Miss Brahms's innocently delivered double entendres. Mrs. Slocombe even gets to speak on the telephone to Ronald Reagan. Capping the scene is the late arrival of Mr. Humphries, who it seems, has been having a private chat with the prime minister herself (he was helping her select a suitable hat for the House of Commons).

The situations are resolved when the Japanese make an inspection of the store, only to find the missing primate ensconced in Rumbold's office. The monkey's bald head and jug ears help facilitate their mistaken notion that he is the middle manager (although we are not told how they know Rumbold is bald with prominent ears) and a rather rude one at that.

"Monkey Business" was almost not aired, due to a general election being called after the show was filmed. The BBC feared the political nature of the episode might influence the election.

EPISODE 6: "LOST AND FOUND" ★★★

Air date: May 27, 1983. Cast: Mr. Humphries (John Inman); Mrs. Slocombe (Mollie Sugden); Capt. Peacock (Frank Thornton); Miss Brahms (Wendy Richard); Mr. Rumbold (Nicholas Smith); Mr. Harman (Arthur English); Mr. Spooner (Mike Berry); Miss Belfridge (Candy Davis); Canteen Manageress (Doremy Vernon); Mr. Winston (Peter Cleall); Customer (Norman Mitchell)

When Mrs. Slocombe's beloved cat goes missing, she turns to Mr. Humphries for comfort.

A pleasant blend of plot and gags, although neither is overwhelmingly inspired. The story is somewhat derivative from earlier episodes that centered on Mrs. Slocombe's pet problems ("Mrs. Slocombe Expects") and her ardor for the fey Mr. Humphries ("The Apartment"). Still, there are enough new twists to keep the punch lines, especially those from the mouth of Mr. Spooner, fresh and entertaining.

The most interesting moments come as Mr. Humphries tries to present Mrs. Slocombe with a new cat to replace her Tiddles. Instead of getting a new cat, Slocombe believes she is receiving a marriage proposal and quickly agrees. Although not thrilled with the prospect of marriage (he faints on the initial realization), Mr. Humphries valiantly soldiers on until Tiddles is found with a litter of six new kittens. This new family responsibility leads Mrs. Slocombe to postpone nuptial plans indefinitely.

Series Ten 1985

EPISODE 1: "GOODBYE MRS. SLOCOMBE" ★★★½

Air date: February 18, 1985. Cast: Mr. Humphries (John Inman); Mrs. Slocombe (Mollie Sugden); Capt. Peacock (Frank Thornton); Miss Brahms (Wendy Richard); Mr. Rumbold (Nicholas Smith); Mr. Harman (Arthur English); Mr. Spooner (Mike Berry); Miss Belfridge (Candy Davis); Canteen Manageress (Doremy Vernon); Miss Featherstone (Joanna Dunham); Customer (Elizabeth Stewart)

Mrs. Slocombe is forced into retirement due to her age and joins the maintenance staff, while the staff schemes to get her reinstated.

Broad comedy in the style that *Are You Being Served?* does best highlights the beginning of the long-running series' final season. Jeremy Lloyd, writing alone, provides an amusing script affording plenty of opportunities for the cast but especially for the two stars, Sugden and Inman. Mollie Sugden is marvelous as forced retirement deflates Slocombe from senior salesperson to charwoman (actually, her character is more likable in the lowly position). As a general maintenance person, Slocombe has a field day, especially when it affords her excuses to lather up Rumbold's bald pate while washing his windows.

Inman has another turn in drag, as Humphries carries out the staff's plot to sabotage Mrs. Slocombe's replacement, Miss Featherstone, by portraying an obstreperous customer. While fun, this scene doesn't really have the impact it might have delivered, since Humphries' woman never provides sufficient motivation to make Featherstone lose her temper.

There are two script inconsistencies, both of which are perpetrated by Rumbold. In the first, the manager asks Peacock to inform Slocombe of her forced retirement, insisting tact isn't his forte. In the previous episode, "Lost and Found," Rumbold insisted that he break bad news to Mrs. Slocombe, arguing exactly the opposite. Later, Rumbold sits down to lunch with the staff on the excuse that the executive dining room is full. Apparently, he forgot that the private dining room was ripped out in "Up Captain Peacock."

Episode 2: "Grounds for Divorce" ★★★

Air date: February 25, 1985. Cast: Mr. Humphries (John Inman); Mrs. Slocombe (Mollie Sugden); Capt. Peacock (Frank Thornton); Miss Brahms (Wendy Richard); Mr. Rumbold (Nicholas Smith); Mr. Harman (Arthur English); Mr. Spooner (Mike Berry); Miss Belfridge (Candy Davis); Miss Bagnold (Maggie Henderson); Mrs. Peacock (Diana Lambert); Glasses Customer (Philip Kendall)

When Miss Bagnold of the accounts department falls madly in love with Captain Peacock, the floorwalker is given an ultimatum by his wife.

A strong entry scripted by Jeremy Lloyd, "Grounds for Divorce" manages to combine a strong, interesting plot with good comedy interjected throughout the episode. Not surprisingly, this works as well as it does since the plot is firmly grounded in the more serious character of Captain Peacock. The ample comedy is supplied by the supporting cast with particularly good bits delivered by John Inman as Mr. Humphries. This marks a return to what John Inman's character does best — support. When called upon to carry a plot, Humphries often falters since his role is not well enough grounded in reality. He does shine, however, in support, without giving up the claim to the starring status that he was afforded in the later seasons.

The plot is a bit thin in logic, particularly when Peacock continually bemoans the fact that his wife has told him that he must decide between staying married to her and going off with Miss Bagnold. At the same time, the character continually complains that his spouse refuses to grant him a divorce.

Still, this is *Are You Being Served?* not *Hamlet*, and this contradiction should be overlooked in the general scheme of things.

Even though he is called upon to drive the plot, Frank Thornton gets plenty of opportunity to engage in his own comedic hijinx. Especially amusing are his repeated romantic entanglements with his inamorata in accounts. Later, in an attempt to cool Miss Bagnold's ardor, the staff arranges for her to catch Peacock and Slocombe in the throes of passion, resulting in a funny practice session between the two store veterans.

Mrs. Peacock, previously played by Diana King, is played by Diana Lambert.

EPISODE 3: "THE HOLD UP" ½

Air date: March 4, 1985. Cast: Mrs. Slocombe (Mollie Sugden); Mr. Humphries (John Inman); Capt. Peacock (Frank Thornton); Miss Brahms (Wendy Richard); Mr. Rumbold (Nicholas Smith); Mr. Harman (Arthur English); Mr. Spooner (Mike Berry); Miss Belfridge (Candy Davis); Burglars (Michael Attwell, Paul Humpoletz); Policeman (Ian Collier)

An evening of stock taking is interrupted by a pair of safecrackers.

Despite attempting an entirely new plot idea, unfortunately "The Hold Up" represents the nadir of *Are You Being Served?* Another episode scripted by Jeremy Lloyd without the assistance of David Croft, "The Hold Up" was conceived as a vehicle for Arthur English to play the spiv role in which he had distinguished himself on the stage. While this is a good idea, it fails with, ironically, English's character being overpowered by the campy performances of John Inman and Mollie Sugden. The starring pair, although regularly called upon to be over the top in their comedy, are so silly here that the slightest shred of believability in the situation is destroyed in the process. With the staff supposedly in a dangerous position, this element is needed to help the premise work. Consequently, half the cast is reacting to the situation as if it were a matter of life or death, while the others are contradicting their colleagues by turning in the silliest turns of their tenure at Grace Brothers. One can sympathize deeply with Nicholas Smith's character, whose reaction to the entire affair is annoyance at having been awakened from a sound sleep to witness such nonsense.

One interesting note: one of the burglars, Michael Attwell, went on to play Wendy Richard's brother in the continuing drama *EastEnders*.

EPISODE 4: "GAMBLING FEVER" ★★½

Air date: March 11, 1985. Cast: Mrs. Slocombe (Mollie Sugden); Mr. Humphries (John Inman); Capt. Peacock (Frank Thornton); Miss Brahms (Wendy Richard); Mr. Rumbold (Nicholas Smith); Mr. Harman (Arthur English); Mr. Spooner (Mike Berry); Miss Belfridge (Candy Davis); Canteen Manageress (Doremy Vernon); Hat Customer (Harriet Reynolds); Seymour (Keith Hodiak)

The staff gambles its bonuses on a horse race.

An interesting, although not particularly funny offering, "Gambling Fever" is highlighted by Frank Thornton's strong performance. Although we have learned many details of Captain Peacock's past—primarily his dubious service record—here we find that the floorwalker is a recovering compulsive gambler. Naturally, his affliction is played purely for laughs here and even spreads to his coworkers as all of the staff members dream of parlaying their annual bonuses into small fortunes by playing the ponies.

Thrown into this fairly strong situation is a repeat contrivance regarding the installation of a modern store security system. Of course, the in-joke is that this system—consisting mainly of secret TV cameras—was previously installed in the store 11 years earlier in an episode from series two. In fact the name of the system, Big Brother, was the title of that earlier episode. Again, writer Jeremy Lloyd trots out the gags of watching what various members of the staff are doing when caught by the hidden cameras. The funniest of these jokes involves Harman, Peacock, and Slocombe observing Rumbold polishing his bald pate in the privacy of his office (it never is explained why a security camera would be installed in a middle manager's office).

The cameras and the gambling plot line are brought together for the episode's climax in which John Inman as Humphries is called upon to mime the call of the big race from another floor while the rest of the staff watches on the monitor. The motivation for this sequence is rather contrived, and ultimately the bit is only sporadically amusing (the best bit comes as Mr. Humphries drops his trousers to indicate "they're off!").

Kudos also go to Arthur English, who effectively shows off his spiv talents as he touts the races, places the bets, and even acts as a pawnbroker when needed. Ironically, the previous episode, "The Hold-Up," had been designed to showcase English's abilities in this area but fails to do so as well as this episode.

Episode 5: "The Night Club" ★★★½

Air date: March 18, 1985. Cast: Mr. Humphries (John Inman); Mrs. Slocombe (Mollie Sugden); Capt. Peacock (Frank Thornton); Miss Brahms (Wendy Richard); Mr. Rumbold (Nicholas Smith); Mr. Harman (Arthur English); Mr. Spooner (Mike Berry); Miss Belfridge (Candy Davis); Canteen Manageress (Doremy Vernon); Seymour (Keith Hodiak); Cinema Patrons (Ron Gatenby, Ronnie Brody)

When Mr. Grace allows the staff to use the store for an after-hours nightclub, the employees collaborate on a cinema advertisement.

It is indicative of just how derivative *Are You Being Served?* had become by this final series when one considers an episode like "The Night Club." Nevertheless, this offering manages to remain fresh and interesting without excessive padding despite the fact that one can trace plot elements back to at least three earlier shows ("It Pays to Advertise," "The Club," and "Calling All Customers"). Its success is testimony to the efforts of Jeremy Lloyd, who took what could have easily been a formula offering and put fresh twists and gags into the mix.

"The Night Club" is essentially a three-act show, with the first two parts covering the most familiar territory. The opening again presents a staff meeting think tank session, although this remains entertaining thanks to (rather than despite) the clever use of old situations (Mrs. Slocombe with another, yet amusing, "pussy" joke and Mr. Humphries once again in drag). The second segment involves the making of the commercial and is the most routine — with Humphries playing the high strung director of the ad forced to work with trying amateurs. The final bit is the freshest and the best. With the ad complete, the staff goes off to the cinema where it will play between pictures. Circumstances conspire against a smooth premiere, however, as the audience, there to watch a French sex film, is rather unsavory. In addition, the picture is lost, forcing the theater to run the ad with only the sound. As a result, what had been a fairly sanitary advertisement for a supper club becomes highly titillating, as the unillustrated dialogue proves to be filled with spicy double entendres.

Much of the inventiveness of "The Night Club" is seen in the little inconsequential gags that help flesh out the episode. There is one that is particularly good as the staff members settle down in their seats at the cinema and take turns putting their arms around one another's shoulders with telling reactions from each other. There is also a fine throwaway gag as Mrs. Slocombe opens her make-up case while preparing for the filming of the ad, and the chest begins playing circus music.

EPISODE 6: "FRIENDS AND NEIGHBORS" ★½

Air date: March 25, 1985. Cast: Mr. Humphries (John Inman); Mrs. Slocombe (Mollie Sugden); Capt. Peacock (Frank Thornton); Miss Brahms (Wendy Richard); Mr. Rumbold (Nicholas Smith); Mr. Harman (Arthur English); Mr. Spooner (Mike Berry); Miss Belfridge (Candy Davis); Canteen Manageress (Doremy Vernon); Mrs. Rumbold (Jean Challis); Mrs. Peacock (Diana Lambert); Hat Customer (Carol Cleveland); Birthday Boy (Felipe Izquierdo)

When the staff requests a travel allowance to meet the high cost of commuting, Mr. Grace rents a trio of rooftop apartments instead.

The inspiration that helped turn recycled situations into fresh comedy in the previous episode had sudden evaporated in the writing of "Friends and Neighbors."

The ploy to have the staff stay overnight in the store (as in "Camping In," "The Apartment," and to a lesser degree "Is It Catching?") seems even more contrived than the previous incarnations of the plot.

Here, instead of making a cozy apartment out of store fixtures (as in the far superior "The Apartment"), we learn that there already were three furnished flats on top of the store. Despite a problem that logically must affect the entire store staff, only the needs of the six stars seem to be addressed by management. The result is that the coworkers soon begin sniping at one another, as the close quarters are exacerbated by the introduction of Mrs. Slocombe's cat and a pair of crying infants who Mr. Humphries is watching. Introducing the dalliances of Captain Peacock and Miss Belfridge shows some promise, but unfortunately this is not fully capitalized upon. Instead, the plot, such as it is, resolves with the rather mechanical use of a Murphy bed that folds into the wall with the pull of a cord. For some unexplained reason, poor Mike Berry is left out of the entire climactic scene, which takes place up in the apartment.

Monty Python fans will recognize Carol Cleveland, the regular female featured player of that otherwise all-male troupe.

EPISODE 7: "THE POP STAR" ★★★

Air date: April 1, 1985. Cast: Mrs. Slocombe (Mollie Sugden); Mr. Humphries (John Inman); Capt. Peacock (Frank Thornton); Miss Brahms (Wendy Richard); Mr. Rumbold (Nicholas Smith); Mr. Harman (Arthur English); Mr. Spooner (Mike Berry); Miss Belfridge (Candy Davis); Canteen Manageress (Doremy Vernon); Around London Host (Nick Ross); Seymour (Keith Hodiak); TV Director (Charles Nicklin); Director's Assistant (Suzy Aitchison); Cleaners (Mary Bradley, Joan Dainty)

Mr. Spooner leaves Grace Brothers after being signed to a recording contract.

Ten seasons of *Are You Being Served?* come to a close with this rather atypical episode. Drawing his inspiration from the real-life pop singing career of Mike Berry, scriptwriter Jeremy Lloyd fashioned the story that effectively brings an end to the Grace Brothers saga. Like the final installment of *Dad's Army*, there is a sense of closure in "The Pop Star." Despite the fact that Berry's character, Bert Spooner, was never afforded a part on a par with the show's established stars, his success as a pop star marks the end of the story, much as Corporal Jones's wedding did in *Dad's Army*. It is somewhat ironic, however, that the long-running series would end on an story focused on a character who was never spotlighted in any previous story.

The episode is largely plot driven, although there are some of the standard mechanical gags that fans had come to expect. The first of these is rather good and involves the taking of a publicity photo of Spooner and the staff for the newspapers. Using the store's antiquated equipment, Mr. Harman accidentally blows up Rumbold's office when he substitutes gunpowder for flash powder. The second gag is less inspired and not nearly as amusing. This routine involves the use of a back-up tape employed during Spooner's TV appearance, when the new pop star loses his voice. Of course, the tape has been recorded at the wrong speed, making Spooner and, more particularly, his backing singers (Slocombe, Humphries, and Brahms) mouth their parts at twice the normal speed.

The Good Life (Good Neighbors)

BBC-TV 1975–1978

There are many funnier television situation comedies than *The Good Life*. Many that employ ensemble casts more effectively. Many that explore the topic of the midlife crisis more imaginatively. Still and all, there are few shows that are as warm, comfortable, and, dare I say it, cozy as this unassuming little gem of a comedy from the team of John Esmonde and Bob Larbey. This tale of suburban self-sufficiency, which was first structured around its primary star (Richard Briers), quickly developed into a quartet effort as the cast became friends, first with each other and then with the viewers who gladly welcomed them weekly into their sitting rooms. While programs like *Steptoe and Son*, *Fawlty Towers*, or *Blackadder* may elicit more laughs, we wouldn't really like to have those characters living next door. The Goods or the Leadbetters, on the other hand, would be welcome at anytime. We feel at home around Tom and Barbara Good's wood-burning stove with this couple who are as commodious as the hand-dyed, homespun sweaters in which they are clothed. Their adventures, although somewhat radical, are still safely suburban and do not alienate middle-class sensibilities. The true charm of this series is not the laughter it generates, but the smiles. Not the comedy it engenders, but the caring for its cast. Although the show's original title, *The Good Life*, was changed for export to the United States (so it would not be confused with a short-lived 1971 Larry Hagman/Donna Mills NBC comedy), the new title, *Good Neighbors* (note the American spelling), is just as, if not more, fitting.

As previously stated, *The Good Life* emanated from the prolific pens of the writing team of John Esmonde and Bob Larbey, who together have accounted for more than 20 sitcoms, beginning in 1966 with the BBC's *Room at the Bottom*. A move to ITV in 1968 proved successful as the pair created the popular school comedy *Please, Sir!* This program not only ran for 57 installments, it also spawned a spinoff titled *The Fenn Street Gang*, which led to its own short-lived prequel, *Bowler*. Given this impressive comedy string, which accounted for more than 100 episodes, the BBC approached the team with a view toward recreating some of their ITV success for the government-run channel.

After writing several series that reflected their south London roots, the pair decided to leave the previously explored areas of youth and base this series on their present lives — particularly that of Larbey. Two years the senior partner, Larbey was reaching his 40th birthday with a degree of introspection. What does a man do with the rest of his life when he reaches 40?" was the pivotal question Larbey posed. Together the team decided to center a show on a man facing the same quandary.

Although Larbey denies that *The Good Life* was designed with Richard Briers in mind as the lead, he admits that the well-known comedy actor was mentioned early in the development of the new show. "He [Briers] was, along with me about to celebrate his fortieth birthday," Larbey noted, "and that's where the idea started."

Briers had seen steady work on British television since 1962, when at the age of 27 he starred in *Brothers in Law*, a 13-episode BBC comedy based on Henry Cecil's book of the same title. His work in *Brothers in Law* served as a springboard to the long-running *Marriage Lines*, which premiered the following year. *Marriage Lines*, subtitled "A Quizzical Look at the Early Days of Married Life," paired Briers and Prunella Scales (the future Sybil Fawlty) as George and Kate Starling. Unfortunately, for all its popularity with the public, *Marriage Lines* left Briers typecast in what the *Radio Times* called a "silly-ass TV image — the chinless, stammering simpleton."

Luckily for Briers, Tom Good, the central character of Esmonde and Larbey's script, was neither a silly ass nor a simpleton. Rather, their protagonist was more firmly based in reality than the average sitcom hero. From the outset, Tom Good is drawn as an average man whom when faced with his midlife crisis, reacts in a rather extraordinary manner. Tired of running in the rat race as a draftsman for a company that manufactures plastic toys for insertion in cereal boxes, Tom decides to go back to the land and try for complete self-sufficiency. With the support of his perky wife, Barbara, Tom decides to attempt his radical experiment from the comfort of their home in Surbiton, a suburb to the south of London.

Unlike the title character in *The Fall and Rise of Reginald Perrin*, David Nobbs's brilliantly absurd series on the same subject, Tom Good's rebellion never strayed far beyond the realms of credulity. Larbey explained to Gordon McGill in a 1975 article that he and Esmonde tried to make the situations believable. "When Briers is worried that the rain might spoil his bean crop, then you should be concerned for him," Larbey elaborated, "and not simply feel that he'll be saved in the next line by the script. You need this reality for the laughs."

True to this premise, the Goods, despite their occasional triumph, rarely advanced beyond barely eking out a living via their chosen lifestyle. In fact, the final regular series entry finds them worse off—through no fault of their own—than when they first began their experiment. Throughout it all, the Goods remain amazingly upbeat and cheerful—at times almost disturbingly so. (Dan Abramson, writing in *British Television*, remarked that compared to Tom and Barbara Good, Dick Van Dyke and Mary Tyler Moore "were something out of Tennessee Williams.")

With Richard Briers chosen for the Tom Good role, the authors and John Howard Davies, the show's producer, needed to find a suitable actress for the plucky wife of this suburban revolutionary. Rather than seek a veteran of the small screen for the part of Barbara Good, the search led to London's West End, where Felicity Kendal was appearing in Alan Ayckbourn's hit comedy *The Norman Conquests*. Kendal recalls in her autobiography, *White Cargo*, that she was first approached by Richard Briers for the part of his on-screen wife when he came backstage one evening after the show. According to Kendal, Briers casually mentioned the new series and nonchalantly asked if she would be interested in reading a few of the scripts. Briers cautioned that the show's subject was rather unconventional but had excellent writers, and at the least would probably be fun to do. Kendal was delighted.

"I had missed out on several television comedy series in the past few months," Kendal wrote years later, "and Richard Briers was already an established star. I thanked him effusively and asked him to 'please, please send me a script'—although I knew I would accept the part even if I hated the script. I needed the work and I liked Richard: I felt at ease with him from the moment I met him."

The following week, Felicity Kendal read and loved the scripts. Meanwhile, producer John Howard Davies attended *The Norman Conquests* to get a final look at his Barbara before casting. While watching Kendal's performance, Davies also noticed the actress playing Sarah, Penelope Keith, and decided she was perfect for Margo Leadbetter, the Goods' snobby neighbor. The final cast member, Paul Eddington, was also recruited from the stage.

Like *Steptoe and Son* before it, *The Good Life* was not burdened with a professional comic anchoring the cast but rather was blessed with professional actors. Larbey, like Galton and Simpson years earlier, called this factor a "huge bonus," which made the writing of the show all the easier. This ensemble of stage actors also helped the chemistry of the cast.

"From the very first day," Kendal wrote, "we slotted into a way of working together that was fun, fast and furious. We were all primarily theatre actors ... all extremely professional, ambitious and hard-working, and our dedication to the show was total."

Kendal recalled that although Briers was the star, the success of *The Good Life* was a team effort. "It was the whole show, not individual applause, that interested us — a rare situation in this business of enlarged egos."

Larbey echoed this sentiment, calling the cast "lovely" and not having "an inflated ego between [sic] them."

Penelope Keith also has fond memories of the cast, especially its lead player. "I shall always hold Richard Briers in enormous affection because he was the person I made my first situation comedy with," Keith told A. S. Berman in *British Television* magazine. "He was a marvelous lead in a company. He'd been a star of situation comedy before the three of us came along, and he was so generous I learned a lot from him."

Ironically, although she played the snooty Margo, Keith confesses that in real life she was closer to the down-to-earth character of Barbara Good. While making the series and living in London, Keith had her own garden and admits she even would have had a goat had the local ordinances allowed it. Keith also recalls creating homemade soups and chutneys for the rest of the company. Larbey, too, remembers Penny Keith's cooking, although not always fondly. At the wrap-up of one of the four series, Larbey relates that the actress made a "screaming hot Chili con Carne ... forgetting to soak the kidney beans first, and causing some rather nasty stomach aches later that night."

While the back-to-nature theme of the show may have been "preaching to the converted" to some of the cast, according to the nature-minded Penelope Keith, it did inspire the star of the series to explore gardening. Larbey relates the tale of Briers trying to grow some runner beans in his backyard. Unfortunately, according to the writer, the beans were planted too close to a tree, which they subsequently climbed, making the vegetables impossible to pick. Felicity Kendal later wrote that Briers was actually the last man in the world who would have attempted Tom Good's experiment in self-sufficiency.

Kendal confesses that she too was cast against type. While to this day her portrayal of Barbara Good makes grown men pine for a similar wife (there are actually Internet websites devoted to Kendal and her sitcom character), the truth was somewhat different. "The idea of my being devoted and a good little loving wife was a bit of a company joke," confessed Kendal in *White Cargo*. Sadly, the actress's marriage fell apart during the production of the series.

The gardens of Briers and Keith aside, once the filming began an exterior had to be found for the homes of the Goods and Leadbetters. While supposedly set in Surbiton, the neighborhood used, Northwood near Harrow in Middlesex; was on the northern outskirts of London, rather than on its southwest side. There, after contracting to use two neighboring gardens (the British term for yard), a BBC crew removed the grass and replaced it with rows of half-grown vegetables and livestock pens to approximate the Good's spread.

"For three weeks we do instant allotments," producer Davies explained to the *Radio Times* in 1976. "The problem was to keep everything alive—planting successful lettuces that would not wilt, propping up rhubarb so that it wouldn't fall down." Davies also recalls that the show's goat added to the logistical problems of the exterior shooting. Luckily, despite the uproar of having a film crew tearing up the neighborhood for nearly a month, the residents took it all in stride. "None of the locals turned a hair," remembers Davies, "they were all very British."

Of course, once filming was completed, the BBC landscaped the property into what Felicity Kendal referred to as "a showcase garden."

Kendal wrote in her memoirs about the difficulties presented by working with livestock: "The pigs never did what they were told, the chickens always squawked at the wrong moment, and the goat was a devil to milk, but we approached these minor problems with humor."

The goat must have truly been a "devil to milk," especially since, as one female viewer complained in a letter to the BBC, it was clear that the animal in question was a male. The correspondence was passed along to Kendal, who informed the woman that she would do many things for her art "but milking a billy goat was not one of them."

With each new season, the cast and crew would return to Northwood and redestruct the neighborhood. "By the last series," wrote Kendal, "the next-door neighbours had had enough and moved, but our hostess was a local star and had taken to plying us with coffee and cake on our first day back."

The Good Life premiered in April 1975 and, like many programs, took some time to become established with viewers. "It started off slowly," Bob Larbey told the author in 1997, "but quickly picked up and became enormously popular."

One of the keys to the success of the series, according to Kendal, was not only the chemistry of the four principals, but the fact that Esmonde and Larbey noticed it and built on it. The writers realized the natural affection of the cast for one another and started incorporating it in their scripts, writing for the "actors and the characters combined."

"We were all a little in love with one another," explained Kendal, "spending weekends together whenever we could. Paul [Eddington] and Dickie [Briers] together were two of the funniest men I have ever met."

Larbey also remembers, as he puts it, "the sheer amount of fun" everyone involved had in making *The Good Life*.

The popularity of the first series in the spring of 1975 paved the way for the second approximately six months later in December of the same year. This, in turn, led to a third series nine months later and the final series six months after that as the program reached "cult status," according to Kendal. Remarkably, all four series of *The Good Life* were produced in a two-year span. A final Christmas special was made for airing on Boxing Day 1977, with the cast brought together one last time in April 1978 for a Royal Command Performance before Queen Elizabeth II. According to her memoirs, Felicity Kendal says they were picked for the honor for the BBC since it was the only clean show being filmed that month. This recollection is probably not accurate, especially since the show had stopped filming a year earlier.

The week of rehearsals leading up to the Royal Command Performance was especially exciting for the cast, although there was also a lot of joking about what would happen if they forgot their lines or messed up in front of Her Majesty and being about banished to the Tower of London. The normal studio's small seats were replaced with large armchairs for the comfort of the special guests. In addition, yards of bunting were strewn about the usually drab studio, and red carpets were laid down over the regular maze of cables and wires. Fortunately, the performance went off without a hitch, and none of the actors were compelled to forfeit their lives.

Although there was popular demand for more adventures featuring the Goods and Leadbetters, Esmonde and Larbey decided four series were enough. "We had written thirty episodes by then," explained Larbey, "and the feeling of all of us was that we should get out while we were on top. Self-sufficiency ideas were getting harder to come by and we didn't want it to turn into a series which was just about two sets of neighbors."

The show had run its natural course and reached a sense of closure with the last regular episode, "Anniversary." In that installment, the Goods are faced with a setback that basically leaves them worse off materially than when they started their experiment in self-sufficiency. In addition, Jerry Leadbetter finally achieves his goal of becoming the managing director of his firm. There really was little else to say or explore. For a time after the production ceased, Paul Eddington and Penelope Keith suggested that the writers create a spinoff for their characters to be called *The Better Life*. This idea was apparently dropped as both performers went on to star in their own tremendously popular series within a matter of years (Eddington's *Yes, Minister* and Keith's *To the Manor Born*).

Now, more than two decades after its initial run, *The Good Life* is still warmly recalled by the many fans it attracted in the late 1970s. Bob Larbey admits that people still ask him if the series will ever be revived. Sadly, with the death of Paul Eddington in 1995, any reunion attempt would be tinged with melancholy. Still, with the passing of time, this warm series manages to be recalled with increasing fondness and continues to run from time to time on various PBS outlets across the United States.

In 1997 CBS/Fox (with the BBC in Great Britain) released a video containing three episodes of the show. Despite the choices being rather odd (the final entry from the first series along with "The Windbreak War" from series three and the 1977 Christmas special), the move was heartening to fans. Also encouraging was the designation on the packaging that this was "volume one," although it took another two years for subsequent tapes to be released. One can only hope that there is still enough of a cult following for this quiet, positive little sitcom to coax all the installments of this genial comedy out of the BBC archives.

THE EPISODES

By John Esmonde and Bob Larbey. Produced by John Howard Davies

Series One 1975

Episode 1: "Plough Your Own Furrow" ★★★½

Air date: April 4, 1975. Cast: Tom Good (Richard Briers); Barbara Good (Felicity Kendal); Jerry Leadbetter (Paul Eddington); Sir (Reginald Marsh); Charles (Norman Atkyns); Brian (Martin Neil)

Tom Good is celebrating his 40th birthday by taking stock of his life. He is a draftsman for JJM Ltd., where he spends his days designing molds for the plastic toys that are put in cereal boxes. He and his wife, Barbara, live in the London suburb of Surbiton, next door to Jerry and Margo Leadbetter. Jerry also works at JJM, as an executive.

Tom complains to Barbara that their lives are cluttered with things but devoid of any real quality. After a night of concerted thought, he announces to Barbara that he wants to work at life itself. Toward this end, he describes a life of self-sufficiency in the suburbs, where they will grow or make everything they can and barter for the rest. After thinking it over, Barbara agrees. The next morning, when Jerry arrives to take Tom to the office, Tom announces he has "sacked" the company, swapped his car for a rotary tiller, and plans to dig up the front yard to put in potatoes.

The Good Life begins with a solid, yet atypical episode. While first episodes are often burdened with the necessary task of introducing the characters, *The Good Life* is more concerned with introducing the philosophy of Tom Good. As with *The Fall and Rise of Reginald Perrin*, this series examines the meaning of life, or at least the deficiency of what tries to pass for meaning in modern society. The writers do a good job of presenting Tom's motivation, while still managing to introduce the main characters as warm and charming individuals, albeit ones about whom little is known.

It is noteworthy that Penelope Keith's character, Margo, doesn't appear in the first episode, except as an off-camera voice arguing with Jerry. While Margo would be a mainstay of the series as a comic foil for Tom, her presence isn't necessary to the establishment of the premise.

A charming formal portrait of the Goods and the Leadbetters. *Top:* Tom Good (Richard Briers), Barbara Good (Felicity Kendal). *Bottom:* Margo Leadbetter (Penelope Keith), Jerry Leadbetter (Paul Eddington). Copyright © BBC.

The most amusing moments in the premiere episode of *The Good Life* also give the viewer insight into Tom Good's motivation. These take place in Jerry's office as he gives Tom a friendly motivational talk on his future with the company. Although we readily understand Jerry's lecture, we can also relate to Tom's reaction. Jerry is essentially asking Tom to grow up and apply himself at the age of 40. Unfortunately, he is earnestly asking his good friend to devote his life to plastic animals that will end up in cereal boxes. Although he is accused of playing Peter Pan, Tom finds the "serious" work trivial and calls the entire practice of prizes in packages "choke-a-child week."

Tom reaches the breaking point when Sir, the company's president, arrives for a conference with Jerry. Jerry suggests that Tom sit in and builds up his friend to Sir. Tom truly tries to take the opportunity, and for a moment he impresses Sir with his knowledge of the latest project — a plastic hippopotamus. When Sir responds to Tom's earnestness, however, and launches into a monologue about thrusting into the "vanguard of world molding," Tom has difficulty suppressing a snicker. Finally, Sir confides to Tom that the planning department, after much study, has decided to follow up the hippo with a giraffe. With great solemnity, Sir puts his arm around Tom and announces that he is considering putting the "giraffe on your plate." Tom nods and excuses himself, then can be heard bursting into gales of laughter just outside the office door.

EPISODE 2: "SAY LITTLE HEN..." ★★★

Air date: April 11, 1975. Cast: Tom Good (Richard Briers); Barbara Good (Felicity Kendal); Jerry Leadbetter (Paul Eddington); Margo Leadbetter (Penelope Keith); Sir (Reginald Marsh); Sir's Wife, Felicity (Moyra Fraser)

After one week of having self-sufficient neighbors, Margo and Jerry are beginning to worry about the Goods. In the meantime, Tom and Barbara are busying themselves converting their greenhouse into a henhouse. That afternoon over drinks at the Leadbetters, Sir offers Tom his job back. Tom refuses, and the gathering degenerates into a clash of philosophies. Jerry invites the Goods to stay for dinner, but Tom boasts that he and Barbara are having a special meal produced from their own resources — one egg.

The second installment of *The Good Life* finds Tom and Barbara well on their way to self-sufficiency. Not only have they planted most of their Surbiton garden, but they have also added chickens to their list of livestock. With things progressing so well, it is a bit odd that the writers would chose to reintroduce Tom's ex-boss so soon with an offer for a job. This could have been incorporated better into the next episode when, for Barbara at least, there is at least a brief temptation to ditch the self-sufficiency scheme. The only motivation presented here for Tom rejoining the rat race is the fact that, after one day, their hens haven't produced any eggs. Rather than being seriously captivated by Sir's offer, Tom merely uses it to restate his reasons for quitting. Still, the episode is well done if not entirely consistent in plotting.

Author Bob Larbey notes that the cast and crew voted one of the chickens in this episode the best actress in the series for the way she opened her beak in terror on cue when Tom was about to shoot her. "It turned out," Larbey reports, "that she suffered from asthma and her 'timing' was nothing more than gasping for breath."

There are quite a number of enjoyable vignettes in "Say Little Hen..." including Jerry giving Tom and his goat a ride back from grazing on the town common and Tom's attempt at killing a chicken. The most notable, however, is the first real appearance of Penelope Keith in the role of Margo Leadbetter. Keith's wonderfully dry and haughty delivery is evident in her first scene. When Jerry explains that he has given Tom and his goat (which the Goods have named Margo) a ride, Margo objects. Margo asks rhetorically why the Goods can't have a dog like most neighbors. Jerry explains that dogs don't have udders. "Jerry," Margo coolly chides, "don't be obtuse."

EPISODE 3: "THE WEAKER SEX?" ★★½

Air date: April 18, 1975. Cast: Tom Good (Richard Briers); Barbara Good (Felicity Kendal); Jerry Leadbetter (Paul Eddington); Margo Leadbetter (Penelope Keith); Sam (Tony Selby); Telephone Man (Paul McDowell)

The Goods barter with Sam, the local rag and bone man, for a rusty old cast iron stove. While Barbara slaves the entire day removing the rust, Tom tries to invent something to keep the birds out of the garden. Barbara finally rebels when Tom cheerfully extols the joys of their new life. Barbara retreats to the

Leadbetters for a drink and some comfort. When Jerry and Margo start quarreling, Barbara leaves, realizing that she is better off with Tom and the rust.

A fairly slim episode but still enjoyable, "The Weaker Sex?" focuses on the issue of morale. Tom is still reveling in their new self-sufficiency, but Barbara rebels when saddled with a less-than-glamorous chore.

A bit of double entendre supplies the biggest laughs in "The Weaker Sex?" Margo, in one of her heavy-handed attempts at charity, offers Barbara an expensive dress as a gift. Barbara refuses it, but as Margo is leaving, Tom accepts the dress. Later, Margo is horrified to learn that Tom wanted the gown not for his wife but for his scarecrow. Margo protests to Tom that everyone will think her taste in clothes is only fit for scarecrows and notes that she won't sleep knowing she's being abused in his garden.

Tom agrees that if she were being abused, she would find it hard to sleep. Margo is not amused and orders Tom to take down her dress or else she'll call the police. Grinning at Margo's unintentional double entendre, Tom agrees since it seems the dress only serves to attract birds anyway.

Tony Selby has a good role as the rag-and-bone (junk) man, who actually has a villa in Spain but adopts Cockney rhyming slang to appear sufficiently colorful for his suburban customers.

EPISODE 4: "PIG'S LIB" ★★★

Air date: April 25, 1975. Cast: Tom Good (Richard Briers); Barbara Good (Felicity Kendal); Jerry Leadbetter (Paul Eddington); Margo Leadbetter (Penelope Keith); Mr. Carter (Robert Gillespie); Window Cleaner (Jonathan Lynn); Shopkeeper (Lionel Walker); Customer (John Lawrence)

When Tom and Barbara get a pair of pigs (Pinky and Perky), Margo complains to Mr. Carter, the head of the civic association. The Goods agree to get rid of the pigs if they trespass into Margo's garden. The next morning, Pinky and Perky tunnel under the fence and are taken away to be destroyed. When Margo finds out what the pigs' fate is to be, she gives the animals a second chance. Tom rushes off to save the pigs before it is too late. When Tom returns with the pigs, Barbara and Margo are jubilant. It is only after the women exit that Tom threatens to turn the pigs into sausages if they ever reveal that they are not the original Pinky and Perky.

This episode illustrates why *Good Neighbors* is such an excellent choice as the American title of *The Good Life.* For all their disagreements with each other, the Goods and the Leadbetters never become disagreeable. This should be especially refreshing for American audiences, which are used to sitcoms where the slightest conflict is an excuse for the lowest insults. Although "Pig's Lib" represents the first of many all-out battles between the neighbors, it remains civil without sacrificing comedy.

There are plenty of fun moments in "Pig's Lib," few of which are directly tied to the actual plot. The first two involve Tom and Barbara's bartering for what they need. In the opening scene, Tom trades a local magazine vendor two eggs for the latest issue of a pig-breeding magazine. Barbara's foray into swapping takes a humorous turn when she informs the window cleaner that she can no longer pay cash for his services. When she suggests another arrangement, the cleaner is at first confused. Barbara remarks that they could try the "oldest form of business in the world." Instead of bartering, however, the man thinks she is suggesting prostitution in return for clean windows. The window cleaner, marvelously portrayed by Jonathan Lynn, goes through a range of facial expressions from confusion to surprise to contemplation to eager lust and finally, to embarrassment when he realizes that Barbara is not suggesting what he thinks she has been suggesting. It is only after the chagrined workman offers to clean the windows free that Barbara realizes what he's been thinking. Fans of *Yes, Minister/Prime Minister* will notice that the window cleaner, Jonathan Lynn, is the cowriter of those other series. At this stage in his career, Lynn divided his time between acting and writing. After *Yes, Prime Minister*, Lynn moved on to direct films.

Another funny scene involves Margo and Barbara getting drunk on Tom's peapod wine (which, according to Tom, has a kick that hurts the back of one's eyes) and playing cards while waiting to see if Tom could save the pigs.

Finally, fans of animal trivia should note that Barbara calls the goat Geraldine in this episode. The goat was previously called Margo in episode two.

EPISODE 5: "THE THING IN THE CELLAR" ★★★★

Air date: May 2, 1975. Cast: Tom Good (Richard Briers); Barbara Good (Felicity Kendal); Jerry Leadbetter (Paul Eddington); Margo Leadbetter (Penelope Keith); Sports Fisherman (Ray Mort)

While Margo and Jerry worry about an impending power worker's strike and subsequent power cut, Tom has built a generator, which will convert their animals' waste into electricity. Tom and Barbara laugh at the threatened power cut and flaunt their generator to their neighbors. The generator breaks down after the Goods have stocked their freezer with fish. Tom takes the thawing bundles over to the Leadbetters only to discover that their freezer is out of commission also due to the power cut.

The first installments have seen Tom Good do a lot of talking about his ingenuity; here we get strong proof in the guise of the effluent generator. The series begins to hit its stride here after four episodes that, in varying degrees, were exposition. "The Thing in the Cellar" introduces plots beyond the quitting of jobs and the setting up of a suburban farm. With this episode, the show gets down to exploring the day-to-day living of the Goods' great experiment in self-sufficiency.

While the plot seems somewhat sparse, "The Thing in the Cellar" is a delight to watch from start to finish. After firmly establishing the characters in the first four episodes, the writing seems to have come into its own, resulting in plenty of good dialogue based on the principals' relationships. The best laughs come from seemingly casual throwaway lines, which work precisely because of the characterizations.

Barbara's first attempt at baking bread results in a loaf that is approximately three feet high. When she first sets it before Tom at lunch, he eyes it with obvious amazement, then recovers to ask his wife what she will be eating.

Jerry is housesitting for the Goods when Margo stops by. He makes minor romantic movements toward her. Margo thaws enough to respond ever so slightly to his overtures, when Jerry realizes the generator has stopped, and he must go investigate. A crestfallen Margo pouts that this will be the last time she plays "the tart" for her husband.

Episode 6: "The Pagan Rite" ★★★½

Air date: May 9, 1975. Cast: Tom Good (Richard Briers); Barbara Good (Felicity Kendal); Jerry Leadbetter (Paul Eddington); Margo Leadbetter (Penelope Keith); Sir Andrew (Reginald Marsh); Sir's Wife, Felicity (Moyra Fraser); Waiter (John Scott Martin)

Sir Andrew, Tom's former boss, asks Tom to accept a freelance assignment. Tom refuses with Barbara's backing. Tom later takes the job in order to finance a "pagan rite"—a luxury overnight stay at a hotel for Barbara and himself. Tom does the work in Jerry's study, but Margo discovers it and informs Barbara. Barbara explodes on Tom until she learns why he did it.

One of the reasons for the popularity of *The Good Life/Good Neighbors* is the genuinely warm rapport between Richard Briers and Felicity Kendal as the Goods. It may seem slightly cloying to say, but they really are a cute couple, who viewers would actually like as next-door neighbors (even with their pigs, chickens, and goats). "The Pagan Rite" is a good example of their compatibility, which manages to be loving without being overly sentimental and is always lighthearted.

There's a marvelously warm scene in which Briers and Kendal cuddle in front of the wood stove and converse about the changes in their lives since self-sufficiency. Barbara confesses that she misses the parties, and at first seems in earnest until she mentions "Liz" jetting in and "Frank" singing "My Way" while sitting on the piano. She concludes with a straight face that such were "simple times" but still fun.

Later, in the hotel's dining room, the Goods enjoy a playfully romantic time, until Barbara learns that Tom was paid three times what their spree is costing. Feeling that he is using the money to subvert their goal of self-sufficiency, Barbara erupts again and dumps Tom's dessert into his lap. Tom presents an expensive piece of jewelry to prove that he has spent the entire sum on their luxury spree. Barbara takes Tom's hands and expresses her undying love for him. He reciprocates verbally, while pushing her hands into her trifle.

Episode 7: "Back to the Wall" ★★★

Air date: May 16, 1975. Cast: Tom Good (Richard Briers); Barbara Good (Felicity Kendal); Jerry Leadbetter (Paul Eddington); Margo Leadbetter (Penelope Keith); Doctor (June Jago); Pub Crowd (Billy Milton, Pamela Manson, Frank Lester, Harry Goodier).

Tom is immobilized with a back injury on the eve of the Goods' first harvest. A storm complicates matters, giving Barbara three days to bring in the harvest before it rots in the mud. Barbara tries to rally their friends to help, but Margo and Jerry are vacationing in Africa, and the others ignore her pleas. Finally, they manage to bring in the harvest when the Leadbetters return early.

The Goods' inaugural harvest is a fitting climax to the show's first series, and although the episode contains more drama than comedy, it is still compelling viewing. "Back to the Wall" also includes Tom Good's first, albeit brief, attack of pessimism at having launched Barbara into his self-sufficiency scheme. Barbara, on the other hand, never wavers, even during 14-hour days, proving that her spirit is the backbone of their self-sufficiency success.

For the first time, we are introduced to other friends and neighbors in a trio of pub scenes. Given their reaction (or lack of reaction) to the Goods' dire circumstances, one is just as glad not to have met them before. Jerry and Margo, however, come through in the pinch and prove yet again why *Good Neighbors* is a fitting title. "Back to the Wall" is the first episode on volume one of the Stateside video of *Good Neighbors.*

With the crisis of bringing in the harvest looming, there are few opportunities for the Goods to provide much comedy. The responsibility for much of this episode's laughs falls into the capably comic hands of Penelope Keith's character. In the opening pub scene, Margo, replete in faux safari gear, enlightens the gathering on her African expertise as she and Jerry get ready to jet to Kenya. Margo explains that the animal migration will be commencing just as they arrive. Tom observes that the herds have good sense.

Later, the African vacation a disaster, the Leadbetters arrive home in time to help with the harvest. Unfortunately, Jerry has broken his foot, and Margo is Margo. As tiny Barbara struggles under 50-pound sacks of potatoes, Tom hobbles around with the use of two canes, and Jerry gets his cast stuck in the muck, Margo flitters around the garden in a designer rain outfit, picking beans one at a time. She then carries each individual bean ten feet through the mud to deposit it in the collecting box. When Tom scolds Margo's inefficiency, Barbara defends her by calling her "weak and feeble." To prove otherwise, Margo swings a sack of spuds onto her shoulders, toppling the others into the mud like dominoes in the process.

Series Two 1975–1976

EPISODE ONE: "JUST MY BILL" ★★½

Air date: December 5, 1975. Cast: Tom Good (Richard Briers); Barbara Good (Felicity Kendal); Margo Leadbetter (Penelope Keith); Jerry Leadbetter (Paul Eddington); Michelangelo Lombardi (Wolfe Morris); Ronny Boxall (Frank Gatliff); Mr. Squires (Blake Butler); Charity Lady (Ruth Kettewell)

After bringing in their harvest, the Goods look forward to earning enough by the sale of their surplus to pay their rates (property taxes). Having failed at wholesale, the Goods attempt to sell the vegetables retail. Barbara sets up shop on the curb until she realizes that not only is it unprofitable, it is illegal. Tom, on the other hand, pulls his trolley through the streets, hawking the merchandise until a local greengrocer has his giant of an assistant chase him off. Defeated, they sell their produce to a restaurant for a lower price. They show up at the tax office with the check from the restaurant and the remainder in coin.

With "Just My Bill," the second series picks up chronologically where the first series ended. Every day presents a new challenge (or crisis) in the lives of Tom and Barbara Good. The triumph of their uphill struggle to harvest their crops leaves them with the problem of selling their surplus to pay their taxes. It is a testimony to the writing of John Esmonde and Bob Larbey that they have balanced out the Goods' victories with their ties and defeats. For most of us life is not a string of triumphs but a continual struggles, for survival in which we sometimes manage to barely make it through another day. In "Just My Bill," the Goods survive — just barely — and that is their victory. Perhaps this is one reason why *The Good Life* is such a well-loved series.

The best moments in "Just My Bill" are saved until the end of the episode. After an uphill fight, Tom and Barbara manage to scrape together the amount due for their rates, plus one penny. To Tom, this achievement proves that they can be self-sufficient, even more so than bringing in their first harvest. Margo reminds him outside the tax office that he has no money; Tom reminds her of the penny. Just then, Barbara excuses herself. A charity worker comes up and asks them both for donations. Tom gives the woman his last penny on earth, proclaiming proudly to Margo that he still survives despite not having a cent to his name. Just as he's lecturing on his total freedom from filthy lucre, Barbara calls out from the doorway of the ladies' room, asking for the penny.

EPISODE 2: "THE GURU OF SURBITON" ★★

Air date: December 12, 1975. Cast: Tom Good (Richard Briers); Barbara Good (Felicity Kendal); Margo Leadbetter (Penelope Keith); Jerry Leadbetter (Paul Eddington); Guy (Bruce Bould); Ruth (Irene Richards)

The Goods are playing host to a pair of college students for a week. The students, Guy and Ruth, are helping Tom clear his allotment in return for room, board, and apparently a seminar in practical philosophy. The students almost worship Tom as a new messiah. Tom is taken with their adulation until he learns that the students plan to purchase the house next door to start a commune.

"The Guru of Surbiton" receives high grades for its concept but, unfortunately, low ones for its actual execution. After all his ardent philosophizing in the introductory episodes of the first season, Tom finally has an audience idealistic enough to fully appreciate him. Regrettably, this concept of throwing Tom and Barbara's practical self-sufficiency in with the rhetorical Communism of two college students fails to gel as one would wish. There are some amusing turns as we watch the students hang on Tom's every utterance, but ultimately the episode falls flat for lack of real conflict or crisis.

The students' adoration of Tom provides the lion's share of the laughs in "The Guru of Surbiton." When Tom and Barbara relax after dinner, Guy and Ruth turn the evening into the sermon on the couch. Their deadly earnestness extends even to the Goods' home-grown food, claiming that before they arrived they'd never eaten food.

"That dinner was *food*," Guy exclaims, apparently referring to the repast's moral content.

"Yes," admits Barbara, "that's what we usually have for dinner."

The students continue in this vein as Tom and Barbara exchange puzzled glances. Guy and Ruth eventually wind up sitting at Tom's feet, anticipating every sound from his lips as if it might be the clue to the meaning of life. By the end of the episode, Ruth has taken to fondling Tom's pullovers (not with him in them).

Fans of *The Fall and Rise of Reginald Perrin* will recognize, under Guy's beard, actor Bruce Bould, who played David Harris-Jones ("Super!") less than a year later.

EPISODE 3: "MR. FIX-IT" ★★★

Air date: December 19, 1975. Cast: Tom Good (Richard Briers); Barbara Good (Felicity Kendal); Margo Leadbetter (Penelope Keith); Jerry Leadbetter (Paul Eddington); Mr. Coles (John Quayle); Deliveryman (Steve Emerson)

When a journalist interviews the Goods for The *Observer* (a prestigious nationwide weekly newspaper), Jerry suggests that Tom and Barbara capitalize on their forthcoming fame by endorsing local shop merchants in exchange for goods. Jerry even offers to strike the deals for them, and they agree. Soon a flood of clothes, tools, and other necessities are streaming into the Goods' home (Jerry also secures a sailboat for himself as his agent's commission). The following Sunday, they learn that the story has been sold to the *Oxonbucks Observer*, a tiny regional paper. Jerry is forced to return the Goods windfall and his sailboat.

The title character, although at first apparently referring to Tom, applies, in this episode at least, to Jerry Leadbetter. However, it is Penelope Keith as Margo Leadbetter who really shines in this offering as her usually reserved character becomes passionate in her attempt to bask in the Goods' limelight. This is also the first mention of Margo's upcoming performance in the local production of *The Sound of Music*. This subplot will provide much mirth over the next few episodes before its hilarious conclusion in "The Mutiny."

Margo's attempts at getting mentioned in the article on the Goods and their unusual lifestyle provide an abundance of amusement in "Mr. Fix-It." When she first learns that a reporter is coming, Margo generously offers to be present to help them. Tom and Barbara politely refuse her offer, causing Margo to seethe and to try even more to be a part of the proceedings.

The next day, when the reporter is taking pictures of Tom and Barbara in the back garden, Margo can be seen in the background over the fence, pantomiming hedge trimming in an attempt to get in each shot. Finally, impeccably coiffured and in heels, Margo climbs a stepladder in her bid to insert herself into the photos.

When the interview moves inside, Margo appears moments later, in a different hairdo and dress, to provide "background information." Her idea of background information, however, turns out to be details on herself, Jerry (whom she refers to as "Jeremy"), her hobbies, and her upcoming performance in the town hall production of *The Sound of Music*.

Tom and Barbara finally intervene to give Margo a mention along with a taste of medicine. They tell the reporter that Margo has been vital to their self-sufficiency scheme. At first, Margo brightens at the attention, but she turns to suffering in silence as the Goods explain that Margo advocated their keeping of pigs and regularly volunteers to chauffeur their goat to grazing in her own car. Finally, Tom compares Margo's support to that of a truss, much to her consternation.

Episode 4: "The Day Peace Broke Out" ★½

Air date: January 2, 1976. Cast: Tom Good (Richard Briers); Barbara Good (Felicity Kendal); Margo Leadbetter (Penelope Keith); Jerry Leadbetter (Paul Eddington); Magistrate (James Cossins); Harry Bennett (Brian Grellis)

Tom winds up in court after assaulting Harry Bennett, a man who has been pilfering leeks from Tom's front garden. At the hearing, the magistrate takes into account the seriousness of the charge given the Goods' unique lifestyle. He fines Bennett £10 and orders Tom bound over for three months (essentially probation). Tom refuses the lenient sentence since it means promising that he will not again use similar force to protect his property. The magistrate sends Tom to prison for 28 days to reconsider.

While not particularly laugh-packed, "The Day Peace Broke Out" is a pleasantly entertaining tale. The main difficulty, however, is not the relative absence of gags but rather Tom's ultimate reconciliation with Harry Bennett, the man who has caused him so much trouble. Although the turnaround makes for a desirable ending, it is sudden, especially given the fact that Tom has just vowed not to forgive the man. That the change is even more drastic than we think is punctuated by Barbara's vitriolic reaction to seeing Bennett in the final scene.

The best moment, however, focuses on Tom's snatching of defeat from the jaws of victory at his court hearing. When the magistrate passes his lenient sentence, he asks Tom if he has anything to say. Tom takes full advantage of the offer, thus digging his own pit. He starts by giving the magistrate a back-handed compliment by telling him that up until now he thought all judges were "pompous old twits." He seals his doom by calling his sentence a "token slap on the wrist." When the magistrate explains the full meaning of the sentence, Tom paints himself into a corner of a prison cell.

The magistrate is well played by James Cossins, who should be familiar as the yacht salesman who Basil Fawlty mistakes for a hotel inspector in the *Fawlty Towers* episode "The Hotel Inspectors."

EPISODE 5: "MUTINY" ★★★★

Air date: January 9, 1976. Cast: Tom Good (Richard Briers); Barbara Good (Felicity Kendal); Margo Leadbetter (Penelope Keith); Jerry Leadbetter (Paul Eddington); Sir Andrew (Reginald Marsh)

Sir asks Jerry to play host to a visiting client the weekend of Margo's performance in *The Sound of Music*. Jerry refuses and is promptly fired. Jerry has difficulty finding a new job. Margo's play is a disaster. Finally, Tom and Barbara invite Sir over to plead for Jerry's job. Although they can't muster a convincing reason for Jerry's reinstatement, they don't need one. Sir reveals that Jerry can have his old job if he comes crawling back. Jerry happily throws dignity to the wind and grovels.

By the sheer number of funny scenes, "Mutiny" ranks as the best installment of the second series. Every situation delights, and no character is left without some good bit to play. It is no surprise that the best episodes of *Good Neighbors* are those in which Penelope Keith's character has a pivotal role. Although Richard Briers is the star of the show (and rightfully so), Felicity Kendal is always wonderfully sparkling, and Paul Eddington is always a welcome presence, Keith is without peer with her perfect comic timing. She regularly steals each scene in which she appears with a grace that makes it seem effortless.

The fun starts right away in "Mutiny" as Tom plays golf with Jerry and Sir. Jerry unashamedly lets Sir cheat while purposely missing his own easy shots. Although Tom is slightly outraged at this, he is far too busy collecting nuts and berries to really care much. The climax of the game comes when Tom pulls a club cover off a shotgun in his golf bag and starts taking shots at passing rabbits.

The scenes leading up to Margo's debut as Fraulein Maria are also gems. Margo is so nervous and upset she can't even remember the correct words to the songs. The source of her anxiety is the fact that one of the Von Trapp boys has a continually runny nose, and the Baron's lederhosen squeak when he walks. Unfortunately, we never actually see any of the show itself.

After the shows Jerry, Tom, and Barbara rush back to the Leadbetters to make ready for the opening night party (they are also scheduled to throw a closing night party the following evening). Before the cast arrives, the three discuss the absolute fiasco that they've just witnessed, including the see-through habits of the nuns, a conductor with his conducting arm in a sling, and Margo's singing of a number from *West Side Story*.

"One can't expect an amateur performance to be perfect. Can one?" Barbara asks rhetorically.

"Not after tonight," Tom agrees.

Soon Margo arrives alone. The mayor has cancelled the one remaining performance since, he reasons, the show is giving Surbiton a bad name. Those holding tickets for the final performance will be told the chandelier in the hall is unsafe and in danger of collapsing.

Although he is unbilled, Tony Page has a brief speaking part in this episode as the Von Trapp child who reminds Margo that the curtain is going up. Page is seen to much better effect as snotty young Harold, who contends that his chips aren't the right shape, in the "Gourmet Night" episode of *Fawlty Towers*.

EPISODE 6: "HOME SWEET HOME" ★★★

Air date: January 16, 1976. Cast: Tom Good (Richard Briers); Barbara Good (Felicity Kendal); Margo Leadbetter (Penelope Keith); Jerry Leadbetter (Paul Eddington); Boar Walker (Edwin Brown); Mrs. Weaver (Charmian May)

After a local farmer takes the Goods to see a small eight-acre farm nearby, Tom can't think of a practical reason not to sell their home and buy the farm. For that matter, neither can Barbara, and the couple starts making plans to move, although secretly neither one wants to move.

This episode proves that for all his talk of practicality, Tom Good is essentially a sentimentalist at heart. Of course, if he were truly practical, he would have sought a small farm upon which to conduct his experiment in the first place. The outcome of this plot gives credence to Jerry Leadbetter's frequent observation that Tom has a deep-seated bent toward self-masochism. Still, without his constitution as it is, Tom would have moved to the country, and we would have been left without a terrific situation comedy.

Early in the episode, Margo announces to the Goods that they have new neighbors, the Weavers. She explains that the Weavers are the right kind of people: charming. Margo goes on to hope that Mrs. Weaver will not be outraged by the Goods' backyard farm, adding that she herself has become accustomed to their experiment in self-sufficiency, and nothing they can do will shock her. With that, Tom reveals that the Boar Walker is coming the following day to "serve Pinky" (mate her). At first, Margo is unsure of what he will be serving the pig, but once she catches on she is stunned, especially since it will all happen in full view of her garden. Margo remarks incredulously that this sort of thing doesn't go on in Surbiton. Tom reasons that it must since that is how little Surbitonites are created.

The episode concludes with a solid laugh as Barbara, angry over Tom's patronizing speech, chases her husband around the yard with an egg. In the front yard, Margo is explaining to Mrs. Weaver what upstanding and dignified neighbors the Goods are despite appearances. Just then the couple in question comes tearing around the corner. Barbara lets her egg fly, Tom ducks, and the hen fruit hits Mrs. Weaver squarely in the arm. Tom and Barbara freeze for a moment, then, like two naughty children who have just broken a window, the couple runs away to hide.

EPISODE 7: "GOING TO POT?" ★★★½

Air date: January 23, 1976. Cast: Tom Good (Richard Briers); Barbara Good (Felicity Kendal); Margo Leadbetter (Penelope Keith); Jerry Leadbetter (Paul Eddington); Mrs. Weaver (Charmian May)

After taking night classes, Tom discovers he is a veritable genius at pottery. Soon he has a small cottage industry going on the strength of word of mouth. Margo and Jerry announce that an upscale Chelsea gallery has agreed to retail Tom's work at lucrative prices. For a moment, Tom and Barbara make plans to expand the business, reconnect the phone, buy a van, and hire an accountant. Their enthusiasm quickly sours, however, when Margo comments that they will be "normal people" again. They realize how close they were to slipping back into the rat race and quickly get out of the pottery business.

The second series ends much like the first, with a crisis that threatens Tom and Barbara Good's dream of a self-sufficient lifestyle. Unlike the formidable task presented them in "Back to the Wall," however, this trial is even more insidious since it comes wrapped in a velvet glove. Again, this episode, like the majority of those in *Good Neighbors*, is well thought out by Esmonde and Larbey and well scripted.

"Going to Pot?" offers Paul Eddington as Jerry some strong supporting scenes and some good laughs at the expense of his on-screen wife. First, Jerry practically begs Margo to join the Goods in their night school classes. It seems that since *The Sound of Music* debacle (see "The Mutiny"), Margo has resigned from the music society, thus robbing Jerry of his one peaceful night at home alone. When Margo enrolls in the pottery class, Jerry is allowed to indulge in the simple pursuits that make enduring Sir and Margo worthwhile: eating curry, listening to pop music, reading trashy paperbacks, and smoking cigars.

Jerry's bliss is short lived, however, when Margo comes home early from the first class and announces she has given it up. She explains that the instructor was a crude "bearded lout," and the class was a breeding ground of "familiarity and bad manners."

In addition, the teacher insisted on calling her "Margie." The grossest insult, however, was when Margo asked what size lump of clay she should use. "He stared — quite unashamedly — at my … breasts and said," Margo relates with horror, "'in your case, Margie, about a 36-B!'"

Jerry manages to offer token outrage, as he muffles a laugh behind his handkerchief.

Series Three 1976

EPISODE 1: "THE EARLY BIRDS" ★★½

Air date: September 10, 1976. Cast: Tom Good (Richard Briers); Barbara Good (Felicity Kendal); Margo Leadbetter (Penelope Keith); Jerry Leadbetter (Paul Eddington)

When Jerry and Margo are awakened one morning at 6 A.M. by the Goods' clambering about in their garden, Tom and Barbara apologize and promise to be less noisy in the early morning hours. Tom hits upon the idea to live by nature's clock: going to sleep at sunset and getting up at sunrise. Unfortunately, when they try the plan, neither sleeps all night. The next evening, the totally exhausted Goods go to bed at eight and quickly fall into a deep sleep. They are awakened later that night by the sounds of a late night party at the Leadbetters. Furious at having their own sleep disturbed after they themselves have vowed to be considerate, the Goods trundle over in their pajamas to complain. Once next door, their ire is disarmed when they learn that it is only 8:30 and they've only been asleep a half hour.

The third series in the Good saga begins with what is essentially a one-joke episode. It's a fine joke but not an uproarious one so, consequently, this is a fine little entry in the series, but nothing spectacular. One wishes that the writers had had the daring to eschew the services of Penelope Keith and Paul Eddington (wonderful as they always are) for this one episode and explore in greater depth the situation of sleeplessness. *One Foot in the Grave* author David Renwick would do this 15 years hence in his frequent one-scene installments of that series. It would be interesting to see Tom Good's character visiting that Meldrewian realm just once. The stream-of-consciousness dialogue that would fill the "Timeless Time" episode of *One Foot in the Grave* is evident here, albeit in seminal form.

The discussion begins with Barbara's comment that they are going to bed while *The Archers* (one of her former radio show favorites) is still on. This wanders into a discussion of some of the show's plot devices before Tom insists that they both settle down for some sleep. Next, Tom's habit of exhaling in grunts bothers Barbara. This leads to Tom's criticism of Barbara's twitchy shoulder, which he likens to a "puppy with a bad dream."

Barbara gives up her quest for Morpheus and starts playing with a portable chess set. Her game is disturbed when Tom drops his pretense of sleep to declare she's cheating. From here on, any attempt at slumber is aborted, and the couple whiles away the night playing chess and compiling their list of Top 20 films.

EPISODE 2: "THE HAPPY EVENT" ★★★½

Air date: September 17, 1976. Cast: Tom Good (Richard Briers); Barbara Good (Felicity Kendal); Margo Leadbetter (Penelope Keith); Jerry Leadbetter (Paul Eddington); Police Constable Hillman (George Innes); Animal Noises (Percy Edwards)

When the Goods' pig Pinky goes into labor in the middle of the night, the Leadbetters are pressed into helping. When a runt is born, Tom suggests that they let nature take its course and do nothing. Barbara rebels, forcing Tom to attempt to save the piglet. Tom and Margo set up first aid while Jerry and Barbara rush off to the hospital for an oxygen tank. On the way to the hospital, they are stopped by a policeman who subsequently gets drawn into the drama. In the end the runt is saved.

"The Happy Event" is an unusual entry of *Good Neighbors* in that it doesn't really get into the meat of the plot until almost halfway through the episode. The first third of the episode makes some valiant, yet unfulfilling, attempts at humor with a routine about planting seeds like icing through a pastry bag and with a bit about Barbara surprising Tom with a secondhand horse, which they cannot keep. Still, when "The Happy Event" finally occurs, matters pick up quickly. The end result is a very good installment in the series.

Guest George Innes is particularly fine as the policeman who is simultaneously kind and helpful to the Goods while being belligerent and officious to the Leadbetters.

When the piglets start coming in the middle of the night, Jerry is dragged into the delivery since he has a utility lamp with an extra long cord. While Tom is busy acting as midwife and Barbara enjoys the wonder of birth, Jerry stands dutifully in his pajamas, holding the light. When Margo arrives, it is less to help than to chide Jerry for rushing out and leaving the front door open. Margo imagines various unsavory characters coming in through the open door to take advantage of her.

After Tom announces that seven piglets have been born thus far, Margo grows uneasy at the prodigious pig procreation. With a curl in her upper lip and not a clue as to the procedures of nature, Margo remarks that seven should be enough. Tom nods, pretending to agree, then tells the pig that she can stop on Margo's authority.

Series coauthor Bob Larbey votes for "The Happy Event" as his favorite episode.

EPISODE 3: "A TUG OF THE FORELOCK" ★★★½

Air date: September 24, 1976. Cast: Tom Good (Richard Briers); Barbara Good (Felicity Kendal); Margo Leadbetter (Penelope Keith); Jerry Leadbetter (Paul Eddington)

Tom decides to convert their rotary cultivator into a motorized cart. To earn the money to run the vehicle, Tom and Barbara offer to work for Margo while her maid and gardener are on holiday. Soon the arrangement proves to be less than satisfactory for both Barbara and Margo. Barbara cannot stand Margo's micromanagement of the housework. Margo, on the other hand, is irritated by the Goods' less-than-servile attitude and fires them after one week.

The title, "A Tug of the Forelock," refers to the servile gesture given by domestics to their masters. Though an antiquated custom, it is still much in vogue in the world of Margo Leadbetter — even when the servants are her best friends, Tom and Barbara Good. This episode does a masterful job of exploring Margo's notions of class distinction. Up to this point in the series, Margo has continued to accept Tom and Barbara as equals, albeit ones that she thinks have lost their way on the path to the upper-middle-class dream. When the Goods briefly become her domestic servants, she expects them to behave as menials and not as friends. This notion is completely foreign to Tom and Barbara and manages to provide interesting and humorous conflict.

The first clue that Margo expects obsequious servants comes when she first agrees to hire the Goods. Jerry, Tom, and Barbara are all making light of the temporary arrangement, but Margo, typically, finds no humor in the situation. When Barbara jokingly agrees not to steal the good silver, Margo is appalled, noting that such impudence is tolerable from friends but not from servants.

Later Margo tells Jerry of the shambles the Goods made of her hosting of the Surbiton Ladies' Conservative Association meeting. She insists that Jerry—as the "master"—deal with the servant problem when the perpetrators enter. Jerry melodramatically threatens to have Tom and Barbara beaten. The Goods enter into the spirit of the jest and respond with feigned deference. Next, they explain that they've come for their wages since they've had to sell eight of their children already. The charade goes on until Margo can stand it no more and storms off in fury.

Episode 4: "I Talk to the Trees" ★★

Air date: October 1, 1976. Cast: Tom Good (Richard Briers); Barbara Good (Felicity Kendal); Margo Leadbetter (Penelope Keith); Jerry Leadbetter (Paul Eddington); Mr. Wakely (Noel Howlett); Mr. Chipchase (Raymond Mason); Acting Chairwoman (Joyce Windsor)

Mr. Wakely, the Goods' allotment neighbor, explains his theory on growing robust plants by talking to them. Tom sets up a scientific experiment to test the theory. His experiment ruins an important meeting of Margo's music society, which in turn causes Margo to inadvertently spoil Tom's experiment. Ultimately, no harm is done as Margo is elected society president based on her pledge that Jerry will donate £200 to the club treasury.

"I Talk to the Trees" features two rather contrived plots that are meant to combine in a rousing finale. Unfortunately, the mixture is rather thin, and of the two, the secondary plot (Margo's music society machinations) proves the stronger and ultimately overpowers the first. Ultimately, one must conclude that the buildup over Tom's plant experiment is really only an excuse used by the writers to have Margo's music society meeting disrupted by Peter Dawson singing "The Bandolero," the record Tom plays to his plants.

The initial setup of the plant experiment provides some laughs, as Tom sets aside one plant for loving conversation, one as a control plant, and one for abusive speech. Next, Tom explains to Barbara that she will be responsible for being the voice of love to the first plant, while he is the voice of hate to the other. When her turn comes to speak lovingly to her plant, Barbara begins to giggle since she has never spoken to a bean before. After she regains her composure, she provides more sexy passion than warm kindness as she speaks to the plant as one would to a lover. Tom notes in his journal that Plant A was subjected to "20 seconds with an oversexed laboratory assistant."

Tom is in the middle of a tirade to his plant when Jerry walks in and witnesses the display. Even after Tom explains the experiment, Jerry persists in mocking it. Jerry finally leaves but only after making sure he has said goodbye to all the individual pieces of furniture in the room.

EPISODE 5: "THE WIND-BREAK WAR" ★★½

Air date: October 8, 1976. Cast: Tom Good (Richard Briers); Barbara Good (Felicity Kendal); Margo Leadbetter (Penelope Keith); Jerry Leadbetter (Paul Eddington); Arthur Bailey (Timothy Bateson); Workmen (Roger Pope, Desmond Cullum-Jones).

A minor fracas erupts when Margo plans to erect a garden windbreak, which will block the sun to the Goods' fruit trees. A string of misunderstandings follows in which the windbreak and the fruit trees are moved back and forth, always to the wrong places. After the problem is finally resolved, the neighbors reconcile over a few bottles of the Goods' peapod wine. Both couples get drunk. Jerry suggests they try to relocate the windbreak themselves. They uproot it but then drop it on Margo's new statue, destroying both it and the windbreak.

"The Wind-Break War" is an oddly paced, somewhat unbalanced entry. Less of a war than a misunderstanding, there is really little dramatic tension to help the episode along. Indeed, what ire there is comes from Tom and Barbara jumping to conclusions and being totally unreasonable. Margo, for all her haughtiness, is shown to be a much more considerate neighbor than the Goods. Oddly, this episode was one of three chosen to be on the BBC video release of *Good Neighbors*. It is an unfortunate choice not only because it isn't one of the more humorous installments of the series, but it also presents the two main characters in a rather unflattering light. The main redeeming quality of the episode is the last third in which the four neighbors get drunk and bare their souls to one another.

The best moments here have little if anything to do with the troublesome windbreak and thus the plot. In two parallel scenes, the four primary cast members make deep confessions — helped along by the peapod burgundy. The first comes while Jerry and Barbara clean up the dinner dishes in the kitchen. Jerry is unable to stand the sexy way that Barbara brushes back her bangs, and he admits to always having a yen for her. Barbara reminds Jerry that she is a married woman. "So am I," Jerry drunkenly concurs.

Jerry then hints at the then-current craze of wife swapping but is forced to admit that both he and Barbara love their respective mates too much to engage in that. The weight of the conversation is lightened when they discover that Jerry has been mistaking the freezer for the dishwasher.

Back in the living room, Tom is attempting to apologize to Margo for his constant teasing of her. Margo interrupts him with the shocking revelation that she is not a "complete woman." Upon further discussion, Tom discovers that Margo is bemoaning her lack of a sense of humor. Tom tries to convince Margo that she has a sense of humor. Unfortunately, he can only manage to tell her that she has a sexy neck before falling off the chair they are sharing.

Later, Margo is delighted when Jerry, Tom, and Barbara destroy her windbreak and her new statue because she can finally see some humor in the situation.

EPISODE 6: "WHOSE FLEAS ARE THESE" ★★★★

Air date: October 15, 1976. Cast: Tom Good (Richard Briers); Barbara Good (Felicity Kendal); Margo Leadbetter (Penelope Keith); Jerry Leadbetter (Paul Eddington); P. V. Balstrode (Michael Robbins); Postman (Ray Dunbobbin)

After the soot in their chimney billows into their kitchen, the Goods are forced to use the Leadbetters' bathtub to clean up. Back home, Barbara discovers she has fleas. Tom assumes the infestation is from the animals and starts giving the animals flea baths. Unfortunately, the Leadbetters also have fleas, presumably brought over when the Goods used their bathtub. Margo is horrified and immediately informs the authorities. A defestation man visits the Goods, examines the fleas, and pronounces them common dog fleas and not a health threat. Further investigation reveals that Margo is the source of the fleas, having brought them home from the sheepdog of her snooty friend Mrs. Dooms-Paterson.

"Whose Fleas Are These" is an episode rich in comic vignettes and is easily the high point of the third series. The script, while not particularly heavy with jokes, still is filled with plenty of humorous dialogue based on situation and characterization. Veteran comic actor Michael Robbins is especially effective as P. V. Balstrode.

American audiences may wonder what all the fuss is about a few fleas. A hint to this mystery is voiced by inspector P. V. Balstrode when he remarks that his family has been in "infestation" back to the time of the bubonic plague, when of course, the black death was spread by fleas.

Almost every scene is a delight. The opening finds the Goods spending a quiet evening in front of their wood stove. Tom laments that most of his countrymen are probably wasting away in front of the television instead of reading a good book. Of course, his dissertation is distracting Barbara from doing just that. Tom, on the other hand, is filling his time playing schoolboy cricket (a mock cricket match played with coins and paper) at the kitchen table. When Barbara investigates his notebook, she finds that her boyish husband is the captain of an imaginary powerhouse team, which regularly trounces such competition as the "International Musicians" and the "World Religious Leaders." Tom himself is the star — of course as any normal ten-year-old would be — averaging 279 runs a game (100 is usually considered outstanding).

There's also an amusing scene in which the Goods arrive covered with soot, hoping to use the Leadbetters' bathtub. Margo initially refuses their request, but Jerry overrides her. Margo offers Tom and Barbara a drink while refusing to allow them beyond the front hall. She serves them as they stand on newspaper, and she makes concerted attempts at small talk. When Jerry returns to announce that their bath is drawn, the Goods go off together. Barbara informs a horrified Margo that she and Tom often take baths with each other. Jerry responds with a grin and leer, suggesting that he would like to give co-bathing a try. "Certainly not!" Margo firmly asserts.

The high point of the episode is the visit from Balstrode, the defestation man. Initially, Balstrode introduces himself as an encyclopedia salesman so as not to cause unnecessary panic among the neighbors. Within moments, we learn that the Balstrodes have been in the vermin business since the Middle Ages, the current Balstrode loves his job, and he can identify the sex of a flea without the aid of magnification. Tom asks how Balstrode can tell the sex of an insect from three feet away. "*Vive la difference*," Balstrode remarks matter-of-factly.

Episode 7: "The Last Posh Frock" ★★★

Air date: October 22, 1976. Cast: Tom Good (Richard Briers); Barbara Good (Felicity Kendal); Margo Leadbetter (Penelope Keith); Jerry Leadbetter (Paul Eddington); Eileen (Liz Robertson); Man in Street (Ronald Nunnery)

After being mistaken for a boy, Barbara tries to get back in touch with her feminine side by putting on her only posh frock, but Tom fails to notice the dress. When he does, he tells her to change since it is impractical for working in the cellar. As she exits to do so, Barbara tears the dress on a nail, ruining the garment. When Tom fails to understand Barbara's upset over the accident, she goes into a brooding depression. Finally, after a stern lecture from Jerry, Tom is made to see the symbolism of Barbara's posh frock. He presents her with a brand-new gown and tells her he sold a few things to afford it.

More dramatic than most episodes and in that respect somewhat reminiscent of "Back to the Wall," "The Last Posh Frock" is a solid installment to close out the third season. Unlike the two previous season closers, this episode doesn't present an obvious threat to the Goods' self-sufficient lifestyle. It does, however, deal with a potentially devastating crisis for Tom, namely the demoralization of his greatest asset: Barbara. This has been explored before in "The Weaker Sex?" of the first series, although not as believably due to the poor motivating situation in that episode. Here, the premise is much more believable since there has been more time for Barbara to reflect on how far she and Tom have come and at what price to her personally. This episode allows us a deeper view into a side of the normally perky Barbara that we have only previously glimpsed. Felicity Kendal provides a first-rate performance as the hurt and raging Barbara.

Series Four 1977

Episode 1: "Away from It All" ★★½

Air date: April 10, 1977. Cast: Tom Good (Richard Briers); Barbara Good (Felicity Kendal); Margo Leadbetter (Penelope Keith); Jerry Leadbetter (Paul Eddington)

With a disappointing second harvest staring them in the face, the Goods become discouraged with their circumstances. Jerry suggests they recuperate and offers them the use of a traveling friend's London penthouse for a weekend, while he and Margo care for their animals. After leaving voluminous instructions, Tom and Barbara leave for London. They are just beginning to enjoy the soft life when they start imagining all sorts of problems that must be going on at home. Soon, they have themselves convinced that Margo is in the hospital and that their goat is dying. They rush home to discover that everything is perfect — well, almost.

Similar to series one's "The Pagan Rite" with enough variation to prevent an exact copy, "Away from It All" explores the Goods' need for relief from their daily grind. While the theme of the Goods' discouragement has been explored before, the cast performs its duties cheerfully enough to keep the episode from appearing too threadbare.

There are some fresh wrinkles. When Margo calls the Goods to report a strange new noise emanating from the generator, both Tom and Barbara overreact. Sounding like Corporal Jones from *Dad's Army*, they both start shouting, "Don't panic!" into the phone to the placid Margo. It is only after Margo is forced to repeat the odd sound — a distasteful request to the cultured Margo — that Tom easily diagnoses the problem. He tells Margo to have Jerry place a drop of oil on the generator's nipple. Margo reacts to this information with a curl of her lip over Tom's careless use of the word *nipple*.

With the generator fixed, Margo starts putting other things right. As she meticulously measures each grain of animal feed, Jerry enters as if he's running from a scuffle. He earnestly declares that despite Margo's orders he doesn't think the goat wants its horns polished. Margo firmly asserts that despite the beast's wishes, it will have polished horns.

Episode 2: "The Green Door" ★★

Air date: April 17, 1977. Cast: Tom Good (Richard Briers); Barbara Good (Felicity Kendal); Margo Leadbetter (Penelope Keith); Jerry Leadbetter (Paul Eddington); Mrs. Holman (Jane Hilary); Miss Thompson (Toria Fuller)

When Margo starts making clandestine visits to a mysterious address in town, Tom and Barbara suspect she is having an affair.

A comedy of suspicion, "The Green Door" is something of a departure from the usual style of the series. In this respect, the episode is fairly disappointing since there is little balance to the premise that Margo is cheating on Jerry. Both Tom and Barbara assume the worst almost simultaneously, Margo remains mum on the subject, and Jerry never finds out anything regarding the plot. Although the authors do a good job of keeping Margo's secret (she is going to a weight loss specialist) until the final moments of the episode, the proceedings might have been funnier if there were a little more tension over Margo's furtive activities.

The best moments of the episode take place in two scenes between the Goods and Jerry. Unable to come up with any explanation but the worst, Tom and Barbara heap comfort and sympathy on Jerry. Unfortunately, Jerry has no idea why he is being commiserated with and comes to the conclusion that his neighbors are even further 'round the bend than he previously suspected.

Episode 3: "Our Speaker Today" ★★★

Air date: April 24, 1977. Cast: Tom Good (Richard Briers); Barbara Good (Felicity Kendal); Margo Leadbetter (Penelope Keith); Jerry Leadbetter (Paul Eddington); Lady Georgette Truscot (Angela Thorne); Remand Home Inmate (Robert Lindsay); Bus Conductor (Colin McCormack); Remand Home Supervisor (Con Chambers)

When Margo's women's group needs a guest speaker at the last minute, Barbara agrees to step in and talk on self-sufficiency. Despite her nervousness and inexperience, Barbara's talk is a success. One of the visitors, Lady Truscot, stops by the Goods' home to ask if Barbara will give her talk at a charity gathering. She agrees and soon is booked into addressing numerous worthy groups. Finally, Barbara quits the speaking circuit when she realizes that Tom can't run their home without her help.

"Our Speaker Today" is a low-key episode yet one with a surprising amount of humor and laughs. Angela Thorne is good as the down-to-earth Lady Truscot. She would appear again with Penelope Keith as her best friend, Marjory Frobisher, for three seasons of *To the Manor Born.*

Margo's attempts at ingratiating herself with Lady Truscot provide more than a few laughs. When she hears that her ladyship is coming to speak to Barbara, she makes Jerry run around ("like a demented flunky") to fetch special refreshments and her cleaning lady. When Lady Truscot arrives, she goes directly to the much less elegant Good home. Margo is nonplused when she and Jerry arrive dressed to the nines and find Lady Truscot sitting in the kitchen drinking Tom's homemade wine. To make matters worse, her ladyship is on familiar terms with the Goods and insists that she be called "George," a liberty that Margo cannot force herself to take.

Later, Tom's need for Barbara becomes acute when he is forced to try and build the new chicken coop alone while she is at a speaking engagement. Tom accidentally leaves the gate open, and their rooster, Lenin, gets loose. Tom chases the bird down the street, where it hops on a bus. He is forced to ride the bus to the next stop then walk back since he doesn't have enough money for a round-trip fare. When Barbara and Lady Truscot return, they find the other chickens loose and Tom gone. After they round up the chickens, Tom returns to explain that he and Lenin have been all the way to Kingston.

Barbara's last speaking engagement at a tough reformatory also provides a surprise chuckle. Tom goes along in anticipation of trouble with the rowdy crowd. When Barbara charms the mob, Tom figures it must be the topic of self-sufficiency that did it. He stops one of the teens to ask why they were so attentive. The boy explains that they weren't interested in the talk but stayed quiet so Barbara wouldn't get nervous and move from her spot. It seems that she was standing in front of a window, and the backlighting allowed them to see through her dress.

Episode 4: "The Weaver's Tale" ★★★

Air date: May 1, 1977. Cast: Tom Good (Richard Briers); Barbara Good (Felicity Kendal); Margo Leadbetter (Penelope Keith); Jerry Leadbetter (Paul Eddington); Salesman (Milton Johns)

Tom spends the profits from the recent soft fruit sale to purchase a loom, then schemes to have Margo buy the necessary spinning wheel to go with it. His plan backfires, however, when the Leadbetters split up over Jerry's refusal to purchase Margo the wheel. Ultimately, Jerry makes peace and gives Margo the spinning wheel. Much to Tom's dismay, however, he discovers that the wheel, while appearing functional, has been converted into a motorized music box.

Strong in plot and in execution, "The Weaver's Tale" provides good opportunities for the entire cast to show off its talents. Disturbing yet amusing at the same time is Tom Good's selfishness at attempting to get a spinning wheel at any cost — even the happiness of his two best friends. It is also interesting to note that, despite his preaching of the practical, Tom is almost as much of an impulse buyer as the frivolous Margo.

When Tom enters the secondhand shop, he immediately spots a used loom. His attempts to purchase the item are hindered by the salesman, who is reluctant to sell anything without his boss being there. Tom finally convinces him to sell the loom but only because its absence will free up enough room in the crammed shop to allow a hot plate on which to make tea.

Episode 5: "Suit Yourself" ★★★½

Air date: May 8, 1977. Cast: Tom Good (Richard Briers); Barbara Good (Felicity Kendal); Margo Leadbetter (Penelope Keith); Jerry Leadbetter (Paul Eddington); Sir (Reginald Marsh); Snetterton (Philip Madoc); Dolby (Terence Conoley); Mrs. Dolby (Patricia Driscoll)

The Goods' latest project is a small home-based textile factory where they turn raw fleece into naturally dyed green fabric. Meanwhile, Jerry reveals that Sir is going to retire and will announce his successor at a dinner with the three primary candidates for his job. In preparation for the event, Jerry has written a detailed expansion plan for JJM.

The night of the dinner, Jerry's confidence melts when he discovers that he has lost his proposal. A waiter arrives to announce that Tom and Barbara have arrived with Jerry's plan. They give it to the grateful Jerry but then are pulled into the dinner by Sir, who thinks they have come to honor him.

With the Goods' self-sufficiency scheme firmly entrenched and them branching out into new fields (weaving), the focus of the series switches to the Leadbetters. While so far the character of Jerry Leadbetter has received the least attention of the four principals, now and for the remaining two shows in the series, Jerry is the center of attention. These last three shows present a linear plot, which builds to a tidy climax for the entire run of *The Good Life/Good Neighbors.*

"Suit Yourself" features dual plots each of which neatly fills half the episode. The first involves the Goods' textile factory, while the second concerns Jerry's chance to become Sir Andrew's successor as managing director at JJM. Both story lines are joined at the end for a hilarious one-joke finish.

Philip Madoc appears as Jerry's chief rival, the slimy Snetterton. Madoc gained lasting fame in the hearts of *Dad's Army* aficionados as the unforgettable U-boat Captain in that series' classic entry "The Deadly Attachment."

The best moment in "Suit Yourself" is the final one. After the three candidates for managing director have maneuvered all evening, their attempts are blunted when Tom arrives. Unable to get away, the Goods join the private party, and Sir starts lavishing great praise on Tom (although he still can't get his name right). Sir honors Tom as the only man who has ever fought him to a draw in a battle of wills. He calls Tom a giant and asserts that if he had stayed with JJM, he would probably be in the running to succeed him. Sir goes on to insist that Tom is just the sort of man he admires, one "with a style all his own." At this point, Sir insists that Tom take off his topcoat. He does, revealing that he is wearing a garish homemade suit in putrid green. Sir bellows in horror before a blackout ending.

Episode 6: "Sweet & Sour Charity" ★★★

Air date: May 15, 1977. Cast: Tom Good (Richard Briers); Barbara Good (Felicity Kendal); Margo Leadbetter (Penelope Keith); Jerry Leadbetter (Paul Eddington)

Margo is outvoted—68 to 1—on the choice of the next production of the music society. She wanted to do the *Merry Widow,* while everyone else picked *Sweet Charity*, which she feels is vulgar and debased. When she is asked to play the leading role of a call girl, she struggles between her morals and the desire to be the star.

Tom learns that his other neighbors, the Weavers, have moved. He also discovers that their oil tank is half full. He covets the oil, which he reasons can be swapped with a local farmer for some straw. Tom justifies taking the oil but is stopped when Barbara insists that it would be stealing. His yearning for the oil is increased when the level of the tank goes down, leading him to believe that someone else is stealing the fuel.

"Sweet & Sour Charity" is a clever title for an episode that examines the struggle between principles and expediency. Both Tom and Margo are faced with tough decisions about whether to give into temptation or hold out for virtue. Ultimately, both characters decide to do the right thing, although with mixed results. Tom's initial outrage that someone else is stealing the oil that he feels is rightfully his to purloin, quickly becomes frustration when he realizes that the fuel is leaking into his garden.

In this entry, we learn that Margo's prudishness extends beyond the public stage and into her bedroom. When the music society's costume designer sends over some sketches, she is outraged by the revealing, tarty designs. Jerry on the other hand is titillated — especially by the black stockings. Margo accuses him of having a fetish. She coolly advises him to see a doctor, as she believes he is in immanent danger of becoming a pervert.

EPISODE 7: "ANNIVERSARY" ★★★

Air date: May 23, 1977. Cast: Tom Good (Richard Briers); Barbara Good (Felicity Kendal); Margo Leadbetter (Penelope Keith); Jerry Leadbetter (Paul Eddington); Sir (Reginald Marsh)

The Goods face yet another crisis of disastrous proportions, while Jerry is elevated to managing director of JJM upon Sir Andrew's retirement.

For a series whose hallmark was geniality and leisurely pacing, the final regular episode of *The Good Life* is packed with drama and several important events. While the latest round of disasters facing Tom and Barbara Good are not particularly disheartening (their goat stops giving milk, and the oil from the previous episode has seeped into their garden, ruining the soil), the senseless trashing of their home by vandals is. This moment, coming as it does at the height of a celebration, provides the singularly most dramatic scenes of the entire series, and it is almost enough to bring the struggle for self-sufficiency to an end.

Jerry too faces his moments, where as it appears his hopes have been dashed. His aspirations to replace Sir Andrew seem to end when Sir takes

Snetterton out for a private dinner. This plot line provides the bulk of the laughs a Margo composes as scathing letter to the *Times* over the injustice of the affair. Later, when Sir arrives to announce that Jerry got the job, he must first endure the combined hostility of the Leadbetters and the Goods.

In a surprise twist, Sir also announces that he plans to follow the Goods' lead by trying his own experiment in self-sufficiency. Of course, his scheme involves a 100-acre estate and a staff of 12 servants. Ironically, most revolutions, Tom Good's included, eventually wind up being adopted, adapted, and assimilated by the very ones being revolted against.

There is a poignant final moment when the four neighbors stand in Tom and Barbara's ransacked living room to raise a toast "to the good life." This scene must have worked better in the original British version since, after all, that is the title of the series — not *Good Neighbors*.

Christmas Special 1977

"Silly, but It's Fun..." ★★★

Air date: December 26, 1977. Cast: Tom Good (Richard Briers); Barbara Good (Felicity Kendal); Margo Leadbetter (Penelope Keith); Jerry Leadbetter (Paul Eddington); Delivery Man (David Battley)

The Goods share their sparse self-sufficient Christmas with the Leadbetters after their expensive Christmas preparations aren't delivered. After a home-grown feast, the couples open crackers that Tom has made out of empty toilet paper tubes and the color supplement and play silly games. Even Margo agrees that it has been the happiest holiday ever. Finally, they exchange gifts. The Goods present Jerry and Margo with tremendously oversized home-woven sweaters, while the Leadbetters surprise Tom and Barbara with a cow.

More than six months after the final series episode, the Goods and the Leadbetters returned for this Boxing Day special. The title is a fairly good summation of the episode, which ostensibly tries to make a point about the meaning of Christmas, without ever really getting close to it. While Tom is shocked to find that all the Leadbetters' holiday trimmings are delivered en masse, the only difference between his celebration and theirs hangs on the philosophy of self-sufficiency, without any true meaning of the season beyond that. Still, it is all fun, despite some of the misplaced earnestness.

The charms of this episode are the little throwaway lines that are indicative of these characters. The abortive delivery of the Leadbetters' Christmas trappings shocks Tom.

"Your Christmas comes in a van," he cries to Margo.

"It's supposed to, Tom," Margo explains matter-of-factly.

Later, when the Goods get ready to go to bed on Christmas Eve, Barbara reveals an interesting holiday tradition by telling Tom that his white beard and red suit are waiting in the drawer. Tom offers mock surprise that Barbara knew that he was the jolly elf who made the annual boudoir visits. "Remembering last Christmas Eve, it had better be," Barbara replies.

Fawlty Towers

BBC-TV 1975, 1979

Explain to the casual acquaintance in the United States that you are writing a book on British situation comedy, and the first response is likely to be: "Oh, you mean like *Benny Hill*?" After explaining that Benny Hill, funny though he was, plied his craft in a variety format, you try to establish common ground by mentioning *Steptoe and Son* or *Dad's Army*. You are met with blank stares ... until you mention *Fawlty Towers*. With those two words, your acquaintance's eyes light up, and a smile forms around the corners of her mouth.

Most people in the United States who have never seen any other Brit-com have seen and enjoyed *Fawlty Towers*. Individuals who couldn't tell Arthur Lowe from the Artful Dodger are familiar with this remarkable creation of John Cleese and Connie Booth. The reason for this is quite simple: *Fawlty Towers* comprises 12 of the funniest comedy episodes ever sprayed across a cathode ray tube. I daresay, many fans of Brit-coms reading this book are aficionados of other series because of *Fawlty Towers*, the success of which on American public television paved the way for other imports. Shows like *The Good Life* (*Good Neighbors*) and *The Fall and Rise of Reginald Perrin* found audiences in the States because *Fawlty* fans were looking for that second strike of comedic lightening. As fine as many of these other shows might be, *Fawlty Towers* is truly unique.

The genesis of *Fawlty Towers* came during some location filming on *Monty Python's Flying Circus*, the show that first brought fame to John Cleese. It was May 1972 (although some accounts place the date a year earlier), and the Python troupe was in Torquay, along the southwestern coast of England. While filming there, Cleese and his compatriots had the displeasure of staying in a hotel (the Gleneagles) run, in Cleese's words, by the "most wonderfully rude man I've ever met." According to Cleese, this proprietor, a Mr. Sinclair, was in a continual state of agitation: the source being his guests. "He thought that guests were sent along to annoy him and to prevent him from running the hotel," Cleese told the *Radio Times* in 1979.

During the course of the Pythons' brief stay, Terry Gilliam was chided for having table manners that were too "American" (he is from Minneapolis, after all), Eric Idle had his luggage thrown into the streets, while the rest of the crew received generally poor treatment.

One night, when they arrived back at the hotel late, the Python crew was met by Sinclair, clearly annoyed at having to wait up for the comedians. "He looked at us with the same look of self-righteous resentment and tacit accusation," Michael Palin recalled, "that I've not seen since my father waited up for me."

The next day, most of the company left for another hotel but not before being threatened with a bill for two full weeks' worth of charges. Palin recalls they left with "lighter hearts," having escaped the discourteous Mr. Sinclair.

While his Python partner may have departed with a lighter heart, John Cleese left the Gleneagles with a fully developed comedy character, one strong enough to carry a series into television history—although he didn't yet realize it. "He [Sinclair] was like Basil," Cleese later told Python biographer Kim Johnson, "but much smaller, a skinny little guy about five foot, four inches, with a large wife who dominated him. We reversed the sizes."

After *Python*, one of Cleese's next assignments was to write, along with Graham Chapman, some episodes for London Weekend Television's *Doctor at Large* series. One of their efforts, a February 1973 episode entitled "No Ill Feelings," was set in a rundown hotel, and Cleese effortlessly based the uncivil manager and his dominating spouse on the couple he had encountered in Torquay. This original incarnation of Basil Fawlty was named George Clifford and was played by Timothy Bateson who, according to Cleese, was very good in the role. LWT producer Humphrey Barclay, who had directed Cleese in the *Footlights Revue* at Cambridge, was similarly impressed by the character. "You know," Barclay advised Cleese, "there's a series about those two characters."

Cleese dismissed the suggestion as the typical thinking of a television producer, always trying to expand a one-off idea into a full-blown series. Another two years went by before Cleese actually sat down with his then-wife, Connie Booth, to try and develop a television series for the BBC. After a few abortive concepts, Cleese recalled the infamous Gleneagles and the irritating Mr. Sinclair, and he realized that Barclay's easily dismissed advice was indeed prophetic. Cleese particularly relished the venue of a hotel in that it made it possible for any funny character he desired to simply come walking in without any ponderous motivation or reason. "We didn't have to explain or set anything up," Cleese recalled in *The First 20 Years of Monty Python.* "It's all very straightforward and conventional, so we could start right away with the jokes."

True to his word, Cleese and Booth's scripts do indeed start right away with jokes with an absolute minimum amount of exposition. What we discover about the regulars in the cast we learn while laughing at their easily recognizable types. As with other classic Brit-coms, such as *Steptoe and Son*, we are not introduced to the staff of Fawlty Towers as much as we are allowed to observe them in midcrisis on what is apparently an average day in their world. Truly, it is difficult from mere observation to tell which is the premiere episode (it is "A Touch of Class"). One of the few clues to what shows came when is not found in the scripts but is evident by the changing architecture of the sets.

Architectural design also is an apt description of the way in which the carefully crafted episodes were scripted. Whereas, by Cleese's own estimate, the average sitcom half hour took ten days to write, each episode of *Fawlty Towers* took around six weeks. And while the average comedy would come in at approximately 65 pages of scripted material, Cleese and Booth turned in close to 120 pages per installment.

"We play it much faster than most people," Cleese explained in 1979, "so there's more to write. We try to cram more plot in too. We are trying for a mini-play rather than the usual sketch."

The Guinness Book of Classic British TV places the average time for scripting a *Fawlty Towers* opus at nearly four months, during which the authors went through around ten separate drafts.

The key to *Fawlty Towers*, of course, are the beautifully conceived plots, which skillfully intertwine divergent characters and situations in a comic symphony that inevitably comes crashing down in a crescendo atop Basil Fawlty by the final fadeout. To keep each carefully drawn plot on track, Cleese and Booth would first outline the story on long rolls of wallpaper, with each separate character's involvement written in a different color of felt marker. Only after the plot reached its final form would the writers go back and drape their marvelous jokes and physical bits over this framework.

"We always plot the scripts first," Cleese confessed to Guy Bellamy prior to the second series premiere, "then we speak the lines until the rhythms are right. Only then do we start to write."

Booth credits their writing routine to Cleese's meticulous thought processes. "John's very thorough," she recalled in 1979. "He has a mathematical mind. He was a law student once and he spent two years teaching in a boys' prep school."

This painstaking attention to detail more than any other factor, accounts for both the quality of the shows and the fact that only 12 episodes were ever produced.

Cleese and Booth have admitted writing the first series of six shows purely for their own pleasure. Producing a ratings hit was not their primary motivation. Apparently, the BBC was also not anticipating a comedy sensation from the new series, since it aired *Fawlty Towers* on BBC 2, the junior channel, on Friday evenings at 9 P.M. When the initial six entries proved to be instant classics, critical smashes, and ratings winners, the BBC and the public naturally expected more episodes. The creators of the show, however, thought they had exhausted the possibilities from the core characters. This, coupled with the fact that the Cleese/Booth marriage was quickly disintegrating (they divorced in August 1978) forestalled the return of the saga to the airwaves.

The basic premise of *Fawlty Towers* is poetically simple: a hotel run by a brusque owner who would rather abuse his guests than serve them. John Cleese as Basil Fawlty plays his part with the perfect blend of hostility and frustration, so the audience is easily able to root for this paragon of rudeness. Lending the needed level of sympathy to Basil is the sublime construction that surrounds him with the irritants necessary for him to produce his pearls of wit. The greatest bane to Basil's existence — even more than the stream of guests expecting a minimal degree of service — is of course his harridan of a wife, Sybil (Prunella Scales). Sybil and Basil's marriage has long had any semblance of affection drained from it. All that is left of their union is a steady flow of fuming antipathy. Most of this hatred flows from Basil toward his spouse, as she definitely rules the roost, much to his constant frustration.

Finding no solace in his marriage, Basil Fawlty is further tormented by Manuel, his bellhop/waiter from Barcelona. In a less finely crafted sitcom one, might expect Basil to pass on his ire to his underling. Basil does try mightily to find some release in abusing Manuel — often physically — but more often than not he actualizes scant comfort in doing so. Manuel, as brought to life by Andrew Sachs, is so wonderfully dense and inept that Basil's attempts at verbal mistreatment bounce off him harmlessly, adding to Basil's ill humor. The only slight comfort, which Basil fails to notice, comes from Polly (Connie Booth), the only fully sane and competent member of the staff.

In addition to the core quartet, *Fawlty Towers* boasted a trio of dotty old-age pensioners as permanent residents. The most prominent of these was Ballard Berkeley as Major Gowen, whose addled mental state only adds to Basil's troubles. Gilly Flower and Renee Roberts as Misses Tibbs and Gatsby provided similar, albeit gentler, non support.

With Cleese and Booth taking such care on the scripts, it comes as no surprise that the execution of their masterpieces demanded similar commitment from the cast. Prunella Scales described the acting chores on *Fawlty Towers* as blissful but demanding. "John, quite rightly, expects very hard work from the cast," Scales told the *Radio Times*. "That's how he achieves the very high standards that he gets. If it's not right, we do it again. But it's nice to work with someone you respect."

Andrew Sachs, in a 1998 interview with *British Television* magazine described Cleese as "a wonderful team man ... if you comported yourself as a professional and did your job properly, John could be wonderfully generous and sensitive."

Sachs, with the often physically demanding role of Manuel, proved himself the consummate trooper. During the first series' "The Wedding Party" episode, the script called for Cleese to strike Sachs with a frying pan. Instead of delivering a glancing blow, Cleese accidentally got closer than he intended with the skillet, leaving the utensil dented from the impact. On another occasion, Cleese almost knocked out Sachs's teeth with a spoon. Despite these close calls, however, the most dangerous encounter for Sachs came during the filming of "The Germans." A scene that required Manuel's jacket to catch fire left Sachs permanently scarred when the acids used to produce the smoking effect burned the actor's shoulders. "In the summer it's the bit that doesn't get brown," Sachs later said, describing the injury. "It looks as if my wings have fallen off."

The BBC compensated Sachs with a £700 settlement.

Notwithstanding the demands of creating the first six episodes, Cleese and Booth gave in to popular demand and began work on a second series in 1976. Other projects, including Cleese's work in the Pythons' *Life of Brian* and Booth's appearance in *The Glass Menagerie*, intervened. The writers' other commitments coupled with their divorce and their exacting standards stretched the hiatus between the two series to four years. At one point, the couple went to Monaco with their daughter with hopes of producing some suitable *Fawlty* material but came back as frustrated as their lead character when they were unable to capture the comic muse.

The first five installments of the second series began airing in February 1979. The final episode, "Basil the Rat," was not seen until late October of that year, owing to a strike at the BBC. Generally, the second series was not quite up to the incredibly high standard set by the first half-dozen episodes of *Fawlty Towers*. Still, even the weaker entries in this series are better-than-average situation comedy fare.

After the second series, Cleese successfully resisted all enticements to continue *Fawlty Towers*. There were rumors of returning the characters for a film in which they would travel to Spain and encounter an Iberian version of Basil. Andrew Sachs, for one, is glad that the series was confined to the 12 shows produced. "I don't think it would have transferred well to the big screen," Sachs speculated almost 12 years after the final show aired. "Nor would it have been likely to work in a two-hour format. Part of the success of *Fawlty Towers* is that it works so perfectly as a half-hour-long small-screen entertainment."

Although John Cleese and Connie Booth were adamant about not continuing *Fawlty Towers*, numerous attempts have been made to translate the classic formula to American television. The first try was called *Snavely* (aka *Chateau Snavely*) and starred Harvey Korman as Henry Snavely, the American version of Basil Fawlty. Together with his Sybil-like wife, Gladys (played by Betty White), he attempted to run a shabby hotel in the Midwest. Manuel's character changed nationality, becoming an Italian named Petro (Frank LaLoggia), while Polly became Connie, a college student working as a waitress (played by Deborah Zon). A pilot was produced and aired in June 1978 on ABC, but it failed to become a series.

Five years later, ABC gave it another try with *Amanda's*, starring Bea Arthur as a female version of Basil, who ran Amanda's by the Sea, a hotel overlooking the Pacific. Originally, the producers of *Amanda's* tried to lure Andrew Sachs to America to repeat his role as a Spanish waiter. "My first response was that 'you have enough Hispanic actors in the United States,'" Sachs told Dan Abramson. "Why should I get the Green Card?"

Sachs decided against taking the role especially when he learned that his contract would have called for a commitment of 36 weeks a year for up to five years. As it turned out, there was little to fear. *Amanda's* aired as a midyear replacement from February 10 to May 26, 1983, but failed to come close to the original it intended to emulate and was dropped from ABC's schedule.

Some — including a Finnish Internet website — have wrongly claimed that the hit 1980s series *Newhart*, starring Bob Newhart, was a *Fawlty Towers* imitation. Aside from both series being set in hotels (*Newhart* is actually in an inn), the two shows have little in common, especially their respective stars' comic styles.

In 1999, yet another attempt was made to recapture the Cleese/Booth formula of hard work and genius. This time, the incarnation was titled *Payne* and starred Emmy Award–winning actor John Larroquette in the title role of Royal Payne (get it?). While Larroquette's talents came closer than any of the other Cleese imitators in recapturing Basil Fawlty, unfortunately, JoBeth Williams as his wife was a pale, forced, and often confused shadow of Sybil. The set for *Payne* looked incredibly like that for *Fawlty Towers*, although for some odd reason it was all reversed from the original (probably Hollywood's attempt at innovation).

The inability of *Fawlty Towers* to be successfully cloned or perpetuated beyond its original inspiration is a tribute to the genius contained in the scant dozen shows created by John Cleese and Connie Booth. While the many fans of the show have to content themselves with only a handful of classic programs, they can also be grateful for a consistently hilarious show that, like the best comedy, stands up well to repeated viewings.

THE EPISODES

By John Cleese and Connie Booth. Directed by John Howard Davies and Bob Spiers. Produced by John Howard Davies and Douglas Argent

Series One 1975

EPISODE 1: "A TOUCH OF CLASS" ★★★½

Air date: September 19, 1975. Cast: Basil Fawlty (John Cleese); Sybil Fawlty (Prunella Scales); Manuel (Andrew Sachs); Polly (Connie Booth); Major Gowen (Ballard Berkeley); Miss Tibbs (Gilly Flower); Miss Gatsby (Renee Roberts); Lord Melbury (Michael Gwynn); Danny Brown (Robin Ellis); Sir Richard Morris (Martin Wyldeck); Mr. Watson (Lionel Wheeler); Mr. Wareing (Terence Conoley); Mr. Mackenzie (David Simeon)

Behind his wife, Sybil's, back Basil Fawlty has placed an expensive advertisement in an upscale magazine to try and attract a better class of clientele to their hotel. Basil's caste system is put to the test, however, when he discovers that Lord Melbury, who he has been fawning over, is actually a con man, while the Cockney guest he has been deriding is in reality a policeman trying to catch Melbury.

Fawlty Towers begins with a bang and truly never lets up on the pace. The first installment in the series, unlike other programs, has little exposition to tell us that it indeed is the premiere episode. The characters arrive well written and fully developed. Within the first few moments we are given strong indications of Basil's idiosyncrasies and the stormy relationships among himself, his wife, his help, and his guests.

"A Touch of Class" is especially good in that it delves into one of Basil Fawlty's primary weaknesses — his desire to be a part of Britain's upper class, or at least cater to it. This is done, as with most episodes of this series, with a clever twist. The noble who Basil dotes over turns out to be a crook, and despite his best efforts, the true peers are repulsed by Basil's lack of class.

Basil's constantly obsequious behavior toward Lord Melbury, especially as juxtaposed against his disdain of commoners, is the source of most of the mirth in "A Touch of Class." For Basil Fawlty, in the case of nobility, there is never any question. A perfect case in point is his illogical defense of Melbury's shabby luggage.

When Sybil remarks that his lordship's suitcases were "tatty," Basil takes up the cause, noting that only real nobility would distinguish itself with such worn luggage.

EPISODE 2: "THE BUILDERS" ★★★★

Air date: September 26, 1975. Cast: Basil Fawlty (John Cleese); Sybil Fawlty (Prunella Scales); Manuel (Andrew Sachs); Polly (Connie Booth); Major

Gowen (Ballard Berkeley); Miss Tibbs (Gilly Flower); Miss Gatsby (Renee Roberts); O'Reilly (David Kelly); Lurphy (Michael Cronin); Jones (Michael Halsey); Kerr (Barney Dorman); Stubbs (James Appleby); Delivery Man (George Lee)

Against Sybil's wishes and without her knowledge, Basil hires O'Reilly, a cheap and inept builder, to do some minor construction work at the hotel. When O'Reilly makes a complete mess of the job, Basil tries to blame Sybil's builder of choice, but she quickly sees through his feeble subterfuge. After Sybil storms out of the hotel, O'Reilly and Basil put the work right — only to place the entire edifice in jeopardy when they inadvertently knock through a supporting wall.

"The Builders" spotlights the second of the major conflicts of *Fawlty Towers*: Basil versus his wife, Sybil. This presumably continuing battle is set against the situation of a minor renovation to the hotel. Sybil wants Stubbs, a professional builder, who charges professional fees, to do the job. Basil on the other hand wants O'Reilly, an incompetent contractor, for the work, mainly because he is cheap. While ostensibly the plot centers on the building, it really is about Basil's ongoing attempts to save a pound, against his wife's knowledge and her wishes.

Prunella Scales shines in this episode and turns in a genuinely shrewish performance, although never is her nagging without justification. She actually gets to release physically some of her built-up hostility, although not toward Basil but directed at the puckish, simple O'Reilly (wonderfully played by David Kelly). Basil presumably knows better.

The episode is also noteworthy for some funny bits by Andrew Sachs as Manuel is left in charge of the hotel. The befuddled Barcelonan takes great pride in swaggering behind the front desk and answering imaginary phone calls as the proprietor of "Manuel Towers."

The situation deteriorates rapidly when Manuel is called upon to deal with real individuals. He mistakenly believes that a man delivering a garden gnome is trying to secure a room for the statue. He hangs up repeatedly on Basil, who is calling in to the hotel. Finally, he manages to get punched in the nose by one of the builders.

Also entertaining is the similarly inadequate O'Reilly, the only change being an Irish accent rather than a Spanish one. O'Reilly's overriding sanguinity clashes wonderfully with Basil's hard-won pessimism.

EPISODE 3: "THE WEDDING PARTY" ★★★

Air date: October 3, 1975. Cast: Basil Fawlty (John Cleese); Sybil Fawlty (Prunella Scales); Manuel (Andrew Sachs); Polly (Connie Booth); Major Gowen (Ballard Berkeley); Miss Tibbs (Gilly Flower); Miss Gatsby (Renee Roberts); Alan (Trevor Adams); Jean (April Walker); Mrs. Peignoir (Yvonne

The staff of Torquay's most inhospitable hotel (1. to r.) Manuel (Andrew Sachs), Polly (Connie Booth), and Sybil Fawlty (Prunella Scales) await the pleasure of another guest as manager Basil Fawlty (John Cleese) provides support and encouragement. Copyright © BBC.

Gilan); Mr. Lloyd (Conrad Phillips); Rachel Lloyd (Diana King); Customer (Jay Neill)

Basil's sense of propriety is stretched to the limit when an unmarried couple asks for a double room. Out of Basil's earshot, we learn that the couple, Alan and Jean, are long-time friends of Polly and are in town for a wedding the next day. To challenge his protestations of decency, Basil is continually embarrassed by situations intimating hanky-panky with Mrs. Peignoir, a French guest, and even Manuel.

"The Wedding Party" employs a favorite *Fawlty Towers* theme: mistaken identity/situation. Basil Fawlty, of course, is a master of the erroneous snap judgment; four of the series' 12 episodes hinge on this device. Another oft-used contrivance, Basil's prudery, rears its head here as well.

The episode has little in the way of the typical verbal humor that is a mainstay of *Fawlty Towers.* Instead it features strong situations played with little exaggeration. John Cleese's ability as an actor is showcased in this episode, as he must run through a full slate of emotions from moral indignation to guilty embarrassment.

Basil, as usual, gets it wrong. This occurs twice with hilarious results in "The Wedding Party." The first time, he upbraids guest Alan for supposedly wanting to find a late-night chemist (drugstore) to buy prophylactics. When Alan explains that he wants to buy some batteries, Basil becomes even more outraged, imagining that the batteries are for some boudoir apparatus. It is only after he registers his full revulsion that Basil realizes the man wants to buy batteries for his electric razor.

The second time is when Basil tries to keep Mrs. Lloyd, Jean's mother, from her room because he believes Mr. Lloyd is fondling a string of strangers there when actually he is hugging his stepdaughter and Polly. Basil takes Mrs. Lloyd on a contrived tour of the kitchen and feigns a leg cramp from a recurrent war wound in an attempt to keep her from her room. Finally he takes the poor woman into a room across the hall from her own on the pretext that it is superior to her own and then apologizes for the fact. When Basil delivers her back to her husband, the woman clings to him for a moment before looking about bewildered and noting that their room is just like the one across the hall.

The best moments, however, come when Basil is found in what seem to be compromising positions with Manuel. What makes the discoveries even harder to take is that they are made by the very persons to whom Basil has purported to be morally superior.

EPISODE 4: "THE HOTEL INSPECTORS" ★★★★

Air date: October 10, 1975. Cast: Basil Fawlty (John Cleese); Sybil Fawlty (Prunella Scales); Polly (Connie Booth); Manuel (Andrew Sachs); Mr. Hutchinson (Bernard Cribbins); Mr. Walt (James Cossins); Major Gowen (Ballard Berkeley); Miss Tibbs (Gilly Flower); Miss Gatsby (Renee Roberts); John (Geoffrey Morris); Brian (Peter Brett)

When Basil learns that hotel inspectors are in town, he wrongly assumes that one guest, the demanding Mr. Hutchinson, is one of them. From that point on, Hutchinson receives the red-carpet treatment, only to have it rescinded when Basil discovers that Hutchinson is in fact a spoon salesman. At that point, Hutchinson receives increasingly uncivil handling from Basil as retaliation for not being a hotel inspector. Basil's vengeance backfires as the real inspectors arrive to witness his gleeful abuse of Hutchinson.

While no hotel inspector would be likely to rate Fawlty Towers a four-star establishment, "The Hotel Inspectors" episode of *Fawlty Towers* achieves that status easily. This installment crackles with good dialogue, broad physical humor, and strong performances from regular cast members and guest stars alike.

Veteran British actor Bernard Cribbins is wonderfully annoying as the fussy, verbose spoon salesman, Mr. Hutchinson. Cribbins has appeared in numerous films, including Alfred Hitchcock's *Frenzy*, and has starred in various British television comedies of his own (none of which have been exported to America). The plot in this episode is somewhat Hitchcockesque itself with its use of mistaken identities and McGuffins (Hitchcock's term for a trick on the audience). Although Basil mistakes Mr. Hutchinson for a hotel inspector, it is obvious to the audience that the more serious Mr. Walt is probably the inspector. This supposition is yanked out in the episode's final moments and delivers a great closing gag in the process.

The previously lauded Bernard Cribbins lends a great deal to the success of "The Hotel Inspectors." His deft delivery of Hutchinson's verbose speeches lends the right degree of lightness, making a potentially annoying character a delight to watch. Hutchinson, as scripted by Cleese and Booth, is the type who is loath to use one or two words when 10 or 20 will suffice. After his initial confrontations with Basil over ordering a taxi and obtaining a town map, Hutchinson further frustrates the innkeeper by trying to reserve a television to watch a documentary on Squawking Bird, the chief of the Blackfoot Indians. Basil first reacts by trying to ignore Hutchinson, then by answering him, hilariously, in the spoon salesman's own florid speaking style.

This episode is also noteworthy since it, along with "Waldorf Salad," takes place in real time.

EPISODE 5: "GOURMET NIGHT" ★★★½

Air date: October 17, 1975. Cast: Basil Fawlty (John Cleese); Sybil Fawlty (Prunella Scales); Manuel (Andrew Sachs); Polly (Connie Booth); Andre (Andre Maranne); Kurt (Steve Plytas); Colonel Hall (Allan Cuthbertson); Mrs. Hall (Ann Way); Mr. Twitchen (Richard Caldicot); Mrs. Twitchen (Betty Huntley-Wright); Major Gowen (Ballard Berkeley); Miss Tibbs (Gilly Flower); Miss Gatsby (Renee Roberts); Mr. Heath (Jeffrey Segal); Mrs. Heath (Elizabeth Benson); Master Heath (Tony Page)

Basil decides to showcase Kurt, his new chef, by holding a gourmet night. Unfortunately, Basil's upscale plans go awry when Kurt becomes drunk to the point of unconsciousness. Basil tries to salvage the evening by ordering duck dinners from a local restaurant but inadvertently winds up with a large trifle instead of the fowl.

In the *Fawlty Towers* series, viewers are treated to the many facets of John Cleese's comic persona. There is his marvelously sharp sarcastic side, his smarmy groveling side, his outrageously silly side. "Gourmet Night" represents Cleese in one of his most amusing moods — blind frustrated rage. One might guess from the title that this is another of Basil's attempts to rub elbows with the upper class, as in episode one. However, the premise of "Gourmet Night" is no half-baked social climbing scheme. Rather the idea — to feature haute cuisine at the hotel — is not only good, it is endorsed by all concerned. This, instead, is a case where everything that can possibly go wrong does so, thus leading to Basil's fits of manic anger.

As funny as the ending of "Gourmet Night" is, it is anticlimactic after the scene that immediately precedes it. When Basil's car breaks down, his own fault for trying to fix it himself, he verbally abuses, threatens, and finally exacts corporal punishment on the errant auto by thrashing it with a small uprooted sapling. This scene is hysterical not only because it is so irrational but also because it is close to the way most of us personify our cars. Basil's beating the vehicle with a tree limb not only is eminently amusing, it is also very satisfying to those of us who have ever dealt with truculent cars.

Aside from the famous car thrashing, "Gourmet Night" also features a wonderful scene that has absolutely nothing to do with the plot. Still, it is classic *Fawlty*, as Basil confronts a spoiled young diner who is eating with his parents. First the boy, Master Ronald Heath, complains that the chips (French fries) are awful, and the eggs look like Basil just laid them. Ronald goes on to point out that the chips are the wrong shape. "Oh, dear, what shape do you usually have?" Basil asks in mock sympathy. "Mickey Mouse shape? Smarty shape? Amphibious landing craft shape? Poke in the eye shape?"

When Basil rhetorically asks if he can get the boy anything else, Ronald asks for some bread and salad cream. Basil points out that there is already freshly made mayonnaise on the table. Ronald contends, however, that Basil's culinary offerings are puke. "Well, at least it's fresh puke," Basil retorts before launching into a scathingly sarcastic tirade on the chef's magical abilities when it comes to opening jars of salad cream.

EPISODE 6: "THE GERMANS" ★★★★

Air date: October 24, 1975. Cast: Basil Fawlty (John Cleese); Sybil Fawlty (Prunella Scales); Sister (Brenda Collins); Doctor (Louis Mahoney); Major Gowen (Ballard Berkeley); Polly (Connie Booth); Manuel (Andrew Sachs); Mr. Sharp (John Lawrence); Mrs. Sharp (Iris Fry); Miss Tibbs (Gilly Flower); Miss Gatsby (Renee Roberts); Large Woman (Claire Davenport); German Guests (Nick Lane, Lisa Bergmayr, Willy Bowman, Dan Gillan)

Sybil instructs Basil to accomplish three relatively easy tasks while she is in the hospital having an ingrown toenail removed: hang a moose head in the lobby, conduct a fire drill, and attend to a visit by a group of Germans. He has astounding difficulty with all three.

One of the occupational hazards of qualitatively rating a program such as *Fawlty Towers* is the danger of running out of stars. A show that sets such a consistently high standard invariably will go beyond itself, thus threatening to demolish any attempts at ranking it. "The Germans" does that. This episode should be put on a list of television programs to be taken to that mythical island where people are forever being shipwrecked with their ten favorite books, CDs, movies, and so on.

Oddly, although it is perhaps the funniest and certainly one of the most popular with fans, it is not a typical episode. The usual character traits and daily frustrations of Basil Fawlty, while in evidence, are not the driving force behind the laughs. Even its title is a bit misleading since the German guests only show up in the show's final third. One imagines that John Cleese and Connie Booth were conjuring up this installment by saying, "Wouldn't it be funny if Basil got to berate some German visitors and blame them for World War II?" Starting with that desired outcome, we can see that everything prior to the punch line is merely there to deliver us to the hilarious conclusion. Of course, this is in no way telegraphed to the viewer, and the escalation of the situation is humorous in and of itself.

To fully convey the highlights of this episode, one would either have to print the entire text of the script or, better still, include the video cassette of it with each book. In any event, here is a brief recap of some of the best moments:

MAJOR GOWEN

The major has two excellent bit of business in "The Germans." The first is a prolonged conversation with Basil on women, Indians, and Germans, in which the topics are continually being shuffled and confused in the major's addled cranium. The second is a delightful routine in which the major believes that the stuffed moose is speaking to him. What he actually hears is Manuel practicing his English from behind the counter while the moose head rests on top. The major's astonished stammering is priceless in reaction to the Moose / Manuel's earnest intonations that he can speak English well since he learned it from a book.

THE FIRE DRILL

This simple semiannual drill is beset by problems from the start. First Basil cannot find the key to the alarm since Sybil has put in the safe. When he goes to retrieve it from the safe, Basil trips the burglar alarm, which naturally the guests mistake for the fire alarm, and they start to vacate the hotel. Basil must then call them back and try to educate them on the difference between the two signals (the fire alarm is a semitone higher). Once everyone is straight on the nuances between the two bells, Basil announces that the alarm will start in 30 seconds. He is annoyed when the guests stand around, waiting for the drill to start, sarcastically noting that they would obviously be waiting in the lobby if a fire were to start.

THE GERMANS

As previously stated, all that goes before in this episode are just devices to deliver the viewer to Basil's confrontation with the Germans. His main mission, at which he fails miserably, is to not mention the war. Of course with his brains scrambled by his concussion, Basil manages to do nothing but bring up the conflict even in response to the most innocuous comments. For example, Basil rewords every item ordered from the lunch menu to correspond to the topic he's trying to avoid. Thus a prawn cocktail reminds Basil of "Eva Prawn" (Eva Braun was Hitler's girlfriend), pickled herring becomes "Hermann Goering," and a cold meat salad naturally is a Colditz salad (Colditz was infamous German POW fortress). When one of the ladies in the group starts crying, Basil asks if there's anything wrong. A German man insists that Basil stop mentioning the war. Basil responds, innocently, that they started the whole conflict by invading Poland.

Finally, Basil attempts to "cheer up" the Germans with jokes about bombers flying over Berlin and raving imitations of Adolph Hitler — complete with the "funny walk." The funny walk is a goosestep straight out of Cleese's *Monty Python* "Ministry of Silly Walks" skit. It receives the biggest ovation of the program.

Series Two 1979

EPISODE 1: "COMMUNICATION PROBLEMS" ★★

Air date: February 19, 1979. Cast: Basil Fawlty (John Cleese); Sybil Fawlty (Prunella Scales); Polly (Connie Booth); Manuel (Andrew Sachs); Mr. Yardley (Mervyn Pascoe); Mrs. Richards (Joan Sanderson); Mr. Firkins (Johnny Shannon); Major Gowen (Ballard Berkeley); Miss Tibbs (Gilly Flower); Miss Gatsby (Renee Roberts); Terry (Brian Hall); Mr. Mackintosh (Bill Bradley); Mr. Kerr (George Lee)

Basil's attempts to play the horses are frustrated by Sybil's disapproving gaze, the major's unreliable memory, and the interruptions of Mrs. Richards, a hard-of-hearing guest. Even though he manages to win £75, Basil ultimately loses it when circumstances conspire against him.

If you have any sympathetic feelings toward Basil Fawlty, "Communication Problems" is a frustrating episode to watch. It is not that the entry is not well written, rather the difficulty is that it is too well written and too well performed. Its situations are so close to real life, its irritations so believable that one can easily feel Basil's pain. Basil struggles throughout the proceedings, as usual, to come out ahead in the game of life. What makes this latest attempt most annoying is that here he almost succeeds.

Joan Sanderson is particularly irksome in the role of Mrs. Richards, again, not because she plays the part poorly, but rather because she is too real for comfort. While there is much fun in the reactions that the hard-of-hearing Richards elicits from others in the cast, she is ultimately too aggravating to laugh at.

As in other episodes, the main conflict is between Basil and Sybil, with an outsider, this time Mrs. Richards, providing the fodder for their battle.

The title refers ostensibly to Mrs. Richards's frugality in refusing to turn up her hearing aid, but on a wider scale it is the basic problem between the Fawlties.

This episode, the first of the second series, also marks the arrival of Brian Hall in the role of Terry, Fawlty Towers' chef.

While, as previously stated, the character of Mrs. Richards tends to grate on the viewer, she does provide the best exchange of the episode. After checking into her room, Mrs. Richards calls for Basil to complain about the view. She protests that for 7 pounds 20 pence a night she expects a better vista than the one she can enjoy from her window. When Basil explains she has a perfectly good view of Torquay, she remarks that it isn't good enough.

Basil asks what Mrs. Richards had hoped to see out the window of a Torquay hotel: Sydney Opera House, the Hanging Gardens of Babylon, or perhaps herds of wildebeest? Mrs. Richards, it seems, expects to see the sea, which Basil contends is plainly visible between the land and the sky.

EPISODE 2: "THE PSYCHIATRIST" ★★★★

Air date: February 26, 1979. Cast: Basil Fawlty (John Cleese); Sybil Fawlty (Prunella Scales); Polly (Connie Booth); Mr. Johnson (Nicky Henson); Dr. Abbott (Basil Henson); Mrs. Abbott (Elspet Gray); Raylene Miles (Luan Peters); Manuel (Andrew Sachs); Terry (Brian Hall); Miss Tibbs (Gilly Flower); Miss Gatsby (Renee Roberts); Major Gowen (Ballard Berkeley); Mrs. Johnson (Aimee Delamain); Girlfriend (Imogen Bickford-Smith)

A guest, Mr. Johnson, has sneaked a girl into his room, and Basil is trying to catch him at his game. Complicating the matter are the facts that no one else seems to have noticed this nor does anyone else seem to care. In the course of trying to catch Johnson, Basil manages only to attract the attention of a visiting psychiatrist and his wife (who think Basil is crazy), a pretty young Australian girl (who thinks Basil is disturbed), and Sybil (who thinks Basil is trying to fondle the Aussie).

Aside from "The Germans," "The Psychiatrist" is probably the funniest installment in the *Fawlty Towers* saga. Unlike "The Germans," however, this episode is much more typical and representative of many of the standard themes of the series. This should come as no surprise since "The Psychiatrist" is, if not a remake, a return to two situations covered in a pair of entries from the first series. The first theme is Basil's obsession with running a hotel in which all his guests will adhere to his own moral standards. This was the predominant topic of "The Wedding Party." The other revisited subject is that of Basil's loathing of common people and his fawning over those of position, first presented in "A Touch of Class." Melding these themes together is Basil's ongoing battle with his wife. The final result is classic misunderstandings facilitated by confused situations and all carried out with split-second timing.

Fans of the first *Blackadder* series may recognize Elspet Gray as the attractive wife of psychiatrist Dr. Abbott. Although it was only four years after appearing in this episode that she played the Queen in that series, her make-up and accent for that latter role presented quite a different appearance from the one displayed here.

Two marvelous exchanges highlight "The Psychiatrist," one verbal and the other physical. The first involves Basil's horror when he learns that his esteemed doctor visitor is a psychiatrist. Basil feels that all psychiatrists are mad, meddlesome individuals who reduce everything to sex. After voicing his opinion to Sybil, Basil waits on the Abbotts, who have been discussing how difficult it must be for innkeepers to take vacations. Understandably, when Dr. Abbott asks Basil how often he and Sybil "manage it," Basil thinks he is discussing their sexual habits.

After regaining his composure, Basil states that he and Sybil are "about average." Dr. Abbott asks what "average" would be. Mrs. Abbott suggests that average is a few times a year. Basil is shocked. Dr. Abbott's guess is that the Fawlties "manage it" once a year, leaving Basil further nonplused. Regaining a modicum of composure, Basil curtly defends his manhood by asserting that he and the wife manage "it" two or three times a week.

The second incident involves Basil's attempts to peer into Johnson's window in hopes of seeing the girl. With the help of Manuel, Basil places a ladder against Johnson's second-story window. Unfortunately, he picks the wrong window, which he discovers when he scales the ladder only to witness the Abbotts getting ready for bed. The ladder falls over, leaving Basil sprawled on the ground. Manuel runs for help and explains to Sybil that Basil has fallen off a ladder. Sybil asks Manuel what Basil was doing on a ladder in the dark. Manuel innocently explains that his boss is merely trying to see the girl through the window. Sybil then storms outside to present Basil with a slap, which succeeds in knocking him back to the ground.

EPISODE 3: "WALDORF SALAD" ★★★½

Air date: March 5, 1979. Cast: Sybil Fawlty (Prunella Scales); Mr. Libson (Anthony Dawes); Basil Fawlty (John Cleese); Mrs. Johnstone (June Ellis); Mr. Johnstone (Terence Conoley); Miss Hare (Dorothy Frere); Miss Gurke (Beatrice Shaw); Mr. Arrad (Norman Bird); Mrs. Arrad (Stella Tanner); Manuel (Andrew Sachs); Polly (Connie Booth); Mrs. Hamilton (Claire Nielson); Mr. Hamilton (Bruce Boa); Terry (Brian Hall); Major Gowen (Ballard Berkeley); Miss Tibbs (Gilly Flower); Miss Gatsby (Renee Roberts)

Mr. and Mrs. Hamilton, an Anglo American couple on holiday, arrive at Fawlty Towers late one evening. Finding that the dining room is closed, Hamilton pays Basil £20 to keep the chef on and have him cook them a hot meal. After some haggling, Basil lets Terry go and pockets the money himself. Basil would have gotten away with his ruse if it were not for Hamilton's insistence on enjoying a Waldorf salad (apples, celery, walnuts, and grapes in mayonnaise) with his dinner. Finally, Basil's charade falls through and the Hamiltons leave, but not before insisting that Basil listen to the complaints of all the other guests. In response, Basil tells the guests off before leaving himself.

The long-running battle between Basil Fawlty and his guests has, for the most part, been a stalemate. In "Waldorf Salad," however, Basil meets his match in the guise of American Harry Hamilton. Still, Basil does not go quietly into that rainy Torquay night, putting up a valiant struggle even when Hamilton rallies the entire registry against him.

"Waldorf Salad" is seminal *Fawlty Towers* and is the most basic examination of the series' original premise: a rude innkeeper who intensely dislikes waiting on his guests. Given this examination of the primal theme, there is little comedy that stems from secondary sources. Manuel and Polly are almost absent, although Manuel does have a funny bit centered around examining a mystery object in a plate of salad.

The byplay between Basil and Hamilton is splendid throughout, with Basil delivering his usual tactic of defense by excuse and hoax to counter Hamilton's demanding, cash-waving, ugly American. Throughout the conflict, Basil carries on staged shouting matches between himself and an imaginary chef for Hamilton's benefit. Another humorous bit involves Hamilton's American idiom — especially the phrase "bust his ass"— which leaves Basil confused. The last time Hamilton uses it, Basil remarks quietly, "Everything's bottoms, isn't it?"

There's also another of Basil's panic-driven rantings, which occurs when he is frantically searching the kitchen for the ingredients for the Waldorf salad. Sybil enters and tries to calm her husband down by telling him to just look. When Sybil announces that she's found the apples, Basil's tirade shifts into high gear. He sarcastically celebrates Sybil's discovery by announcing they'll throw an apple party, with each guest bringing a piece of the fruit to cram down each other's throat.

The climax of the episode finds Basil forced to defend his hotel's service before Hamilton and the guests. Basil at first intimidates his clientele into agreeing that they are satisfied with their stay, then launches into a patriotic speech about the superiority of British values. His oration is cut short, however, when Mr. Johnstone pipes up that he is not at all satisfied. Basil quickly drops his noble tone and, reverting to form, verbally abuses Johnstone and proves Hamilton's point.

EPISODE 4: "THE KIPPER AND THE CORPSE" ★★★★

Air date: March 12, 1979. Cast: Mrs. Chase (Mavis Pugh); Major Gowen (Ballard Berkeley); Basil Fawlty (John Cleese); Sybil Fawlty (Prunella Scales);

Manuel (Andrew Sachs); Dr. Price (Geoffrey Palmer); Guest (Len Marten); Mr. Leeman (Derek Royle); Mr. Xerxes (Robert McBain); Mr. Zebedee (Raymond Mason); Miss Young (Pamela Buchner); Polly (Connie Booth); Terry (Brian Hall); Miss Tibbs (Gilly Flower); Miss Gatsby (Renee Roberts); Mr. White (Richard Davies); Mrs. White (Elizabeth Benson); Mr. Ingrams (Charles McKeown)

With a hotel full of guests, Basil Fawlty's life is further complicated when one of them, Mr. Leeman, dies in his sleep. Before the undertaker can come to collect the body, Basil, Manuel, and Polly must spend the entire morning hiding the corpse from the other guests. The deceased is shuttled from his room, to another guest's room, into a closet, to the office, then outside, into the kitchen, into a laundry basket, onto a laundry truck, off the truck, back to the original room, back to the other guest's room, and finally onto an umbrella stand. When the rest of the guests finally discover the corpse, Basil hides himself in a laundry basket and goes off on the next truck.

"The Kipper and the Corpse" is a hysterical exercise in the sort of fast-paced farce usually present in a Marx Brothers or Preston Sturges comedy. Beginning with the simplest of premises — the death of a guest — the episode becomes one prolonged attempt to hide the event from the other patrons.

It is surprising in an episode so rife with physical comedy that one finds some of the best dialogue of the series as well. Cleese and Booth have outdone themselves, not only supplying the characters with funny things to do but with equally amusing things to say while doing them. Here are some of the standouts.

Basil has trouble with Mr. Leeman alive and dead. When the obviously ill guest requests breakfast in bed for the following morning, Sybil is quite sympathetic and graciously takes his order. Basil seethes at what he sees as mollycoddling and responds in his usual sarcastic style. After Sybil has noted Mr. Leeman's choices, down to his preferred morning newspaper, Basil asks his own questions, snidely inquiring as to the type of wood he would like his breakfast tray made of. Basil then sends the guest off to bed with the recommendation that he sleep with his mouth open so he can be fed his breakfast while he sleeps.

Basil is even more annoyed the next morning when he delivers the now-dead Leeman's breakfast, and the corpse fails to express gratitude. Basil takes his silence for rudeness. Ultimately, Polly discovers Leeman's final state when she delivers some milk. When Dr. Price is called upstairs to officiate over the body, he questions Basil's failure to notice the deceased's condition. In his defense, Basil sarcastically offers to change the name of the hotel to the "hotel for people who have a better than 50 percent chance of making it through the night."

Adding wonderful support to the generated pandemonium are two familiar actors to fans of Brit-coms. The first is Geoffrey Palmer as the dour, sausage-craving Dr. Price. Palmer has made guest appearances in roughly half of the series covered in this book and had a regular role in the *Reggie Perrin* series. The second is veteran actress Mavis Pugh as the canine-pandering Mrs. Chase. *Dad's Army* devotees may remember her as Lady Maltby in the "Captain's Car" installment.

EPISODE 5: "THE ANNIVERSARY" ★½

Air date: March 26, 1979. Cast: Polly (Connie Booth); Terry (Brian Hall); Manuel (Andrew Sachs); Sybil Fawlty (Prunella Scales); Basil Fawlty (John Cleese); Roger (Ken Campbell); Alice (Una Stubbs); Virginia (Pat Keen); Arthur (Robert Arnold); Reg (Roger Hume); Kitty (Denyse Alexander); Major Gowen (Ballard Berkley); Audrey (Christine Shaw); Miss Tibbs (Gilly Flower); Miss Gatsby (Renee Roberts)

Basil plans a surprise get-together with friends on his and Sybil's wedding anniversary. Unfortunately, when he pretends to have forgotten the date, Sybil storms out just before the guests are to arrive. Rather than tell the truth, Basil goes to great lengths to convince the party that Sybil is seriously ill and cannot have visitors.

"The Anniversary" gives great insight into the reasons for the success of *Fawlty Towers*. Ironically, it provides this by being one of the least amusing installments in the series. While basically sound in its plot, writing, and execution, the main ingredient is missing — the series' driving premise, Basil's utter disdain for the hotel and its guests. Since there are no guests (aside from the major and the two ladies) present nor any hotel business to tend to, Basil Fawlty's major irritants are not present. There is always the battle between him and Sybil, but oddly in this episode he is trying to do something nice for her. When Sybil thinks Basil has forgotten their anniversary, she is more hurt than combative and leaves. The main plot then involves Basil trying to conceal the fact that Sybil has walked out on him. This motivation is rather weak, however, since the truth is not embarrassing to Basil. Consequently, "The Anniversary" is probably the weakest entry in the *Fawlty Towers* canon.

This episode is noteworthy in that the viewers finally meet Audrey, Sybil's best friend, who is frequently spoken to on the phone but until now never actually seen. One can only guess that she is not a friend of both the Fawlties since Basil has not invited her to the anniversary party.

There are some good moments in "The Anniversary." Ken Campbell as Roger, Basil's wisecracking friend, has most of the best lines. Aside from this, the biggest laughs come in the final moments. In this respect, this episode is more like the typical British situation comedy, which builds up its premise throughout to supply one big punch line.

After Basil has told his friends that Sybil is sick in bed, one last couple arrives to announce that they have just seen Sybil driving around town. Basil contends it is a woman from up north who is a dead ringer for her, including the fact that they both drive the same make of automobile. In the show's final minute, after the guests have just been to see Sybil in bed (Polly in disguise), the real Sybil enters the lobby. For a split second, everyone is stunned. Basil is the first to regain his wits and introduces himself to Sybil as if she were her own double. He then leads his confused wife into the kitchen while asking how things are up north. Once in the kitchen, he places a dazed Sybil into the cupboard and locks her inside before going out and saying goodbye to his guests.

Episode 6: "Basil the Rat" ★★★½

Air date: October 25, 1979. Cast: Sybil Fawlty (Prunella Scales); Basil Fawlty (John Cleese); Mr. Carnegie (John Quarmby); Polly (Connie Booth); Terry (Brian Hall); Manuel (Andrew Sachs); Miss Tibbs (Gilly Flower); Miss Gatsby (Renee Roberts); Guest (Stuart Sherwin); Major Gowen (Ballard Berkeley); Mr. Taylor (James Taylor); Mrs. Taylor (Melody Lang); Ronald (David Neville); Quentina (Sabina Franklyn)

After a visit from the health inspector, Basil has 24 hours to bring the hotel into compliance or be shut down. Complicating matters is the discovery that Manuel has been keeping a pet rat (named Basil), which he believes is a rare Siberian hamster.

The next day, everything is ready for reinspection, when Basil-the-rat escapes and returns to the hotel. While the inspector looks over the hotel, Basil and the staff furtively search for the missing animal. In an attempt to bait the rodent, Basil laces a piece of veal with rat poison. Unfortunately, the poisoned veal gets mixed in with the rest of the meat. After completing his duties, the inspector decides to stay for lunch and orders the veal. Finally, after some close misses with tainted veal, the inspector finishes his lunch with a tin of biscuits containing Basil-the-rat.

Fawlty Towers returns to form for its final episode, "Basil the Rat," which features plenty of the series' signature devices, including frantic action, confused situations, strong dialogue, and another panic attack for Basil Fawlty.

Fittingly, the final moment of the episode, and so the whole series, is also a gem. The inspector has asked for the biscuit tin. With Sybil and Basil standing alongside, Polly brings the tin to the inspector and lifts off the lids, revealing Basil-the-rat. The inspector sits in stunned silence, staring at the rodent. After a moment, Basil decides to bluff it out by asking if the gentleman would care for a rat. Polly takes the tin back to the kitchen as the inspector stares into space, obviously wondering if he is seeing things. Sybil calmly pours the inspector's coffee as the inspector attempts to speak. Polly then returns with the same tin, minus the rat, and represents the cookies as if nothing is out of the ordinary. As the confused inspector quietly takes a biscuit, Sybil speaks conversationally of the weather, while in the background Manuel drags out Basil, who has finally fainted under the strain of the day.

The Fall and Rise of Reginald Perrin

BBC-TV 1976–1979

There is little that has gone before that can prepare one for *The Fall and Rise of Reginald Perrin.* This classic slice of television is a combination theater of the absurd and sitcom, which simultaneously assaults and soothes. The viewer is confronted with the hard cruelties of modern society (especially to those trapped in the corporate culture), then relieved of the angst when the demons of the same are exposed as sheer foolishness. All this is deftly accomplished within a framework of plots that spin increasingly out of control with characters that provide the broadest possible targets. In short, the world of Reggie Perrin is a maddening place in which one would never want to be trapped, but it is a sheer delight to observe from the outside.

Bringing this lunacy successfully to the small screen was the joint triumph of its author, David Nobbs, and its star, Leonard Rossiter. Together the author and the actor managed to break out of the predictability and the constraints of the sitcom genre — and soar. Anything could happen from moment to moment in Nobbs's lunatic scripts, from poisoning a fishing derby with loganberry syrup, to a man marrying his own widow incognito, to somebody making a fortune selling square hula hoops. And although he was not the author's original choice for the part, today it is difficult to imagine anyone else bringing such a sense of desperate logic to Reggie Perrin's insanity than the brilliantly manic Rossiter.

Reginald Iolanthe Perrin almost came to television in a much different form than the incarnation that would become a classic. The germ of Perrin first came to David Nobbs in 1974, when the BBC was planning a series of TV plays focusing on current social problems. Already a working television writer for such programs as *The Two Ronnies* and the author of three novels, Nobbs was asked to submit a 30-minute play for the series. In response the author provided an outline about a corporate executive who is driven crazy by his job. The producers rejected the scenario, citing that it hadn't addressed a relevant problem of contemporary life. Nobbs also feels that the fact that he had pitched it as a comedy worked against it. The rejection, however, turned out to be a blessing in disguise. "If the BBC had not turned down this idea — an executive in a food firm being driven mad by the rat race — the books and the series might never have happened," Nobbs explained to the author in 1998.

Undaunted, Nobbs expanded his one-page treatment into a novel entitled *The Death of Reginald Perrin*. After shopping the book to more than a dozen publishers and completely overhauling the second half (in the first draft, Reggie winds up in an asylum), Reggie's tale was finally sold and published in 1975. Attracting good reviews and solid sales, *The Death of Reginald Perrin* was soon coaxed onto the small screen.

The first offer, however, was not to David Nobbs's liking. Granada TV had suggested adapting the novel into three 90-minute programs with comedian Ronnie Barker in the title role. While Nobbs liked the notion of the talented Barker in the role (the stocky actor also more closely fit the physical description of Reggie given in the novel), his agent thought that turning the work into three plays was a mistake. "My agent was convinced that there was a sitcom in it," recalled Nobbs. "I had not seen this as a possibility. My agent sent it to Jimmy Gilbert, then Head of Comedy at the BBC, and he liked the idea instantly. Sometimes agents earn their 10 percent!"

When Nobbs met with Gilbert, the comedy chief asked who the author envisioned in the lead. When Nobbs suggested Ronnie Barker, Gilbert nodded and said: "Fine! Leonard Rossiter it is then." Later, Nobbs discovered that Barker was already tied up with two BBC series (*Porridge* and *Open All Hours*), while Gilbert was trying to land Rossiter for the BBC after the latter's ringing success in ITV's *Rising Damp*. Aside from Rossiter, the majority of the cast was chosen by John Howard Davies, the producer of the pilot episode (the main exception being Geoffrey Palmer in the role of Jimmy, who was selected for the part by Gareth Gwenlan, the show's primary producer).

In retrospect, Nobbs saw the perfection in casting Rossiter as Reggie Perrin. "I know of nobody who did better double-takes," said Nobbs in Robert Tanitch's biography of Rossiter. "He was brilliant at throwaways and at visual jokes. His timing was faultless. His use of body was excellent. He knew exactly where to put the inflection for comic effect. He had above all the rare capacity to be extremely fast and extremely subtle at the same time. Yet none of these devices interfered with his ability ... to present a real human being whose plight could touch us deeply."

The then 50-year-old Leonard Rossiter was Reggie Perrin, or at least he might have been had he not decided to become an actor in 1954. Prior to that decision, Rossiter spent six years as a clerk in the claims and accidents department of an insurance company. While not exactly Sunshine Desserts (the fictional company for which Reggie Perrin worked), one can imagine Rossiter reacting the same way after 20 years or so had he remained there.

David Nobbs tells a story that illustrates well the similar mind processes of the actor and the character who he portrayed. While the series was on location in Oxfordshire, Leonard Rossiter arrived at the hotel where the cast and crew were to stay. Immediately upon checking in, the landlord informed the actor that they didn't furnish front door keys and locked the door promptly at 11.

"Thank you for your thoughtfulness," replied Rossiter politely, "It was nice of you to tell me that before I wasted time and energy walking upstairs." With that, he picked up his suitcase and walked out of the hotel for another one across the way.

Later that evening, the entire cast and crew, about 70 people, gathered in the hotel bar. Rossiter was the last to arrive and loudly announced to the thirsty throng that the drinks would be on him. The landlord brightened, anticipating a huge bar bill.

"Oh, incidentally," added Rossiter in his most Perrinesque fashion, "we're having the drinks in a pub across the green. It seems a very nice place."

With that, the entire assemblage marched out, leaving the bar deserted.

"Reggie would have been proud," notes David Nobbs.

Aside from his offbeat sense of humor, Rossiter could be difficult to work with at times. "Leonard was a perfectionist," recalled Nobbs to the author in 1998, "not always easy to work with, though I always found him very good company socially."

In addition, Nobbs remembers that while Rossiter was a stimulating person to be around, one always had to be on one's mettle. The first time the pair met, Rossiter tried to annoy Nobbs by expressing that he couldn't wait to bring Reggie Perrin to life, then adding that the book was the "second best comic novel by an English writer I've read recently."

Pauline Yates, brought on board to play Elizabeth, Reggie's wife, called Rossiter "an actor's actor." "He was a perfectionist in his work," Yates told Robert Tanitch. "He always knew all his words, all his cues, and in filming all his bits of clothing for continuity; he often caught lazy costume or props people out and he was always right."

Geoffrey Palmer, who played brother-in-law Jimmy, recalled that Rossiter would, when necessary for the outcome of a successful show, tell others how to do their job or even do it for them. "In three series," notes Palmer, "he was never wrong."

While it may seem that such attention to detail on the part of the show's star could lead to a tense professional relationship, those who worked on *The Fall and Rise of Reginald Perrin* recall it as a rewarding experience. "It was," according to Geoffrey Palmer, "the happiest company I have ever worked with and a lot of the credit for that must be his [Rossiter's]."

"It was one of the happiest casts I have ever worked with," echoed Bruce Bould, who played David Harris-Jones, "and Len led it brilliantly."

Apparently the *Perrin* company was so much fun to be around that even David Nobbs took to hanging around, although his work as the show's writer was for all intents finished. He remarked that this was more "for pleasure than to be of great influence." Often, however, Nobbs would be pressed into service to write some extra dialogue when a scene was in danger of running short. This happened quite often, it seems, due to the fact that Leonard Rossiter spoke his lines much more rapidly than the average actor.

"His delivery was extremely fast," Nobbs explained to Richard Webber in that author's *The Life and Legacy of Reginald Perrin*, "and other people took their cue from him, so I ended up writing what would have been 35 minutes on any other production."

On one occasion Nobbs arrived at a location to be told by the production staff there was a problem with the script. The author asked what the trouble was. "Your line says 'Well, we've got a lovely day for it, anyway,'" Nobbs was told, "and it's raining."

"How about changing the line to 'Well, we haven't got a very nice day for it?'" suggested the writer.

"Brilliant," was the sincere reaction to the obvious solution. "Thank goodness you came!"

Another time, during the filming of the first series, Nobbs encountered Leonard Rossiter in his Martin Wellbourne disguise for the first time. "I stood next to him on the catering wagon steps, and didn't recognize him," explained Nobbs. "He roared with laughter when I made some polite remark as to someone I didn't know."

The series also boasted a fine supporting cast. The aforementioned Pauline Yates played the patient and ultra-understanding wife of the unpredictable Reggie Perrin. That the actress brought out those characteristics successfully is attested to by the fact that Yates received most of her fan mail from middle-aged men, all of whom wished they could have a wife like Reggie's.

In the key role of the pompous, overbearing, cliché-spouting C.J., Reggie's boss, pilot producer John Howard Davies called upon character actor John Barron. Barron was sent a copy of the original novel while on location with a TV production in Manchester, along with an offer to play C.J. "I was reaching for the phone as I finished the last page," Barron told the author in 1998. "I usually play upper-class establishment figures, and in this case I think I played it 'straight.' Anyway, the writing was so expert and economical that only a very poor actor could have gone wrong!"

After close to 60 years as an actor, John Barron cites *Reggie Perrin* as the highlight of all his television work. "Middle-aged parents kept coming up to me saying: 'I didn't get where I am today without...,'" Barron told Richard Webber, recalling his and perhaps the series' best known catch phrase.

Next in the cast was Geoffrey Palmer as Jimmy, Elizabeth's brother. Jimmy, who had his own catch phrase ("Cock-up on the catering front"), usually delivered his lines in a clipped military style, reflecting the lifetime he had spent in his country's armed services. At first though, Palmer confesses that he had trouble getting the portrayal of Jimmy right. "Gradually," Palmer confessed to Richard Webber, "I realized the character had to be stronger and bigger in his blundering incompetence — he couldn't be bland."

Once Palmer had his characterization of Jimmy down, he ran with it, making what began as a lesser character one of the more memorable in the series. The character became so well liked that David Nobbs adapted Jimmy into Major Harry Truscott for another program, *Fairly Secret Army*, which ran for two seasons in the mid–1980s on Britain's Channel Four.

Rounding out the excellent supporting cast were Trevor Adams and Bruce Bould as Tony Webster and David Harris-Jones, the up-and-coming but essentially hollow young executives at Sunshine Desserts. Sue Nicholls played Joan Greengross, Reggie's secretary about whom he fantasizes regularly but with whom he fails to have a successful affair (in the book, Reggie succeeds). Tim Preece managed to make Tom, Reggie's dull son-in-law, an interesting and amusing character for the first two seasons. Preece had to hand the reins of the character over to another actor, Leslie Schofield, when other commitments made it impossible for him to appear in the third series. Sally-Jane Spencer was fine as Tom's wife, Linda, while John Horsley, as Doc Morrisey, lent a wonderful sense of befuddled failure to his character.

Following the airing of the first series, there was little response from the BBC. The show had been pitted against strong competition on ITV, leaving its author to wonder how it had been received. Nobbs need not have worried, as he soon discovered while waiting for an elevator at a hotel in Leeds. There he overheard complete strangers exchanging catch phrases from the show, and he knew they had connected with their audience. (The show did spawn an amazing number of catch phrases and variations of them.) Still the show was never an unqualified ratings success. The most-watched installments could only claim just under 11 million viewers, which is rather meager compared to top-rated shows, which usually draw upward of 27 million. Those who understood Reggie, however, represented a devoted core of fans.

At first there weren't any immediate plans for a second series, especially since the novel (and, of course, the first series) had come to so neat a conclusion. At producer Gareth Gwenlan's request, Nobbs went to devise a possible way to bring back the entire cast of characters for a sequel. Happily, Nobbs did, picking up the story where it had been neatly tied up, then unraveling it all with a new set of complications. The second series was also initially brought to life as a novel (*The Return of Reginald Perrin*) and takes the premise to even wilder heights of lunacy. Nobbs himself prefers the second novel and series to the first. "The first was the heart of the matter; it was the dilemma that kicked off the extreme actions Reggie was to take," explained Nobbs in *The Life and Legacy of Reginald Perrin*. "The second saw the series hit its peak in respect of invention."

In the first series, Reggie Perrin revolted against his corporate existence by faking his own suicide, then coming back to interact with his friends and loved ones disguised as someone else. It was all pretty revolutionary but still rather confined to his small circle of acquaintances. In the second series, Reggie rebels against society as a whole as he opens Grot, a store that guarantees to sell nothing but rubbish at exorbitant prices. It is this fantastic plot invention that led to some of the best installments of all three series of *Reggie Perrin*. David Nobbs personally counts episodes four through seven (the Grot episodes) of season two as his favorites (his other favorite is episode five of the first series in which Reggie delivers a drunken speech to a fruit conference).

The quality of the second series naturally called for a third to be made, although it also made sustaining the high standard that much more difficult. Again a novel (*The Better World of Reginald Perrin*) paved the way for the television series. This time Reggie takes the fortune he made with Grot and opens a suburban commune staffed by his friends and family. Aside from some interesting new characters, the most notable being a crazed Scottish chef named McBlane (played by Joseph Brady and utterer of the immortal insult "Up yer clunge!"), the third series failed to live up to the standard of its predecessors.

"The show's run ended because we felt that the third series was not quite as good as the first two," explained David Nobbs to the author. "Leonard Rossiter insisted that I do a novel first each time before he agreed to do the show, as he felt (rightly) that this was a reason for it having greater depth than many sitcoms."

The end of *Reginald Perrin* was not permanent, however. As with most quality comedies produced in Great Britain, there was an American producer who wanted to adapt it for U.S. audiences. Despite the fact that the British originals had already been aired on PBS and had attracted something of a cult following, in 1983 an American version was mounted. Titled simply *Reggie*, the American edition starred Richard Mulligan as Reggie Potter. David Nobbs had been offered a hand in adapting his work for audiences across the pond but declined.

"I had already worked the material twice, as book and series, and wanted to move on to new things," Nobbs wrote to the author. "I also wasn't confident about writing for America and I had an enormous respect for American comic expertise — sadly, I think this was not justified in this particular case."

Reggie ran its lone six episodes on ABC as a late summer replacement series. Unfortunately it was in most respects the opposite of its British predecessor. Whereas the original had been fast-paced and funny, the American version was slow and not nearly as humorous. The American version even managed to destroy the indestructible character of C.J. Instead of translating the captain of industry intact, *Reggie* found him a young whiz kid! Aside from these glaring faults, Nobbs sees the reason for the American version's failure in the basic motivation. "The series failed, I feel, because the reasons for Reggie's eccentricity and desperation were not sufficiently established."

The world of Reggie Perrin received a fatal jolt the year after the disastrous *Reggie* had played on American television with the tragic death of Leonard Rossiter. Rossiter had been appearing in the play *Loot* (which ironically is about death) when he died in his dressing room in London's Lyric Theatre in the middle of a performance. The cause of death was a congenital heart defect. Rossiter was only 58.

Although the death of the man inseparably linked with the character of Reggie Perrin would have seemed to put any speculation regarding a revival of the classic series to rest, it was not so. Following his work on *Reginald Perrin*, David Nobbs had gone on to write more novels and television series, most for the BBC's competitors. Wanting to coax the uniquely talented author back to the BBC, producer Gwenlan offered Nobbs carte blanche to create any series he chose. Nobbs suggested a return to *Reggie Perrin*. At first, Gwenlan thought the idea ill advised, until the author pointed out that he didn't want to make a series with a replacement for Leonard Rossiter. Instead, Nobbs pitched the notion of what would happen to the rest of the characters after Reggie's death. Again, Nobbs wrote a novel (*The Legacy of Reginald Perrin*) upon which to base the television series. While the middle-aged Nobbs had focused on the problems of middle-aged executives in the mid–1970s, 20 years later the new series concentrated on the problems of those reaching retirement age. The original cast all agreed to have another go at it, except for Trevor Adams, who the producers thought was unavailable and living in Australia (he wasn't and said so in a bitter newspaper interview when the series first aired).

Unfortunately, although it still had some clever touches (Reggie dies when a billboard advertising his life insurer falls on him), 1996's *The Legacy of Reginald Perrin* missed the mark rather broadly. The problem is not Nobbs's skills as a writer; rather, he was too good a writer in creating such a strong central character to begin with. The characters are compelled to earn a secret inheritance that Reggie has bequeathed, but they must carry out a totally absurd act to do so. Eventually the characters join forces to begin a pensioners' movement, which culminates in a march on London. While there is still some inspired silliness, most of the time the dialogue keeps harking back to the memory of Reggie. Pauline Yates's character, in particular, is constantly urging her compatriots on by telling them to do "what Reggie would have done." As a result the viewer winds up missing the deceased fictional character more than the other fictional characters do.

John Barron, who reprised his role of C.J., summed it up best when he told the author that the *Legacy* series "may have been a bit of a gamble, but Leonard apart, the rest of us seemed to have survived the 20 years and much enjoyed coming together again."

Despite the title of the last series, the legacy of Reginald Iolanthe Perrin is not a financial treasure waiting to be claimed. Rather, it is a rich wealth of comedy as close as the latest rerun or videotape. This should come as great comfort to anyone who has ever run in the rat race, struggled with the frustrations of modern society, or just needed a good laugh.

THE EPISODES

By David Nobbs. Produced by Gareth Gwenlan and John Howard Davies

Series One 1976

EPISODE 1 ★★★★

Air date: September 8, 1976. Cast: Reginald Perrin (Leonard Rossiter); Elizabeth Perrin (Pauline Yates); C.J. (John Barron); Joan Greengross (Sue Nicholls); Doc Morrisey (John Horsley); Tony Webster (Trevor Adams); Morris Coates (Roland MacLeod); David Harris-Jones (Bruce Bould); Esther Pigeon (Jacki Piper); Peter Cartwright (Terence Conoley); Ron Napier (Norman Mitchell); Waiter (Ray Marioni)

Reginald Perrin lives in the London suburb of Norbiton, commutes to his executive job at Sunshine Desserts on a train that is invariably 11 minutes late, has an overbearing, cliché-spouting boss, and is close to the end of his rope. Reggie's drastic mental state surfaces one morning when he can't speak of his mother-in-law without employing the word *hippopotamus* followed by a vivid mental picture of the same beast. In addition, he starts to fantasize on a variety of subjects from flashing the neighbors, to having sex with his secretary, to roller skating to work wearing a kilt and a balaklava.

At the office, Reggie is in charge of the company's new project: a line of exotically flavored ice creams. A test session of the flavors is of little help since,

Another exciting day at Sunshine Desserts struggling over exoctic ices. Reggie Perrin (Leonard Rossiter, left) dictates a memo to his distracting secretary Joan (Sue Nicholls). Copyright © BBC.

owing to a computer glitch, the three most popular flavors are "Bookends, Pumice Stone, and West Germany."

Finally, the pressure to conform to his daily routine becomes too great, and Reggie starts to rebel. He dismisses the attendees at an important meeting by telling them he can't be bothered, and he goes to lunch in an Italian restaurant where he orders ravioli for all three courses of the meal.

Welcome to the absurd world of Reginald Iolanthe Perrin. David Nobbs's script, based on his own literary creation, provides a wonderful encapsulation of each of the quirky characters who inhabit the land of Sunshine Desserts. We are quickly brought up to speed by being afforded a three-day glimpse of Mr. Perrin's humdrum existence, thus allowing us to fully sympathize with the drastic twists and turns to which the protagonist will subject us over the course of three series. The characters, most of them broad parodies of familiar types, are firmly established, usually through the repetition of their favorite phrases.

The premiere episode is so rich in Perrin detail and flavor one hardly knows where to begin in spotlighting favorites. Some of the standout scenes are the examination with Doc Morrisey, the exotic ice cream tasting, and the advertising meeting. Little details, such as C.J.'s flatulent chairs (I wish I knew where you could buy such furniture) and Reggie's fantasy of running longingly across a field toward Joan while sensuously licking an ice cream cone are merely tiny gems thrown in along the way.

Episode 2 ★★★

Air date: September 15, 1976. Cast: Reginald Perrin (Leonard Rossiter); Elizabeth Perrin (Pauline Yates); Peter Cartwright (Terence Conoley); Joan Greengross (Sue Nicholls); Tony Webster (Trevor Adams); David Harris-Jones (Bruce Bould); Doc Morrisey (John Horsley); C.J. (John Barron); Jimmy (Geoffrey Palmer); Linda (Sally-Jane Spencer); Tom (Tim Preece); Tea Lady (Penny Leatherbarrow); Children (Abigail Morgan, Robert Hillier)

Elizabeth suggests that Reggie needs a month-long holiday to combat his current malaise. Reggie agrees and the next day asks C.J. for the time off. Instead of a month, however, Reggie is only given the afternoon to recuperate.

The next day, Reggie seethes as he is forced to drive around a safari park with his daughter, son-in-law, and grandchildren. Finally, the car breaks down in the lion section. Able to stand no more, Reggie gets out of the car in full view of the lions. The lion charges, and Reggie barely manages to return safely to the vehicle.

The second installment of *The Fall and Rise of Reginald Perrin* affords us our first real view of the pressures Reggie encounters in his home. While these are certainly secondary to what he must endure at Sunshine Desserts, they still are enough, coupled with his other problems, to drive him into the face of man-eating lions.

Although he is progressively inching closer to a complete collapse, Reggie still has a firm grip on the absurdity of the business world. He is informed that Tony and David will arrive at any moment to receive their sales territories for the new exotic ice cream line. Undaunted, Reggie takes two area maps. On the first, he traces a large circle using a wastepaper basket; on the second he traces the territory using his secretary's purse — including the strap. When the two junior executives arrive Reggie, with Joan's purse still draped over his wrist, calmly explains that the territories were carefully determined by a computer analysis of market studies. Tony studies his map and announces that 20 percent of his territory is in the sea. Reggie explains this will allow him to forge new sales to the previously untapped markets of trawlers, dredges, and submarines.

Major characters, such as Reggie's flaky son-in-law, Tom, and his overly earnest military brother-in-law, Jimmy, are introduced to good comic effect. Jimmy should be familiar to viewers, as veteran actor Geoffrey Palmer appeared as a guest on a number of popular shows, including *Fawlty Towers* and *Blackadder Goes Forth*. More notably, Palmer starred in *Butterflies* and *As Time Goes By*, both of which have had successful Stateside runs.

EPISODE 3 ★★★½

Air date: September 22, 1976. Cast: Reginald Perrin (Leonard Rossiter); Elizabeth Perrin (Pauline Yates); Joan Greengross (Sue Nicholls); Tom (Tim Preece); Mark (David Warwick); Jimmy (Geoffrey Palmer)

In an attempt to relieve his stress, Reggie decides to finally act upon his fantasy and have an affair with his secretary. With his wife away visiting her mother on Sunday, Reggie asks Joan over under the pretext of getting some important work done.

When Joan arrives, Reggie nervously kisses her, only to find that his advance is passionately returned by Joan, who has harbored a similar fantasy about Reggie. She leads Reggie up to the spare room, but Reggie has second thoughts. The tryst is interrupted when a steady stream of relatives comes to call unexpectedly. Reggie nervously entertains his unwanted guests downstairs while Joan waits upstairs in bed. Finally, Reggie rushes upstairs and tells Joan she had better leave by crawling down the drainpipe.

Unable to find any release with his own wife in episode two, here Reggie Perrin takes a bold step toward having an affair with Joan. Leonard Rossiter turns in one of his most hilarious performances in this installment, playing the nervous straying husband for all it's worth. Ultimately, Reggie realizes that sex is not going to repair his shattered nerves and backs down. It is quite possible, as she stated in the previous episode, that Elizabeth does truly understand her husband's problems since it is she who wisely sends a bevy of family members to keep Reggie from consummating the unwanted affair.

The delight of this episode is not so much in the situation but rather in Rossiter's adept performance. A lesser actor might have denigrated this opportunity into standard farce. Reggie manages to keep his unexpected visitors from entering the bedroom in which he has deposited Joan by a variety of silly excuses. The best of these is that the spare room is filled with top secret dessert experiments, the most covert of which is a nonstick, nonwobbling jelly.

EPISODE 4 ★★★½

Air date: September 29, 1976. Cast: Reginald Perrin (Leonard Rossiter); Elizabeth Perrin (Pauline Yates); Peter Cartwright (Terence Conoley); Joan Greengross (Sue Nicholls); C.J. (John Barron); Mr. Campbell-Lewiston (Tim Barrett); Tony Webster (Trevor Adams); David Harris-Jones (Bruce Bould); Davina Letts-Wilkinson (Virginia Balfour); Mrs. C.J. (Dorothy Frere); Uncle Percy Spillinger (Tony Sympson); Doc Morrisey (John Horsley)

Reggie's strange behavior is becoming more brazen everyday. With his wife away tending to her sick mother, Reggie decides not to cancel a dinner party with C.J. and his wife. Instead he invites a combination of guests guaranteed to clash with each other and decides not to serve any food but plenty of alcohol.

The next day David Harris-Jones wakes up at Reggie's and learns that not only did he get drunk, but he also dropped his trousers to reveal his Beethoven underwear. At the office, C.J. calls Reggie in to have a discussion on standards after discovering that one of his subordinates is wearing Beethoven underwear. After a ridiculous inquiry into the matter, the issue is dropped.

Reggie ends his day by meeting with the company's German representative, who turns out to be a disliked old school acquaintance, Campbell-Lewiston.

Through a series of humorous vignettes, episode four manages to move Reggie Perrin closer to his crisis point. Having failed to find an outlet via sex in episode three, Reggie throws all restraint to the wind and behaves just as it pleases him. This is made easier since Elizabeth is away with the hippopotamus/mother-in-law. Ultimately, however, this does little to satisfy Reggie, and he spends the morose evenings after his wild days trying to talk to Elizabeth on the phone. Unfortunately, every time he calls he manages to wake her up, leaving him apologetic and comfortless.

The episode is grounded on three funny scenes: the no-dinner dinner party, the meeting concerning the Beethoven underwear, and Reggie's meeting/confrontation with Campbell-Lewiston.

At the party the guests, including Reggie's dirty old Uncle Percy, are uncomfortably trying to mingle despite the fact that they have nothing in common except they all are eager for a dinner that will never be served. Only Reggie is enjoying himself— immensely — as he leads the guests around to various locations where they anticipate the food might finally be.

The conference on David Harris-Jones's Beethoven underwear is also a super send-up of business meetings that have nothing to do with business. The scene — as with most of the meetings ever held at Sunshine Desserts — should be all too familiar to anyone who has spent more than a few days working in the corporate world.

The meeting with Campbell-Lewiston is also a delight, thanks primarily to Rossiter's delivery of Nobbs's script. With effortless rapid delivery, Rossiter slips outrageous insults into sentences containing otherwise mundane business figures. He also manages to accuse the man of breaking wind and not cleaning his teeth properly by the time he finishes. Trying to make sense of the attack, Campbell-Lewiston asks if it isn't perhaps a new middle-management test. Reggie agrees, smiling, and suggests he try it out on his German clients.

EPISODE 5 ★★★½

Air date: October 6, 1976. Cast: Reginald Perrin (Leonard Rossiter); Elizabeth Perrin (Pauline Yates); Peter Cartwright (Terence Conoley); Joan Greengross (Sue Nicholls); C.J. (John Barron); Tony Webster (Trevor Adams); David Harris-Jones (Bruce Bould); Doc Morrisey (John Horsley); Dr. Hump (Dennis Ramsden); Elwyn Watkins (Tenniel Evans); Bill (John Rudling)

Having reached the crisis point, Reggie decides to give his speech before the British Fruit Association, attend C.J.'s annual fishing outing, then disappear.

Reggie arrives at the Fruit Association conference, but instead of delivering his planned stinging indictment of society, Reggie gives a mostly incomprehensible speech due to a combination of tranquilizers and wine. Ultimately, he is dragged from the platform by his friends and coworkers.

After the speech debacle, Reggie sneaks away to Sunshine Desserts, requisitions a dessert tanker (shaped like a giant gelatin mold), and drives down to C.J.'s country estate. The next morning Reggie sabotages the fishing derby by pumping loganberry concentrate into the stream.

Reggie drives the tanker to the seaside where, that night, he changes clothes, puts on false whiskers and a wig and strolls off to start a new life.

After building up to it for four episodes, Perrin takes the drastic step of faking his own suicide and starting life anew. The fifth episode is something of a transitional installment, bridging Reggie's angst and his search for a new life. His speech, delivered drunk, is still a succinct presentation of the Perrin philosophy, although not at all understood by its audience (if it had been, Reggie wouldn't have been driven to the point of desperation). The fishing derby sabotage is somewhat anticlimactic, coming as it does between the speech and the bittersweet seaside scene.

The speech itself is a good mix of the incoherent and lucid with many gems floating in his stream-of-consciousness ramblings. Reggie bemoans a life wasted trying to sell desserts instead of enjoying nature, then announces that all the parking meters in London have come down with "Dutch Parking Meter Disease." He then comes down to his core belief, which is essentially that he doesn't know (or care) about anything. This he defends as a noble and peaceful philosophy since the impassive rarely start wars, nor is there wide-scale persecution of the "apathetic by the bone idle." It is at the same time humorous and highly illustrative of the plight of the post modern man.

Episode 6 ★½

Air date: October 13, 1976. Cast: Reginald Perrin (Leonard Rossiter); Elizabeth Perrin (Pauline Yates); C.J. (John Barron); David Harris-Jones (Bruce Bould); Tony Webster (Trevor Adams); Linda (Sally-Jane Spencer); Jean Timpkins (Anne Cunningham); Mr. Deacon (Ken Wynne); Mrs. Deacon (Hilary Mason); Miss Pershore (Charmian May); Mr. Thorneycroft (Roger Brierley); Barmaid (Pamela Manson); Henry Possett (John Forbes-Robertson); Landlord (David Millet); Neighbor (Vi Kane); Waiter (Hamilton McLeod); Major (Bob Sutherland)

Having successfully staged his suicide, Reggie travels through a variety of towns in an assortment of identities, looking for a place to establish a new life. After a month he winds up back in his own area and spends his days stalking his old stomping grounds. Reggie soon learns that Elizabeth is being courted by his old rival, Henry Possett.

Disguised with a pair of buckteeth, Reggie gets a room in a rundown boardinghouse and finds a job as a manual laborer. After being approached sexually by his spinster neighbor, Reggie decides he wants to go back to his old life but doesn't know how to do it. He visits his daughter, Linda, who agrees to break the news to Elizabeth. Elizabeth stops by, but before Linda can tell her Reggie is alive, she announces that she is going to marry Henry Possett.

Episode six finds the thought-to-be-late Reginald Perrin searching for a new life and identity. Unfortunately, this installment wanders a bit, taking the entire episode to establish the fact that Reggie misses his wife and would like at least part of his old life back. There is less amusement than one would imagine as Reggie tries a variety of disguises and accents, and one is left with the impression that this is a somewhat mundane stretch in the road between two exciting locations.

After exploring a variety of exotic alter egos (an Australian, an explorer, an Italian), Reggie decides to find work as Donald Potts, a straggly-haired, raspy-voiced, bucktoothed bloke from the lower classes. He attends an interview for work with the Parks Department and manages to paint the worst possible picture of himself. He admits to spending six months in jail for embezzlement.

The interviewer is ecstatic with Reggie's answers, explaining that he's fed up with bright college graduates. He remarks that Reggie is just the type he's been looking for—a shiftless, nefarious drunk.

His delight it turns out is because the job isn't landscaping in the city park, as Reggie assumed, but working in the sewage reclamation works. On his first day on the job, Reggie quickly falls into the sewage.

EPISODE 7 ★★★★

Air date: October 20, 1976. Cast: Reginald Perrin (Leonard Rossiter); Elizabeth Perrin (Pauline Yates); C.J. (John Barron); Joan Greengross (Sue Nicholls); Jimmy (Geoffrey Palmer); Tony Webster (Trevor Adams); David Harris-Jones (Bruce Bould); Linda (Sally-Jane Spencer); Tom (Tim Preece); Miss Pershore (Charmian May); Vicar (Gerald Sim); Mark (David Warwick); Henry Possett (John Forbes-Robertson); Mrs. C.J. (Dorothy Frere); Waiter (Peter MacKriel)

Disguised as Martin Welbourne, an old friend of Reggie's who has been in Brazil for the past 25 years, Reggie attends his own memorial service.

Elizabeth sees through the curly wig and beard disguise, although she tells no one. Elizabeth invites Martin for a day in the country. Soon the two fall in love (or at least express it since they are already in love, unbeknownst to the other). Elizabeth tells Martin she has broken off her engagement to Henry Possett for him. Martin proposes and Elizabeth accepts.

Deeply affected by Reggie's death, C.J. hires Martin to head the new Reggie Perrin Memorial Foundation created to make the employees happy.

At a party to celebrate the engagement, Linda tells Elizabeth that Martin is actually Reggie. Elizabeth admits she's known all along but isn't going to tell Reggie since he's happier as Martin, and it's fun.

The final episode of the first series is — to quote the words of Tony Webster and David Harris-Jones — "great" and "super." Episode seven is so full of zany lines and concepts that the entire half hour is a non stop joy. After trying to establish an alter ego, Reggie hits upon Martin Welbourne, who is essentially Reggie. This allows Reggie to behave like himself among his family and friends while still enjoying the benefits achieved by faking his suicide. Of course, this is all made possible by Elizabeth — beautifully played by Pauline Yates — who, yet again, proves that she really does understand Reggie.

As good as the entire episode is, the best scene is easily the one in which Elizabeth has fun at Reggie's expense by commenting that Martin's gestures and mannerisms are so incredibly similar to those of her deceased husband. Martin nervously paces around, suddenly self-conscious of every move he is making.

Next, Elizabeth remarks on how well Martin knows the layout of the house, including the location of the bathroom, without being told. Martin explains that Reggie, obsessed with giving Martin the layout of his home, conveyed this information in his letters.

Finally, Elizabeth questions Martin about his family and his past. Not having thought of such things when he first donned the wig and beard, Reggie fabricates a ridiculous history for Martin, with each point being sillier than the preceding one.

Series Two 1977

Episode 1 ★★★½

Air date: September 21, 1977. Cast: Reginald Perrin (Leonard Rossiter); Elizabeth Perrin (Pauline Yates); C.J. (John Barron); Joan Greengross (Sue Nicholls); David Harris-Jones (Bruce Bould); Tony Webster (Trevor Adams); Linda (Sally-Jane Spencer); Tom (Tim Preece); Jimmy (Geoffrey Palmer); Doc Morrisey (John Horsley); Owen Lewis (David Rowley); GPO Engineer (Ken Barker); Man at Telephone Box (Derek Deadman)

Reggie hates his new life as Martin Welbourne. His days consist of consciously not doing things as he would have previously and running his own memorial foundation. Unable to keep up the charade any longer, Reggie tells Elizabeth the truth (which, of course, she has known all along). Elizabeth invites the family over, and they are also told. The next day Reggie must continue to be Martin Welbourne at work or risk being fired.

Martin goes to see the recently rehired Doc Morrisey, who quickly figures out his secret identity and rushes to tell C.J. C.J. is not happy with the revelation, and he fires both Reggie and Doc. Reggie goes home, happy to be rid of Sunshine Desserts, and confident that he can get a new job. In the final scene Reggie, in disguise, is tending swine in a piggery.

The opening show of the second series finds Reggie Perrin in a similar state to the first show of the first series. Although he has managed to regain all that he lost by staging his own suicide, Reggie finds that maintaining a separate identity is tiresome at best. When Reggie finally reveals he is alive, the reaction is general relief that the charade is over. In actuality, more characters than not already had seen through Reggie's disguise. Oddly, the person who praised Reggie most highly in death is the one most angry to discover he is alive: C.J.

As Martin Welbourne, Reggie must meet with each employee on a monthly basis to see how happy he or she is. One such meeting is with the timid, nervous David Harris-Jones. In a wonderful performance by Bruce Bould, David fumbles and stutters uncontrollably to declare that the new employee policy has made him a more self-confident and decisive individual.

If putting up with meetings like that weren't enough, Reggie starts to hate his Martin Welbourne role since it involves pretending to enjoy things he hates, such as martinis, mutton casserole, and long walks after dinner. On one of these strolls with Elizabeth, Martin/Reggie is suddenly aware that his beard is coming off. He grabs the false whiskers in panic. When Elizabeth asks what's wrong, Martin claims he has a touch of indigestion in his face.

Unfortunately, the only one he tells of his dissatisfaction is a utility worker. In a running gag, Martin walks around the corner on his way to work and suddenly shouts that he hates Martin Welbourne. The abruptness of the declaration causes a utility worker to fall down his manhole on two consecutive days. On the third day, Martin stops to apologize to the man. The worker graciously disregards the outburst, then asks who Martin Welbourne is. "I am!" Reggie announces as he walks away, causing the man to tumble down the hole a third time.

EPISODE 2 ★★½

Air date: September 28, 1977. Cast: Reginald Perrin (Leonard Rossiter); Elizabeth Perrin (Pauline Yates); C.J. (John Barron); Mr. Pelham (Glynn Edwards); Joan Greengross (Sue Nicholls); David Harris-Jones (Bruce Bould); Tony Webster (Trevor Adams); Linda (Sally-Jane Spencer); Tom (Tim Preece); Peter Cartwright (Terence Conoley); House buyer (Christopher Lawrence); Clerk at Labour Exchange (Ralph Watson); Girl at Bus Stop (Helen Bernat)

Unbeknownst to Reggie, Elizabeth lands a job at Sunshine Desserts as a secretary to Tony and David. Elizabeth tells Reggie she is working for the

British Basket Company, but Reggie is suspicious, having never heard of such a firm. Soon the Perrins settle into a new routine of Elizabeth going to the office and Reggie keeping house.

C.J. attempts to have an affair with Elizabeth by asking her over to his house on a Saturday when his wife is away on the pretext of doing some filing. At the last minute, C.J. gets cold feet and produces some paperwork for them to file.

Unable to quell his suspicions any longer and suspecting his wife of having an affair, Reggie follows Elizabeth on Monday morning and discovers she is working at Sunshine.

A conscious reversal of roles and situations from the first shows of the first series, this episode finds Elizabeth working at Sunshine Desserts while Reggie tends house. There are some amusing moments as Reggie plays the dutiful housewife — remember, this was 1977, when such a situation was still fodder for comedy — sending his wife off to work exactly as she used to send him. The only difference is that in the Britain of the late 1970s, Elizabeth is only a typist, not an executive. There is also a tilt at an affair, but unlike her husband, Elizabeth — again, indicative of the times but also the character — is the pursued not the pursuer. Unlike Joan Greengross, however, Elizabeth has no trouble rejecting the advances of her boss, even when he tells her that friends call him "Bunny."

The only flaw in this installment is the somewhat tiresome repetition of action with little plot advancement.

When Elizabeth goes to see C.J. at his request, she informs Reggie's former employer that he's working at a piggery. C.J. replies — with a pantomime sincerity that only a top-level executive could muster — that the corporate world's loss is the "porkers' gain."

Rather than tell Reggie that she is working for the firm that drove him over the edge, Elizabeth makes up a fantastic story —à la the Martin Welbourne chronicles — about her employer. Her boss is a Scottish-Hungarian, former heavyweight boxer with a wooden leg, who drinks like a fish. Reggie dutifully swallows the story at face value (a common courtesy on *The Fall and Rise of Reginald Perrin*) but questions Elizabeth's veracity when he discovers there is no listing for the British Basket Company in the phone book. Elizabeth explains that it had its listing removed so as not to be confused with the other BBC.

Reggie's attempts at keeping house are as poor as Elizabeth's attempts at fabrication. Everyday when Elizabeth returns home, Reggie is vacuuming — or at least he has the machine running — while doing something else: reading the paper, drinking, or watching children's programs on television. At the sound of Elizabeth coming in the front door, he quickly hides the evidence of his real activity and leaps to the vacuum cleaner. While his extra-cleaning activities vary, his menu never does. Each night for dinner, Reggie serves risotto.

EPISODE 3 ★★★

Air date: October 5, 1977. Cast: Reginald Perrin (Leonard Rossiter); Elizabeth Perrin (Pauline Yates); C.J. (John Barron); Mr. Pelham (Glynn Edwards); Jimmy (Geoffrey Palmer); Linda (Sally-Jane Spencer); Tom (Tim Preece); Joan Greengross (Sue Nicholls); Tony Webster (Trevor Adams); David Harris-Jones (Bruce Bould)

At the piggery, Mr. Pelham informs Reggie that he knows his entire history and fires him for deceiving him. At Sunshine Desserts, C.J. fires Elizabeth for rewriting a letter to a complaining customer that admits that their products are overpriced "synthetic rubbish." Having been sacked on the same day, Elizabeth and Reggie agree to work together on their next venture. Elizabeth suggests they open a shop and make things to sell in it. Reggie sarcastically attacks the idea as simplistic.

Jimmy stops by to offer Reggie a secret job. When Reggie meets him at a secret location, Jimmy shows him a box of rifles and suggests that he join a paramilitary group devoted to fighting just about everyone else in society. Reggie calls the idea rubbish, then suddenly gets a brainstorm, and rushes home. Reggie excitedly tells Elizabeth that they will open her suggested shop, and they will make and sell rubbish. He tells her they will call the store "Grot," and its slogan will be "Everything in this shop is guaranteed absolutely useless."

Just as the first series steadily marched toward its main event (Reggie's staged suicide), so the second season of *The Fall and Rise of Reginald Perrin* moves toward its goal: the establishment of the Grot shops. The first is Reggie's rejection of his middle-class, corporate life and his attempt to leave it. The second is rejection of it by vigorously playing the game with the intent to mock it.

There are some good and varied scenes in this episode. The excellent comic actor Geoffrey Palmer, as Jimmy, finally gets an opportunity to shine in the scene in which he explains his secret war to fight anarchy. The only disappointment in the episode is Elizabeth's revelation that she planned to get fired and have an affair as an object lesson to Reggie. The affair, of course, never really happened, nor was the notion of dallying with C.J. attractive to her. Still one wishes that she had written admissions of Sunshine's "soggy sponges" for the sheer pleasure of admitting it.

Reggie's best moments in the third episode of the second season are with employers, past and present. When Reggie confronts C.J. about Elizabeth's affair, C.J. has just finished blowing kisses into the phone to Elizabeth. In the face of an irate husband, however, the usually blustering C.J. is quickly deflated. Not having gotten where he is by being deflated, C.J. throws Reggie off the scent by admitting that he saw Elizabeth and Tony Webster in compromising positions. Reggie asks for details.

C.J. confesses that he caught Tony dictating and Elizabeth taking notes from opposite ends of the room. Reggie fails to see what is scandalous about that. "Suspiciously unsuspicious," C.J. concludes in yet another perfect parody of corporate logic.

EPISODE 4 ★★★½

Air date: October 12, 1977. Cast: Reginald Perrin (Leonard Rossiter); Elizabeth Perrin (Pauline Yates); C.J. (John Barron); Linda (Sally-Jane Spencer); Tom (Tim Preece); David Harris-Jones (Bruce Bould); Tony Webster (Trevor Adams); Joan Greengross (Sue Nicholls); Morris Coates (Roland MacLeod); Esther Pigeon (Jacki Piper); Miss Erith (Joan Blackham); Peter Cartwright (Terence Conoley); Mr. Milford (Edward Dentith); Wine Buyer (Michael Bilton); Housewife (Cynthia Etherington); Well-Dressed Man (Del Derrick); Elderly Lady (Beatrice Shaw); Woman with Fur (Gilly Flower)

Reggie goes to see C.J. for a personal loan to start the Grot shop. C.J. willingly writes him a check for £30,000 when he thinks Reggie is blackmailing him over his attempted affair with Elizabeth.

Grot opens and is an immediate success from its first day of business. Two years goes by, and Grot expands to 44 stores with a manufacturing firm (Perrin Products) that supplies its worthless merchandise. Reggie now goes to work at Perrin House, his own modern office building. He has hired David Harris-Jones and other former Sunshine Dessert employees, who have been fired as that firm slowly goes bankrupt.

Although two years elapse in this episode, there is little character development. Most of this installment is concerned with the founding and growth of the Grot shops, Reggie's ultimate rage against the consumer culture. While this episode is tremendous fun, it unfortunately is somewhat akin to a Sunshine Dessert. Like one of those exotic ice creams, it is a sweet treat to view Reggie's rise juxtaposed against C.J.'s failure, but ultimately it provides scant nourishment.

Reggie's successful launching of Grot provides most of the laughs in this fun-filled episode. Starting out, Reggie does his own advertising by writing slogans on posterboard. With such catchy phrases as "Hundreds of gift ideas for people you hate" and "Gifts for people with no taste," Grot is assured of success.

After Grot becomes a resounding triumph, Reggie spends his days with his staff devising new useless items to be manufactured for the shops. Here, for posterity, are a few of the better-selling Grot items: a silent long-playing album entitled *Laryngitis in 30 Lands*; rubber razor blades for nervous shavers; porous waterbeds; upright models of the Leaning Tower of Pisa; slanted models of the Eiffel Tower; mousetraps made entirely of cheese; heat-resistant saucepans; elastic tow ropes for motorists you hate; salt and pepper shakers with no holes; oversized egg cups; non stick glue; and a Dutch-to-Dutch translating dictionary for sale in Holland.

Episode 5

★★½

Air date: October 19, 1977. Cast: Reginald Perrin (Leonard Rossiter); Elizabeth Perrin (Pauline Yates); C.J. (John Barron); Joan Greengross (Sue Nicholls); Tony Webster (Trevor Adams); David Harris-Jones (Bruce Bould); Miss Erith (Joan Blackham)

When Grot continues to grow, Reggie agrees to let Elizabeth come to work beginning June 1st. That is also the day that all Reggie's former Sunshine Dessert colleagues begin working for him, unbeknownst to one another. When they all find out they are working with each other again, but in reversed roles, Reggie is amused. Reggie's amusement fades, however, when he realizes that he's beginning to talk like C.J. and has started seeing the hippo again when his mother-in-law is mentioned.

As wonderfully silly as the success of Grot is, the novelty begins to wear thin rather rapidly (as one would expect of a Grot product). While it is satisfying to see Reggie in command of the individuals who once made his life miserable, this is not the place for our hero. David Nobbs must have realized this also, as he comes to the same conclusion. If Reggie is to best C.J., he must do it by becoming another C.J., as he starts to do by episode's end. The lesson: to beat an adversary at his own game, one must become better at the game than he is, thus you must be like him — only more so.

C.J.'s job interview with Reggie is a treat for anyone who has ever dreamed of turning the tables on an overbearing employer. In anticipation of the interview, Reggie purchases a special flatulent chair. When C.J. sits down, he is visibly shaken by the noise the chair. Reggie delights in forcing his ex-boss to get up and down no fewer than three times to repeat the sound.

When Reggie asks C.J. if he could work for him, the former head of Sunshine Desserts replies in typical form. "I've always taken great pains not to talk in clichés," C.J. begins. "Mrs. C.J. and I have always avoided clichés like the plague. A cliché to me is like a red rag to a bull."

Finally, C.J. uses yet another cliché to agree to take the job.

Reggie concludes the interview by pointing out that the ashtray C.J. has been holding in his lap is bottomless (another Grot product), and his cigar ashes are now all over his trousers.

Episode 6

★★★½

Air date: October 26, 1977. Cast: Reginald Perrin (Leonard Rossiter); Elizabeth Perrin (Pauline Yates); C.J. (John Barron); Jimmy (Geoffrey Palmer); Doc Morrisey (John Horsley); Seamus Finnegan (Derry Power); Joan Greengross (Sue Nicholls); Tom (Tim Preece); Linda (Sally-Jane Spencer); David Harris-Jones (Bruce Bould); Tony Webster (Trevor Adams); Gladys (Sheila Bernette); Arthur (Ken Morley); Adam (Robert Hillier); Jocasta (Abigail Morgan)

Tired of being a tycoon, Reggie sets out to secretly destroy Grot by employing incompetents in key positions. The first hired is hypochondriac

Doc Morrisey as head of forward planning. Next Reggie meets Seamus Finnegan, a common Irish laborer, in a pub and immediately hires him as administrative officer of the company. A disastrous family holiday makes Reggie realize that Tom is the perfect poor choice to be head of advertising for Grot. When brother-in-law Jimmy's secret paramilitary army deserts him, Reggie makes him head of creative thinking.

Unfortunately, all these horrible decisions result in record profits. Reggie fears that he will go on to success after success and die a rich, lonely, mad man. In a last-ditch effort to destroy Grot, Reggie announces that he will have to start behaving eccentrically.

Strong on plot, episode six succeeds on the well-designed execution of a simple situation. Reggie's final joke against society, Grot, has turned out to be a great success and a bane to his existence. Only a genius who built a fortune selling rubbish could devise such a clever, surefire way to destroy it. Unfortunately, as David Harris-Jones's character pointed out in series one, predictability is often an unpredictable thing.

Geoffrey Palmer and John Horsley are back after too long an absence, as are Reggie's insufferable grandchildren, Adam and Jocasta.

Derry Power's performance as Seamus Finnegan, the leprechaun of a laborer who is actually an organizational genius, is a delight. Seamus quickly figures out how to save the company thousands, while seeing into Reggie's secret schemes of destruction and all the while insisting to be a simple Irishman from "the land of the bogs and the little people."

Jimmy also has some good scenes as he takes Reggie to the headquarters of his secret army. After blindfolding Reggie and taking him on a rather circuitous journey, they arrive at an abandoned farm. Unable to find any of his army, Jimmy takes Reggie on a tour of the farm. He points out a haystack, which supposedly conceals 300 rifles, and milkcans purported to be filled with grenades. Upon closer inspection, Reggie discovers they are only a haystack and empty milkcans. Jimmy points out a cowpat that he insists is a disguised plastic explosive. Reggie picks it up to learn the turd isn't disguised at all. Finally, a crestfallen Jimmy realizes that his men have taken the weapons and deserted him. Jimmy concludes in his clipped military style that he would shoot himself if only the others hadn't absconded with the guns.

Episode 7 ★★★★

Air date: November 2, 1977. Cast: Reginald Perrin (Leonard Rossiter); Elizabeth Perrin (Pauline Yates); C.J. (John Barron); Jimmy (Geoffrey Palmer); Doc Morrisey (John Horsley); Joan Greengross (Sue Nicholls); Tom (Tim Preece); Linda (Sally-Jane Spencer); David Harris-Jones (Bruce Bould); Tony Webster (Trevor Adams); Colin Pillock (Timothy Carlton); Sheridan Honeydew (Blain Fairman); Peregrine Trembleby (Neville Barber); Mr. Lisburn (Keith Smith); Mr. Herbert (David Rowlands)

Reggie makes good on his plan to try to ruin Grot by behaving eccentrically. First he grants three "exclusive" television interviews to BBC 1, 2, and ITV on three consecutive nights. Despite his best worst efforts, each appearance is interpreted as a triumph. He also tries behaving more erratically, to no avail, since he now has a reputation for being an eccentric genius.

In an attempt to shock those around him, Reggie makes a pass at a male manager of one of his shops. Rather than outraging the man, he finds his overtures welcome. In one last supreme effort, Reggie walks through his neighborhood dressed as a woman. Everyone treats him normally.

Reggie informs Elizabeth that he would like to fake a suicide again, but he won't do it without her. She reluctantly agrees. At the seaside they change into old clothes and buckteeth and shuffle off to become Mr. and Mrs. Gossamer. The next morning they are stopped by a panhandler, who turns out to be C.J. in similar disguise. He points to the beach, where they see dozens of men and women faking their suicides.

Reggie Perrin comes full circle and again decides to stage his suicide. If there is anything his previous experience has taught him, however, it is not to leave behind that which is most important to him. He takes Elizabeth along. After they have done the deed, they discover that Reggie's experiences have given impetus to dozens more who are tired of being in the rat race.

The final installment of the second season proves that even eccentricity can become routine and predictable. Throughout the episode, Reggie predicts the reactions of those around him — especially David Harris-Jones in some very funny takes — but is surprised when they can do likewise to him. The point? Anything done enough can creep into the realm of "normal" behavior.

Reggie also gives some hysterically funny television interviews. The first, a BBC 1 show known as *Pillock Talk*, features host Colin Pillock. The aggressive Pillock tries to corner Reggie by accusing him of being a con man who is bilking the public via the Grot shops. Reggie counters that he admits all of the items are rubbish, and in fact, he is providing a valuable public service. Reggie explains that he makes people feel prosperous when they spend money on useless items. When Pillock tries to force Reggie into admitting that Grot's prices are high, Reggie vehemently denies it before clarifying that the prices aren't high but exorbitant. Next, Reggie quickly turns the tables and begins asking personal questions of an increasingly unnerved Pillock.

Unfortunately, his appearance on *Pillock Talk* makes Reggie something of a hero. The next night on ITV's *The World Tomorrow Today*, Reggie actively contradicts the statements he made the previous night. Not only that, but he keeps mentioning his interview on *Pillock Talk* after being specifically asked not to, then tells the viewers to switch to a movie on BBC 1 after his interview is over. In light of his contradicting statements, the host, Sheridan Honeydew, accuses Reggie of lying. Reggie agrees, confessing that he is a "congenial liar."

Honeydew corrects him, noting the word is "congenital." Reggie reaffirms he is a congenial liar, since he enjoys doing it.

Series Three 1978–1979

EPISODE 1 ★★★

Air date: November 29, 1978. Cast: Reginald Perrin (Leonard Rossiter); Elizabeth Perrin (Pauline Yates); C.J. (John Barron); Doc Morrisey (John Horsley); Tony Webster (Trevor Adams); Joan Greengross (Sue Nicholls); David Harris-Jones (Bruce Bould); Tom (Leslie Schofield); Linda (Sally-Jane Spencer); Prue Harris-Jones (Theresa Watson); Big Man in Bank (Brian Coburn); Little Man in Bank (George Trevor); Bank Clerk (David Hanson); Barman (Leslie Rhodes); Indian in Park (Ali Baba); Adam (Robert Hillier); Jocasta (Abigail Morgan)

After less than a day as Mr. and Mrs. Gossamer, Reggie and Elizabeth decide to go back to their old lives, sell Grot, and enjoy their wealth. While admitting his new life is sheer bliss, Reggie concludes that it isn't enough. He wants to devise a brilliant idea to better the world and leave his mark on mankind.

Reggie conceives of a commune for middle-aged, middle-class people after witnessing a fight in a bank line. The commune, to be called "Perrin's," will be located in a normal middle-class house, in a normal neighborhood. Guests will stay as long as they like and pay whatever they wish. Reggie fills the staff with all his old friends from Sunshine Desserts, along with his daughter and son-in-law.

Series three begins a few minutes after the end of series two, and soon, despite a second faked suicide, all the characters are reunited. This episode introduces David Harris-Jones's wife, Prue. Prue is well suited to her skittish husband. She wears outfits identical to his, has the same habit of responding to everything with "super," and can usually be found clinging to his arm (almost as if she were holding him up).

Although the character is the same, Leslie Schofield replaces Tim Preece as Reggie's son-in-law, Tom. Preece would return to the role he originated for 1996's *The Legacy of Reginald Perrin*. Although they are listed in the credits, neither Adam nor Jocasta appear in this episode.

The episode features a wonderful parody bit in which Reggie telephones Mrs. C.J. in an attempt to locate her husband. To shorten the exposition, he repeats everything she says for the benefit of the audience who can't hear her side of the conversation. Then, the exposition lapses into a parody of the device. "Yes," Reggie says into the phone, "I know I'm repeating everything you're saying … yes, I know it's irritating … yes, I know I'm still doing it."

C.J., it seems, is still tramping around disguised as a panhandler. Reggie finds him busking (performing as a street musician) for people waiting in cinema queues. Despite C.J.'s long hair, Reggie recognizes his former boss as he accompanies himself on the banjo, singing songs whose lyrics are comprised of his usual clichés.

Tony Webster's return is marked by a new catch phrase. Insisting that he's—"still the kiddy," Tony has dropped "great" and replaced it with the more ludicrous—"City, Arizona" (as in "Tony Webster is Success City, Arizona").

Episode 2 ★★★

Air date: December 6, 1978. Cast: Reginald Perrin (Leonard Rossiter); Elizabeth Perrin (Pauline Yates); C.J. (John Barron); Doc Morrisey (John Horsley); Tony Webster (Trevor Adams); Joan Greengross (Sue Nicholls); David Harris-Jones (Bruce Bould); Tom (Leslie Schofield); Linda (Sally-Jane Spencer); Prue Harris-Jones (Theresa Watson); Jimmy (Geoffrey Palmer); McBlane (Joseph Brady); Mr. Penfold (Arnold Peters); Mrs. Hollies (Joyce Windsor); Mr. Babbacombe (James Warrior); Passerby on Canal Towpath (Stewart Quentin Holmes)

Reggie puts the staff members through a three-month training period during which they will learn to be more pleasant people. Reggie also hires McBlane as chef and Jimmy to be the group's commando of good works. The commune's neighbors come by to complain about the noise, the cars, and the tents. Reggie dismisses their grievances by promising them that the congestion will multiply when guests actually start arriving.

After three months the staff is ready, but they only have one initial guest. The man, a lonely undertaker named Babbacombe, has come to Perrin's to be with other people. Rather than disappoint him, Reggie has half the staff assume the roles of other guests. Mr. Babbacombe quickly sees through the ruse and leaves.

Although not at all cohesive in its plotting (even for a *Reggie Perrin* episode), this installment manages to be a good entry in the series on the strength of its laugh content. There is so much happening here that the end result never quite gels.

Episode two features two welcome additions. The first is the return of Geoffrey Palmer's character, Jimmy. Reggie finds Jimmy running a fleet of excursion canal boats. Unfortunately, as with his secret army, Jimmy is soon out of business when his partner absconds with the firm's assets. The second addition is Joseph Brady as McBlane, the unintelligible Scottish cook. Every utterance from McBlane's mouth is either an oath, a complaint, or an insult, the most lucid of which is "Up yer clunge!"

There are some funny moments as the staff attempts to grow into its unfamiliar assignments by practicing on one another. At one point, Doc Morrissey works on his psychology skills by doing a word association drill with Tony Webster. When Doc offers the word "table tennis," the randy Tony counters with "sex." In another session, Doc offers the word "sex" in a similar exercise with C.J. The blustering C.J., of course, responds by associating it with "table tennis."

Aside from their professional duties, the staff members must also take their turns with the household chores. This is particularly trying for C.J., who is assigned the task of caring for the commune's three children. A clearly annoyed C.J. interrupts one staff meeting to characteristically declare that he didn't get where he is today by having green frogs placed down his trousers. He then pulls a stuffed Kermit doll from his pants, evidently put there by a truculent Adam or Jocasta.

When half the staff must pose as guests for the benefit of Mr. Babbacombe, confusion ensues. Aside from wearing ridiculous disguises, they can't remember who they are. Doc keeps responding when his name is mentioned, although for the purposes of the ruse Jimmy is supposed to be the doctor. Unfortunately, Jimmy's only previous experience with doctors was confined to the military. When he is called upon, instead of giving psychological advice, he tells the room to stay away from the local call girls.

Elizabeth and Joan also forget their roles, and both claim to be the same person. C.J., on the other hand, transparently tries to make Babbacombe feel needed by explaining that he too has no friends and wishes he were dead so he could use the services of an undertaker.

The whole hilarious charade comes crashing down when Mr. Babbacombe sees through David Harris-Jones's disguise of a drug-crazed roadie for a rock band.

Episode 3

★½

Air date: December 13, 1978. Cast: Reginald Perrin (Leonard Rossiter); Elizabeth Perrin (Pauline Yates); C.J. (John Barron); Doc Morrisey (John Horsley); Tony Webster (Trevor Adams); Joan Greengross (Sue Nicholls); David Harris-Jones (Bruce Bould); Tom (Leslie Schofield); Linda (Sally-Jane Spencer); Prue Harris-Jones (Theresa Watson); Jimmy (Geoffrey Palmer); Mr. Pelham (Glynn Edwards); Thruxton Appleby (Leslie Sands); Bernard Trilling (Frederick Jaeger); McBlane (Joseph Brady); Arthur Nobles (Ronald Pember); Hilary Meadows (Sally Lahee)

After advertising, Perrin's doubles its guest bookings to two. The first is Reggie's old employer from the pig farm, Mr. Pelham. Pelham's business is booming, but he finds this disturbing since the thought of meat now revolts him. The second guest is Thruxton Appleby, an obnoxious textile tycoon who wants to be likable. Reggie decides that Appleby's cure rests in treating him as rudely as he treats others. He enlists C.J.'s aid to deflate the tycoon's ego.

Soon, other guests start arriving, the most notable one being Mr. Trilling, the head of the comedy department for a television network, who has lost his sense of humor. Trilling is soon cured when he begins to laugh at the ridiculousness of his own malady.

At episode's end, Reggie announces that both Pelham and Appleby have left happier people. As payment, Appleby has given £1,000 while Pelham has provided a year's supply of pork chops.

After a shaky start Perrin's starts to catch on in this rather disappointing episode. Unfortunately, this installment and the one immediately following represent the difficulty in executing what must have seemed like a surefire concept. While the notion of Reggie Perrin running a commune to soothe the psyches of the middle-aged and middle class is initially amusing, the actual running of it is rather mundane. Reggie is too much like a fish out of water, or rather, too much one in water to be funny. This is what he *should* be doing, rather than creating exotic ices or selling absolute rubbish, and therefore he is little more than the gatekeeper at the asylum, rather than its main inmate.

The main comedy set piece of this episode is a rather prolonged role-playing skit that C.J. conducts on the subject of industrial negotiations. While C.J. insists that the exercise be realistic, he insists on playing the secretary to the boss, one Cynthia Jones. The role playing goes rather poorly with the industrialist Appleby playing the part of the labor negotiator; while a laborer, Mr. Nobles, takes the part of management. It seems that the participants are too eager to take the others' points of view.

Episode 4 ★

Air date: December 20, 1978. Cast: Reginald Perrin (Leonard Rossiter); Elizabeth Perrin (Pauline Yates); C.J. (John Barron); Doc Morrisey (John Horsley); Tony Webster (Trevor Adams); Joan (Sue Nicholls); David Harris-Jones (Bruce Bould); Tom (Leslie Schofield); Linda (Sally-Jane Spencer); Prue Harris-Jones (Theresa Watson); Jimmy (Geoffrey Palmer); McBlane (Joseph Brady); Mr. Dent (Robert Gillespie); Mr. Winstanley (Peter Schofield); Factory Owner (David Ellison); Insurance Salesman (Bunny May); Ethel Merman (Janet Davies); Edwards (Peter Hill); Mr. Jenkins (Michael Segal); Mr. Pennell (Andrew Johns); Youth (Peter Roberts); Shy Vet (Frank Baker)

Perrin's commune is a great success and bursting at the seams. The only opposition comes from Mr. Dent from the Botchly Borough Council, who attempts to shut Reggie down on the claim that he is running a business from a residence. Dent quickly asks to join the commune when he realizes the pathetic state of his duties. A week later, Mr. Winstanley, Dent's boss, arrives looking for him. He too is persuaded to stay along with two subsequent council members who come looking for their missing comrades.

At Mr. Winstanley's suggestion, the staff and guests hold a communal evening of sharing folk songs, stories, and experiences. Unfortunately, this goes poorly. The event ends in a communal touching session, which the cook, McBlane, takes for some sort of orgy. Reggie confesses to Elizabeth that he is finally deeply contented but is worried that his bliss is too good to last. With that admission, a piece of the ceiling falls on him.

Episode four is the nadir in the saga of *Reginald Perrin*. The primary problem is the lack of conflict to make the episode interesting. The commune is succeeding, what little resistance there is easily handled, and even Reggie admits he is content and happy at last. Unfortunately, even a steady stream of odd clients (this episode boasts the largest cast in all three series) with humorous maladies is not enough to make a successful episode. Even when Grot was a huge success, there was still a story created by Reggie's internal anxiety over what he had wrought. Fortunately, the series rebounds quickly in the final three installments.

While the communal evening has some good moments, it is all rather too labored to sustain any real interest. The best moment, such as it is, comes when Tom suggests another non violent sport: boxing. A bout is staged between the heavyweight Mr. Wilkins and the flyweight Mr. Dent. Rather than trade blows, the two men dance around the ring, punching themselves. The bout ends with Wilkins beating himself by a knockout, while Dent beats himself on points.

Janet Davies, *Dad's Army* regular Mavis Pike, makes a guest appearance as Ethel Merman, the housewife who is tired of hearing jokes about her name.

Episode 5 ★★½

Air date: December 27, 1978. Cast: Reginald Perrin (Leonard Rossiter); Elizabeth Perrin (Pauline Yates); C.J. (John Barron); Doc Morrisey (John Horsley); Jimmy (Geoffrey Palmer); Tony Webster (Trevor Adams); Joan (Sue Nicholls); David Harris-Jones (Bruce Bould); Tom (Leslie Schofield); Linda (Sally-Jane Spencer); Prue Harris-Jones (Theresa Watson); McBlane (Joseph Brady); Clive "Lofty" Anstruther (Terence Alexander); Deborah Swiffham (Hilary Tindall); Colin Pillock (Timothy Carlton); Glenn Higgins (Vincent Brimble); Johnson (Gordon Case); Shy Vet (Frank Baker); Superintendent (Kenneth Watson); Merchant Banker (Leslie Glazer)

After another appearance by Reggie on the television program *Pillock Talk* bookings begin to rise at the commune. Soon, however, the community is beset by two crises that shake it to the core. The first is a series of thefts of money and valuables (even McBlane reports a stolen "clegle of gunges"). The thefts ultimately cause a mass exodus of guests. The robberies end when the thief—Clive "Lofty" Anstruther, Jimmy's ex-partner in the secret army—moves on after having stolen everything worth taking.

The second crisis involves a woman, Deborah Swiffham, who tries to seduce every male member of the staff. Reggie bemoans the chaos that has beset them. Elizabeth consoles him by noting that at least it cannot get worse.

Following two substandard installments, episode five recovers to provide some interesting situations and many good laughs. Not surprisingly, much of the humor comes from the character of Jimmy. Especially in the third series, it seems that the bigger part allotted for Major James Anderson (retired), the better the episode. This episode provides him plenty of room to perform, featuring, as it does, the appearance of "Lofty" Anstruther, the man who embezzled away Jimmy's secret army.

In a hilarious scene, Reggie takes Jimmy to a local pub to break the news. He asks Jimmy if he is a forgiving soul. Jimmy insists that he is. Reggie tells him that Lofty has joined the community, and Jimmy goes wild. Reggie calms Jimmy down and tells him that this is a test for the community and Jimmy's own personal Everest. Jimmy promises to be civil and to try to forgive Anstruther.

Lofty enters and confesses the embezzlement. He goes on to confess that he never was even in the army. Jimmy concedes that if everyone were in the army there would be nobody left to wave goodbye. Ultimately, Jimmy forgives Lofty, citing that he is suffering from a "cock-up on the character front," adding that it's not Lofty's fault that he's a "lousy, rotten, stinking, yellow, thieving swine."

EPISODE 6 ★★★

Air date: January 3, 1979. Cast: Reginald Perrin (Leonard Rossiter); Elizabeth Perrin (Pauline Yates); C.J. (John Barron); Doc Morrisey (John Horsley); Jimmy (Geoffrey Palmer); Tony Webster (Trevor Adams); Joan (Sue Nicholls); David Harris-Jones (Bruce Bould); Tom (Leslie Schofield); Linda (Sally-Jane Spencer); Prue Harris-Jones (Theresa Watson); McBlane (Joseph Brady); Seamus Finnegan (Derry Power); Mrs. E. Blythe-Erpingham (Joan Peart); Landlord (Jonathan Fryer); Driver (Leslie Adams)

Elizabeth fears that Reggie is trying to destroy the commune by becoming increasingly sarcastic and rude. Guests start leaving in droves when Reggie gets in a series of arguments with McBlane, the details of which end up in the tabloid press.

Reggie meets former Grot employee Seamus Finnegan in a pub. Seamus warns him that he has heard rumors that a group of local thugs is going to raid Perrin's in retaliation for Jimmy's anti-crime campaign. Given the news of the threat, all the guests decide to leave. The staff votes to stay and fight. At Reggie's urging, Jimmy is voted military commander for the defense of the commune. Disguised as trees, the staff awaits the arrival of the thugs on the planned night of the raid. When no toughs show up, they go inside to celebrate. Just then, the thugs arrive. The commune is shattered, and all the staff members are brought home in an ambulance.

The humor increases as the commune rapidly begins to disintegrate here in episode six. There are some slow spots — particularly a transparent plot line involving Doc Morrisey's discovery of a miracle tonic — but the community's effort to defend itself more than compensates to make this a good entry in the series.

When Jimmy suggests that the staff don disguises to lay in wait for the thugs, he offers several options for camouflage, including molehills and compost heaps. This second suggestion is particularly offensive to C.J., who responds with an amazing, yet characteristic diatribe. "I'm told," he says in a rare moment of self-realization, "I keep saying 'I didn't get where I am today by … whatever it is.' If so, I'm sorry. I'll try not to use this phrase again. However, if I didn't get where I am today by one thing above all other things I didn't get where I am today, I didn't get where I am today disguised as half a compost heap!"

Later while celebrating the nonarrival of the mob, C.J. reveals that he is writing a novel about ants (a parody of the late seventies' bestselling *Watership Down* about rabbits). C.J. explains that he is considering numerous titles, all of which are purloined from other sources, including *Watership Ant*, *Lord of the Ants*, *Ant of the Flies*, and *No Sex Please, We're Ants.* He starts to read an excerpt of the novel when the thugs actually arrive, much to Reggie's relief, who prefers a beating to a sampling of C.J.'s literary talent.

EPISODE 7 ★★★½

Air date: January 10, 1979. Cast: Reginald Perrin (Leonard Rossiter); Elizabeth Perrin (Pauline Yates); C.J. (John Barron); Doc Morrisey (John Horsley); Jimmy (Geoffrey Palmer); Tony Webster (Trevor Adams); Joan (Sue Nicholls); David Harris-Jones (Bruce Bould); Tom (Leslie Schofield); Linda (Sally-Jane Spencer); Prue Harris-Jones (Theresa Watson); Mr. Fennel (John Quayle); Iris Hoddle (Linda Cunningham); Muscroft (Terence Woodfield); Rosewall (David Sparks)

Perrin's disbands, and Reggie bids farewell to the staff. Reggie is surprised to receive a letter from the personnel head of Amalgamated Aerosols, inviting him to come in for an interview. Arriving for the interview, Reggie is stunned to discover that the company's managing director is C.J.'s brother, F.J. Reggie begins work at Amalgamated Aerosols and quickly realizes he is in exactly the same situation that nearly drove him mad at Sunshine Desserts. The greatest shock comes when he discovers that he reports directly to C.J., who is in charge of air fresheners. After sabotaging a fragrance smelling, Reggie dictates a letter confessing that he is the guilty party. He then asks his secretary for the times of trains to the Dorset coast, as he daydreams about running naked into the sea.

The final installment in the world of Reginald Perrin brings the story full circle. With the commune in ruins, Reggie returns to the corporate world, only to find himself exactly where he started his odyssey.

In the end Reggie (and we viewers) are left with two conflicting messages on the meaning of these three remarkable series. The first summation is delivered eloquently by Tom, who tells Reggie that "a dream is over, but because of that dream reality will never be the same again." This beautiful summation of course is quickly proven false, since Reggie returns to the rat race without nary a change in it.

A more grim, yet realistic approach is offered by C.J., who basically tells Reggie that the grass isn't greener on the other side of the fence, and wise is the man who can come to that realization.

Reggie's meeting with C.J.'s brother, F.J. (John Barron, disguised with glasses and a toupee) is a delight. F.J. is exactly like his brother, only more so it seems, since F.J. developed most of the techniques adopted by his sibling. F. explains that C. (as the brothers refer to each other) is too soft, as he makes Reggie rise up and down in the specially designed flatulent chair (F.J.'s invention, it turns out).

At one point F.J. invites Reggie and his wife over to sample Mrs. F.J.'s specialty, which, he proclaims, is "Lobster Thermostat." Reggie nods patronizingly, as F.J. explains that the dish is so called since it must be served at a precise temperature. Suddenly F.J. corrects himself, asserting that the item in question is really called Lobster Thermidor, and there is no such thing as Lobster Thermostat.

When Reggie affirms that he knew that F.J. had gotten it wrong, F.J. demands to know why he didn't say so.

"Because," F.J. begins, answering his own question, "you thought I was a pretentious, ignorant oaf who had got it wrong."

"That's it exactly," Reggie confesses blithely.

Another bright spot and a direct throwback to the exotic ice creams testing in the series' first episode is the fragrance testing. This time, however, Reggie is the cause of the disaster, not an errant computer. C.J. announces that someone has tainted the results by asserting that all ten samples smelled like "Bolivian Unicyclist's Jock Strap."

Bless Me, Father

London Weekend Television 1978–1981

During the initial research for this book, I was sitting in an English pub enjoying a convivial chat with a few native experts on the field of British comedy. We were discussing the planned volume on the best shows England has sent Stateside and what shows were to be included. Most of the proposed selections were met with nods and hearty assent, except one: *Bless Me, Father*. One of my companions remarked that the series hadn't been aired in Great Britain since its initial run. The other chap quickly added that the reason was that in the prevailing opinion it hadn't been very funny.

I was rather stunned by this assessment since I had always counted the series about a pair of Catholic priests as one of the finest, most subtly crafted sitcoms I had seen. Frankly, I thought it ironic that this understated jewel of a comedy had not been seen in the land that spawned it for almost 20 years. *Bless Me, Father*, the semi-autobiographical series by Peter De Rosa is largely forgotten today by the general public in England. The show, however, has been exported by LWT and plays intermittently around the globe, captivating fans with its gentle whimsy.

The origins of *Bless Me, Father* date from 1971, when Peter De Rosa left the Roman Catholic priesthood after more than 20 years of service due to mental anguish over the papal ban on contraception. From the church, the middle-aged De Rosa went to work for BBC radio as a program producer. While doing a series of shows on author James Herriot, De Rosa was encouraged to write a fictional account of his years as a priest. That these accounts were mostly fictionalized is borne out by the fact that most of his years in the priesthood were spent as a seminary professor.

De Rosa wrote the book (and its subsequent sequels) under the pseudonym of Neil Boyd (the name he also gave to one of the main characters). De Rosa chose to work under a nom de plume for several reasons, which he outlined in a 1977 interview with the *Sunday Independent*. First, he was following the advice of James Herriot, who thought the practice advisable. Next, De Rosa had written ten previous books — all studies of theology — under his own name and didn't want his usual readers being conned into buying his work of fiction thinking they were getting something else entirely.

"The third thing," explained De Rosa, "is that if I wrote under my own name people might think it was autobiographical in every way and they might say 'Good Heavens, I told him that as a priest and now he's gone and put it in a book.'"

The book was an immediate success. Contracts for sequels and the offer for De Rosa to write a television adaptation allowed the former priest to quit work at the BBC and become a full-time writer. His new acclaim as a fiction writer led De Rosa to write the television series under his own name, although the credits note that the shows are based on the books by Neil Boyd.

The television series, and the book upon which they were based, chronicled the experiences of two priests. The older of the pair, Father Duddleswell, was a product of the old school and was a playful combination of saint and rogue. Duddleswell's young curate, Neil Boyd, was fresh out of seminary and something of a holy innocent, learning the facts of ecclesiastical life from his mentor. According to the author, these two were, in ways, adaptations of himself. "I sometimes say," explained De Rosa to the author in 1997, "Father Neil was myself when young, Father Duddleswell myself as I then was [in 1977]. If Father D was based on anyone it was on my first parish priest, an Irishman."

According to a 1977 interview, De Rosa also included elements of the first priest he had ever met in the mix that became Father Duddleswell. "He took me onto the altar at the age of four," recalled De Rosa to Brendan Martin. "He was of the old stock."

De Rosa's first priest was the inspiration for at least one of the *Bless Me, Father* tales, the one told in the episode "A Back to Front Wedding." In that installment from the second series, Duddleswell is watching a movie in a theater when an urgent message is delivered over the public address system that he must return to his parish to marry a waiting couple. The actual event from which it was taken involved the real priest going to a sporting match.

"In those days," recounts Peter De Rosa, "they didn't have microphones and loudspeakers so halfway through the match someone came 'round with a big board held up to the crowd. It bore a poster reading: 'Would Father So-and-So please return to his church where the bride and the groom are waiting.'"

With such rich inspiration for his main character, De Rosa had hoped that an august actor would assume the lead in the series, which was to be produced by London Weekend Television. The author's first choice to play the irascible Father Duddleswell was Alec Guinness. The scripts for the first season were dispatched to the Academy Award–winning actor, who turned them down.

"He liked the scripts," noted Peter De Rosa, "but said he had never (then) played a religious part." This wasn't entirely true, since the versatile Guinness had portrayed no less a clergyman than a bishop in the 1949 film *Kind Hearts and Coronets*. Probably closer to the truth is De Rosa's opinion that the actor did not want to commit himself to a television series at that time.

While the notion of Alec Guinness as Charles Clement Duddleswell is intriguing, one cannot be disappointed in the second choice for the role. Arthur Lowe, fresh from his nine-year triumph as Captain Mainwaring in *Dad's Army*, was offered the part next and selected it from the many offers on his plate. (Lowe also accepted one of the other sitcoms offered: the title role in Roy Clarke's *Potter*, which ran almost concurrently with *Bless Me, Father*.) Lowe's son, Stephen, recalled that his father approached the role with great relish.

"Arthur polished his Irish brogue about the house and slipped into the character of Father Duddleswell for the series," wrote Stephen Lowe in his biography of his father. "He loved the character, took real pleasure in him."

According to Stephen Lowe, Arthur became Duddleswell as he became "wholly absorbed in the character."

With the keystone to the television adaptation in place, the rest of the series was cast. For the part of Father Neil, 19-year-old Daniel Abineri was picked. From an acting family (his father, John Abineri, and brother Sebastian Abineri both preceded him in the profession), Abineri, despite his youth, was not exactly a novice. Two years prior to being chosen to play Father Duddleswell's curate, Daniel Abineri appeared in the television play *Best of Enemies*. This exposure helped him land a role in the film *International Velvet*, in which the young actor had the distinction of giving Tatum O'Neal her first screen kiss. Although admittingly that Abineri looked right for the part, Peter De Rosa wasn't always thrilled with the performance of his Father Neil. The author said that Abineri was allowed to "overact at times" but lays this fault as much at the feet of director David Askey.

Rounding out the regular cast was actress Gabrielle Daye as Mrs. Pring, Duddleswell's long-term, long-suffering housekeeper and verbal sparring partner. Augmenting the cast on a regular basis were Patrick McAlinney as Dr. Daley, Father Duddleswell's closest friend and the town's boozy physician; Sheila Keith as the intimidating Mother Stephen; and David Ryall as Billy Buzzle, the local bookie and the priest's neighbor. All three provided wonderful support and interacted well with the show's star, Arthur Lowe. In fact, one of the few flaws of *Bless Me, Father* is that the secondary regulars are not used in every episode.

"If I were writing the series today," noted Peter De Rosa in 1997, "I would make sure that all the main characters came into every episode. I did not do that at first. My excuse is: I never liked or watched sitcoms on TV. Nor had I ever seen an episode made until my own first one."

For sitcom novice De Rosa, watching the actors bringing his characters to life was something of a revelation — especially the marvelous Arthur Lowe. To De Rosa, the most memorable instance came during the pilot episode when Father Duddleswell gives an impromptu eulogy over the grave of his predecessor. The author described Lowe's performance as "a new dimension opening before your eyes."

David Ryall, who played the spiv Billy Buzzle, also recalls that working with Lowe was a wonderful experience. At times, however, filming could be difficult due to Lowe's suffering from an advanced form of narcolepsy. The disorder caused the actor to fall asleep in an instant if there wasn't enough going on around him to hold his attention. By the time he did *Bless Me, Father*, Lowe's narcolepsy had reached what his son called a more "sinister" level. "He would nod off— cut out would be a better description — in midsentence or midaction," remembered Stephen Lowe.

David Ryall recounts, "Arthur was suffering from a malady at the time which caused him to drop off to sleep without warning. Sometimes in the middle of rehearsing a scene. And David Askey, the director, would say gently but firmly, 'Arthur!' And he would wake and continue from exactly where he left off. He was an extraordinarily kind and funny man, and the sort of actor who can make you laugh simply by coming through a door."

Bless Me, Father premiered on London Weekend Television on Sunday, September 24, 1978, and was well received. A second series followed a year later, with a third in the summer of 1981. Based on the success of the program and the wealth of material from which Peter De Rosa could draw (by this time "Neil Boyd" had penned three more *Father* books), it seemed like the show would enjoy a long run. Unfortunately, this was not to be. On April 15, 1982, while plans were progressing for the fourth series of *Bless Me, Father*, Arthur Lowe died after suffering a stroke in the dressing room of the Alexandra Theatre in Birmingham. He was 66 years old. With the death of Lowe, *Bless Me, Father* came to an end, which is just as well since it is hard to imagine another actor taking the part (or wanting to) after Lowe had left his indelible stamp upon it. (*Potter*, Arthur Lowe's other series running at the time, did attempt another season with another actor in the title role, without success)

As previously stated, the reputation and remembrance of *Bless Me, Father* has suffered greatly from years of neglect in Great Britain (Lowe's son calls the series "dated"), but there is hope. In his excellent reference work, *Radio Times*

Guide to TV Comedy, Mark Lewisohn extols this series as a "hidden gem in Britain's sitcom archives." Perhaps such praise may finally provoke broadcasters in the United Kingdom to give the show a fresh airing. One can only hope so, for the merriment of millions would indeed be greatly blessed by the amiable antics of Fathers Duddleswell and Boyd.

THE EPISODES

Peter De Rosa. Produced and Directed by David Askey.

Series One 1978

Episode 1: "Baptism of Fire" ★★★½

Air date: September 24, 1978. Cast: Father Duddleswell (Arthur Lowe); Father Boyd (Daniel Abineri); Mrs. Pring (Gabrielle Daye); Jeremy (Kevin Collins); Child at Confessional [voice only] (Susan Sheridan)

Father Neil Boyd arrives at the parish of St. Jude's to take up his duties as the curate to Father Duddleswell.

The premiere episode does an exemplary job of introducing the show's three main characters: Father Duddleswell (Arthur Lowe); his curate, Father Neil Boyd (Daniel Abineri); and their housekeeper, Mrs. Pring (Gabrielle Daye). Although other characters, such as neighbor Billy Buzzle, Dr. Daley, and the Reverend Mother Stephen, would play wonderful recurring roles over the rest of the series, author Peter De Rosa wisely reserves the premiere episode for his stars, and not a scene is wasted.

All the dialogue, while witty throughout, does double duty to establish the playful irascibility of Father Duddleswell and the often sharp, while never nasty, give and take between him and his long-term housekeeper, Mrs. Pring. There is a feeling that the viewer has walked in on an ongoing battle. The only character who will develop much beyond this first episode is Father Neil Boyd. As the newcomer to the household, Father Neil takes a few episodes to establish his rapport with the others, which is to be expected. In fact, it is Father Neil's arrival that helps the viewer gain a glimpse into the history of the other characters. He is, in effect, our eyes, through which we discover the characters inhabiting the parish of St. Jude's. This allows the writing to be consistently humorous without bogging down in excessive exposition. The episode's title refers to young Father Neil's first day at St. Jude's and the gauntlet to which Father Duddleswell subjects him in order to discover his new curate's mettle.

Father Duddleswell's mischievous verbal sparring with Father Neil is one of the most delightful components of the first episode. Arthur Lowe is masterful in instantly establishing the lovable yet exasperating Irish priest. A good instance of this byplay comes in a scene in which Father Neil tries to discover the time of lunch.

Episode 2: "The Parish Bazaar" ★★★

Air date: October 1, 1978. Cast: Father Duddleswell (Arthur Lowe); Father Boyd (Daniel Abineri); Mrs. Pring (Gabrielle Daye); Dr. Daley (Patrick McAlinney); Billy Buzzle (David Ryall); Tim Fogarty (James Duggan); Sarah Sneezum (Ann Wrigg); George Lloyd (David Crosse); Maureen (Nora Connolly); Little Boy (Neil Hayden)

Father Duddleswell urges the parish to have faith in order to make the annual bazaar a financial success.

Having firmly established its three principal characters in the series' first episode, the second serving of *Bless Me, Father* introduces two of the show's most endearing recurring players: Billy Buzzle and Dr. Daley. The two characters help define Father Duddleswell, with one (Buzzle) being his closest adversary and the other (Daley) his closest friend. Billy Buzzle's role in this episode is brief, and he is more fully introduced in the next episode (often that episode, "The Bell of St. Jude," is shown second in American syndication). Another high point of "The Parish Bazaar" is the first of the marvelous Irish dialect duets between Arthur Lowe and Patrick McAlinney.

"The Parish Bazaar," like the best episodes of the *Bless Me, Father* series, concentrates on a strong story line, upon which writer Peter De Rosa's consistently witty dialogue is hung. The plot revolves around the faith of Father Duddleswell versus the unbelief of everyone else. The object of the Irish clergyman's belief is the successful outcome of St. Jude's annual fundraising bazaar which is vital to the shoring up of the church's emaciated bank account.

Father Duddleswell affirms his faith in the Almighty by declaring that this year they will raise the hefty sum of £600. Father Neil suggests they rent a marquee (a tent) to guard against the possibility of rain. Father D explains it is cheaper to have the widows and orphans pray for the right weather.

While Father Duddleswell makes an appeal from the pulpit for donated items for the bazaar's rummage sale, he especially urges the congregation to have faith and pray for "perfect weather," that they might reach their lofty goal. Father D continues to show his faith by again rejecting Father Neil's urgings to rent a marquee and by turning down Billy Buzzle's offer of running a betting booth at the bazaar. The priest insists they can meet their goal without falling back on the tools of disbelief.

The day of the bazaar dawns with threatening skies. Father Duddleswell opens the bazaar by urging the volunteer workers to continue in faith. Before he can finish his remarks, however, the skies open up, and within minutes the entire bazaar is blown away in a torrent of wind and rain. Within days, however, Father Duddleswell begins to reap the rewards of his faith.

"The Parish Bazaar" offers the only insight into Father's Duddleswell's interaction with the laity and church government. In a brief but clever scene, the bazaar committee meets to officially set this year's goal. While Father D pretends to only be a casual participant, he quickly steers the committee to his desired end. One member proposes that they aim at £250 as they did last year. Another member cautions that even that stretched them to their limit. Father D stuns them all by repeating his suggestion of £600.

"600 pounds!" they all cry in disbelief.

Father D nods, readily accepting their shock for assent, and adjourns the gathering.

Episode 3: "The Bell of St. Jude's" ★★★

Air date: October 8, 1978. Cast: Father Duddleswell (Arthur Lowe); Father Boyd (Daniel Abineri); Mrs. Pring (Gabrielle Daye); Bishop O'Reilly (Derek Francis); Billy Buzzle (David Ryall); Dr. Daley (Patrick McAlinney); Monsignor (Oliver Maguire)

Father Duddleswell feuds with his neighbor, Billy Buzzle. The main weapons of the battle: pigeons, bells, and roosters.

The first of the Duddleswell-Buzzle feuds is the primary attraction in this episode and as such there are plenty of classic Duddleswellisms on the topic of loving one's neighbors. "When Jesus said, 'love your neighbor as yourself,'" Father D asks Father Neil at one point, "do you think he also meant the folks next door?"

Later, when Billy Buzzle reminds the priest that he is supposed to love his nearby resident, Father Duddleswell concedes that he loves Buzzle as a Christian, but is resolved to go no further.

The feud erupts over Buzzle's pigeons, specifically their use of Father D's congregation for "target practice." When diplomacy fails, Father D decides to install a bell in the church tower to drive the birds away. Once the bell is operational, it not only disposes of the birds but Billy Buzzle's sleep. Buzzle appeals to Father D to ring the bell later in the morning, but the priest refuses. In retaliation, Buzzle buys two roosters with the intent of keeping Father D awake.

This episode also treats us to a visit by Bishop O'Reilly, who comes to dedicate the bell. In a hilarious scene, the bishop's convocation is interrupted when Buzzle's black Labrador enters the church and menaces O'Reilly, but then, instead of biting him, the dog decides to sit on the bishop's lap. Later the often-inebriated Dr. Daley, warmly brought to life by Patrick McAlinney, gives the bishop his own special benediction. In one of the episode's (and indeed the series') best lines, the good doctor wishes that luck stick to his lordship "like a beggar from the bog!"

Episode 4: "The Doomsday Chair" ★★★★

Air date: October 15, 1978. Cast: Father Duddleswell (Arthur Lowe); Father Boyd (Daniel Abineri); Mrs. Pring (Gabrielle Daye); Fred Bowlby (Peter Bowles); Mrs. Bowlby (Phyllis McMahon); Paddy (Eugene Geasley); Barmaid (Christianne Halstead)

Father Duddleswell seeks to destroy a local superstition surrounding a chair, which supposedly leads to the death of any one foolish enough to sit upon it.

While other episodes of the series may have had more finely woven plot lines and others sharper dialogue, "The Doomsday Chair" stands out as a consistently fine and funny example of the superlative qualities that made *Bless Me, Father* a great Brit-com. Simple yet imaginative, the plot, like "The Seal of Confession," turns on one central theme of faith. Instead of the comfort provided by the sanctity of confession, "The Doomsday Chair" explores the unrest caused by superstition. This is one of the few episodes, aside from the show's premiere, which does not include the support of Billy Buzzle, Dr. Daley, or the still-to-be-introduced Mother Stephen. As a result, the humor emanates primarily from the situation and not from the established characters.

While none of the more familiar secondary cast members are present, Peter Bowles provides a strong foil to Father Duddleswell in the role of pub keeper Fred Bowlby. Bowles, a veteran of many other British shows, is probably best remembered by American audiences for his leading part as nouveau riche Richard DeVere in *To the Manor Born* and for the title role in *The Irish R.M.* (shown Stateside on *Masterpiece Theater*).

Pub keeper Bowlby has a vested interest in perpetuating the myth of his doomsday chair, since it provides a steady stream of curiosity seekers to his bar. To keep the legend alive, Bowlby presents Father Duddleswell with an offer of £100 to sit in the fatal piece of furniture, which supposedly brings death within seven days of someone resting on it.

Father D vows to put an end to the superstition and announces that he intends to sit in the doomsday chair that night and every night for a week until the curse is disproved.

As the week goes on, Father Duddleswell gets bolder and more famous with each successive trip to the doomsday chair. Toward the end of the week, the ritual turns into a vespers service, complete with hymns, vestments, and, according to Father D, "the most Catholic thing of all"—a collection plate. These scenes in the pub and the carnival atmosphere they generate are the highlights of the episode. It is especially humorous to see Arthur Lowe's Duddleswell increasingly enjoying the worldly air he's created while supposedly on a spiritual quest.

By the final night, reporters, patrons, and curiosity seekers pack the pub, while an overflow crowd listens to the proceedings on the porch via a loudspeaker system. Now wearing his most ornate surplice, Father D sits down and proclaims the curse defeated — but a few unsettling surprises are added to his victory.

Episode 5: "Father and Mother" ★★★

Air date: October 22, 1978. Cast: Father Duddleswell (Arthur Lowe); Father Boyd (Daniel Abineri); Mrs. Pring (Gabrielle Daye); Bishop O'Reilly (Derek Francis); Fred Dobie (Clive Swift); Mother Stephen (Sheila Keith); Auctioneer (Timothy Kightley)

Father Duddleswell finds a rare painting underneath a gruesome portrait of the convent's mother foundress but must battle Mother Stephen for the ownership of it.

"Father and Mother" introduces the last of the regular supporting cast of *Bless Me, Father* and perhaps Father Duddleswell's most formidable adversary, the Reverend Mother Stephen. Head of the nearby convent, Mother Stephen, marvelously brought to the small screen by Sheila Keith, is an imposing figure, physically and morally. Throughout the episodes in which she appears, there are few people who are not intimidated by her mere presence. Only the bishop (who has the authority of his office to shield him) and Father Neil (who takes boyish delight in bouncing sophomoric comebacks off of her) do not seem overly threatened by this superior mother superior.

"Father and Mother" also affords the viewer the only glimpse into the austere lair of the celebrated Reverend Mother Stephen. In a marvelously timed scene in this setting, an intimidated Father Duddleswell tries to make spiritual small talk with Mother Stephen, while she fires back with terse, frosty replies. This scene also establishes the duality of the church hierarchy when Mother Stephen informs Father D that she is referring her cause to the highest authority. Father D reasons this to be God, but Mother Stephen clarifies that she is appealing to the bishop.

The plot itself features many clever twists and surprises and is well presented. At the center of the struggle over the ownership of the painting is the belief that it is the only surviving image of the convent's mother foundress. As such, the artwork is vital to the nun's campaign of having the foundress declared a saint by the pope. Later, after the bishop decides to sell the painting and split the proceeds (leaving most for himself), Father Duddleswell is amused to learn that there is an inexhaustible supply of the portraits in a French convent. To prove it, the convent has sent him one as proof. Sensing another masterpiece may be under it, Father D quickly scrapes away the top layer to confirm his suspicions. With the new painting firmly in his ownership, Duddleswell calls the local art dealer, planning to start a campaign for his own canonization with the proceeds.

Fans of Brit-coms should recognize Clive Swift in the role of art dealer Fred Dobie. Swift was still more than a decade away from contending with his own intimidating woman as the long-suffering husband to Patricia Routledge in the hit series *Keeping Up Appearances.*

Episode 6: "The Tennis Match" ★

Air date: October 29, 1978. Cast: Father Duddleswell (Arthur Lowe); Father Boyd (Daniel Abineri); Mrs. Pring (Gabrielle Daye); Dr. Daley (Patrick McAlinney); Albert Appleby (John Ringham); Probble (Gerald Cross); Pinkerton (Geoffery Drew); Biggins (Bernard Gallagher); Mrs. Probble (Sally Lahee)

To become the personal chaplain for the town's first Catholic mayor, Father Duddleswell must first agree to play in the annual tennis match against the Anglicans.

"The Tennis Match" is easily the weakest entry in the first series and probably one of the least satisfying shows of all three seasons. This is not to say that "The Tennis Match" does not have its moments; it does. Some of its individual scenes (Dr. Daley's medical examination of Father Duddleswell is particularly hilarious) stand with the best of *Bless Me, Father.* The downfall of the episode is the light in which the usually lovable, although vexatious, Father D is cast. Twice during "The Tennis Match" (once during a practice session with Father Neil and again in the final scene), the Irish priest comes across as more irritating than impish. These scenes are perhaps the only experiential examples viewers have of how annoying Father Duddleswell must be to his adversaries in the show. Still, even at its weakest, this episode of *Bless Me, Father* is more than fair entertainment.

"The Tennis Match" does feature two strong comic scenes. The first is the inaugural reception during which Father D manages to offend almost every guest. When Mrs. Probble, the Anglican priest's wife, expresses gladness that the Catholics and Anglicans are learning to pray together, Father D disagrees, stating that they were praying with him, not the other way around.

"That is a very fine distinction," the Rev. Probble observes.

"I'm glad you appreciate it," Father Duddleswell nods.

Father D closes the affair by offering a toast that, the largely Protestant gathering discovers is not to the new mayor, as they were led to believe, but to the pope!

The second standout is the previously mentioned scene in which Father D attempts to receive a medical excuse from Dr. Daley. The byplay, although probably a reworking of most doctor sketches ever done in vaudeville and music halls through the years, is consistently first-class foolery thanks to the delivery of comic veterans Arthur Lowe and Patrick McAlinney. After being bribed with repeated whiskeys, the doctor writes out the excuse. It is only after Dr. Daley departs that Father D reads it and discovers that it is not his release, but a prescription for "three large whiskeys and a stiff game of tennis."

EPISODE 7: "THE SEAL OF CONFESSION" ★★★★

Air date: November 5, 1978. Cast: Father Duddleswell (Arthur Lowe); Father Boyd (Daniel Abineri); Mrs. Pring (Gabrielle Daye); Dr. Daley (Patrick McAlinney); Bottesford (Patrick Newell); Miss Flanagan (Dorothy Frere); Mrs. Rollings (Pamela Ruddock); Conroy (Jeffrey Segal); Nellie (Primi Townsend); Mrs. Conroy (Elizabeth Morgan)

The sanctity of confession is compromised when Father Duddleswell ventures into the new soundproof confessional boxes wearing the church's new wireless microphone.

"The Seal of Confession" is a simple story filled out with numerous amusing vignettes that somehow are all related to the script's basic premise. From Father Neil's instruction of the overly inquisitive Mrs. Rollings, a convert to Catholicism, to Father Duddleswell's running needle of his curate's extravagance for enjoying a plate of expensive strawberries all the show's elements tie into the theme of the sanctity of a priest's confessional vow. It is a testament to the writing of Peter De Rosa that he blends all these diverse threads and manages to end the half-hour's entertainment with a strong climax that employs physical and verbal humor simultaneously.

"The Seal of Confession" finds St. Jude's in desperate need of a new loudspeaker system and new confessional boxes. The confessional boxes are a particularly pressing need since Mrs. Conroy, the wife of the local butcher, has been overheard confessing an affair with Mr. Bottesford, the town's undertaker. Once installed, Father Duddleswell mistakenly takes the microphone into the box just as Mrs. Conroy is coming to unburden herself of her sins. With her confession being broadcast to a full sanctuary, Father Neil and Mr. Conroy begin a mad dash around the sanctuary, attempting to turn off the loudspeakers, while Mr. Bottesford makes a hasty exit.

The episode's best scenes involve the two parish priests and their reasoning over the finer points of the Catholic faith with two different women. The first of these concerns Father Neil's attempts to explain the forgiveness of God to Mrs. Rollings. When the convert asks if God would allow a penitent murderer or thief into heaven, the young priest assures her that it is God's nature to be merciful. Still apprehensive, Mrs. Rollings fears that, forgiveness aside, heaven doesn't sound like a safe place for children.

When Mrs. Rollings becomes too inquisitive, Father Duddleswell steps in and informs her that *why* is a "nasty little Protestant word." He warns her that if she wants to ask so many questions she should go to the Anglican priest to be instructed in unbelief, adding there she can "why, why, why" to her heart's content.

The second exchange is a wonderful bit of nonsense between Father Duddleswell and Mrs. Conroy on why chicken is considered meat while eggs are not. Unfortunately, this priceless exchange often takes repeated viewing to fully understand since it is the background conversation that takes place in the confessional while Father Neil is scrambling around the sanctuary trying to disconnect the microphones.

Series Two 1979–1980

EPISODE ONE: "BLESSINGS FROM HEAVEN" ★★½

Air date: November 11, 1979. Cast: Father Duddleswell (Arthur Lowe); Father Boyd (Daniel Abineri); Mrs. Pring (Gabrielle Daye); Dr. Daley (Patrick McAlinney); Mother Stephen (Sheila Keith); Billy Buzzle (David Ryall); Canon Mahoney (Shay Gorman); Young Lady (Rosie Collins)

When a previously barren woman conceives, Father Duddleswell and Mother Stephen battle for the exclusive rights to the miracle.

"Blessings from Heaven" is concerned with the subject of miracles and, when viewed by itself, is a good entry in the series. When viewed against the next show in the series, ("Father Neil's First Miracle"), some inconsistencies appear in just how Father Duddleswell's character views the miraculous. In "Blessings from Heaven," he is hoping against hope in the miraculous properties of his garden rain barrel, while in the next episode he uses elementary chemistry to produce his own. Another inconsistency in the script of "Blessings from Heaven" is that Father Duddleswell claims that his holy water has caused a barren woman to conceive a child. Throughout the episode, he states the fact that she is now six months pregnant, while at other times he repeats that he gave her the water only three months before. All this criticism is, of course, just the nitpicking of a devoted fan of the series. The episode is packed with wonderful dialogue, all the main supporting characters are present and in top form; and Father Neil begins to display some of the assiduous asides that help give his character its full dimension.

The best moments of the episode occur as Father D's own yearning for profit and power get the better of him. When he imagines that he may have his own supply of miraculous holy water resting in his back garden, he quickly envisions a shrine along the lines of Lourdes. Billy Buzzle is soon on board Duddleswell's miracle express, as he too sees the monetary potential in the affair. The two adversaries become partners with Buzzle supplying bottles for the holy rainwater and providing advice on how to spruce up the church for the expected stream of pilgrims (including his suggestion for a "jazzier statue of Our Lady").

There are also some good moments as Father Duddleswell battles Mother Stephen over the credit for the miracle. Father D's rainwater aside, the reverend mother claims that the miracle is the result of giving the pregnant woman a relic from the mother foundress's tibia. It seems that Mother Stephen must establish three miracles for the foundress in order to help her cause for canonization.

Father Duddleswell's visions of a shrine come crashing down as the bishop declares that Catholic miracles are against the law in Protestant England. The bishop's opinion of the holy water is further influenced by the fact that one sip of the stuff lands him in the hospital with a bout of dysentery.

EPISODE 2: "FATHER NEIL'S FIRST MIRACLE" ★★★

Air date: November 18, 1979. Cast: Father Duddleswell (Arthur Lowe); Father Boyd (Daniel Abineri); Mrs. Pring (Gabrielle Daye); Nurse Owen (Phoebe Nicholls); Mr. Ofori (Lionel Ngakane); Mr. Affram (Christopher Asante); Matron (Barbara Hicks); Dr. Spinks (Nicholas LePrevost); Billy Buzzle (David Ryall)

When Father Duddleswell appoints Father Neil as hospital chaplain, his first case is to cure a man suffering from a witch doctor's curse.

"Father Neil's First Miracle" is an episode in the mold of "The Doomsday Chair." The plot is simple and straightforward and, like that earlier show, centers on the dispelling of deadly superstitions. In both episodes, curses are overcome by Father Duddleswell's guile more than via his faith. One last comparison: both, while containing less witty repartee than the average episode, are highly enjoyable thanks to the strength of the story and performances.

The plot revolves around one of the hospital's African patients, Mr. Ofori. It seems that Ofori had been cursed by the local witch doctor while on the Gold Coast. Consequently, he believes his blood is boiling and that he will soon die. He refuses to eat and is quickly fulfilling the curse. The attending physician, Ofori's grandson, and a nurse all urge Father Neil to put on a comparable show to that of the witch doctor in order to make Ofori believe he is healed.

There are some memorable moments as Father Neil begins his hospital duties only to discover his own version of Duddleswell's Mother Stephen in the guise of the hospital Matron. On their first encounter, Matron sternly warns the curate to stick to ministering to souls, since all the patients' bodies belong to her. This sets up some good tension in the episode, as it appears that everyone in the hospital — including the doctors — walk in fear of this formidable woman, effectively portrayed by Barbara Hicks. Later, when Father Neil confesses he may not be able to help Ofori since to do so would impinge on Matron's territory, Duddleswell reminds his assistant that Jesus went all over Palestine healing the sick. Father Neil agrees but adds that the Lord didn't have Matron to contend with back then.

With the help of Father D and Billy Buzzle, in a wonderfully hammy performance by David Ryall, a modern miracle is manufactured in the episode's humorous finale.

EPISODE 3: "FATAL LADY" ★★½

Air date: November 25, 1979. Cast: Father Duddleswell (Arthur Lowe); Father Boyd (Daniel Abineri); Mrs. Pring (Gabrielle Daye); Mrs. Carlin (Maggie Flint); Miss Davenport (Barbara Young); Maid (Anne Bruzac)

Father Neil becomes ruffled when a rich spinster begins showing him excessive attention.

"Fatal Lady" is the first of a few of shows that concentrate primarily on the character of Father Neil Boyd. Coincidentally or not, these episodes ("Fatal Lady," "The Heart of a Curate," and "Things Are Not What They Seem") all concern Father Neil and a woman. Father Duddleswell and Mrs. Pring's characters are almost relegated to supporting roles. These episodes allow Daniel Abineri a chance to prove his strength as an actor, outside of the formidable shadow of Arthur Lowe. Barbara Young proves an excellent foil in the frivolous yet devout title role.

When the parish's richest woman, Miss Davenport, returns from Monte Carlo, Father D is exultant, but Father Neil is less so when she starts paying too much attention to him. Soon, Father Neil is being called away from more important duties to attend to such flighty whims as blessing her sick canary (this bit is especially funny, since the nearest appropriate prayer in his book is for the launching of an airplane). All the time his curate is pandering to Miss Davenport, Father Duddleswell is urging, then ordering, his young charge on to each new indignity.

In one exchange, after Father Neil bristles at accepting the rich woman's generous donations, Duddleswell reminds his curate that although St. Paul bids them to be fools for Christ, it doesn't mean they have to be "blithering idiots." He talks about having sympathy for the rich since, in his inimitable Irish logic, they are just the same as the poor, only with more money. The episode reaches a satisfying climax as the mystery of Miss Davenport's inordinate attention is revealed to a much-relieved Father Neil.

Arthur Lowe does have some good scenes, particularly when he describes his own similar women problems back when he was a young curate with hair and a waistline. He relates with more than a little pride the story of one woman in particular who parked outside his window, hoping for a quick glimpse of him; she even went so far as to covet one of his cassock buttons as a relic. Duddleswell's ego is deflated, however, as he is compelled to confess that soon after showering him with all that adulation the woman was committed to an institution.

EPISODE 4: "THE HEART OF A CURATE" ★★½

Air date: December 9, 1979. Cast: Father Duddleswell (Arthur Lowe); Father Boyd (Daniel Abineri); Mrs. Pring (Gabrielle Daye); Johnny Downes (Daniel Gerroll); Dr. Daley (Patrick McAlinney); Nurse Owen (Phoebe Nicholls); Mother Stephen (Sheila Keith)

When Father Neil enters the hospital to have his appendix removed, he falls in love with a pretty young nurse.

This episode makes up the second of the aforementioned trio of shows spotlighting Father Neil. After receiving the unwanted attentions of Miss Davenport in the previous episode, in "The Heart of a Curate," Father Neil has his own heart broken. Although the character of Father Duddleswell is, for the second straight episode, not the catalyst for the plot, Arthur Lowe manages to carry a lion's share of the laughs of this episode (and some of its more tender moments as well). Phoebe Nicholls makes her second appearance in the part of Nurse Owen (the first was in "Father Neil's First Miracle"), and Daniel Gerroll debuts as Johnny Downes, a role repeated in "Things Are Not What They Seem." Overall, the episode is an entertaining mix of humor and sentiment, including a charming piece on his birthplace by the usually comic Dr. Daley.

Most of the dramatic content of this installment centers on Father Duddleswell's fears that his curate will be lost to him by marrying. This is a well-established possibility, especially as a former seminary classmate, the aforementioned Johnny Downes, reenters Neil's life, now married. Although Father Neil struggles with the notion and eventually resolves the issue without Father D's assistance, he does take a devilish pleasure in teasing the old priest. Duddleswell on the other hand, is forced to admit his deep affection for his curate before realizing that his concern is an item of amusement.

With Father Neil carrying the more sober elements of the episode, the rest of the cast provides good comic relief. Sheila Keith, as Mother Stephen, has a particularly funny turn as she visits the ailing young curate in the hospital. With the warmth of a grave digger, she kneels by his bedside, announcing she has come to pray for him. Upon rising, Mother Stephen declares that his recovery is assured. To aid her prayers, the mother superior also presents Father Neil with an apple pie with, it is later discovered, a rosary baked inside. The imposing nun's visit gives Duddleswell quite a shock, however, as he enters and at first mistakes Mother Stephen for the angel of death hovering over his assistant's bed.

EPISODE 5: "ALL AT SEA" ★★★

Air date: December 16, 1979. Cast: Father Duddleswell (Arthur Lowe); Father Boyd (Daniel Abineri); Mrs. Pring (Gabrielle Daye); Captain Kent (John Bryans); Pinkerton (Geoffrey Drew); Dr. Daley (Patrick McAlliney); Freddie Williams (Geoffrey Palmer); Skipper (Andrew Downie)

Father Duddleswell battles with the Anglicans for the right to bury an old sailor, then discovers that the man wanted to be buried at sea.

"All at Sea" is an interesting entry in the series from a number of aspects. First, it is one of the better plot-driven *Bless Me, Father* scripts in the vein of "The Doomsday Chair." However, unlike that episode, which spotlights the more virtuous side of Father Duddleswell, the driving force in this script is the oft-besetting sin of greed. Unlike other shows that display the Irish priest in a less than glowing light ("The Tennis Match"), Father D's motivation for profit, although clear, is not overpowering, and ultimately he behaves in a manner befitting his vocation.

The primary motivation for Father Duddleswell's quest to bury the departed sailor is a £400 insurance policy. Once he wins the burial rights with the help of Dr. Daley, Duddleswell sadly discovers the deceased's final wishes. The action then shifts to the search for a cheap undertaker who has experience in sea interments. Father D settles for cheap alone when he finds one who also gives "divvy stamps" (dividend or trading stamps). Soon the cost skyrockets as the seagoing funeral encounters new expenses and some rather funny complications. In the end, of course, Duddleswell is completely frustrated in his hopes of realizing a profit on the affair.

"All at Sea" provides a strong guest-starring opportunity for Geoffrey Palmer in the part of undertaker Freddie Williams. Probably best known to American audiences for his regular roles in *The Fall and Rise of Reginald Perrin*, *Butterflies*, and, most recently, *As Time Goes By*, Palmer also made guest appearances in the *Fawlty Towers* and *Blackadder* series. His usual dry delivery and dour appearance are made to order for this assignment.

Lastly, "All at Sea" has the distinction of having the most location shooting of any *Bless Me, Father* episode. As the title suggests, the better part of the location work was done at sea. Ironically, although Father Duddleswell is averse to sea travel, his alter ego, Arthur Lowe, was the proud owner of a steam yacht.

EPISODE 6: "THE SEASON OF GOODWILL" ★★★½

Air date: December 23, 1979. Cast: Father Duddleswell (Arthur Lowe); Father Boyd (Daniel Abineri); Mrs. Pring (Gabrielle Daye); Billy Buzzle (David Ryall); Dr. Daley (Patrick McAlinney); Mr. Wilkins (Charles Lamb)

Father Duddleswell has trouble keeping his annual Yuletide pledge to be kind to all living creatures.

"The Season of Goodwill," the *Bless Me, Father* Christmas episode, is a fine entry in the series. Revolving around the premise of Father Neil's attempts to break Father Duddleswell's annual attempts at saintliness, the show is filled with good dialogue built on a sound plot. The standout of the proceedings, of course, is Arthur Lowe, who delivers a sustained slow burn, which rises steadily throughout the episode to a full boil by the conclusion.

The main source of delight is the fact that, as Mrs. Pring puts it, Father Duddleswell is hard enough to live with when he's his usual bad self, but when he's good he's impossible. In light of this, the housekeeper and the curate decide to break Father D's Christmas resolution by taking advantage of his seasonal "good nature." In the next weeks, Father Neil especially hammers away at his superior's sweeter disposition. In rapid succession, the curate finishes Father D's punch lines, forces him to buy unwanted raffle tickets, take his hospital rounds, and administer communion at the seamen's home at 6:15 in the morning.

Next, the mayor asks Father D to give out the presents at the annual old-age pensioners' Christmas party. Father Duddleswell considers it an honor, until he learns that he must do the duty in a Father Christmas (Santa Claus) suit. At the party, the unwilling Father Christmas hands out mufflers and gloves to even more unwilling senior citizens. He even has difficulty in leading the party in seasonal songs. The party is enlivened with the arrival of Billy Buzzle and his black Labrador, Pontius.

The climax of the episode comes at Christmas Eve midnight mass, where Father Neil delivers his coup de grace and finally returns his superior to his normal temperament.

EPISODE 7: "A BACK TO FRONT WEDDING" ★★★

Air date: January 6, 1980. Cast: Father Duddleswell (Arthur Lowe); Father Boyd (Daniel Abineri); Mrs. Pring (Gabrielle Daye); Cinema Manager (Charles Pemberton); Cashier (Penny Ryder); Best Man (Derek Hollis); Richard Faber (Alan Cheesman); Wanda French (Rowena Roberts); Mrs. Faber (Anne Robson); Mrs. French (Ruth Holden); Dr. Daley (Patrick McAlliney); Maid (Polly Miller)

Father Duddleswell compels a bride and groom to hold their reception before the marriage ceremony when he forgets about the nuptials and takes Father Neil to the movies.

A very enjoyable entry to cap off the second season of *Bless Me, Father*, "A Back to Front Wedding" is an interesting mix of comedy derived from both the situation and some extraneous sources. The plot itself, involving Father's Duddleswell's inadvertent forgetting of an afternoon wedding, is quite clever — especially in regard to the roguish priest's faking of personal injury in order to put the wedding party back into a celebratory mood. The twists do not end here, however, as again, by Father D's error, he discovers he has sent the happy couple off on their honeymoon not legally wed. This is due to the fact that he performed the wedding outside the hours permitted by the law. Not in the practice of sending couples off to begin their wedded bliss in sin, Father D and Father Neil must make a rather unorthodox and correspondingly humorous visit to a hotel bridal suite to set matters right.

The entire catalyst for the back-to-front ceremony is also quite funny in its own right. After a full morning of performing weddings, Father Duddleswell announces that he is treating Father Neil to a movie in the next town that afternoon. When the priests arrive at the cinema, however, it turns out that the party is Father Neil's treat, since the elder priest has forgotten his wallet. The duo sit down to enjoy the 1949 classic *Kind Hearts and Coronets*. During one scene, in which Alec Guinness is playing a clergyman, Father Duddleswell offers his unique brand of film criticism to his young assistant. He informs his young assistant that anyone can play an Anglican minister on the screen since Anglicans aren't "real priests like us." Despite Father Neil's objections, Father D continues to liken his Anglican counterparts to "clowns who prefer churches to circus rings." The hilarious acid commentary continues when Duddleswell mistakenly takes the screen priest's surplice for a barber's sheet.

Earlier in the episode, Duddleswell has similarly rough criticism for Mrs. Pring. The many weddings of late serve to remind the housekeeper of her own days as a young and pretty bride. "Ping," Duddleswell suddenly expostulates, interrupting the reminiscence.

When he is asked what the sound means, Duddleswell explains that it was the sound of his imagination snapping at the strain of recalling such a thought.

One interesting note about this episode is the film that Father Duddleswell and Father Neil go to see. *Kind Hearts and Coronets*, aside from being a classic Ealing comedy, and one of Alec Guinness's first big hits, was also the film debut of Arthur Lowe. Lowe plays the part of the reporter in the last scene of the picture. Of course, in "A Back to Front Wedding," Father Duddleswell is forced to leave before the end of the movie, depriving him of a chance to be as critical of his own performance as he is of Guinness's.

Series Three 1981

EPISODE 1: "THINGS ARE NOT WHAT THEY SEEM" ★★½

Air date: July 5, 1981. Cast: Father Duddleswell (Arthur Lowe); Father Boyd (Daniel Abineri); Mrs. Pring (Gabrielle Daye); Hugh (Jim Wiggins); Father Jim (Mike McCabe); Father Tom (Michael Troughton); Father Bob (Steven Mann); Barmaid (Liza Flanagan); Land Girl (Diana Weston); Molly Downes (Henrieta Baynes); Johnny Downes (Daniel Gerroll); Mother Stephen (Sheila Keith)

Father Duddleswell's lesson to Father Neil — that things are not always what they seem — is driven home when the curate is accused of having an affair with a married woman.

"Thing Are Not What They Seem" is another storydriven episode, although it is not as strong in its comedy as some of the others like it in the series. This may be due to the fact that it is also the third episode that investigates Father Neil's relationship to the opposite sex. While all of Father Neil's "love interests" have been either unobtainable or undesirable (and are ultimately unconscionable due to his devotion to his priestly vows), they do allow a glimpse back into the sensitivity of a character who has grown tremendously in self-assurance and jocosity since the earlier shows. Like the other strongly plotted episodes, particularly those centered on Father Neil, most of the humor comes from the fringes of the proceedings.

This episode affords a glimpse into Father Neil's pre-priestly life, as he meets a group of his former seminary classmates for a day's outing. Unfortunately, it seems that Neil, despite working for the challenging Duddleswell, is the only one entirely happy with his vocation. One classmate complains bitterly about his parish priest, while another confesses that he has fallen in love and is seriously pondering dropping out of the priesthood. The plot thickens as Father Neil starts counseling Molly Downes, the wife of another ex-classmate (Johnny Downes of "The Heart of a Curate"), who believes her husband is having an affair. Neil's clandestine counseling leads to similar charges being leveled against him by various parish meddlers. By the episode's end, the numerous plot lines are shown to be intertwined and are easily sorted out, proving the show's title premise.

"Things Are Not What They Seem" features a good running gag between Father D and Father Neil involving the older priest's attempts at giving his curate some golf clubs. The first incarnation of the gift comes as Duddleswell presents a decrepit bag containing even more dilapidated clubs. When Father Neil refuses the gift, Father D accuses him of being too proud to accept the ancient clubs. The problem is more ingrained than pride, Neil explains, noting that the clubs are right-handed and he is a lefty. Father D is especially annoyed, seeing that his generosity cost him approximately 60 cents. Later in the episode, the older priest tries to set the mistake right by handing Father Neil a new bag filled with a full set of clubs and covers. When Father Neil removes the covers, however, he discovers that the entire bag is filled with left-handed putters. A chagrined Father D confesses that the shop let him have the set at a bargain price.

EPISODE 2: "WOMEN" ★★½

Air date: July 12, 1981. Cast: Father Duddleswell (Arthur Lowe); Father Boyd (Daniel Abineri); Mrs. Pring (Gabrielle Daye); Helen (Carolyn Pickles); Billy Buzzle (David Ryall); Mother Stephen (Sheila Keith); Mrs. Rollings (Pamela Ruddock)

When Mrs. Pring finds a previously unread note from her late husband, she takes a short sabbatical, forcing Father Duddleswell and Father Neil to fend for themselves.

The title refers to the exasperated proclamations made by both Father Duddleswell and Father Neil in this episode. While the priests must contend with the formidable Mother Stephen and the difficult convert Mrs. Rollings, the show really belongs to Gabrielle Daye as Mrs. Pring. "Women" is without a doubt the housekeeper's episode in the limelight. It is the only installment in which we see Mrs. Pring's kitchen and are given any insight into her character beyond her 20-year war with Father D. From this aspect, the episode is to Mrs. P what "The Heart of a Curate" was to the part of Father Neil. In fact, both have similar endings, with Father Duddleswell being compelled to bare his emotions and admit how fond and dependent he is on the subject in question. Not surprisingly, while in "The Heart of a Curate," Mrs. Pring abets Father Neil, in "Women," the young priest conspires with the housekeeper to force Father D's hand. This is all done in an amusing fashion by making Father Duddleswell believe that Billy Buzzle has romantic designs on his housekeeper.

Aside from revealing Father D's true feelings for his housekeeper, "Women" also gives the viewer a detailed glimpse into Mrs. Pring's past. The show opens on her birthday and 35th wedding anniversary. Mrs. Pring explains to Father Neil that she was married to her Ted during World War I, while he was on leave. After a two-week honeymoon, he returned to the front. Soon after, she discovered that she was expecting and wrote to tell Ted. The letter was returned unopened, however, with the rest of his personal effects when he was killed in action. Mrs. Pring gave birth to a daughter, Helen, who she raised alone, until she became "housekeeper for the little ogre of this castle." Father D doted on Helen, who returned the affection by calling the priest "Uncle Charlie."

Some of the better moments in the episode come without "women," as the two priests are left to manage running the presbytery on their own. Father D assigns himself the chores of cooking and laundry, while Father Neil is left with keeping the house tidy. Each day's lunch, aside from being served at least three hours late, is composed of potato soup and boiled eggs. Father Neil complains that the soup is cold and the potatoes raw. In response, Father D runs his finger across the dusty table, which his curate was supposed to have cleaned. The only consolation is the perfect job done on the laundry, which is little surprise after Father D confesses he's been sending the washing out to be done.

EPISODE 3: "BEDDINGS AND WEDDINGS" ★★★

Air date: July 19, 1981. Cast: Father Duddleswell (Arthur Lowe); Father Boyd (Daniel Abineri); Mrs. Pring (Gabrielle Daye); Dr. Daley (Patrick McAlliney); Batty Holohan (Anthony Douse); Dympna Tutty (Rynagh O'Grady); Tommy Turner (Antony Brown); Bottesford (Patrick Newell); Beryl Turner (Peggy Ann Jones)

Father Neil starts a counseling group for married couples but attracts only undertakers to the sessions.

A fine episode, "Beddings and Weddings" marks a return to the quality level achieved in the previous seasons of the program. After two less-than-par offerings, this one scores well, not only with jokes but with a good strong plot that manages to hold the viewer's interest through various twists and surprises.

When Father Neil begins his group for married couples, he is immediately frustrated when only two people show up—both of whom are men and undertakers. The first, Tommy Turner, drolly portrayed by Antony Brown, is a victim of a loveless marriage. It seems that Turner was cajoled into matrimony 25 years earlier in order to keep his job. The other, Bottesford, has been abandoned by his wife (she probably ran off with the butcher; see "The Seal of Confession"). There is some witty byplay as the two funeral directors commiserate on the state of their marriages and their occupational pitfalls. After a brief time, Father Neil is convinced that Bottesford is only there in an attempt to get Turner to work for him, but this is only the first wrinkle in a story line filled with surprises. By the episode's end, it turns out that Bottesford was actually after Beryl, Turner's wife, with whom he runs off, leaving a grateful husband behind.

Early in the proceedings there are some good moments as Father Neil counsels an older couple on the eve of their wedding. He expresses doubts about the prospects for the marriage, especially since the bride, Dympna Tutty, has taken a vow of chastity. Given the Catholic beliefs on procreation, Father Neil remarks that the impending union would be a sham. This leads Father Duddleswell to slyly observe that in the Catholic faith everything is forbidden until it becomes compulsory. Happily, by the second day of the honeymoon, the bride is telephoning Duddleswell long distance to be released from her self-imposed vow.

EPISODE 4: "FIRE AND BRIMSTONE" ★½

Air date: July 26, 1981. Cast: Father Duddleswell (Arthur Lowe); Father Boyd (Daniel Abineri); Mrs. Pring (Gabrielle Daye); Mrs. Rollings (Pamela Ruddock); Mrs. Hughes (Caroline Goodman); Children in Church (Mark Burdis, Natalie Collins, Joseph Daniels, Sam Davies, David Doyle, Anna Hayes, Mark Luxford, Lee MacDonald, Mark Monero, Dicon Murray, Melissa Wilks); Mr. Bingley (Ernest Jennings); Billy Buzzle (David Ryall); Mother Stephen (Sheila Keith); Mrs. Baxter (Linda Renwick); Mr. Probble (Gerald Cross); Mr. Pinkerton (Geoffrey Drew)

Father Duddleswell tries to bring a dying former Catholic back to the church.

"Fire and Brimstone" is a rather disappointing entry in the series. Although there is plenty of clever dialogue, the plot is almost nonexistent. The little story that exists is only introduced halfway through the episode. Otherwise, it seems that the whole program is a weak vehicle for various jokes and observations about hell. Consequently, most of the scenes are unrelated to the others. Not surprisingly, this episode sports the largest supporting cast of all three seasons, since new characters are paraded in and out to give their opinions on the subject and to receive Father Duddleswell's musings in return.

The best observations on the hereafter come in an exchange between Father D and Mrs. Pring. After asking Father D if he's ordered his coal, the housekeeper remarks that an eternity in hell would be a great injustice, seeing as she has endured 20 years with the ornery priest. Father D shoots back that after 20 years with Mrs. Pring an eternity in hell would be a "blessed relief."

The plot, such as it is, involves Jimmy Baxter, a little boy in Father Neil's catechism class. It seems his grandfather, J. J. Bingley, is close to death, and Jimmy fears he will not go to heaven. After Bingley's first wife left him, he remarried outside the church, and subsequently he became an avowed atheist and Communist. Despite Father D's efforts and Mother Stephen's prayers, Bingley remains unmoved to the end. After his passing, however, both the priest and the nun reveal the flaws of their own theology when they confess that the return of Bingley to the fold was never really necessary.

Duddleswell remarks that he would give the last rites to a pet turtle to make a little boy happy. Father Neil is understandably confused by these statements. Despite the fact that they are supposedly motivated by compassion, they indicate that neither spiritual leader actually believes what they have so ardently been preaching throughout the episode. More consistent, and much more entertaining, are Billy Buzzle's views on the subject, which are aired in an ecumenical discussion on hell — one of the episode's highlights.

EPISODE 5: "A LEGEND COMES TO STAY" ★★★

Air date: August 2, 1981. Cast: Father Duddleswell (Arthur Lowe); Father Boyd (Daniel Abineri); Mrs. Pring (Gabrielle Daye); Mother Stephen (Sheila Keith); Billy Buzzle (David Ryall); Dr. Daley (Patrick McAlinney); Father Abe (Peter Copley); Lord Mitchin (Mischa de la Motte); Fireman (David Purcell)

Aged Father Abe, Duddleswell's first parish priest, with whom he served as curate, comes for a visit.

Short on plot, "A Legend Comes to Stay" offers more of a character study than a story. The primary character is the elderly Father Abraham Cody, for whom Father Duddleswell labored 15 years as a curate. While enjoyable, this particular show does not lend itself well to close scrutiny or even to description. Most of the scenes, while bristling with good dialogue, reveal the relationships between the various characters and as such do not fit easily into the thin story. The humor, of which there is plenty, is culled from two sources: the established cast engaging in typical give and take and Father Abe's fond abuse of his former curate. Aside from Peter Copley's role as the 85-year-old priest and a few lines by a lord and a fireman, the only players are the three stars and the three primary supporting characters.

The episode begins as Father Duddleswell receives a note from Father Abe Cody, announcing his imminent arrival. Father Abe now resides in the old priests' home. The note, however, is somewhat late, as its arrival coincides with that of Father Abe, who is waiting in the study, where he is smoking a big black cigar and yelling to be served whiskey. He delights in referring to Father D alternately as his "little Charlie" and "a sloppy little curate." Aside from whiskey, cigars, and badgering "little Charlie," Father Abe also has a passion for gambling, although he knows little about horses. He quickly establishes communications with the parish's nearest bookie, Billy Buzzle. Father D asks Buzzle to pass along any money the ancient priest wagers, and he will take responsibility in the event that he happens to have a winner — an arrangement that inevitably backfires on the priest.

Later, with Father D confined to bed with a bad back, Father Abe proceeds to turn St. Jude's upside down. First, he drives out a churchful of penitents waiting for confession because it is suppertime (although he does offer to hear serious sins immediately), then he baptizes a little boy, christening him "Mary Jane." Next, he burns a hole in the church carpet when he swings the thurible (incense container) too high, causing the charcoal to fly out. Finally, the elderly priest manages to lock Father Neil and a scandalized Mother Stephen in the church.

The episode concludes with some pathos as the 85-year-old priest takes ill and seems to be on the verge of death. Fortunately, however, after a desperate vigil, the priest recovers enough for a final joke before the ending credits.

EPISODE 6: "PORGY AND BESS" ★★★½

Air date: August 9, 1981. Cast: Father Duddleswell (Arthur Lowe); Father Boyd (Daniel Abineri); Mrs. Pring (Gabrielle Daye); Billy Buzzle (David Ryall); Dr. Daley (Patrick McAlinney); Greg Summers (Dave Calderhead); Mr. Tippett (Vyvian Hall); Judge Turnbull (Arnold Peters); Mr. Flack (David Beale); Clerk of the Court (Lennard Pearce); Mr. Banks (Richard Syms)

Billy Buzzle takes Father Duddleswell to court when the priest kidnaps one of his pigs.

In this, the second-to-last episode of *Bless Me, Father*, the series almost turns palindromic — mirroring the third entry of the first season. "Porgy and Bess" is another battle royal between Father Duddleswell and his "best enemy," Billy Buzzle, in the style of "The Bell of St. Jude's." Both episodes feature battles begun when Buzzle's love of animals (pigeons and pigs) disrupts his neighbor's household. Instead of being a mere remake of the earlier program, however, "Porgy and Bess" brings a satisfying closure to the continuing war between the two men. While the episode ends with the promise of more battles, at least the viewer is left with the impression that the combat is more sporting than vitriolic.

The bulk of the episode is taken up with Father D's repeated attempts to have Buzzle remove the pigs and their offensive odor. This escalates from simple arguing and cajoling to stronger measures, such as throwing rocks through Buzzle's windows and tossing a carving knife at a pig. Finally, the priest kidnaps one of the animals in an amusing nighttime raid and removes it to a nearby farm.

With Porgy safely out of olfactory range, Father Duddleswell becomes rather fond of the beast, visiting it often and arranging for veterinary care. Buzzle, on the other hand, is beside himself and can be heard calling for Porgy throughout the neighborhood. Father D decides to return the pig but receives a call from the farm informing him that Porgy has suddenly died. Buzzle retaliates by suing him.

The trial sequence provides some amusing moments. Father D arrives in court wearing a rather garish and poorly knotted necktie, since the bishop has refused to let him wear his clerical collar to the proceedings. On the stand, the priest testifies that he was actually fond of the deceased pig. Upon cross-examination, however, Father Duddleswell contradicts himself, calling Porgy "playful" and then admitting he threw knives at the animal, while not wanting to harm the pig.

Peter De Rosa manages to wrap up the feud and the episode well with some clever and surprising twists. Although no one could know it at the time, since a fourth series had been planned, this episode brings the relationship between Duddleswell and Buzzle to a nice resolution.

EPISODE 7: "A MIXED-UP MARRIAGE" ★½

Air date: August 16, 1981. Cast: Father Duddleswell (Arthur Lowe); Father Boyd (Daniel Abineri); Mrs. Pring (Gabrielle Daye); Mother Stephen (Sheila Keith); Rabbi Rosen (Cyril Shaps); Mr. Goldman (Benny Lee); Christine Hammond (Julia Chambers); Isaac Rosen (Gary Brown); Mr. Pinkerton (Geoffrey Drew)

When a rabbi's son wants to marry a Catholic girl, Father Duddleswell and Rabbi Rosen intervene.

Bless Me, Father ends its three-season run with this rather weak entry, which is certainly not representative of the overall quality of the series. "A Mixed-Up Marriage" is cast from the same mold as "Fire and Brimstone," in that it introduces a dogma, which is initially vehemently supported by Father Duddleswell, only to be cast aside by show's end for reasons of sentimentality. Whereas "Fire and Brimstone" examined damnation, here the subject is interfaith marriages. Some life is injected into the proceedings by the amusing performance of Cyril Shaps as Rabbi Manny Rosen, but unfortunately his character is written as too much of a stereotype to be completely enjoyable. Still, there is such a good rapport between the rabbi and Father Duddleswell that one wishes the character had been included in other episodes and afforded more depth. Another flaw in this episode is the repetition of punch lines, with one in particular (a reference to either the rabbi converting the priest or the priest converting the rabbi) trotted out no fewer than three times. Father Neil has a major part in the proceedings as the voice of conciliation, although his advice tends to gloss over some of the challenges inherent in interfaith marriages.

The better moments in the episode occur as the priest and the rabbi enjoy their newfound friendship, which quickly blossoms into something of a mutual admiration society. By the episode's end, Duddleswell warmly confesses that Rabbi Rosen is almost nice enough to be a Catholic.

"Thank you, Charlie," the rabbi replies, adding, "and if you ever decide to turn Jewish, I will see you suffer no pain."

Benny Lee appears in this episode, which was made at approximately the same time that he was appearing as Mr. Klein in three episodes of *Are You Being Served?*

Yes, Minister

BBC-TV 1980–1984

Yes, Prime Minister

BBC-TV 1986–1988

Yes, Minister and, to a lesser degree, its sequel, *Yes, Prime Minister*, comprise some of the most clever, most intelligent writing to ever grace a sitcom in Britain or indeed in any country. It was enjoyed not only by the viewing audience but by critics and, perhaps most tellingly, by the very politicians it lampooned. The key to the success of both series lay in their scripts, which offered an inside view of the workings of the British government.

As scripted by Antony Jay and Jonathan Lynn, the show proved to be shrewd and clever without being intimidating to the average viewer. At the same time, the writers, provided a primer to the bureaucracy that had grown up around British parliamentary government without ever talking down to its audience. That *Yes, Minister* could do all this and still be funny and entertaining confirms its deserved place in the pantheon of great Brit-coms.

Yes, Minister had its genesis in the meeting of its creators, Jay and Lynn. The pair first met while working at Video Arts, the comedic training film company begun by John Cleese (*Monty Python's Flying Circus*, *Fawlty Towers*) in the 1970s. Lynn, a Cambridge contemporary of Cleese, had his first nationwide exposure appearing in and cowriting *Footlights '64*, an ITV sketch special featuring the best and brightest comic talent that university had to offer. From there Lynn worked as both a writer and performer on a variety of television programs. These included *Doctor at Large* (both writing and performing), *The Liver Birds* (performing), *On the Buses* (writing), and ITV's *My Brother's Keeper* (which he cowrote and costarred in with George Layton). Lynn can also be seen in a small turn as a window cleaner who mistakenly thinks Felicity Kendal is willing to trade sex for his services in the "Pig's Lib" episode of *The Good Life*.

Unlike his future partner, Antony Jay had focused his pre–*Minister* efforts exclusively on the writing side of the business. More politically minded than Lynn, Jay's most notable early work had been as a writer on such erudite satires as *That Was the Week That Was* and *The Frost Report* (both of which also included the scripting talents of Cleese). While attending a 1972 lecture, Jay first realized the unique relationship that existed between government politicians and the civil servants who supposedly were there to serve them. Mainly, Jay discovered that there was a vast difference between ministry policy and a minister's policy. Ministers came and went with each successive government, but the civil servants wielded the more entrenched power behind the scenes. With this revelation, Jay's mind began fomenting the possibility of a comedy based on such a relationship.

Upon meeting Lynn at Video Arts, Jay found the perfect comedy balance to his knowledge of politics. Using the published diaries of Crossman, along with personal anecdotes culled from some government insiders, Jay and Lynn completed their pilot script in 1977 and sold it to the BBC. Unlike America, where upcoming elections often inspire more political satire, in Britain the BBC usually shies away from the genre during campaign seasons due to the fact that it is government funded and avoids jeopardizing its subsidy by appearing biased. Consequently, the project was put on hold until after an upcoming national election.

The basic premise of the series — and just about every installment thereof— was the relationship between Jim Hacker, a new minister (akin to a cabinet secretary in the U.S. federal government) for the Department of Administrative Affairs, and his permanent secretary (the top civil servant in the department), Sir Humphrey Appleby. Lynn saw their interaction as something of a governmental Bertie Wooster and Jeeves, in that the servant was smarter than his master. Adding a new twist to P. G. Wodehouse's classic duo, however, was the fact that not only was Sir Humphrey more intelligent than the well-meaning but often obtuse Hacker, he also had a touch of Machiavellin to him. Thus, whereas Jeeves always used his brains to the benefit of his slower-witted boss, Sir Humphrey almost never did — except on the rare occasion when it would benefit him first. Starting with the notion that ministers come and go with each new government but permanent secretaries are, well, more or less permanent, each installment saw Humphrey trying to keep the reform-minded Hacker from tinkering with his private kingdom.

Caught between the pair was another civil servant, Bernard Woolley, who had the job of being Hacker's private secretary. The Woolley character was a masterstroke of construction, creating a generally likable, intelligent, albeit slightly naive buffer between the two leads. The fact that Bernard works directly for Hacker, although he is also accountable to Humphrey as a civil servant, provided many amusing situations. Bernard's general naivete also provided ripe opportunities for the hard and cynical Humphrey to provide his minion an education. These scenes usually took on the flavor of C. S. Lewis's *Screwtape Letters* in which a veteran demon advises an apprentice on the intricacies of damning a soul. In effect Bernard became the representative of the audience, allowing the writers to explain the inner workings of the British government to the viewer through him.

Casting the three primary players was the work of then-head of BBC comedy, John Howard Davies. For the top-billed part of the Honorable James Hacker, Davies tapped Paul Eddington. Eddington had just come off four seasons of the popular *The Good Life* (*Good Neighbors*) in which he played Jerry, the husband of Penelope Keith's Margo. A devout Quaker, Eddington got into acting during the Second World War when his conscientious objector status landed him in ENSA (essentially the British version of the USO), entertaining the fighting men. After the war, Eddington went into repertory theater, where he built up a solid resume. It wasn't until *The Good Life*, however, that Eddington's considerable comic talents received a national televised audience. The role of Jerry Leadbetter, which had also been cast by John Howard Davies, made Paul Eddington a welcomed household name.

For the pivotal role of the nefarious Sir Humphrey, Davies selected Nigel Hawthorne. While not nearly as well known as his costar, Hawthorne also had a solid reputation in the profession earned through years of hard work, some of them rather lean. As a young man, Hawthorne had arrived in England from South Africa with only £12 in his pocket. Against his father's wishes, Hawthorne had left home to pursue a stage career. His father, a respected doctor, had wanted young Nigel to train for a career in the diplomatic service. While playing a permanent secretary in Whitehall was not quite the same, it was close enough to diplomacy to be ironic. Unlike most, who saw Sir Humphrey as an arch-schemer, Nigel Hawthorne chose to play the part with a touch of insanity.

"He is raving mad of course," Hawthorne confessed to the *Radio Times* in 1986. "Obsessive about his job. He'd do anything to keep control. In fact, he does go mad in one episode [probably "The Key"]. Quite mad." (This approach to Sir Humphrey proved to be good practice for Hawthorne's title role in *The Madness of King George*, which earned him an Academy Award nomination for best actor in 1995.)

Derek Fowlds was chosen for the part of Bernard Woolley. Although Fowlds had appeared in a variety of sketch programs and one-off comedies, the actor was most recognizable as the straight man for ten years to Basil Brush, a fox puppet that was one of the best-liked stars of the BBC's children's programming. Perhaps feeding lines to a wisecracking fox for a decade was just the training Fowlds needed to support the wily Sir Humphrey. In any event, Fowlds, although he looked a little old, especially in later seasons, to be playing an uninitiated civil servant, more than proved his worth in support of Eddington and Hawthorne.

When the first episode of *Yes, Minister* was produced, the director, Stuart Allen, wanted the writers to add more jokes to the script. Thankfully, Jay and Lynn refused, allowing the situations and the characters to provide the ample humor. After this pilot offering, the directing reins were turned over to Sydney Lotterby for the remaining six programs of the first series. That the show would instantly become a series was not a foregone conclusion at the time since, as Lotterby has pointed out to the author, the material was seen to be "somewhat esoteric for a comedy." Indeed, the first series of scripts were examined by Lady Falkender, the secretary to former Prime Minister Harold Wilson, for political accuracy, a detail not afforded the usual situation comedy.

From the outset *Yes, Minister* was a ratings and critical success. Surprisingly, the series had its biggest fans inside the halls of power at Whitehall. Since no political party was ever mentioned, speculation about which side could claim the bumbling Jim Hacker ran high. Some thought Hacker represented the new Labour, while others pointed to the more conservative policies he favored and placed him on the Tory side of the aisle. As time went on, the prevailing opinion shifted, placing Hacker as a Conservative, especially since that was the party in power for the whole of the show's run. Still, even when politicians were certain they were the model for Hacker (as the majority of cabinet ministers thought), the program was generally loved.

Margaret Thatcher, the prime minister during both series, praised the show on television and even appeared in a skit with Paul Eddington and Nigel Hawthorne before a live audience at the National Viewers and Listeners Association. Thatcher gave a further endorsement of the show in the conservative *Telegraph* when she noted: "Its clearly observed portrayal of what goes on in the corridors of power has given me hours of pure joy."

It is little wonder that *Yes, Minister* was so dead-on in its spoofing of those corridors since more than 50 government insiders contributed true anecdotes to Jay and Lynn during the show's run.

Not everyone inside Whitehall admired the show, however. Predictably, the only segment of the government chafed were the civil servants, but who could blame them, represented (albeit accurately by most accounts) by such a scoundrel as Humphrey Appleby? Further salt was rubbed into the wounds when the civil service minister began referring to his permanent secretary as "Sir Humphrey."

Civil service complaints aside, *Yes, Minister* managed to accumulate awards and accolades as easily as Sir Humphrey picked up new honors from the semiannual honors list. The show won the (BAFTA) British Academy of Film and Television Arts Award for best comedy during each of its three years of eligibility. In addition, the program was similarly honored by the Broadcasting Press Council and the TV and Radio Industry Club, among others. In 1986 as the first series of *Yes, Prime Minister* was launched, both Eddington and Hawthorne were cited in the New Year's honours list. The following year, Antony Jay was knighted.

Buoyed by the success of the first three series, in 1984 Jay and Lynn decided to elevate Hacker to prime minister in a Christmas season special that paved the way for *Yes, Prime Minister* approximately one year later. (Hacker, true to form, stumbled into the top spot quite by accident in a script that almost predicted John Major's rise to power four years later.) While still impeccably written, unfortunately the 16 shows of the sequel were not as well received by critics. It was, after all, quite amusing and believable to imagine a fool like Hacker as a cabinet minister. To see the same man as prime minister, however, was rather unsettling to many. The fault lay not in the material itself but rather that it came as a follow-up to the universally praised *Yes, Minister.* (In the United States, the entire run of *Yes, Prime Minister* was available on video years before *Yes, Minister*, thus preventing any comparison of the two shows. For those who experienced the characters in this reverse order, the second group of shows holds up well.)

Yes, Prime Minister also saw the further development of Sir Humphrey or at least one of his funniest routines. Almost from the start, Humphrey was the master of the obscure evasive answer. The character of the permanent secretary would employ the device whenever Hacker came too close to discovering the truth about a topic. Successfully executed, the answer would effectively return Hacker to the realm of the totally mystified. By the time the sequel series was being written, Jay and Lynn had developed these answers to the level of an art form, making them not only full of jargon and bureaucratic gobbledygook but also incredibly long. In the mouth of a lesser actor they would have been rendered impotent, but in the skillful charge of Nigel Hawthorne they were marvelously funny.

Sydney Lotterby, who directed all of *Yes, Prime Minister*, recalled that one time Hawthorne's drive for perfection in these speeches resulted in some slight embarrassment for the program, which had similarly high standards. Hawthorne's speech, which had become a staple, even a highlight, of each show did not go as well in the taping as it had in rehearsals. Although it was good enough to satisfy most present, by the end of the taping, Hawthorne asked to retake the scene.

"The cameras were repositioned," explained Lotterby to the author in 1998, "Nigel changed into the clothes he was wearing for that scene and we did the sentence again. This time it was perfect. When I came to edit the program I noticed that although the sentence was perfect Nigel had the wrong tie on!"

In deference to Hawthorne's wishes, Lotterby decided to use the perfect performance with the wrong tie. "If the audience is watching that," reasoned the director, "then they're watching the wrong thing."

When the show was aired, Lotterby was flooded with letters, some containing old ties, all complaining about the error.

"Moral," according to Sydney Lotterby, "even in classic entertainment never underestimate what your audience is looking at!"

The offending scene was reshot the following week to avoid any further complaints during reruns and video releases.

THE EPISODES

***Yes, Minister**—by Antony Jay and Jonathan Lynn. Produced and Directed by Sydney Lotterby, Stuart Allen, and Peter Whitmore.*

Series One 1980

EPISODE 1: "OPEN GOVERNMENT" ★★★½

Air date: February 25, 1980. Cast: Jim Hacker (Paul Eddington); Sir Humphrey Appleby (Nigel Hawthorne); Bernard Woolley (Derek Fowlds). With John Nettleton; Edward Jewesbury; Diana Hoddinott; Neil Fitzwilliam; Norman Mitchell; David Moran; Fraser Kerr

After years in the opposition, Member of Parliament Jim Hacker's party has won a general election and is back in power. Hacker is given the potentially dead-end cabinet post of minister for Administrative Affairs.

Hacker's first goal is the implementation of his party's "open government" plan to keep the public informed of the government's actions. Despite Hacker's notions to the contrary, the permanent secretary of the department, Sir Humphrey Appleby, is quickly on the way to having him "house trained."

Ultimately, Humphrey manages to quash the open government plan by contriving a situation that makes its implementation politically disastrous to Hacker.

"Open Government" effectively establishes the pattern for the majority of the episodes in *Yes, Minister* and its sequel, *Yes, Prime Minister*. Jim Hacker resolutely but naively tries to implement the policies of his party and effect change in government. Working hard to maintain the status quo for the civil service is the department's permanent secretary, Sir Humphrey Appleby. Caught between Hacker and Appleby is Bernard Woolley, Hacker's private secretary, who is also a member of the civil service.

Although he doesn't realize it, Hacker is definitely in over his head when paired against Sir Humphrey, as shown in their first formal meeting. Humphrey recalls that Hacker grilled him with some tough questions during a hearing the previous year. Hacker patronizingly admits that being a Member of Parliament necessitates asking tough questions, to which Humphrey deftly replies that being in government means not answering them. Hacker is taken aback and comments that Humphrey did answer all his questions. Humphrey smiles and remarks he's glad Hacker thought so.

Later, there is a deliciously cynical scene in which Humphrey and the cabinet secretary educate Bernard on the undesirability of open government. The cabinet secretary informs Bernard that you can be open or have government, but not both. The pair conclude by telling Bernard that secrecy is the only thing that protects the politicians from becoming laughingstocks, while they, the civil servants, actually run the government.

Episode 2: "The Official Visit" ★★★

Air date: March 3, 1980. Cast: Jim Hacker (Paul Eddington); Sir Humphrey Appleby (Nigel Hawthorne); Bernard Woolley (Derek Fowlds). With Tenniel Evans; John Savident; Thomas Baptiste; Robert Dougall; Anthony Carrick

A visit by the president of Buranda is put in jeopardy when the government of that nation is ousted and replaced by Colonel Selim Mohammed in a military coup. The colonel, however, announces he will make the trip. Upon his arrival Hacker immediately recognizes Selim Mohammed as his old classmate from the university, Charlie Umtali.

In what amounts to political blackmail, Charlie threatens to deliver an embarrassing speech on British colonialism. Hacker quickly learns that the price of defusing the speech is an interest-free loan of £50 million with which to buy British oil equipment.

Lest anyone think that Jim Hacker is a complete fumbler and putty in the hands of Sir Humphrey, Lynn and Jay have wisely given him occasional stalemates (and, rarely, victories) in the pair's jousting. "The Official Visit" is the first of these.

"The Official Visit" is also noteworthy for containing one of the few physical comedy displays in the entire series. The routine, which is reminiscent of the stateroom scene in the Marx Brothers' *Night at the Opera,* occurs in Jim Hacker's tiny sleeper compartment on a train bound for Scotland. When a crisis suddenly arises, Hacker, who is in the process of taking off his trousers, quickly finds himself crammed in with five other cabinet members and advisors. This slapstick, coupled with the series' usual urbane dialogue, helps make the bit a standout.

This episode also marks a valuable lesson for the new minister. With Hacker swamped under a load of paperwork, Bernard suggests that all he need do is transfer the mountain of correspondence from the in box to the out box

The Right Honorable James Hacker (Paul Eddington, seated) scans the papers for yet another political scandal as the Machiavellian Sir Humphry (Nigel Hawthorne, left) and the dutiful Bernard Woolley (Derek Fowlds) look on. Copyright © BBC.

and let the civil service send an official reply. Bernard explains that the standard draft thanks the correspondent for his letter and says the matter is under consideration or, in some cases, under active consideration. Hacker asks what the difference is between the two. Bernard explains that "under consideration" means the file has been lost while "under active consideration" means they're trying to find it.

EPISODE 3: "THE ECONOMY DRIVE" ★★★½

Air date: March 10, 1980. Cast: Jim Hacker (Paul Eddington); Sir Humphrey Appleby (Nigel Hawthorne); Bernard Woolley (Derek Fowlds). With John Savident; Milton Johns; Diana Hoddinott; Neil Fitzwilliam; Pat Keen; Patricia Shakesby; William Lawford; Norman Tipton; Frank Tregear

After being the focus of an article on waste in government, Jim Hacker insists that economies must be made in the department. Hacker orders that the problem be studied and savings found. In a sly move, Humphrey urges Hacker to lead by example, and Hacker jumps at the bait, losing most of his secretarial staff and perks of power in the process.

A brilliant execution of the series' basic situation, "The Economy Drive" features Hacker being trapped by his own initiatives while Humphrey subtly steers him toward the status quo. Here, the overarching motivation behind Hacker's actions is the politician's absolute dread of bad press.

In a droll scene, Humphrey explains to Bernard that since the civil service does not make profits or losses, the only way it can measure its effectiveness is by increasing the size of its budgets and staffs.

An equally entertaining bit has the shrewd Humphrey blocking a plan to sell a government building to save money. Humphrey points out that the building cannot be sold because of its three-level reinforced basement. Hacker fails to see the significance of the structure, even after Humphrey explains that it is there in case of nuclear war.

Hacker fails to see why government must continue if the rest of society is annihilated. With perfect civil service logic, Humphrey explains that the need for government doesn't end with a society's destruction, adding that annihilation is a bleak enough prospect without compounding it with anarchy. Hacker coyly asks if they plan to rein in any insurgent ashes.

Milton Johns, who appeared as the reluctant loom salesman in *Good Neighbors*, makes a similarly effective guest spot here as the trade union leader.

Episode 4: "Big Brother" ★★★★

Air date: March 17, 1980. Cast: Jim Hacker (Paul Eddington); Sir Humphrey Appleby (Nigel Hawthorne); Bernard Woolley (Derek Fowlds). With Robert Urquhart; Robert McKenzie; Frederick Jaeger; Diana Hoddinott; Neil Fitzwilliam; Andrew Lane; Sheila Ferns; Matthew Roberton

Hacker presses Humphrey to establish safeguards on the National Data Base to avoid intrusions by the civil service on average citizens. Humphrey patronizingly agrees to comply with Hacker's wishes but then sets up an impossible set of hurdles that the new edict must clear. Hacker learns how to scale the hurdles after a short course on Humphrey's tactics from his predecessor.

As described by Bernard Woolley, "Big Brother" is a rare checkmate by Jim Hacker in his never ending struggle with Sir Humphrey and the civil service. The service, after all, is the real opposition in government, as Hacker himself explains in this episode. The other political party is merely the "opposition in exile," while the civil service is the "opposition in residence."

Hacker's infrequent complete victories are like a rich dessert. They are delicious and indeed welcome, but they cannot be indulged in too frequently, lest they lose their appeal. Fortunately, the authors of *Yes, Minister* keep their viewers on a strict diet, allowing them such a treat as this on a limited basis. Still, this episode is sweet and terribly satisfying for those who have the least bit of sympathy toward the Honorable James Hacker.

In an enlightening scene, Tom Sargent explains to Hacker about Humphrey's five-step process of "creative inertia," designed to postpone a project indefinitely. He ends his lesson by telling Hacker that any important documents on the data base issue will be hidden at the bottom of the last work box he is given that evening. Armed with this information, Hacker delights in waking Humphrey at two in the morning to announce he's just found the paper on the Data Base.

The next morning, Hacker sits down to discuss the immediate implementation of safeguards and gleefully brushes each of Humphrey's five stalling tactics aside, ticking them off in his notebook as he goes. Humphrey's chagrin is total.

This episode also features one of the few acknowledgments that Humphrey is married, indeed, that he even has a personal life away from the civil service.

EPISODE 5: "THE WRITING ON THE WALL" ★★★

Air date: March 24, 1980. Cast: Jim Hacker (Paul Eddington); Sir Humphrey Appleby (Nigel Hawthorne); Bernard Woolley (Derek Fowlds). With Daniel Moynihan; Tenniel Evans; John Savident; Neil Fitzwilliam

In the midst of their usual power struggle, Hacker and Humphrey are both stunned to learn that a proposal has been put forth to eliminate the Department for Administrative Affairs — theirs! Although each blames the other for the crisis, Hacker and Humphrey agree to work together for a possible solution to save their careers.

Strong in story line, "The Writing on the Wall" follows logically after "Big Brother" with a more confident Jim Hacker trying to capitalize on his first victory over Sir Humphrey. The authors have cleverly taken the edge off of Hacker's advantage in this episode by concocting a plot that forces the two men to become real allies, albeit briefly. Humphrey's sincere suggestion, proffered in the heat of the crisis, that they work together — something they supposedly have been doing all along — is a rather open admission that until this point they have been doing anything but that. Also interesting is the confirmation that Hacker, for all his earnest talk of cutting back on the size of government, is as big an opportunist as Humphrey when his own neck is on the line.

This episode also marks the introduction of Bernard's irritating (to those around him) but humorous pedantic observations on the misuses of the phrases of others. This excellent little device provides depth to the character while supplying many laughs.

Aside from these corrections, "The Writing on the Wall" features some excellent obfuscation by Sir Humphrey. Frustrated by Humphrey's incessant clouding via language, Hacker demands Humphrey supply a simple yes or no to the question of whether or not he thinks the civil service is overstaffed. His reply is a classic, lengthy discourse, which is even more vague and evasive than his usual answers.

EPISODE 6: "THE RIGHT TO KNOW" ★★½

Air date: March 31, 1980. Cast: Jim Hacker (Paul Eddington); Sir Humphrey Appleby (Nigel Hawthorne); Bernard Woolley (Derek Fowlds). With John Savident; Diana Hoddinott; Gerry Cowper; Harriet Reynolds; Roger Elliott

When Hacker's daughter threatens to take part in a nude environmental protest of her father's policies, Hacker learns the hard way that there are some things that it is better for a minister not to know.

After completely besting Sir Humphrey Appleby in "Big Brother" and allying with him in "The Writing on the Wall," in "The Right to Know," Jim Hacker's fortunes have gradually shifted back to where they began. While Lynn and Jay wisely have made Hacker an underdog in his own department (who but the Machiavellian Humphrey could make one feel sorry for a politician?), they have also been careful not to make him too sympathetic a figure. They allow him his occasional advantage, then return him to falter again under the skillful attack of his permanent secretary.

This episode also affords a rare glimpse into Hacker's home life. While the inclusion of his daughter here is the device upon which the plot turns, it is fortunately not often used. As a whole, the scenes with Hacker's daughter detract from the better scenes in Whitehall.

Some of the episode's best moments come as Humphrey furthers Bernard's education on the ways of government. He reminds Bernard that the civil service — specifically, Sir Humphrey — is there to run the department. Hacker's role, as defined by Humphrey, is to advocate their policies to the public, steer their legislation through Parliament, and fight the cabinet for the funds they need.

Later, Humphrey and one of his colleagues cynically explain to Bernard how to effectively kill unwanted programs. The trick, Humphrey explains, is to label it as "courageous." Whereas a controversial decision, Humphrey notes, only indicates that a politician will lose votes, a courageous one means he will lose an election.

EPISODE 7: "JOBS FOR THE BOYS" ★★★½

Air date: April 7, 1980. Cast: Jim Hacker (Paul Eddington); Sir Humphrey Appleby (Nigel Hawthorne); Bernard Woolley (Derek Fowlds). With Richard Vernon; Neil Fitzwilliam; Arthur Lox; Richard Davies; Brian Hawksley; John D. Collins; Charles McKeown

Against Humphrey's advice, Hacker publicly trumpets the Solihull project, a joint building venture between the government and the private sector. Only after he takes credit for the project does Hacker begin to suspect that something is amiss.

The first series of *Yes, Minister* ends with a clever and well-written episode, which effectively completes Jim Hacker's initiation into the reality of running a governmental department. Again, as in "The Writing on the Wall," Hacker is forced to ally with Humphrey to save his political neck. The primary difference in this episode is that Hacker is more comfortable, almost resigned to playing the civil service's game by their rules. This effectively goes against what he so stridently crusaded for in the series' premiere — it is even in direct opposition to his own political advisor — and one must conclude that Humphrey's "house training" of his new minister is, if not complete, progressing smoothly.

In one particularly telling exchange, Bernard is upset that Sir Humphrey doesn't plan on informing the minister of the impending crisis in Solihull. Humphrey insists that keeping Hacker in the dark is the only possible policy since, like a secret agent, he may be captured and tortured — not by terrorists, but by reporters from the BBC.

Still, Bernard is unconvinced of Sir Humphrey's wisdom and wonders if the affair isn't actually a cover-up like Watergate. Humphrey assures him it is entirely different since Watergate happened in America.

Series Two 1981

Episode 1: "The Compassionate Society" ★★★

Air date: February 23, 1981. Cast: Jim Hacker (Paul Eddington); Sir Humphrey Appleby (Nigel Hawthorne); Bernard Woolley (Derek Fowlds); with John Barron; Norman Bird; Rosemary Frankau; Stephen Tate; Arthur Cox; Lindy Alexander; Robert Dougall

After Hacker learns that there is a new local hospital, St. Edward's, that is fully staffed with administrators and union employees but has no medical personnel or patients, he orders Humphrey to fire half the existing staff and open some wards at St. Edward's. Loath to comply with any directive that would reduce administrative staff, Humphrey secretly plots for a firebrand union leader to be transferred to St. Edward's to block the cuts.

The second series begins on a strong note with another episode that ties together divergent story lines to reach its conclusion. Gone is Neil Fitzwilliam, in the semiregular role of Frank Weisel, after being effectively written out in the final show of the first series. Without his political advisor, Hacker must now act solely as his own conscience, which he does well when lucid enough under Humphrey's constant barrage of ploys designed to keep him off balance.

The episode itself is a stinging commentary on the state of compassion in the modern industrial society. As Humphrey so convincingly explains, the goal of modern compassion is not actually to minister to those in need but to make everyone else feel like they are caring and compassionate.

Hacker is quite amusing as the lone voice crying out in the wilderness over the ludicrousness of staffing a hospital without any patients or doctors. He is appalled that 500 administrators are running St. Edward's. His outrage only grows when Humphrey gives a detailed explanation of the staff's duties. Humphrey concludes his report by arguing that the 500 people running St. Edward's are seriously overworked and need an additional 150 individuals to assist them.

Humphrey's claims are born out when Hacker visits the hospital to find empty wards while the offices bustle with activity. When Mrs. Rogers, the administrator of the facility, proudly shows Hacker their state-of-the-art medical equipment, he asks her if she isn't bothered by its disuse. She answers that she is pleased since the lack of patients will probably extend the equipment's life. She concludes her tour by asserting that St. Edward's is one of the best-run hospitals in the country and is up for an award for most hygienic hospital.

John Barron, C.J. of *Reggie Perrin* fame, appears in this episode as the permanent secretary of the Department of Health and Social Security.

Episode 2: "Doing the Honours" ★★★★

Air date: March 2, 1981. Cast: Jim Hacker (Paul Eddington); Sir Humphrey Appleby (Nigel Hawthorne); Bernard Woolley (Derek Fowlds). With Frank Middlemass; John Nettleton; William Fox; John Pennington; Margo Johns; Anne Maxwell

After a futile meeting on trimming the department budget, Bernard privately suggests that Hacker tie all future honours to actual job performance — specifically, that Hacker not approve the upcoming honours candidates unless they manage to pare their budgets by at least 5 percent. It is up to Humphrey to kill the revolutionary plan before it spreads throughout the bureaucracy.

An excellent installment not only in story and dialogue but also by virtue of the fact that each of the three principals has his own scene in which to showcase his acting talents. Eddington, Hawthorne, and Fowlds take full advantage of their opportunities to display their characters in atypical and previously unexplored situations.

The title refers to the semiannual honours list, when individuals are granted new orders and titles of nobility. As pointed out in the episode, most persons receiving honours are given them after some noteworthy achievement, while civil servants, on the other hand, are granted them regularly as the highest form of perk. Sir Humphrey, therefore, received his knighthood for long years of service in the bureaucracy.

Sir Humphrey's audience with Sir Arnold is a gem of understated anxiety. Intimating that Humphrey's recent performance is lacking, Sir Arnold delivers what in civil service lingo is a stinging rebuke. Sir Arnold starts by informing Humphrey that he isn't actually reprimanding him, which, in the argot of the bureaucracy, is itself a harsh censure. Shaken, Humphrey tries to keep a brave face, but his attempts at lightheartedness begin to crack under the strain. The heaviest blow comes when Sir Arnold informs him that "some people" might not think Humphrey's actions were sound. Humphrey staggers out of the meeting visibly shaken under the harsh criticism.

Later, Bernard gives his boss (and the viewers) a crash course on the honour system as it relates to civil servants. In what essentially amounts to a monologue, Bernard humorously explains the various degrees of knighthood. For example, he points out that civil servants in the foreign office are first awarded a CMG (the Cross of St. Michael and St. George), then a KCMG (Knight of…), then finally a GCMG (Grand Cross of…). Bernard notes, however, that these letter designations are interpreted quite differently inside the civil service. CMG, he points out, means "Call Me God," KCMG means "Kindly Call Me God," and GCMG stands for "God Calls Me God."

Hacker also has a good scene during a private dinner thrown for him by the master of Baillie College. His drunken ramblings at the dinner table are a tour de force by Paul Eddington. Hacker fully believes himself to be in command of the situation, while his sober host toys with him by dangling honorary doctorates before his glassy eyes. Hacker's finest moments come when defending the notion that the honorary law doctorate should go to a politician (namely himself) rather than a judge. He derides judges, while reminding them that he doesn't even have the power to throw Humphrey in jail. Humphrey sits aghast at the revelation that if Hacker had the authority he would be sent off to three years in "the Scrubs."

Episode 3: "The Death List" ★★

Air date: March 9, 1981. Cast: Jim Hacker (Paul Eddington); Sir Humphrey Appleby (Nigel Hawthorne); Bernard Woolley (Derek Fowlds). With Graeme Garden; Diana Hoddinott; Ivor Roberts; Colin McCormack; Michael Keating; Jay Neill

Hacker is outraged when he learns that he was a subject of government surveillance while his party was in opposition. Now in control of all the government's bugging equipment through his position as minister for Administrative Affairs, Hacker orders that strict safeguards be placed on future intrusions into the privacy of the public. Hacker's civil libertarian stance falters, however, when he learns that his name has been discovered on a terrorist group's death list.

From an honours list to a death list, the third episode takes the second series in a rather disappointing direction: into implausibility. The overly simple plot is hampered by the fact that it just isn't believable that the ineffectual Jim Hacker would be one of only three names on a radical group's assassination list. Even Bernard, upon learning of the threat, comments on its irrationality, noting that the minister is so "harmless." Normally, such a leap of credibility would be an easy bound for a situation comedy but not so for *Yes, Minister*, which is so firmly grounded—albeit with tongue in cheek—in real life. Perhaps this would have played better if used in the subsequent series, in which Hacker becomes the prime minister.

One of the better moments comes early in the episode. Hacker is annoyed by the report in *Private Eye* that sheds light on the fact that he is in charge of all surveillance equipment. The report ends with a pun, describing Hacker as the "government's chief bugger" (a rather pejorative appellation).

Hacker, unaware that he had providence over the equipment, asks Humphrey if the statement is true. "Which Minister?" Humphrey asks straight-faced.

Later, Humphrey tries to defend wire tapping as a necessary weapon in the battle against organized crime. Hacker wants to know if Humphrey lumps politicians into that category as well. The permanent secretary smiles coyly before conceding that politicians only represent disorganized crime.

Episode 4: "The Greasy Pole" ★★½

Air date: March 16, 1981. Cast: Jim Hacker (Paul Eddington); Sir Humphrey Appleby (Nigel Hawthorne); Bernard Woolley (Derek Fowlds). With Brenda Blethyn; Freddie Earlle; Jerome Willis; Geoffrey Toone; Robert Dougall; Sheila Fay; Maureen Stevens; Lindy Alexander

Hacker's enthusiastic support for the approval of Propanol, a new chemical compound, quickly withers when he learns that Propanol is a potential political hot potato. To extricate himself from the controversy and outflank Humphrey, who is pushing for Propanol's endorsement, Hacker must resort to subterfuge worthy of Humphrey himself.

The second episode in which Hacker clearly outmaneuvers the slippery Sir Humphrey, "The Greasy Pole" is not nearly as satisfying as the first instance of the device, which was introduced in "Big Brother." The primary reason is that Hacker's cause and Humphrey's desires are reversed. On the surface, at least, Humphrey seems to advocate doing the right thing on the grounds that it *is* right. One keeps waiting for the other shoe to drop to reveal Humphrey's vested interest in the position he is advocating, but it never does.

Hacker, on the other hand, although originally amenable to Humphrey's suggestions, quickly shies away when he discovers they are not politically expedient. This situation is further muddied since it is never clearly explained which position is in fact correct. The result is a decision that Humphrey calls the worst he has ever seen in government, while Hacker simultaneously hails it as the best he has ever made politically.

One clever device echoes Hacker's original triumph over Humphrey in "Big Brother" but with a new twist. In the earlier episode, Hacker bests his permanent secretary by referring to pointers given to him by his predecessor. Here, he obtains similar results by using strategies given to him by none other than Humphrey himself!

There are some good moments when Joan Littler, a member of Parliament from Hacker's party, comes to voice her opposition to the Propanol plant, which will be situated in her constituency. Littler, Humphrey, Hacker, and Bernard all engage in a heated debate on the safety of the chemical until they finally realize that none of them knows the slightest bit about chemistry. They do not even understand the simplest chemical terms, such as *compound* and *inert*. When Humphrey asserts that the new compound is inert, he is pressed for an explanation of the term. Fumbling, Humphrey explains that *inert* means "not 'ert."

"Wouldn't 'ert a fly," Bernard quietly adds after a moment of befuddled silence.

Next they attempt to tackle the term *compound*. Humphrey notes that they all know what compound interest is, and since that is "a jolly good thing to enjoy," any chemical compound must be correspondingly welcome.

Episode 5: "The Devil You Know" ★★★

Air date: March 23, 1981. Cast: Jim Hacker (Paul Eddington); Sir Humphrey Appleby (Nigel Hawthorne); Bernard Woolley (Derek Fowlds). With John Nettleton; Diana Hoddinott; Arthur Cox

With a cabinet reshuffle rumored to be imminent, Hacker is horrified over not knowing whether he will be promoted, demoted, or ignored in the shake-up. Sir Humphrey is pleased with the prospect of Hacker moving on (since Hacker is beginning to get a grasp of his department) and a novice moving into the Department for Administrative Affairs. His delight turns to dread, however, when he learns that Hacker's replacement is even more undesirable. The adversaries must quickly devise a political triumph to shore up Hacker's incumbency.

After managing to successfully block Hacker's attempts at reform at almost every turn, "The Devil You Know" puts Humphrey in the position of having to cooperate and even manufacture results for his minister. Similar in theme to episode five of the first series, "The Writing on the Wall," there is enough variation to keep the situation fresh and entertaining.

There is an amusing running gag throughout the episode involving a paranoid Hacker desperately seeking reassurance from those closest to him concerning his job performance. Rather than comfort, however, the best Hacker manages to elicit from each person polled is a halfhearted "all right." Finally, Hacker queries Bernard, his most loyal supporter and sincere well-wisher. Hacker admits that Humphrey's blocking efforts have contributed to his lackluster "all right" performance. He concludes by asking if "all right" is good enough. "Well," Bernard begins before pausing for a moment of intense thought, "it's all right."

After they have successfully allied to keep the status quo, Humphrey admits he would be sorry to see Hacker go. Hacker takes this admission as a display of personal warmth. He agrees that they have developed a fondness akin to a hostage and his captor.

When Bernard asks which of them is the terrorist, each man points to the other and asserts, "He is."

Their newfound camaraderie is short-lived, however, after Bernard lets it slip that Humphrey's motivation was due not to an affection for Hacker but a fear of Basil Corbett, Hacker's proposed successor.

Episode 6: "The Quality of Life" ★★★½

Air date: March 30, 1981. Cast: Jim Hacker (Paul Eddington); Sir Humphrey Appleby (Nigel Hawthorne); Bernard Woolley (Derek Fowlds). With Richard Vernon; Peter Cellier; Antony Carrick; Zulema Dene; Rex Robinson; Roger Martin; Sue Lawley

In his eternal quest for publicity, Hacker visits a city farm, an inner city project created to bring a taste of rural life to urban children. Once there, he is compelled on camera to pledge his help to get the farm's leases renewed. Unbeknownst to Hacker, he has just been tricked by Humphrey into signing away the city farm's lease to make room for a parking lot for tax collectors.

The pattern set by the first series continues with Hacker firmly back under Humphrey's control after besting him two episodes earlier ("The Greasy Pole"), with a transitional cooperation installment ("The Devil You Know") in between. Fortunately the crispness of the writing and the excellent performances keep the recipe from even a hint of staleness.

Richard Vernon is back as the wonderfully addled Sir Desmond Glazebrook ("Jobs for the Boys"), the bank chairman who doesn't understand a word of the *Financial Times* but faithfully carries it around with him since he is expected to do so. Sharp-eyed viewers may recognize Peter Cellier from his intermittent role as the Major on *Keeping Up Appearances.*

During a meeting over the construction of an office skyscraper, Hacker derides Glazebrook for his typical banker's tunnel vision in regards to his profit margin. Attempting to evoke shame, Hacker asks the banker if he ever thinks of anything but money. "No. Why?" Sir Desmond replies with a clear conscience.

Hacker inquires about the building's effect on the environment. Glazebrook obtusely promises to make the building part of the environment, adding, "It's bound to be, once it's there, isn't it?"

Later, there is a wonderful commentary on the art of political rhetoric when Hacker addresses the gathering at the city farm. He earnestly launches into his speech, not realizing until the second paragraph that it is the address he gave the previous night to a gathering of architects. Embarrassed, he excuses himself for the error, finds the correct speech, and then delivers it only to reveal it is virtually identical except for the mention of the intended audience.

EPISODE 7: "A QUESTION OF LOYALTY" ★★★½

Air date: April 6, 1981. Cast: Jim Hacker (Paul Eddington); Sir Humphrey Appleby (Nigel Hawthorne); Bernard Woolley (Derek Fowlds). With Judy Parfitt; Nigel Stock; John Pennington; Rosemary Williams; Anthony Dawes; John Rolfe

Hacker and Humphrey agree to work as a team to deflect criticism from a select committee of Parliament. Hacker's cooperative tone changes, however, when the prime minister's special political advisor makes it clear to him that he has become a pawn of the civil service.

If it was not known that another full season of *Yes, Minister* and another series of *Yes, Prime Minister* followed, one would almost guess that "A Question of Loyalty" was the last installment in the adventures of the Honorable James Hacker. This episode has a definite finality about it. After wrestling with Sir Humphrey (and mostly losing), Hacker finally bests his permanent secretary in a quick, decisive, and delicious stroke. Again, as with every instance in which Hacker finds himself holding the upper hand, he does so with help, which is seemingly the only way he can outsmart the wily Humphrey.

While "A Question of Loyalty" is rich with the usual cynical insights into the workings of modern bureaucracies, its best moments are the performances of Paul Eddington and Nigel Hawthorne as Hacker and Humphrey appear before the select committee. Both supply their usual excellent turn with Hacker being a portrait of stammering confusion, while Humphrey is the epitome of confident falsehood. As good as these performances are, however, the real treat of the episode comes during their joint appearance when the roles are reversed. It is a delight for fans of the series to see Hacker finally in control, addressing the committee in Churchillian tones, while Humphrey, utterly surprised, writhes and whimpers as the worm turns.

Later, back at the office, Humphrey bitterly predicts a backlash from the prime minister toward Hacker. Instead, however, Hacker receives a personally handwritten note from the PM, inviting him down for lunch at his country retreat. Hacker asserts that his loyalty has been rewarded. Humphrey sneers at Hacker's talk of loyalty in light of his performance before the committee. Hacker smiles and asserts that he supported Humphrey in the same way Humphrey has always supported him.

Series Three 1982

EPISODE 1: "EQUAL OPPORTUNITIES" ★★★½

Air date: November 11, 1982. Cast: Jim Hacker (Paul Eddington); Sir Humphrey Appleby (Nigel Hawthorne); Bernard Woolley (Derek Fowlds). With Eleanor Bron; John Nettleton; Diana Hoddinott; Talla Hayes; Richard Simpson; Peter Howell; Jeffrey Segal; Donald Pelmear

In a rare attempt at striking a blow for principle and positive change, Hacker tries to impose a 25 percent hiring quota for women. Understandably, Humphrey and the rest of his civil service cronies bristle at any move that would upset their status quo.

An intelligent and witty study of the issue of feminism, "Equal Opportunities" manages to offer a number of clever turns in its plot with a rather surprising and ironic ending. That it manages to do so without ever becoming patronizing or resorting to sloganeering is a credit to the authors. Typically, neither Hacker, who is advocating the promotion of women, nor Humphrey, who is trying to block the edict, actually cares much about the gender they are battling over.

Hacker is prompted to advance the career of female civil servants when he realizes that he has scored no actual achievements during his tenure as a minister. This revelation is all the more amusing coming as it does during an interview by a teenager for her school paper. Humphrey, on the other hand, is loath to do anything to upset the current apple cart, upon which he and his old school chums are comfortably resting. There is a telling scene in which the permanent secretaries meet and agree in principle to promote the cause of women, then each manages to find pressing reasons why such a move should not apply to his department.

The best moments are reserved for the ending in which Hacker and Humphrey inform Sarah Harrison (Eleanor Bron) that she is being promoted to deputy secretary. Rather than being grateful or even pleased, Harrison informs them that she is resigning to take a more lucrative position in the private sector where she will actually be judged on her worth as an individual.

This episode also contains a classic moment unrelated to the plot. While reviewing paperwork, Bernard designates a worthless piece of correspondence as "CGSM," which he explains is civil service code for a "consignment of geriatric shoe menders" or, in plainer terms, "a load of old cobblers," the rather pithy British metaphor for a lot of baloney.

Episode 2: "The Challenge" ★★★

Air date: November 18, 1982. Cast: Jim Hacker (Paul Eddington); Sir Humphrey Appleby (Nigel Hawthorne); Bernard Woolley (Derek Fowlds). With John Nettleton; Ian Lavender; Doug Fisher; Moray Watson; Stuart Sherwin; Frank Tregear; Ludovic Kennedy

When Hacker's administrative authority is expanded to include local governments, Humphrey must quash any reform initiatives before they rebound on Whitehall.

This straightforward entry finds Jim Hacker suddenly the chief bureaucrat in Britain thanks to an administrative reorganization. At first, Hacker earnestly sets out to wield his new power, only to be admonished by Humphrey that the only reason he pushed for Hacker's new authority was that he never actually thought Hacker would try to use it. Aside from this new responsibility, it is still the same old Hacker, however, as the relative ease with which Humphrey manages to control his minister attests.

There is a wonderfully ironic bit when Hacker is put on the spot in an interview with BBC reporter Ludovic Kennedy. Caught off guard, Hacker reverts to spouting the same civil service excuses he rejected in the previous episode. Kennedy reminds Hacker that under his initiative to downsize government, his own department has grown by almost 10 percent. Taking a page from Humphrey's book, Hacker confidently states that more staff must be hired to tackle the task of reducing the head count! Later Hacker tries again to employ one of Humphrey's tactics — the long, winding, jargon-laden sentence. Unfortunately for Hacker, he gets so tangled up in his own explanation that he forgets the question before he can reach his conclusion.

The addition of the local authorities to Hacker's department also gives him a new ally in the guise of Dr. Richard Cartwright, an economist absorbed into the DAA in the reorganization. Cartwright's character gives Hacker his first real support in his battles with Humphrey since the part of Frank Weisel was written out at the end of the first series. Less combative than the political Weisel, Cartwright provides an even more threatening opponent to Humphrey in that his recommendations are based on logic and common sense — anathema to a lifelong bureaucrat like Sir Humphrey. Despite his gray hair, mustache, and glasses, Cartwright should be familiar to fans of *Dad's Army* as none other than their beloved Private Pike: Ian Lavender.

Episode 3: "The Skeleton in the Cupboard" ★★★★

Air date: November 25, 1982. Cast: Jim Hacker (Paul Eddington); Sir Humphrey Appleby (Nigel Hawthorne); Bernard Woolley (Derek Fowlds). With Ian Lavender; Donald Gee; John Pennington; Rosemary Williams

Jim Hacker thwarts Humphrey's latest scheme when he learns that a £40 million blunder from the civil servant's past is coming back to haunt him.

Like "Big Brother" and "The Greasy Pole" in the previous two seasons, "The Skeleton in the Cupboard" provides Nigel Hawthorne's normally cool, Machiavellian Sir Humphrey with his annual opportunity to squirm. He does so magnificently as his character must use all of his serpentine skills to wriggle out of a snare he himself laid 30 years previously. Interestingly, however, Humphrey is so shaken that his grand career may be over that he fails to extricate himself by cunning. In a refreshing twist, Humphrey is forced to throw himself on Hacker's mercy — a circumstance that the minister enjoys with great relish and thinly disguised amusement.

The only regret in this wonderfully funny episode is the wish that Hacker could have gotten a little more mileage out of Humphrey's predicament, settling it seems, for a rather weak concession from his permanent secretary. Still, it is great fun to watch Hacker and Bernard attempting to control their laughter when they learn it was Humphrey who effectively gave away a £40 million military base by writing a flawed contract as a young civil servant. The greatest plaudits must go to Nigel Hawthorne for his weak-kneed reactions, his distracted preoccupation, and his woeful blubberings as the ghosts from his long-distant past rise up and take aim at his career.

Prior to Humphrey's undoing, which occurs in the second half of the episode, there is a marvelous scene in which Hacker goes on a "walkabout" through his own department in search of some facts. This sort of activity is strictly forbidden in Humphrey's world, since it means a potential loss of control over his minister. When Humphrey manages to track down the errant Hacker, he condescendingly chides him much as one would scold a child who has wandered into the street. This scene effectively sets up Humphrey's own downfall, making it all the more delicious to Hacker — and to us.

Episode 4: "The Moral Dimension" ★★★

Air date: December 2, 1982. Cast: Jim Hacker (Paul Eddington); Sir Humphrey Appleby (Nigel Hawthorne); Bernard Woolley (Derek Fowlds). With Diana Hoddinott; Antony Carrick; April Walker; Sam Dastor; Vic Tablian; Walter Randall; Michael Sharvell-Martin

After Humphrey and Bernard are caught in lies, Hacker refuses to cover up for them to the press — that is, until he too is found in the same situation.

One of the more sitcomlike entries in the *Yes, Minister* series, "The Moral Dimension" features a more linear plot with fewer twists than usual. One can actually see where this one is going from the start. Nevertheless, it is a tribute to the caliber of Lynn and Jay's writing that even under such circumstances their barbed pens still manage to provide a witty and entertaining script.

The setting for the episode is a trip to the fictitious Arab nation of Qumran for the signing of an export contract. Once there, Bernard discovers that Sir Humphrey has had to bribe the Qumranis as a normal part of the negotiations. Also, Bernard has had a rare 17th-century gift jar valued at under £50 in order to allow Hacker's wife to keep the present she received from her hosts. When rumors of both incidents start appearing in the London press, Hacker is appalled even though both subterfuges were perpetrated to his benefit. Still, since he had no knowledge of either ploy, he announces he is going to take the moral high ground and tell the truth if asked. Hacker's high ground turns out to be built of the same shifting sand as his two subordinates', however, when Humphrey threatens to disclose Hacker's smuggling of alcoholic beverages into the Qumrani palace.

"The Moral Dimension" uncovers the relatively close positions held by the amoral (Humphrey) and the moral person who fails to live up to his own standards (Hacker). In practical terms, Hacker ultimately comes out lower than Humphrey, due to his pompous sanctimony, which quickly crumbles at the first sign of pressure. The final moment is the most telling as Hacker tries to warm up to his two colleagues after threatening to expose them moments before. Predictably, his newfound chumminess is greeted coolly.

There are a number of good gags outside of the usual mold in this episode. The first is a sight gag that shows a long queue of civil servants boarding the plane in London for the junket to Qumran. Hacker is shocked to find they are all accompanying him, but Humphrey deftly justifies their holiday. At the reception in Qumran, Hacker has arranged for booze to be dispensed in a special communications room. This necessitates frequent trips to the room under the guise of reading emergency communiqués from such correspondents as Mr. Haig, Mr. Walker, and Mr. Smirnoff. Finally, there is the humorous sight of Sir Humphrey arrayed in Arab robes for the reception.

Episode 5: "The Bed of Nails" ★★½

Air date: December 9, 1982. Cast: Jim Hacker (Paul Eddington); Sir Humphrey Appleby (Nigel Hawthorne); Bernard Woolley (Derek Fowlds). With John Nettleton; Nigel Stock; David Firth; Peter Dennis; Robert East; David Rose

Hacker is honored to be named "supremo" in charge of formulating a comprehensive national transportation plan until he learns the post is actually a political hot potato.

Oliver Hardy once remarked, concerning his own screen character, that there was no one dumber than a dumb guy who thinks he's smart. Jim Hacker, with some reservations, falls squarely into this category. Although Hacker is obviously not stupid, he certainly is at a disadvantage among the professional cynics and sharpies in the political and civil servant spheres through which he must circulate. In this installment, we see that Hacker is viewed as something of a patsy by those above him. Indeed, the prime minister's chief advisor and the cabinet secretary disguise their booby trap with the impressive title of "transport supremo" in order make Hacker fall for it, which he quickly does. In private, however, they both (along with Humphrey later on) refer to the appointment as "transport muggins" (*muggins* is British slang for a sucker).

"The Bed of Nails" is an interesting departure in the *Yes, Minister* series in that it has the usually opposing realms of politics and civil service joining forces to foist an unsavory appointment on the unsuspecting Hacker. In turn, Hacker is rescued from this pitfall by his usual adversary, Sir Humphrey Appleby. As in other episodes in which Hacker and Humphrey must pull together, it is an enjoyable exercise if for nothing else than its novelty.

Unlike other episodes of this ilk, however, Humphrey's motivation is severely lacking. The permanent secretary's adverse reaction to news of Hacker's assignment is oddly given as, he points out, the fallout from the position will entirely land on Hacker. Humphrey then goes on to state that his primary purpose is to protect his boss's backside. Given his past machinations, this latest assertion of Humphrey's is somewhat hard to believe. Two episodes later, in "The Middle-Class Rip-Off," Humphrey tells Bernard that he is opposed to anything that would improve Hacker's popularity and thus assure his reelection. He also states in that episode that any move that brings added responsibility to his department is welcome.

Fortunately, by the end of the episode, with Humphrey's (and Bernard's) able assistance, Hacker manages to turn the tables and return "The Bed of Nails."

EPISODE 6: "THE WHISKEY PRIEST" ★★★★

Air date: December 16, 1982. Cast: Jim Hacker (Paul Eddington); Sir Humphrey Appleby (Nigel Hawthorne); Bernard Woolley (Derek Fowlds). With John Fortune; Diana Hoddinott; Edward Jewesbury

Hacker is forced to choose between principle and expediency when he learns that British- made technological weapons are finding their way into the hands of terrorists.

There are funnier episodes of *Yes, Minister* but none finer than "The Whiskey Priest." Indeed, this insightful installment is a quintessential example of the type of thought-provoking humor at which Jay and Lynn excel. While most entries in the series are a struggle between Hacker and his civil service nemesis, Sir Humphrey, here the real battle is inside the soul of the hapless Hacker.

The episode opens with Hacker at home reading a book on Winston Churchill's wilderness years, as he waits for the arrival of a secret guest, Major Saunders. Saunders has asked for a clandestine audience to discuss a matter of great importance. As he reads, Hacker imagines himself another Churchill, ready to expose the government's ineptitude. He entertains this fantasy until his wife dutifully reminds him that, unlike Churchill, his party *is* in control of the government. Later, after the arrival of Saunders, Hacker obtusely continues his cloak-and-dagger charade, stressing their need to be cautious lest the government has bugged them. Again, Hacker is reminded that *he* is the minister in charge of the government's surveillance operations.

The best scene occurs next, as Hacker announces to Humphrey that he plans to inform the prime minister of the news that British arms are falling into terrorist hands. Humphrey adamantly argues against the PM being told — primarily on the grounds that the revelation is none of their concern. Hacker, however, is convinced of the basic moral wrongness of the situation and accuses Humphrey of operating in a moral vacuum. The resulting debate is quite stimulating and cleverly presented with compelling arguments being made both by

Hacker (basically, governments are established to do what is right) and Humphrey (government is not about morality but stability). In the end, Humphrey is benign and, rather than being amoral, is more reflective of the moral compartmentalization of the postmodern man. There is, however, a wonderful little scene in which Humphrey tutors the ethically confused Bernard on how to thwart Hacker's crusade. One is reminded of C. S. Lewis's classic *The Screwtape Letters*. In this brief exchange, Humphrey is playing the senior demon, Screwtape, advising the novice, Wormwood, on how to corrupt a Christian soul.

Ultimately, Hacker is forced by the pressures of expediency to retreat from his moral high ground while still appearing to offer a sop to his cherished ideals. For this, his wife understandingly dubs him a "whiskey priest," that is, one who may do the wrong thing but at least recognizes it as such. Perhaps it is this revelation that makes the episode so touching to the rest of us — who fall into the same priesthood.

EPISODE 7: "THE MIDDLE-CLASS RIP-OFF" ★★★

Air date: December 23, 1982. Cast: Jim Hacker (Paul Eddington); Sir Humphrey Appleby (Nigel Hawthorne); Bernard Woolley (Derek Fowlds). With John Nettleton; John Barron; Patrick O'Connell; Derek Benfield

When Hacker tries to save his constituency's popular football team by selling its unpopular art gallery, he meets stiff opposition from Humphrey and the cultural elite.

The final episode of *Yes, Minister* takes a form similar to that of some of the series' best entries: the stimulating discussion. Here the topic for dramatic debate is that of subsidy of the arts versus support for pastimes with more mass appeal. Hacker, quite predictably since he is a politician and therefore covetous of popularity, is attempting to save his local football (soccer) team. His plan, which would necessitate the selling of a rather third-rate art gallery, is seen as the thin end of the wedge by Humphrey and his civil service pals, who not incidentally are eager patrons of the arts. This sets up the episode's main joust as Humphrey snobbishly asserts that the arts must be supported since that is what the public needs, although they will never want it. Hacker's response focuses on the argument that the arts are a rip-off by the educated middle class (hence the title) against the rest of society.

The writing seems to weigh in on Hacker's side of the argument, with Humphrey and his cronies (one played by *Reggie Perrin*'s John Barron) portrayed in a most unsympathetic light as they enjoy their favorite cultural diversions at public expense. Hacker also has some good retorts to Humphrey's arguments for preserving British culture, when he points out that most of the Royal Opera's presentations are German and Italian. There is also a funny moment when Humphrey insists he must end the debate to attend another function. As it turns out, he must go home and dress for the opera — or, as Hacker drolly comments, a "works outing."

Bernard has some good moments in "The Middle-Class Rip-Off," primarily in support of Hacker (unbeknownst to Sir Humphrey, of course). He also provides Hacker his main route of escape after Humphrey thwarts his plan to save the football team.

Christmas Special 1984

"Party Games" Unavailable for Viewing

Air date: December 27, 1984.

Two years after the final episode of the regular airing of *Yes, Minister* and one year prior to *Yes, Prime Minister* came this hour-long special covering the transition of the bumbling Jim Hacker from minister for Administrative Affairs to prime minister of Great Britain. This highly unlikely event occurred thanks to the behind-the-scenes machinations of Sir Humphrey and a ludicrous political victory over the Eurosausage. Although it seemed a bit of a stretch at the time, Lynn and Jay's script managed to be somewhat prophetic in light of John Major's uncomfortably similar rise to power after Margaret Thatcher's resignation.

THE EPISODES

Yes, Prime Minister— *By Antony Jay and Jonathan Lynn. Produced and Directed by Sydney Lotterby*

Series One 1986

Episode 1: "The Grand Design" ★★★★

Air date: January 9, 1986. Cast: Jim Hacker (Paul Eddington); Sir Humphrey Appleby (Nigel Hawthorne); Bernard Woolley (Derek Fowlds). With Frederick Treves; Oscar Quitak; Diana Hoddinott; Barry Stanton; Jonathan Stephens; Miranda Forbes

Hacker tries to make his mark as the new prime minister in one bold move. His "grand design" is to cancel the Trident nuclear program and replace it with military conscription thus solving the problems of defense, education, and unemployment.

Yes, Prime Minister begins in much the same fashion as its forerunner with "The Grand Design" being very close in tone and theme to "Open

Government" of six years earlier. Both episodes present a victory-flushed Hacker attempting to jump into his new position with both feet and start making bold, innovative changes. Of course he runs firmly into the status quo — led of course by Sir Humphrey — and little policy is ever enacted. As was often the case in the past, Hacker's statesmanlike schemes are easily defeated by appealing to his politician's ego. In this instance, Humphrey masterfully maneuvers his desire to keep the Trident missile program by noting that its cancellation would ruin Hacker's chance for a photo opportunity with the president of the United States.

Jay and Lynn's satirical pens are sharp throughout the episode, providing many occasions for cynical laughs along with some thought-provoking dialogue. Particularly interesting is an exchange between Hacker and Professor Rosenblum, the government's chief scientific advisor, regarding when Hacker would dare to use nuclear weapons. The chief outcome of this stimulating exercise is Hacker's realization that he probably wouldn't. Humphrey's reaction to this realization is that a nuclear deterrent (or at least the façade of one) must be maintained. Humphrey's position prompts a wonderfully humorous exchange in which he concedes that the Russians *probably* know that Hacker *probably* wouldn't use nukes, although they couldn't *certainly* know that he *probably* wouldn't.

Juxtaposed against these deep issues (and providing perspective) is Hacker's problems adjusting to life at Number 10 Downing Street. His main struggle is trying to get lunch, an almost impossible undertaking since his residence is a private one located in a public building. Hacker quickly learns that there are no arrangements to provide the prime minister with servants, and he cannot afford a cook on his PM's salary. This issue is cleverly solved by Humphrey, who presents Hacker with a cook and manages to pass it off as a precedent that will make his mark in the history books.

EPISODE 2: "THE MINISTERIAL BROADCAST" ★★★

Air date: January 16, 1986. Cast: Jim Hacker (Paul Eddington); Sir Humphrey Appleby (Nigel Hawthorne); Bernard Woolley (Derek Fowlds). With John Wells; Barry Stanton; Brian Gwaspari; Carolyn Lyster

Sir Humphrey works behind the scenes to prevent Hacker from announcing his grand design scheme during a television speech.

A slim story line supplemented with some uncharacteristic physical humor help make "The Ministerial Broadcast" a highly pleasurable series entry. Humphrey is adamantly opposed to Hacker's new defense plan and has little difficulty in steering him away from actually introducing it to the nation. In his patent style, Humphrey cleverly gets Hacker's cabinet to reverse itself by adroitly handling the various ministers through their permanent secretaries. The only other challenge to Humphrey is to provide an answer to a national poll, which favors a return to conscription. He handles this easily by commissioning his own poll, which as he illustrates to Bernard in a wonderfully cynical bit, can be manipulated to provide any desired result.

Plot aside, Paul Eddington provides most of the laughs through a pair of comic turns. In the first he combats (not very well) the effects of jet lag upon his return from his summit in America. During his more lucid moments in this scene, he informs Bernard that his trip has been a resounding success but only on the basis that it has generated vast media coverage. One is left with the uneasy suspicion that most high-level statesmanship is conducted on such a shallow level.

The bulk of the episode — a full third — is taken up with Hacker's rehearsal for his broadcast. Here, Hacker shines in all his political glory as he earnestly tries to appear as all things to all people. One case in point is the decision whether or not to wear his glasses. Their inclusion, according to the director, makes Hacker look authoritative, while their absence makes him look warm and friendly. With his boss unable to make up his mind, Bernard suggests he start sporting a monocle.

EPISODE 3: "THE SMOKE SCREEN" ★★★½

Air date: January 23, 1986. Cast: Jim Hacker (Paul Eddington); Sir Humphrey Appleby (Nigel Hawthorne); Bernard Woolley (Derek Fowlds). With John Barron; Clive Merrison; Peter Cellier; Bill Wallis; Brian Hawksley

Hacker toys with the idea of banning smoking to provide the necessary leverage to push through a tax cut.

A fine episode, "The Smoke Screen" is ostensibly about the maneuvering of politics and government, served up around a debate about the health risks of smoking. As the title suggests, Hacker's backing of an antitobacco campaign is just an artifice, which he plans on jettisoning after obtaining his real goal of tax reduction. The ploy is effective since smoking brings in more than £4 billion each year against the £1 billion Hacker wants to wrest from the Treasury in tax relief.

The bumbling Jim Hacker comes into his own politically in "The Smoke Screen." Here, for the first time, he wields some of the power that comes with his position and actually puts together some duplicitous machinations worthy of Humphrey Appleby. Of course, Jay and Lynn are wise not to let Hacker fully grow into his new job, and by the episode's end he is forced to enlist Humphrey's aid to make his plan work. The cat's-paw in all this is the highly principled minister for Health, Peter Thorn, whom Hacker uses quite callously. One can almost see Thorn as an earlier version of Hacker before his slow erosion via political expediency ("The Whiskey Priest"). By the end of the episode Thorn begins his own selling out ("Jobs for the Boys"), although he doesn't realize it at the time.

The civil service is rarely seen in a much more imperious light than in this episode. Particularly telling is the permanent treasury secretary, Frank Gordon's (Peter Cellier), disdain at the prospect of a tax cut. Gordon haughtily refers to the funds as "our money," despite the fact that it has been collected from the taxpayers. Humphrey later informs Hacker, somewhat condescendingly, that it is the Treasury's business to collect as much money as it can, regardless of any actual need the government may have of the funds.

In addition to the careful plotting (this episode marks a return to the more twisting story lines familiar in *Yes, Minister*), "The Smoke Screen" features some funny dialogue, including an exchange between Hacker and Humphrey in which the cabinet secretary "foresees all sorts of unforeseen problems." When pressed for examples, Humphrey replies that if he could foresee them they wouldn't be unforeseen. "But you said you could foresee them," Hacker counters.

Here as well is Humphrey's cynical argument that smoking fatalities are actually good for the nation since the victims' premature deaths cost Britain less than having to care for them in their old age.

"The Smoke Screen" features a trio of actors who should be familiar to fans of other British shows. While both John Barron and Peter Cellier appeared in *Yes, Minister*, they are probably better known for their work on *Reggie Perrin* and *Keeping Up Appearances*, respectively. Bill Wallis, who turns in a bright comic turn as the wheezing minister for Sport, may be recognized as a reappearing fixture on the *Blackadder* series.

Episode 4: "The Key" ★★★★

Air date: January 30, 1986. Cast: Jim Hacker (Paul Eddington); Sir Humphrey Appleby (Nigel Hawthorne); Bernard Woolley (Derek Fowlds). With Peter Cellier; Deborah Norton; Victor Winding

When Sir Humphrey's controlling manner becomes too intrusive, Hacker takes measures to rein in his cabinet secretary.

The best of the once-per-series episodes devoted to the humbling of Sir Humphrey Appleby, "The Key" is a splendidly funny entry. Aside from the obvious satisfaction of seeing the oily Humphrey get his occasional comeuppance, the highlight of these forays is the relish that Nigel Hawthorne brings to his part in these episodes. Usually the picture of calm and control, these entries provide hilarious examples of Hawthorne's obvious enjoyment at displaying his character's flappable side.

What makes "The Key" especially potent in its genre are the twin threats presented to Humphrey. Not only must he contend with the psychological threat of having the leadership of the civil service taken away from him by Hacker, Humphrey must deal with the embarrassment of being physically barred from Number 10 Downing Street. Since technically Humphrey works at the address next door, Hacker is well within his prerogative to have the locks changed to bar unwanted interruptions by his cabinet secretary. Making matters infinitely worse for Humphrey is the fact that Hacker gives the relatively lowly Bernard the authority to execute the ban. Derek Fowlds gives a particularly humorous turn as he concurrently displays both fearful reluctance and long-awaited delight in seeing his civil service boss reach his wit's end. In the episode's marvelous climax, Humphrey is reduced to shinnying along the window ledge in a desperate attempt to gain access to the address of power.

The impetus for these bold moves is the character of Dorothy Wainwright, Hacker's political advisor, introduced in this installment. A vast improvement over the same basic character function in the guise of *Yes, Minister*'s Frank Weisel, Dorothy provides Hacker with a strong counter to Humphrey. This fact is not lost on Humphrey either. While Humphrey displayed mere disdain for Weisel, he shows a grudging respect for Wainwright, calling her "dear lady" to her face while reserving a disparaging "that woman" for her absence. The character, well played by Deborah Norton, supplies Eddington's hilariously deficient prime minister with a much-needed source of brains and backbone.

Director Sydney Lotterby notes that this episode received an especially good reaction from viewers due to Sir Humphrey receiving such a thorough comeuppance. Lotterby also notes that the "broader" nature of the comedy in "The Key" added to the installment's popularity.

EPISODE 5: "A REAL PARTNERSHIP" ★★★

Air date: February 6, 1986. Cast: Jim Hacker (Paul Eddington); Sir Humphrey Appleby (Nigel Hawthorne); Bernard Woolley (Derek Fowlds). With John Nettleton; Peter Cellier; Deborah Norton; Diana Hoddinott

Sir Humphrey manages to push through a civil service pay increase in the middle of a financial crisis and look like a hero for doing so.

As bravura as Nigel Hawthorne's performance in "The Key" was, "A Real Partnership" is truly a tour de force for his character, Sir Humphrey Appleby. This episode shows him at his Machiavellian best (or worse). The serpentine Humphrey does not slither through this installment totally unperturbed, however. In fact, at several instances he almost loses his tenuous grip on events. Still, with a little advice from above (John Nettleton returns as the former cabinet secretary, Sir Arnold) and a well-placed tip-off from below (Bernard) Humphrey manages not only to keep his equilibrium but to carry the day.

The title refers to Hacker's assessment of Humphrey's actions in the proceedings, which he sincerely believes are in the best interest of the nation. In actuality, of course, Humphrey's machinations are carried out in his own best interests. Truly, the cabinet secretary manages to backstab his cohead of the civil service, Sir Frank (Peter Cellier), while looking statesmanlike doing so.

There is a particularly amusing scene in which Sir Frank is blindsided by grueling questions from the PM and Dorothy Wainwright concerning the proposed pay raise. Frank fumbles and sweats under the barrage, while Humphrey sits placidly on the accuser's side of the table with an almost beatific visage. After Frank retreats, Humphrey makes his own "modest" proposal for a pay increase, which in effect is the same whopping 43 percent raise, only carefully hidden by accounting tricks. Not only does Hacker swallow the bait, but he heaps great praise on Humphrey.

The final score by Humphrey comes as he introduces a plan to tie politicians' salaries to those in the civil service. Under this scheme, Hacker is actually paid a lower grade than Humphrey himself—which Hacker happily accepts, seeing as it is an increase. The move puts Hacker back symbolically in Humphrey's pocket, where, for purposes of the series, he really does belong after all.

Episode 6: "A Victory for Democracy" ★★★

Air date: February 13, 1986. Cast: Jim Hacker (Paul Eddington); Sir Humphrey Appleby (Nigel Hawthorne); Bernard Woolley (Derek Fowlds). With Clive Francis; Ronald Humes; Donald Pickering; David De Keyser

Hacker attempts to do the right thing in the field of foreign policy in spite of the protests of the Foreign Office.

"A Victory for Democracy" is also quite a victory for Hacker. Indeed, in this episode he actually appears decisive and statesmanlike, although, as in most cases where the prime minister displays such flashes of brilliance, he is borrowing somebody else's flash powder. Here Hacker appropriates the brains and strategy of the Israeli ambassador to get the job done—although he carries out his necessary part superbly, much to the chagrin of the Foreign Office.

Alluded to in various episodes, "A Victory for Democracy" represents the first appearance of any of the minions from the Foreign Office. As hinted at in the past, the FO employees, as represented by two of its more senior civil servants, are the smuggest, most cynical members of the service. They, in the guise of Dick Wharton, permanent secretary, and Luke, Hacker's private secretary for Foreign Affairs (read: Foreign Office spy), make even the oily Sir Humphrey seem benign by comparison. One vainglorious assertion made by the Foreign Office is that politicians cannot be trusted to make diplomatic policy since their tenures are relatively short. The assertion is that careful planning in the field can take a century—and we are left with the impression that these mandarins somehow expect to be around in a hundred years' time to continue their policies. A testament to the pejorative colors in which these characters are painted is the fact that only Humphrey feels comfortable with them. Luke in particular is so smarmy that Bernard is ill at ease in his presence.

The plot turns on a fictitious Commonwealth member, St. George's Island, which is under the imminent threat of a hostile Marxist coup supported by Islamic and Communist states. Hacker tries to avert the takeover, against the protest of the Foreign Office, which would prefer a Communist revolution to any action — decisive or otherwise. There is one humorous moment when Hacker first realizes the composition of the FO and asks Bernard if it in fact is "full of Communists and pinkos." The ever-pedantic Bernard denies the assertion in the strongest terms, then clarifies that the Foreign Office isn't quite full of the unsavory types.

In the end Hacker carries the day with a dose of gunboat diplomacy carried out behind the backs of the career diplomats. Perhaps the full moral strength of his victory is the reason why Sir Humphrey only appears in this episode as something of a cheerleader for the Foreign Office. Such a decisive win over Humphrey could definitely upset the balance of the series. Hacker is rewarded for his diplomatic coup by being caricatured in the closing credits as the British lion, rather than the usual sketch of him as Britannia.

EPISODE 7: "THE BISHOP'S GAMBIT" ★★½

Air date: February 20, 1986. Cast: Jim Hacker (Paul Eddington); Sir Humphrey Appleby (Nigel Hawthorne); Bernard Woolley (Derek Fowlds). With Frank Middlemass; William Fox; Ronnie Stevens; Donald Pickering; Diana Hoddinott

Hacker's recommendation of a candidate to become bishop of Bury St. Edmunds is clandestinely made for him by Sir Humphrey.

A rather routine episode (which for this sterling series still means head and shoulders above most of the competition), "The Bishop's Gambit" serves as Lynn and Jay's primer on the Church of England. As such the entry provides many enlightening discussions on the condition of state-sponsored faith in Britain, with many clever and cynical one-liners to illuminate the way. There are several parallel plots, all of which converge for a tidy ending.

"The Bishop's Gambit" is also notable for the number of previous episodes to which it refers. One of the secondary plots involves a British nurse held in fictitious Qumran for possessing a bottle of alcoholic drink. This was the same imaginary nation Hacker visited in "The Moral Dimension," where he smuggled intoxicating beverages into a diplomatic function. The other plot is also supported by a previous locale, this one Baillie College, Humphrey's alma mater.

It may come as something of a shock to American viewers that the number one politician in England has the power to appoint (technically, recommend to the Crown) high church offices. In this case, and supposedly in all instances, the "choice" is actually a fait accompli with Hacker picking the candidate as one would select a card in a magician's trick (as Hacker and Bernard coyly observe, the choice is usually a "knave" or a "queen"). Still, Hacker tries, with his wife acting as his conscience, to recommend a candidate who actually believes in God. He does succeed in rejecting all the official Church of England choices, only to willingly choose the man Humphrey wanted all along.

Much of the humor comes at the expense of the Church of England, although not at its Christian roots. The few candidates who are true followers of Christ seem to be the logical choice for Hacker, although he is carefully steered clear of them for more theologically "modernist" (atheistic) clerics. Bernard succinctly notes that the perfect candidate for a bishopric is a "socialist and a socialite," since the C of E has primarily become a social club. The true villains in this piece, if there are any, are the church leaders who have lost sight of their calling (or indeed never really understood it in the first place). Theirs is a deserved condemnation delivered up smugly by the amoral civil servants who, although often cynical devils, are at least true to their pronounced vocations.

EPISODE 8: "ONE OF US" ★★

Air date: February 27, 1986. Cast: Jim Hacker (Paul Eddington); Sir Humphrey Appleby (Nigel Hawthorne); Bernard Woolley (Derek Fowlds). With Michael Aldridge; John Nettleton; John Normington; Diana Hoddinott; Martin Muncaster; Miranda Forbes

The revelation that a former head of MI-5 (the counterespionage service) was passing secrets to the Soviets brings allegations that Sir Humphrey is either a spy or grossly incompetent.

Borrowing the two segments of its plots from previous episodes, "One of Us" proves one of the weaker entries in the *Yes, Prime Minister* series primarily on the basis of its repetition. The first device, a human interest story (an orphan's dog is lost on the artillery range on Salisbury Plain) with which Hacker has seemingly little to do, recalls the side plot of the nurse in "The Bishop's Gambit." The episode's primary driver, the accusations against Humphrey that he conducted a shoddy investigation years earlier, is immediately reminiscent of the excellent "The Skeleton in the Cupboard" from the third series of *Yes, Minister*. Unfortunately, although the dialogue is still good and the entry is entertaining, it does have the feel of secondhand goods.

The story is set in motion when it is learned that the late Sir John Halstead, former head of MI-5 was an active Soviet agent. Although such allegations were brought to the fore years earlier, they were dispelled after an internal investigation by Sir Humphrey. In his defense, Humphrey blithely explains that internal investigations are always not supposed to find any wrongdoing. Unlike previous episodes in which Humphrey is caught in a difficult situation, here he displays little abject horror (except at the prospect of being put on an indefinite "gardening leave"). What does make Humphrey's predicament somewhat fresher is the inclusion of his former boss, Sir Arnold, the equation. In masterful style, Sir Arnold manages to distance himself from his protégé before finally coming to his rescue. These scenes are both humorous and unsettling as they show the serpentine Humphrey to be more fallible than previously thought. We can accept one tremendous blunder in Humphrey's past ("The Skeleton in the Cupboard"), but two major gaffes make us wonder if in fact he is more of clay than just his feet. One blunder is an interesting role reversal (Humphrey becoming Hacker); a second suggests a trend.

Ultimately, Humphrey extricates himself easily and via a rather obvious ploy. Still, there are some amusing scenes where Hacker gleefully needles Humphrey with the memo that exonerates him. Unfortunately, these are not enough to rescue the entire episode.

Series Two 1987–1988

Episode 1: "Man Overboard" ★★½

Air date: December 3, 1987. Cast: Jim Hacker (Paul Eddington); Sir Humphrey Appleby (Nigel Hawthorne); Bernard Woolley (Derek Fowlds). With John Nettleton; Michael Byrne; Frederick Treves; Peter Cartwright; David Glover; David Conville; Philip Antony; Philip Blaine; Geoffrey Cousins; Hilary Field

Humphrey causes Hacker to believe that a member of his cabinet is plotting against him in order to kill a plan to relocate some military bases.

Verbally sharp with a fairly straightforward plot, "Man Overboard" plays out like Shakespeare's *Othello*, with Sir Humphrey blithely sowing the seeds of doubt like Iago to Hacker's hapless, unsuspecting Moor. Like *Othello*, the drama results in a death, or at least the death of a career, but the episode is saved from being a tragedy by a surprise twist executed in its final moments.

Humphrey is at his conniving best as he slithers semantically around the proceedings, doing his dirty work while managing to keep his hands clean and a look of total innocence on his face. What makes this episode less than satisfying, however, is the complete and ill-founded trust Hacker puts in Humphrey, although as mentioned previously, he does manage to unwittingly reverse the civil servant's victory in the end.

The plot involves a plan by the employment secretary to move some military installations to northern England in order to alleviate unemployment in that region. Humphrey and most of his counterparts in the Ministry of Defense bristle at the notion since they consider the north the hinterlands and are loath to consider banishing civil servants so far from London. There is considerable sport made of the prevailing opinion that such a relocation would move all concerned (military wives and career civil servants) too far from such centers of the universe as Wimbledon and Harrod's. In order to kill the plan, which

Hacker enthusiastically supports, Humphrey gladly spreads the lie (by subtle implication) that the plan's author is also plotting a coup against Hacker. Hacker obediently rises to the bait with his political paranoia in full bloom.

As previously mentioned, this installment features some clever verbal byplay, especially between Sir Humphrey and Bernard. There is a particularly involved exchange in which Humphrey deftly argues that he needs to know everything, no matter how confidential, in order that he may judge whether or not he needs to know it.

EPISODE 2: "OFFICIAL SECRETS" ★★★½

Air date: December 10, 1987. Cast: Jim Hacker (Paul Eddington); Sir Humphrey Appleby (Nigel Hawthorne); Bernard Woolley (Derek Fowlds). With Antony Carrick; Jeffry Wickham; Denis Lill; Tom Bowles; Sadie Hamilton; James Newall; Michael Shallard

When his predecessor's memoirs are less than complimentary to him, Hacker attempts to censor the offending passages under the Official Secrets Act.

As clever verbally as the preceding episode, "Official Secrets" is ultimately more satisfying on the basis of a stronger plot with more for all three leads to do. Whereas "Man Overboard" featured the machinations of Sir Humphrey to the neglect of his costars, here everyone is given his due. It is especially fun to see more than usual attention given to Derek Fowlds's character of Bernard. The meek personal secretary has several good scenes, including two turns to display his penchant for the pedantic.

The plot turns on the upcoming release of the previous prime minister's memoirs, which first must be cleared by the government to ensure that they do not divulge any secrets that would jeopardize national security. While his cabinet colleagues see no damage, Hacker is frantic to strike out numerous unfavorable references to himself, including one chapter entitled "The Two Faces of Jim Hacker." Essentially, his predecessor paints Hacker as the same dim-witted political chameleon that viewers have come to appreciate over the previous four series of shows.

While Hacker is content to be easily led by his handler, Humphrey, on momentous issues of the age, he is not one to sit idly by when his day-to-day popularity is endangered. Unfortunately, news of Hacker's attempt to excise the offending passages leaks to the press. What follows is a humorous exercise in spin, semantics, and slur (of anyone daring to besmirch Hacker). Humphrey is quite effective in a detached advisory role and can be seen subtly smirking at his boss's foundering attempts to court a suspicious press establishment.

One of the installment's better scenes involves Humphrey instructing Bernard on how to write the minutes of a meeting to reflect what Hacker wants on the permanent record, as opposed to what actually happened. Bernard is faced with an ethical crisis, explaining to Humphrey that he wants a clear conscience in the matter. Humphrey chides his protégé's desire for inner morals (asking Bernard when he "acquired a taste for luxury") then nimbly shows Bernard how to totally reverse the actual record via a string of half-truths. Later, Bernard also has the opportunity to add to Hacker's woes when he is cornered by the press and tricked into saying that the prime minister is above the law.

The events of this enjoyable half hour are neatly wrapped up when Hacker follows the advice of Humphrey to distract the press by expelling a huge contingent of Soviet diplomats under the pretext that they are spies. This tactic is only accepted after a scheme to start a small war is rejected as overkill — but only slightly.

EPISODE 3: "A DIPLOMATIC INCIDENT" ★★★★

Air date: December 17, 1987. Cast: Jim Hacker (Paul Eddington); Sir Humphrey Appleby (Nigel Hawthorne); Bernard Woolley (Derek Fowlds). With Diana Hoddinott; Christopher Benjamin; Nicholas Courtney; Robert East; Mansel David; Alan Downer; Bill Bailey; Raymond Brody; David King; William Lawford

The French try to gain an advantage in negotiations for the Channel tunnel by precipitating a diplomatic incident with a dog.

An excellent episode, "A Diplomatic Incident" bristles with fast-paced and funny dialogue wrapped around clever situations. Jay and Lynn keep the plot boiling along at a rapid clip, thickening it every few moments with new twists, including some imported from previous episodes. Such continuity between episodes helps to add a touch of authenticity to the show. This is also one of those rare episodes in which Humphrey is actually both being civil and serving his boss. This is due to the fact that Hacker and Humphrey easily unite in the face of a common foe: the French. Still, rare as it is, the partnership is an enjoyable departure and helps add a unique touch to the entry.

The proceedings open with Hacker eager to get the treaty for the Channel tunnel finalized — not of course for the sake of progress, but so he can have his picture taken at the ground-breaking ceremony. Humphrey cautions that the negotiations are a matter for professionals and not politicians and illustrates his point by quizzing the P.M. on some of the sticking points. One thing both men can agree upon is that the French will attempt some underhanded ploy to get the advantage of their British partners.

The death of Hacker's predecessor brings the next turn to the plot. The state funeral will bring a visit from the president of France, who insists upon bringing a puppy along as a gift to the queen. The present is actually a bargaining wedge, since Britain has strict quarantine laws. The French also insist upon having their own police accompany their head of state, a request that seems plausible after a bomb is discovered in the French embassy in London. All works out in the end, as Hacker learns that the French actually planted the bomb in their own embassy to embarrass their allies. With the shoe on the other foot, Hacker has little trouble wrapping up the affair and the negotiations.

Paul Eddington is marvelous throughout "A Diplomatic Incident" with his best moments coming as he learns that his predecessor has just died. Moments before, while discussing the man's troublesome memoirs ("Official Secrets"), Hacker vows to give him no further help or honors while he is in office. Upon hearing of the man's demise, Hacker breaks into a wide grin before catching himself and changing his elation to heartfelt remorse. Hacker delights in arranging a state funeral, seeing it as another chance to look statesmanlike as he hosts representatives from around the globe. At one point, he discusses TV coverage of the event, noting to Humphrey that he would like constant frontal coverage of his pew. Humphrey points out that this would necessitate removing the archbishop from the pulpit to accommodate a camera. In a funny exchange, Hacker seriously questions the archbishop's motives in denying himself optimum TV coverage.

Derek Fowlds also has a good bit as he tries to coordinate a state funeral, while balancing the possible inflammatory situation over the French and their puppy. In a rapid-fire scene with meticulous delivery, Fowlds manages to deliver enough jokes on the international arena, event logistics, and dogs to fill a single episode of a lesser sitcom.

This is arguably the best episode in the *Yes, Prime Minister* series.

EPISODE 4: "A CONFLICT OF INTEREST" ★★★

Air date: December 31, 1987. Cast: Jim Hacker (Paul Eddington); Sir Humphrey Appleby (Nigel Hawthorne); Bernard Woolley (Derek Fowlds). With Richard Vernon; Deborah Norton; Peter Cellier; Louis Mahoney; Miranda Forbes

Hacker must choose between appointing an honest man to become the governor of the Bank of England or selecting a fool who will help cover up a growing scandal.

Reminiscent of the style and structure of *Yes, Minister*, "A Conflict of Interest" features a more involved plot and more behind-the-scenes manipulations by Humphrey than in recent episodes of *Yes, Prime Minister*. Indeed, Hacker himself seems to return to the more idealistic form he presented when a freshman minister — wanting to do the right thing rather than opting for the most expedient action.

The episode also brings back Richard Vernon in the role of the woolly-brained Sir Desmond Glazebrook. Last seen six years earlier in the second series of *Yes, Minister* ("The Quality of Life"), Vernon adds his wonderful portrayal of the dim-witted financier to the proceedings. After so long an absence, it is reassuring to know that Glazebrook is one of the few men of power in Britain slower on the uptake than the title character. Also returning to the cast are Peter Cellier and Deborah Norton, neither of whom has appeared since episode five of the first series of *Yes, Prime Minister.*

The plot revolves around a scandal brewing in The City (London's financial district). In order to successfully cover up the mess, which indirectly involves his friend Glazebrook, Humphrey must prevent Hacker from appointing the wrong man as head of the Bank of England. Hacker's first choice for the job is an honest, highly capable man, exactly the wrong person from Humphrey's point of view. In fact, to successfully quash any embarrassing scandal, the ideal candidate is Glazebrook himself.

In another bit that recalls the earlier episode, Humphrey instructs Bernard on how to successfully destroy a good man's reputation and thus ruin his chances for an appointment. He slyly explains his four-step process for damning a saint while appearing to praise him (the best point is the first in which he explains that you firmly get behind the man, since you have to get behind someone before you can stab him in the back). The lesson concludes with a brief primer on how to ruin anyone's reputation based on his marital status: if he is single suggest he is homosexual; if he is married suggest he is an adulterer; if he is obviously happily married suggest he is puritanical.

In the end, as in most cases, Humphrey triumphs as Hacker quickly sheds any remaining shred of courage to grasp at fleeting political expediency. We wouldn't have it any other way.

EPISODE 5: "POWER TO THE PEOPLE" ★★½

Air date: January 7, 1988. Cast: Jim Hacker (Paul Eddington); Sir Humphrey Appleby (Nigel Hawthorne); Bernard Woolley (Derek Fowlds). With Gwen Taylor; Deborah Norton; John Nettleton; Diana Hoddinott; Jonathan Adams; Miranda Forbes

Hacker considers a bold initiative to reform local government until he realizes that too much democracy is not a good thing.

A return to topics explored in *Yes, Minister*'s "The Challenge," "Power to the People' manages to be entertaining but without any genuinely new material. Britain's system of local authority, which Hacker believes to be run by "morons," is again proving nettlesome, especially one revolutionary councilwoman, who has announced that she is cutting off financial and administrative support to her own police force.

Gwen Taylor is refreshing as Agnes Moorehead, a radical from a local council, whose bread and butter is anarchy and confrontation. When this area councilwoman starts making waves all the way up to Downing Street, Hacker insists she must be dealt with immediately. Rather than draw her fire for himself, the prime minister puts a mortified Sir Humphrey on the case of impeding the loose cannon. Nigel Hawthorne turns in a splendid performance as he tries to gingerly handle the woman, only to find the tables quickly turned. In their first confrontation, Moorehead leaves Humphrey totally cowed.

Into this volatile situation, Dorothy Wainwright, Hacker's political advisor, introduces a plan that would totally overhaul local government by making politics a neighborhood responsibility — true grassroots democracy. Hacker embraces the scheme, seeing his place in history as a great reformer. Humphrey, not dependent on the polls or history books, sees it as yet another thin end of a wedge aimed directly at his cushy status quo.

The greatest weakness in "Power to the People" is that a large amount of discussion is spent trying to figure out how to kill a plan that is unanimously opposed by everyone once it is fully understood — thus eliminating any need for clever machinations, which are Humphrey's hallmark. Once Moorehead, the original cause of the problem, hears the proposal, she immediately recognizes that it would mean the end to her power by media advocacy. She quickly folds and strikes an unlikely partnership with Humphrey. For his part, Hacker wants no part of the arrangement either since it would effectively end party politics and his own power.

Episode 6: "A Patron of the Arts" ★★★

Air date: January 14, 1988. Cast: Jim Hacker (Paul Eddington); Sir Humphrey Appleby (Nigel Hawthorne); Bernard Woolley (Derek Fowlds). With John Bird; Deborah Norton; Antony Carrick; Diana Hoddinott; Geoffrey Beevers; Martin Milman; Myfanwy Talog; David Rose

Hacker anticipates a chilly reception when he is scheduled to present the British Theatre Awards on the same day that his budget is announced, granting a smaller-than-hoped-for allocation for the arts.

Another return to previously explored territory as Hacker's tenure runs out, "A Patron of the Arts" explores themes similar to those in "The Middle-Class Rip-Off." This is not just a carbon copy of that episode of six years prior, however. Whereas "Rip-Off" was heavily steeped in philosophical arguments on the funding of the arts, here we see the practical implications of the policy as it affects politicians, artists, and the public. Again, there is the implication that most arts funding goes for unpopular plays produced as a pastime for the upper middle classes.

The episode opens with Hacker on the horns of a dilemma. He has agreed to speak at the Theatre Awards banquet, then later realizes it will occur just after his unpopular arts budget is revealed. The budget, he fears, will result in a snide and hostile introduction from the managing director of the National Theatre. Humphrey, as in the previous episode on the same theme, is a strong proponent of arts subsidies — especially since he is on the National Theatre's board of directors.

In a wonderfully wicked scene, Humphrey lunches with the managing director and coyly manages to reveal the as-yet-unannounced arts grant. Then, to make sure that he can cause his boss the maximum amount of embarrassment in hopes of increasing the grant, Humphrey supplies lists of humiliating government boondoggles. This litany of government waste is provided ostensibly as examples of what not to mention in any introduction of the prime minister.

Later, after the managing director makes his threats, Hacker's political advisor, Wainwright, suggests an innovative solution that will allow the budget for productions to be increased but will radically change the face of the National Theatre. As in "Power to the People," Hacker's opponents quickly become tamed when faced with losing their little seats of power.

Score this one as a rare complete victory for Hacker although, as usual, with outside help. Bernard gets some fine opportunities in this episode for some unintentional digs at his boss as well as some good pedantic ramblings. There is an especially telling bit in the opening scene in which the private secretary warns Hacker not to associate with phony actors, lest the public make the connection between them and politicians.

EPISODE 7: "THE NATIONAL EDUCATION SERVICE" ★★½

Air date: January 21, 1988. Cast: Jim Hacker (Paul Eddington); Sir Humphrey Appleby (Nigel Hawthorne); Bernard Woolley (Derek Fowlds). With Deborah Norton; John Nettleton; Diana Hoddinott; Peter Cartwright; Jerome Willis

Hacker sets out to improve the state of British education by abolishing the centralized Department of Education and Science and establishing more parental choice in the process.

After eight years and 36 episodes, the misadventures of Jim Hacker in government land are beginning to wear a little thin. This is not to say that the dialogue is less crackling. On the contrary, by the end of this final season, Humphrey's obfuscating explanations have risen to the level of an art form, and Bernard's pedantic interruptions contain even more minutiae. The topics, except for some occasional minor rehashing, are still relevant and provoke lively debate and deep reflection. The primary problem, most evident here in "The National Education Service," is that the structure upon which all this wonderful business is hung is becoming obvious. While it is arguable that the series has always been formulaic, by the end of the run it is becoming glaringly so.

Most of "The National Education Service" is a debate on the deplorable state of public education in Great Britain, although it is set up by Jay and Lynn as a rather one-sided argument. Of course, any initiative by Hacker to move power away from the national government is met with fierce opposition from

Humphrey, but here even Humphrey must grudgingly admit (but not to Hacker) that the plan makes perfect sense. For his part, Humphrey must attack the plan for the harm it would do to the teachers' unions and the bureaucrats, while being careful to hide the fact that it would be a boon to parents and children. There are some good moments when Humphrey asserts that parents are not qualified to choose a school for their own children, but in the next breath he proudly admits that his parents were responsible for sending him to the finest educational establishments. He defends this illogic by firmly declaring that "parents are the worst people to bring up children!" One suspects that Sir Humphrey's double standard is the usual practice of politicians and policymakers, who support public education publicly, decry school choice vociferously, then quietly send their own children to the best possible private schools (a practice not reserved to England, eh, Mr. Clinton?).

Ultimately, Hacker's bold plan (actually springing from the mind of Dorothy Wainwright, his political advisor) is defeated not on the basis of its merits, but because it would be politically inexpedient to enact it.

Episode 8: "The Tangled Web" ★★★★

Air date: January 28, 1988. Cast: Jim Hacker (Paul Eddington); Sir Humphrey Appleby (Nigel Hawthorne); Bernard Woolley (Derek Fowlds). With Ludovic Kennedy; Geoffrey Drew

In a rare display of honesty, Humphrey takes the moral high road when Hacker asks him to lie, until it later becomes personally expedient for him to do so.

At the end of a final season that proved to be less sharp than its predecessors, it is heartening to see Hacker, Humphrey, and Woolley pass into the ether in such a marvelous vehicle as "The Tangled Web." Fittingly, this last installment spotlights the three principal players with only BBC interviewer Ludovic Kennedy (previously seen in *Yes, Minister*'s, "The Challenge") and a bit player to support them. It is especially gratifying to see Paul Eddington have the meatiest part afforded him in the final series. For their parts, Nigel Hawthorne is given his last chance to play Sir Humphrey in his obligatory foot-caught-in-the-door routine, while Derek Fowlds shines as he definitively answers the question "Whose side is Bernard really on?"

The plot turns on Hacker making an unequivocal statement (that the government is not bugging members of Parliament) in the House of Commons, which he later discovers is untrue. When informed of his embarrassing and potentially damaging gaffe by Humphrey, Hacker demands to know why he wasn't informed. The pat civil service answer, of course, is that he doesn't need to know everything. At first, one expects a revisiting of themes from such earlier installments as "The Right to Know" and "Big Brother," but this is not the case. Instead, Humphrey, when called upon to back up his boss, decides to tell the truth. This actually isn't a departure for the Machiavellian's Machiavelli, since he is not a habitual deceiver; he only lies when it profits him. Here, since he could care less about Hacker's fate, Humphrey delights in sermonizing to the desperate prime minister. By the end of the episode, however, Humphrey finds himself in a similar fix to which Hacker deliciously responds by repeating back the same smug admonitions to him.

There is a wonderful scene that occurs before Humphrey's appearance on a radio interview program. Hacker coaches his cabinet secretary on tactics useful in handling media questions, but Humphrey only patronizingly listens, believing the media to be as easy to tame as politicians. When Humphrey falls for one of the oldest tricks in the book (by Hacker's own estimation) and gives potentially career-ending statements to the BBC, Hacker is especially gleeful. Of course, the two adversaries are again thrust into a position of mutual back scratching to extricate themselves from their predicaments. Only Bernard, in his most proactive maneuvering, manages to come out of the tangled web unscathed. In fact, the often-timorous private secretary is almost exultant and can barely hide his joy over being instrumental in bringing Humphrey to heel.

BLACKADDER

BBC-TV 1983, 1986, 1987, 1989

The hilarious *Blackadder* saga marks the perfect adaptation of Britain's alternative comedy movement to the wider situation-comedy format. Iconoclastic, usually rude, often childish, shocking, and most important, comical, the "movement" was the punk generation's finding of its funny bone. As *Monty Python* ten years before had managed to work itself from cult status into the mainstream of entertainment, so youngbloods such as Rik Mayall and Ben Elton began bringing their comedy to television in the early 1980s. The first rumblings of this more cynical approach to humor appeared in 1979 with the shocking sketch program *Not the Nine O'Clock News*.

This series, which replaced *Fawlty Towers* in the schedule (and incidentally was introduced by Cleese in his Basil Fawlty character), introduced Rowan Atkinson to a mass audience. *Not the Nine O'Clock News* ran for four series, after which its cast members reasoned that they had worked the rapid-paced format for all it was worth, and they moved on to new projects. Rowan Atkinson, who had done sketch and toured in his own one-man show, decided to try his hand at a different type of situation comedy.

With the help of old college friend and collaborator Richard Curtis, Atkinson created what some have termed a situation tragedy, *The Black Adder*. The premise was simple yet at the same time quite intelligent. Set in 1485, the series asserts that the standard English history regarding Richard III is wrong. Instead of murdering his two nephews in the Tower of London, Richard was a kindly relative. In addition, although Richard III was killed at the battle of Bosworth

Field, his family, led by his nephew Richard, duke of York, carried the day, and the duke became Richard IV. Their hated opponent, Henry Tudor, did not succeed in toppling them until 13 years later, when, as Henry VII, he had the calendars changed to hide the fact of Richard IV's reign.

With this revisionist backdrop in place, the writers made Atkinson the shiftless, power-hungry, but ultimately dim-witted, young son of Richard IV, Edmund. Edmund, who in his scheming for his father's throne renames himself "The Black Adder," is joined in his plots by his even more stupid friend, Percy (Tim McInnerny), and his personal squire, Baldrick (Tony Robinson). Together, the three find increasingly convoluted ways to seize power, which, thanks to their ineptness and bad fortune, always are frustrated.

Producing chores on *The Black Adder* fell to John Lloyd, who had done similar duty on *Not the Nine O'Clock News*. Lloyd explained to Albert Hunt of the *Radio Times* that one of the main inspirations for the historical series was the desire to get away from the more topical humor of the previous series. Instead of spoofing politicians and modern problems, the laughs stemmed from more vital struggles.

"People in the late 15th century lived with violent death as a matter of course. When a plague arrived up to a third of the population could be wiped out in a few months," said Lloyd. "This is a comedy dealing with matters of enormous seriousness."

Consequently, even though the comedy was broad, the producer and writers decided to sprinkle dramatic actors in the cast, along with those from the comedy field. The most notable of these was Brian Blessed, who brought great vigor to the role of the bombastic warrior Richard IV. Although he had earned his reputation appearing in crime dramas (the BBC's *Z Cars*) and straight historical dramas (*I Claudius*), Blessed took to the broad role of the king with a gusto that makes him appear to be having the time of his life in the part.

"We want everybody to act it for real," explained cowriter Curtis to the *Radio Times* in 1983. "We want it to be dramatic, exciting, and consequently absurd."

To give the series a degree of realism rarely seen in a sitcom, the shows were filmed on location on the private estate of the duke of Northumberland (including the Alnwick Castle), some 35 miles north of New Castle in northern England. In addition, the ambitious project employed 65 extras, most for the battle scenes, and a dozen horses. As a result, the finished exterior work had a bleak, medieval look about it. The atmosphere of the series, according to Rowan Atkinson, was planned as a part of the comedy.

"We've found that if you set jokes in a very hard and nasty background, the jokes actually become funnier," noted the star and cowriter to Albert Hunt.

Years later, in 1996, Atkinson confessed to Jim Slotek of the *Toronto Sun* that the humor of *The Black Adder* was highly steeped in British history, perhaps too highly. "I'm amazed that anyone outside the British public school system could possibly understand what half of it is," admitted Atkinson. "Even I don't understand all of it, I relied on Richard [Curtis] for a lot of it."

Still, for all the meticulous preparation, the best moments in The *Black Adder* proved to be those stemming from the absurd characters, as many of the historical jokes (and probably most in the case of American audiences) are lost on the audience. The result was an interesting but ultimately unsatisfying series. The first series did manage to capture a young audience, which tuned in mainly to see Atkinson. In addition to the youth audience, *The Black Adder* also managed to win an international Emmy Award in the popular arts category. The award helped convince the BBC to commission a second series in the saga, although not before its creators performed some fine tuning on their vehicle.

A number of changes took place between *The Black Adder* and *Blackadder II*, which helped turn the series from interesting, flawed comedy to an unqualified classic. The first shift involved the main character. In the first series, Edmund had been scheming, cringing, and, above all, stupid. The second series retained the character's Machiavellian bent but made Edmund Blackadder (now spelled as one word, having achieved surname status) intelligent. Correspondingly, Baldrick, who had been the brightest chum in the first series, was made the thickest in the second. In addition, Baldrick was demoted in station (from squire to dogsbody) and in the level of his personal hygiene. Only Percy remained essentially unchanged in temperament and brains.

The character change was the key ingredient that helped to make the series become something of the *Fawlty Towers* of the 1980s, at least as far as the relationships among the characters were concerned. The Edmund Blackadder of *Blackadder II* (as well as in the subsequent incarnations of the series) is much like Basil Fawlty in a period piece. Both characters scheme and plot but are ultimately frustrated by those above them and below them. Baldrick is essentially Manuel, only more broadly played. Unlike Basil Fawlty, however, Edmund Blackadder is completely surrounded by idiots, not only as friends, but also as those in power with whom he must contend. The second series found Edmund even further from power but still near the throne as Lord Blackadder, one of the favorites of the silly and childish Queen Elizabeth I (Miranda Richardson). Given the queen's flighty nature, one of Blackadder's main pursuits is staying on his temperamental sovereign's good side and thus retaining his head. Also on board to scatter tacks in his path is Stephen Fry as his rival, Lord Melchett.

Another major change that helped the series tremendously was the addition of Ben Elton to the writing staff. Elton's major success up to this time had been as coauthor of *The Young Ones* earlier in the decade. With Curtis and Elton together (Atkinson stepped down from his writing duties), the dialogue crackled with fast-paced, hilarious lines, especially for the new incarnation of the title character. This suited Atkinson, who proved especially adept at the verbal assault.

With the second series essentially dialogue driven, it was also decided that the show should dispense with the extensive exterior shooting that had been a hallmark of the first show. Apart from a few location shoots (most notably in the first episode, "Bells"), the show was taped before a studio audience. Changing his stance of a few years earlier, Atkinson defended the move, noting that the action got in the way of the comedy. Not only did the new format bolster the humor, it also dramatically reduced the price tag for *Blackadder II* over that of its predecessor, but the move almost came too late. On the eve of production, Michael Grade, the new controller at BBC 1, cancelled the series. The decision came when Grade analyzed the cost of the first series versus the viewers it had attracted. Of course no one had bothered to inform Grade that the new series would be much less expensive to shoot due to the fact that there would be almost no location work. In view of this, *Blackadder II* was reinstated and went on to far surpass its predecessor and become a genuine hit.

With the success of the second series, a third group of six episodes in the family saga was a foregone conclusion. A year and a half later, in the autumn of 1987, *Blackadder the Third* appeared with a change to the basic cast. Tim McInnery, who had played Percy in the first two series, had decided to bow out of the third. Also known for his work in Shakespearean roles, McInnerny was fearful of being typecast as the hopelessly obtuse Percy. (McInnerny later made a guest appearance as half of the Scarlet Pimpernel in the "Nob and Nobility" episode.) The absence of Percy actually helped make *Blackadder the Third* a much more tightly constructed series. Without Percy's utter stupidity around, the writers (again Curtis and Elton) bestowed the characteristics upon Hugh Laurie, playing the Prince Regent who would ultimately become King George IV. The move was a masterstroke, essentially frustrating the Blackadder character by not only having him deal with a complete idiot but also forcing him to be subservient to the fool. Edmund Blackadder, presumably another bastard descendant of the original, was no longer a member of the aristocracy as in the first two series but had, by the Georgian period when the series is set, sunk to the level of the butler to the prince. The struggles of the main character therefore are even more basic and thus easier for the audience to sympathize with. In the first series the focus is Edmund's schemes to become king. In the second, he tries to retain his position in the court of a childish and petulant queen. Here, he tries to rise above his lowly position and find himself a more comfortable life.

While Blackadder had sunk considerably in the roughly 200 years that ensued between the second and third series, Baldrick had not. Being essentially at the bottom of the ladder, or actually under it, the latest generation of Baldrick was still groveling away with the hopes of some day owning his own turnip.

The tighter format of *Blackadder the Third* (as well as the success of the second series) paved the way for more guest stars in historical roles. The best of these included Robbie Coltrane as Dr. Samuel Johnson, Stephen Fry as the Duke of Wellington, and the aforementioned Tim McInnerny as the Scarlet Pimpernel. This reliance on guests also helped keep *Blackadder the Third* much livelier since in addition to the three regular players, each episode featured fresh and varied characters.

Following the success of *Blackadder the Third*, which won a BAFTA Award as best light entertainment series of the year, there was a two-year interval before the final *Blackadder* series. This time was not idly spent, however, as two *Blackadder* specials appeared in 1988. The first of these was a regression back to the time of the English Civil War and Charles I. *Blackadder: The Cavalier Years* was a 15-minute skit filmed for inclusion in Britain's *Comic Relief* telethon. In the demi-episode, Sir Edmund Blackadder is the last remaining faithful nobleman to King Charles (hilariously portrayed by Stephen Fry doing a turn more reminiscent of the current Prince Charles than the ill-fated monarch). Baldrick is still performing his usual duties, while Warren Clarke plays Oliver Cromwell. The cavalier version of *Blackadder* probably accounts for how the Blackadders lost their titled status.

Two days before Christmas 1988 saw the airing of *Blackadder's Christmas Carol*, an amusing spoof of Dickens' classic with a clever twist. Here, instead of a hardened evil Scrooge being shown the error of his ways, the only kindly Blackadder descendant is given a glimpse into the history of his wicked ancestors. Rather than being inspired to continue on his virtuous path, the Victorian version of Blackadder is himself turned to a more heinous way.

After the streamlined cast of *Blackadder the Third*, Curtis and Elton came back with the largest regular supporting cast yet for the final installment of the saga, 1989's *Blackadder Goes Forth*. This time around, Edmund Blackadder was a captain in the British army, stationed in the trenches of France during the First World War. Tony Robinson was there as his ever-loyal, ever thick-witted batsman (essentially an officer's assistant), Private Baldrick. Hugh Laurie was also there, basically unchanged from his incarnation in the third series, as Lieutenant George Colthurst St. Barleigh, an exuberant but still terribly idiotic twit. Supporting these frontline troops back at headquarters were Stephen Fry, this time as the raving mad General Hogmanay Melchett, and Tim McInnerny as the sniveling, scheming Captain Darling.

While the comedy remained as crisp as ever — especially the sharp-tongued assaults on the hapless Baldrick — there was also a strong tragic undercurrent to the humor. Providing this drama was the fact that the character now was plotting on an episode by episode basis to preserve his very life from the insanity of trench warfare. This was no more evident than in the final episode in which Blackadder, Baldrick, St. Barleigh, and Darling are sent over the top in a suicidal attack. Although viewers of the series were used to grim endings (all three of the previous series ended with main characters dying, two in mass killings), here the historical immediacy of the event made the finale that much more chilling. In addition, previously the characters had perished primarily as a result of their own actions. In *Blackadder Goes Forth*, however, the cast is sent to its doom as mere cannon fodder for a senseless war machine.

Even before the fourth series had finished its run on the BBC, it was being clearly stated that this would be the last of, despite the series winning another BAFTA Award.

"It's not me who wants to throw it all away," explained producer John Lloyd to Patrick Stoddard in *The Times* (London), "It's the writers. Things do get very tense by the end of a series, because everyone involved in the thing is very clever, and very funny, and they all want to push the scripts along."

In the same article, Richard Curtis agreed that, despite the great talent assembled for each series of *Blackadder*, he wanted some time away from his coworkers of the past few years. "Everybody on the show thinks they can put in good jokes, despite the fact that Ben Elton and I think there are already quite a few good ones in there to start with," explained Curtis. "It does usually end up funnier, but it's time to do something over which I have more control."

In addition to being generally worn out from the property, the writers also saw a dearth of promising new eras in which to drop the next Blackadder. Besides being too much a repeat of the First World War situation, a WWII Blackadder might have hit too close to home and offended too many viewers. A year after the final episode, however, Curtis told the *Radio Times* that a fifth *Blackadder* was still a long shot bet. "The chances of a new series are about the same as the chances of Blackadder working for charity and Baldrick doing ads for Camay," joked the cowriter of some of the best television comedy of the 1980s. But Curtis did offer two possible suggestions for another series.

"If there was a fifth, the two most charming suggestions so far are *The Blackadder Five*, with Rowan as a 60s entrepreneur ... and Bald Rick [sic] as the drummer of his very dodgy band. The other was *Blackadder in the Fifth* with Stephen Fry as Headmaster, Hugh Laurie as Head Boy, Rowan as a jolly nasty bully and Baldrick as his fag."

Although the prospect of seeing such a humorous cast reassembled is tempting, it is just as well that it has not come to fruition — at least not in the ten years since *Blackadder Goes Forth*. After the impact of the final series, any further attempts would seem weaker in comparison, and without sufficient creative motivation the talented participants could appear to merely be going through the motions to recapture an era in television comedy that was truly special.

THE EPISODES

The Black Adder— *By Richard Curtis and Rowan Atkinson. Directed by Martin Shardlow. Produced by John Lloyd*

Episode One: "The Foretelling" ★★

Air date: June 15, 1983. Cast in Order of Precedence: Richard III (Peter Cook); Richard IV (Brian Blessed); Henry VII (Peter Benson); Harry, Prince of Wales (Robert East); Edmund, Duke of Edinburgh (Rowan Atkinson); Percy, Duke of Northumberland (Tim McInnerny); Queen (Elspet Gray); Painter (Philip Kendall); Goneral (Kathleen St. John); Regan (Barbara Miller); Cordelia (Gretchen Franklin); Baldrick (Tony Robinson)

It is the eve of the battle of Bosworth Field and all is well in the court of Richard III, except for one individual. Edmund, great-nephew to the king, is disgruntled over his prospects for advancement. Despite this, he and his painfully slow-witted chum, Percy, boast of glory they will earn in battle against the Tudors. One of the cup bearers, Baldrick, catches Edmund's eye, and he elevates him to the post of his personal squire.

Edmund, Percy, and Baldrick arrive at the battle late due to oversleeping. Once he arrives at Bosworth Field, Edmund kills Richard III, who he mistakes for a horse thief.

Not content with being a prince, Edmund schemes to become king.

The first episode of *The Black Adder*, like many series' introductory entries, is long on exposition. Although a valiant attempt is made to integrate comedy into the proceedings, the episode falls short of the level of humor achieved by some of the other shows in the series. The reason for this, aside from the needed introductions, is that most of the first episode, indeed the entire *Black Adder* series, is based on the show's premise. The main joke here is the concept that recorded history has gotten the facts wrong, and these are the true details. Full appreciation then is predicated on the viewer having some familiarity with English history and, especially in the first episode, some knowledge of Shakespeare's *Richard III*. It is such knowledge that brings out the full scope of what writers Curtis and Atkinson were attempting: broad parody based on historical drama. Unfortunately, for most American audiences, some of the jokes will be lost.

In a brief prologue to the episode, and indeed the entire series, a narrator explains that Henry Tudor (King Henry VII) rewrote history to put his predecessor, Richard III, in the worst possible light. Instead of Richard killing his two nephews in the Tower of London as history rumors, we are told that he was a kind and playful uncle (of course this ignores the fact that one of the princes held claim to the throne before Richard III). The narrator goes on to explain that Henry Tudor did not ascend to the throne after Richard's death

By the third incarnation of the Blackadder saga Edmund Blackadder (Rowan Atkinson, left) had been reduced to being a servant for the witless Prince Regent (Hugh Laurie, right), while the hapless Baldrick (Tony Robinson, bottom, as usual) retained his lowly position. Copyright © BBC.

at the battle of Bosworth Field but rather his nephew, Richard IV, took the crown. These buried facts are finally to be brought to light in the saga of *The Black Adder*.

"The Foretelling" has the advantage of a strong guest star in the person of well-known British comic actor Peter Cook. Although less familiar to American audiences than his former partner, Dudley Moore, the rangy Cook should be recognized by some for his sketch work with the Beyond the Fringe troupe and for such films as *Bedazzled* (with Moore) and *The Secret Policeman's Other Ball.*

In perhaps the funniest scene of the introductory episode, Edmund's older brother, Harry, stops by to tabulate the battle averages. When he asks Edmund who he killed, Edmund replies he killed no one. Informed that this will probably mean forfeiting a Legion of Honor, Edmund foolishly clarifies that he didn't kill the king. With Percy and Baldrick prompting from the side, Edmund regains his composure and announces that he killed 450 peasants. Unfortunately, peasants only count in the case of a tie.

Episode 2: "Born to Be King" ★★½

Air date: June 22, 1983. Cast in Geographical Order: Laird of Roxburgh, Selkirk and Peebles (Rowan Atkinson); Richard XII of Scotland (Brian Blessed); McAngus, Duke of Argyll (Alex Norton); Percy, Duke of Northumberland (Tim McInnerny); Gertrude, Queen of Flanders (Elspet Gray); Harry, Prince of Wales (Robert East); Baldrick, Bachelor of the Parish of Ghigwell (Tony Robinson); Jumping Jew of Jerusalem (Angus Deayton); Celia, Countess of Cheltenham (Joolia Cappleman); Sir Dominick Prique of Stratford (Martin Clarke); 2nd Wooferoonie (Martin Soan); 3rd Wooferoonie (Malcolm Hardee); Messenger (David Runn)

When it appears that King Richard has died during a crusade, Edmund conspires with McAngus, the duke of Argyll, to prove Harry a bastard, thus making himself king.

The second episode of *The Black Adder* is a noticeable improvement over the series' premiere. Much of this is due to the fact that the script is not burdened with the exposition that was a necessary part of episode one. Still, the writing has not yet fully gelled to the point of the later episodes. The main strength of "Born to Be King" is in the wonderfully broad performance of guest star Alex Norton as McAngus, Duke of Argyll.

This episode also marks the first appearance of semiregular cast member David Runn as the Messenger. The rotund Runn, who appears in three episodes total, is amusing in his small part of the dull-witted herald, who not only delivers messages but also unconsciously mimics the gestures of those with whom he comes in contact.

Fans of *One Foot in the Grave* will note that one of the Jumping Jews of Jerusalem (the only one with a speaking part) is played by Angus Deayton, who went on to play Patrick, Victor Meldrew's belligerent neighbor in that series.

One last note for those unfamiliar with medieval entertainment: the Morris dance, which Edmund so vehemently loathes, is traditionally performed by six men, a fool, another man with a cardboard hobby horse around his middle, and a boy dressed as Maid Marian. The dance, which originally recounted the Robin Hood legend, became popular toward the end of the 15th century, was later outlawed by the Puritans, and revived at the turn of the 20th century. Bear-baiting involved watching dogs attack a captive bear.

Edmund's attempts at trying to arrange a suitable entertainment for St. Leonard's Day make the best scene of the series' second episode. Aside from the fact that he fancies himself an archvillain, Edmund's task is made the more difficult because he hates all the popular diversions of his day — especially Morris dancing. He describes the folk dance as "the most fatuous, 10th rate entertainment ever devised by man. Forty effeminate blacksmiths, waving bits of cloth they've just wiped their noses on."

Episode 3: "The Archbishop" ★★★½

Air date: June 29, 1983. Cast in Order of Reverence: Herbert, Archbishop of Canterbury (Paul McDowell); Godfrey, Archbishop of Canterbury (Arthur Hewlett); Percy, Bishop of Ramsgate (Tim McInnerny); William, Bishop of London (Arthur Hewlett); Mother Superior (Joyce Grant); Sister Sara (Carolyn Colquohoun); Harry, Prince of Wales (Robert East); Queen (Elspet Gray); Duke of Winchester (Russell Enoch); Cain, Peasant (Bert Parnaby); Abel, Peasant (Roy Evans); Messenger (David Runn); Sir Justin deBoinod (Bill Wallis); Sir George deBoeuf (David Delve); Lord Graveney (Leslie Sands); Brother Baldrick (Tony Robinson); King Richard IV (Brian Blessed); Edmund, Archbishop of Canterbury (Rowan Atkinson)

King Richard is continually losing the estates of dying nobles to the church. Frustrated by his losses, the king has taken to killing each archbishop of Canterbury who succeeds in wresting lands from his clutches. In an attempt to solve his ecclesiastical problems, the king announces that Edmund will be the next Archbishop. His reign is imperiled, however, after a pair of drunken knights mistakenly think the King wants Edmund assassinated.

After feeling its way in the first two episodes, *The Black Adder* takes a great leap in the third episode. Although this cohesiveness falters by the series' final programs, the promise is shown and the foundation laid for the subsequent histories in the saga of this sinister, yet silly family line.

The strength of "The Archbishop" rests firmly on its script, primarily the dialogue. There are many good bits, the standouts being Edmund's convincing the dying noble on the benefits of an eternity in hell and Baldrick's inventory of curses and indulgences. As with the best of all *Blackadder* episodes from all four series, these scenes could stand alone and are funny even when read.

For those unfamiliar with ecclesiastical history, the multiple references to multiple pontiffs (two and three popes, respectively) speak to actual times in church history when there were competing claimants to St. Peter's throne (with illegitimate postulants being labeled antipopes).

Two scenes stand out in "The Archbishop," both concern Edmund's unique grasp of ecclesiastical doctrines and practices. The first is Edmund's description of the benefits of hell to the dying Lord Graveney. He explains that heaven is reserved for those individuals who go in for more sedate pastimes, such as praying and tending house plants. Conversely, according to Edmund, hell is perfect for those who enjoy rape, torture, and pillage.

The other bit involves the medieval church's system of pardons and curses available at graduated prices. For example, for two pebbles an offender can purchase a pardon for talking with his mouth full. The top of the line features a pardon for everything up to and including dismembering friends and relatives. The curses run similarly. For half an egg one can purchase a curse so that an onion falls on your enemy's head, while the premier curse goes for four ducats and includes the wish that one's enemy's head will "fall off at an awkward moment."

EPISODE 4: "THE QUEEN OF SPAIN'S BEARD" ★★★★

Air date: July 6, 1983. Cast in Affable Order: Edmund, Duke of Edinburgh (Rowan Atkinson); King Richard IV (Brian Blessed); Queen (Elspet Gray); Harry, Prince of Wales (Robert East); Percy (Tim McInnerny); Baldrick (Tony Robinson); Infanta Maria Escalosa of Spain (Miriam Margolyes); Don Speckingleesh, Interpreter (Jim Broadbent); Mrs. Applebottom (Jane Freeman); Rev. Lloyd (John Rapley); Mr. Applebottom (Howard Lew Lewis); Lord Cheswick (Stephen Tate); 1st Messenger (Kenn Wells); 2nd Messenger (Richard Mitchley); 3rd and 4th Messengers (David Runn); Archbishop (Willoughby

Goddard); Princess Leia of Hungary (Natasha King); Lady on Ramparts (Harriet Keevil)

In order to forge victorious alliances, Richard has decided that Edmund will marry the Spanish Infanta in order to cement an alliance between Spain and England against the French. When the Infanta arrives, however, she is short, extremely plump, and rather ugly. The King, eager to seal his alliance, announces the wedding will take place the next day. Edmund immediately looks for a plan that will release him from his impending marriage.

In the fourth episode of *The Black Adder*, the series reaches its apex. "The Queen of Spain's Beard" hits the mark of historical parody that presumably creators Richard Curtis and Rowan Atkinson had been aiming for all along. The episode is filled with all the best elements. There are generous helpings of clever dialogue, broad physical comedy, and general all-about silliness. There are also two fine guest performances from Miriam Margolyes as the Infanta Jim Broadbent as and Don Speckingleesh, her fatuous interpreter. In addition the supporting cast members are given plenty to do, and all shine in their respective duties.

Perhaps part of the success of this episode and "The Archbishop" lies in the fact that both have little outdoor filmed scenes aside from links. While there is no inherent amusement in studio performances versus those on film, the type of sketch comedy that *The Black Adder* thrives on is a verbal style, which does not depend upon location. The best of Curtis and Atkinson's lines can be enjoyed without the enhancement of site, costumes, or props. While the outdoor scenes used in the first *Blackadder* series are handsomely mounted, any comedy in them is usually visual and not as well done as the show's verbal wit. It is interesting to note that the other three series do not use out-of-the-studio scenes — even *Blackadder Goes Forth*, in which much of the action takes place in a trench.

While "The Queen of Spain's Beard" is rife with highlights, two of the best exchanges have little to do with the plot. The first is a scene between Edmund and Percy, as the latter attempts some flattering small talk on the subject of Edmund's bride-to-be. "You know they do say," Percy begins, "the Infanta's eyes are more beautiful than the famous stone of Galveston."

When pressed on this famous stone, Percy explains that it is incredibly blue and from Galveston. Edmund inquires further to learn that neither Percy, nor anyone he knows, has seen this stone or the Infanta's eyes with which to compare them.

"So, what you're telling me, Percy," Edmund concludes, "is that something you have never seen is slightly less blue than something else you have never seen."

In another amusing side scene, the Infanta, via her interpreter, asks the Queen about English men. The Queen explains that most Englishmen prefer the company of animals and other men. She adds, however, that they only want one thing from their women — a pudding made from bread, butter, and raisins. The sex-crazed princess suggests that surely they must want one other thing. The Queen agrees and adds that Englishmen also enjoy custard. Not interested in Englishmen's snacking habits, the Infanta asks specifically what Edmund likes in bed. His mother replies that Edmund enjoys warm milk and cinnamon in bed.

EPISODE 5: "THE WITCHSMELLER PURSUIVANT" ★

Air date: July 13, 1983. Cast in Order of Witchiness: Great Grumbledook (Rowan Atkinson); Witchsmeller Pursuivant (Frank Finlay); Witch Queen (Elspet Gray); Percy, a Witch (Tim McInnerny); Baldrick, a Witch (Tony Robinson); Ross, a Lord (Richard Murdoch); Angus, a Lord (Valentine Dyall); Fife, a Lord (Peter Schofield); Soft, a Guard (Stephen Frost); Anon, a Guard (Mark Arden); Daft Red, a Peasant (Perry Benson); Dim Cain, a Peasant (Bert Parnaby); Dumb Abel, a Peasant (Roy Evans); Dopey Jack, a Peasant (Forbes Collins); Officer, an Officer (Patrick Duncan); Jane Firkettle (Barbara Miller); Princess Leia (Natasha King); Piers, a Yeoman (Howard Lew Lewis); Mrs. Kield, a Goodwife (Sarah Thomas); Mrs. Tyler, a Goodwife (Louise Gold); Richard IV, A King (Brian Blessed); Stuntman (Gareth Milne)

The black plague has returned to England. To make matters worse, King Richard has been stricken with an illness that makes him even more violent than usual. The King's council is of the opinion that the recent string of ill fortune is because an evil spirit possesses the King. They urge Edmund to hire the Witchsmeller Pursuivant. The Witchsmeller tries to ingratiate himself with the council and concurrently thwart Edmund's skepticism by placing Edmund on trial for witchcraft.

After its two strongest offerings, *The Black Adder* series serves up its weakest entry in "The Witchsmeller Pursuivant." The main problem is that the episode just isn't all that funny. Aside from some fairly amusing courtroom exchanges, much of the fault lies at the feet of guest star Frank Finlay in the title role.

Finlay's portrayal of the ranting, maniacal witch hunter passes beyond the bounds of parody, even beyond satire. Instead of being comical, the character is evil and ultimately tiresome. This is especially surprising given Finlay's credentials as an actor. Fundamentally a stage actor, Finlay was featured in many films. His performance as Iago in the 1965 version of *Othello* won him an Academy Award nomination. Perhaps it was Finlay's well-won reputation that landed him the role of the Witchsmeller, when less of an actor but more of a comic may have been called for. Finlay is given star status in the opening titles.

Another flaw in the episode is the use of devices not used elsewhere in the series. The first is Baldrick's unexplained ability to physically transport himself and his friends to another part of the castle. The second is the Queen's skill at witchcraft, which is used to resolve the episode's plot. The weakness in using these ploys is that no similar plot devices are employed or even hinted at in the other five shows of the series. They introduce a fantasy element in a program that heretofore has kept itself rooted firmly in reality, albeit very silly reality.

What few highlights there are in this uneven offering come in the trial scene. At one point the Witchsmeller accuses Edmund of being overly familiar with his cat, Bubbles, which the Witchsmeller insists is short for "Beelzebubbles." Edmund admits that he was talking to the cat but, he contends, only to ask the feline if she wanted some milk. The Witchsmeller persistently hounds Edmund as to what he meant by "milk."

A frustrated Edmund cries that he meant, "bloody milk," leaving the prosecution to note that he fed the cat blood mixed with milk.

Edmund's horse, Black Satin, is also brought in to testify that he has joined his master in satanic orgies. When the horse fails to speak, the Witchsmeller accuses the animal of hiding the truth.

Episode 6: "The Black Seal" ★★

Air date: July 20, 1983. Cast in Order of Disappearance: Murdered Lord (John Carlisle); Cain, a Blind Beggar (Bert Parnaby); Able, a Blind Beggar (Roy Evans); Trusting Father (Forbes Collins); Person of Unrestricted Growth (Des Webb); Retired Morris Dancer (John Barrard); Mad Gerald (Himself); Pigeon Vendor (Perry Benson); Friar Bellows (Paul Brooke); Jack Large (Big Mick); Three Fingered Pete (Roger Sloman); Guy of Glastonbury (Patrick Malahide); Sir Wilfred Death (John Hallam); Hawk (Patrick Allen); Sean, the Irish Bastard (Ron Cook); Harry, Prince of Wales (Robert East); Queen (Elspet Gray); King Richard IV (Brian Blessed); Flat Adder (Rowan Atkinson); Baldrick (Tony Robinson); Percy the Poisoner (Tim McInnerny); Stuntman (Gareth Milne)

It is St. Juniper's Day 1498 and, by tradition, King Richard IV has gathered his kinfolk to bestow honors upon them. Whereas his eldest son, Harry, is lavished with additional honors and titles, Edmund has his only substantial title (duke of Edinburgh) stripped from him. Left only with the title of Warden of the Royal Privy, Edmund decides it is time to rid his life of all the "chaff." His main means to this end is to fire his only acquaintances, Percy and Baldrick. Having done this, he leaves the castle to organize the most desperate band of villains England has ever known in hopes of capturing the throne and installing himself as king.

The final installment of *The Black Adder* is a departure from the rest of the series in that the supporting cast is for all intents and purposes jettisoned. Except for the first scene and final scene, nothing is seen of Tony Robinson, Tim McInnerny, Brian Blessed, Robert East, or Elspet Gray. Ironically, in this and the previous episode, each of the cast of regulars is given a visual and credit in the opening title sequence.

This final episode also sets a rather gruesome precedent, which carries forward into the other installments of the *Blackadder* saga: the demise of its main characters. In this first series, Edmund is mutilated to the brink of death (but drinks poison before he can die from his injuries), and the entire court and royal family swallows poisoned wine. Only Percy (who put the poison in the wine) and Baldrick are left alive. This helps to set history back on course, since presumably, with the death of the Plantagenets, Henry Tudor can finally assume the throne of England. The other series also end grimly, although not always with good cause, except perhaps that it was the writers' macabre way of bringing each series to closure.

Blackadder II

By Richard Curtis and Ben Elton. Directed by Mandie Fletcher. Produced by John Lloyd

EPISODE 1: "BELLS" ★★★

Air date: January 9, 1986. Cast: Edmund Blackadder (Rowan Atkinson); Lord Percy (Tim McInnerny); Baldrick (Tony Robinson); Queen Elizabeth I (Miranda Richardson); Lord Melchett (Stephen Fry); Nursie (Patsy Byrne); Kate (Gabrielle Glaister); Flashheart (Rik Mayall); Dr. Leech (John Grillo); Kate's Father (Edward Jewesbury); Wisewoman (Barbara Miller); Young Crone (Sadie Shimmin)

To support her aged father by means other than prostitution, Kate decides to disguise herself as a teenaged boy and seek employment in London. Calling herself "Bob," she finds a position as the servant of Lord Edmund Blackadder, displacing his lifelong menial, Baldrick. Edmund finds himself strangely attracted to Bob, which worries him greatly. Finally, Blackadder decides to fire Bob. When he does, she reveals her true gender and Edmund immediately proposes. When the best man, Edmund's flamboyant school chum, Flashheart, arrives however he manages to insult or assault the guests and steal the bride.

"Bells" is a bright start to what would prove a witty, well-written series. Aside from introducing the principal cast members, this episode also features Brit-com star Rik Mayall (*The Young Ones, Bottom, The New Statesman*) in his first appearance as the flamboyant, egotistical, oversexed Flashheart. He would reprise the role a few centuries later in *Blackadder Goes Forth*. Barbara Miller (Wisewoman) played similar roles in the first and fifth episodes of *The Black Adder* series.

"Bells" is full of good scenes, many of which go to Tim McInnerny's hopelessly thick Percy. When Bob arrives, Edmund instinctively (although not consciously) sees through her disguise, but Percy roughhouses with her as if she were a genuine young "roister-doister." Later, Percy has similar problems when the grimy and bearded Baldrick is being fitted for a gown in anticipation of being Kate's maid of honor. Percy cozies up to Baldrick as Edmund watches in disbelief. As Baldrick plays coy (any positive attention is welcome to him), Percy succeeds in eliciting a kiss from the servant. It is only after Edmund explains that Percy's vision of loveliness is Baldrick in a dress does Percy's ardor turn to revulsion.

Edmund's visit to the Wisewoman is amusing also. After explaining he is in love with his boy servant, the crone gives him three options. First, he can kill Bob. Second, he can kill himself. Rejecting these, Edmund is given a final option, which will allow him to enjoy his servant and assure that they will never be found out: kill everyone else in the entire world.

Episode 2: "Head" ★★★½

Air date: January 16, 1986. Cast: Edmund Blackadder (Rowan Atkinson); Lord Percy (Tim McInnerny); Baldrick (Tony Robinson); Queen Elizabeth I (Miranda Richardson); Lord Melchett (Stephen Fry); Nursie (Patsy Byrne); Lady Farrow (Holly de Jong); Gaoler Ploppy (Bill Wallis); Mrs. Ploppy (Linda Polan); Earl Farrow (Patrick Duncan)

Edmund is appointed lord high executioner, a thankless job that most appointees rarely survive for a week. Edmund's first executive decision in his new job is to move Wednesday's executions to Monday, so that he and the staff can have the middle of the week off. Problems arise when Edmund learns that not only has the staff executed a man early but also the wrong man at that—one that the Queen has decided to pardon.

"Head" is slightly better than its predecessor in the series if only because the characters are better defined. Miranda Richardson's portrayal of Queen Elizabeth I is especially improved upon from the first episode, making her the marvelously petulant, silly, and childish monarch who would elevate *Blackadder II* to new heights of entertainment.

Bill Wallis's Ploppy, son of Ploppy the Slopper, has come down quite a bit from the first series of the saga in which he played one of the killer knights in "The Archbishop." There's a wonderfully silly exchange when Edmund meets his execution staff, which includes the jailer, Ploppy; the last meal cook, Mrs. Ploppy (no relation); and the executioner, Baldrick, who announces he is willing to change his name to Ploppy to help foster a family atmosphere.

Ploppy explains to Edmund that it was from his father that he inherited his array of fascinating skin ailments. Edmund congratulates Ploppy, noting that even in their age of pestilence and abnormality, Ploppy has achieved new levels of repulsiveness.

"I would shake your hand," Edmund observes, "but I fear it would come off."

"There's not many bosses would be that considerate, sir" is Ploppy's heartfelt reply.

EPISODE 3: "POTATO" ★★★★

Air date: January 23, 1986. Cast: Edmund Blackadder (Rowan Atkinson); Lord Percy (Tim McInnerny); Baldrick (Tony Robinson); Queen Elizabeth I (Miranda Richardson); Lord Melchett (Stephen Fry); Nursie (Patsy Byrne); Captain Rum (Tom Baker); Sir Walter Raleigh (Simon Jones)

All of England is celebrating the return of explorer Walter Raleigh. Everyone except Edmund, who feels that Raleigh is terribly overrated and smells of fish. To put an end to Raleigh's boasting, Edmund claims he will lead his own dangerous expedition. Once on their way, Edmund explains to Percy and Baldrick that he intends their cruise to actually be a six-month holiday in France. They soon discover that their captain only knows how to sail around the Isle of Wight; in addition he has no crew. Soon they are hopelessly lost at sea.

With "Potato" *Blackadder II* ascends to its zenith, and although all the episodes in the series are funny and entertaining, this is the best. Perhaps it is because "Potato" manages to integrate historical farce into its story better than any of the other five entries. This ploy, which is presumably the cornerstone of the entire saga, is especially well done throughout most of *Blackadder the Third.*

Fans of British sci-fi TV should enjoy seeing Simon Jones doing a very able turn as Sir Walter Raleigh and Tom Baker completely and marvelously over the top as Captain Rum, the madman Blackadder hires to captain his expedition. Jones played Arthur Dent on *Hitchhiker's Guide to the Galaxy*, while of course Baker was the fourth incarnation of Doctor Who.

Blackadder's meeting with the eccentric Captain Rum is silly and thus entertaining. Upon agreeing to hire his ship, Blackadder offers Rum his hand to seal the arrangement. "You have a woman's hand!" Rum bellows as he strokes Blackadder's appendage, adding that by his estimation Edmund's delicate digits have never performed hard shipboard labor.

Blackadder admits the statement to be true. From there, the Captain makes similar observations regarding Edmund's supposedly feminine skin, purse, mouth, and legs. Each remark is sillier than the one preceding it, including a wager that the purse had "never been used as a rowing boat" for shipwrecked mariners.

EPISODE 4: "MONEY" ★★★½

Air date: February 6, 1986. Cast: Edmund Blackadder (Rowan Atkinson); Lord Percy (Tim McInnerny); Baldrick (Tony Robinson); Queen Elizabeth I (Miranda Richardson); Lord Melchett (Stephen Fry); Nursie (Patsy Byrne);

Bishop of Bath and Wells (Ronald Lacey); Mollie (Cassie Stuart); Mrs. Pants (Leslie Nicol); Arthur (John Pierce Jones); Mad Beggar (Tony Aitken); Leonardo Acropolis (Philip Pope); Messenger (Piers Ibbotson); Mr. Pants (Barry Craine)

Edmund's £1,000 loan from the sadistic Bishop of Bath and Wells has come due. The Bishop informs him that if Edmund does not pay by sundown, he will be impaled with a spike up the bottom. Unfortunately, Edmund only has £85 to his name, which launches him on a frantic scramble for some life-saving cash.

A small step down from "Potato," "Money" is nevertheless very funny with a sturdy, simple plot filled with a number of interesting twists and turns. It also features a wide array of interesting characters from Ronald Lacey's "baby-eating" Bishop, to Cassie Stuart's "reasonably priced" prostitute, to Tony Aitken's Beggar taken right out of *King Lear*. In fact the only member of the larger-than-average cast not to have a funny part is Piers Ibbotson in an incidental role as the Messenger.

Edmund's attempts to earn £1,000 via prostituting Baldrick are woefully inept and wonderfully amusing. As Baldrick stands in the fog holding a sign that reads "Get It Here," a burly sailor approaches. He offers Baldrick a penny in return for a kiss, but Edmund refuses to let his servant work so cheaply. It turns out the sailor, named Arthur, is homesick and misses his mother's affection. Finally, they work out an arrangement for tuppence for which the sailor will get a kiss on the cheek and a bedtime story. After a children's story about a squirrel, Arthur is quite touched but quickly recovers to lecherously ask Edmund the price of a "good hard shag."

There's also a glimpse into the real estate tactics of the Elizabethan era as Edmund shows his home to Mr. and Mrs. Pants. Mrs. Pants asks about the privies. Edmund describes the facilities as the "very latest in front-wall, fresh-air orifices, combined with a wide-capacity gutter installation below."

From this, the prospective buyer rightly concludes one must go out the windows. Edmund admits as much, clinching the sale since the Pantses can't stand those dirty indoor bathrooms.

Episode 5: "Beer" ★★½

Air date: February 13, 1986. Cast: Edmund Blackadder (Rowan Atkinson); Lord Percy (Tim McInnerny); Baldrick (Tony Robinson); Queen Elizabeth I (Miranda Richardson); Lord Melchett (Stephen Fry); Nursie (Patsy Byrne); Lady Whiteadder (Miriam Margolyes); Simon Partridge (Hugh Laurie); Geoffrey Piddle (Roger Blake); Monk (William Hootkins); Lord Whiteadder (Daniel Thorndike)

Edmund's rich puritanical aunt and uncle are coming to dinner to discuss his inheritance. Unfortunately, Edmund is goaded into having a drinking party and contest with Melchett the same evening. Unable to postpone either, Edmund holds the diametrically opposed gatherings simultaneously across the hall from one another.

Probably the weakest entry in *Blackadder II* (which is akin to being the worst Rembrandt), "Beer" is still entertaining television and is only weak in comparison to the other episodes. Still, the proceedings build up to a rather predictable climax, and there is less of the sharp dialogue one has come to expect from Curtis and Elton.

Hugh Laurie makes his first appearance in the *Blackadder* saga and would appear in every episode hence except for the specials. Uncharacteristically, he is largely one-dimensional and wasted in this part.

Although in this episode she appears as a chaste character, Miriam Margolyes should be recognizable as the actress who added such lusty verve to the part of the Spanish Infanta in *The Blackadder.*

Most of the episode involves Edmund's harried shuttling back and forth between the dinner and drinking parties, and this quickly becomes predictable. The best moments in the episode come prior to this and involve Baldrick.

The first bit concerns Baldrick wearing a headpiece, which leaves a piece of cheese dangling in front of his mouth. Baldrick informs his master that the device is a mousetrap. Baldrick explains that he lies on the floor with his mouth open and waits for the rodents to run in. Later in the episode Baldrick returns wearing the same contraption save with a mouse dangling where the cheese had previously been. Baldrick relates to his confounded employer that he is tired of an all-mouse diet and is attempting to move up to cats.

EPISODE 6: "CHAINS" ★★★½

Air date: February 20, 1986. Cast: Edmund Blackadder (Rowan Atkinson); Lord Percy (Tim McInnerny); Baldrick (Tony Robinson); Queen Elizabeth I (Miranda Richardson); Lord Melchett (Stephen Fry); Nursie (Patsy Byrne); Prince Ludwig (Hugh Laurie); Torturer (Max Harvey); 1st Guard (Mark Arden); 2nd Guard (Lee Corners)

A rash of kidnapping spreads across England, with Blackadder and Melchett the latest victims. The pair soon discover they are captives of German Prince Ludwig, an archvillain and master of disguise with plans to dominate the world. When the Queen decides to save the ransom money and throw a fancy dress party instead, Blackadder and Melchett agree to betray her in return for their lives. Ludwig, leaves to hatch his plot, but the two prisoners quickly escape from their stupidly methodical guards. Edmund enters the party in time to stab Ludwig who has come to the gala disguised as Nursie dressed in a cow costume. Ludwig vows his revenge as he escapes. After the closing titles, a brief epilogue reveals that the main characters have been slaughtered and Ludwig has assumed the throne disguised as the Queen.

Although it has the same gruesome outcome as *The Black Adder*, *Blackadder II* manages to maintain its nonsensical tone right up to the final credits. In fact, it seems that the series has ended well for the main characters until a brief scene tagged on after the credits reveals the true ending. It seems that this was added almost out of principle. In any event, even this carnage is amusing, unlike the somber coda to the first series.

Hugh Laurie is back in a much meatier role than was given to him in "Beer." Unfortunately, as in the final episode of *The Black Adder*, Tim McInnerny and Tony Robinson have much smaller parts in which to display their comic talents.

One of the more clever bits involves Edmund and his Spanish torturer attempting to trade insults despite their inability to speak each other's language. They bridge their communication gap with an impudent game of charades.

The character of Prince Ludwig also supplies his share of fun. Ludwig is the sort of villain one usually sees in a James Bond film, only here he is in Elizabethan times. A master of disguise, over the course of the episode Ludwig reveals to Blackadder, Melchett, and the Queen that he was Big Sally, the waitress; Flossie, the sheep; and Shorty-Greasy-Spot-Spot, the stable boy.

For all the buffoonery packed into "Chains," perhaps the biggest audience laugh is generated by a throwaway line. At the party the Queen finds Baldrick sitting in the corner with two pencils stuck up his nostrils. When the Queen inquires what Baldrick is supposed to be, he deadpans that he has come as a pencil box.

Blackadder the Third

By Richard Curtis and Ben Elton. Directed by Mandie Fletcher. Produced by John Lloyd

EPISODE 1: "DISH AND DISHONESTY" ★★★½

Air date: September 17, 1987. Cast: Edmund Blackadder (Rowan Atkinson); Baldrick (Tony Robinson); Prince Regent (Hugh Laurie); Mrs. Miggins (Helen Atkinson-Wood); Mr. Vincent Hanna (Vincent Hanna); Sir Talbot Buxomly (Denis Lill); Pitt the Younger (Simon Osborne); Ivor Biggun (Geoff McGivern); Pitt the Even Younger (Master Dominic Martelli)

When the prepubescent Pitt the Younger becomes prime minister, he names the three primary targets of his administration: Napoleon, his old geography teacher, and the Prince Regent. He notes that the Prince has spent £59,000 on socks alone and suggests that Parliament withdraw its funding.

To avert a household financial crisis, Edmund Blackadder, the Prince's butler, decides they must win a key seat in Parliament.

The excellent *Black Adder the Third* series begins with a foray into the realm of 18th-century British politics. Although the humor of the script is sufficiently strong to enjoy without a degree in European history, some of the finer points will be lost without at least a cursory knowledge.

First and most relevant for the rest of the series is the role of the Prince Regent. Hugh Laurie's character, Prince George, is the eldest son of King George III. Although his father's first bout with insanity would occur in roughly the span of time represented in the series (the late 1700s), George would not actually become Prince Regent until 1811. He then served as Regent for nine years until his father's death.

The references to Pitt the Elder and Younger are based on the father and son prime ministers, both named William. Although their terms of service as inferred from the script follow directly upon one an other, this was not the case. The real Pitt the Elder served from 1756 to 1761. He died in 1778. Pitt the Younger was first prime minister from 1783 to 1801. The term "the Younger" is appropriate not only because his father was prominent in politics but also because he first became prime minister at the youthful age of 24. The script makes great fun of Pitt's tender age and his schoolboy insecurities and exaggerates them to great comic effect.

The historical references conflict so wildly in this episode that it makes it pointless to attempt to give them any weight. For example, Pitt became prime minister in 1783, but he names Napoleon as a threat, although Napoleon would not ascend to power for another 12 years. He also rails against a Prince Regent who would not become one for another 28 years. Still, this is historical farce at its broadest and, ultimately, who cares?

The high points of the first episode are many. When they need a pliable soul to do their bidding in Parliament, Blackadder feels Baldrick is the perfect candidate to run. While helping Baldrick fill out his application for office, however, Blackadder encounters trouble from the first question: name. Baldrick isn't sure but guesses his first name is "Sod off," since that is how his childhood playmates used to greet his arrival. Blackadder shortens his full name to simply "S. Baldrick" for the application.

Next, he asks what Baldrick's minimum bribe level would be. Not wanting to price himself out of the market, Baldrick announces he could be had for one turnip.

It is here that we learn the overriding obsession in Baldrick's life is turnips. In an attempt to fathom his dogsbody's value system, Blackadder asks what Baldrick would do with £1,000 pounds. Baldrick replies wistfully that he would purchase a little turnip of his own. When Blackadder ups the supposition to a million pounds, Baldrick becomes more serious, stating he would buy a large turnip in the country.

Episode 2: "Ink and Incapability" ★★★★

Air date: September 24, 1987. Cast: Edmund Blackadder (Rowan Atkinson); Baldrick (Tony Robinson); Prince Regent (Hugh Laurie); Dr. Samuel Johnson (Robbie Coltrane); Mrs. Miggins (Helen Atkinson-Wood); Shelley (Lee Cornes); Byron (Steve Steen); Coleridge (Jim Sweeney)

In order to raise his dismal intellectual reputation, the Prince decides to sponsor the latest work of Dr. Samuel Johnson: the first English dictionary. Unfortunately, no one in the Prince's household can see the value of such a book, and the only manuscript is burned by Baldrick to start a fire. Blackadder must attempt to reproduce in one weekend what took Dr. Johnson ten years to complete or face a painful death at the hands of England's literary community.

After politics in the first episode, the second installment of *Blackadder the Third* delves into the world of 18th-century letters. It is a stroke of genius on the part of Curtis and Elton to juxtapose that era's literary giants with their ridiculous, inane characters Prince George and Baldrick. As is the usual case with the Blackadders, Edmund is cool toward the greatness that surrounds him and feigns boredom to cover his jealousy.

Historically, Dr. Samuel Johnson's *Dictionary* only took eight years to write, instead of the ten claimed here. The book was sponsored by a group of booksellers, not the Prince Regent. Johnson was not a contemporary of Byron (b. 1788) or Shelley (b. 1792) since both were born after Johnson died in 1784. He could have possibly known Samuel Taylor Coleridge, but this too is unlikely, since Coleridge was only 12 when Johnson passed away.

Robbie Coltrane is excellent as the brilliant and pompous Samuel Johnson. The only thing that makes his performance that much more glowing is its teaming with Hugh Laurie's vacuous Prince Regent. It is delightful to witness the exchanges between England's greatest mind and its most obtuse.

"I celebrated last night the encyclopedic implementation of my premeditated orchestration of demotic Anglo-Saxon," Johnson announces upon his arrival.

The Prince nods and grins for a moment before admitting he hasn't understood a word of Johnson's sentence. Dr. Johnson tries to restate his description of the *Dictionary*, but the Prince is still lost, although he admits it sounds "damn saucy," especially the bit about being given some "Norman tongue."

Dr. Johnson's frustration over the Prince's response is only compounded by Blackadder's attempts to unnerve his confidence that the work is all-inclusive. Blackadder does this by dropping ersatz but realistic sounding words, such as "contrafribularities, phrasmotic, and interphrastically."

Episode 3: "Nob and Nobility" ★★★½

Air date: October 1, 1987. Cast: Edmund Blackadder (Rowan Atkinson); Baldrick (Tony Robinson); Prince Regent (Hugh Laurie); Mrs. Miggins (Helen

Atkinson-Wood); Lord Topper (Tim McInnerny); Lord Smedley (Nigel Planer); Ambassador (Chris Barrie)

All of London is agog over the exploits of the Scarlet Pimpernel — all except Edmund Blackadder, that is. In order to silence a pair of the Prince's foppish friends, Edmund accepts a wager that he can go to France, rescue a doomed aristocrat, and bring him back alive. Edmund and Baldrick set off for a week amid the dangers of the revolution but actually spend the seven days peacefully in the kitchen. Before returning to his duties, Blackadder picks up an expatriated French aristocrat — one Count de Frou Frou — at Mrs. Miggins' Pie Shop. When Edmund and Baldrick bring de Frou Frou to the French embassy, it turns out that the revolutionaries have extended their grasp across the Channel. All three are imprisoned with execution scheduled for the morning.

After two episodes that were historically intensive, the third episode of the series turns to fiction for its plot material. Borrowing from Baroness Emmuska Orczy's novel, "Nob and Nobility" returns to life the Scarlet Pimpernel — the outwardly foppish English aristocrat who saves victims from the French Revolution. Not only do Curtis and Elton borrow from Orczy's classic but from themselves. The plot here has more than passing similarities to not one but two installments of *Blackadder II*. Blackadder's jealousy of the hero of the day (here the Scarlet Pimpernel; in *Blackadder II*'s "Potato," Sir Walter Raleigh) causes him to boast that he can duplicate the heroics. In both, Blackadder plans only to pretend to accomplish what he has boasted he would do. The device of being kidnapped by foreigners was also used in the second series' "Chains," although there it was the primary plot, not a secondary one as it is in "Nob and Nobility." All this aside, the authors' reusing their own plots doesn't seem to hurt as this episode is well scripted, well performed, and has plenty of laughs.

One of the strengths of "Nob and Nobility" is certainly its supporting cast. Tim McInnerny is on hand for his only appearance in *Blackadder the Third*. He does his usual funny turn as half of the duo that performs the Pimpernel's daring duties. The other fop/hero is well played by Nigel Planer. Planer was one of the title characters in Ben Elton's *The Young Ones* earlier in the decade. Finally, the revolutionary-turned-ambassador is humorous portrayed by Chris Barrie, who at the time of this episode's airing was less than six months away from his role as Rimmer on the cult favorite *Red Dwarf*.

One thing British comedy lampoons extremely well is the French. Although this was touched upon in "The Black Seal" episode of *The Black Adder*, it reaches full flower in "Nob and Nobility," as Edmund cringes at his country's newfound fascination with anything French. Even Mrs. Miggins' Pie Shop is overrun with French aristocrats, French food, and French phrases. "Bonjour, monsieur," Mrs. Miggins cackles as she greets Edmund, adding for his enlightenment, "It's French!"

"So is eating frogs, cruelty to geese, and urinating in the street, but that's no reason to inflict it on the rest of us," Edmund sneers.

Episode 4: "Sense and Senility" ★★★★

Air date: October 8, 1987. Cast: Edmund Blackadder (Rowan Atkinson); Baldrick (Tony Robinson); Prince Regent (Hugh Laurie); Keanrick (Hugh Paddick); Mossop (Kenneth Conner); Mrs. Miggins (Helen Atkinson-Wood); Anarchist (Ben Elton)

When an anarchist attacks the Prince one evening at the theater, Blackadder suggests that the Prince placate the oppressed masses by delivering a speech designed to show he is a sensitive regent. The Prince agrees to present a speech written by Edmund but insists that Keanrick and Mossop, two hammy actors, instruct him on its delivery.

If comedy is to be judged on the basis of sheer laugh production, then "Sense and Senility" is easily the zenith of *Blackadder the Third.* Curtis and Elton have provided a simple yet sturdy premise and fleshed it out with a script that is both clever and silly. As with all the entries in this third incarnation of *Blackadder*, the supporting cast — namely Hugh Paddick and Kenneth Conner — is wonderful. Although they are not as well known to American audiences as some of the other supporting cast members from this series, both Paddick and Conner have appeared in numerous British comedies. Conner may be recognizable to fans of *'Allo, 'Allo*, and the *Carry On* films. Cowriter Ben Elton appears briefly as an anarchist who lobs a bomb at Prince George.

Although "Sense and Senility" is laugh-out-loud funny from start to finish (and arguably the best of all the *Blackadders*), there are some standout moments. First, there is idiotic Prince George's inability to distinguish between real life and acting. Thus, when he witnesses a murder on the stage, George interrupts the play to call for the arrest of the actors. When the play is over and an anarchist lobs a bomb at him, George catches the device and believes that it is part of the show. His powerlessness to grasp the concept of theater continues even after the bomb goes off.

The efforts of Paddick and Conner as the overly dramatic actors are wonderful. They first arrive at the palace just after Edmund has explained to Baldrick that it is extremely bad luck to mention Shakespeare's *Macbeth* to an actor. Of course after he ushers them in, Blackadder ignores his own admonition and utters "Macbeth" as often as he can. Each time he does, the actors are compelled to go through an elaborate ritual to exorcise the ill fortune brought on by the mention of "the Scottish play." The rite includes a round of patty-caking while chanting (as best as I can tell, although I have heard different translations of the rapidly spoken lines), "Hot potato, off his drawers, pluck to make amends." This last phrase is punctuated by each actor twisting the other's nose. Although it is oft repeated this silly bit never loses its comic effect.

The actors' actual elocution lesson for Prince George is also wonderful. As they attempt to replicate their own horrendous style, they instruct the Prince to effect a ridiculous stance in which his feet are far apart and his groin is thrust far forward.

Finally, the session ends with a lesson in how to roar before speaking in order to evoke the proper sense of respect from the audience. George's roar turns out to be an uncontrollable bellow, which of course the pair praise excessively — as one tends to do when critiquing royalty. The Prince puts the stance and the ear-splitting roar together, only to revert to a sedate delivery to read: "Unaccustomed as I am to public speaking..."

EPISODE 5: "AMY AND AMIABILITY" ★★★½

Air date: October 15, 1987. Cast: Edmund Blackadder (Rowan Atkinson); Baldrick (Tony Robinson); Prince Regent (Hugh Laurie); Mrs. Miggins (Helen Atkinson-Wood); Amy Hardwood (Miranda Richardson); Sally Cheapside (Barbara Horne); Duke of Cheapside (Roger Avon)

Seeking to quickly regain their financial solvency, Edmund recommends the Prince marry into wealth. After a tireless search Edmund discovers a worthy bride: Amy Hardwood, the daughter of an industrialist. The courtship of the Prince is fraught with difficulty since Amy is a delicate "fluffy bunny" of a girl, and the Prince merely wants to make rude sex talk to her, followed, he hopes, by rude sex.

"Amy and Amiability," like "Nob and Nobility," concerns itself with another of the romantic figures of the late 18th-century: the highwayman. Oddly, however, it is this portion of the plot that presents its weakest link. A good two-thirds of the episode revolves around the attempt to marry Prince George to the overly sugary Amy Hardwood. This, coupled with Blackadder's try at highway robbery (with Baldrick in harness as his horse, Quicksilver), provides as much laughter as any *Blackadder* installments. Unfortunately, what should provide a climax to the hilarity — the revelation that the saccharine Amy is in reality a notorious highwayman — is ultimately anticlimactic.

Miranda Richardson, who played Queen Elizabeth in *Blackadder II*, is very funny as the icky Amy but not as humorous as the bandit.

As stated above, Edmund's efforts to procure a wealthy wife for the Prince Regent provide abundant mirth for much of the episode. When the Prince first resigns himself to the idea of marriage, he is quite particular about the type of woman he would wed. "They've got to be lovers, laughers, dancers..."

"And bonkers," Edmund adds.

Unfortunately, during Edmund's search of the 262 princesses in Europe, he finds that 165 are over 80, 47 are under 10, and 39 are insane. These last 39 would have been perfect save for the fact that they all got married the previous week to the same horse. From the 262, only two are left. One is a terrible shrew, which leaves only the Grand Duchess of Turin, who is disqualified on the basis of having actually met the Prince.

Ultimately Edmund gives up his quest for a royal pairing and settles on the daughter of an industrialist who has more mills than the Prince has brain cells — seven to be precise. Edmund informs the Prince of his candidate, and George decides to begin the wooing with a letter announcing his intentions. After dictating a note in which the Prince calls his prospective bride a "saucy young trollop" and a "lucky tart" and urges her to come around with a naughty negligee and lots of money, Edmund decides he had better handle the courtship.

There is a particularly riotous scene in which the Prince comes to serenade Amy with poetry. Fortunately Blackadder accompanies him, thus narrowly preventing the Prince from reciting "Harold the Horny Hunter" and making good on his promise to deliver a consignment of "German sausage."

While Amy waits on her balcony, Edmund recites sticky love rhymes with his hand firmly clamped over the Prince's mouth. The ploy succeeds in fooling Amy, who proclaims George the "snugglie wuggliest lambkin in the whole of Toyland."

The ruse finally falls apart when she invites "Prince Cuddlykitten" to scale the ivy to her balcony, causing George to boisterously proclaim it to be "sausage time."

EPISODE 6: "DUEL AND DUALITY" ★★★½

Air date: October 22, 1987. Cast: Edmund Blackadder (Rowan Atkinson); Baldrick (Tony Robinson); Prince Regent (Hugh Laurie); Mrs. Miggins (Helen Atkinson-Wood); Duke of Wellington (Stephen Fry); King George III (Gertan Klauber)

When Prince George takes sexual advantage of the Duke of Wellington's nieces, the Duke challenges the Prince to a duel. This means certain death for the Prince. Baldrick suggests that the Prince get someone to take his place, then recommends Blackadder. When the Duke calls on the Prince prior to the duel, Edmund and George switch places. The Duke, expecting an idiot of a regent, is impressed with Blackadder's playing of the Prince and regrets he will have to kill him. George, on the other hand, annoys Wellington to no end and receives several beatings at his hand.

During the duel — which incidentally is waged with cannons — Edmund is struck down. After a brief death scene, Edmund discovers he has been saved by a metal cigarillo case given him earlier by Wellington. George arrives to announce what fun the whole exercise has been. Unable to suffer him any more, Wellington shoots George. The King arrives, takes Edmund to be his son (due to his madness), and leaves with Edmund and Wellington to enjoy dinner. Baldrick starts a soliloquy to the dead George, who recovers to announce that he too had a cigarillo box. As he reaches into his vest for the case, George realizes that he left it on his dresser and quickly dies.

Blackadder the Third, one of the most consistently funny series on either side of the Atlantic, finishes its brief run as strongly as it began. Unlike any of the other title characters in the saga, this one manages to survive the final episode. Not only that, but he apparently takes the place of the Prince Regent and, one assumes, will become King.

After a respite of three episodes, the series also returns to the realm of history with a visit from the Duke of Wellington. Apparently this installment takes place in the midst of the Napoleonic Wars, as Blackadder himself suggests that Nelson position his fleet at Trafalgar. As in the series' other historic presentations, this one is rife with errors, which are quickly overlooked amidst the laughter. Stephen Fry makes a memorable (albeit a touch overbearing) appearance as the Iron Duke, making him the last of the three supporting regulars from *Blackadder II* to guest star in the subsequent series.

Following many references to him in the first five episodes, we finally get a brief glimpse at the mad King George III. His royal lunacy does not disappoint. What is somewhat disappointing, however, is Rowan Atkinson's uncredited appearance as his own Scottish twin cousin. Mad MacAdder has little to do and is not really essential to the plot.

By far the best moments in "Duel and Duality" involve Edmund's swapping roles with the Prince to face the irate, blustering Duke of Wellington. Blackadder suggests that he and the Prince exchange coats and wigs to effect the charade. The Prince agrees and mentions that it is just like that story, "The Prince and the Porpoise." (Although it would be almost 100 years before Mark Twain penned *The Prince and the Pauper*.)

Not only does George have difficulty understanding that a porpoise will not be joining them in their scheme, he cannot even grasp the proper way to address a Prince. Blackadder reminds him that George must treat him as if he were the Prince.

When Wellington arrives, the fun begins in earnest as the Duke enjoys beating up George for the slightest infractions. The climax of this physical scene comes when the Duke punches George in the nose and Edmund gently corrects him for it. Wellington contends that he hardly touched George and proceeds to demonstrate a hard punch on the hapless George. Blackadder joins in with his interpretation of what constitutes hard and soft blows. Soon the two men are pummeling George around the drawing room as they debate what constitutes cruelty to servants.

One last note: in England a Wellington (or Wellie) is a rubber boot. This bit of trivia is essential to fully enjoy the Duke's warning to the Prince: "When a man soils a Wellington, he puts his foot in it."

Comic Relief Special

Blackadder: "The Cavalier Years" ★★★½

Richard Curtis and Ben Elton—Air date: February 8, 1988. Cast: Sir Edmund Blackadder (Rowan Atkinson); Baldrick (Tony Robinson); Charles I (Stephen Fry); Oliver Cromwell (Warren Clarke)

As the last faithful subject of Charles I, Blackadder tries in vain to save the doomed sovereign's life before ultimately becoming his executioner.

Taking a leap backwards, from the period of *Blackadder the Third*, this 15-minute sketch provides a hilarious slant to the English Civil War. Essentially, the characters of Blackadder and Baldrick are the same as in the third series (and for that matter the second) and do not disappoint in this new historical setting. At the outset, Blackadder is trying to save the king's life from Cromwell and the Roundheads, although Baldrick's obtuseness dooms this venture almost from the start. With his own life in jeopardy from taking the wrong stance in the Civil War, Blackadder quickly reverts to form and finds a way to save his own neck and turn a profit as well.

The true inspiration in this Curtis/Elton farce is the construction of the Charles I character. Although it would be lost on most American audiences, Stephen Fry's interpretation of the ill-fated King is actually a hilarious imitation of a much more recent Charles: the Prince of Wales. Fry's affectations are quite hilarious as the King politely converses with Cromwell, the man after his life, as the current Charles would chat with an ordinary worker during a public relations appearance at a factory. When he is informed by Cromwell that he, Cromwell, is now the lord protector of England, Charles asks, "What does a lord protector do?" Given the grim answer, Charles, with patronizing enthusiasm, replies, "Fascinating."

Christmas Special 1988

"Blackadder's Christmas Carol" ★★★

Richard Curtis and Ben Elton. Directed by Richard Boden. Produced by John Lloyd—Air date: December 23, 1988. Cast: Blackadders (Rowan Atkinson); Baldricks (Tony Robinson); Queens Elizabeth I/Asphyxia XIX (Miranda Richardson); Lords Melchett/Fondo (Stephen Fry); Princes Regent/Pigmot (Hugh Laurie); Spirit of Christmas (Robbie Coltrane); Queen Victoria (Miriam Margolyes); Prince Albert (Jim Broadbent); Nursie/Bernard (Patsy Byrne); Beadle (Denis Lill); Mrs. Scratchit (Pauline Melville); Lord Nelson (Philip Pope); Millicent (Nicola Bryant); Ralph (Ramsay Gilderdale); Enormous Orphans (David Barber, Erkan Mustafa, David Nunn)

The Spirit of Christmas affords the one benevolent Blackadder a glimpse at the fiends in his family's past and future.

A 45-minute holiday special, "Blackadder's Christmas Carol" puts a nice twist on the usual Dickens story yet doesn't quite fulfill the promise of its premise. Given the history of the Blackadders, it is a clever stroke on the part of Curtis and Elton to make the Victorian version "the kindest and loveliest man" in Great Britain. Even as such, Ebenezer Blackadder manages to be a funny character, delivering the usual barbs his ancestors did but without malice behind them. It is the setup, then, rather than the payoff that entertains most here. Once the Spirit of Christmas arrives to show Ebenezer the cads of the clan's past, the going slows considerably.

The first flashback shows the Elizabethan Blackadder managing to get Melchett a beheading for Christmas (although this couldn't have happened since Melchett dies in the final episode of the series along with the other characters). The second vision shows the Regency Blackadder trying to trick Prince George out of his Christmas presents. Neither is as inspired as the series from which they are drawn. The final visitation shows two views of the distant future: one if Ebenezer remains a kind man, the other if he doesn't. Unlike Scrooge, the exercise only proves to this current Blackadder that "bad guys have all the fun." Duly convinced, Blackadder turns mean and thus forfeits a prize that was to have been granted him by Queen Victoria.

Blackadder Goes Forth

By Richard Curtis and Ben Elton. Directed by Richard Boden. Produced by John Lloyd

Episode 1: "Captain Cook" ★★★

Air date: September 28, 1989. Cast: Captain Edmund Blackadder (Rowan Atkinson); Private S. Baldrick (Tony Robinson); General Sir Anthony Cecil Hogmanay Melchett (Stephen Fry); Lieutenant the Honorable George Colthurst St. Barleigh (Hugh Laurie); Captain Kevin Darling (Tim McInnerny)

Captain Edmund Blackadder's relatively safe existence in the trenches is about to be endangered by an upcoming attack on the German lines. In an effort to avoid this almost certain death, Blackadder tries to earn a transfer to Paris, first by becoming a magazine illustrator, then a chef.

"Captain Cook" manages to introduce plenty of good exposition for the remaining five installments but unfortunately is rather uninspired in exploiting its own premise. The plot — revolves as do all in this final *Blackadder* series — around Edmund's attempts to avoid going "over the top" from his trench to certain death at the hands of the Germans. In this premiere installment, the clever plan of disguising themselves as cooks is introduced in the first few minutes, then totally discarded until the last few minutes. The main attempt to get off the front lines — and thus the focus of the episode — is via painting.

Some of the humor is more than a little distasteful as Baldrick gives detailed descriptions of his recipes for ersatz dishes made with dog turds, cat vomit, and rats. While passages are presented with some wit, they elicit groans from members of the live audience. Later, the jokes are repeated almost verbatim as Melchett and Darling dine on the repulsive repast.

The best moments in "Captain Cook," as in most *Blackadder* escapades, are those brimming with inspired silliness. General Melchett's discourses on strategy and tactics are marvelous for their utter lack of any sense. He confidently plans the 19th in a series of suicidal full frontal attacks against entrenched positions. His reasoning is that after 18 such miserable failures, the enemy will never suspect that they would try them again.

In a similar vein of illogic, Edmund ventures into no-man's land with St. Barleighand Baldrick to make sketches of the German fortifications. As the trio crawls into a foxhole, Edmund inquires as to their position. George consults his map and notes they are in an area rife with mushrooms. When Edmund informs him that a military map is not likely to list the more noteworthy fungi of the region, George refers to the map's legend. There he discovers that the mushroomlike symbol denotes "mine." George concludes that the mushrooms are the property of the man who drew the map.

Episode 2: "Corporal Punishment" ★★★

Air date: October 5, 1989. Cast: Captain Edmund Blackadder (Rowan Atkinson); Private S. Baldrick (Tony Robinson); General Sir Anthony Cecil Hogmanay Melchett (Stephen Fry); Lieutenant the Honorable George Colthurst St. Barleigh (Hugh Laurie); Captain Kevin Darling (Tim McInnerny); Corporal Perkins (Jeremy Hardy); Corporal Jones (Stephen Frost); Private Fraser (Lee Cornes); Private Robinson (Paul Mark Elliott); Private Tipplewick (Jeremy Gittins)

A communications problem is further exacerbated when Blackadder shoots and eats a carrier pigeon. This is especially serious since the shooting of carrier pigeons has just become an offense punishable by death. To make matters even worse, the pigeon in question was Speckled Jim, a close personal friend of General Melchett.

Due to an error in messages, Edmund must have George as his defense counsel. It hardly matters, however, since Melchett is the judge. Blackadder is found guilty and is sentenced to death by firing squad.

A slight improvement over "Captain Cook," primarily on the strength of its plotting, "Corporal Punishment" still gives its best moments over to supporting players — most notably Stephen Fry as the ridiculous General Melchett.

Although secondnotch *Blackadder* is still better than most television comedy, this episode underlines one of the primary faults of the entire series: the title character. Here Captain Blackadder faces his imminent death at the hands of the firing squad in the same way he faces his almost certain death at the hands of the Germans throughout the series. In both instances, the character reacts with a bored resignation that robs him of motivation. There is little of the diabolic cunning that marked his ancestors. Fortunately there is still plenty of humor from the rest of the talented cast, but one wishes the star had outshone them all.

The kangaroo court scene has some funny moments, particularly from the characters of Baldrick and General Melchett. As Baldrick shuffles to take the stand, Blackadder quietly advises him to deny everything. Baldrick nods and obeys totally. On the stand he denies his name, his occupation, and even the identity of George.

Melchett is equally ludicrous on the stand, appearing as the main witness for the prosecution while concurrently serving as the judge. He tearfully mourns the loss of his precious boyhood pigeon, then breaks into hysterics when pointing out the culprit. Finally, as is often his wont, Melchett shifts gears completely, returning to a semblance of sanity as he proceeds to the next item of business.

Baldrick shines again as he delivers an escape kit to Blackadder in prison. The first indispensable item is a tiny duck decoy. Baldrick explains that if he is pursued near water, Blackadder can balance the decoy on his head as a brilliant disguise. Blackadder delves further into the bag and pulls out a pencil and a trumpet. Baldrick explains he has included the pencil so Edmund can write him a postcard telling him how the escape went. The trumpet is there in case Edmund has to "win favor with a difficult child" during his escape.

Jeremy Gittins, appearing here as Private Tipplewick of the firing squad, should be recognizable to fans of *Keeping Up Appearances*, in which he played Hyacinth Bucket's long-suffering Vicar.

EPISODE 3: "MAJOR STAR" ★★★½

Air date: October 12, 1989. Cast: Captain Edmund Blackadder (Rowan Atkinson); Private S. Baldrick (Tony Robinson); General Sir Anthony Cecil Hogmanay Melchett (Stephen Fry); Lieutenant the Honorable George Colthurst St. Barleigh (Hugh Laurie); Captain Kevin Darling (Tim McInnerny); Driver Parkhurst (Gabrielle Glaister)

With hopes of returning to London, Blackadder agrees to organize a morale-building troop show, despite his loathing of such theatrics. Edmund barely manages to arrange a shell of an entertainment, the star of which is George in drag. General Melchett, believing George to actually be a woman, is smitten by the show's star and announces the undertaking a success. Before the show can go to London, however, Melchett asks to escort the lovely "Georgina" to the regimental ball.

"Major Star" is one of the most entertaining entries in the *Blackadder Goes Forth* saga, which is not surprising since it capably borrows from many sources. Plot elements (female and male impersonation and amateurs putting on shows) are culled from such sources as *Some Like It Hot*, *Victor/Victoria*, and indeed even previous *Blackadders* ("Born to Be King" from *The Black Adder* and "Bells" from *Blackadder II*). This is not a criticism since most of these plots are at least as old as Shakespeare, and they are presented here with wonderful silliness. Gabrielle Glaister reprises her role of Bob from the first episode of *Blackadder II*.

There are some historical gaffes, almost obligatory it seems when any real life references are introduced in *Blackadder*. First, General Melchett's plan for a show is an attempt to boost morale after the Russians leave the war. The show then is made unnecessary by the end of the episode when it is announced that the Americans have entered the conflict. In reality, while the first Russian Revolution resulted in the overthrow of the czar in March 1917, the country did not actually make peace with Germany until 1918, after the Communist regime took power. The Americans, on the other hand, declared war in April of 1917.

The second error involves Edmund sending a telegram to Charlie Chaplin care of the Sennett Studios. While Chaplin began his film career with Sennett, by 1917 he had changed studios twice and was making films for Mutual. Lastly, Melchett accuses Baldrick of doing a bad imitation of Buster Keaton. This is odd, since Keaton only began making films in late April 1917 and would not be a star of his own films until after he served in the war.

Baldrick has some funny bits in "Major Star," particularly when he attempts to perfect his Charlie Chaplin imitation on the strength of his ability to keep a dead slug perched on his upper lip.

General Melchett also provides interesting interludes as he falls hopelessly in love with the "gorgeous Georgina." Melchett rehearses the sweet nothings he intends to use on his "darling" Georgina, as Captain Darling helps him get ready for the ball.

Later, in a scene right out of *Some Like It Hot*, George tells Blackadder about his wonderful evening of romance in the arms of the General. He concludes by confessing that Melchett proposed marriage to him, and he accepted. Blackadder is incredulous.

In his own defense, George explains that he didn't feel he could refuse the offer since to do so would be disobeying a superior officer and could lead to court-martial. Edmund sarcastically reasons that the General isn't likely to give George a medal after he lifts his bride's frock on their wedding night to discover "the last turkey in the shop."

Episode 4: "Private Plane" ★★★★

Air date: October 19, 1989. Cast: Captain Edmund Blackadder (Rowan Atkinson); Private S. Baldrick (Tony Robinson); General Sir Anthony Cecil Hogmanay Melchett (Stephen Fry); Lieutenant the Honorable George Colthurst St. Barleigh (Hugh Laurie); Captain Kevin Darling (Tim McInnerny); Squadron Commander Lord Flashheart (Rik Mayall); Baron Von Richthoven (Adrian Edmondson); Lieutenant Von Gerhardt (Hugo E. Blick); Driver Parkhurst (Gabrielle Glaister)

Flying ace Lord Flashheart drops in on Blackadder's trench when his plane runs out of gas. Flashheart thrills George and Baldrick with tales of his exploits but is dismissed by Blackadder as a "git." Before he leaves, Flashheart urges George to join his flying corps. After thinking it over, Edmund decides to apply to the Royal Flying Corps along with George. During their first day of flight school, the pair learn that 20 minutes is the average life expectancy of a new pilot. In less than ten minutes, they are up in their own planes. Edmund has the disadvantage of having Baldrick as his navigator, and the pair are quickly shot down and imprisoned by the Germans.

The manic pace of "Private Plane" helps the episode soar into the heights of laughter. If this isn't the funniest installment of *Blackadder Goes Forth*, it certainly is one of the most appreciated — especially by its studio audience, which often interrupts its own howls of laughter to break into spontaneous applause. Again, most of the adulation is for the supporting players and, in this case, the guest star: Rik Mayall. Mayall returns as the flamboyant, usually hysterical, always vulgar Flashheart, the descendant of the man who stole Edmund's bride in the second series' "Bells." As successful as Mayall's performance is here, he is topped by his costar from *The Young Ones*, Adrian Edmondson, who is especially funny as the Red Baron who loves talking of honor and the British sense of humor more than flying. Ultimately, it is his verbosity that leads to his being shot by the man of action, Flashheart (it is this action that scores the biggest laugh with the audience).

The sexually voracious Lord Flashheart provides the greatest share of the punch lines in "Private Plane." Witness the exchange in flight class, where Flashheart instructs his pupils to treat their planes like they do their women, which means getting "inside her five times a day and taking her to heaven and back." Edmondson, in his Von Richthoven role, provides the other highlights. As he confronts his prisoners (Blackadder and Baldrick), the Red Baron is most taken with the English sense of humor — especially their reliance on bathroom jokes. "How lucky you English are to find the toilet so amusing," the Baron states with earnest admiration. "For us, it is a mundane functional item. For you, the basis of an entire culture."

Episode 5: "General Hospital" ★★★

Air date: October 26, 1989. Cast: Captain Edmund Blackadder (Rowan Atkinson); Private S. Baldrick (Tony Robinson); General Sir Anthony Cecil

Hogmanay Melchett (Stephen Fry); Lieutenant the Honorable George Colthurst St. Barleigh (Hugh Laurie); Captain Kevin Darling (Tim McInnerny); Nurse Mary (Miranda Richardson); Brigadier Smith (Bill Wallis)

A bomb hit lands George in the hospital. At the same time General Melchett asks Blackadder to find the spy who has been leaking British secrets to the Germans from the same hospital. After three weeks of shagging Nurse Mary in her office, Blackadder announces that she is the spy. Melchett immediately orders her shot. It is only after she is led out that Edmund discovers that the source of the leaks is George, who used the time in hospital to write his uncle in Munich.

Sandwiched as it is between the two best installments of the series, "General Hospital" tends to get easily overlooked. Still it is average *Blackadder*, which translates to better-than-average anything else. Miranda Richardson is back in the series, although she is not nearly as effective as she was in her guest role in *Blackadder the Third*. Another familiar face, albeit heavily bandaged, is Bill Wallis in the role of the wounded spy. Wallis turns in a funny performance, as he did in *Blackadder II* as Ploppy, son of Ploppy.

Blackadder's torture of Darling for torture's sake is quite amusing, including Darling protesting that he is as "British as Queen Victoria." Edmund correctly concludes then that Darling's father was German, he is half-German, and he is married to a German.

The best moment in "General Hospital," however, is a totally absurd slice of silliness served up with dead earnestness by Stephen Fry as General Melchett. When Edmund and Nurse Mary return to headquarters to report to the General on the hunt for the spy, Nurse Mary mentions that she suspects Captain Darling may be the spy on the basis of the fact that he "pooh-poohed" Blackadder's efforts at counterespionage.

To the General, pooh-poohing is a court-martial offense. When Blackadder insists that the pooh-poohing was only incidental to the case, Melchett disagrees.

"If there's one thing I've learned from being in the army," Melchett begins as he launches into his most loony digression, "it's never ignore a pooh-pooh. I knew a major — got pooh-poohed — made the mistake of ignoring the pooh-pooh. He pooh-poohed it. Fatal error, because it turned out all along that the soldier who pooh-poohed him had been pooh-poohing a lot of other officers, who pooh-poohed their pooh-poohs. In the end we had to disband the regiment. Morale totally destroyed ... by pooh-pooh."

EPISODE 6: "GOODBYEEE" ★★★★

Air date: November 2, 1989. Cast: Captain Edmund Blackadder (Rowan Atkinson); Private S. Baldrick (Tony Robinson); General Sir Anthony Cecil Hogmanay Melchett (Stephen Fry); Lieutenant the Honorable George

Colthurst St. Barleigh (Hugh Laurie); Captain Kevin Darling (Tim McInnerny). Special Guest: Brass Hat Field Marshall Sir Douglas Haig (Geoffrey Palmer)

After dodging it for two and a half years Blackadder, George, and Baldrick are finally ordered to go over the top. The next morning, despite their most desperate efforts to avoid the offensive, Edmund, George, Baldrick, and Darling scramble out of their trench to a quick, violent death.

"Goodbyeee" ends the centuries-old saga of the Blackadder clan. Oddly, for four series that have evoked as much laughter as any other in the history of television, their finale is more effective for its drama. As with other programs that have consciously produced finales, the *Blackadders* finish with a show that is wistful, reflective, and one of the most gripping endings any television show has ever had — comedy or drama.

Rowan Atkinson turns in his best performance of *Blackadder Goes Forth* as he drops the comic edge with which his Blackadders have always faced death and speaks with philosophical resignation over Edmund's fate. In fact, all of the main characters have moments in which they are less silly and more realistic. George and Baldrick become less the simpletons, Darling is more sympathetic, and Melchett illustrates the deadly danger of having a madman in command.

The opening titles come full circle from the first episode of the first series. In "The Foretelling," Peter Cook was given special guest status in the role of Richard III. In "Goodbyeee," Geoffrey Palmer receives special notice in the opening credits for his portrayal of Field Marshall Haig. Although this ties the two ends together neatly, it is more likely that here the credit is given first since there are no end credits, just a ghostly fadeout.

The most memorable moments from "Goodbyeee" are, as previously stated, dramatic in nature. Edmund's discussion of the causes of the war and his military career, George's reciting of the fate of his school chums, and even Melchett's sending of Darling to his doom; although all are sprinkled with wit, all are ultimately more melancholy than merry.

At one point George and Baldrick plan a postwar reunion that will never happen. George urges Baldrick to motor down to his family's country home to relive their old army days. Edmund interprets this to mean sitting in a water-filled ditch in the garden while George's gamekeeper takes potshots at them.

Finally, when the fatal attack is launched and our heroes rush into no-man's land, the action is shown in slow motion. As the bombs burst around them, they slowly fade away. Their Flanders trench also dissolves into a field of wildflowers. The effect is chilling.

Mr. Bean

ITV Tiger Television/ Tiger Aspect 1990–1995

Mr. Bean is not your average situation comedy, at least not in the way that genre is usually defined. The program does not have a regular cast aside from its title character (although he does have a semiregular girlfriend). There are no witty dialogue or clever jokes or any of the other verbal elements that are key aspects of most other sitcoms. Yet *Mr. Bean* is virtually pure situation comedy — and nothing but. After the introduction of Rowan Atkinson's odd creature in the first episode, the remaining installments do little but examine him in different situations. Other shows, such as *Steptoe and Son* and *Keeping Up Appearances,* may more properly be designated "character comedies" since they focus primarily on the nuances of their casts. We learn little about Mr. Bean, although from the outset he is almost universally recognizable, at least to anyone who has ever spent more than ten minutes in the company of a self-centered, bored, yet creative child.

Mr. Bean is both wonderfully imaginative and terribly immature entertainment. The show's best moments recall a lost remnant of silent comedy's golden era — which may have been captured by aliens and transported to the 1990s. Atkinson's *Bean* is a blend of several comedy styles. Bean himself is akin to an aggressive Harry Langdon, an emotionally arrested Buster Keaton, or even a Chaplin with all the stops and restraints removed. He is especially like Chaplin and Langdon in his (albeit infrequent) use of pathos. Unlike those two clowns, however, any sympathy Bean may elicit from his audience is quickly dispelled by a cruel rejoinder, which dissipates any tender feeling. This leads to the primary weakness of the character and, consequently, the program as a whole — its mean and often childish streak.

Mark Lewisohn in his *Radio Times Guide to TV Comedy* rightly observes that another strong influence upon the Bean character is the post–World War II French comedian Jacques Tati and his sublime Monsieur Hulot. Like Monsieur Hulot, Mr. Bean, although operating in a world of sound, rarely makes much noise himself. Also like Hulot, the word most often uttered by the normally mute character is his own last name. Where the two creations part company, however, is in their view of childhood — or more likely their interpretation of childlikeness. Both men are obviously childlike, although Bean often reflects the crueler side of preadolescence. Both Hulot and Bean will usually run away frightened from a disaster they have caused, although Hulot took no delight in causing mayhem. Bean often does. Hulot has innocence; Bean has innocence but is halfway to losing it. Simply put, Monsieur Hulot is a five-year-old in a man's body, while his counterpart from across the Channel is around nine or ten.

Mr. Bean's birth (or perhaps it is more appropriate to say his arrested development) was rooted in Rowan Atkinson's appearances at the 1977 Edinburgh Festival. After Atkinson's success on the BBC's *Not the Nine O'Clock News* opened the way for a 1981 stage tour, the childish character came along as part of the comic's repertoire. During these series of performances, the comic actor would do mostly pantomime bits, which capitalized on his ability to make outrageous faces and play physical comedy. The personality of Bean further gelled into a childish man, a hopelessly inept individual that caught on with the live audiences. Atkinson describes his creation as himself at a younger age. "He's me as a 10-year-old boy, grossly exaggerated, I hope," Atkinson explained to Louis B. Hobson in 1997, "but I definitely recognize that he grew out of me. I can call him up so quickly and naturally whenever I need him on stage. I can always get a laugh when I summon him."

At first, the clueless character didn't have a name, although when he did finally get around to christening the odd fellow, Atkinson instinctively knew the character had to share his title with a vegetable. After abortive attempts with Mr. Cauliflower and Mr. Cabbage, Mr. Bean was tried and not found wanting.

In 1983, Atkinson created the first *Blackadder* show with Richard Curtis, thus beginning a successful series that would run for the remainder of the decade. After the final screening of *Blackadder Goes Forth* in 1989, however, the comic sought a new direction for his talents. After the highly verbal nature of *Blackadder*, the natural inclination was to go back to the practically mute Mr. Bean.

Instead of building a regular series around the character, Atkinson and Curtis decided to let Mr. Bean seep out in small doses. The reasoning behind this was twofold. First, the mass television audience would be introduced to the character gradually, and second, the writers wouldn't have to use all their ideas for *Bean* in one initial series. The first episode was aired on New Year's Day in 1990 and was scripted by Atkinson, Curtis, and Ben Elton (coauthor with Curtis of the final three *Blackadder* series). The initial episode was an immediate success, winning not only high ratings but also the prestigious Golden Rose at the Montreux TV Festival. The second episode, "The Return of Mr. Bean," followed 11 months later. The first anniversary of *Mr. Bean* was celebrated with the airing of "The Curse of Mr. Bean." Like the original program, this third episode was also a prize winner, copping an International Emmy Award.

Ten more episodes were produced and aired on the average of two per year. Each episode begins with the now-familiar beam of light dropping a confused Mr. Bean onto a darkened London street. Before the spastic creature skitters out of the frame, a celestial choir is heard exulting: "Ecce homo qui est farba" (Behold the man who is a bean). The exact source of the ray is never established, leaving the viewer to speculate. This man-who-is-a-bean has either been placed where he is by aliens (perhaps after experimentation) or by God (maybe as divine revenge for the Fall). Either way, one can assume Bean has been plopped down in England by a more intelligent force that either is trying to annoy the rest of the human race with this creature or has run out of patience dealing with the character itself.

In addition to the 13 episodes created for television, a 14th segment, "Hair by Mr. Bean of London," was produced and released directly to video. Atkinson has also trotted out his surefire laugh-getter in a number of other venues. Three of these were incarnations of the *Comic Relief* charitable concerts (1991, 1993, 1995). In 1993, to promote the release of the first *Mr. Bean* video, the character appeared on the BBC's *Live & Kicking*, a Saturday morning children's program. Mr. Bean also proved quite adept at hawking other products than his own videos and hired out for a number of commercials. The most notable of these was an ad in Britain for M&M candies in which Bean bowled one of the larger-than-life spokescandies down a bowling alley by accident.

Despite only airing 13 episodes, *Mr. Bean* proved to be a ratings bonanza not only in the U.K. but around the world. The mute figure is a natural for export to non–English-speaking countries and has been sold to more than 70 nations. In addition, the short nature of the average routine (essentially a one-reel short) makes *Mr. Bean* well suited to play on airplanes and in shopping centers.

"I never thought I could make Germans laugh, but Mr. Bean has done it," remarked Rowan Atkinson in an article published in the *Calgary Sun*. "Even the staid Japanese find him amusing, though they don't react as vociferously as the Germans."

Atkinson, a rather private individual, finds the international success of *Mr. Bean* a little intimidating. His first taste of the global acceptance of the character came in 1995 when he was mobbed in a number of cities, including Berlin, Amsterdam, and Toronto while promoting the *Bean* videos. Atkinson's fame is less daunting at home, which is why for the most part the comic chooses to remain in England. "When people encounter me in Britain, they do a double take," related Atkinson. "They're not stunned. It's just that it takes a second or two to realize who they've just seen."

One of the most Bean-resistant markets has been the United States, where the program, like its star, has a small but devoted following. Initially, *Mr. Bean* was broadcast in the U.S. on cable's Home Box Office, but the premium channel didn't give *Bean* the wide exposure afforded in other countries. Next, the episodes shifted to PBS, and then they were segmented and aired over the Fox Family Channel as a regular part of an anthology show of imported comedy clips.

Not surprisingly, given the limited success of *Mr. Bean* in the United States, that America was one of the last to see the release of *Bean*, the international hit film. The movie, which was released in 1997, already had earned more than $100 million worldwide before finally opening in the United States in November of that year. While the film was something of an event in other countries, it was not so in the States. "America didn't want a little British comedy plunked down in the middle of their blockbuster summer," Atkinson told Louis B. Hobson, "so we had no choice but to open in the autumn."

Bean, the movie, is a mixed affair, reworking a number of bits from the original 13 episodes, often without sufficient motivation (one glaring example is the inclusion of the turkey gag from "Merry Christmas, Mr. Bean" in a scene concocted merely as an excuse to cram the routine into the film). In their favor, Atkinson, Robin Driscoll, and Curtis have managed to transport a character usually used in ten-minute routines into a full-length feature film. (Not always an easy task, as the producers of films based on *Saturday Night Live* skits can attest.) The primary weakness in the feature-length *Bean*, however, is not the title character, but those who have to react to him sympathetically at times. On the whole, however, the film will not disappoint fans of the television program.

Still, the best platform for the broad humor of *Mr. Bean* is still the original 13 television programs and the extra portions, all of which are abundantly available (it seems they are repackaged annually!) on video.

"He's an incredibly selfish man," sums up Rowan Atkinson on the subject of Bean. "That's essentially what he is."

While this estimation of the fey Mr. Bean may be accurate, it is not entirely true. Certainly, the character has shared financially with his alter ego, making Atkinson a millionaire many times over. In addition, Bean has shared the valuable gift of laughter and entertainment with audiences eager for both around the world.

THE EPISODES

By Richard Curtis, Rowan Atkinson, Robin Driscoll, and Ben Elton (additional material by Paul Weiland and Andrew Clifford). Directed by John Howard Davies, John Birkin, and Paul Weiland. Produced by John Howard Davies, Sue Vertue, and Peter Bennett-Jones

"MR. BEAN" ★★★

Air date: January 1, 1990. Cast: Mr. Bean (Rowan Atkinson); Student (Paul Brown); the Invigilator (Rudolph Walker); Blind Man (Roger Sloman); Church Organist (Howard Goodall); Mr. Sprout (Richard Briers)

In the first sketch, Mr. Bean takes an exam. After the test begins he discovers to his horror that the subject is calculus, while he has studied for trigonometry.

Next, Bean goes to the beach. When he starts to change into his bathing suit, he notices a lone man in sunglasses, sitting on the beach staring at him. Self-consciously, he manages to put the trunks on over his pants, then wriggle out of his pants while still wearing the bathing suit.

In the final bit, Mr. Bean goes to church. There he encounters a myriad of troubles, including having to blow his nose without a handkerchief (he uses the inside of his jacket pocket), falling asleep, and trying to unwrap and eat a piece of candy without attracting attention.

The introductory incarnation of Mr. Bean presents him in three separate sketches of varying quality. The first bit, while the strongest, is the least believable due to its setting. While we are never led to believe that Mr. Bean is not intelligent, it is a bit of a surprise to see him taking an exam at a university. Throughout the rest of the episodes, we indeed see flashes of genius from the title character, but one would guess any brilliance he possesses is innate and not cultivated in the halls of academia.

The premiere episode also presents the running gag of Mr. Bean's occasional encounters with the three-wheeled blue Reliant Robin automobile. He encounters the vehicle here three times, managing to run it off the road, tip it over, and bump it from its parking space. Bean does this with the help of his Austin Mini, although here the car is orange, not the yellow-and-black model that would become a familiar fixture in future episodes.

There is a wonderful insight into Mr. Bean's character in the opening moment of the exam sketch. When the student seated next to him pulls out a pen and places it on the desk, Mr. Bean follows suit. Next the student pulls out a reserve pen and places it next to his first one; Bean matches him. Then, in a gesture left over from preadolescence, Mr. Bean elaborately removes a third pen from his jacket. Three more pens follow, each removed with the same flourish. Next, Mr. Bean reaches into the other side of his jacket and pulls out a handful of pens. In a final proof of his superior preparation, Bean opens his briefcase to remove a toy policeman, a bendable Pink Panther doll, and an alarm clock.

The church scene also provides some good moments, the best of which is Mr. Bean's attempt to join the congregation in the singing of "All Creatures of Our God and King." Unfortunately, he doesn't have a hymnal. Rather than share with his neighbor, Bean manages to mutter along with the verses. When it comes to the more familiar alleluias of the chorus, however, Bean proudly bellows them at the top of his lungs, although never quite managing the difficult timing of the final alleluia.

Richard Briers, Tom Good of the 1970s sitcom *The Good Life* (*Good Neighbors*), makes a guest appearance as the unfortunate worshipper who shares a pew with Bean. Rudolph Walker, who would appear with Atkinson in *The Thin Blue Line* later in the decade, is the exam proctor in the first sequence.

"THE RETURN OF MR. BEAN" ★★★½

Air date: November 5, 1990. Cast: Mr. Bean (Rowan Atkinson); Busker (Dave O'Higgins); Customer (Paul McDowell); Checkout Manager (William VanDyck); Maitre D' (John Junkin); Waiter (Roger Lloyd Pack); Violinist (Steve McNicholas); Cinema Manager (Robin Driscoll); Waitress (Matilda Ziegler); Royal (Tina Maskell)

Sketch one finds Mr. Bean on a shopping trip to a department store to try out his new American Express card.

The second routine takes place in an elegant restaurant, which Mr. Bean has visited to celebrate his birthday. The problems begin in earnest when Bean orders steak tartar without realizing it is raw ground beef.

The final vignette occurs in the lobby of a London cinema during a royal premiere of a film. Mr. Bean, one of the ushers, waits in line with his coworkers for the royal party to arrive. He busies himself by practicing bowing, brushing his teeth with his finger, and flossing with a thread stolen from the apron of the girl standing beside him.

"The Return of Mr. Bean" presents three more sketches that place the extraordinary Bean in ordinary situations. This second episode was written by Richard Curtis, Rowan Atkinson, and Robin Driscoll, who replaced Ben Elton in the triumvirate. Driscoll also appears in the final skit as the manager with the dubious honor of having Mr. Bean on his staff (aside from the feature film, this is the only time Bean is seen working).

Matilda Ziegler appears as the cinema waitress in the final skit, although in future installments she plays Bean's dowdy girlfriend.

While initially the sequence in the department store promises much, it soon becomes repetitious, as does the final bit in the cinema lobby. This leaves the restaurant scene to provide the highest share of innovative gags.

Upon arriving at his table, Mr. Bean writes out, seals, and addresses a greeting card, presumably for a guest who has not yet arrived. After placing the card aside, Bean looks around absently for a few moments, only to discover the card, which, it turns out, is for him. He opens it with surprise and gratitude.

When his steak tartar arrives, Mr. Bean examines it carefully. He sniffs it and even listens to it in hopes of solving the mystery of the raw meat. Finally, he endeavors to try the dish, only to wretch in a style similar to a five-year-old forced to eat liver.

Unwilling to acknowledge his ignorance of the item or ruin his festive birthday meal, Bean decides to hide the raw meat around the table. He puts some in the tiny flower vase, some in the sugar bowl under the sugar, some inside his roll, and some under his plate. Running out of convenient hiding spots, he manages to secrete the rest in the back of the Violinist's trousers and in a woman's handbag. After Bean has completed this, the waiter accidentally spills a tray onto Bean's table. The manager comes by to apologize. Bean takes the opportunity afforded him by the accident to reveal all the hidden meat and blame its farflung locations on the waiter. The manager leads Mr. Bean to a new table, where he is presented with a fresh plate of steak tartar.

"The Curse of Mr. Bean" ★★½

Air date: January 1, 1991. Cast: Mr. Bean (Rowan Atkinson); Pool Attendant (Angus Deayton); Man on Park Bench (Angus Deayton); Girlfriend (Matilda Ziegler)

Mr. Bean visits a public pool and winds up trapped at the top of the high diving platform when he is afraid to jump.

In the middle sequence, Mr. Bean makes his lunch on a park bench from a variety of ingredients (including live sardines, which he beats to death) that he extracts from his coat.

Bean accompanies his girlfriend to a *Nightmare on Elm Street* film in the final sequence. He spends the time before the movie making horrific faces at her and the other patrons, only to be terrified himself when the film begins.

Another three sketches penned by Driscoll, Curtis, and Atkinson. Although they are not up to the standard set by the first two installments, there are still plenty of inventive gags. The pool sequence is reminiscent of a similar scene in Buster Keaton's 1928 film *The Cameraman* (especially the bit where Bean loses his bathing suit), while Rowan Atkinson manages to add some new business of his own. The freshest bits involve two routines that employ Mr. Bean's distinctive yellow-and-black Austin Mini, which appears for the first time in the series.

When Mr. Bean finds that he hasn't enough money to leave the automated parking garage, he drives over to the entrance in hopes of sneaking out when another car enters. The gate drops down before he can get out, however, prompting Bean to pull a heavy trash wagon onto the sensor in the floor to raise the gate. Unfortunately, he fails to get back to his car before the entrance is closed again. Finally, he backs up his Austin Mini along the aisle facing the entrance gate. When a car finally approaches, he guns the engine, manages to force the other vehicle out of the way, and makes his escape. The other vehicle, of course, turns out to be that little blue three-wheeled Reliant Robin, which is toppled over in the process.

Later, in a clever bridging sequence, Bean and the Mini are forced to stop at a red light. As he waits impatiently, Bean notices a cyclist who stops at the light, dismounts, and then pushes his bike around the turn. Bean follows suit, climbing out of his tiny car, pushing it around the corner, then getting in and going on his way.

Matilda Ziegler makes her first of numerous appearances as Bean's plain, often exasperated girlfriend. Angus Deayton, most familiar as Victor Meldrew's neighbor in *One Foot in the Grave*, appears with and without mustache in two separate roles.

"Mr. Bean Goes to Town" ★★★

Air date: October 15, 1991. Cast: Mr. Bean (Rowan Atkinson); Camera Thief (Nick Hancock); Police Sergeant (Robin Driscoll); Shoe Salesman (Dursley McLinden); Girlfriend (Matilda Ziegler); Eddie Spangle (Alan Shaxon); Monique (Julia Howson); Musicians (Howard Goodall, Richard Marcangelo); Disco Dancers (Mark Kahn, Phil Nice)

Mr. Bean buys a television but has trouble getting a clear picture.

In the second sketch, Bean has his camera stolen when he gives it to a man to take his picture. Bean catches the thief by putting a wire trash basket over his head. Later, in the police line-up, Bean cannot successfully identify the thief until all the candidates have trash baskets placed over their heads.

Next, Mr. Bean gets something in his shoe while walking through town. He takes off his shoe and places it on the hood of a car while he balances against a lamppost. The car drives off, leaving him to hop after it on one foot. He hops around town, chasing the vehicle, until finally he dives in front of it to retrieve his shoe.

In the final scene, Mr. Bean meets his girlfriend at a nightclub. After ruining a magician's act and embarrassing his girlfriend in the process, he follows her into the club's disco to wreak further mayhem.

Four separate vignettes are presented here. The first and the third are the strongest, while the second and fourth are rather routine.

In the first bit, Mr. Bean's new television set only delivers a clear picture when he holds the portable antenna a few inches off the floor to the left of the set. Unfortunately, he can't see the picture from that angle, and whenever he cranes his neck toward the set it reverts to static.

Carefully drawing his curtains, Bean strips down to his underwear and dresses a chair with his clothes in an attempt to replicate himself in the necessary spot. It fails to work until he climbs into the empty television crate, removes his underwear, and places it down his pants on the chair. Finally, he settles down, naked but happy, in the crate to enjoy his new set. Just then the timer on his room's electric meter expires, plunging him into darkness and turning off the set.

Second appearances are made both by coauthor Robin Driscoll (as the Police Sergeant) and by musical composer Howard Goodall (as one of the musicians in Club Phut).

"The Trouble with Mr. Bean" ★★★★

Air date: January 1, 1992. Cast: Mr. Bean (Rowan Atkinson); Dentist (Richard Wilson); Traffic Warden (Caroline Quentin); Schoolboy (Sam Mead); His Mum (Christine Ellerbeck); Dental Nurse (Bridget Brammall); Boy in Park (Hugo Mendez); Man in Wheelchair (Michael Godley); Car Thief (Nathan Lewis)

Despite a number of alarm clocks (including one contrivance that drips water on his feet when it is time to wake up), Mr. Bean oversleeps and finds he only has ten minutes to get to a dentist appointment. Rather than waste any more time, Bean gets dressed in the car while driving. Once in the dental chair, Bean manages to knock out the dentist by accidentally stabbing him with the novocaine needle. Instead of leaving, Bean drills and fills his own teeth.

In a second sketch, Mr. Bean takes a picnic to the park. There he helps a boy fix his radio-controlled boat, and inadvertently makes it control a nearby motorized wheelchair in the bargain. Next, he sets out his picnic (consisting of a lone cupcake) but is soon driven away by a fly.

"The Trouble with Mr. Bean" is a breakthrough episode. With its almost total reliance on visual gags, *Mr. Bean* has often been compared to silent comedy. This episode presents an almost perfect silent two-reeler in its first 20 minutes. Not surprisingly, the clever sight gags concocted by Driscoll, Curtis, and Atkinson play better when presented on a linear plot line rather than in brief situations.

This growth can be likened to the movement of Chaplin, Keaton, or Lloyd from one-reel comedies to those double the length. The extra length necessitated the inclusion of plots, which in turn served to enhance the gags. Future episodes, such as "Merry Christmas, Mr. Bean," "Mind the Baby, Mr. Bean," and "Mr. Bean in Room 426," will further develop this positive trend.

Mr. Bean's dressing while driving to the dentist is a gem of sight comedy, the highlight of which is when he brushes his teeth in the car's side mirror with his neck craned outside the vehicle. When it comes to rinsing out the toothpaste, Bean reaches out, re-angles the windshield washer jet, and squirts the fluid into his mouth.

Once in the dental chair, Mr. Bean plays with the controls, raising and lowering the contraption while the dentist's back is turned. Next, he discovers the device used to suction saliva from the mouth. Intrigued, Bean manages to catch his tongue with the instrument before turning the device to such practical applications as vacuuming his jacket and sucking up all of the dentist's morning juice.

After he has knocked out the dentist, Bean examines the X-ray and decides to drill his own cavity. He carefully counts out the teeth, drills, and fills it. Only then does he realize that the X-ray holder swivels left to right. Unsure if he has drilled the right tooth, he counts in the opposite direction, then drills and fills that tooth. Next he discovers that the bracket holding the X-ray also flips vertically. Unwilling to let the job go undone, he completes work on two more teeth. The dentist awakens just as he is finishing.

And, yes, that bearded dentist is Richard Wilson, who plays Victor Meldrew on *One Foot in the Grave.*

"Mr. Bean Rides Again" ★★½

Air date: February 17, 1992. Cast: Mr. Bean (Rowan Atkinson); Heart Attack Man (Roger Sloman); Lady with Letter (Su Douglas); Postman (John Rolfe); Laughing Man (Stephen Frost); Ticket Inspector (Nick Hancock); Air Hostess (Eryl Maynard); Young Boy (Hugo Mendez)

While waiting for a bus, Mr. Bean tries to revive a heart attack victim.

Next, Mr. Bean stops to mail a letter. After accidentally swallowing his last stamp, Bean steals one from a woman's envelope. He then is forced to hide in the mailbox when the woman returns after finding her discarded letter.

The third skit finds Mr. Bean packing for a trip. He discovers his tiny suitcase is too small and makes the necessary adjustments. These include taking a washcloth instead of a full-sized towel, breaking his toothbrush in half, and cutting the legs off his trousers to make shorts. After doing this, he discovers an identical pair of shorts and a much larger suitcase. Rather than repack, Bean merely places the smaller case inside the larger.

On a train, Mr. Bean tries to read his book, while another passenger roars hysterically at his own book.

Finally, Mr. Bean tries to amuse an ill little boy on a plane.

Five sketches, some of them related, combine to fill "Mr. Bean Rides Again." The series' predilection for exploring the boundaries of bad taste is especially evident in this installment. There are some initially funny, but ultimately disturbing images that involve Mr. Bean's attempts at reviving a heart attack victim, then using an ambulance to jump start his own car, leaving the emergency vehicle stranded. The final blackout gag, involving an exploding bag of vomit, also sinks lower than it needs to.

One of the better gags is also one of the simplest. Mr. Bean struggles to read while his compartment mate on the train laughs loudly. Bean attempts to block the noise by placing his fingers in his ears. Next, he sticks his tie in his ears and pulls his jacket over his head (making it necessary to shine a flashlight in the neck hole to see his book). Finally, he succeeds when he clogs his ears with discarded chewing gum from under the seat. The ploy works so well that he fails to hear the conductor asking for tickets. When the man taps him on the shoulder, Bean is so startled that he hurls his book and ticket out the window.

Stephen Frost, who played the genial leader of the firing squad in *Blackadder Goes Forth* ("Corporal Punishment"), is effective as the laughing man on the train.

"MERRY CHRISTMAS, MR. BEAN" ★★★★

Air date: December 29, 1992. Cast: Mr. Bean (Rowan Atkinson); Irma Gobb (Matilda Ziegler). With C. J. Allen; Owen Brenman; John Warner; Lee Barrett; Chris Sanders; Jonathan Stratt; Carol Singers from Sylvia Young's School

Mr. Bean spends Christmas Eve buying the preparations for his holiday. While in town he meets Irma, his girlfriend, who shows him a display of diamond rings in a jewelry store window. She retreats excitedly as Bean goes into the shop to make a purchase. The next day Irma is disappointed to learn that Bean has purchased the advertising display from the window, rather than the ring.

Robin Driscoll, Richard Curtis, and Rowan Atkinson combined to create a Christmas gift that is far and away the finest and funniest *Mr. Bean* episode. The story line well supports the numerous and inventive gag situations, and while some of the routines hark back to previous episodes (Bean must test Christmas decorations before he purchases them and sends Christmas cards to himself), they are in the minority. There is also a degree of cruelty, especially toward Bean's girlfriend, although this is not outside the bounds of the character's established personality.

While this episode brims with clever touches, the two best involve Bean's playing with a store window nativity display and, later, wrestling with a giant turkey. In the first bit, Mr. Bean is distracted by a nativity scene in the department store and begins to play with the display. First, he sets the cow to mooing, while causing the ceramic Joseph to shush the beast lest he wake the Christ child. Next the sheep starts bleating only to be silenced by Mary, followed by one of the Wise Men developing a nasty cough. The scene is disturbed by an invasion of toy sheep, which a toy shepherd and his dog round up and send off in the back of a toy truck. The silliness begins in earnest when a toy Dalek invades, followed by a tyrannosaurus rex. Soon, the Dalek and tanks from the German and British armies join together to fight the dinosaur. Finally, Bean has an angel suspended from a helicopter airlift the holy family to the safety and quiet of a nearby doll house.

The next day, while stuffing the holiday turkey, Bean loses his watch inside the bird. As he attempts to retrieve the watch, Bean gets the giant bird stuck on his head. Just then his girlfriend arrives; Bean staggers around his apartment looking for the door like a cross between the Elephant Man and the scientist from *The Fly*. Finally, they succeed in removing the poultry by tying it to a coal scuttle and dropping it out the window. Unfortunately, the turkey goes out the window as well, and the couple is forced to have peanut butter sandwiches for dinner.

Matilda Ziegler's girlfriend character is finally given a name (although with a handle like "Irma Gobb" perhaps she would have preferred to remain nameless). Owen Brenman, who plays Nick Swainey on *One Foot in the Grave*, appears briefly as a department store clerk.

"Mr. Bean in Room 426" ★★½

Air date: February 17, 1993. Cast: Mr. Bean (Rowan Atkinson). With Michael Fenton Stevens; Roger Brierley; Matthew Ashforde; Danny la Rue

Mr. Bean arrives at a resort hotel. Upon registering, he immediately begins an inexplicable rivalry with the man who has the room next door to his. Bean must register more quickly, get to the room first, and even eat more and faster than the other guest.

At the hotel's buffet, Mr. Bean gets food poisoning when he eats some bad oysters while in competition with his neighbor. Unfortunately, Bean has proudly finished his trayful of the bacteria-laden mollusks before the other man discovers they are past their prime.

Later that night, Bean manages to lock himself out of his room while completely naked.

Although the exploitation of a single premise is a welcome respite, "Mr. Bean in Room 426" proves to be one of the series' weaker forays into this realm. There are some good gags but not enough to carry the episode. There is also an unfortunate recurring gag at the expense of the elderly.

There is a good scene when Mr. Bean unpacks. First he removes his blindfolded teddy bear from his suitcase. After taking off the blindfold, he shows the "surprised" bear around the room before making a bed for him in the nightstand drawer. Unfortunately, he accidentally takes the stuffed animal's head off while closing the drawer.

Next, he pulls out a set of curtains from home and hangs them over the hotel's drapes. A matching lampshade soon follows the curtains. Finally, Bean pulls a giant drill from his luggage and begins remodeling in earnest. By the time he is finished, Bean has managed to fill all the walls with paintings and photographs he has brought from home.

The drill also comes in handy when Bean is unable to find his bathroom. With his ear to the wall he hears the sound of running water. Soon he has drilled an opening into his neighbor's bathroom. Bean enjoys a bath while the room's occupant and the hotel manager try to determine how the bathroom door has become locked from the inside.

This episode was not scheduled to be aired at this time but was shown in place of "Mind the Baby, Mr. Bean," due to a recent child murder that had unsettled Britain.

Michael Fenton Stevens, who also appeared in *The Legacy of Reginald Perrin*, plays Mr. Bean's rival next door at the hotel. *Jeeves and Wooster* fans should recognize Roger Brierley, who played Sir Roderick Glossop in that series. Finally, veteran British female impersonator Danny la Rue appears as himself.

"Do It Yourself, Mr. Bean" ★★★½

Air date: January 10, 1994. Cast: Mr. Bean (Rowan Atkinson). With Robert Austin; Simon Godley; Helen Burns; David Stoll; Colin McFarlane; Rupert Vansittart; Andy Greenhalgh

It is New Year's Eve 1993, and Mr. Bean is preparing a party for two friends, Rupert and Hubert. While he has carefully made newspaper hats for each guest — including his teddy bear — Bean has forgotten refreshments. After the pair arrives, he hastily creates snacks by dipping twigs into yeast extract and concocts wine by pouring sugar into vinegar.

The next day Mr. Bean rushes to a department store to buy a mechanical reclining chair at the January half-price sale. Exiting the store, Mr. Bean is forced to put the recliner on top of his car, then to drive the vehicle from atop it when he overfills the passenger compartment with redecorating supplies.

Back at his apartment, Bean rearranges his furniture, cuts new holes in his walls, and finally devises a new, faster way of painting.

A somewhat linear although still episodic entry, "Do It Yourself, Mr. Bean" chronicles a series of unrelated events, which happen on two consecutive days. A certain amount of sympathy is generated for Mr. Bean as we finally are introduced to two of his acquaintances (aside from his girlfriend). The pair, Rupert and Hubert, can hardly be described as friends as they deceive Bean in order to leave his New Year's Eve party early. Of course, their behavior is somewhat justified given the "refreshments" served to them. The entire scene is reminiscent of a similar failed party in Chaplin's *The Gold Rush*, although with much less emotional impact.

Still, it seems for every moment that elicits the audience's sympathy for Mr. Bean, there is a counterbalancing act that repulses. At the January sale, Bean malevolently crushes a woman in the recliner he wants to buy, then turns up the store's music so her husband cannot hear his wife's screams for help.

Although Mr. Bean's drive home on the top of his car is amusing to see, the best moments come in the final redecorating sequence. Bean starts out by moving his furniture to accommodate his new chair. Then he realizes that he has moved a table from its convenient spot under the hatchway to his kitchen. Rather than rearrange the furniture again, Bean uses a saw to cut a new hatch on the other side of the kitchen. He manages to cut through frames, pictures, wallpaper, and the phone line in the process. When he finishes, Bean inserts the removed and mismatched portion of wall into the old hatch.

Next he tries to paint his room. When the bristles fall out of his brush, he shoves the handle up his teddy's backside and starts using his beloved friend as a substitute. This proves to be slightly messy, however, leading Bean to carefully wrap everything (including individual grapes) in newspaper. Bean then places a jumbo firecracker in a bucket of paint and lights it. He runs into the hall and around the corner to await the explosion. Just then one of his guests from the previous night returns to retrieve his hat. The firecracker goes off, and Bean comes back into his apartment. He discovers a mysterious set of paint footprints leading out of his door. The room, however, is perfectly bathed in fresh white paint, except for one area in the outline of a man reaching for a hat.

"Mind the Baby, Mr. Bean" ★★★

Air date: April 25, 1994. Cast: Mr. Bean (Rowan Atkinson). With Susie McKenna; Andy Bradford; Nick Scott; Lydia Henderson-Boyle; Anthony Hambling

While visiting an amusement pier, Mr. Bean is left caring for an infant after the baby's carriage becomes inadvertently linked to his car's bumper. After a few failed attempts at trying to fob the baby off on someone else, Bean resigns himself to the responsibility.

A good execution of a single situation, "Mind the Baby, Mr. Bean" suffers from a number of weak points, which keep it from being a total success. First and foremost is the premise itself. Although Mr. Bean is shown to be caring toward the baby, he quickly proves that his version of care is potentially dangerous toward the child. While we know that the child is never in any real peril, it is still unsettling to watch at times.

The second major flaw is the unfortunate reverting to gags of questionable taste. When Bean changes the baby's diaper, the item soon gets propelled around the park into the various faces of unsuspecting patrons. Ultimately the soiled nappy lands atop a candy apple just as a man is about to bite into it. Not fare for the weak of stomach.

One of the more frantic gags finds Bean winning a goldfish by cheating at a dart game. He proudly shows the fish to the baby, then realizes the plastic bag is leaking. Bean rushes around wildly looking for more water but can find none. Ultimately he places the precious remaining water and its occupant into his mouth. He then continues to enjoy the fun fair with his cheeks bulging with water and fish. Despite the stares of onlookers, Bean momentarily forgets the fish while playing at a bingo arcade. He wins, which forces him to yell out "Bingo," and swallows the goldfish in the process. Bean is stunned for a moment until the fish comes shooting out of his mouth, across the room, and into a bowl with another prize goldfish.

"Back to School, Mr. Bean" ★★½

Air date: October 26, 1994. Cast: Mr. Bean (Rowan Atkinson). With Suzanne Bertish; Lucy Fleming; Al Hunter Ashton; David Schneider; John Barrard; John Clegg; Sam Driscoll; Tracey Roberts; Harriet Eastcott; Sarah Milo; Chris Ryan; Rupert Bates; Chris Driscoll

Mr. Bean visits an adult education open house. Upon arriving he secures a reserved parking spot by pushing a car identical to his out of its place. Once inside Bean causes a number of disturbances, most notably blowing up the chemistry lab and dyeing a small boy blue in the process.

Bean exits the school to discover his car has been moved to the middle of the parking lot. He starts for the car but stops to purchase a cupcake. While he savors the dessert, a tank crushes his Austin Mini as part of a demonstration (the reserved parking spot was for the car designated for destruction). Upon discovering his car flattened, Bean is stunned but regains his composure when he happily salvages his padlock from the wreckage.

Some good gags prevail, despite the fact that the installment contains more than the usual amount of mean-spiritedness that often mars Bean's adventures. One sequence in particular shows Bean's callous disregard for others, rendering it fully unfunny. In this scene, Mr. Bean manages to wreck a philatelist's collection, ruin a calligrapher's book, and almost set fire to another man's matchstick model. These acts are not malicious in themselves but become so when Bean wreaks his havoc with mocking contempt. Later in the episode, when Bean suffers a severe loss by his own machinations, it is hard to feel sympathy for the character.

One of the better jokes occurs early in the episode when Mr. Bean encounters a platoon of soldiers being drilled by their sergeant. While the sergeant is absent, Bean accidentally discovers that the soldiers respond to his coughs as if they were subtle yet definite commands. Standing behind them, Bean delights in moving the unit via his grumbles, hacks, and murmmurs. Finally, he leaves the men standing on one foot with their hands in the air and their fingers waving effetely. At this point the sergeant returns and irately demands an explanation from his silly soldiers.

Later, when Mr. Bean stumbles into an art class, he enjoys drawing a still life of some fruit. While he is engrossed in sketching a banana, however, the model changes — with a nude woman taking the place of the bowl of fruit. Bean recoils in embarrassment when he realizes that the two melons he has just sketched are not melons after all. He quickly transforms his half-finished picture into a portrait of a face (with the banana becoming the nose and the "melons" the eyes), but the art instructor insists that he draw the entire body. Bean overcomes his reluctance to look at the nude by retreating to the ceramics portion of the room and fashioning a clay brassiere for the woman to wear.

"Tee Off, Mr. Bean" ★★★½

Air date: September 20, 1995. Additional material by Andrew Clifford. Cast: Mr. Bean (Rowan Atkinson). With Jacqueline Defferary; Grant Master; David Battley; Marilyn Finlay

Mr. Bean does his laundry while having to contend with a bully who is also a black belt in karate (the man is there washing his ghee). Mr. Bean's attempts to remain unobtrusive are made all the more difficult when he takes off his trousers to put his underwear in the wash and inadvertently replaces his trousers with a woman's skirt.

The second sketch finds Mr. Bean playing a game of miniature golf. After acing the difficult first hole, Bean knocks his ball out of bounds on the ridiculously simple second hole. He starts to pick up the ball but is cautioned against it by the watchful attendant. Thus begins Bean's odyssey around the town and surrounding countryside as he bashes the ball about in a Herculean attempt to get back on the course. Night is falling when he completes the hole, which he dutifully scores on his card as a "3,427."

"Tee Off, Mr. Bean" presents two unrelated skits, both of above average quality for the series. The first is probably the stronger of the pair on the basis of its gags and situation, while the other tends to be somewhat predictable at times.

The laundromat routine is especially satisfying in that it gives the often-malevolent Mr. Bean a worthy adversary to battle against. Rather than venting his subjuvenile wrath on the elderly, infirm, or someone chosen at random, here Bean must do battle against a bully. The fight and the results, given his opponent, are thus much more gratifying.

Mr. Bean's adventure in the skirt begins when he counts out his underwear and realizes he will not have enough for the week without washing the pair he is wearing. He discreetly ducks behind a partition to remove his trousers and places them on the counter. While he takes off his briefs, a woman mechanically scoops his trousers up and puts them in with her load. Bean reaches back for what he thinks are his trousers but emerges in a floor-length skirt identical in color to his own garment. He nonchalantly walks back to his seat, oblivious to the situation, until he goes to cross his legs. Horrified upon discovering the truth, Bean attempts to hide the skirt by carefully tucking it between his legs, thus giving the illusion that it is actually a pair of trousers. Properly tucked, he hobbles around the laundromat with his legs firmly locked together as he searches in vain for his trousers.

Later, when Bean substitutes his cup of coffee for the bully's bleach, all is well until the bully notices his wash is turning brown. He angrily eyes Bean as the prime suspect in the affair, forcing Bean to casually blow on the paper cup of bleach as if it were hot coffee. The bully is not satisfied that Bean is innocent until he actually witnesses him drinking the whitening agent. Bean does so insouciantly, until the bully turns away, allowing him to react as one would expect after just having been compelled to swallow bleach.

"Goodnight, Mr. Bean" ★½

Air date: October 31, 1995. Cast: Mr. Bean (Rowan Atkinson). With Suzy Aitchison; Elizabeth Bennett; Rupert Bates; Penelope Nice; Rupert Vansittart

Mr. Bean visits a hospital emergency room when he gets a small teapot stuck on his fist. Rather than wait his turn, Bean schemes to take advantage of the other patients to get served first.

The second sequence features Mr. Bean's attempt at photographing himself with a royal guardsman.

The final sequence shows Mr. Bean's bedtime routine and his efforts to combat insomnia.

A forgettable collection of gags in three separate situations, except for the rather nasty tone set in the first two sequences. Bean's attempts at getting ahead in a hospital emergency queue are humorous but spoiled by his insistence on mocking the elderly and infirm. Fortunately, he doesn't succeed, but the gags still lose some of their humor in the process. His humiliation of the guardsman in the second bit also becomes tiresome and rather mean-spirited. One almost wishes the stoic soldier would lose his temper and punch Bean.

The least contrived and therefore the best gags are in the final scene. After cleaning his teeth and ears with his electric toothbrush, Mr. Bean climbs into bed with his teddy bear. He enjoys a picture book with the stuffed animal until he realizes the bear isn't getting the jokes. He lovingly puts the bear's wire-rimmed glasses on him so his tiny friend can enjoy the book too.

When it comes time to put out the light, Bean reaches into a bedside drawer filled with light bulbs and an air pistol. He uses the pistol to shoot out the ceiling fixture and presumably will replace the bulb in the morning from his large stock.

Next, Bean has difficulty getting to sleep. When a cat yowls beneath his window, Bean dons a makeshift dog disguise to frighten the feline away. After a number of failed attempts, Bean succeeds in getting to sleep by taking out a large photograph of a flock of sheep. He starts counting the sheep but keeps losing his place. Finally, he manages to get an accurate count by using his pocket calculator. Upon hitting the total key, Bean suddenly drops into a dead sleep.

"Hair by Mr. Bean of London" ★★★

Direct to video. Additional material by Richard Curtis. Cast: Mr. Bean (Rowan Atkinson). With Chris Driscoll; Frederick Treves; Tony Haase; Susie McKenna; Jamie Yeates; Colin Wells; C. J. Allen; Matthew Ashforde; Robin Driscoll

First, Mr. Bean takes up haircutting when a barber leaves him unsupervised in his shop.

In the second skit, Bean visits a country fair where he and his teddy bear enter a pet show.

Finally, Bean attempts to sneak past a railway exit when he loses his ticket.

A homogeneous blend of skits, "Hair by Mr. Bean of London" provides good laughs throughout. The best is delivered first, as Bean takes over a barber shop when the proprietor is summoned into the next room for a phone call. Left to himself, Bean soon is mistaken for the barber by a trio of customers. The first, a boy dropped off by his mother, is somewhat apprehensive about Bean working on his mop, especially when he gingerly snips off one hair at a time. At first, Bean approaches each hair as if he were attempting to defuse a bomb — carefully holding out one hair at a time before snipping it off, then heaving a sigh of relief at the successful severing. Next Bean works his magic with a bowl and then with an unwieldy set of electric trimmers. The results leave the boy looking like something akin to Henry V with a reverse Mohawk — which it turns out the lad is quite happy to sport.

The other clients, two men, receive similarly damaging dos, which go unnoticed until after they leave the shop. When the customers return, concurrent with the barber getting off the phone, Bean makes a clever retreat disguised as Prince Charles.

The middle segment contains some good gags, although the best of these are more charming than inventive. The highlight of this sequence involves Bean entering his teddy in a pet show, where he manages to win first prize (in England this entails a red ribbon, rather than a blue). This is achieved by simple virtue of the stuffed bear's amazing obedience. One nice feature of this skit is the reaction of the pet show's audience, which is entirely composed of children. While the adult judges of the show are rather annoyed and confused by Bean's entry, the children truly appreciate and root for this adult who is a refugee from their world. It is one of the few times that Bean is allowed to bask in the glow of his peers' understanding.

One Foot in the Grave

BBC-TV 1990–1997

In many respects comedy is like chocolate. The majority of the public enjoys chocolate very much — especially when it is sweet and light. There are some, however, who prefer their chocolate dark, with little sugar added. Those who don't like dark chocolate find it bitter and unpalatable. To its aficionados, however, it is much more rich and closer to the original article.

The majority of comedy is sweetened up considerably as well. It is processed and softened to remove much of the bitterness inherent in the real life situations from which it originated. There are those who like their comedy dark, however. Unsweetened. For this minority there is nothing better than a comedy that delivers its humor filled with the pith and marrow of real life. David Renwick's *One Foot in the Grave* is such a comedy — dark and rich, with no added sugars or flavorings. It is definitely not a series for every taste — particularly in America, where we tend to like our laughs whipped into a frothy meringue. For those who have the right comedy taste buds to appreciate it, though, it is absolutely delicious.

One Foot in the Grave chronicles the daily frustrations of one man, Victor Meldrew, a 60-year-old, who in the show's premiere episode is given early retirement from his job as a security guard/receptionist. From this beginning, many mistakenly believe that the show is about aging or retirement but this assumption misses the point entirely. For the program is not primarily about those topics, although they are naturally touched upon. Rather *One Foot in the Grave* is about the frustrations of modern life, as seen through the most sensitive man on the planet. Victor Meldrew is an everyman but one who has somehow gotten only the worst of it, continually, throughout his life. (Somewhere presumably there is his mirror image everyman, who is having a perpetually wonderful time.)

One imagines that Victor is who Tom Good (*The Good Life*) or Reggie Perrin (*The Fall and Rise of Reginald Perrin*) would have wound up being in 20 years — had they not staged their midlife rebellions. Most of us, however, do not dig up our backyards to become suburban farmers or fake our own suicides and come back to life to become retail tycoons. Most of us are like Victor Meldrew, subjected to taking what life dishes out and swallowing it. That is why for many, *One Foot in the Grave* is disquieting, it offers potent doses of real life hilariously presented but still disturbing. For those who still believe that they are entitled to their own happy endings as inalienable rights, it can be quite bothersome.

Victor Meldrew is a man who is twice injured by falling walls. Once when they tumble on him through no fault of his own (except for standing under them) and the second time when he shoves them back in retaliation, only giving them a chance to hit him again. Because of the lifelong calamity to which he has been subjected, Victor Meldrew has developed into a man who must spit back the bile continually fed to him by the rest of the world merely to survive. Victor's curmudgeonly reputation is so widespread that at one point an enemy posts a letter addressed merely to "that cretin in the cap," and the piece of mail arrives in record time.

Many, again especially in the United States, dismiss the show because the main character appears so nasty on the surface. Actually, Meldrew is probably one of the more feeling persons ever portrayed on a sitcom. Among other traits, he has a tremendous sense of justice, which usually prompts him to take the law into his own hands to right a perceived wrong. Invariably, this backfires terribly — except in the episode "Hearts of Darkness," in which Victor's vigilante activities succeed with chilling results.

Complementing Victor Meldrew perfectly is his long-suffering wife, Margaret, who simultaneously loves and is infuriated by her husband. In one episode, "Warm Champagne," Margaret toys with the idea of having an affair, but ultimately doesn't go through with it, telling her inamorata that she could not bear to see Victor hurt. "He's the most sensitive person I ever met, and that's why I love him," Margaret explains, before adding, "and that's why I constantly want to ram his head through a television screen."

One Foot in the Grave is the creation of author David Renwick. After years of contributing to some of Britain's finest sketch shows (including *Not the Nine O'Clock News* and *The Two Ronnies*), Renwick and his partner, Andrew Marshall, created the dark sitcom *Whoops Apocalypse* in 1982 for London Weekend Television. This acclaimed series of six shows was followed by a feature film of the same name. While less successful than its televised forerunner, the film did make use of a Scottish actor, Richard Wilson. During the filming of *Whoops Apocalypse*, while observing Wilson, Renwick first hit upon the character of Victor Meldrew.

Wilson who was playing the foreign secretary in the black political comedy, had a scene in which he was to be crucified on the field of a football stadium. The action required the actor to be strapped to the cross, then hauled upright. Years later, Wilson remembers the filming was "bloody excruciating." What made the experience all the more intolerable was that the film's director was intent on doing 20 takes in an attempt to get the perfect cinematic effect of the cross against the setting sun.

David Renwick watched as the director ignored his actor while trying to get his aesthetic sunset on film. "As the cross went up and down, up and down," recalled Renwick to James Roose-Evans, "you could see the irritability etched on Richard's face every time that cross went up. Oh, no, he was not a very happy man!"

The image of this constantly crucified man became the defining trait of Victor Meldrew.

Strangely, while other lead actors in popular series may seem as if their roles were tailormade for their particular talents, this is usually not the case. It is hard to believe that Arthur Lowe was not the first choice for either Captain Mainwaring (*Dad's Army*) or Father Duddleswell (*Bless Me, Father*), or that Roy Clarke did not create Hyacinth Bucket (*Keeping Up Appearances*) with Patricia Routledge in mind. With his first glimpse of Richard Wilson under torturous conditions, however, David Renwick thought of no other actor when creating Victor Meldrew. It is unthinkable, given the actor's perfection for the role, but the partnership of Renwick, Wilson, and Meldrew almost never saw the light of day.

Aside from his appearance in Renwick's film, Richard Wilson, born Iain Carmichael Wilson, had been an increasingly familiar face to British audiences since leaving a career at Paddington General Hospital as a laboratory technician at the age of 27 to become an actor. The aspiring thespian delayed a career on the stage due to a lack of confidence. "I thought people would laugh at me if I told them I wanted to be an actor," Wilson explained in 1990, "and indeed they did. I once told my amateur dramatics teacher at school that I'd like to try being an actor. She said, 'Don't be stupid, Wilson, you can't speak properly.' And I believed her."

Ironically, it was Wilson's distinctive speaking style that won him the praise and gratitude of his collaborators on *One Foot in the Grave*. Both author Renwick and director Susan Belbin appreciated his unique diction. Belbin described Wilson's speech as biting off words "with gusto." Renwick admits that not only was Wilson the sole inspiration for Victor Meldrew, Wilson also continued to inspire him. "The writing," Renwick told Roose-Evans, "has become cross-fertilized by Richard's performance."

After his strong supporting roles in such comedy series as *My Good Woman*, *Hot Metal* (cowritten by Renwick), and *Only When I Laugh*, the *Radio Times* referred to Wilson as "arguably the best-known unknown actor in the country." Wilson may have remained unknown had he followed his first instincts regarding the three scripts the BBC head of comedy sent him for a new series by David Renwick. "I read the scripts and I really didn't fancy them at all," Wilson confessed to Roose-Evans. "I didn't think they were all that good, and I thought Victor was rubbish because I felt he was too angry for too long. I couldn't imagine the audience would believe in him."

Another factor that gave Wilson pause was that Victor Meldrew was scripted as a man of 60, while the actor was only in his early fifties. Consequently, Wilson wrote to Renwick and politely told the author thanks, but no thanks. Renwick, having crafted the tortured Mr. Meldrew with Wilson as his template, asked if the actor would read three more scripts, those completing the first series. Wilson did, began to see the character in the light Renwick intended, and agreed to star in *One Foot in the Grave.*

Indeed, Wilson's initial reaction to the first three scripts had some validity, for they are arguably the weakest in the bunch (although still better than most other sitcoms running at the time). The second half of the first season does give more direction and definition to the author's expectations for the program, especially with regard to the complexity of Victor Meldrew. *One Foot in the Grave* is not a series about old people (such as *Waiting for God*). Rather, it is about a hapless individual who just happens to be older. Renwick himself noted that he made Meldrew a man forced into early retirement because he thought it would give him more freedom to explore different situations. It also gave Victor greater motivation for his constant railing against the injustices hurled toward him.

"He becomes a grumpy old so-and-so because society treats him like a cast-off," Wilson told Ian Woodward in the *Radio Times* just prior to the premiere of the first series. "It's what a lot of people are going through in these days of redundancies, only Victor's not very good at dealing with it."

In the same interview, Wilson expressed hopes that the viewers would take to the character and the show, stating that he thought it was "quite funny, quite an anarchic series" and "quite surreal."

Unfortunately, especially given the themes of the first two shows (forced retirement and death) the public mainly saw *One Foot in the Grave* as a dark show about aging (rather than a dark show about a tormented soul). The first ratings were in the neighborhood of 9 million viewers — not bad, but certainly not in the range needed to qualify as a solid hit. As the first series was repeated, and a second series quickly produced later the same year (1990), the quality of Renwick's meticulously crafted plots and Wilson's skill in the main role became evident to a much wider audience.

Certainly much of the success of the show must also go to actress Annette Crosbie in the pivotal role of Victor's wife, Margaret. In a comedy that runs so close to the precipice of tragedy as does *One Foot in the Grave*, how the main character's spouse reacts to the proceedings is almost as important as how the lead reacts. As stated before, *One Foot in the Grave* has parallels to shows like *The Good Life* or *Reggie Perrin*; it reflects similar situations, only without the optimism that buoyed those shows. To make Margaret Meldrew cheerfully supportive, as was Barbara Good, or an unconditional succorer like Elizabeth Perrin, would have struck a sour note in such a finely crafted comedy. Margaret is supportive, but in a more realistic sense and then only up to a point. She loves her husband but still at times would love to put his cranium through the television screen. She often tries to insulate Victor from impending tragedy — but mostly to preserve her own peace and sanity.

Annette Crosbie plays this integral part to perfection, providing just the right balance of affection and frustration. Had she been too sympathetic, her own character would have been cardboard, thus ruining the needed basis in reality. Had she been too much a harridan — as say, a Sybil Fawlty — the character of Victor would lose the sympathy he needs. In casting the part, the producers turned to Crosbie, an actress with little comedy experience. In fact the role of the working wife (Margaret works in a florist shop, another reminder to Victor that he no longer has a job) was quite a departure for Crosbie, who won BAFTA (British Academy of Film and Television Arts) Awards for playing Catherine of Aragon in the *Six Wives of Henry the VIII* and Queen Victoria in *Edward VII*. Like Richard Wilson, Crosbie is also a Scot, a heritage that seemed to help make their stage marriage appear more believable.

"When you're thought of as a straight actress," Crosbie told Wilson's biographer, "there's a certain respect. Nowadays people come up to me in the street and ask me how I can bear to live with an awful man like Victor — as though I really were married to him. Margaret's a saint really. I don't know why she's not on tranquilizers."

Whether or not Margaret Meldrew ever needed tranquilizers, some of the series' viewers apparently have to soothe themselves after they react angrily to the show. As could be expected with a comedy program that treats the heavier subjects of life with the weight usually offered in a drama or documentary, *One Foot in the Grave* is often the target of criticism from those who don't like their humor dark. "David's humor is very black," reasoned Wilson to Roose-Evans. "He often takes things to the edge, but he knows how to make people laugh."

Perhaps the actor would be better to qualify that to "most people" since the program often was the target of complaints from offended viewers. Some leaders of retirees' organizations have accused the series of making fun of the elderly (even though Victor is not technically a senior citizen). Animal rights activists protested the first season's "The Valley of Fear," which showed a cat being frozen stiff after wandering into the Meldrews' freezer. Others bristled when the second series' "We Have Put Her Living in the Tomb" featured Victor accidentally incinerating a live tortoise, with another of the same type of pet later being buried alive.

The fourth season's "Hearts of Darkness" generated the most complaints, however, as it depicted inmates of a retirement home being abused by the staff. That episode is particularly chilling, as we see Victor Meldrew's swift revenge on behalf of the abused patients. In this, and other instances, however, the author never endorses or encourages the macabre situations. Rather, Renwick uses them to illustrate deeper points about human behavior and social responsibilities.

In defending his show to the chairman of the BBC, Renwick wrote: "You will always offend even though you don't set out to. Horror and comedy are closely related. Disasters are always funny when they're happening to other people."

Later, Renwick explained in a general announcement, which was drafted to answer complaints about his program, that while *One Foot in the Grave* doesn't intentionally set out to shock people, the nature of the reality-based comedy makes it difficult not to offend someone.

Despite the handful of dissatisfied viewers, by the end of its second season *One Foot in the Grave* had started to develop a cult following. The first 12 episodes were followed by two double-length Christmas specials in 1990 and 1991, both of which further honed the querulous Mr. Meldrew's character into what the *Radio Times* described as "the man who has turned irritability into an art form."

Successful third and fourth series in 1992 and 1993 led to Victor Meldrew being featured in a seven-minute sketch in a *Comedy Relief* special. The otherwise unreleased bit shows Victor contemplating life while taking a bath. As expected, Victor's bath is interrupted by an annoying telephone call.

From the brief *Comedy Relief* appearance, the next incarnation of Meldrew came in the ambitious but slightly disappointing feature-length television film *One Foot in the Algarve*, in which the Meldrews vacation in Portugal. A year later, viewers were treated to another Christmas present from David Renwick in the form of "The Man Who Blew Away." This 40-minute special could also be considered the kickoff show for the fifth season, which commenced one week later but contained only five episodes rather than the usual six.

By the fifth season, the episodes, which arguably hit their firmest stride in the third and fourth seasons, began to show signs of slippage. The fifth would be the last series, as Victor and Margaret were relegated to yearly appearances in Christmas specials. This new approach helped prevent the complex formula from fraying around the edges, while keeping the quality up to the higher standard that viewers had come to expect from Renwick

As of this writing, "Endgame," a 70-minute installment that aired on Christmas evening 1997, has been the most recent word from Victor Meldrew. Since then both Renwick and director Susan Belbin have been busy with *Jonathan Creek*, a detective series that the author describes as a "British Columbo." After much prodding by the comedy-starved BBC, it was announced in the spring of 1999 that Renwick had once again agreed to create a fresh series for his inimitable creation, Victor Meldrew. It will indeed be a treat to once again hear from the man whose tortured existence can be encapsulated in his own quote: "One thing you can be sure about life: just when you think that things are never ever going to get better, they suddenly get worse."

Poor Meldrew. They always do get worse for him but, thankfully, for the viewer, they also get funnier.

THE EPISODES

By David Renwick. Directed by: Susan Belbin, Sydney Lotterby, and Christine Gernon. Produced by Susan Belbin and Esta Charkham

Series One 1990

EPISODE 1: "ALIVE AND BURIED" ★★½

Air date: January 4, 1990. Cast: Victor Meldrew (Richard Wilson); Margaret Meldrew (Annette Crosbie); Mrs. Inglis (Susie Blake); Mrs. Jellis (Valerie Minfie); Mrs. Warboys (Doreen Mantle); Nick (Owen Brenman); Garage Manager (Nick Maloney); Police Officer (Simon Greenall)

After 26 years as a security guard/receptionist, 60-year-old Victor Meldrew is replaced by an electronic box and forced into early retirement. Suddenly Victor is given all the time in the world and nothing with which to fill it. After Victor is mistakenly arrested on the charge of trying to procure a call girl, Margaret tries to assure her husband that he still has his whole life ahead of him. Victor glumly agrees that this is what scares him most of all.

The first episode of *One Foot in the Grave* does a fair job of introducing the premise and main characters. For American viewers, however, who have usually had their first taste of Victor Meldrew via the second series, there is often something missing. In this initial installment the marvelous Meldrew is not as sharp, not as aggressive as he would become in the later series. Here he is more compliant, less willing to act (beyond a humorous verbal complaint) when suffering a wrong. At one point in this first episode he enters a service garage to announce that he is Victor Meldrew, "the Crimson Avenger." The more developed Victor would only announce that (if at all) after he had plotted his revenge. (Perhaps the later shows are funnier because more befalls Victor when his own schemes to right wrongs backfire on him and compound his misery.)

Victor's initial attempts at puttering around the house start to drive him up the wall the first day of his retirement. By 9 A.M. he is already counting the hours until bedtime. He also catches himself going to the toilet every 15 minutes just to have something to do. He quickly catches himself since he is afraid he will become a "toilet junkie" and be forced to have his fly soldered shut as a treatment.

Victor's restlessness is interrupted by a visit from Nick (who will become his neighbor in subsequent series) from the Outward Bound Senior Transport Program. Victor throws him out but is forced to accept his services the next day. Victor does a wonderful slow boil in the back seat of Nick's car, wedged between two aged women. While Victor frets about being late for his interview, the congenial Nick takes extra care to give a syrupy commentary on all the points of interest along the way, including geraniums and women's hats. The ride from hell is prolonged even further when the car stalls and the elderly passengers must get out and push it down a hill to get it going again. Later when Victor's car breaks down on his way back from the Senior Center, he encounters Nick's car being pushed again by a group of retirees — one of whom has to use a walker.

EPISODE 2: "THE BIG SLEEP" ★½

Air date: January 11, 1990. Cast: Victor Meldrew (Richard Wilson); Margaret Meldrew (Annette Crosbie); Window Cleaner (Faye Maguire); 1st Jehovah's Witness (Christopher Saul); 2nd Jehovah's Witness (David Peart); Keep Fit Instructress (Kay Adshead); Len (Leonard Lowe); Michael (Danny O'Dea); Elspeth (Hilary Mason); Nurse (Pamela Lane); Make-Up Girl (Lisa Bluthal); Dr. Snellgrove (Helen Fraser); Radio DJ (Colin Ward-Lewis)

In an attempt to relieve Victor's malaise, Margaret enrolls them both in a senior citizens' exercise class. Unfortunately, the Keep Fit Instructress has a coronary while demonstrating yoga and dies. By the end of the episode Victor imagines that he has died after waking up from a nap in his fog-shrouded backyard. When he encounters a man in a white beard, Victor takes the man to be his maker. Rather than being awestruck, however, Victor chides God for allowing so much frustration in his life.

After delving into the anxieties of forced retirement in its premiere episode, the second installment of *One Foot in the Grave* takes a deeper step into

Only the luckless, querulous Victor Meldrew (Richard Wilson) could find himself buried in his own garden to be discovered by his neighbor and nemesis Patrick (Angus Deayton). Copyright © BBC.

the dark topic of death. Even for a series that is often a black comedy, this episode gets a bit grim with depression often winning out over any humor that is generated. As with "Alive and Buried," "The Big Sleep" (a euphemism for death) concentrates on one theme, which is then illustrated through Victor Meldrew. This serves to put the focus on the topic, which often makes the situations too close for comfort. Later episodes make Victor the center of the show, with any themes introduced being on the periphery and more easily laughed at.

Very sharp eyes may spot Reggie Perrin's landlady, Mrs. Deacon (Hilary Mason) as Elspeth, the woman whose plastic hip locks in exercise class.

Despite the grim nature of the topic, there are some humorous moments, most of which come in the form of one-liners from Victor Meldrew. At the start of the episode Victor explains that a book on coping with retirement advises that recalling pleasant memories can control depression. He then grimly announces that he's been trying to conjure up a happy memory for a fortnight with no success.

Episode 3: "The Valley of Fear" ★★★½

Air date: January 18, 1990. Cast: Victor Meldrew (Richard Wilson); Margaret Meldrew (Annette Crosbie); Mrs. Warboys (Doreen Mantle); Mrs. Birkett (Gabrielle Blunt); Plumber (Christopher Ryan); Plumber's Assistant (David Keys); George (Walter Sparrow); Mr. Prout (Peter Corey); Market Stall-holder (Jonathan Kydd); 1st Yob (Jake Wood); 2nd Yob (Joseph Wright); Bowls Player (Donald Bisset)

After being mugged, Victor Meldrew tries to organize a citizens' crime prevention group to fight crime. Rather than curb crime, it only emboldens Mrs. Warboys to start carrying a hand grenade in her purse. Worst of all, Victor inadvertently conducts his own armed robbery by episode's end.

While a vast improvement over the first two episodes, "The Valley of Fear" still presents some rather grim situations, but the strength of its humor overcomes potentially depressing reactions from the audience. Victor is mugged, finds a dead cat in his freezer, locks an elderly woman in his attic for 24 hours, and commits armed robbery, but thanks to David Renwick's script, none of this becomes too morose since it remains firmly anchored to the main character's world. Instead of passively witnessing tragedies, Victor now fights back despite his best intentions becomes part of the problem he is combating. In this way the horrors of daily life can be translated through Victor Meldrew, rather than be presented in the raw as straight social commentary.

As offensive as it might seem to find a cat frozen in one's freezer, the tragedy is truly hilarious when it's Victor Meldrew's freezer. Victor discovers the animal and quickly accuses Margaret of leaving the door open. Margaret is justifiably horrified, noting that she has suddenly come over "all cold." "*You've* come over all cold," Victor replies, picking up the stiff feline.

Margaret wonders how long it's been there. Victor sarcastically answers that he'll look for the animal's sell-by date.

Finally, in true Meldrew resignation, Victor looks at the only apparent bright side to the morbid affair. He remarks that it's a good thing they didn't have a full-sized freezer chest since he'd probably have been left with a frozen mammoth.

Episode 4: "I'll Retire to Bedlam" ★★★

Air date: January 25, 1990. Cast: Victor Meldrew (Richard Wilson); Margaret Meldrew (Annette Crosbie); Iris (Rebecca Stevens); Mr. Gillespie (Roger Hammond); Mr. Jellinek (John Bluthal); Eye Clinic Nurse (Cecily Hobbs); Mr. Parslow (Norman Lumsden); Old Lady (Evie Garratt); TV Producer (Victoria Hasted); Cleaner (Joolia Cappleman); Mr. Davidson (Jim Barclay); Dylan

(Edward Harris); Elliott (Simon Bright); Hospital Nurse (John Cassady); Hospital Doctor (Heather Canning); Tory MP (Tony Mathews)

Victor Meldrew is menaced by bees, young children, and political candidates. Later, Victor is rushed to the hospital with abdominal pains. An orderly enters Victor's examination room to announce his appendix must come out, then begins shaving his lower torso and genitals in preparation. The orderly seems to be doing a professional job, until he starts explaining to Victor that he has been shopping for real estate on the moon. The doctor enters and urges Victor not to make any sudden moves while the madman continues shaving his groin.

Primarily a commentary on the state of Britain's national health system, "I'll Retire to Bedlam" make its points without sacrificing its entertainment value. As in the previous episode, David Renwick has managed to be satirical by concentrating on Victor Meldrew's personal pitfalls, rather than by taking too broad an aim at his intended targets.

Some of the better moments in *One Foot in the Grave* are those in which Victor makes his endless commentaries on pet peeves. One of his greatest frustrations is the litter that passersby lob over the fence into his back garden. This steady stream of refuse led him to declare in the premiere episode that he was thinking of compiling a volume entitled "The Observer's Book of Crap on Your Front Lawn."

In this episode he can't sleep for wondering how three Twix wrappers managed to land on his lawn in one day. He sarcastically reasons that they must be coming from the

"Planet Twix in the star system Flat Lager Can."

Later in the episode Victor rants about the inability of toilet paper manufacturers to align the perforations on both sheets of two-ply paper. He stalks off to repair the defect on the sewing machine before Margaret stops him.

EPISODE 5: "THE ETERNAL QUADRANGLE" ★★★½

Air date: February 1, 1990. Cast: Victor Meldrew (Richard Wilson); Margaret Meldrew (Annette Crosbie); Art Teacher (Angus MacKay); Mrs. Mauleverer (Gillian Barge); Harold Wharton (John Barrard); Carpet-Fitter (David Battley); Leonard (Peter Copley)

Margaret becomes jealous when she learns that Victor has been sketching a nude woman in his evening art class. She is further incensed when she discovers that Victor not only gave the model, a divorcee named Mrs. Mauleverer, a ride home, but he also has agreed to do odd jobs around the woman's home. Out of spite Margaret fosters a relationship with Harold Wharton, a quiet little retiree.

The first real exploration of the marriage of Victor and Margaret Meldrew, "The Eternal Quadrangle" introduces a theme that will be revisited throughout subsequent series of *One Foot in the Grave*. As in future episodes the outcome is essentially the same: Victor often drives Margaret to the brink of infidelity without her actually succumbing to temptation, while Victor comes close to stumbling many times himself, without seeking or even being aware of it.

Victor Meldrew, as he confesses in series five's "Rearranging the Dust," has only ever had eyes for Margaret and never doubts her fidelity. In fact when Harold Wharton cautiously courts Margaret under Victor's nose in this episode by sending her flowers, Victor interprets it as an attempt to show him up as a gardener. Here, as in future temptations, the Meldrew marriage survives, which is a blessing not only to Victor and Margaret, but also to us viewers. Where would we be without the long-suffering Margaret and her marvelous reactions to her husband's latest mishaps?

Margaret's outburst of jealousy is quite funny as she confronts Victor over his drawing of the nude model. She is especially angry that he insisted on drawing breasts on her. Victor defensively asks if he was supposed to ask the model to slip them off until he finished his sketch.

His wife's ire grows, however, when she discovers that Victor gave the model a ride home. While Margaret keeps referring to her as that "nude woman," Victor tries to explain that she only was naked while modeling. Finally, Margaret asks if he let the model sit in the car's passenger seat. Victor sarcastically asserts that he tied the woman to the luggage rack.

There's also some good work done by Peter Copley as Leonard, Mrs. Mauleverer's aged father. As Victor tries to vacuum the living room, Leonard enters from the opposite side of the room with a vacuum cleaner of his own. It seems that Leonard resents Victor's presence since he feels he can still manage to do the work despite his advanced age. Soon the two men are faced off, banging their extension wands against each other like two hockey players fighting over a puck. Mrs. Mauleverer enters to try and calm her father but only manages to incite him to suck his toupee off into the vacuum in an act of defiance.

Leonard returns later in the episode as his daughter is sketching Victor upside down for a portrait of the crucifixion of St. Peter. Leonard complains again that Victor's services are not needed, adding in a wonderful throwaway line, "I could have done that standing on my head."

EPISODE 6: "THE RETURN OF THE SPECKLED BAND" ★★★

Air date: February 8, 1990. Cast: Victor Meldrew (Richard Wilson); Margaret Meldrew (Annette Crosbie); Mrs. Warboys (Doreen Mantle); Electricity Man (Clive Mantle); Mr. Berenger (John Cater); Garden Center Manager (Lloyd McGuire); Dustman (Willie Ross)

The Meldrews are getting ready to go on a vacation to Athens but first must run a gamut of Meldrewian situations. The worst of these involves Victor inadvertently bringing home an escaped giant python from the gardening center.

The final episode of the introductory season is rather typical fare by *One Foot in the Grave* standards. "The Return of the Speckled Band" offers the usual mistaken situations and unforeseen mishaps. One new twist is the element of suspense in the guise of a seven-foot python on the loose in the Meldrews' home. Unfortunately, they never discover the snake, although the episode finishes with the promise of almost certain detection by Victor, presumably at the most inopportune moment. This is somewhat of a letdown after such a careful buildup of the situation. Perhaps author Renwick thought our imaginations would resolve the suspense much more vividly than any actual filmed sequence could.

There is a good recurring gag in "The Return of the Speckled Band," when Victor is given an ill-fitting homburg hat as a gift from the obtuse Mrs. Warboys. She explains that the lid used to belong to her late Uncle Edwin. Mrs. Warboys remarks they had intended to bury Edwin in the hat but reasoned that it would be foolish to waste it on a corpse when she could give it to Victor.

Later, Victor throws out the hat, only to have the trashman return it to him in exchange for a reward. Finally, Victor throws the hat in a rented dumpster down the street. The hat returns in a parcel the next morning, along with an irate letter from a neighbor warning Victor about dumping his trash in their hired receptacle. Victor comments that he would bury the homburg in his backyard, except that he fears a stranger would give it back to him in Athens.

Series Two 1990

EPISODE 1: "IN LUTON AIRPORT NO ONE CAN HEAR YOU SCREAM" ★★★½

Air date: October 4, 1990. Cast: Victor Meldrew (Richard Wilson); Margaret Meldrew (Annette Crosbie); Mrs. Warboys (Doreen Mantle); Irate Neighbours (Michael Robbins, Doremy Vernon); Nick Swainey (Owen Brenman); Mr. Prout (Peter Corey); Mr. Drewitt (Michael Bilton)

Victor and Margaret return from a disastrous holiday in Greece only to be informed by Mrs. Warboys that their house has been demolished while they were away. Six months later the Meldrews finally move into a new home. Their new neighbor, Nick Swainey, tells Victor some unsettling but vague stories about the gory demise of the previous owner.

Once settled, Victor and Margaret throw a housewarming party, but nobody comes. After two hours, Victor finds that his housewarming guests are indeed having a party but in the wrong house.

"In Luton Airport No One Can Hear You Scream" is a marvelously funny beginning to the second round of woes in the life and retirement of Victor Meldrew. Picking up where the first series left off, David Renwick then wipes the slate clean, giving the Meldrews a new home and a new neighbor.

The addition of Owen Brenman's Nick Swainey to the regular cast is inspired. After appearing as the cheerfully patronizing man from the elder transport program in the premiere episode, Swainey is reintroduced here. In addition to his previous persona, the character is now endowed with a subtle deranged edge. He hints about his previous neighbor's bloody death, watches Freddie Kruger videos, and purportedly lives with his elderly mother, who Victor never sees. The mixture gives Nick a definite air of being a suburban Norman Bates.

One of the funnier bits is purely expository, as Mrs. Warboys describes the fate of the Meldrews home. It seems that a fire started when some children put some firecrackers through Victor's letterbox. When a neighbor tried to call the fire brigade she got the wrong number, and a trio of men in gorilla suits from the Singing Telegram Company arrived instead. Next, the fire was extinguished, saving the shell of the house. That was when the hurricane struck. Finally, the place had to be demolished when parts of it started collapsing on people in the street.

If being homeless weren't bad enough, the Meldrews soon discover that their luggage has been hopelessly lost, leaving them with only the clothes they are wearing. Six months later, Victor receives one sock back from the airline.

EPISODE 2: "WE HAVE PUT HER LIVING IN THE TOMB" ★★★★

Air date: October 11, 1990. Cast: Victor Meldrew (Richard Wilson); Margaret Meldrew (Annette Crosbie); Jennifer (Sarah Mortimer); Mrs. Warboys (Doreen Mantle); Sky TV Salesman (Andrew Powell); Car Park Attendant (Malcolm Frederick)

Victor returns from the hardware store with a sample book of wallpapers only to discover that his paint estimate is written on the back of a suicide note penned by the deceased husband of the woman who runs the shop.

Next, the Meldrews babysit pet tortoise and ultimately wind up incinerating the animal, and they also inadvertently cause its replacement to be buried alive.

Situations fly by and intertwine furiously yet almost effortlessly in "We Have Put Her Living in the Tomb," making the episode almost the highlight of the entire series — indeed it is quintessential *One Foot in the Grave.* From Victor's opening argument over the phone with his dry cleaners, to an unexplained, yet terribly funny running gag that has Victor yelling about pastry in his sleep, to a lingering smell left on Victor by a solvent, there are masterstrokes throughout the episode.

The climax to all this lunacy is reached when Victor must take a urine sample to the clinic. Victor sterilizes an old bottle that previously held tranquilizers. Before he can fill the bottle, Victor falls asleep on the couch while browsing the wallpaper sample book. Mrs. Warboys enters to discover Victor on the couch, the empty tranquilizer container, and the suicide note written on the back of the estimate from the shop. Unable to stir Victor from his deep slumber, she assumes the worst and drags Victor off to the bathroom where he finally awakens when she puts her fingers down his throat.

"We Have Put Her Living in the Tomb" was chosen as the template for the premiere episode of the American series *Cosby*. Unfortunately, the piece suffered greatly in the translation, underlining the differences between American and British television and humor. One of the main differences, and indeed the one that takes the backbone from the plot, is that where Victor accidentally kills a pet tortoise in his care, Bill Cosby's character only almost kills it. The animal lives, thus robbing the situation of its punch. The humor lies not in burning a tortoise to death — which certainly would be cruel by itself— but in the resulting plot complications and the final dark gag.

Apparently, the powers that be at CBS, creative and otherwise, have a difficult time understanding the building of a comedy situation, and they think a smoking turtle is a funny gag all by itself. To make matters even more ridiculous, at the time of *Cosby*'s airing there was considerable controversy over showing the tortoise being abused and a disclaimer was issued by the network — thus the making of the show became far more humorous than the show itself.

EPISODE 3: "DRAMATIC FEVER" ★★★★

Air date: October 18, 1990. Cast: Victor Meldrew (Richard Wilson); Margaret Meldrew (Annette Crosbie); Plumber (Dick Sullivan); Plumber's Mate (Billy Clarke); Postman (Mark Baxter); Hilary (Maggie Ollerenshaw); Graham (Gareth Armstrong); Martin (Bill Monks); Desiree Gibson (Fleur Chandler); Jasper Gibson (Terry Taplin); Gerry (Geoff Parry). With the voices of John Sessions and Chris Emmett

Margaret's joining of the local theatrical group results in the Meldrews being invited to a dinner party. Meanwhile, Victor is playing vigilante again after he witnesses a burly construction worker littering. In his bid for justice, Victor fills the man's sports car with garbage. Unfortunately, Victor dumps the trash in the wrong car.

Later in the week the Meldrews arrive at the party to discover that they were not asked to attend as guests but as caterers. To make matters worse, one of the guests is the owner of the car despoiled by Victor. Although he did not witness the act, the car's owner found some discarded slides of Victor amidst the trash.

As in the previous episode, author David Renwick weaves another masterful ballet of mistakes and mishaps in "Dramatic Fever." In addition to the usual hilarity, however, we also catch a glimpse of the sensitive underside of the crusty Victor Meldrew. Throughout the episode Victor is working on a situation comedy pilot for a BBC contest. He chuckles to himself as he fine tunes his script, while keeping its contents a secret until he finishes. Finally, he allows Margaret to read the opus. She pronounces the work "absolute dribble." Victor quietly remarks that he enjoyed the writing and had hoped he finally found something at which he was good. Margaret tries to retract her harsh critique but later finds the script torn to pieces.

Victor Meldrew apparently would be his own best audience for *One Foot in the Grave*, for although he suffers through his life, it is filled with situations that he finds amusing. When he goes to Margaret's play rehearsal, Victor mistakes a tragic accident for a riotous black comedy. He watches the proceedings disinterestedly until a workman falls from the catwalk through a greenhouse set. Thinking it is part of the play, Victor begins chuckling to himself as the players scramble to rescue the injured man. As the real life mishaps escalate, Victor laughs all the more and even takes out a bag of candy to add to his enjoyment.

Only after Victor begins applauding in grateful appreciation of the scene he has just witnessed do the cast members realize there is someone in the darkened auditorium. Hoping beyond hope, Margaret peers into the black, then correctly guesses: "Victor?"

Ironically, Margaret later criticizes Victor's attempt at comedy writing for having too many outlandish situations that don't reflect real life.

EPISODE 4: "WHO WILL BUY?" ★★★½

Air date: October 25, 1990. Cast: Victor Meldrew (Richard Wilson); Margaret Meldrew (Annette Crosbie); Toy Salesman (William Vanderpuye); Nick Swainey (Owen Brenman); Pippa (Janine Duvitski); Patrick (Angus Deayton); Jill Archer (Patricia Greene); Albert (Jimmy Jewel)

Margaret befriends a lonely old blind man when she delivers some flowers to him by mistake, while Victor revives his ventriloquism act with his sawdust-leaking dummy, Cuthbert.

By the end of the episode both of these activities result in surprising outcomes — one comic and the other tragic.

With its stinging commentary on consumerism, "Who Will Buy?" is simultaneously one of the most hilarious and most tragic pieces of sitcom ever broadcast. Perhaps with the exception of the last episode of *Blackadder Goes Forth* (which has the added impact of being that series' final testament), this episode's final moment presents the most chilling coda in television comedy.

This episode also introduces the Meldrews' other next-door neighbors: Patrick and Pippa. Although it is only barely suggested here, Patrick will provide Victor with a much-needed personal adversary.

Perhaps the comic high point of the episode comes when the timorous Pippa arrives to drive Victor to one of his ventriloquist performances. Letting herself in, Pippa overhears Victor shouting on the phone with a local repair shop while holding his ventriloquist's dummy. Unfortunately, from her angle, it appears that he is giving the severe lecture to Cuthbert the dummy.

After the show Pippa helps Victor carry his paraphernalia back into the house. Victor asks her to take the dummy into the downstairs toilet, adding that he's ready to burst. Not realizing Victor is referring to the dummy's sawdust stuffing and wanting to humor her neighbor, Pippa takes Cuthbert into the bathroom where she dutifully holds him over the toilet, shakes him out, zips him up, then flushes. Victor and Margaret watch in dumbfounded silence as Pippa hands Cuthbert back, then runs out the door.

Episode 5: "Love and Death" ★★★½

Air date: November 1, 1990. Cast: Victor Meldrew (Richard Wilson); Margaret Meldrew (Annette Crosbie); Elderly Lady on Train (Myrtle Devenish); April Bluett (Georgina Hale); Vince Bluett (Stephen Lewis); Petra (Leigh Samuels); Marie (Patricia Martinelli); Rusty (Peter Burroughs); Policeman (Paul Mari)

Victor and Margaret visit their friends April and Vince Bluett, who run a seaside boardinghouse. In one disastrous weekend everything goes wrong, with both Victor and Margaret believing they have been forced into infidelity by their hosts.

"Love and Death" is filled with so many improbable situations and mistaken perceptions, it is a wonder that it all fits into a 30-minute episode. Victor Meldrew takes a trip to the seashore that turns out to be a nightmarish version of *Mr. Hulot's Holiday*. Unlike Jacques Tati's inimitable Mr. Hulot, who walks through the scenery sparking odd events, Meldrew's only aim is to make it through a simple weekend without having the scenery fall on him. Thankfully, he fails.

April's annoying habit of laughing at everything Victor says is established early in the episode and provides much mirth. Soon after arriving, Victor strides in to supper to announce that there is a dead seagull in the upstairs toilet. April laughs, even after Victor twice insists that he isn't joking. After finally believing Victor's assertion, April reasons that the bird must have flown in the window and fallen in the bowl. In a wonderful blend of sarcasm and disbelief of April's obtuseness, Victor answers that he didn't think the seagull had come out of someone's bottom.

The next day, Vince proudly presents Victor with a marble headstone, which he carved himself. Despite the quality of the stone and the obvious craftsmanship, Victor is less than thrilled with the chilling gift. Sensing Victor's lack of enthusiasm, Vince asks if Victor perhaps already has a headstone.

The funniest situation, however, is Victor gluing a plastic cup to his head. Unaware that Margaret has just reattached the bottom of the drinking cup with super glue, Victor enters and pours a bottle of beer into the vessel. He then lies on the bed, while cooling his face with the cold cup. Finally, he rests the bottom of the cup on his forehead. Margaret enters, but the epoxy has already set. He tries to get up, but Margaret cautions that doing so will spill beer all over the place. Victor complains that he can't stay in the prone position indefinitely and compares himself to a "bedridden Dalek."

Episode 6: "Timeless Time" ★★

Air date: November 8, 1990. Cast: Victor Meldrew (Richard Wilson); Margaret Meldrew (Annette Crosbie)

Victor cannot sleep and eventually spreads his insomnia to Margaret. The couple talk about various things, from the mysteries of the universe to the first time they slept together.

In between discussions, Victor must twice turn off his ultrasensitive car alarm — once when an owl defecates on it, the second time when a cat sits on the hood. While returning from the second trip, Victor accidentally loses his slipper and inadvertently replaces it with a dead hedgehog.

The couple never do get to sleep. When the first morning sparrow begins to chirp, Victor yells at it to shut up.

The first of a series of one-set episodes played out in real time, "Timeless Time" is a valiant attempt that doesn't quite work. The main problem perhaps is that while the situation is well suited for the type of stream-of-consciousness dialog presented here, it is not all that conducive for comedy.

The best moments in the episode are dramatic in nature. Margaret offers a tender soliloquy toward the end that comments on the brevity of a lifetime. The Meldrews' son, Stuart, who apparently died tragically while still a child, is also mentioned for the first time.

At one point, while staring at the ceiling, Victor develops his theory that nothing really exists. He reasons that the future hasn't happened, and the past is already gone, leaving only the present. But the present is extremely fleeting also, since as soon as it occurs it becomes the past. He then proves his point by repeatedly noting that every sentence he is speaking is quickly becoming the past. He does this until Margaret turns on the light and tells him to shut up.

Christmas Special 1990

"Who's Listening?" ★★★½

Air date: December 27, 1990. Cast: Victor Meldrew (Richard Wilson); Margaret Meldrew (Annette Crosbie); Mrs. Warboys (Doreen Mantle); Mrs. Burridge (Cathy Shipton); Reverend Croker (Geoffrey Chater); Pippa (Janine Duvitski); Patrick (Angus Deayton); Adam Burridge (Chase Marks); Ted (Bob Appleby); Starkey (Enn Reitel)

Just before the holiday, the Meldrews' home is overrun with 263 garden gnomes when Victor mistakenly puts the item number in the quantity space on the order form.

Pippa's father, the Reverend Croker, a minister who is quitting because of a crisis of faith, spends some time with Victor and Margaret while waiting for his daughter to come home. To illustrate his loss of faith in God, the Reverend Croker tells them of Mrs. Burridge, one of his parishioners whose husband was just killed in a fiery car crash on the way to a business trip. He explains that although Mrs. Burridge, a devout Christian, has not lost her faith through the incident, he has.

After being held hostage by a homeless man on Christmas day, Victor returns home to wonder if there is any use in believing in anything or if anyone — Father Christmas or God — is really listening. Across town young Adam Burridge waits in the snow for his father to return. Suddenly his father appears, and the family shares a joyous reunion.

The next day, Mrs. Warboys explains to Margaret that Mr. Burridge took an earlier flight on his business trip, and his car was stolen from the airport car park. While the thieves were joyriding, the car and its occupants were burned beyond recognition in the crash.

A fine holiday treat for fans of *One Foot in the Grave*, "Who's Listening?" manages to reaffirm the Christmas message of hope and faith without letting any of the cheer reach the beleaguered Victor Meldrew. Given his trend toward black comedy and grim endings ("Who Will Buy?"), it is a pleasant surprise that author David Renwick did not opt for this route, although at times it definitely seems that is the direction the special is taking. Although the Reverend Croker discards his faith, and Victor Meldrew wonders who's listening, those who, hoping against all hope, cling to their beliefs (Mrs. Burridge in God and her son in Father Christmas) are ultimately much richer for it.

By far the best moments are reserved for Victor and the gnomes who have overrun his home. At one point Victor absentmindedly brings one of the grinning statues to bed with him before he realizes his mistake and chides the gnome for it. In the end any hopes of Victor getting a refund for the gnomes is dashed when Patrick mows the little men down with a machine gun (the one taken from the homeless man) in retaliation for Victor ruining his bottle of rare £800 wine.

Christmas Special 1991

"The Man in the Long Black Coat" ★★★

Air date: December 30, 1991. Cast: Victor Meldrew (Richard Wilson); Margaret Meldrew (Annette Crosbie); Patrick (Angus Deayton); Pippa (Janine Duvitski); Receptionist (Cecily Hobbs); Nick Swainey (Owen Brenman);

Mr. Killick (Michael Robbins); Mervyn Whale (Special Guest Appearance by Eric Idle)

Seven months after Patrick machine gunned his garden gnomes, Victor Meldrew is still feuding with his neighbor. Patrick's main weapons of irritation are yellow post-it notes, upon which he writes complaints before sticking them to Victor's back gate. Victor's latest ploy has been an attempt to teach a local cat to vomit in Patrick's garden.

The latest irritant to Patrick, and indeed the whole neighborhood, is apile of horse manure sitting on Victor's curb. It seems that Victor purchased the fertilizer from a mysterious man in a long black coat for use on his allotment garden. Instead of delivering the manure to the allotment, however, the man brought it to Victor's house.

Later, when it is discovered that the excrement is radioactive, the allotment association dumps Victor's entire garden in front of his house.

Victor and Patrick reconcile briefly, however, when the Meldrews rush Patrick to the hospital when Pippa suffers a miscarriage.

Shown at Christmastime but not really a holiday special, "The Man in the Long Black Coat" picks up the story line where "Who's Listening?" left off. The special is essentially a prolonged series entry filled with the usual misadventures that viewers have come to expect from Victor Meldrew.

While the plot centers on Victor's battles with Patrick, ironically, all the hard feelings between the two men are precipitated by misunderstandings. Both wives wonder how to effect reconciliation between the pair but never really attempt one. The tragic ending provides a brief truce, but as events in subsequent seasons will prove, it in no way signals a halt of hostilities.

Both neighbors think it a deliberate act when Victor trips and lands headlong in the fresh cement of Patrick's front walk, leaving a deep, full-sized impression of himself.

Later, Victor asks if Patrick plans on filling in the walkway. Patrick sarcastically replies that he's preserving the impression as the first in a memorial of neighbors' faces in concrete.

Days later Margaret accidentally puts Patrick's ginseng capsules in her purse and Victor mistakes them for his hemorrhoid suppository prescription. When Margaret discovers the error, she quickly returns the remaining capsules to Patrick, who has been searching for them. "I looked in most places," he tells Pippa, "it's fair to say I never dreamed of looking there."

Pippa figures out how Margaret took the capsules by accident, but Patrick is not placated. He decides that a law should be passed labeling most items with the warning: "Caution! This product should not be shoved up Victor Meldrew's rectum."

Monty Python's Eric Idle, who wrote and sang the show's title theme, appears to good effect as a quirky health inspector.

Series Three 1992

Episode 1: "Monday Morning Will Be Fine" ★★★★

Air date: February 2, 1992. Cast: Victor Meldrew (Richard Wilson); Margaret Meldrew (Annette Crosbie); Jack Aylesbury (Tony Millan); Pat Aylesbury (Jan Ravens); Billy (Richard Davies); Meg (Diana Coupland); Chippie Joe (Jonathan Kydd); Detective Gannis (James Hickish); Detective Diller (Nick Ball); Sales Assistant (Helen Patrick)

Burglars steal most of the Meldrews' furniture, including their television set. Victor asserts that they are better off without the TV and tells Margaret he is tempted to not buy a new one. By the end of the week, however, Margaret is desperate for a new set, if only to keep Victor out of the myriad of troubles caused by his new video-free existence.

"Monday Morning Will Be Fine" is a perfect example of situation comedy. The episode moves smoothly from happenstance to mis-happenstance, with no reliance on jokes or gags that are not directly related to the plot. The entire half hour fits together neatly from an apparent jumble of seemingly unrelated pieces, much as the jigsaw puzzle upon which Victor works in this episode. A gem of writing and execution.

One of the funnier situations involves Victor running into Billy, an old schoolmate, at a pub. The reminiscing turns to odd characters they once knew, and Billy distastefully recalls a "bastard" named Victor Meldrew. Billy then begins calling Victor "Steve" and remembers how similar he was in appearance to Victor Meldrew. At this point, Margaret enters with Meg, a coworker. It seems that Billy is Meg's fiancé, so Victor must continue to be Steve in order to support the lie that Margaret has fabricated to avoid going to the couple's upcoming wedding. Ultimately, Billy gives everyone a ride home, which includes dropping "Steve" miles away from Victor's house. Victor is forced to walk home in the rain, which results in a severe case of laryngitis.

This perfect episode ends with Margaret buying a new television to keep Victor out of any more trouble. She pleads with the assistant for a Saturday delivery. While the assistant goes to arrange a delivery time, however, Margaret looks at the previews for Saturday night's TV lineup on the display models. "You've Been Framed," a home video blooper show, features a clip of a bird's nest and eggs falling on Victor's head. The assistant returns to tell Margaret that Saturday delivery can be arranged. Margaret decides they should wait until Monday morning.

Episode 2: "Dreamland" ★★

Air date: February 9, 1992. Cast: Victor Meldrew (Richard Wilson); Margaret Meldrew (Annette Crosbie); Mrs. Warboys (Doreen Mantle); Nick Swainey (Owen Brenman); Elderly Lady (Damaris Hayman); Policewoman (Julie Hewlett); Ladies in Tea Shop (Barbara Grant, Annette Kerr); Tramp (Enn Reitel)

Margaret has been having a recurring nightmare in which she is waiting to be hanged for battering to death a balding old man with gray hair. When a last-minute reprieve sets her free on the grounds of justifiable homicide, she refuses to leave the jail and clings to her cell. Assuming that the man is Victor, she takes delight in ridiculing him to others.

The next evening Margaret turns up missing. Phone calls by Victor and Mrs. Warboys reveal that she never arrived at work that morning, and no one has seen her. The next day the police discover her coat down by the canal and assume the worst.

An interesting but not always successful foray into psychology, "Dreamland" finds Margaret beset by recurring dreams. As a result she becomes unfeeling and at times even cruel to Victor. This leads to the unusual circumstance of Margaret getting on Victor's nerves, rather than the other way around.

Later, Margaret's explanation of her disappearance (she went on a two-day bus trip) and the memories it revived is a tour de force by Annette Crosbie in a performance that surpasses the similar scene in "Timeless Time." Recalling the trip to the Dreamland amusement park on their third anniversary, Margaret remembers how she and Victor were trapped in the hall of mirrors for an hour. She especially recalls Victor remarking that he was content to stay trapped and look at the reflections of his wife.

The entire episode is told as a series of flashbacks narrated by Mrs. Warboys to two women in a tea shop. By the end of the story, which contains some personal details on the Meldrews, Mrs. Warboys excuses herself and reminds the women that they have been told this story in the strictest confidence. After she exits we find out that the women were total strangers to her.

Episode 3: "The Broken Reflection" ★★★★

Air date: February 16, 1992. Cast: Victor Meldrew (Richard Wilson); Margaret Meldrew (Annette Crosbie); Chinese Youth (Paul Courtenay Hugh); Chinese Girl (Sulin Looi); Chinese Chef (Vincent Wong); Patrick (Angus Deayton); Pippa (Janine Duvitski); Sales Representative (Jim Sweeney); Toddler (Michael Jones); Young Mother (Ruth Burton); Workman (Peter Hepelthwaite); Alfred (Richard Pearson)

Victor's brother, Alfred, comes to visit from New Zealand. Although Victor hasn't seen him in 25 years, he dreads the visit, likening it to two weeks cooped up in the house with Stan Laurel. Alf's visit is made all the more trying since he has become hard of hearing, making it necessary for the impatient Victor to repeat everything he says twice.

More successful than "Dreamland," "The Broken Reflection" treads on similar territory. Examining Victor's love/hate relationship with his brother, David Renwick makes his point well with plenty of strong comedy situations interspersed along the way. Victor learns the lesson that we often despise those closest to us for the ways that they remind us of our own similar failings.

Margaret gets a sample of Alf's brand of dopiness when she picks him up at the airport. She spots him in the crowd, sitting calmly, reading a newspaper with his hat on fire (he absentmindedly tapped out his pipe onto the hat). That evening Alfred accidentally ruins dinner when he inadvertently tucks the tablecloth into his shirt as a napkin then gets up, pulling everything off the table. In the middle of the night Victor and Margaret are awakened by a crash. "Don't tell me," guesses Victor, "he accidentally napalmed his underpants."

Not quite. Returning from a bathroom visit, Alf attacked the full-length mirror, having mistaken his own reflection for an intruder.

Aside from the main plot line, there are numerous story lines that weave in and out of the episode to supply an amazing amount of laughs. Patrick and Pippa keep catching Victor in the middle of seemingly inexplicable behavior just when they are entrusting him to water their plants while they go on vacation. The climax to these strange events begins when Victor, while watering the plants next door, spots two young women throwing trash on Patrick's front lawn. He leans out the window to yell at them, then watches to see where one of them lives. Victor then takes some trash and shoves it through the woman's letterbox. A few days later, Margaret allows a workman to attach a hose to the Meldrews' kitchen faucet. The man turns out to be the husband of the woman who got the trash through the letterbox. Together they uncoil the hose out the back gate, down the alley, around the corner, and into Patrick's letterbox (since that is where they think Victor lives). Later Patrick returns to find his downstairs flooded. Angrily he follows the hose to Victor's kitchen. He turns the water off, as Victor enters innocently and asks if anything is wrong. Patrick has just one question for the confused Victor: how is Victor going to get the end of the hosepipe out of his rear end?

EPISODE 4: "THE BEAST IN THE CAGE" ★★★½

Air date: February 23, 1992. Cast: Victor Meldrew (Richard Wilson); Margaret Meldrew (Annette Crosbie); Mrs. Warboys (Doreen Mantle); Salmon (Trevor Byfield); Lisa (Lousie DuPrey); Carol (Tish Allen). With the voices of Eric Idle and John DuPrez

A bank holiday outing turns into four and a half hours of "unfettered misery" as the Meldrews and Mrs. Warboys get caught in a horrific traffic jam. During the half hour it takes to play out the episode, their car moves less than 15 yards.

The second foray into a one-set, real-time episode, "The Beast in the Cage" works much better than "Timeless Time." This installment features a situation with much more opportunity for interaction and thus more conflict for the querulous Meldrew. Just like "Timeless Time," this episode features a philosophical climax this time delivered by Victor. He relates life to a drive on a highway, which for the first 50 miles is done at top speed but which eventually grinds to a complete halt.

Soon the relative peace is broken when the inhabitants of the cars on either side of them move up in their lanes and begin carrying on a conversation through Victor's car. The topic soon turns suggestive as the man in one car tries to pick up the girls in the other. Victor interrupts, and a brief verbal skirmish ensues before Margaret rolls up the windows.

Finally, Victor tries to break the monotony by putting a tape into the stereo. Instead of big bands, he gets a beautifully arranged a capella ode to Victor by the garage mechanics (voiced by title theme composers Eric Idle and John DuPrez) sung to the tune of the hymn "Guide Me, O Thou Great Jehovah." The Meldrews sit in stunned silence until Mrs. Warboys comments that for mechanics the pair carry a tune well.

EPISODE 5: "BEWARE THE TRICKSTER ON THE ROOF" ★★★

Air date: March 1, 1992. Cast: Victor Meldrew (Richard Wilson); Margaret Meldrew (Annette Crosbie); Patrick (Angus Deayton); Pippa (Janine Duvitski); Nick Swainey (Owen Brenman); Young Wife (Britt Morrow); Mrs. Skimpson (Hilda Braid); the Cyclist (Steve Perry); Mr. Tildsley (Peter Aubrey); Wife (Louise Kerr). With the voice of John Challis

Victor Meldrew's already ill-fated existence is made worse when Nick Swainey gives him a scorpion encased in a glass paperweight as a souvenir from his holiday in North Africa. Swainey kiddingly explains that the insect is supposed to bring bad luck.

Immediately new disasters begin happening to the Meldrews.

An examination of good luck and bad luck, "Beware the Trickster on the Roof" concludes that what brings Victor Meldrew nothing but trouble turns out to be a great blessing in the hands of others. Actually, the events that supposedly stem from Victor's possession of a North African scorpion are somewhat routine, even mild compared to some of his misfortunes. Ultimately, it is intimated that Victor's trials are caused by the item referred to in the episode's title. "The trickster on the roof" turns out to be the television aerial across from the Meldrews' house, which Victor swears is grinning at him malevolently.

Another good bit involves Patrick and Pippa desperately trying to sell their home to get away from Victor. Unfortunately he inadvertently keeps scaring away their prospective buyers. Victor tries to save money on a child's present by reconstructing a teddy bear from discarded stuffed animals. Margaret is horrified at the result, calling it "the Abominable Dr. Phibes in a fur coat" and the hideous product of a diseased mind. Victor reluctantly throws his handiwork into the trash. There the child of some prospective buyers finds the beast and is so traumatized that his parents carry him screaming from the property.

Later in the episode, Victor gets a call from one of the burglars who robbed his house in "Monday Morning Will Be Fine." The man asks Victor if he still has the manual to former video recorder, since they're having trouble figuring out the 14-day timer. After sarcastically telling the burglar to send over the sofa cushions if they need cleaning, Victor hangs up. He then crosses to the upstairs window, opens it, and starts yelling obscenities at the burglars, wherever they might be. Unfortunately, another pair of house hunters is coming up Patrick's walk. They beat a hasty retreat.

EPISODE 6: "THE WORST HORROR OF ALL" ★★★★

Air date: March 8, 1992. Cast: Victor Meldrew (Richard Wilson); Margaret Meldrew (Annette Crosbie); Mrs. Warboys (Doreen Mantle); Window Cleaner (Harold Goodwin); Wilfred (John Rutland); Mildred (Jean Challis); Ronnie (Gordon Peters); Warm-Up Man (Bobby Bragg); Man in Taxi (William Chubb); Woman in Taxi (Rowan Suart); Man in Wheelchair (Geoffrey Fordham-Barnett)

The Meldrews take a concussion victim to the taping of a television show after mistaking him for Mrs. Warboys's cousin Wilfred. In addition, they desperately try to avoid "the worst horror of all," a visit from their friends Ronnie and Mildred — the world's most boring couple. The episode concludes with Victor starting and losing a job as a hotel doorman.

"Seventy-two hours of non stop madness, misery and mayhem beyond all belief" is Victor Meldrew's assessment of the events that take place in this episode. His assessment is fairly accurate, except that he omitted hilarity, humor, and hysterics. "The Worst Horror of All" sustains the excellent caliber of comedy presented throughout most of the third season.

This installment also features one of the first instances of Victor's vigilante heroics finally going right. His timing and execution of his own brand of justice is so well done that the act elicits rousing applause from the studio audience. The incident occurs on the first morning of Victor's job as a doorman. When Victor fails to give instant service to an arrogant man and his girlfriend, he receives a severe and humiliating upbraiding. While the man goes on about Victor's sloppiness and bad manners, Victor watches a man in a wheelchair struggling to get into his car. Regaining his perspective, Victor begins a sincere apology, which turns sarcastic when he apologizes for having to throw the man's toupee down the storm drain. With that, Victor flings the man's hairpiece down the nearest sewer grate and storms off.

In an unrelated but hilarious bit, Victor hires a dumpster to cart away the remains of his demolished shed. He explains to Margaret that he has carefully arranged the rubbish in order to prevent neighbors from filling his bin with their trash. According to Victor, someone invariably dumps a busted mattress in other peoples' rented dumpsters.

The next morning, Victor looks out his window to find that someone has placed an entire Citroen automobile in the dumpster. If this wasn't outrageous enough, upon closer inspection he finds that there is a busted mattress shoved in the car's back seat.

Series Four 1993

Episode 1: "The Pit and the Pendulum" ★★★

Air date: January 31, 1993. Cast: Victor Meldrew (Richard Wilson); Margaret Meldrew (Annette Crosbie); Patrick (Angus Deayton); Pippa (Janine Duvitski); Kazanzi (Daniel Peacock); Daughter (Sarah Bolden). With the voice of Katharine Page

Victor is having Mr. Kazanzi do some work in his garden. He is having him dig a pit next to his back fence in order to cut off the roots of Patrick's cherry tree. Victor claims the tree is stealing the moisture from his garden. Aside from stretching one day's work into a week, Kazanzi annoys Victor by spending most of his time lewdly flirting with all the females in the neighborhood.

Basically a one-situation episode — rare for *One Foot in the Grave*— but still funny. It is almost as if the author started with the problem of how to get Victor Meldrew buried up to his neck in his garden and worked backward from there. After enduring Kazanzi's flirtatious manner for a week, Victor returns home one afternoon to find the workman in his living room apparently in the act of helping a teenage girl out of her jeans. Victor grabs the girl and is pushing her out, when Kazanzi grabs him. The girl turns out to be Kazanzi's daughter, struggling into her tight jeans after using the Meldrews' bathroom.

Margaret comes home to find the pit filled in and Victor buried up to his neck in it. The sight of Victor Meldrew, complete with his signature tweed cap on his head, buried up to his neck in his garden is priceless. By the time Margaret discovers him Victor has had enough time to consider his situation and is quite resigned to it. When Margaret wonders aloud what to do, Victor turns sarcastic. "Spread some fertilizer around my neck," he suggests, "and wait 'til I come up in the spring."

As in many of the series' entries, there are some darker and philosophical moments. These revolve around the death of Margaret's mother and her clumsy answering machine message, which turns chillingly appropriate by the episode's conclusion.

Episode 2: "Descent into the Maelstrom" ★★½

Air date: February 7, 1993. Cast: Victor Meldrew (Richard Wilson); Margaret Meldrew (Annette Crosbie); Mrs. Warboys (Doreen Mantle); Nick Swainey (Owen Brenman); Unemployed Man (Stephen Ley); Andrea Temple (Helen Lederer); Woman (Joanna Bacon); Mrs. Ashcroft (Laura Cox)

Margaret collapses from nervous exhaustion, which, according to the doctor, has been building up over the last 35 years (the length of time she's been married to Victor). Her recuperation is anything but peaceful as she is cared for by Victor.

By the fourth series of *One Foot in the Grave*, fans should know all too well that Victor Meldrew is a constant complainer about everything that happens to him. Lest we should think that Meldrew's frustration is entirely self-centered, David Renwick has written a group of episodes that spotlight Victor's altruistic side. Here, and especially in the following installment, we see Victor take it on the chin for others. In "Descent into the Maelstrom," he chooses to have Margaret heap abuse on him rather than shatter her mistaken opinion of a fondly remembered acquaintance.

Still, Victor manages to fill Margaret's recuperation with enough material for another nervous breakdown. First, he accidentally gives their rented VCR to a panhandler, thinking the man is from the electronics shop. Later in the episode, the grateful man returns with a friend, who is inadvertently given another VCR and the Meldrews' car before Margaret realizes what her husband has done.

Next, Mrs. Warboys returns from the dry cleaners with Victor's dress suit, only she has brought back a gorilla costume instead. She obtusely blames the cleaners for mixing up the tickets. Victor explains the mix-up to Nick Swainey, who offers to loan Victor a suit for a party he's attending. When Victor returns, however, he discovers that instead of loaning him a dress suit, his goofy neighbor has given him another gorilla costume.

Episode 3: "Hearts of Darkness" ★★★

Air date: February 14, 1993. Cast: Victor Meldrew (Richard Wilson); Margaret Meldrew (Annette Crosbie); Nick Swainey (Owen Brenman); Mrs. Warboys (Doreen Mantle); Mr. Gorshin (Bill Gavin); Sonia (Arabella Weir); Miss Lander (Janet Henfrey); Rachel (Melody Brown); Martin (Nick Scott); Mrs. Endicott (Katharine Page); Officials (Marcia Myrie, Seymour Matthews)

The Meldrews, Mrs. Warboys, and Nick Swainey go on an outing in the country. After taking a wrong turn in a hired rowboat they become lost in a swamp. They manage to find their way out of the swamp only to be lost in the woods. With nightfall approaching, Victor goes off on his own to find help and comes upon a retirement home. When he learns that the staff routinely abuses the retirees, Victor decides to take justice into his own hands.

The ultimate example of Victor playing the vigilante avenger, "Hearts of Darkness" does not introduce its primary story until almost two-thirds through the episode. The opening sequences are funny, although usual series fare that do not prepare us for the stunning, disturbing, and ultimately macabre ending. Stuck in a swamp, the Meldrews, Mrs. Warboys, and Mr. Swainey play Trivial Pursuit. After 40 minutes Victor halts the game because only Mrs. Warboys has had a turn. It seems that the generally addle-brained Mrs. Warboys is something of a genius on trivia (including such obscure subjects as the smell of a gazelle's excrement).

Once out of the swamp, the merry band walks along a forest road as it begins to rain. Luckily, they discover an abandoned contractor's van and climb in out of the rain. When they try to emerge, however, Victor and Mrs. Warboys discover their feet are welded together inside a bag of cement. In seems they fell asleep with their feet on top of a broken bag of the cement and the van's roof leaked.

The most memorable moment in this installment involves Victor's remedy for the nursing home horrors he discovers. With the inmates' help, Victor drugs the staff and the director. After carrying the staff members outside, Victor tells the elderly folks that he will send the authorities around the next day. The next day the authorities arrive in response to an anonymous call. They find evidence of abuse but cannot find any trace of the staff. They reason that rather than face criminal charges they have all scattered. As the authorities drive away, they fail to hear the faint cries for help coming from inside the scarecrows in the field where Victor has bound and gagged the abusers.

Ultimately, the episode proves that Victor Meldrew's heart is not dark, although his brand of justice is swift and severe.

EPISODE 4: "WARM CHAMPAGNE" ★★★★

Air date: February 21, 1993. Cast: Victor Meldrew (Richard Wilson); Margaret Meldrew (Annette Crosbie); Patrick (Angus Deayton); Pippa (Janine Duvitski); 1st Boy (Anthony Watson); 2nd Boy (Simon Long); Ambulancewoman (Susan Barnard); Ambulanceman (Alan Cooke); Mrs. Staveacre (Georgina Beer); Ben (Tristram Jellinek)

Unable to stand the steady stream of Meldrewian disasters, Margaret succumbs to temptation and agrees to have dinner with Ben, a man she met on vacation. After briefly entertaining the notion of an affair, Margaret rejects Ben. She returns home to find Victor in bed with an old crone, who was mistakenly put there by an ambulance crew after getting their addresses mixed up.

A priceless episode that supplies abundant laughs along with a fair share of drama as the long-suffering Margaret Meldrew contemplates cheating on Victor. She is driven to the brink of infidelity but resists the temptation when her intended partner delivers an all-too-accurate criticism of Victor. Annette Crosbie proves once again that she is a marvelous actress in her speech explaining why Margaret loves Victor.

The episode begins with the Meldrews returning from a holiday at the beach to find that neighborhood boys have broken their front window. Victor yells at the boys, who are riding by on their bicycles. The boys threaten to have their father fix Victor. He dares them to. The next morning Victor is speechless when he opens his front door and sees a beautifully painted hanging sign, such as one would find outside a pub, on a pole in his front lawn. The sign includes a vivid color painting of a sneering Victor surrounded by the words "The Pain in the Arse." It seems the boys' father is a sign painter.

Thankfully, after a few episodes' lull, the battle between Victor and Patrick begins afresh as Patrick launches a new offensive. Victor returns home from vacation to learn that Patrick's dog has swallowed the key to his shed. Patrick is more than willing to help recover the key. Toward this end he has saved all of the dog's excrement in a bag and has even supplied Victor with a pair of rubber gloves.

Later, in the episode's climax, Victor and Margaret find the ancient old woman sleeping on Margaret's side of the bed. In perhaps the biggest laugh in the series, Victor stammers, trying to figure out who he has been sleeping with, then confesses, "I thought it was you."

"This is the end to a perfect week," Margaret announces "You come home and find your husband has taken up necrophilia."

Episode 5: "The Trial" ★★★★

Air date: February 28, 1993. Cast: Victor Meldrew (Richard Wilson)

Victor is forced to wait inside on a rainy afternoon for a jury duty call.

A one-man tour de force by Richard Wilson as Victor Meldrew, "The Trial" is the most successful of the one-set, real-time episodes of *One Foot in the Grave*. The audience is afforded a steady, 30-minute glimpse into the mind of Meldrew as he paces about the house desperately trying to pass the time. The results range from inquisitive reflection (Q: What makes you yawn? A: Anything starring Robert Mitchum), to philosophical self-examination (Why does Victor gladly kill wood louses while catching daddy long legs and taking them outside?), to out-and-out frustration (trying to solve a cryptic crossword puzzle with impossible clues). Boredom was never so funny.

Alone, with no company aside from his own hypochondria, Victor's mind runs amuck. He first imagines that he has contracted lockjaw from a cut received off a plastic card. When he goes to look up lockjaw in his medical dictionary, however, he finds an entry on colon tumors that makes his brain race even faster — especially when he reads that the disease features no symptoms in the early stages.

"That's exactly what I've got," Victor notes, observing his lack of symptoms.

Later, Victor goes to use the downstairs toilet and starts exclaiming wildly. He rushes to the phone to call the local nursery. It seems they delivered a yucca plant early in the day, and Victor told the boy to put the plant in the downstairs toilet. He walks into the room to see that the five-foot yucca has been transplanted to the bowl itself. Victor asks the manager if he's supposed to cock his leg against the plant like a Yorkshire terrier every time he needs to go.

Finally, Victor is shattered when he discovers a new mole on his stomach. He quickly builds the blemish into a life-threatening affliction until he examines a baby picture of himself and discovers he has had the mole his entire life. Relief washes over Victor, as he promises to immediately turn over a new leaf. The new leaf survives all of 30 seconds and is quickly blown away when Victor discovers a lost toupee baked into his loaf of bread.

Episode 6: "Secret of the Seven Sorcerers" ★★★½

Air date: March 7, 1993. Cast: Victor Meldrew (Richard Wilson); Margaret Meldrew (Annette Crosbie); Mrs. Warboys (Doreen Mantle); Fire Officer (Chris Walker); Nick Swainey (Owen Brenman); Window Cleaner (John Cassady); Patrick (Angus Deayton); Pippa (Janine Duvitski); Magician (Simon Fisher-Becker); Fire Officer (Vincent Leigh)

A typical day at the Meldrew house: the telephone only works for incoming calls, one of Victor's neighbors keeps sending in false alarms to the fire brigade on his location, and one of the members of his magician's club gets left for hours locked in a trunk. On the other side, however, Patrick and Pippa are coming over for dinner in hopes of Patrick mending his relationship with Victor.

A good entry filled with the odd occurrences and happenstance that make *One Foot in the Grave* such a gem. One is left with the impression that this may originally have been envisioned as the last of the 30-minute episodes since there is a sense of finality about things. Mrs. Warboys's marriage ends, and a major effort to reconcile with Patrick and Pippa goes irretrievably poorly. Almost two years would pass before series five would begin, and then it would only have five episodes.

One of the more memorable bits occurs when Mrs. Warboys fretfully informs Margaret that her husband may be having an affair. In light of this terrible news, all Victor can do is laugh uproariously. It seems that as Mrs. Warboys pours out her heart to Margaret on the couch, Victor is listening to a comedy cassette (*Monty Python*'s "Spam" skit) via headphones two feet away in his easy chair. The scene is beautifully timed, as each new outburst of laughter from Victor is precisely juxtaposed against each new revelation from the distraught Mrs. Warboys.

"Secret of the Seven Sorcerers" is also noteworthy since after 25 episodes it is the first to feature all four of the regular supporting players.

Television Movie 1993

One Foot in the Algarve ★★

Air date: December 26, 1993. Cast: Victor Meldrew (Richard Wilson); Margaret Meldrew (Annette Crosbie); Mrs. Warboys (Doreen Mantle); Martin Trout (Peter Cook); Lady on Plane (Joan Sims); Afonso (Edward de Souza);

Humphrey (Louis Mahoney); Hugo (Eamonn Walker); Shirley (Louise Duprey); Glaswegian (Craig Ferguson); Isabella (Anna Nicholas); Old Man (Benjamin Falcao); Waitress (Margarida Rodrigues); Policemen (Augusto Portela, Eduardo Viana); Farmworkers (Jose Gomes, Jorge Parente); Fisherman (Andre Maia); Coastguard (Jorge Sequerra); Mortuary Attendant (Joao D'Auila); Mortuary Assistant (Maria D'Aires); Photo Shop Owner (Luis Zagalo); Maria (Lidia Franco); Cabbie (Joao Lagarto)

The Meldrews accompany Mrs. Warboys on a holiday to Portugal's Algarve region where she is going to meet Afonso, a long-time pen pal. Unbeknownst to them they are followed to the region by freelance photographer Martin Trout, who is trying to retrieve a valuable roll of film that has accidentally found its way into Margaret's handbag. After meeting Afonso, however, Victor is skeptical about him, especially after hearing the mysterious events leading up to the disappearance of his first wife. Nevertheless, a romance quickly develops between Afonso and Mrs. Warboys.

As with most feature-length versions of popular situation comedies, this Boxing Day special is disappointing when compared to the show upon which it was based. The primary problem with *One Foot in the Algarve* is padding. Its triple-length running time contains little more material than is found in a normal series installment. There are some moments, and Peter Cook as Trout does get a chance to perform some good physical comedy, but the lasting impression is one of emptiness.

Especially missed in this feature is Angus Deayton as Patrick, Victor Meldrew's archneighbor. The author has tried to substitute another interesting holiday neighbor — a boxer who has lost his killer instinct — but the relationship is somewhat contrived. Still, there are some good moments as the fighter quickly regains his urge to pummel after a few days in close proximity to Meldrew.

One of the better, although telegraphed, gags comes early in the proceedings. En route to their rented villa, the trio are stopped by the local police. The police, who speak no English, apparently arrest them and lock them in a miserable, filthy prison cell. After languishing unattended in the cell for three days, Margaret discovers that their "prison" is in reality their rented villa.

Another good running incident involves Victor's use of a new aftershave lotion, which apparently is only pleasingly aromatic to him and any donkey within three-quarters of a mile. Soon, Victor is surrounded by the beasts.

Christmas Special 1994

"The Man Who Blew Away" ★★★

Air date: December 25, 1994. Cast: Victor Meldrew (Richard Wilson); Margaret Meldrew (Annette Crosbie); Pippa (Janine Duvitski); Patrick (Angus Deayton); Mr. Foskett (Brian Murphy); Ian Grimwade (Daniel Smith); Neil Grimwade (Ryan O'Leary).

Victor Meldrew has been tormented of late by a prankster. The perpetrator has built a scowling snowman outside his alley, dangled false severed arms from his dustbin, and dropped a frog through his letterbox. The Meldrews' weekend is further disrupted when the people across the street throw one of their infamous all-night parties. When the affair finally breaks up the next dawn, Victor has only managed an hour of sleep. Margaret consoles him with the fact that it is Sunday, and he can sleep late. Just then Mr. Foskett, a suicidal bore who met the Meldrews on holiday 17 years earlier, decides to keep his promise to visit them some day.

Airing on Christmas Day, "The Man Who Blew Away" is a rather grim holiday package, dealing as it does with the topic of suicide. This is not to say that the episode is without humor, since it has some wonderfully funny moments, or that it contains any material outside the black realm of *One Foot in the Grave.*

The laughs begin in earnest when Victor tries to divert his attention from the recent string of pranks played on him by opening a Christmas cracker. Inside he finds a rather personalized riddle: "What's the difference between Victor Meldrew and a chef who keeps dropping his pancakes? Answer: They're both useless tossers!"

Aside from the fact that he is now being harassed through Christmas favors, Victor is annoyed that the riddle is illogical since it begins by asking the difference, then states a similarity.

Later, Victor pours over new car brochures, trying decide on a replacement for his old car, which was stolen three months earlier. After having nothing but trouble with the previous vehicle, he and Margaret consider the theft a blessing. They are eagerly looking forward to finally receiving a check from an insurance company after a lifetime of paying premiums. In the midst of their discussion they receive a call telling them that a lumberjack has discovered their car in the middle of a forest in Finland. Annoyed and frustrated at the prospect of getting the troublesome auto back, Victor lifts his head heavenward and thanks "Saint Total Bastard, the patron saint of insurance companies!"

Next door, Patrick has his own problems as he prepares for an important presentation to prospective clients. He and Pippa drive to the meeting, while also giving Margaret a lift into town. Once there, Pippa casually mentions to Margaret that a pair of Victor's underwear blew off the line and over the fence into their yard. She noticed they were not Patrick's since they had a blue stripe and promises to return them later. Patrick is horrified, since he mistakenly put on the garment. He suddenly is unable to move under the realization that he is going into the most important business meeting of his life wearing Victor Meldrew's underpants. With his clients watching, Pippa helps Patrick move stiff-legged across the street, while he likens the experience to that of John Hurt in the film *Alien*, when that actor had an extraterrestrial in his belly.

At around 40 minutes, "The Man Who Blew Away" is only slightly longer than the standard episode and could almost be considered the first show of the fifth season, as the fifth series would start exactly one week after this special and only contained five episodes rather than the usual six.

Series Five 1995

EPISODE 1: "ONLY A STORY" ★★★½

Air date: January 1, 1995. Cast: Victor Meldrew (Richard Wilson); Margaret Meldrew (Annette Crosbie), Mrs. Warboys (Doreen Mantle); Nick Swainey (Owen Brenman); Reporter (Steve Humphrey)

Flooded out of her basement apartment by a week's worth of rain, Mrs. Warboys is forced to become a house guest of the Meldrews. The arrangement is not sitting well with Margaret, who quickly tires of her friend's comments on her housekeeping. Victor, on the other hand, is remarkably placid thanks to his weekly sessions with a reflexologist, who relaxes him by manipulating his feet with her little finger.

After a hiatus of almost two years, Victor Meldrew and company return to the regular series format with an episode that espouses the quintessential *One Foot in the Grave* philosophy. The title itself is the thesis. After watching a particularly baffling mystery program, Victor and Mrs. Warboys debate the meaning of various clues and occurrences. While Victor is annoyed by these hints that have no apparent connection, Mrs. Warboys blithely dismisses it as "only a story." Victor insists, however, that a story has to have a point, it cannot be just a bizarre string of events that occur for no apparent reason. Margaret asks why this can't happen — since apparently that is what their life is. Victor still contends that life has to have logic behind it, otherwise nothing would make sense.

Despite his new method of coping, Victor is annoyed by the shoddy service supplied by the editor of his local newspaper. When Victor sends a letter to the editor, his name is inadvertently switched with Polly the Penguin's in a nearby zoo article. After he sends in a subsequent letter to complain about that, his name and address is swapped with the editor's, leaving him in the unenviable position of appearing to be the paper's editor. He soon starts receiving sacks of mail complaining about a variety of topics. The most notable is the paper's recent decision to run a surveillance photo of a local politician's homosexual tryst.

Later Margaret reads an article on a local housewife who has turned to prostitution to relieve her ennui. In the article the woman describes her kinkier customers, including one older man who merely likes to lie back and close his eyes while she strokes the bottoms of his feet with her breasts. Margaret quickly makes the connection between the woman and Victor's "reflexologist," but Victor can't figure out how the misunderstanding occurred.

Victor goes upstairs to apply ointment to his sore rear end (perforated when he sat on a rusty meat rack left on his chair by Mrs. Warboys), while Margaret turns on the television. She is horrified to see Victor, live in the bedroom, on a local news program. She looks out the window and sees the TV crew filming in their upstairs window with the use of a crane. On screen a reporter chides Victor, supposedly the editor of the local paper, for invading the privacy of the politician. The reporter wonders if Victor can take it as well as he dishes it out, as Victor, unaware of the crew, drops his drawers for the folks at home.

Episode 2: "The Affair of the Hollow Lady" ★★★

Air date: January 8, 1995. Cast: Victor Meldrew (Richard Wilson); Margaret Meldrew (Annette Crosbie); Nurse (Richard Lumsden); Woman in Hospital (Edna Monterel); Mrs. Warboys (Doreen Mantle); Millicent (Barbara Windsor); Laverick (Nick Maloney)

After paying £260 for a new, more secure lock system, the Meldrews have constant difficulty getting in or out of their home. Finally, they resort to climbing in and out of the windows, while Victor tries in vain for days to get the locksmith to come and fix the problem. As if being unable to use his door were not enough, Victor suspects that Millicent, the local greengrocer, is wrapping his vegetables in a suggestive manner. Margaret laughs the notion off, remarking that the woman must be desperate. When Millicent makes a delivery, however, Margaret suspiciously witnesses her flirting firsthand.

After Margaret's near affair in "Warm Champagne," Victor gets his chance in "The Affair of the Hollow Lady," although unlike his spouse he neither seeks nor entertains the notion. The title refers not only to the woman who has set her sights on Victor but also to a full-sized wax statue of the dotty Mrs. Warboys. Mrs. Warboys receives the statue as the first prize in a contest. Given the choice of £500 or a full-sized waxed replica of herself, Mrs. Warboys obviously chooses the latter.

When the waxwork arrives, it is delivered to the Meldrews' house. They quickly cover up the frightening dummy with a lampshade before relegating it to the spare bedroom. When Mrs. Warboys finally sees the statue her excited anticipation quickly turns to disgust at her silly vanity, and she terms the thing "hideous." Margaret agrees but notes it is a very good likeness.

Typically well written, the episode provides the usual share of laughs, although one can't help feeling that this has all been seen before. Perhaps, after almost 30 episodes, we're beginning to expect the unexpected and thus are less surprised when it happens. There's a good instance of Victor exacting revenge against the untrustworthy locksmith, but even this is less satisfying than his toupee-tossing incident in "The Worst Horror of All."

After waiting for days for the locksmith, Victor decides to take matters into his own hands. He visits the man, Laverick, at home on his day off. Laverick answers the door in his robe and promises to send someone around the next day. Tired of promises, Victor shuts the man's front door, then swipes the key and closes the porch door, effectively locking him inside his entryway. Laverick pleads for Victor to put the key through the letterbox, to which Victor readily agrees. He places the key inside an envelope, addresses it to Laverick, then goes off to mail it, announcing that with the first class stamp the key should come back in a few days.

Episode 3: "Rearranging the Dust" ★½

Air date: January 15, 1995. Cast: Victor Meldrew (Richard Wilson); Margaret Meldrew (Annette Crosbie). With Antony Sher; Damaris Hayman; Valerie Minifie; Laura Cox

Victor and Margaret are in the waiting room of their solicitor in anticipation of their appointment to draw up wills. While Margaret contentedly reads a magazine, Victor counts the leaves on an artificial plant (1,592), manages to get chewing gum and bird droppings on the end of his nose, and breaks or upsets the room's table, barometer, and venetian blinds. Several odd people pass through — including one man with a fetish for spraying various parts of his body with an aerosol can — all of whom are called for their appointments ahead of the Meldrews.

The last and arguably the weakest of the one-set, real-time examinations of boredom, "Rearranging the Dust" is similar in outline to the first foray into this area, "Timeless Time." Again, Victor is confined to a relatively small area and drives Margaret closer to insanity while trying to relieve his own ennui.

While the episode does have several good laughs, they are almost entirely centered around bodily functions and in poor taste and soon become tiresome. The redeeming feature of the exercise is another thoughtful reminiscence by Annette Crosbie, this one shedding light on how she and Victor came to be a couple. Especially effective is her admission that Victor was not her first, or second, or even third choice as a mate. To this revelation, Victor quietly confesses that she was always his first selection.

This disclosure comes at the episode's end when Margaret mentions that it was 37 years ago that week that she and Victor first had sex. She romantically relates the story of the party at which she first saw a dashing young man. After smiling at him all evening from across the room, Margaret took advantage of a power outage to grab the object of her desire and take him out into the garden for passion. It was only after they returned to the party and the lights came back on that she discovered that she had snatched away Victor by mistake.

Episode 4: "Hole in the Sky" ★★★½

Air date: January 22, 1995. Cast: Victor Meldrew (Richard Wilson); Margaret Meldrew (Annette Crosbie); Pippa (Janine Duvitski); Patrick (Angus Deayton); McKendrick Twins (Christopher Ryan); Mrs. Stewkley (Hilary Mason); Mr. Stewkley (Peter Tuddenham); Geoffrey Croker (Michael Fenton Stevens)

Victor Meldrew's latest interest in retirement is exotic seafood cookery. Aside from bringing the authorities around after they mistake the aromas emanating from his kitchen for a blockwide gas leak, this latest Meldrewian foray has Margaret suffering again. She likens Victor's new uses for fish as something out of *The Quartermass Experiment*, the classic British sci-fi series. This, coupled with Victor's preoccupation with a marionette of a Dutch girl, is driving Margaret up the wall. The final blow comes when she loses her job, leaving her with the horrifying prospect of becoming just like her husband.

The strongest episode of the fifth season, one wishes that "Hole in the Sky" had been moved back one episode, as it is a fitting bookend to the regular series' premiere of more than five years earlier, "Alive and Buried." Here, the focus is on Margaret Meldrew, who is forced to make her own adjustments just as it seems that her husband is finally finding new — albeit bizarre — ways to occupy his retirement.

The continuing feud between Victor and Patrick is hilariously revisited. If Patrick thought that wearing Victor Meldrew's underpants was horrific ("The Man Who Blew Away"), he encounters his greatest nightmare when he is compelled to have dinner with his querulous next-door neighbor. The meal has been arranged by Pippa and Margaret in one last-ditch attempt to sort out the feud between their husbands. Of course the meeting is an utter disaster, which begins with the two men going to an Armenian restaurant in which none of the staff speaks English. Thanks to Pippa's request that Victor and Patrick be given an intimate table at which they may discuss personal affairs, the staff think the two men are lovers.

As if being given one bowl of soup with two spoons weren't bad enough, the two enemies are compelled to share one long, phallic sausage, which they must concurrently nibble at until their lips meet in the middle. Next, the staff joins them for a romantic souvenir photo of the occasion, in which Victor and Patrick are made to hold hands. Their evening is made complete by a visit from the Gypsy violinist, who insists on serenading them. "It would have been cruel just to tell him to bugger off," Patrick explains to Pippa as he relates the details of the disaster, "so we told him to bugger off."

Michael Fenton Stevens appears as Pippa's brother. The following year he would become a regular on *The Legacy of Reginald Perrin* as Joan Greengross's beau, Hank.

EPISODE 5: "THE EXTERMINATING ANGEL" ★★★

Air date: January 29, 1995. Cast: Victor Meldrew (Richard Wilson); Margaret Meldrew (Annette Crosbie); Nick Swainey (Owen Brenman); Tania (Anita Chellamah); Lewis Atterbury (John Bird); Ronnie (Gordon Peters); Mildred (Barbara Ashcroft); Roy (Ronald Leigh-Hunt); Ruth (Annette Kerr); Dentist (Jennie Stoller). Stunts: Steve Whyment, Lex Milloy

Thanks to yet another contractor's shoddy work, Victor's back is scalding in the shower. Luckily, Tania, Nick Swainey's mother's nurse, is next door and quickly responds with first aid. As Tania leaves, Margaret notices that the nurse and Nick are mutually attracted to each other. Nick gets up enough courage to ask out Tania, and she accepts. Nick is elated, but ultimately his romantic hopes are dashed.

Meanwhile, Victor gets a job as driver for Lewis Atterbury, a rich businessman. Victor is hired as Lewis's chauffeur and introduced to his three children: the BMW, the Mercedes, and the Jaguar. Within three days Victor manages to destroy all three cars in freak accidents.

This last regular installment of *One Foot in the Grave* is standard fare for this excellent series but still not quite up to the pinnacles attained in the second, third, and fourth seasons. The series goes out with a bang, at least in terms of material destruction and budget.

For all its mangling of machines, "The Exterminating Angel" does offer a quick glimpse into the heart of the Meldrews' daffy neighbor, Nick Swainey. One always suspected that a shy and sensitive soul resided behind that ever-cheerful disposition and in this episode it is bared. Unfortunately, this examination is too brief, ending almost before it begins with unanswered questions — a bit like life.

"The Exterminating Angel" is also notable for its small touches and throw-away gags. The episode begins with Victor looking like Bugs Bunny thanks to a set of temporary crowns. Later, when he is scalded by the shower, Victor lies naked, face down on his bed, covered with bags of frozen vegetables for relief. When the nurse arrives, she recoils in surprise — not at the condition of Victor's burn, but rather that the local store carries a certain type of frozen produce.

Christmas Special 1995

"THE WISDOM OF THE WITCH" ★★★★

Air date: December 25, 1995. Cast: Victor Meldrew (Richard Wilson); Margaret Meldrew (Annette Crosbie); Pippa (Janine Duvitski); Patrick (Angus Deayton); Melvin (Phil Daniels); Lorna (Rachel Bell); Christine (Joanne Engelsman); Tunstall (Bruce Byron); Gridley (Peter McNally); Postman (Peter Terry); Party Guest (Virginie Gilchrist); American (Tony Sibbald); Edwin (Boris)

A local soothsayer predicts that Victor will be visited by a plague of devils and come to a sudden and untimely end. The prophecy seems to be coming true when Victor is snowbound in a remote old house with his enemy, Patrick, and a giant spider named Edwin.

A good plot line with plenty of the twists that fans of *One Foot in the Grave* have come to expect. Perhaps the biggest news is that after years of trying, the Trenches (Patrick and Pippa) have finally succeeded in selling their house next door to the querulous Victor Meldrew. Rather than his troubles ending, Patrick's are only just beginning when he learns that a homicidal maniac is stalking him after being falsely told that Patrick slept with the man's girlfriend.

Through a series of mishaps, Patrick is locked in Victor's trunk by the would-be killer. Unaware of the stowaway, Victor takes Patrick along on a trip to the home of Margaret's recently deceased aunt, where the two are snowbound. In some well-written business the two long-time adversaries actually become friendly, although their camaraderie is short-lived given the usual Meldrew luck. Angus Deayton is particularly good as he is afforded his most substantial turn in the always-rewarding role of Patrick. Deayton probably has at least half of the laughs and the screen time, and he makes the most of the opportunity.

Aside from the plot there are some good unrelated bits including Victor taking a job on a nearby farm as a handyman. The first assignment is finding the farmer's lost wedding ring in a newly plowed field. Only after a week of search does Victor learn there is no ring, and he has been hired to be a living scarecrow. The scene in which Victor relates the scheme to Margaret and Pippa is one of the most hysterical of the series as the ladies fight the urge to laugh in the face of his ranting. In another gag, the audience learns that Patrick has been sticking pins into a trenchcoat-and-cap-clad doll — his way of relieving the stress of living next door to Victor Meldrew.

As during other times in the run of this often black comedy, the viewer is led to believe that one of the major characters is dead. Here it is Victor that is assumed dead from the special's framing device, which opens and closes the installment with Margaret at the graveside of Victor Meldrew. By the end of the show, however, it is explained that Victor received his name from his father, thus clearing up the misdirection.

Christmas Special 1996

"Starbound" ★★★½

Air date: December 26, 1996. Cast: Victor Meldrew (Richard Wilson); Margaret Meldrew (Annette Crosbie); Mrs. Warboys (Doreen Mantle); Patrick (Angus Deayton); Pippa (Janine Duvitski); Nick (Owen Brenman); Vargrant

& Millichope (Ray Winstone); Mrs. Blanchard (Lucy Davis); Primary School Teacher (Roli Okorodudu); Dog Owner (Elizabeth Chambers); Fenella Fortune (Rula Lenska)

When Victor becomes uncharacteristically cheery, Margaret starts to think it is a result of contact with visitors from outer space.

A marvelous presentation of misdirection throughout, along with the usual Meldrewian disasters, combine for another splendid *One Foot in the Grave* Christmas special. Every element neatly fits together in David Renwick's tight script, with nary a moment wasted along the way. The entire supporting cast is also in place, including Patrick and Pippa, even though the couple moved away in the previous special. Thankfully, the costars are all given plenty of opportunity to strut their own quirkinesses. Nick Swainey is preoccupied with his mother, who by her own account is being taken on nightly visits to Neptune. Patrick is working for a new boss — Rula Lenska in an effective guest spot — who insists on fondling him. Mrs. Warboys is raped (off camera) by a German shepherd, as some sort of cosmic payback for boring people to tears with her endless tales of her vacation to Los Angeles. (In a funny side bit, she shows her slides, which feature the dotty woman rubbing elbows with an endless stream of superstars.)

Despite the wealth of material afforded the supporting players, stars Wilson and Crosbie still get the bulk of the laughs, of which there are many. The best plots involve Victor inadvertently advertising his services as a recycler of used surgical appliances, then having his home overrun with discarded artificial limbs, corsets, and trusses. The other features Victor excitedly preparing to adopt a dog after Mrs. Warboys urges him to do so, only to find out that the animal is dead and stuffed. The reaction has Meldrew employing some of his finest sarcasm as he plays to perfection off of Warboys's impenetrable obtuseness.

The finale presents some fine physical destruction as the remarkably giddy Victor (the reason for which I'll not give away) manages to wreak havoc on a business conference, Patrick's career, and an impressive glass house with a simple riding lawnmower. The motivation for it all makes perfect sense but only in retrospect, after the viewer has enjoyed a clever mystery along the way.

Christmas Special 1997

"Endgame" ★★★

Air date: December 25, 1997. Cast: Victor Meldrew (Richard Wilson); Margaret Meldrew (Annette Crosbie); Derek (Tim Brooke-Taylor); Betty (Marian McLoughlin); Nick (Owen Brenman); Mrs. Kahn (Usha Patel); DI Rickles (Norman Eshley); Archie (Ian Redford); Rambler (Robin Davies); Dr. Clarke (Christopher Robbie); Doctor (Regina Freedman); Mr. Kahn (Arif Hussein). With Matthew Whittle; Ian Swann; Alisdair Ross; Nicholas Moore; Coral Lorne

Victor buys a used mobile home, only to find out that it has a haunted history. Also, Victor manages to inadvertently kidnap the mother of a wealthy businessman while simultaneously driving his new neighbor toward a nervous breakdown.

"Endgame" is the last in a trilogy of *One Foot in the Grave* Christmas specials that ran after the series had ceased regular production. As such, the hour-long format is beginning to wear a little thin by this go-round, with little to justify the additional length. The material really doesn't build up to any climax and could have just as easily been divided into two half-hour episodes. As "The Wisdom of the Witch" two years earlier, the viewer is once again led to believe that one of the main characters has died. In that 1995 special, it was Victor. Here, it is Margaret, although David Renwick had already toyed with that situation in "Dreamland" back in series three.

Along the way there are the usual Victor Meldrew mishaps although none top what has already happened before to this constantly set-upon character. For the first time in many episodes, there are neither Patrick, Pippa, nor Mrs. Warboys to add to the mixture. One assumes Patrick is finally living peacefully somewhere far from his former neighbor. The only regular on hand is Nick Swainey, who is mainly there for narrative purposes and supplies none of his usual quirkiness. New neighbors are introduced, another husband and wife. The man, Tim Brooke-Taylor, may be recognizable to fans of British comedy as one-third of *The Goodies* team. This new couple soon finds itself stumbling into the same situations that had long ago made Patrick and Pippa leery about living next door to Victor.

There is one classic visual in which Victor tries to rid himself of his haunted camper by unhitching it from his car and allowing it to roll freely towards, a cliff. Upon reaching the precipice the mobile home stops on the edge. As Victor wanders over to it to examine why it stopped, over his shoulder the camera reveals that his car is now freewheeling at a different angle toward the same bluff. Victor watches in last-minute horror as his Ford goes crashing over the edge to the rocky beach below. It is a moment of which Buster Keaton would be proud, especially as it recalls a similarly constructed gag in that comedian's short *One Week*.

This episode was the first not directed by Susan Belbin; Christine Gernon is guiding from behind the camera.

Keeping Up Appearances

BBC-TV 1990-1995

Unlike their American counterparts, the author in British television is afforded much more credit and control in the creation of situation comedy. The writer not only originates a property, but also is essentially its owner throughout its creative history. Rare is the American situation comedy writer who is well known outside of the circle of peers and critics. In the U.K., however, the author's name usually stands alone immediately after the title. Thus have been fostered the long and rewarding careers of such teams as Galton and Simpson (*Steptoe and Son* and *Hancock*), Croft and Perry (*Dad's Army* and *It Ain't Half Hot Mum*), Croft and Lloyd (*Are You Being Served?* and *'Allo, 'Allo*), and Dick Clement and Ian La Frenais (*The Likely Lads, Whatever Happened to the Likely Lads* and *Porridge*), and individual writers, including Johnny Speight (*Till Death Us Do Part*) and John Sullivan (*Citizen Smith* and *Only Fools and Horses*). But in terms of sheer volume of work and ratings success, the name Roy Clarke stands out from all the rest. The prolific Clarke is responsible for more than a dozen series. Among these are some of Britain's most popular shows, including the hilarious *Open All Hours* (starring Ronnie Barker) and the incredibly long-running *Last of the Summer Wine* (25 years and 162 episodes). It comes as something of a surprise then that Roy Clarke's biggest hit in America is *Keeping Up Appearances*, which although it is well liked in the British Isles, is by no means Clarke's best.

Why then is *Keeping Up Appearances* so successful as an import to America while other Clarke sitcoms are virtually unknown on the western side of the pond? Most likely the answer lies in the success of another Anglo import, *Are You Being Served?*, although the shows are in many respects very different. The common thread running between the two, however, is that both shows are built around strong, easily identified character types. While the characters in *Keeping Up Appearances* rarely behave as broadly or bawdily as those in the employ of Grace Brothers' department store, they are still meticulously drawn at the outset and remain constant throughout the run of the series. Like in that other show, the characters in *Keeping Up Appearances* arrive in the pilot fully formed. We as viewers learn little more about them than we are shown in the first episode. They do not necessarily grow, but they are constantly reinforced with each subsequent installment. Again, this strikes a comforting chord in the American psyche, providing good entertainment with little effort needed to keep up with the plot.

Consequently, *Keeping Up Appearances* is similar to *Are You Being Served?* It is long on character and relatively short on plot. It is difficult with the average episode of *Keeping Up Appearances* to even distinguish among the series of the shows (except for the first series, which featured a different actress in the role of Rose and didn't yet have the character of Emmet). Often one has to wait until five and sometimes ten minutes into the show to find a plot. Much of the running time is taken up with the characters — primarily the leading lady — going through variations on familiar set pieces. This is not to criticize *Keeping Up Appearances* as overly repetitious, since the writer almost always offers subtle twists and clever dialogue (usually peppered with hilarious retorts and observations) to maintain freshness. It does indicate, however, that the show is adept at exploring and revisiting the familiar, rather than launching into new situations. The show's director/producer and one of its stars told the author that their favorite and most memorable episodes were those that featured the characters in unfamiliar settings, perhaps indicating that they too had difficulty distinguishing among the more average episodes. Even Clive Swift, who played Richard in the series, confessed to *British Television* magazine that the basic premise for the show was "very simple," and its primary joke was "oft repeated."

Unfortunately, one of the strengths of the show is also one of its drawbacks. Roy Clarke's meticulous attention to character detail and dialogue early in many episodes often leaves the plot, when it is introduced, hurried and rushed to a hasty resolution.

A former schoolteacher, Roy Clarke began his television writing career by contributing to various drama series. Clarke made the jump to comedy in 1970 with an hour-long comedy for ITV entitled *The Misfit*, which ran for 13 episodes over two years. In 1973 Clarke hit his stride when he created *Last of the Summer Wine* for the BBC. This series chronicled the adventures of three retired men in the Yorkshire town of Holmfirth as they explored their second childhood. To say *Last of the Summer Wine* became something of an institution is putting it mildly. The series racked up more than 160 installments, more than any other British situation comedy. Not content to rest on his laurels, Clarke continued to create other series while personally scripting every episode of his long-running hit.

In 1990, after 20 years in the business, Clarke conceived of the idea for a series based around a socially ambitious, overbearing, middle-aged woman named Hyacinth Bucket. "I came up with the idea for *Keeping Up Appearances* by way of the character of Hyacinth," Clarke told the author in 1997. "She's legion. Everybody knows one. They're marvelous fun (from a distance) but you wouldn't want to spend your life with one."

Complementing the character of Hyacinth, Clarke created a hapless, henpecked husband who *has* spent his life with this insufferable woman: Richard Bucket.

Hyacinth Bucket (pronounced "Bouquet," borrowing a venerable W. C. Fields gag from his classics *It's a Gift* and *The Bank Dick*) is something of a female hurricane. Like the relentless storm, Hyacinth overpowers those she comes in contact with to such a degree that those who know her rarely try to reason with her. Rather, the best course of action to take when one sees Hyacinth approaching is to run and hide, which is precisely what otherwise dignified men and women do with often-hilarious results.

To balance out the status-seeking main character and her sympathy-evoking spouse, Clarke invented her slovenly family, which includes a gone-to-seed sister named Daisy; Onslow, Daisy's bone-lazy lout of a husband; and Rose, a middle-aged nymphomaniac sister. This trio lives on a nearby (much too nearby for Hyacinth's comfort) council estate (government-subsidized housing) with the brood's patriarch, Daddy, a senile war veteran who still thinks the Blitz is in full swing.

As with the preponderance of his characters, Clarke's creations here are well thought out and carefully drawn, emerging from the outset as meticulously crafted types with whom the audience can easily identify. The writer received his inspiration from real life. "I think the characters are all based partially on actual people," explained Clarke. "Not perhaps one but built up from bits of observation."

With the pilot script completed, Clarke submitted it to the head of comedy at the BBC, who promptly turned it over to Harold Snoad, television writer, director, and producer, for an opinion. "I read it that same day over a lunchtime sandwich," Snoad explained to the author in 1998, "and I could immediately see the possibilities. Later that afternoon I reported back saying that I was very interested and in my role of producer/director I would like to make the episode I had been given to read as a pilot."

Although it may seem difficult to believe after having seen actress Patricia Routledge in the role of Hyacinth Bucket, the part was not originally written for her (although, according to fellow cast member Clive Swift, the actress thought it was). The task of casting fell to Harold Snoad. To fill the lead role, the producer began an alphabetical search of casting books with a particular type of actress in mind. "Basically," writes Snoad, "I was very anxious that the person I cast was, in herself, a bit of a stately galleon — both in build and presence. I didn't want to finish up with someone 'lightweight' who — in their attempt to take on board the facets of the character might make it become a caricature."

The producer had searched *A* through *Q* of the casting directories with only a few possibles jotted down, until he came to *R*. There Snoad saw a photograph of Patricia Routledge and knew at first glance he had found his Hyacinth.

Despite seeming as if she had been born for the role of Hyacinth, Patricia Routledge actually had only intermittent sitcom experience before *Keeping Up Appearances*. Primarily a stage actress and a member of the Royal Shakespeare Company, Routledge had made only a few guest appearances on television (most notably in the "Seance in a Wet Rag-and-Bone Yard" episode from the final season of *Steptoe and Son*). The actress had her first and only other starring sitcom role in a six-episode series for ITV entitled *Marjorie and Men*, in which she played the title role.

For the part of Richard Bucket, producer Snoad chose Clive Swift, an actor with whom he had worked before. Like his costar, Swift was also an alumnus of the RSC, where he had played mostly comic roles, although he had never been a regular in a sitcom. As first presented to him by Snoad, the role offered Swift few lines. "Harold said, 'Now look, there's this part of the husband ... He just says "Yes, dear, no dear, you're wanted on the phone," and I don't know if you're interested,'" recalled Swift to *British Television* magazine.

Despite the seemingly slim role, Swift considered the company with whom he would be working, primarily Clarke, Snoad, and Routledge. "I thought to myself," said Swift, "well, this is Harold Snoad who started as a boy on *Dad's Army* and has directed several successful sitcoms. The writer is Roy Clarke who had had *Last of the Summer Wine* going for twenty years! And this is Patricia Routledge who I'd never worked with, but I'd admired whenever I'd seen her on the stage."

Thankfully, Swift accepted the pivotal role of Richard. The actor brought the right blend of weariness and suppressed rebellion to the part, keeping it from becoming just another stereotypically henpecked husband.

Another key cast member also initially had his part pitched to him as similarly slim. Although he had never worked with him, Harold Snoad asked Geoffrey Hughes to read for the part of the shiftless Onslow, Hyacinth's primary bane. "At that stage," recalled Hughes in an interview with the author,

"Onslow only had four lines, but as they were all tags to gags I decided to do it."

Harold Snoad also remembers being attracted to Hughes because of his girth, which would play well against the imposing presence of Routledge. "I could see that the combination of those two could work extremely well — not only because of their undoubted talents, but their slightly 'larger' proportions!"

Rounding out the cast were veteran comedy actresses Judy Cornwell as sister Daisy and Josephine Tewson as Hyacinth's skittish and beleaguered neighbor, Elizabeth. Both brought considerable comic depth to their roles and proved excellent foils for Routledge and Hughes.

For the part of Rose, the rather tarty sister, Harold Snoad originally envisioned Mary Millar. Unfortunately, at the time of the pilot Millar was appearing in the West End in *Phantom of the Opera* and was not available. Instead, the producer cast Shirley Stelfox in the part for the first series. The following year, for the second series, it was Stelfox who was unavailable. Happily, however, Millar was then free to assume the part of Rose, who she played for the remainder of the series. Millar, aside from being more believable physically as Rose, also provided a manic sense of desperation to her part, which helped the audience understand the character's man-chasing proclivities.

Other additions to the cast included David Griffin as Elizabeth's brother, Emmet. Like Millar, Griffin joined the series at the beginning of the second series and provided another outlet for Hyacinth Bucket's many idiosyncrasies. Jeremy Gittins played a semiregular role as the Vicar. His casting by Harold Snoad inspired author Clarke to include some previously unconsidered situations. "I thought it would be rather nice to get away from the traditional, middle-aged Vicar," explained Snoad, "and cast someone younger and good looking. A fact that Roy Clarke instantly grabbed hold of with regard to Rose's interest in him."

One of the more interesting characters was often spoken of but never seen — the Bucket's college-aged son, Sheridan. At least once each episode, Hyacinth would have a one-sided conversation with their son, who it was intimated was gay, a fact that clearly eluded his mother, despite some rather overwhelming evidence. Clive Swift mentions in his interview with *British Television*'s A. S. Berman that the cast suggested a Christmas special in which Hyacinth and Richard travel to London to visit their son. "I think that the button was going to be that, of course, he wasn't there or we missed him or he'd moved or something," explained Swift. "We still weren't going to see him."

Swift went on to reason that the idea was never used due to the fact that Roy Clarke doesn't like anyone suggesting material to him. "We kept thinking of hundreds of story lines that never materialized," said Swift, "which is a pity." (Harold Snoad did manage to supply at least one idea to Clarke: the basic idea for the episode in series five in which Richard buys Hyacinth a home burglar alarm.)

With the cast in place, director Snoad started scouting for the exterior locations to be used in the series. Often this chore is handled by an assistant, but Snoad preferred doing the initial legwork himself (a task to which he brought considerable experience, having done the same duties for David Croft years earlier on *Dad's Army*). "In any series you always look first for a frequently used location and/or the one likely to be the most difficult — and then (for convenience) find the others in the same vicinity," Snoad told the author. "In the case of *Keeping Up Appearances* I could see that the 'down market' home and surrounding area required for Onslow's was likely to be tricky because you have to ensure that you use a location over which you can maintain control (in the nicest possible way) during the actual filming. When I discovered the short cul de sac which I eventually used I immediately knew that this would make it much easier to 'control' — and I was right."

In a case of life imitating art, the key exterior locations of Onslow's house and the Bucket residence were found about a mile apart. Both sites are on the outskirts of the city of Coventry. Fans who wish to scout Hyacinth's home will find it located on Heather Road in an area called Binley Wood.

With a successful pilot in hand, the BBC soon commissioned another five shows to round out what would be the first series. While producer/director Snoad cautioned his cast that it often took several series for a program to catch on with the audience, happily *Keeping Up Appearances* found its mark rather quickly.

"By about the third or fourth episode, we got ratings of over 14 million," recalled Clive Swift. These were very respectable numbers in a nation with a population of around 60 million inhabitants and indicative that the show was a hit. A second series of ten shows was authorized in short order. "It had taken off so quickly," said Swift to *British Television*, "that was the unusual thing. It was just cleverer and wittier than quite a lot of them."

Clive Swift also attributes Roy Clarke's inclusion of several economic classes in the show with the ratings success of *Keeping Up Appearances*. "Not only did we manage to get the middle class and the working class thing inside one family, but it is also a family show that the kids love. A big percentage of our audience was children."

No doubt the younger viewers were attracted by the numerous physical comedy pieces written into the show by Clarke for Patricia Routledge. The actress's ability to play broad knockabout inspired Clarke to seek out ways to exploit this unique talent. "I think Pat Routledge is not only a talented actress but she's a brilliant physical clown," explained Clarke in 1997. "Consequently I tend to enjoy the episodes where she's able to display this. The boating episode springs to mind." (This episode from the third series, which features Hyacinth falling into a river, is also one of Harold Snoad's favorite bits.)

Off-camera, the fine cast worked well together, and although few had worked together before most knew and respected the others' previous work. Geoffrey Hughes recalls: "I had only worked with one member of the cast before, Shirley Stelfox, the original Rose. I did know everyone else's work. I think part of the success of the show was that we all had a great respect for each other's work."

"The cast [was] great," admitted Harold Snoad, "and although it was hard work it was a very happy show to work on and, for some reason, not a lot used to go wrong."

One of the primary reasons for such a smooth schedule, according to Clive Swift, was the professionalism of the cast. They did have their fun, however, but this was usually at the read-throughs of the episodes. Swift explained to *British Television*, "Once the tape is rolling it's too expensive to crack up, and you don't get any prizes for cocking up a take. Although obviously we're only human. There were the odd giggles."

Unfortunately, the happy atmosphere experienced during the taping of the shows didn't carry over into the relationship between the writer and the show's director/producer. "My recollections of the making of *Keeping Up Appearances* are all unpleasant," confessed Roy Clarke to the author. "It was the most battle-driven show I've ever been the writer of."

Apparently most of the conflict stemmed from the differing theories between Clarke and Snoad as to how much involvement there should be by a writer of a sitcom. "I'm never involved in the filming of my stuff," admitted Clarke. "I feel all my work's been done by then."

While Roy Clarke may have felt his contribution ended with the submission of each script, Harold Snoad disagreed. "It is an accepted part of the job of the producer/director to discuss with the writer any element of the script which he feels doesn't quite work—or perhaps could be better or stronger," explained Snoad. "Unfortunately Roy never accepted this basic fact."

According to Snoad, when he or Routledge thought a particular bit of Clarke's script didn't work, the writer refused to make any revisions. As a result the unusable passages had to be revised by Snoad himself. The producer recalled in a 1998 interview, "Because the BBC bosses agreed with me that something 'didn't work' or was totally unbelievable (all good comedy needs to start from a credible basis) and because Patricia Routledge refused point blank to play some of Roy's material, there was no other way to get the show on the road than for me to rewrite certain elements and, at times, write replacement scenes—unpaid I might add!"

Although the added chore of doing script rewrites may have been annoying, at least the show didn't suffer. Aside from being an experienced producer and director, Snoad also cowrote three radio series (including the radio adaptation of *Dad's Army* and the radio sequel to that series, *It Sticks Out Half a Mile*) and one television comedy.

Despite this less-than-ideal working relationship, both Snoad and Clarke agree that the final product was a good one. "The producer and I were always miles apart in our ideas," stated Clarke, "but because it worked so well finally, we're still speaking to each other."

"Fortunately," echoed Snoad, "our combined talents meant that we finished up with some very strong episodes. Interestingly he [Clarke] very seldom commented on the material that wasn't his in the various episodes."

With strong ratings in the United Kingdom, *Keeping Up Appearances* enjoyed a new series each autumn for four consecutive years. This is especially remarkable when one considers that series one through five of *Keeping Up Appearances* ran almost concurrently with seasons 12, 13, 14, 15, and 17 of Clarke's other hit, *Last of the Summer Wine*. Both shows appeared on BBC 1 on Sunday evenings, making it something of a bonanza for Roy Clarke fans. Interestingly, neither series ran in the fall of 1994, although *Summer Wine*'s 16th season did run a few months later in early 1995. The reason for the absence of a new series of *Keeping Up Appearances* in 1994 was the unavailability of Patricia Routledge, although a Christmas special was produced.

In all, there were 45 installments of the series, including 42 half-hour episodes, one 50-minute Christmas special, and the hour-long Christmas special filmed on the *Queen Elizabeth II*. There was also one short segment with the characters that aired in November 1995 as part of the *Children in Need* special, although this has not played in the United States.

Even with continued success in Great Britain and a growing audience in the United States, *Keeping Up Appearances* concluded its run after the 1995 Christmas special. The primary reason for ending the popular series was Routledge feeling that she had had enough.

Following the end of its run, the show went on to become one of the more popular Brit-coms in America, a fact that both surprises and delights Roy Clarke and Harold Snoad. The show was so well received that it spawned a limited release on video as well as a tongue-in-cheek guide to etiquette according to Hyacinth Bucket. Snoad produced a special compilation for the American market with linking sequences by Geoffrey Hughes and Judy Cornwell, reprising their roles as Onslow and Daisy.

Like most other successful Brit-coms, there have been rumors of an American adaptation, although this (like many American translations) would be ill advised. The main argument against an American *Keeping Up Appearances* is the rather uniquely British nature of Hyacinth Bucket. There really isn't an easily recognizable American counterpart to her. In fact, American fans of the show often have a mistaken appreciation for the main character, as Harold Snoad explains: "From conversations I have had with various Americans and the BBC's staff in New York plus the fan letters I receive the success of the series in the States seems to revolve around the fact that Hyacinth is, to the American viewer, the epitification of the upper middle class British lady."

According to Snoad, and anyone familiar with the type Hyacinth is satirizing, this clearly isn't the case. Still, the show's producer/director indicates that it doesn't really matter, as long as the American audience finds the show entertaining. Apparently, if the program's steady run on PBS since its premiere there in the mid–1990s is any indication, Hyacinth Bucket's Stateside audience finds it very entertaining.

THE EPISODES

By Roy Clarke. Produced and Directed by Harold Snoad

Series One 1990

EPISODE 1 ★★

Air date: October 29, 1990. Cast: Hyacinth (Patricia Routledge); Richard (Clive Swift); Liz (Josephine Tewson); Daisy (Judy Cornwell); Onslow (Geoffrey Hughes); Rose (Shirley Stelfox); Doctor (Bruce Alexander); Major (Peter Cellier); Postman (Leo Dolan); Meter Man (Paul Toothill); Mr. Oxley (James Ottaway)

Hyacinth Bucket (pronounced "Bouquet") is in the midst of preparations for one of her candlelight suppers when her sister Daisy calls to say that their father is in the hospital after an accident caused by his habit of chasing women.

While the premiere episode carefully cuts the template for almost every subsequent installment in the series, it ultimately is disappointing. What is lacking is a continuing plot to drive this installment. Although most *Keeping Up Appearances* story lines are paper thin, they do provide the motivational slices of bread between which the real meat of this series (the familiar but humorous routines) is then sandwiched. Here we have a beginning but no real ending. The formula is not followed, and the resulting concoction is flat.

All the routines are here: the morning confrontation with the mailman (often switched with the milkman to give the other fellow a rest), Hyacinth's beautifully executed one-sided conversations (especially with the unseen Violet and Sheridan) on her "private, slimline, white telephone," and the tea break with Liz. Also featured are the wonderfully funny sequences at Onslow, Daisy, and Rose's home. Hyacinth likens her family's neighborhood to Beirut. Daisy, Onslow, and Rose are similarly unexcited about Hyacinth's visit, calling her the "Queen Mother." They make a halfhearted attempt at straightening up their filthy, mismatched, yet oddly comfortable living room. After Hyacinth and Richard arrive (Richard chauffeurs his wife everywhere), Hyacinth quickly sends her husband outside when the details become too embarrassing.

EPISODE 2 ★★★

Air date: November 5, 1990. Cast: Hyacinth (Patricia Routledge); Richard (Clive Swift); Liz (Josephine Tewson); Daisy (Judy Cornwell); Onslow (Geoffrey Hughes); Rose (Shirley Stelfox); Vicar (Jeremy Gittins); Vicar's Wife (Marion Barron); Gypsy (Eileen Davies); Passerby (Jill O'Hare)

Hyacinth's meticulous preparations for afternoon tea and light refreshments with the new Vicar and his Wife are dashed when Rose's latest star-crossed love affair spills over into the occasion.

Much more satisfying than the first episode, this installment follows the pattern that defines the majority of the series' shows: Hyacinth plans a social event; a family crisis arises; she struggles to keep the two situations separate; the final clash.

Aside from meeting the semiregular characters of the Vicar and his Wife, Onslow's patchwork, backfiring automobile is also introduced. Also, after a brief career as a revolutionary in the first episode, Hyacinth's beloved Sheridan veers clearly off into the alternative lifestyle that is apparent to everyone but his mother.

There is a good opening sequence in which the protocol-sensitive Hyacinth chides Richard for raising his arms in public while gardening in the front yard. She then informs him that if he insists on perspiring while he works he had better labor in the back garden away from the full view of the public.

Later, while trying to counsel Rose over the phone, Hyacinth asks her wayward sister what could possibly happen once a week on a Wednesday afternoon to make her latest lover, Mr. Hepplewhite, so important to Rose. In a magnificent bit of mugging, Hyacinth listens as Rose apparently explains the lurid details. First Hyacinth's eyebrows shoot up, then they quickly plummet in a painful squint, then her eyes twitch. Finally, she has heard enough. "I'm not standing here," Hyacinth informs Rose, "surrounded by expensive wallpaper to be given details like that."

EPISODE 3 ★★★½

Air date: November 12, 1990. Cast: Hyacinth (Patricia Routledge); Richard (Clive Swift); Daisy (Judy Cornwell); Onslow (Geoffrey Hughes); Liz (Josephine Tewson); Rose (Shirley Stelfox); Angry woman (Liz Gebhardt); Car Park Attendant (Eric Carte); Stately Home Visitors (Les Clack, Stella Kemball); His Lordship (Michael Bilton)

Hyacinth's plans to rub elbows with the aristocracy while on a tour of stately Carldon Hall are thwarted when her shabby relatives turn up at the estate.

Henpecked Richard Bucket (Clive Swift, left) stands aside his pretentious spouse, Hyacinth (Patricia Routledge) in a posed still from this popular Roy Clark vehicle. Copyright © BBC.

This episode gives Clive Swift's character, the thoroughly beleaguered Richard Bucket, his first real chance to shine. In addition, the principal characters appear much more comfortable in their roles, especially Patricia Routledge, whose reactions have quickly achieved the level of a female Oliver Hardy. She has been given more physical comedy, as well, including the recurring routine of falling into the hedge after being surprised by Onslow's dog.

This episode also provides the first of many examples of Hyacinth's passenger seat–driving technique. After Richard asks his wife which route they want to take to the country, Hyacinth comments that such a decision is up to him. After Richard turns to take one route, however, Hyacinth firmly states she would have chosen the other. Richard is forced to turn around in a service station, running over the bell and summoning the attendant as he drives through. Hyacinth then decides they should go and see Daddy before going to the country, thus compelling Richard to drive through the same gas station. She changes her mind twice more, resulting in other turns through the station. Next, Hyacinth displays her invaluable assistance as Richard's navigator, as she commands her husband to be wary of parked lorries and pedestrians on the opposite side of the street

Actor Michael Bilton (His Lordship) must be quite accustomed to strangers in his house. He also played the old man in whose house Victor Meldrew's guests party by mistake in *One Foot in the Grave*'s "In Luton Airport No One Can Hear You Scream," as well as Ned on *To the Manor Born*.

EPISODE 4 ★★★

Air date: November 19, 1990. Cast: Hyacinth (Patricia Routledge); Richard (Clive Swift); Liz (Josephine Tewson); Daisy (Judy Cornwell); Onslow (Geoffrey Hughes); Rose (Shirley Stelfox); Daddy's Fiancée (Gretchen Franklin); Councillor Nugent (Charmian May); Mr. Duxbury (Norman Lovett); His Mate (Denis Bond); Postman (Leo Dolan)

Hyacinth's stint at the charity shop coincides with that of the prestigious Mrs. Nugent. Her well-formulated plans to impress the proper Mrs. Nugent are jeopardized when Rose arrives to donate a bag full of racy lingerie.

The first full-scale exhibition of the marvelous physical clowning of Patricia Routledge, this episode finds Hyacinth scaling walls in her futile attempts to preserve her false dignity. Routledge's skill in this area adds immensely to the series, not just for the actual physical execution of the gags, but since it emphasizes the irony of the character, who performs deeds that are totally embarrassing while trying to support a façade made of vain boasts and verbal assertions.

Hyacinth's scaling of the garden wall is without a doubt the crowning comedic achievement of this episode. Rather than let Elizabeth see Daisy's real home, Hyacinth has Liz drop her off in front of a much more fashionable property. Then Hyacinth ducks around the back of the house (literally walking like a duck with a broken leg in an attempt at stealth) to find that the backyard is surrounded by a ten-foot brick wall. She climbs over some gardening equipment to the top of the potting shed then, by standing on some oversized flowerpots, struggles over the wall. The comedic effect is even greater given that the whole exercise is carried out by a plump woman in a floral print dress, hat, and gloves. In the last stages of her ascent, Hyacinth is observed by the homeowners, who watch aghast from their second floor window. She then proceeds through back alleys to Daisy's house. Of course she repeats the feat upon her return, again with the people watching in even greater astonishment as this bizarre sight has occurred twice in the same day.

The dour Mrs. Nugent is played by the versatile Charmian May, who also played the spinsterish Miss Pershore in the first series of *The Fall and Rise of Reginald Perrin* and the suburban Mrs. Weaver in the second series of *The Good Life*.

EPISODE 5

★★★½

Air date: November 26, 1990. Cast: Hyacinth (Patricia Routledge); Richard (Clive Swift); Liz (Josephine Tewson); Daisy (Judy Cornwell); Onslow (Geoffrey Hughes); Rose (Shirley Stelfox); Vicar (Jeremy Gittins); Milkman (Robert Rawles); Mrs. East (Jeanne Mockford); Mrs. Dobson (Tricia Thorns); Neighbor (Ian Burford); Youth (Jonny Lee Miller); Ladies at Church (Linda James, Pamela Abbott)

Fearing that Onslow doesn't love her anymore, Daisy borrows Rose's 17-year-old boyfriend and introduces him to Onslow as her "toyboy."

A very good episode, with a great deal of the humor coming from an exploration of Daisy and Onslow's relationship, this installment marks a turning point in the way Daisy is presented. In the previous episodes her tone toward her husband was one of muted antagonism. In the future Daisy will be painted as more love struck, yet unsatisfied, which, given the object of her affections, presents much grist for the humor mill.

This episode also introduces a familiar routine that will become a staple of *Keeping Up Appearances*: the avoidance of Hyacinth by just about everyone but her own family. In fact, most of the extras in this installment are here to dive, duck, and hide upon even the hint that Hyacinth is about to appear. When Hyacinth arrives at the church hall, a lookout warns the rest of the ladies, and the entire group rushes off to hide. Later, after being brought back out by Liz, the women suffer as Hyacinth takes charge of the luncheon preparations. She carries on a steady monologue on the wonders of Sheridan, only pausing to deliver backhanded comments on the food items the other women have brought. Even the Vicar tries unsuccessfully to sneak past.

The comic high point of the episode, however, comes when Daisy informs Onslow that she is in love with a 17-year-old. Onslow remarks that he is disgusted, not by Daisy's affair, but by the fact that she is interrupting his television viewing to announce it. When Daisy ushers the youth into the room, Onslow recognizes the lad as one of Rose's boyfriends, but Rose explains that she gave him to Daisy. Unruffled, Onslow asks if the boy is old enough to smoke. The kid pulls out some cigarettes. Onslow takes one, but the toyboy insists that he keep the whole pack. Encouraged by this display of generosity, Onslow hopefully asks if Daisy can keep the youth interested until he reaches drinking age.

Episode 6 ★★

Air date: December 3, 1990. Cast: Hyacinth (Patricia Routledge); Richard (Clive Swift); Daisy (Judy Cornwell); Onslow (Geoffrey Hughes); Liz (Josephine Tewson); Rose (Shirley Stelfox); Vicar (Gerald Sim); Reg (Bruce Bennett); Dennis (Jonathan Fryer); Mrs. Midgely (Patricia Leach); Hippies (Rick Friend, Richard Ashton); Stephanie (Laura Shavin)

Hyacinth and Richard attend the christening of their niece Stephanie's baby. The ceremony is particularly nettlesome to Hyacinth since the child has been born out of wedlock. Once the family arrives at the church, the affair quickly degenerates.

The final episode of the first season fails primarily because it lacks real opportunity for Hyacinth to lose face in the eyes of those whose approval she covets. Here she is surrounded by her family, who embarrass her anyway, so while she is uncomfortable, she is never actually ashamed. Her wish from the beginning of the episode, that they not be discovered at the family event, comes true — when it needs not to.

The much-talked-of fourth sister, Violet, makes an appearance but is only seen from a distance. This is also the only appearance of Daisy and Onslow's daughter, Stephanie.

Series Two 1991

Episode 1 ★★★

Air date: September 1, 1991. Cast: Hyacinth (Patricia Routledge); Richard (Clive Swift); Daisy (Judy Cornwell); Liz (Josephine Tewson); Onslow (Geoffrey Hughes); Rose (Mary Millar); Emmet (David Griffin); Milkman (Robert Rawles)

Hyacinth notices a strange man coming out of Elizabeth's house dressed only in a towel. She immediately assumes the worst and bemoans the loss of property values in the area due to the "illicit love nest" next door.

Buoyed by the success of the first season, the second season of *Keeping Up Appearances* is a full ten episodes in length. Despite a popular first run, two changes are evident here, both of which add to the show. The first is the casting of Mary Millar in the part of Rose, the youngest of the four sisters. Millar's performance along with her overall appearance help give her character a gullibility and naivete that lend credence and an air of innocent melodrama to Rose's many affairs.

The second change is the welcome addition of David Griffin in the role of Emmet, Liz's brother. Emmet, wisely made a producer of amateur operettas, not only provides good opportunities by virtue of his profession but gives Liz someone to play off aside from Hyacinth.

In an attempt to gather more information about the strange man, Hyacinth coaches the long-suffering Richard through an elaborate drill of leaving for the office and returning again so that he may get a better look at Elizabeth's house. First, Richard walks ten feet from the door, turns and waves goodbye, while scanning Liz's house. Next, he is instructed to begin to walk away, then stop and pretend he has forgotten something in order that he might repeat the exercise. Patricia Routledge's broad stage directions here are truly hilarious and must be seen to be appreciated, along with Clive Swift's marvelous interpretations of the same.

EPISODE 2 ★★★

Air date: September 8, 1991. Cast: Hyacinth (Patricia Routledge); Richard (Clive Swift); Daisy (Judy Cornwell); Elizabeth (Josephine Tewson); Onslow (Geoffrey Hughes); Rose (Mary Millar); Emmet (David Griffin); Mrs. Fortescue (Jean Anderson); Pub Customer (Leonard Lowe); Neighbor (Michael Burrell)

The elderly Mrs. Fortescue calls Hyacinth to request a ride into town. Richard, however, is reluctant to kowtow to the woman after she hit him with her cane in church.

Somewhat plodding and seemingly disjointed at the outset, this episode quickly congeals for a strong ending. Again, there is some fine physical work by Routledge, although some of the better supporting characters are given little to do. This episode also gives more definition to the peripheal character of Bruce, sister Violet's husband. While Bruce's predilection for kinkiness was introduced in the premiere episode, here it blossoms into full-blown cross-dressing with an actual sighting of the party in question.

Before Richard can drive someone as important socially as Mrs. Fortescue, he must submit to lengthy training from Hyacinth. The hapless husband endures coaching on how to walk, open the door, escort the woman, smile, and even how to ring the doorbell. With the preliminaries done, Hyacinth proceeds to the eventuality of having to converse with Mrs. Fortescue while driving. She asks Richard what he usually discusses while driving. Richard replies that usually Hyacinth talks while he listens. After a moment to ponder this veiled insult, Hyacinth brightens and concludes they won't tamper with their successful system.

Routledge delivers some more good physical comedy in the pub scene. While Hyacinth refuses to enter the pub, she is burning with curiosity outside climbs a window cleaner's ladder in an attempt to peek inside. When a pair of acquaintances stroll by, she uses the ladder to climb on the back of a parked flatbed truck and scramble under its tarpaulin. Before she can climb back down, however, the driver returns and drives off. As the truck goes down the street Hyacinth can be seen by all around (including her two acquaintances), standing on the flatbed, screaming for the driver to stop.

EPISODE 3 ★★★½

Air date: September 15, 1991. Cast: Hyacinth (Patricia Routledge); Richard (Clive Swift); Elizabeth (Josephine Tewson); Daisy (Judy Cornwell); Onslow (Geoffrey Hughes); Rose (Mary Millar); Emmet (David Griffin); Boris (Dicken Ashworth); Mr. Helliwell (Gregory Cox); Man with Dog (Stuart Sherwin)

Hyacinth's latest candlelight supper is ruined when most of the guests manage to find convenient excuses to avoid the affair. With only Elizabeth and Emmet attending, the supper is ruined when Rose and two of her boyfriends pick Hyacinth's doorstep for a fistfight.

Stronger than its predecessors in the second series primarily on the basis of some very funny dialogue, episode three presents one of the often spoken of, but heretofore never seen, candlelight suppers. The plot is slim but amply filled with good situations.

Most of the clever lines go to Onslow, who does not have any interaction with Hyacinth in this episode. This is an important leap in the development of his character, who is becoming a marvelously humorous personality in his own right, rather than merely a foil for Hyacinth. Thanks to watching *Open University* on television, Onslow has become something of a philosopher, and he uses his new depth as an excuse to stay even later in bed to ponder man's deep-seated yearning to understand the mysteries of the universe. When Daisy asks what mysteries Onslow is pondering, he replies that the main one is why she keeps her knee in his back while he's trying to sleep.

Later, Daisy, upset by Onslow's earlier pondering, asks her husband if the universe really is meaningless. He admits he is beginning to think so, especially after witnessing Daisy wearing a see-through negligee over an undershirt.

Richard also has some good moments. As he dutifully polishes the silver, Hyacinth chides him for grunting while toiling. Hyacinth wonders why humans have not yet risen above uttering such guttural sounds, to which Richard teasingly replies that they're merely mammals.

"Richard," Hyacinth replies in dead earnestness and perfect alliteration, "what a thing to say to somebody with a solid silver, self-cleaning sauce separator!"

EPISODE 4 ★★½

Air date: September 22, 1991. Cast: Hyacinth (Patricia Routledge); Richard (Clive Swift); Daisy (Judy Cornwell); Onslow (Geoffrey Hughes); Rose (Mary Millar); Major (Peter Cellier); Hotel Guests (Dinah Sheridan, Bernard Archard); Receptionist (Sally Hughes); Porters (Christopher Mitchell, Eamonn Clarke); Chambermaid (Sharon White)

Richard and Hyacinth travel to a golf resort at the invitation of the Major. Hyacinth spends most of her time annoying the receptionist and the other guests but ultimately is embarrassed by the appearance of Rose, Onslow, and Daisy.

A rather dull beginning is well resuscitated by a much livelier ending. Much of this is thanks to the arrival in the final 15 minutes of Onslow and Daisy. As gifted a comedian as Patricia Routledge is, she is quickly tiresome in the role of Hyacinth without an imagined crisis to react to — usually something involving her less seemly relatives. Unfortunately, for most of this episode she is left to wander about a resort hotel inflicting herself on others, rather than being inflicted upon.

The Major returns for his first appearance since the premiere episode, repeating his efforts to violate the proper Hyacinth. Even in the middle of being sexually accosted, Hyacinth strives to keep up appearances. After she frees herself from the Major's salacious clutches Hyacinth retreats into a pasture by climbing over a fence. "I love you, Mrs. Bucket," the Major cries after her.

"It's Bouquet," Hyacinth corrects as she struggles to retain her dignity while scaling the fence in a dress.

EPISODE 5 ★★★★

Air date: September 29, 1991. Cast: Hyacinth (Patricia Routledge); Richard (Clive Swift); Elizabeth (Josephine Tewson); Daisy (Judy Cornwell); Onslow (Geoffrey Hughes); Rose (Mary Millar); Emmet (David Griffin); Registrar (Helen Christie); Committee Chairman (Simon Merrick); Committee Member (Robert McBain); Missionary (Brendan O'Hea)

Hyacinth continually interrupts Richard in the middle of an important meeting with a series of family crises, including Daddy's suspected elopement and brother-in-law Bruce sulking up a tree (because Violet won't share her party dresses with him).

Filled with good dialogue built around the perfect execution of stock situations, this episode is quintessential *Keeping Up Appearances*. There are fine scenes in which Hyacinth inflicts herself on others (Elizabeth and a hapless Missionary) beautifully balanced against numerous humorous occasions where she struggles through potentially embarrassing events. Both Richard and Onslow are seen toiling at their places of work only to be dragged away by their respective wives. In Onslow's case, however, his "office" is the inside of a betting parlor. Every cast member, with the possible exception of Rose, has good opportunity to shine — even the elusive Violet and Bruce are given a scene, albeit out of sight, up a tree.

Emmet manages to derive a measure of revenge on Hyacinth when he diverts a door-to-door Christian Missionary to her home. Rather than bringing enlightenment to Hyacinth, the Missionary finds that he is the one being preached to and tries frantically to leave. As he struggles toward the door, Hyacinth gives him some parting words of advice concerning his choice of socks, noting that polka dots are sufficiently Christian for a man of his calling. As the Missionary finally starts on his way, Hyacinth asks him to remind

God in his prayers of the high quality of furnishings that he has been privileged to enjoy while visiting.

EPISODE 6 ★★★½

Air date: October 6, 1991. Cast: Hyacinth (Patricia Routledge); Richard (Clive Swift); Daisy (Judy Cornwell); Elizabeth (Josephine Tewson); Onslow (Geoffrey Hughes); Rose (Mary Millar); Emmet (David Griffin); Major (Peter Cellier); Vicar (Jeremy Gittins); His Wife (Marion Barron); Jeweler (Anthony Davis); Committee Member (Robert McBain); Mr. Maranopolous (Ivan Santon)

Hyacinth is dreading being invited to Onslow's birthday party almost as much as he dreads having her come. She changes her tune, however, when she learns that Rose's new boyfriend, Mr. Maranopolis, a well-to-do Greek gentleman, will be picking up the celebrants in his limousine. She is mortified to learn, however, that the foreign suitor has earned his wealth as an undertaker and that his limousine is actually a hearse.

The majority of the fun in this good entry stems from Hyacinth's leaping to conclusions about Rose's new boyfriend — a habit begun in the previous episode — then trying to remain composed when her dreams are dashed.

One of the biggest laughs in this strongly plotted episode has nothing to do with the story. It occurs when Onslow is watching TV with the dog across his lap while he eats chips (fries). He kindly shares the chips with the animal, even letting it have the first bite on a particularly large piece, before finishing it himself.

Later, thinking she is going to be picked up by a limousine, Hyacinth invites friends over to witness the event. She discovers the vehicle is a hearse before her guests do and quickly waves the car around the block. While the hearse circles repeatedly in front of the house, Hyacinth first tries to dismiss her guests. Having failed this, with the party milling around in her front yard, Hyacinth attempts to divert her guests' gaze from the vehicle. On one pass she excitedly has the entire party look up on the roof to admire their new lead flashing, which, according to Hyacinth, came from a disused monastery in Toulouse. The next go-round she is less successful, and the guests get a good look at the hearse, bowing respectfully as it continues up the street.

EPISODE 7 ★★★

Air date: October 13, 1991. Cast: Hyacinth (Patricia Routledge); Richard (Clive Swift); Elizabeth (Josephine Tewson); Daisy (Judy Cornwell); Onslow (Geoffrey Hughes); Rose (Mary Millar); Emmet (David Griffin); Vicar (Jeremy Gittins); His Wife (Marion Barron); Mr. Penworthy (Nigel Williams)

Hyacinth is thrilled at the prospect of Richard accepting early retirement. Richard, however, is deeply distressed over the same prospect since it means spending all his days with her.

This episode is an especially good vehicle for Clive Swift in the role of the long-suffering Richard and Mary Millar in the often-overlooked part of Rose. Interesting for its investigation of how Hyacinth reacts to the personal traumas of those around her (she ignores them), this installment finds a number of the supporting cast members at their breaking points. In a major plot move, Richard is first faced with the horrifying prospect of early retirement, while Rose contemplates giving up men for the life of a nun. Even Emmet finally snaps under the pressure of prolonged exposure to Hyacinth. Despite the fact that Emmet launches into a tirade in front of her eyes, Hyacinth fails to see that she is the cause of the outburst.

Troubled by chronic wrong numbers for the Chinese take-away restaurant, Hyacinth orders Richard to telephone the Chinese ambassador to remedy the situation. Despite the obvious ludicrousness of her request, Richard dutifully agrees and places the call. While Richard is on the phone, Hyacinth takes great delight in going into the street to request that passersby remain as quiet as possible while her husband is talking with the Chinese ambassador. Returning inside, Hyacinth is not at all disappointed that Richard only left a message on the embassy's answering machine, interpreting the act as one that places her husband on "chatting terms" with the high-ranking diplomat.

There's also a clever little sight gag when the Vicar's Wife interrupts her husband's ringing of the church bells to announce that Hyacinth is on the way. With the bells ringing in melodious tones, we see the wife run into the bell tower. After a moment, the Vicar can be heard crying, "The Bucket woman!" The bells continue to ring but now in a sour cacophony.

EPISODE 8 ★½

Air date: October 20, 1991. Cast: Hyacinth (Patricia Routledge); Richard (Clive Swift); Elizabeth (Josephine Tewson); Daisy (Judy Cornwell); Onslow (Geoffrey Hughes); Rose (Mary Millar); Emmet (David Griffin); Councillor Nugent (Charmian May); Frank (Robert McBain); Insurance Salesman (John Owens); Store Official (John Pennington); His Assistant (David Warwick)

Onslow, Daisy, and Rose arrive on Hyacinth's doorstep — necessitating her shoving guests Elizabeth and Emmet out the back door — to announce that Daddy is being held hostage. It seems that a local department store is detaining him until a £235 bill is paid for items he purchased in their toy department. Hyacinth telephones Richard, instructing him to meet them at the store with his checkbook.

A rather uninspired entry padded with inconsequential situations already explored in previous episodes. There are some bits of information here that may be of interest to diehard fans (such as the first mention of Emmet's last name, Hawksworth, and a definitive listing of the four sisters' birth order: Hyacinth, Daisy, Violet, and Rose), but these hardly generate any laughs.

Richard manages to continue to milk the prospect of early retirement to good effect, and there is a humorous cameo by Violet's oddball husband, Bruce. Aside from these standout moments — along with Daddy's cavorting in a spacesuit — there is little to recommend here.

Perhaps the most amusing moment is provided in a climactic, yet almost throwaway gag concerning Bruce. Leaving his cross-dressing hobby by the wayside momentarily, Bruce decides to drum up publicity for his turf account's business by dressing like a jockey and trotting through town with a papier-mâché horse around his waist. Although mentioned early, this sight provides the final gag. Having just defused a potentially embarrassing situation with Daddy, Hyacinth is shocked to discover Bruce galloping down the street outside the department store waving cheerily to the passersby and urging on his pantomime steed, Thunderbolt.

EPISODE 9 ★★

Air date: October 27, 1991. Cast: Hyacinth (Patricia Routledge); Richard (Clive Swift); Daisy (Judy Cornwell); Elizabeth (Josephine Tewson); Onslow (Geoffrey Hughes); Rose (Mary Millar); Emmet (David Griffin); Van Driver (Nick Burnell); Driver's Mate (David Keller)

Hyacinth is all aflutter over the impending arrival of her new three-piece living room suite. She is especially desirous that one of her neighbors witness the delivery and be envious.

A good concept with a thin but viable plot, this episode just doesn't quite live up to its potential. The central theme of the series is vigorously explored here but unfortunately with not enough input from the supporting cast to disarm Hyacinth's irritating qualities.

Aside from a pair of humorous, one-sided phone conversations by Hyacinth with Violet and Sheridan, the best moments in this episode come when Hyacinth tries to urge Onslow to move his old truck. Not wanting to openly offend her relatives, Hyacinth pretends she is giving directions to strangers in the off chance that the neighbors are watching. Onslow, Daisy, and Rose stand with their mouths agape as Hyacinth quietly tries to tell them to come back later, while making broad and quite hilarious gestures designed to look like motoring instructions. The trio finally leave, convinced that Hyacinth has finally lost her mind.

EPISODE 10 ★★½

Air date: November 3, 1991. Cast: Hyacinth (Patricia Routledge); Richard (Clive Swift); Daisy (Judy Cornwell); Elizabeth (Josephine Tewson); Onslow (Geoffrey Hughes); Rose (Mary Millar); Emmet (David Griffin); Vicar (Jeremy Gittins); His Wife (Marion Barron)

Hyacinth decides to take Daddy on a picnic. The picnic turns into a mad car chase, however, when Daddy commandeers Richard's car. The rest of the family piles into Onslow's car and follows in hot pursuit around the town and into the countryside.

Operating on a slim premise, this episode is ultimately redeemed by a lively car chase sequence in the finale. As good as this ending is, however, it doesn't help resolve the plot. In fact, the chase itself is unresolved, leaving one wondering about the welfare of one of the main characters.

This episode also marks the first time that Hyacinth shows that she holds out a glimmer of hope for her youngest sister, Rose. While Rose's predilection for dating married men embarrasses Hyacinth to no end, here (and in the next episode) Hyacinth is encouraged when she believes her sister may be getting ready to settle down with a man of means. Of course this is not the case, and Hyacinth does what she can to bring a swift termination to the affair.

While in hot pursuit of the speeding Daddy, Richard can only worry about what will happen to his car. Hyacinth, on the other hand, has the proper perspective. "Impulsive Daddy," she frets as they race along, "I hope he's not going to drive at speeds incompatible with my cut glass condiment set."

Christmas Special 1991

★★★

Air date: December 25, 1991. Cast: Hyacinth (Patricia Routledge); Richard (Clive Swift); Daisy (Judy Cornwell); Elizabeth (Josephine Tewson); Onslow (Geoffrey Hughes); Rose (Mary Millar); Emmet (David Griffin); Vicar (Jeremy Gittins)

Hyacinth arranges for Richard to play Father Christmas for a senior citizens' party at the church hall.

This 1991 holiday offering is like many Christmas presents in that it delights upon opening but ultimately fails to sustain its initial joy. To put it more plainly, the best moments of this half-hour special come during its first half. There are some wonderful touches, including Onslow proudly showing off the Christmas decorations he has created inside the abandoned car perpetually rotting away in his front garden. (The deep-thinking Onslow explains that the display is his contribution to the world of abstract art.) Hyacinth dressing up the reluctant Richard as Father Christmas also supplies a generous bit of laughter, as does Richard's subsequent escape to Emmet's house in the costume, where both men proceed to get tipsy on holiday cheer in liquid form. Elizabeth masquerading as Richard in the Father Christmas outfit also provides some merriment, especially her brother's admonition that to fool Hyacinth in the disguise she merely has to "listen like Richard."

The best moments, however, come as Rose awaits her new boyfriend, Mr. Sudbury, who, according to Rose, is a marvelous dancer. As she stands outside their dilapidated home with Daisy and Onslow, the resplendently dressed

Mr. Sudbury comes prancing down the alleyway like some sort of third-rate Fred Astaire. As Onslow watches in a combination of disgust and amazement, Rose and her paramour perform earnest, albeit clumsy dance routines around the council estate as if they were skipping through an MGM musical. Daisy apparently appreciates the display much more than her husband and shows her excitement by unconsciously rubbing Onslow's bare arm with suppressed romantic intensity.

Unfortunately, after these high points, the rest of the affair becomes rather routine and even hurried as the special resorts to plot devices seen in other episodes.

Series Three 1992

Episode 1 ★★★

Air date: September 6, 1992. Cast: Hyacinth (Patricia Routledge); Richard (Clive Swift); Elizabeth (Josephine Tewson); Daisy (Judy Cornwell); Onslow (Geoffrey Hughes); Rose (Mary Millar); Emmet (David Griffin); Richard's Boss (Ivor Daniels); Milkman (Robert Rawles); Roger (Jon Glover)

While Richard faces his last day on the job, Hyacinth paves the way for his future by inviting an influential woman to tea.

Rather slim on plot but still with enough comedy to carry the day, the premiere episode of the third season centers on Richard's early retirement. First hinted at in the seventh episode of the second series, this is the first day of the rest of his life that Richard has been dreading more than any other.

Clive Swift does a splendid job portraying a man overwrought with enough quiet desperation to fill a psych ward. The first ten minutes of the episode find Richard so preoccupied with his impending fate that he cannot function properly. Unable to complete even simple tasks like shaving or leaving the house, poor Richard continually has to be ushered in the right direction by Hyacinth. At one point Hyacinth puts her husband in the car, then walks into the street to direct his reverse. After stridently waving him on, she notices that he is frozen behind the wheel like a zombie. When she goes to retrieve him, Richard finally snaps out of his catatonia and greets Hyacinth as if he were returning rather than leaving.

When Richard gets to work the thin veneer of his composure finally splinters as he first offers, then pleads, then begs to be kept on in any capacity available. As good as this is, it is somewhat anticlimactic since we don't see Richard again for the remainder of the episode, even though it still has a good half to run. One can only guess that he left work to find solace in a pub before facing a life sentence with Hyacinth.

Hyacinth has some good scenes, although most are repetitions of the standard routines so well engrained in the series by this point. The one standout bit involves a large black Newfoundland dog that plants itself in the middle of Hyacinth's driveway and refuses to budge. The dog has been left there by Roger, Rose's boyfriend. With the wife of a local frozen food magnate coming for tea, Hyacinth and Elizabeth try in vain to move the dog before she arrives. The dog finally does move but only to chase the arriving visitor's dog, dragging Hyacinth along in the process.

EPISODE 2 ★★★

Air date: September 13, 1992. Cast: Hyacinth (Patricia Routledge); Richard (Clive Swift); Daisy (Judy Cornwell); Elizabeth (Josephine Tewson); Onslow (Geoffrey Hughes); Rose (Mary Millar); Emmet (David Griffin); Vicar (Jeremy Gittins); Postman (David Janson)

Hyacinth's search for Iron Age remains are interrupted by another crisis in Rose's love life.

There's quite a bit of fun to be had in this offering, but unfortunately there are also some tantalizing possibilities that are never quite explored. The bits that are exploited are done so to their full potential, including some of the best opportunities that Mary Millar as Rose has in the entire series. As usual, Rose is pining away over her romantic situation, finally locking herself in her room and calling for the cute Vicar for spiritual comfort. At one point, Rose is driven to wearing a sexy black teddy in addition to a black veil (she explains that it is because she is both mourning and ready for excitement). There is some especially good verbal byplay between Rose and Onslow.

The comic climax comes as Hyacinth forces Richard to climb a ladder for a glimpse into Rose's room, then accidentally pushes it out from under him.

The initial plot concerns Hyacinth's futile search throughout the countryside for Iron Age remains with the hapless Richard in tow. Although this segment has some amusing moments, they fall fairly flat. Afterward, however, there is promise of more as Hyacinth wonders why Richard is suddenly acting strangely, while at the same time Emmet is counseling him to act irrationally to add interest to his retirement. To help him along this path, Emmet joins Richard in some impromptu headstands alongside the road, much to Hyacinth's mortification. One is left hoping for more along this line, but regrettably there is no more.

EPISODE 3 ★★★½

Air date: September 20, 1992. Cast: Hyacinth (Patricia Routledge); Richard (Clive Swift); Daisy (Judy Cornwell); Elizabeth (Josephine Tewson); Onslow (Geoffrey Hughes); Rose (Mary Millar); Emmet (David Griffin); Dorian (Royce Mills); Bunty (Marcia Warren); Neighbor (Ian Burford)

Hyacinth and Richard borrow Violet's country home for the weekend.

Plenty of fresh material, new situations, and new characters make this a splendid entry in a strong season of shows. There is an especially nice twist regarding the arrival of Onslow and his entourage at the end of the episode. Usually, this occurrence is a cause for great embarrassment on the part of Hyacinth as she is trying to put on airs before influential people. Here, however, Hyacinth falls in with Bunty and Dorian, a socially well-placed but extremely eccentric couple. When Onslow, Daisy, and the rest arrive, they find the usually decorous Hyacinth congaing around the lawn with Bunty and Dorian. It is fun to see the lower-class relatives somewhat embarrassed and more than a little confused by this display.

There are also many good touches to the proceedings before the Buckets actually leave home. Despite the fact that Violet's country home is fully furnished, Hyacinth insists upon taking a full range of her own china and ornaments. Aside from giving Richard the back-breaking task of loading all this paraphernalia, it also makes the neighbors think Hyacinth is taking an extended holiday. The prospect of any hiatus from Hyacinth brings the entire neighborhood out to gleefully wave goodbye. Misconstruing the spontaneous outburst, Hyacinth vows to Richard that they will never move in light of what her presence means to the rest of the neighborhood.

Marcia Warren is good as Bunty, the eccentric country neighbor. She comes calling fresh from hunting in search of her dog, when she encounters Richard unloading the car. Bunty asks Richard if he has seen a bitch, eliciting one of the biggest laughs of the episode as he turns slowly to stare in Hyacinth's direction. Royce Mills, as Dorian, also provides some humor as yet another demented middle-aged male who finds the stout Mrs. Bucket sexually irresistible.

EPISODE 4 ★★★

Air date: September 27, 1992. Cast: Hyacinth (Patricia Routledge); Richard (Clive Swift); Elizabeth (Josephine Tewson); Daisy (Judy Cornwell); Onslow (Geoffrey Hughes); Rose (Mary Millar); Emmet (David Griffin); Vicar (Jeremy Gittins); Vicar's Wife (Marion Barron); Waitress (Karen Chatwin)

Hyacinth makes a show of collecting expensive holiday brochures in order to keep up with an acquaintance who is going on a Caribbean vacation.

An amusing little episode containing two basic story lines that converge nicely for the finale. The first involves the familiar theme of Hyacinth trying to impress the neighbors, specifically one rival who is going on an expensive holiday. This of course calls for a visit to the local travel agency, despite Richard's assertions that they can't afford a luxury trip. Oddly, and somewhat out of character, Hyacinth for once agrees with her hapless hubby, and instead of the visit escalating into a costly tour, Hyacinth emerges with only opulent-looking brochures. This leads to some of the better humor of the installment, as Hyacinth must go to great lengths to have the travel pamphlets noticed by the right people. In one incident she purposely throws the brochures out the car window as they are passing one acquaintance on the street, then orders Richard to stop so she can retrieve and display the books to the woman.

The second plot centers on Onslow's determination to do some charity work — meaning he schemes to find a way to give Richard a little freedom from Hyacinth. Unfortunately, this sequence, while welcome, is a little disappointing. The end results are only that Richard has a nice afternoon in a pub playing billiards with Onslow and returns to his wife slightly tipsy. The character of Rose also figures prominently in this episode, as she arrives, much to Hyacinth's mortification, for a church cleaning day dressed in something suitable for a French maid. The cleaning day exercise also provides some laughs, especially when Hyacinth outmaneuvers herself into volunteering to clean the lavatories.

EPISODE 5 ★★★½

Air date: October 4, 1992. Cast: Hyacinth (Patricia Routledge); Richard (Clive Swift); Elizabeth (Josephine Tewson); Daisy (Judy Cornwell); Onslow (Geoffrey Hughes); Rose (Mary Millar); Emmet (David Griffin); Mrs. Nugent (Charmian May); Policemen (Jonathan Stratt, Matthew Long)

Hyacinth urges Richard to become a filmmaker to fill his idle retirement time.

If there were any doubts as to why Richard Bucket approached his early retirement with more than a little trepidation, they are easily dispelled with this consistently entertaining episode. The martyred husband, expertly portrayed by Clive Swift, illustrates clearly that his only desire is to get a bit of peace from the constant blare of his wife. After being sent out for the umpteenth morning to care for an already perfect garden, Richard longingly yearns for the solitude of a solo sail around the globe (even this brief reverie is dispelled by Hyacinth's argument that there would be no one there to wash his shirts). As a solution, Hyacinth orders Richard to go film something with his new video camera (a retirement gift) with specific orders to return by tea time with a minor masterpiece.

Hyacinth's need for cinematic brilliance by the afternoon is driven by her desire to try to impress (yet again) Councillor Nugent. This time Hyacinth is hoping to be appointed to Mrs. Nugent's committee, although she has no idea what the committee's work is. Entering into the mix is Onslow, laboring mightily to try and find a way to alleviate Richard's retirement ordeal.

Roy Clarke manages to bring all these elements back together for a highly comedic conclusion, with a few policemen thrown in for good measure. There is also some good physical comedy involving Hyacinth and Elizabeth, especially one bit in which the jittery Liz nervously tosses one of her neighbor's Royal Dalton cups (with the hand-painted periwinkles) across the room, necessitating a split-second reaction and diving catch by Hyacinth.

Episode 6

★½

Air date: October 11, 1992. Cast: Hyacinth (Patricia Routledge); Richard (Clive Swift); Elizabeth (Josephine Tewson); Daisy (Judy Cornwell); Onslow (Geoffrey Hughes); Rose (Mary Millar); Emmet (David Griffin); Vicar (Jeremy Gittins); Mrs. Lennox (Jennifer Daniel); Mr. Finchley (Nicholas Bennett)

Hyacinth's introduction into the world of art is disrupted when Daddy decides to join the French Foreign Legion.

A disappointing entry, especially coming as it does in the midst of such a vibrant season of offerings. The primary weakness here is one of unfulfilled promise. The author sets up many potentially hilarious situations and impending disasters but then never delivers on their promise. One keeps expecting the divergent plot lines to join up for a rousing finish, but at best they only briefly touch without tying the knot. Perhaps each situation is given too much of a buildup, necessitating the rushed ending, or perhaps we are supposed to imagine what mishaps will follow the closing credits. The end result, however, is like that of a hungry diner being allowed to read the menu and to smell the delicious aromas, then being ushered out of the restaurant.

There are many promising setups here. The first is Hyacinth's intention to attend a small local art exhibit. As usual, news of her intention strikes fear into the hearts of the neighbors who also have notions of attending. For his part, Richard brings home an armful of books on art, seeing as both he and his wife are neophytes in the world of painting. Hyacinth, however, busies herself with much more important preparations, such as deciding which hat to wear.

Add to this base the revelation that Daddy has run away again, this time to join the Foreign Legion. Soon, Rose and her latest lover, Mr. Finchley, are out looking for him in the latter's van, which is equipped with roof-mounted loudspeakers. The loudspeakers are accidentally switched on, broadcasting the couple's amorous escapades. Onslow and Daisy also join the hunt, but only after Onslow refuses to take advantage of their rarely empty house to make sexual advances of his own, much to his wife's disappointment. Ultimately, Hyacinth and Richard find Daddy and are forced to bring him to the exhibition. Unfortunately, these tantalizing bits fail to converge, leaving Hyacinth only moderately inconvenienced rather than completely flustered and embarrassed.

Episode 7

★★★★

Air date: October 18, 1992. Cast: Hyacinth (Patricia Routledge); Richard (Clive Swift); Elizabeth (Josephine Tewson); Daisy (Judy Cornwell); Onslow (Geoffrey Hughes); Rose (Mary Millar); Emmet (David Griffin); TV Repairman (Tony Aitken); Sales Assistant (Ian Collier); Youth (Nicholas Boyce)

Hyacinth's plans for a nautical buffet on a borrowed yacht go awry.

A simple, straightforward story line helps make this one of the best entries of the entire series. The plot and premise of the episode are so serviceable that this is one of the few instances where the other side of Hyacinth's family (Daisy, Onslow, and Rose) are given too much to do. Their contribution is almost negligible and is quite unnecessary in view of the strength of the main situation.

Hyacinth and Richard have been given the use of a boat for the weekend by the father of their son's "friend." Of course Hyacinth quickly envisions a luxury cabin cruiser and makes elaborate plans for a nautical buffet. In her quest for perfection, Hyacinth insists on stopping at a men's store on the way to the yacht and outfitting Richard in suitably nautical togs, including white shorts and a captain's hat. She also tries to heighten the flavor of the experience by tossing seafaring terms about whenever possible. As amusing as all of this is, it is only the warm-up to the episode's climactic scene.

There is some truly hilarious knockabout comedy as the couple arrives at the mooring and discovers that the yacht, regally named *Contessa II*, is in fact the smallest, shabbiest old tub in the yard. Richard mentions that the boat looks even worse in comparison to its more luxurious neighbors, prompting Hyacinth to insist that he move it to a more favorable mooring. In some business worthy of Laurel and Hardy, Richard tries to maneuver the craft while Hyacinth gives the orders and navigates. Unfortunately, Richard knows next to nothing about boats, a deficiency that Hyacinth tries to overcome by delivering her orders more authoritatively. The highlights to this marvelous scene come as Hyacinth uses her hapless husband's back as a plank to board the ship and of course when she finally succumbs to the inevitable and falls in the drink.

This episode is one of the personal favorites of director/producer Harold Snoad.

Series Four 1993

EPISODE 1 ★★★½

Air date: September 5, 1993. Cast: Hyacinth (Patricia Routledge); Richard (Clive Swift); Elizabeth (Josephine Tewson); Daisy (Judy Cornwell); Onslow (Geoffrey Hughes); Rose (Mary Millar); Emmet (David Griffin); Millburn (Frederick Jaeger); His Companion (Joe Dunlop); Postman (David Janson); Pillion Rider (Michael L. Blair)

Hyacinth schemes to make Richard a golf course hero in order to impress a local captain of industry.

The premiere entry of series four breaks away from the usual format of *Keeping Up Appearances* with this consistently amusing offering. The primary difference here is that there really is only one plot, instead of two that may or may not intertwine at the end. Onslow and Daisy are recruited by Hyacinth as an integral part of her plan, rather than appearing as an intrusion or embarrassment to her. This approach helps to ensure that the story line is fully exploited and resolved. The result is a good episode full of entertainment with a strong final gag to wrap up things.

The plot begins from the opening scene as Hyacinth sees a job posting in the morning paper for a managing director at Frosticles, a local frozen food firm. She thinks the position is ideally suited (as far as prestige is concerned) for Richard, despite the fact that he is not qualified for the job. Eschewing the application process, Hyacinth hatches a plot to make Richard look "ruthlessly efficient" to Mr. Millburn, the owner of Frosticles.

The plan is ridiculously simple and just simply ridiculous: Onslow is recruited to appear on the golf course as a menacing lout, who Richard will forcibly eject in full view of Mr. Millburn. Hyacinth's enlistment of the brother-in-law who she usually avoids is quite funny, as is Onslow's involvement in the plot. For his part, Onslow has no idea why he has been hired (for a month's supply of beer and crisps, with a future option for large amounts of frozen food) to merely stand on the golf course. Daisy tags along, but waiting in the woods only rekindles fond memories of when she and her husband used to play Tarzan and Jane in similar surroundings while courting. In a good surprise twist, Hyacinth's plan actually succeeds, until some real thugs arrive after Richard's first display of forcefulness.

EPISODE 2 ★★½

Air date: September 12, 1993. Cast: Hyacinth (Patricia Routledge); Richard (Clive Swift); Daisy (Judy Cornwell); Elizabeth (Josephine Tewson); Onslow (Geoffrey Hughes); Rose (Mary Millar); Emmet (David Griffin); Estate Agent (Denis Bond); Yokel (Barrie Gosney); His Wife (Liz Daniels)

Hyacinth's search for a small country cottage soon expands to include expensive estates, much to Richard's chagrin.

More leisurely paced than some recent episodes, this entry begins Hyacinth's quest for a rural retreat. This theme will occupy no fewer than three episodes of the seven presented in this fourth series.

The primary disappointment in this episode is the relatively small parts allotted to Onslow, Daisy, and Rose. Early in the proceedings their plot line is introduced — Rose announces that she is starting her tell-all autobiography — but unfortunately after one return glimpse we see no more of these wonderful characters. This is more the pity since there are some humorous moments as Rose hunkers down to the task of writing her memoirs, but first she must ask Onslow how to spell *memoirs*. Her husband's command of spelling evokes new admiration from Daisy as she is convinced that she married an intellectual. One wishes the potential of these scenes had been further exploited.

The main plot is quite good, with Hyacinth leading the luckless Richard on a hunt for a country home, which grows increasingly grandiose and expensive. To complicate Richard's woes, Hyacinth also believes that her husband is in the throes of a midlife crisis based on his inability to decide which hat she should wear. Richard gets back some of his own on this score as he manages to tease his wife (without her knowing, of course) on the topic. There are also some funny touches as Hyacinth adapts her brand of driving assistance to the country (instead of cautioning Richard in regard to pedestrians and parked lorries, she warns of fenced-in cows and stationary shrubbery).

The episode builds to a good slapstick climax when the Buckets visit a prospective estate but are less than enthused to discover that their guide through the home is a country bumpkin who they mistook for a village idiot a few moments earlier. The Yokel, as Hyacinth dubs him, is almost unintelligible through his rural accent but does manage to communicate clearly through some unwelcome body language that he fancies Hyacinth. When Richard manages to get stuck in the house's attic, the man takes full advantage of the situation and begins his pursuit of Hyacinth in earnest.

EPISODE 3 ★★★★

Air date: September 19, 1993. Cast: Hyacinth (Patricia Routledge); Richard (Clive Swift); Daisy (Judy Cornwell); Elizabeth (Josephine Tewson); Onslow (Geoffrey Hughes); Rose (Mary Millar); Emmet (David Griffin); C. P. Benedict (Paul Williamson); Cashier (Clovissa Newcombe)

Hyacinth invents a new form of barbecue while her sister Daisy worries that Onslow is seeing another woman.

Often when I'm introducing a friend to a Brit-com I try to select an episode that provides all the best the show has to offer, presented in the best light. This offering from the fourth season is probably the choice I would make to usher a neophyte into the world of Hyacinth Bucket. Roy Clarke is to be commended for integrating the usual elements present in each episode and some of the series' best dialogue, all of which is woven in and out of two marvelously balanced plots.

The plots feature two of the four sisters in crisis. Hyacinth is driven to distraction by the fact that her neighbors, the Barker-Finches, have attracted a minor celebrity (*the* Douglas Chater, a local cement supplier) to a barbecue. Daisy, on the other hand, is obsessed with the notion that the sedentary Onslow is having an affair. Both crises of course are the products of their imaginations, leading one to wonder if paranoia runs in the family. Daisy's fear is especially humorous, what with Onslow barely being able to drag himself from bed in time to watch racing on the telly. Still, seeing her beloved slob through lovestruck eyes, Daisy insists that her husband exudes a raw animal magnetism that all women must find as irresistible as she does.

The running time is evenly divided between the two story lines, with the scenes alternating as they go through phases of discovery, strategy, and resolution of the problems. Unfortunately for Hyacinth, and in the best *Keeping*

Up Appearances fashion, Daisy's attempt at resolution destroys Hyacinth's. Both Daisy and Hyacinth attack their issues with imagination. Hyacinth invents her own local celebrity (to match the first one she made of the cement vendor) out of the owner of the nearby garden center, reasoning that he must be famous since he's been on television. Daisy is no less creative, as she, with Rose's help, sets about reinventing herself with a glittery makeover.

Hyacinth is also given two new excellent catch phrases to add to such ones as the "white, slim-line telephone" and her "Royal Dalton with the hand-painted periwinkles." First she replaces Richard's favorite breakfast food (corn flakes) with an unappetizing "exclusive, high-fiber, European breakfast cereal," chosen because the package was endorsed with the crest of the Dutch royal family. The other invention is her new twist on the standard barbecue: "the outdoors-indoors luxury barbecue with finger buffet." This event is created by cramming one's dining room with enough plants that it resembles a piece of the Amazon rain forest. As executed by Hyacinth, it adds tremendously to the finish of a very funny episode.

EPISODE 4 ★★★

Air date: September 26, 1993. Cast: Hyacinth (Patricia Routledge); Richard (Clive Swift); Elizabeth (Josephine Tewson); Daisy (Judy Cornwell); Onslow (Geoffrey Hughes); Rose (Mary Millar); Emmet (David Griffin); Commodore (Nigel Davenport); Vicar (Jeremy Gittins); Chairlady (Geraldine Newman); Committee Members (Linda James, Liz Edmiston); Lady at Luncheon (Ann Davies); Passenger (Leonard Lowe); Station Manager (Donald T. Allen); Ticket Clerk (Gordon Peters); Lady at Station (Irene Sharp); houseowner (John Barrard)

Hyacinth volunteers to pick up the guest speaker of the ladies' luncheon at the train station and escort him to the event.

Patricia Routledge's Hyacinth has never been more energetic as she anticipates playing host to the ladies' club's guest, the Commodore, renowned for his solo sailing exploits. The fact that the man, who is never actually named, has an impressive title is enough for Hyacinth, who quickly volunteers to fetch him at the station. Of course in true Hyacinth fashion, that simple task soon becomes expanded with plans for entertaining the Commodore at home, culminating in a lifelong friendship.

Roy Clarke pulls a surprise with his scripting. Early in the episode the author sets up what seems to be a stock situation just ripe for picking, namely, that the Commodore is a notorious drinker and womanizer. Rather than deliver this as the main thrust of the episode, however, Clarke teases the viewer with the premise, then prolongs the delivery. Instead of the imagined scenes of Hyacinth wrestling with a drunken amorous sailor, she is forced to rush around the local train stations searching in vain for the guest of honor. These twists are quite fruitful, as she aggravates not only the long-suffering Richard but a panoply of railway workers, passengers, and finally the Vicar (in one of his better appearances). The anticipated groping scene with the Commodore is finally played out but only in the final moments and in an unforeseen venue that adds humor to what has grown to become a regular show routine.

There is also a fresh variation on the long-running routine of Elizabeth coming for coffee. This time Emmet is forced into the klatch, resulting in some of the better moments that character has been afforded since he first arrived on the scene in the second series.

The only weakness of the episode is, unfortunately, quite glaring. Again, it appears that there was too much plot for the allotted time, and as in the past, the Onslow/Daisy/Rose story suffers. For its part, the trio has some funny sequences in the early going, but the three are not seen past the episode's halfway point. Onslow especially has some good lines as he ponders why (as he has been told on *Open University*) if humans have 98 percent of their genes in common with apes, he wants a cigarette when he awakens instead of a banana. Next, when Daisy complains of her husband's chronic bone-idleness, Onslow replies that his laziness is a "philosophical position," and he is in the midst of making a statement. Later, Onslow winds up helping Rose sell jewelry door to door. On his first call, the homeowner mistakes Onslow's sales technique for a robbery attempt.

EPISODE 5 ★★½

Air date: October 3, 1993. Cast: Hyacinth (Patricia Routledge); Richard (Clive Swift); Elizabeth (Josephine Tewson); Daisy (Judy Cornwell); Onslow (Geoffrey Hughes); Rose (Mary Millar); Emmet (David Griffin); Constable (John Phythian); Eric (Terrence Hardiman); Estate Agent (Jennifer Clulow); Sir Edward (John Arnatt); Sergeant Watkins (Eric Carte); Driver (Stuart Fell); Daddy (George Webb)

Hyacinth shops for a country home while Richard retrieves her father from the police station.

An uneven offering, this episode's secondary plot (the one not featuring Patricia Routledge) provides more laughs than the primary one. The main story involves Hyacinth resuming her search for a second home in the country (first pursued in series four, episode two). There is some good preliminary humor and the anticipation of a better payoff than actually is delivered, as the Buckets' preparation to house hunt are interrupted by a call from a local Constable. It seems that Daddy has reverted to WWII form and has been performing sentry duty in front of the town hall again. Hyacinth has her best moments in this opening sequence, as she is appalled that the neighbors may see a uniformed policeman leaving her home. To remedy the situation, she suggests that the cop leave with a blanket draped over his head and upper body. Failing to achieve this, she coaches him to smile broadly to signal to any onlookers that the visit is a happy and social one. Intent on searching for her country retreat, Hyacinth dispatches Richard to the police station to fetch her father, while she goes with Elizabeth. This sequence, especially with Richard's pleas to his wife not to buy anything, especially anything large or expensive, sets us up for the big laugh that never materializes. True, Hyacinth does visit an expensive estate and does indicate to Richard that she has made a real estate transaction, but the explanation is so rushed that the comic potential is cut short by the time constraints of the half-hour episode. Like many episodes in the series, the possibilities are sacrificed by the author's pacing of the material.

As stated, the best moments are delivered sans Hyacinth as Clive Swift provides some amusing turns as he collects Daddy at the police station. Under Hyacinth's instructions not to be seen entering the station, Richard is compelled to attempt the maneuver in a trenchcoat and sunglasses. Unfortunately, however, every time he nears his objective, an acquaintance crops up, making it necessary for him to overshoot his target and walk around the block again. George Webb as Daddy is finally given an end credit, since he finally is given a speaking part. There's also a good Onslow moment, as he is disturbed from the important business of eating crisps in bed by Daisy and Rose. The pair frantically tell him that Daddy is missing, but Onslow remains calm and asks for details. After being told that his father-in-law could have been gone for hours, Onslow placidly returns to his crisps, adding that a physical search is futile since the trail has gone cold.

Episode 6 ★★★★

Air date: October 10, 1993. Cast: Hyacinth (Patricia Routledge); Richard (Clive Swift); Elizabeth (Josephine Tewson); Daisy (Judy Cornwell); Onslow (Geoffrey Hughes); Rose (Mary Millar); Emmet (David Griffin); Postman (David Janson); Milkman (Robert Rawles); Visitor (Helen Dorward)

Hyacinth and Richard find their new apartment retreat in the country more than a little confining.

Sometimes it seems that the average episode of *Keeping Up Appearances* is less satisfying than it could be, only because the viewer identifies too closely with the plight of Hyacinth's victims. After watching Hyacinth terrorize those nice people around her for 25 minutes, too often any retribution forthcoming is rushed into the final five minutes of the program. For those who have salivated to see poetic justice served to the Bucket woman, this is the episode for you. Filled with humorous details, this installment is a continuous parade of Hyacinth on the receiving end.

The episode begins with Hyacinth and Richard now moved into the tiny apartment they bought in a country mansion. Unfortunately their pocketbook relegated them to little more than a warren under the mansion's attic, which is reached only after an exhausting climb to the top. While Richard compares their new digs to those of bats, Hyacinth is still blinded by the quality of the address and refers to the mini-flat as "Old World bijou."

While the Buckets suffer (they continually bang their heads against the sloped walls and low ceilings), the rest of their world is enjoying a Hyacinth-free holiday as the Milkman, Postman, and especially Emmet relish their peace. Emmet's peace is short-lived, however, as he and his sister are invited to tea at the country estate. There is a hilarious scene as Hyacinth, wearing riding clothes complete with jodhpurs, meets Emmet and Elizabeth on the road to the estate. Hyacinth of course has worn the items only for purposes of appearance, but she is dismayed to learn that Emmet is similarly dressed since he is an actual horseman. Compelled to continue her charade, Hyacinth winds up on the back of a rather spirited jumping horse, much to the delight of Emmet, who knew, but never let on, that the bane of his life never rode before.

From here the episode builds to a strong finish as guests and family arrive for tea in the new apartment. When Emmet's head accidentally gets wedged in the sloping ceiling of the living room, Hyacinth diverts the other guests into the minuscule kitchen. No fewer than six people are soon crammed into the space, which isn't even comfortable for one. In a bit reminiscent of similar scenes in the Marx Brothers' *A Night at the Opera*, Buster Keaton's *The Cameraman*, and Laurel and Hardy's *Our Wife* and *The Flying Deuces*, the hapless inhabitants of the kitchen are condensed so tightly that ultimately the emergency squad must be called to free them.

EPISODE 7 ★★

Air date: October 17, 1993. Cast: Hyacinth (Patricia Routledge); Richard (Clive Swift); Daisy (Judy Cornwell); Elizabeth (Josephine Tewson); Onslow (Geoffrey Hughes); Rose (Mary Millar); Emmet (David Griffin); Vicar (Jeremy Gittins); Postman (David Janson); Mrs. Drummond (Sue Lloyd); Driver (Pamela Abbott); Daddy (George Webb)

Hyacinth volunteers Richard to fix the electrical system at the church hall, despite the fact that he knows nothing about the subject.

A leisurely paced, slightly plotted series entry, this episode wanders pleasantly along before closing with a flashy show of pyrotechnics in the final minutes. The best moments in the installment are afforded Richard, who must attempt to tackle electrical repairs. Hyacinth confidently offered the church her husband's expertise on the basis of the fact that he once fixed their Christmas tree lights by tightening a loose bulb. Once Richard ventures into the church hall crawl space, he discovers the Vicar, who is hiding from Hyacinth but explains that he often likes to use the remote locale for meditating. By episode's end the crawl space refugees also include Onslow (complete with a six-pack of beer) and Emmet, all presumably hiding from the Bucket woman.

While working on the lights — the end result of his efforts being the aforementioned explosions in the finale — Richard admits he too has a favorite hiding place from Hyacinth. Without a convenient crawl space, Richard confesses he spends large amounts of his time in the bathroom reading.

This episode is also noteworthy in that it offers a nearsighting of the elusive Sheridan, the Buckets' son. As he rides away in a taxi, Hyacinth stands on the curb, waving a tearful goodbye. Upon returning to the house, she expresses concern to Richard about their son's latest college endeavor: membership in the Workers' Revolutionary Vanguard. Of course, Hyacinth's concern is not about the revolutionary nature of the organization but rather the status. She feels Sheridan would be better served to join the Executives' Revolutionary Vanguard.

There is also a good, albeit brief, Daisy/Onslow moment, as the couple discusses an event from their honeymoon that almost ended their marriage before it could begin. It seems that on their wedding night, Onslow discovered a secret hidden in Daisy's past. After teasing the audience with what sounds like some sort of wild affair, the mystery is disclosed: Daisy is a fan of the Liverpool football team, a loyalty that is perilously close to grounds for divorce to Onslow.

Christmas Special 1993

★★★★

Air date: December 25, 1993. Cast: Hyacinth (Patricia Routledge); Richard (Clive Swift); Daisy (Judy Cornwell); Onslow (Geoffrey Hughes); Elizabeth (Josephine Tewson); Emmet (David Griffin); Rose (Mary Millar); Postman (David Janson); Check-in-Girl (Alice MacDonald); Ship's Officer (Michael Cochrane); Restaurant Manager (Bernard Holley); Holiday-Maker (Barry Bethell); Port Official (Mark Brignal). Guest Appearances by the Band of the Welsh Fusiliers; Lindsay Frost; the Mark Joyce Showband; and Lord Lichfield

Hyacinth and Richard take a cruise on the *Queen Elizabeth II* unaware that Daisy and Onslow have won a luxury tour on the same voyage.

Based on an idea by Harold Snoad, this hour-long Christmas special is also the favorite episode of the series' producer/director. The cruise is a wonderfully comical exploration of two basic situations, both of which are fully exploited. Indeed, the show is so well divided between the two segments that it is often aired as two separate but consecutive episodes when American stations present it.

The first half concerns Hyacinth and Richard's preparations leading up to their cruise on the *QEII*. More accurately, most of the preparations are Hyacinth's as she packs enough suitcases to outfit an expeditionary force. It is Richard's thankless job to haul the luggage around throughout the first 30 minutes. The fun (or trouble, depending on how you view it) begins in earnest when Hyacinth directs Richard to leave the highway leading them to Southampton. Soon the couple is horribly lost and finally winds up stuck in a muddy field. At this point Hyacinth, impeccably overdressed, is compelled to get out and push. In a humorous vignette, she forgets herself and threatens revenge on "Richard Bucket," pronouncing their last name as the pail, rather than the flower arrangement. When they do finally arrive at the dock, it is just in time to watch the ship sail away, despite Hyacinth's orders that it turn around.

There are also some good moments as the Buckets fly ahead to Copenhagen to meet the ship at its next port. Hyacinth feels quite safe in the Danish capital, until she realizes that the Danes are the same nation that pillaged and raped England during the Middle Ages. From then on she insists on huddling with Richard on the pier as she bolsters their courage by singing "Rule Britannia."

Once on board the *QEII*, Hyacinth busies herself with a nonstop round of changing clothes. This activity quickly ceases when Hyacinth sees Daisy and Onslow climbing down from a lifeboat (they were receiving a VIP tour of the ship). Sure that they are stowaways, she begins a shipwide search for her relations, hoping to find them before the authorities do. There are some fine comic turns in this sequence, as Hyacinth and Richard, posing as joggers, dash madly about the *QEII*. The sequence also serves as something of a travelogue for Cunard, a feature that Snoad has remarked helped to add a special experience for viewers who may never get to travel on a luxury liner.

After the truth about Onslow's prize is revealed, it almost bothers Hyacinth as much as if he had been a stowaway. Once she sees the recognition and acclaim being lavished on her brother-in-law, however, Hyacinth relents and joins him for a lively comic dance to cap off the special.

As usual, the best lines of the episode go to Onslow. At one point the ever-frustrated Daisy reminds her insouciant husband that cruises are supposed to stir romantic feelings, to which Onslow responds that such feelings aren't compulsory. The best joke of the proceedings comes toward the end as Onslow complains about his luxury accommodations, particularly dining at the captain's table, which he likens to eating with the crew. Not surprisingly, this episode is also a favorite of Geoffrey Hughes, who called it "great fun to do as we filmed while the ship was doing a cruise of the northern capitals."

Christmas Special 1994

★★★★

Air date: December 26, 1994. Cast: Hyacinth (Patricia Routledge); Richard (Clive Swift); Elizabeth (Josephine Tewson); Daisy (Judy Cornwell); Onslow

(Geoffrey Hughes); Rose (Mary Millar); Emmet (David Griffin); Vicar (Jeremy Gittins); Salesman (Trevor Bannister); customer (Andrew Bicknell); His Wife (Caroline Strong); Mr. Mawsby (Preston Lockwood); Daddy (George Webb)

Richard's simple case of athlete's foot swells to become gout to please the social-climbing Hyacinth. Meanwhile, Daddy disappears after renting out his bed to a strange man.

After a year's hiatus, *Keeping Up Appearances* returns with this quintessential episode in the form of an hour-long special. This excellent installment makes crystal clear the flaw inherent in so many of the series' weaker episodes — length. While twice the running time of the majority of episodes, there isn't really any more material here, only more time to allow it to reach its full potential. All the usual routines and familiar bits are here — from Hyacinth compelling visitors to remove their shoes, to an absolutely wonderful playing of the morning coffee shtick. Now, however, there is no rush to the proceedings. Consequently, given the time to work at its proper pace, work it does and marvelously so.

The leisurely plot lines are some of the best of the entire series. The first involves Hyacinth's plans for a complete kitchen remodeling, especially her insistence upon a countertop covered with a discontinued color described as "Angel Gabriel Blue" (she even consults the Vicar as to the ecclesiastical authenticity of the shade). The quest becomes more involved when Hyacinth visits the kitchen showroom with an array of food samples to test the stain resistance of the surfaces. Another revolves around the latest disappearance of the aged Daddy. This time, however, before he departed Daddy rented his bed to the mysterious Mr. Mawsby.

The most comical device, however, is reserved for the long-suffering Richard. A visit to the doctor reveals that Richard has athlete's foot. Hyacinth is mortified at the prospect of having a husband with such a common disease (the fact that Richard also describes it as a fungus only makes matters worse). To cope, Hyacinth decides that Richard is suffering from the "painful but polite" gout. For the rest of the episode, Clive Swift does some fine physical clowning as he hobbles about on his overly bandaged foot, including some difficult turns behind the wheel of his sedan.

Also adding to the fun is the inclusion of Trevor Bannister (Mr. Lucas from *Are You Being Served?*) as the beleaguered kitchen salesman. Bannister's nervous tics and heavy sighs are perfectly placed, along with his surprise appearance later in the episode.

Series Five 1995

Episode 1 ★★

Air date: September 3, 1995. Cast: Hyacinth (Patricia Routledge); Richard (Clive Swift); Elizabeth (Josephine Tewson); Daisy (Judy Cornwell); Onslow

(Geoffrey Hughes); Rose (Mary Millar); Emmet (David Griffin); Vicar (Jeremy Gittins); Vicar's Wife (Marion Barron); Mr. Farrini (Angus Lennie); Mr. Cooper Bassett (Derek Waring); Mrs. Lomax (Rita Davies); Sergeant (Eric Carte); Inspector (John Darrell); Lady Helper (Sheila Rennie)

Hyacinth volunteers to chaperone senior citizens on a church outing to the seashore.

The premiere episode of the fifth season is much like the fun fair in which most of the action takes place. There is much action, noise, color, and amusement, but ultimately it leaves one feeling more exhausted than exhilarated.

The entry begins with promise. The Vicar posts a notice for volunteers for the seaside excursion, then recoils in horror to notice that Hyacinth's are the first pair of eyes to see the advert. With the prospect of sharing a van with the Bucket woman for the 60-mile trek, the Vicar wisely decides to put Hyacinth in charge of the second van. He further simplifies his life by assigning all the problem travelers to Hyacinth's care. Aside from Richard, who is pressed into service as the van's driver, and Elizabeth, the van includes Mr. Farrini, a randy Italian banished from the main group because he can't keep his hands off the ladies, and Mrs. Lomax, a wraithlike woman suffering from motion sickness. Both of these guests are amusing for the most part. Mrs. Lomax's condition keeps forcing Richard to stop by the roadside, although she regains her health long enough to consume three sundaes and cotton candy at their destination. Most of the mirth in the latter part of the episode is provided by Mr. Farrini, who naturally, is yet another older gent captivated by the plump Mrs. Bucket. The majority of the fun fair scenes involve Mr. Farrini chasing Hyacinth through a variety of rides and amusements with the climax coming as he succeeds in handcuffing himself to the object of his desire on the ghost train ride (a dark ride perfect for stolen kisses). Patricia Routledge plays well off the character of Farrini, especially in the employment of a running gag in which she imitates the amorous laugh of the leering Italian.

Unfortunately, the poorer relations (Onslow, Daisy, and Rose) are given little to do in this offering, and as is the case in such situations, their contribution is missed.

Episode Two ★★★

Air date: September 10, 1995. Cast: Hyacinth (Patricia Routledge); Richard (Clive Swift); Daisy (Judy Cornwell); Elizabeth (Josephine Tewson); Onslow (Geoffrey Hughes); Rose (Mary Millar); Emmet (David Griffin); Postman (David Janson); Town Hall Official (Ivor Danvers); Mrs. Donaghue (Jean Harvey); Boy (Kyle Wicks)

Hyacinth makes plans to attend the lord mayor's annual fancy dress ball.

A mixed offering, this episode presents a number of interesting situations executed with varying degrees of success. The best involves Hyacinth's desire to attend the lord mayor's fancy dress ball. However, since Richard has retired, he is no longer an employee of the town and is therefore not automatically included on the guest list. This provides some potentially amusing business when Hyacinth dispatches her spouse back to his former place of work to secure an invitation. For all the embarrassment Richard displays at having to complete this chore, the invitation is obtained easily as a matter of routine, leaving one wondering what the buildup was all about.

The secondary plot, involving Rose's engagement to a Polish man, provides some good moments but, oddly, not for Rose. This latest betrothal affords Daisy and Onslow some humorous reminiscing about their own engagement, while it also serves to stoke the ever-unquenched flames of poor Daisy's passion. At one point Daisy is beside herself with joy and admits that the source of her delight is knowing that Onslow is all hers. To this confession the lethargic Onslow responds by reminding his wife that he is "not just a plaything." The identity of Rose's intended is a variation on the joke used in series three, episode three, in which Daddy took up with a woman who is called "Mrs. Thing" due to the unpronounceability of her name. The Polish man has a similarly confusing arrangement of consonants in his name, leaving him to be referred to as "Mr. What's-it," although Rose prefers to call him "Cuddly Chops."

As stated above, the best moments revolve around Hyacinth's actual plans for the fancy dress ball, particularly her choices of costumes. Her previous years' disguises included Cleopatra to Richard's Marc Anthony (a disappointment since he wasn't brutal enough) and her Robin Hood to Richard's Friar Tuck (that year, son Sheridan was disappointed since he wasn't allowed to attend as Maid Marian). This year Hyacinth decides to go as Marie Antoinette, while Richard cheerfully suggests that he may go as the executioner. Hyacinth's ultimate costume for the fancy dress ball, although comical in appearance, may not be familiar to American audiences. She is dressed as Boadicea, the queen of the Iceni, a tribe of ancient Britain, who after her army was defeated by the Romans in 62 A.D., took poison rather than live conquered. Of course, Hyacinth's plans to impress are thwarted when at least three other women show up in the same costume.

EPISODE 3 ★★★★

Air date: September 17, 1995. Cast: Hyacinth (Patricia Routledge); Richard (Clive Swift); Daisy (Judy Cornwell); Elizabeth (Josephine Tewson); Onslow (Geoffrey Hughes); Rose (Mary Millar); Emmet (David Griffin); Vicar (Jeremy Gittins); Postman (David Janson); Security Representative (Ian Lavender); Engineers (Graham Root, Ben De Winter); Daddy (George Webb); the Elderly Lady (Margaret Towner)

Richard tries to conceal the fact that he's forgotten their wedding anniversary by presenting Hyacinth with a home alarm system.

A tidy little plot, well conceived and well executed, with a good strong punch line to top it off, marks the third entry of the final season. This episode is probably the best showcase in the series for the considerable talents of Clive Swift. Starting with a premise that haunts every husband — forgetting an important date, such as an anniversary — Swift as Richard Bucket goes through the gamut of reactions before the plot plays out. At first Richard is confused regarding Hyacinth's cheery mood, not knowing it is fostered by the anticipation of receiving an anniversary gift. Once he realizes he's forgotten his nuptial date (by overhearing Hyacinth's complaint to the post office for losing the expected gift), Richard goes through a series of agonizing gyrations anticipating the tongue lashing he will receive. Next, there is relief when he seizes upon the idea of giving Hyacinth the security system and his apparent success at executing the cover-up of his error. Finally, the installment ends with the agony of being found out when, hilariously, Richard trips the alarm and can't remember the security code (their anniversary date) that will disarm it.

Patricia Routledge turns in one of her better performances as Hyacinth. There is an especially good scene with Elizabeth in which she happily relates that Richard is sending in a team of specialists to "alarm her" for her anniversary. Her incessant hounding of the Security Representative (amusingly portrayed by Ian Lavender, *Dad's Army*'s Private Pike) over such details as the color of the alarm (dusty pink to match a stately home she once visited) and the sound (hopefully a siren to match that of the *QEII*) is a highlight.

Surprisingly, the subplot featuring the other side of the family is mostly extraneous and could have been done without. The only real notable feature of this side story — involving Daddy's contention that his bedroom is haunted — is the extended speaking role it affords the usually silent George Webb.

This episode is another one of producer/director Harold Snoad's favorites and deservedly so.

EPISODE 4 ★★★½

Air date: September 24, 1995. Cast: Hyacinth (Patricia Routledge); Richard (Clive Swift); Daisy (Judy Cornwell); Elizabeth (Josephine Tewson); Onslow (Geoffrey Hughes); Rose (Mary Millar); Emmet (David Griffin); Vicar (Jeremy Gittins); Vicar's wife (Marion Barron); Postman (David Janson); Violet (Anna Dawson); Lock-Keeper (Steve Morley)

Hyacinth's plans for a "waterside supper with riparian entertainments" go awry.

Only a slow start keeps this delightful entry from being one of the best the series has to offer. Once rolling, however, the laughs come in droves in this episode, which was shot largely on location. A drive in the country inspires Hyacinth to translate one of her infamous candlelight suppers to the side of a river. Once home the Bucket woman pours over a dictionary to confirm that she does indeed want "riparian entertainments."

Unable to beg off from the outing, the Vicar and his Wife, along with Liz and Emmet, form the rear end of the caravan that Hyacinth leads to her selected locale. The entire affair soon takes on something of a safari flavor. First, unsettled by the effect a bumpy dirt road may be having on her chinaware, Hyacinth gets out of the car and leads the autos on foot as she personally scouts out the smoothest path. Next, the hapless band is forced by their hostess to act as pack animals to transport the food and furniture to the dining site. Once they arrive at Hyacinth's chosen locale, they discover a dredger is quickly depositing muck on the site. Next, the expedition takes to the water in a trio of rowboats, seeking a new spot for supper. There are some good gags when they must navigate a canal lock, as well as a rousing good finish involving Hyacinth losing face in front of the baser side of the family. Of course, any episode that unites Hyacinth and water is bound to wind up with Patricia Routledge soaked. Rather than just dunk the actress in the river, there is a nice surprising twist to accomplish what is expected.

Episode 5 ★★½

Air date: October 1, 1995. Cast: Hyacinth (Patricia Routledge); Richard (Clive Swift); Elizabeth (Josephine Tewson); Daisy (Judy Cornwell); Onslow (Geoffrey Hughes); Rose (Mary Millar); Emmet (David Griffin); Vicar (Jeremy Gittins); Vicar's Wife (Marion Barron); Violet (Anna Dawson); Misses Pilsworth (Lois Penson, Clare Kelly); Bruce (John Evitts)

Hyacinth buys Richard a pair of skis for his birthday, despite the fact that he has no interest in the sport.

Better in concept than in actual execution, this episode presents some good ideas that never come to a full boil. Once again Roy Clarke concocts too much material for the 30 minutes allotted him, leaving a number of situations unrealized. Most of these loose ends, as usual, fall on the other side of Hyacinth's family; this time the unresolved plot is about Rose.

Rose has met a born-again Christian in a pub (on his night off, Onslow guesses) and is considering a religious conversion to further her relationship with the man. This premise itself generates many good lines of dialogue as the cast members discuss the implications of life after death. Two in particular tie their view of the afterlife to their current marriages. While staring at the bone-idle Onslow, Daisy hopes for life after death, noting there hasn't been much for her before it. For his part, Richard casts a pitiful glance toward his spouse as she confidently asserts that they will be bonded together for all eternity. Despite all this, this side plot fails to fully play out, with Rose's hopes for a consultation with the "dishy Vicar" sidetracked.

The main plot certainly lives up to the series' title as Hyacinth presents Richard with a pair of skis for the sole purpose of having them displayed on the top of his car. While Richard declares his utter lack of interest in skiing, Hyacinth carries on as if their entire purpose is to let the neighbors see them — and of course, for her, this is so.

Violet and Bruce make one of their rare appearances as the Buckets drop by to borrow Bruce's ski rack. This marks Violet's most significant appearance in the series, as she is distraught over the state of her marriage. Hyacinth naturally urges her sister not to divorce her husband since to do so would forfeit the comfort and security of having a Mercedes.

Episode 6 ★★★★

Air date: October 8, 1995. Cast: Hyacinth (Patricia Routledge); Richard (Clive Swift); Elizabeth (Josephine Tewson); Daisy (Judy Cornwell); Onslow (Geoffrey Hughes); Rose (Mary Millar); Emmet (David Griffin); His Lordship (Bruce Montague); Auctioneer (David Simeon); Auction Assistant (David Ashford); Mrs. Braddock (Jessica James); His Lordship's Servant (Colin Stepney)

Hyacinth attends a country estate sale. Meanwhile Onslow, Daisy, and Rose must contend with Mrs. Braddock, another woman Daddy has promised to marry.

This is a delightful series entry, reminiscent of some earlier episodes but with fresh plot twists, especially in the ending. Surprisingly, all the major elements of the plot have been used before: visiting a country estate, Richard getting lost under Hyacinth's navigation, people desperately trying to avoid Hyacinth in public, Daddy promising matrimony. What makes this episode so enjoyable, however, is not the individual elements but the skillful blending of them into a satisfying whole that is well balanced. None of the story lines suddenly takes over to the neglect of the others, and the two main ones come neatly together for the finale.

The Hyacinth story involves the Buckets' visit to an estate auction. While Hyacinth can't wait for the sale, Richard is so nervous that his wife will overspend at the event that he finds it impossible to sleep the night before. Once they actually arrive at the auction, there is some good broad humor as Richard physically restrains Hyacinth from bidding on the overpriced items — an especially daunting task since she wants to bid on everything merely because it belonged to an aristocrat. Finally, Hyacinth is unleashed to bid £10 on six bottles of the "dowager Lady Ursula's homemade gooseberry wine." Ironically, the wine, only of value to Hyacinth because of its aristocratic connection, winds up ruining one of her precious few opportunities to socialize with a lord.

The estate piece also gives Elizabeth and Emmet a rare opportunity to do something aside from cowering in their home and talking about Hyacinth. The brother and sister also attend the auction, unaware that their overbearing neighbor is there. Hearing her voice from afar, the duo immediately scurries, supposedly off the premises. Later, however, toward the end of the auction, a dressing screen is removed from the side of the room for bidding to reveal Liz and Emmet crouching sheepishly behind it in full view of Hyacinth.

The Onslow/Daisy/Rose plot features some funny moments as well, with the trio trying to contend with the slightly barmy Mrs. Braddock. Known to bite people, Mrs. Braddock supplants Onslow's dog from its home in the rusty car body on the front lawn. This sets up a good variation on a standard series gag when Hyacinth, drunk from the gooseberry wine, comes to share the vintage with her relatives.

Episode 7 ★★★½

Air date: October 15, 1995. Cast: Hyacinth (Patricia Routledge); Richard (Clive Swift); Elizabeth (Josephine Tewson); Daisy (Judy Cornwell); Onslow (Geoffrey Hughes); Rose (Mary Millar); Emmet (David Griffin); Vicar (Jeremy Gittins)

Hyacinth angles to get a part in Emmet's production of *The Boyfriend*, while Daisy tries to sexually entice Onslow, and Daddy prepares to defend his house to the last man.

This episode represents that rarest of *Keeping Up Appearances* phenomena: the plots are actually resolved well before the closing credits. Rather than leave story lines dangling, this show actually has something of an epilogue, which while related to one of the plots, is not vital to its resolution. Part of the reason for this is author Clarke's decision to pace Hyacinth's narrative more leisurely and have it continue in the next installment of the Bucket saga. This formula works so well that it is a pity it hasn't been done in more of the series' entries.

While ostensibly the primary focus, Hyacinth's attempts to land a part for which she is 30 years too old in Emmet's upcoming show take a comic back seat to the goings-on at Onslow's house. This story opens with Daisy bringing breakfast in bed to a justifiably suspicious Onslow, who guesses he is being primed to do his biannual garden work. When Daisy informs him that they have the house to themselves and the pampering is a warm-up to romance, Onslow quickly volunteers to do the gardening instead. A few minutes later, Daisy is back in a red lace number, jiggling to a cassette tape of "The Stripper." After watching his wife's fertility dance, Onslow has one question: "Any more bacon?" Daisy is dispatched to the store to purchase more of Onslow's porcine idea of foreplay. These are some of the funniest exchanges in the entire series between the sexually disinterested Onslow and the ever-hopeful Daisy.

Daisy's hopes for romance are dashed when Daddy returns in full World War II gear, fixes a bayonet to his rifle, and announces that the house is off limits as a restricted military area. The majority of the episode's remainder is taken up with the attempts to disarm Daddy, a feat humorously accomplished by Hyacinth, who puts her musical aspirations on hold for the moment to do so.

With the plot resolved, there is a wonderful little coda of parallel scenes in which Hyacinth and Daisy, and Richard and Onslow discuss the conjugal aspects of long-term marriages. Hyacinth advises her sister to get more things to polish, while Onslow admires Richard's courage for sleeping in the same bed with Hyacinth. The bit is a nice condensation of some of the basic themes of the series, leaving one with the distinct message that the slob Onslow is the most contented of the principals.

Episode 8 ★★

Air date: October 22, 1995. Cast: Hyacinth (Patricia Routledge); Richard (Clive Swift); Elizabeth (Josephine Tewson); Daisy (Judy Cornwell); Onslow (Geoffrey Hughes); Rose (Mary Millar); Emmet (David Griffin); Vicar (Jeremy Gittins); the Vicar's Wife (Marion Barron); Man in Phone Box (Jack Smethurst); Violet (Anna Dawson); Bruce (John Evitts); Dancers (Jenny Morton, Alexandra Howard, Anna Bolt)

Hyacinth combines her attempts to land a part in *The Boyfriend* with a barbecue she hosts at Violet's house.

Some funny moments are set adrift in this leisurely paced, somewhat aimless episode. Unfortunately, while continuing the story line from the last episode was good for that over plotted entry, it doesn't leave enough direction for this succeeding installment. Picking up on the theme established in the previous episode (Hyacinth's efforts to force her way into Emmet's amateur theatrical production), the Bucket woman tries to hijack a rehearsal of the show. The highlight of this portion of the installment has Emmet and the Vicar (the show is being rehearsed in the church hall) fleeing upon hearing Hyacinth approaching, leaving three innocent chorus girls alone to face her. After just a few moments of Hyacinth's voice instruction, the girls also run. All five are later found cowering in the dark crawl space underneath the stage by the Vicar's Wife, who is more than a little suspicious at her discovery.

The finale also provides some laughs, as Hyacinth tries to conduct a barbecue for her friends at Violet's house. Hyacinth tries to conceal the fact that Violet and Bruce are having a raucous row by leading the guests in overpowering renditions of "There'll Always Be an England" and "Rule Britannia." While these moments are funny, they are offset by the rather feeble motivation for everyone to be at Violet's in the first place, thus blunting the comic effect.

The best moment by far comes in a side gag in which Hyacinth tries to use a roadside telephone box. When a man innocently enters the box moments before her, Hyacinth rudely tries to order him from the phone. At first the man is polite, but he turns understandably annoyed when she begins banging on the sides of the box. Finally, she tells Richard to forcibly eject the caller, but instead of complying Richard rebels. In a marvelous moment that was five years in the making, Richard ignores his wife's request and commands Hyacinth to return to the car. Stunned, a cowed Hyacinth complies. Later, after recovering, she chides Richard for *his* impatience and lack of consideration toward others.

Episode 9 ★★★

Air date: October 29, 1995. Cast: Hyacinth (Patricia Routledge); Richard (Clive Swift); Daisy (Judy Cornwell); Elizabeth (Josephine Tewson); Onslow (Geoffrey Hughes); Rose (Mary Millar); Emmet (David Griffin); Salesman (Timothy Carlton); Sergeant (John Pennington)

After coming in second at a craft fair to Lydia Hawkesworth, Hyacinth hijacks a Rolls Royce in an attempt to appear more affluent than the winner.

Another one of those satisfying episodes in which Hyacinth's careful schemes go disastrously awry. Although this is one of the last regular installments of the series, its return to the basic premise of the show is more reminiscent of some of the first season's offerings -particularly series one, episode three. In fact, some of the bits are almost taken verbatim from that episode.

The new twist that keeps the rest of the proceedings fresh is rather inspired. When Hyacinth loses the flower-arranging competition to Mrs. Hawkesworth, she also happens to note that the champion drives a larger car than the Buckets' sedan. Ironically, since he will be the recipient of almost all the ensuing grief, Richard categorically denies their need for a new car, thus placing the notion firmly on the path of his wife's one-track mind. The next day, Richard innocently allows Hyacinth to guide him to a car dealership that is selling a Rolls Royce. As her husband protests, Hyacinth deftly manages to steer him from not even wanting to touch the £115,000 vehicle to commandeering it away from the showroom for a jaunt into the country. This sequence is particularly well scripted, and one sympathizes deeply with Richard, almost wanting to shout out warnings to him as he is led to ruin by degrees. Thankfully, Hyacinth's machinations come to naught, leaving her with quite the opposite effect she had planned and causing her maximum embarrassment.

Episode 10 ★★★

Air date: November 5, 1995. Cast: Hyacinth (Patricia Routledge); Richard (Clive Swift); Daisy (Judy Cornwell); Elizabeth (Josephine Tewson); Onslow (Geoffrey Hughes); Rose (Mary Millar); Emmet (David Griffin); Milkman (Robert Rawles); His Assistant (John Waterhouse); Richard's Friend (Ian Burford)

Hyacinth advertises her services as a social hostess but quickly quits the business after meeting her first clients.

A nice little offering, this episode marks the last of the regularly scheduled adventures of Hyacinth Bucket with a compact plot, fully explored and exploited. All of the comedy stems from the basic premise — that Hyacinth is going into business as a social consultant — and the final gag manages to top it all off nicely. The Onslow/Daisy/Rose subplot is also good, providing fine balance to the proceedings.

Advertising her services (which she refers to as "scintillating socializing") leaves Hyacinth on needles and pins all morning in anticipation of the flood of clients that will soon be calling on her. She wakes Richard at the crack of dawn in order to be up when the paper arrives. When it finally does arrive, there is an amusing bit in which Hyacinth must chase the paperboy in order to retrieve the paper (the last time they had a face-to-face encounter, Hyacinth forced the lad to clean his ears). There are also some laughs to be had when Hyacinth compels her husband to sit in the hallway so he can be right next to the phone, not even allowing him to come into the kitchen for a coffee.

The lower-class plot involves Daisy trying to pin down a long-faded memory of a pink dress once worn to one of Rose's engagement parties (according to Onslow, Rose has had more engagements than he's had bags of crisps). The dress is special to Daisy because Onslow tore it off her in the last fit of passion he ever experienced. In a humorous exchange, Onslow has great difficulty recalling the incident, then finally concludes that if he ever tore off one of Daisy's frocks, it must have been because it was on fire. Undeterred, Daisy and Rose spend the rest of the episode searching through the boxes of photographs of Rose's former fiancés.

Christmas Special 1995

★★★½

Air date: December 26, 1995. Cast: Hyacinth (Patricia Routledge); Richard (Clive Swift); Elizabeth (Josephine Tewson); Daisy (Judy Cornwell); Onslow (Geoffrey Hughes); Rose (Mary Millar); Emmet (David Griffin); Vicar (Jeremy Gittins); Vicar's Wife (Marion Barron)

When Hyacinth takes over the running of the church's pageant, all the volunteers suddenly disappear.

This last hurrah of the long-running situation comedy is a fitting send-off with many of the familiar themes revisited for one last time. Not as constitutive as the previous year's special, there are still many good moments left in the character of Hyacinth Bucket. While not exactly surprising — perhaps that is the strength of Roy Clarke's scripts — the proceedings do not disappoint in providing their well-placed laughs.

As in the past, whenever Hyacinth approaches the church hall, any and all volunteers quickly take shelter from the hurricane force of the woman. Left without any other players for her historical pageant, Hyacinth — who reserves the lead for herself, naturally — presses her hapless friends and loved ones into the gap. There are some amusing moments as Richard, Elizabeth, Emmet, and the others are forced into the awkward costumes. By the end, the entire fiasco proves itself just that — all in time for the closing credits.

CHEF!

BBC-TV 1993–1996

On first encountering *Chef!* one is immediately aware of the parallels between it and *Fawlty Towers*, the classic Brit-com of almost 20 years earlier. Both shows feature highstrung, usually sarcastic protagonists in service industries. Both are vehicles personally conceived by their stars. Both employ often intricate literary plots. These similarities aside, the programs are really quite different. Whereas *Fawlty Towers* was inspired by a real-life, rude, and inept hotel proprietor, the main impetus for *Chef!* came from actual professional chefs, who were all the trendy rage in the early 1990s. Basil Fawlty is funny because he's rude and pompous while having absolutely no right to be due to his own ineptitude. Gareth Blackstock, the title character of *Chef!* on the other hand, is rude and pompous while believing he has every mandate to be that way. Chef Blackstock of Le Chateau Anglais is the consummate professional with an ego to match.

Chef! was not a typical vehicle for its creator, comedian Lenny Henry. Born in 1958, Lenny Henry had an impact on the comedy world while still in his teens when he appeared on *New Faces*, a talent competition program similar to America's *Star Search*. What he lacked in polish in his celebrity impersonations, the young Henry more than made up for with self-assurance and enthusiasm. Buoyed by this early success, Henry left school and devoted himself to becoming a full-time comedian. After some initial rough going, Henry landed a part on *The Fosters*, an ITV sitcom that was an Anglicized version of the popular American import *Good Times*. After learning the rudiments of acting on *The Fosters*, Lenny Henry's next leap was to a Saturday morning children's show entitled *Tiswas*. On this program, Henry started developing his own characters rather than merely impersonating other people.

In the summer of 1981, Lenny Henry became a comedian to be reckoned with when he appeared on *Three of a Kind*, a fast-paced, hit-or-miss sketch comedy series, which also served to make fellow performer Tracey Ullman a star. With the end of *Three of a Kind* in 1983, Henry had no trouble finding work, and he starred in a string of specials and series throughout the rest of the decade. Most of these programs were of the stand-up and sketch variety, although Henry did appear in a series of six comedy plays (*Lenny Henry Tonite*) in 1986. *The Lenny Henry Show* (1987–1988) found him starring in a sitcom for the first time, although the program only survived two seasons.

In 1990, when Henry was in Hollywood making the film *True Identity*, that he read an article in a British paper that caught his attention. "I used to get the papers and the magazines from England sent over to me cause I was homesick," Henry told *British Television Magazine*, "and I was reading a lot of articles about the new breed of superchefs. In Britain there are people like Marco Pierre Wight and Nico LeDennis and Raymond Blance, and I was reading these stories about them being complete prima donnas — sending people out of the restaurant for ordering salt before they've tasted the food and drinking the wrong wine with the wrong dish and I just thought it was funny."

Playing a dictatorial chef would be a departure from Henry's usual characterizations, which had been based on sympathy, comic appearance, and memorable lines. "It's not just me with a silly wig and a catch phrase," Henry told the *Radio Times* in early 1993. "This time it's got a good narrative structure and it's got the words, and I'm a great lover of words."

The "words" to which Henry was referring were supplied — in the first two series at least — by Peter Tilbury. Tilbury was a veteran comedy writer who had previously created ITV's longest running sitcom, *Shelley*, as well as writing and starring in three series of *It Takes a Worried Man* (also for ITV).

From Henry's premise, Tilbury fashioned the character Gareth Blackstock, the perfectionist master chef of Le Chateau Anglais, an exclusive restaurant in the English countryside (exteriors of Le Chateau were filmed at Nether Wincheendon House in Oxfordshire).

Despite there being a precedent in British comedy for unsympathetic leading characters (Basil Fawlty, Alf Garnett, Edmund Blackadder, etc.), Henry was concerned that Gareth Blackstock might not be accepted. "The big challenge was to convince people that this kind of person deserved a place in their hearts," Henry told the *Dallas Morning News* in 1997. "I'm playing a character that's unlike me in that he's dysfunctional, he's a depressive, he's incredibly obessional. Gareth is quite a serious person. He says things that are witty and articulate but he really has no idea he's being funny — that's his key."

Sharing in Blackstock's life — what little of it there is outside of his single-minded devotion to his food craft — is his attractive wife, Janice, portrayed by actress Caroline Lee Johnson. A newcomer to the ranks of situation comedy, Johnson provided a depth of performance that lent an often-disturbing reality to the proceedings. Similar in looks and style to Phylicia Rashad, Johnson as Janice Blackstock constantly reminds the viewer of the demands and strains of being married to a dictatorial workaholic. While this may sound counterproductive to comedy, the hard edge (albeit justified) presented by Johnson's character helped temper the similar tone of Henry's. Her dissatisfaction with her husband's consecration to his career, coupled with her own intelligence, underscored the fact that outside of the kitchen, the great chef was actually rather an inept individual.

The final member of to the regular cast was Roger Griffiths in the role of Everton, Blackstock's hapless but lovable (to the audience at least) kitchen help. Everton is the most sympathetic of the main characters, and he provides a constant source of annoyance for the blustering chef.

Chef! was commissioned as a series by the BBC and was shot on film rather than tape for its first two seasons. This gave the show a classier look but often proved time consuming since it involved more location shooting. "It might look nice," conceded Henry, "but the aesthetic of it didn't really add up to a simplicity of life."

As a result, the third season was shot on videotape.

Premiering in January 1993, *Chef!* attracted a different audience from previous Lenny Henry vehicles, primarily due to the fact that the show was about the life of a chef. Fans of the culinary arts, who usually eschewed comedies for cooking shows, were tuning in to watch. From a technical standpoint, at least, these viewers were not disappointed. To help provide culinary authenticity, the producers hired Paul Headman, a chef from a hotel in Birmingham, to prepare the dishes used on the show. Despite looking delectable, however, few gourmets would have enjoyed Headman's creations. "You have to cook stuff that looks great," related Henry to the *Dallas Morning News*, "but you can't really eat it because it has to stay under the lights." As a result, the taste-tempting entrees would be preserved with sealing wax and plastics in order not to melt instantly under the harsh filming conditions.

In addition, Lenny Henry also had to learn the basics of cooking by working in a professional kitchen, chopping vegetables, among other things. "They gave me this tray of rabbits," recalled Henry to the *Radio Times*, "and said 'sort that lot out.' I had to take the insides out and chop off the little bunny-wunny tails."

Henry noticed that the higher tone of *Chef!* exposed him to a wider audience than he previously thought possible. Now, at his live shows, the black comic was finding that the crowd contained more than a few middle-aged and middle-class people.

The favorable response to the first series was capitalized on with a Christmas special later in 1993 and a second offering of shows in the fall of 1994.

Aside from the three established regulars, the rest of the supporting staff—essentially the kitchen staff—was replaced. This was logical, Henry explained, since that was what would happen in a real kitchen. The second series introduced a number of new characters, the most important one being Gustave. Comically played by the rotund Ian McNeice, Gustave was a well-respected chef who had fallen on hard times due to a drinking problem. Although he was featured prominently in three of the episodes in the second series, the character was not utilized at all in the other four shows. A disappointing response to the second season — at least in terms of ratings as compared to the first — led to a reappraisal of the entire show.

"I thought the writing was very good," reflected Lenny Henry to *British Television*, "but the way it was placed in the schedule might not have been complementary."

Consequently, there was a two-year hiatus before the third series appeared on small screens around Britain, with a revamped strategy. First, the look of the show changed — with filming out and video in. Second, the supporting cast was given a more prominent role. Rather than having Gareth's world filled with a kitchen staff of frightened little assistants, the chef had to contend with some rather strong competition. Gareth, through his own extravagant spending, was forced to sell the restaurant, opening the way for the nouveau riche but quite common northerner, Cyril (Dave Hill). This gave Gareth the ultimate irritant to which he could react — someone in authority over him without any of the class he tried to project. The character of Gustave was retained, although now he was played by Jeff Nutall. Nutall gave Gustave a more sarcastic edge, which proved good in support, especially when played off Savannah (Lorelei King), a transplanted California chef. Rounding out the new company was Renee (Sophie Walker), the flighty daughter of Cyril, fobbed off on Gareth's staff by her father.

"I wanted this series to be slightly more ensemble," explained Henry. "It felt like it was weighted slightly too much on Gareth in the first two series, so now the characters have more comedic weight."

The other major change in the third series was shifting the focus away from what Henry termed "food comedies" toward ones based more on the lives of the characters. The first show of the third series accomplished this in jarring style with Janice leaving Gareth. Thus, Gareth is shaken to his core, even in his professional arena, the one domain in which he had always reigned supreme. This ploy helped make the third season more linear — almost soap opera–like — especially as the main characters fell in and out of love with one another. To bring these changes to life were new writers Geoff Deane and Paul Makin, who alternated the scripting responsibilities (and collaborated on one episode). While this new format took a little time to hit its stride, by the third episode the new formula had reached a nice consistent level.

THE EPISODES

By Peter Tilbury, Paul Makin, and Geoff Deane. Directed by John Birkin and Dewi Humphrey. Produced by Charlie Hanson

Series One 1993

EPISODE 1: "PERSONNEL" ★★★½

Air date: January 28, 1993. Cast: Gareth (Lenny Henry); Janice (Caroline Lee Johnson); Lucinda (Claire Skinner); Everton (Roger Griffiths); Piers (Gary Parker); Otto (Erkan Mustafa); Greg (William Ivory); Manager (Peter Tilbury)

Demanding, tyrannical chef Gareth Blackstock is informed by management that he must cut his budget by 15 percent. The next day Everton, a former classmate of Gareth, appears and begs for the chance to learn cooking under the great Blackstock. In return, he offers to work without wages, solving the crisis for the time being.

"Personnel" belongs to that rare breed of introductory episodes that helps to distinguish a great show from one that is less than great. The premiere installment of *Chef!* provides the necessary exposition while simultaneously being as entertaining as the shows that follow. Within two minutes of the opening credits, we are given an essential grasp of Gareth Blackstock's character, and although this initial snapshot is further fleshed out later, it is all we need to enjoy the show and understand its premise.

For those viewers who always wondered what a television writer looked like, wonder no more. The actor playing the manager is Peter Tilbury, author of the show. While Tilbury's character is fired for his incompetence at managing Le Chateau Anglais, Tilbury himself could not be accused of the same for his writing.

The first five minutes of the episode are wonderful for exposition but also for their sheer laugh content. The entire opening is a veritable barrage of insults and harangues leveled by the Chef at his hapless staff. Gareth criticizes everything his palate tastes or his eye sees. Only moments later, however, after he is asked to cut his staff, do we learn the truth. Chef's kitchen staff has been handpicked from a long list of applicants and is the best in Britain.

EPISODE 2: "BEYOND THE PASS" ★★★★

Air date: February 4, 1993. Cast: Gareth (Lenny Henry); Janice (Caroline Lee Johnson); Everton (Roger Griffiths); Lucinda (Claire Skinner); Lola (Elizabeth Bennett); Piers (Gary Parker); Otto (Erkan Mustafa); Derek (Matthew Byam Shaw); Bank Manager (Geoffrey McGivern); Diners (Rupert Vansittart, Shelley Minto)

Gareth and his wife, Janice, attempt to purchase the foundering Le Chateau Anglais, but Janice explains that one of the reasons its has struggled financially is Gareth's ignorance of money matters.

La Chateau Anglais' Chef, Gareth Blackstock (Lenny Henry, center) surrounded by his kitchen staff from series one of *Chef! Left to Right:* Otto (Erkan Mustapha), Everton (Roger Griffiths), Piers (Gary Parker), and Lucinda (Claire Skinner). Copyright © BBC.

"Beyond the Pass" refers to the real world outside of Chef Gareth Blackstock's kitchen (the "pass" being the rack where dishes are constructed before being picked up by the waiters). This episode shows us that while Gareth is the arrogant supreme ruler of his kitchen, he is rather thick concerning everything beyond the realm of food.

There's so much in "Beyond the Pass" that one wonders where to begin. In the first few moments Gareth confronts Derek, the sommelier (wine steward), over his attempts to economize. After deeming his less-expensive choice "denture cleaner," Chef focuses his attack on Derek, explaining that he is at the bottom rung of the social order — just below "creeping things" and people who eat instant soup.

Similarly, Gareth's ranting in the Bank Manager's office is excellent. In response to a normal review, he personally blames the Bank Manager for everything from foreclosing on the needy to creating crises in the Third World and South Africa.

The best routine in the episode, and perhaps in the entire series, is Gareth's reaction to the request of a diner for salt. Gareth is walking through the dining room when one of the patrons makes the mistake of addressing him as one would a waiter (Gareth's regular term for waiters is "the morons"). The gentleman asks for salt. To Chef this is akin to glancing at the Mona Lisa, then asking Leonardo for some fingerpaints. At first Gareth tries to compose himself, but soon his dam of restraint bursts loose with a beautifully sarcastic flood. Gareth offers the gentleman not only salt but a full range of loathsome condiments from salad cream and barbecue sauce to Tabasco and a package of potato chips.

This bit, which is seemingly unrelated to the plot, connects with the final scene, in which the Bank Manager visits Le Chateau Anglais to finalize the loan. Gareth serves him a special dish; the manager smells it appreciatively, praises it, then asks for the salt. Gareth turns toward the camera with a hilariously apoplectic grimace.

EPISODE 3: "SUBJECT TO CONTRACT" ★★★

Air date: February 11, 1993. Cast: Gareth (Lenny Henry); Janice (Caroline Lee Johnson); Lucinda (Claire Skinner); Everton (Roger Griffiths); Piers (Gary Parker); Otto (Erkan Mustafa); Bank Manager (Geoffrey McGivern); Receiver (Tam Dean Burn); Ginnie (Sophie Thursfield); Toby (Ben Forster); Photographer (Sean Gasgoigne)

In an effort to increase business, Janice arranges for the local newspaper to do an article on Gareth. Instead of asking pertinent questions about cuisine, however, the silly reporter only wants to know Gareth's age, marital details, and star sign.

"Subject to Contract" is an enjoyable but rather scattered episode. Rather than presenting a neatly resolved plot, this installment is more along the lines of a continuance of the Blackstocks' adventures (à la *As Time Goes By*). There is still plenty of comedy, but the episode will be more meaningful if one has seen the previous two episodes in the series.

With a reporter and photographer on the way, Gareth becomes even more paranoid and critical of his staff's cleaning regimen. He gushes forth with a fountain of sarcasm. Next, Gareth discovers Everton preparing food with a bandage-less cut on his finger, which causes him to wonder aloud why they don't serve a "dollop of botchilized toxin" with each dish and be done with it.

EPISODE 4: "THE BIG CHEESE" ★★★★

Air date: February 25, 1993. Cast: Gareth (Lenny Henry); Janice (Caroline Lee Johnson); Everton (Roger Griffiths); Lucinda (Claire Skinner); Lola (Elizabeth Bennett); Piers (Gary Parker); Otto (Erkan Mustafa); Sebastian (Derek Hutchinson); Fishman (George Kahn); Hodgkin (Eugene Cheese); Police Sergeant (Al Ashton). Special Guest: Allbert Roux (Himself)

Gareth prepares feverishly when he learns that Allbert Roux, England's finest chef, is coming to lunch at Le Chateau Anglais. For the crowning touch to the meal, Gareth wants to serve Roux some "real, nasty, bareback, no safety net, unpasteurized Stilton" cheese. Unfortunately, the cheese is no longer legally sold in its natural form due to health restrictions, leading Gareth on a desperate search for the illicit fromage.

There are actually two cheeses referred to in the title. The first is Allbert Roux, the real-life chef. The second is some illegal Stilton. This episode is interesting because for the first time we see how Gareth reacts to someone he admires. Roux's impending visit sends the otherwise confident, self-assured, egotistic Chef into fits of doubt and fear. The only possible flaw to an otherwise excellent episode is the telegraphing of the final punch line. Whereas Gareth is surprised that Roux should ask for his Stilton source, he should not be, nor should the viewer. Gareth has spent the entire morning hunting down farmers and bribing policemen to secure the cheese. If it is that important to him, it certainly will be impressive to Roux.

Many good scenes highlight "The Big Cheese." The first is the opening in which Janice rails at Gareth for spending his day off in the kitchen preparing salmon mousse. Her fury climaxes with her literally ripping into the mousse with her fingers. When she pauses to lick her digits clean, her ire melts under the sensual delight of the dish. Her ecstasy turns to harsh criticism, though, when she learns it is for Roux. She then helps Gareth perfect the recipe.

Gareth's conversation with the cheese merchant is also enlightening, not only for its entertainment value but for its glimpse into the fact that many of the greatest delicacies are also dangerous to consume. When the merchant explains that unpasteurized Stilton is no longer sold because of the bugs, Gareth responds that he is fully aware of the bugs. He adds that really fine cheese is essentially bad milk with bugs and mold. Gareth then informs him that if a few of his customers die from eating such things as real Stilton, at least they will die happily.

EPISODE 5: "FAME IS THE SPUR" ★★★½

Air date: March 4, 1993. Cast: Gareth (Lenny Henry); Janice (Caroline Lee Johnson); Lola (Elizabeth Bennett); Everton (Roger Griffiths); Lucinda (Claire Skinner); Piers (Gary Parker); Otto (Erkan Mustafa); Colin (Trevor Peacock); Kevin (Kevin Allen); Nicholas (Simon Slater); Cameraman (Kiff Diamond); Floor Manager (Tim James)

To promote the restaurant, Janice arranges two newspaper interviews and a television documentary for Gareth.

"Fame Is the Spur" reintroduces a theme touched upon in "Subject to Contract," the media. While it was only a secondary plot in that episode, apparently Peter Tilbury saw enough potential to investigate the theme in more depth. Fortunately he did, since for sheer laughs this may be the champion of the first series of *Chef!*

Undoubtedly, that film crew with all its equipment seen at the end of "Fame Is the Spur" is the actual crew of *Chef!*

Much of Gareth's ire, left over from his encounter with journalists in episode three, comes roaring to the surface here. After spending his much-needed day off pandering to reporters' inane questions, Gareth bursts into the kitchen the following morning, railing against an imaginary brigade of journalists armed with more inane questions.

From there Gareth must endure another interview, this evidently the worst of all as a tabloid reporter mashes his carefully presented food together, calls Gareth "Chief," and intimates that he would rather be collecting Gareth's tax returns and nude photos of Janice to make the story really interesting.

Finally, when Everton accidentally sets the crayfish free, there's some funny dialogue as Gareth asks if he's a plant from the "animal liberation front," or if he just wanted to race the crustaceans. When the staff members start searching for the animals, Everton begins calling them as one would a dog.

EPISODE 6: "RICE AND PEAS" ★★★

Air date: March 11, 1993. Cast: Gareth (Lenny Henry); Janice (Caroline Lee Johnson); Lola (Elizabeth Bennett); Everton (Roger Griffiths); Lucinda (Claire Skinner); Piers (Gary Parker); Otto (Erkan Mustafa); Justin (Oliver Samuels)

Gareth submits to learning Caribbean cuisine from Everton in an attempt to impress his estranged father.

"Rice and Peas" is noteworthy for what it does not do. In an American sitcom in which the main plot device was the reunion of an estranged father and son, one would expect conflict followed ultimately by reconciliation before the fadeout. "Rice and Peas" surprises in that it does not follow this route but rather uses the plot device to investigate a more important (to the series) relationship. In past episodes, Gareth has had to admit his ignorance to bankers and to kowtow to journalists. Here, in an attempt to impress his father, he must humble himself before one of the lowest of the low on his scale of creatures: the inept Everton. In a way the results are more interesting than hilarious but still good viewing.

The opening scene presents Gareth's worse nightmare: a diner has sent back his meal untouched. Gareth wonders hopefully if the perpetrator of this culinary crime is perhaps an errant Freemason whose tongue has been ripped out after he revealed his lodge's secrets.

Soon the patron enters the kitchen to rattle off a litany of complaints: the food is worse than pig slops, the portions are too small, the prices too high, and the cuisine is French. After he finishes his tirade (the style of which is a good cue to the man's identity), Gareth pauses for a moment before saying, "Hello, Dad."

Later, upon studying Caribbean dishes, Gareth tries them out on Janice. After sampling some inedible soup, Janice urges Gareth to ask Everton to teach him. Gareth refuses and comments that he is on the verge of firing his lowest, most incompetent assistant. After listing Everton's faults, he presents the next dish: cowfoot and beans.

Janice notes that toad-in-the-hole hasn't really any toad in it, so perhaps cowfoot and beans is similarly misnamed. "So what's in cowfoot and beans?" she asks optimistically.

"Cowfoot and beans," is the hope-dashing reply.

After one painfully awful mouthful, Gareth develops a quick amnesia and cheerfully decides to ask Everton to teach him Caribbean cooking.

Christmas Special 1993

"A BIRD IN THE HAND" ★★★

Air date: December 24, 1993. Cast: Gareth (Lenny Henry); Janice (Caroline Lee Johnson); Lucinda (Claire Skinner); Everton (Roger Griffiths); Piers (Gary Parker); Otto (Erkan Mustafa); Mrs. Courtenay (Vivian Pickles)

Gareth conducts a frantic search of the countryside for the source of the perfect turkey for Christmas dinner.

A solid, if somewhat predictable, plot-driven episode, "A Bird in the Hand" revisits several themes previously explored. Gareth and Janice quarrel with one another for interloping on the other's domain (Janice orders around the kitchen staff, while Gareth tries feebly to negotiate for the best price on ingredients). There is also the mad dash for the perfect ingredients, as previously witnessed in "The Big Cheese." Still, there are enough new twists employed to keep the resulting dish fresh. The final joke is especially good, injecting a bit of irony into the Yuletide festivities.

There is little sentiment, but this is in keeping with the theme that those who work on Christmas are supplying others with enjoyment, not necessarily experiencing it for themselves.

Series Two 1994

EPISODE 1: "A RIVER RUNS THRU IT" ★★★

Air date: September 8, 1994. Cast: Gareth (Lenny Henry); Janice (Caroline Lee Johnson); Everton (Roger Griffiths); Gustave (Ian McNeice); Alice (Hilary Lyon); Debra (Pui Fan Lee); Donald (Gary Bakewell); Crispin (Tim Matthews); Alphonse (Jean Luc Rebaliati); Tariq (Antony Zaki); Health Inspector (John Surman)

Due to a shortage of capable kitchen staff, Gareth is forced to review resumes. One reference leaps out from his past: Gustave LaRoche, a once-great chef. Gareth finds LaRoche working in a small village French restaurant in one of the seedier parts of the town. Although he wonders why Gustave — who is really an Englishman named Gary Lansdown — would be working in a tiny restaurant, after sampling his talents Gareth hires him immediately and makes him sous chef. Soon, while Gareth is enjoying a day off fishing, Gustave's Achilles' heel becomes apparent: alcohol. Gustave, it seems, is in the habit of passing out on the floor after a few bottles of wine.

Upon first watching the premiere episode of the second season of *Chef!* devotees of the program are usually surprised to see that the kitchen staff, except for the hapless Everton, has been fully overhauled. This is due most to the attempt at reality in the framing of the show. Whereas the staff of, say, *Fawlty Towers* is frozen in time, a restaurant like Le Chateau Anglais would be expected to have regular turnover as apprentice chefs came, learned, and moved along.

The episode seems to introduce a major new character, Gustave. Unfortunately, while Gustave is at the center of this episode, he does not have a large part in the second season despite this promising beginning. Gustave only appears in two of the six remaining shows in this season, while being mentioned in a third. This is regrettable since many of the themes delved into in the first season are rehashed in the second. An expansion of Gustave's character could have been a way to prevent some of the staleness that plagues some of the weaker episodes.

Although the plot of "A River Runs Thru It" is seasoned more with drama, there is a funny scene in which Gareth and Janice take a day off in the country: Gareth to go fishing, Janice to read by the riverside. Looking quite out of place in his fishing regalia complete with waders, Gareth remarks unconvincingly that he loves fishing. Unfortunately, he never catches any fish due, he reasons, to his "patent fish-repelling waders." Finally, when he does get a bite, Gareth manages to trip and fall into the stream, causing his waders to quickly fill with water. In some good physical business, Gareth waddles gelatinously to the land, his legs bowed out under the weight of the water while Janice tries unsuccessfully not to laugh.

Janice notices that the fish is still on the line and picks up the rod and reel. Gareth plops down in Janice's chair, only to release a Niagara of liquid in the process. Soon, Janice is pulling in a giant trout, while Gareth feebly delves into his wife's novel.

EPISODE 2: "TIME FLIES" ★★

Air date: September 15, 1994. Cast: Gareth (Lenny Henry); Janice (Caroline Lee Johnson); Gustave (Ian McNeice); Donald (Gary Bakewell); Alphonse (Jean Luc Rebaliati); Crispin (Tim Matthews); Debra (Pui Fan Lee); Bank Manager (Geoff McGivern); Ms. Lanning (Emma Bernard); Nicky Patel (Kulvinder Ghir); Addison (Dominic Mafham)

Gareth is thrown into a panic when Janice announces that there is an outside possibility that she may be pregnant. Although he is not openly averse to having children, Gareth has always taken the stand that starting a family was something that needed to be postponed until a later date.

With Le Chateau Anglais in financial difficulty, Janice suggests they take on outside investors. Later, the Blackstocks meet with prospective investors. Gareth initially dismisses them as yuppies who want to introduce microwaves and boil-in-the-bag meals. However, when the investors present him with a prototype of a retail frozen dinner with his picture on the box, Gareth softens to their ideas. The meeting is interrupted when Janice learns that she is not pregnant, causing Gareth to feel both relieved and disappointed.

In many respects, "Time Flies" is similar to "Beyond the Pass," the second show from the first series of *Chef!* The theme, again, is Gareth's inability to exercise the same dominion of the world beyond his kitchen as he does in his natural surrounding. Unfortunately little new territory is explored here, and the majority of the jokes revolve around Gareth taking an absolute stand with Janice, then reversing it in public to her frustration. The problem of finances crops up again, as in "Beyond the Pass," and Geoff McGivern is back as the beleaguered Bank Manager who must suffer a similar harangue from Gareth. The one new wrinkle to the proceedings is the subject of the Blackstocks having children. This theme supplies most of the laughs.

Everton (Roger Griffiths) is strangely absent from this episode, as is the newly introduced character of Alice.

There are some amusing moments when Gareth, faced with the slight possibility of being a father, starts calling exclusive schools for rate information. He is astounded to learn that the tuition fees are triple what he estimated. In addition he is further shocked by miscellaneous charges for uniforms and games. It is at this last figure that he finally explodes, asking what type of games are included in the exorbitant fee: grand prix auto racing? Alpine paragliding? Or perhaps, he concludes, they play battleship with actual dreadnoughts?

Gareth's outrage is severely curbed, however, when he discloses that he is the chef of Le Chateau Anglais. The person on the other end remarks that they have eaten there, then begins to complain of *his* outrageous prices.

There are also some interesting moments as Gareth tries to create a signature dish for the restaurant. Each new culinary creation is met with disdain from Gustave, until finally Gareth wins him over with a final attempt. Gustave raves over it until he realizes that Gareth has put together a hightone version of a traditional English breakfast after he gets the idea from the Bank Manager.

Episode 3: "Do the Right Thing" ★★★½

Air date: September 22, 1994. Cast: Gareth (Lenny Henry); Janice (Caroline Lee Johnson); Everton (Roger Griffiths); Crispin (Tim Matthews); Debra (Pui Fan Lee); Donald (Gary Bakewell); Health Inspector (John Surman); Sidney

Filkins (Mark Long); P. C. Bosworth (Robert Gwilym); Waterman (Richard Cordery); Bailiff (Paul Trussell)

Gareth obtains wild partridges from a poacher and in the process becomes a suspect, then a customer of the local police and game authorities.

A most satisfying episode, mainly on the strength of its plot, "Do the Right Thing" is fast-paced and engaging comedy. Like the previous episode, which revisited themes explored in the first series, "Do the Right Thing" returns to ground covered in "The Big Cheese." Fortunately, whereas the previous episode was disappointing in that it repeated routines and situations verbatim, here new twists have been added.

There is more than a little cynicism in the plot, which presents almost everyone (except the Health Inspector) as trying to operate outside the law to his or her own advantage. Ironically, the only individual who is acting according to his claims is the poacher. He, however, is soon muscled out of the proceeding by the real spivs.

One of the funnier scenes involves Gareth, Janice, and Everton driving into the woods to meet Sidney Filkins, the poacher. They wait in the car amidst the trees until they receive a call on the car phone. In a bit reminiscent of some thriller films' instructions on a ransom drop, Gareth is told to come alone along a path deeper in the woods. At this point he realizes he is hopelessly lost outside the kitchen and must have Janice sketch him a likeness of an oak leaf so he knows where to turn. He still manages to lose his path and struggles through the undergrowth until he emerges at his desired location. Before continuing, he pauses to give the bushes a scornful kick.

Episode 4: "A Diploma of Miseries" ★★½

Air date: September 29, 1994. Cast: Gareth (Lenny Henry); Janice (Caroline Lee Johnson); Everton (Roger Griffiths); Anita Lawrence (Frances Barber); Debra (Pui Fan Lee) Crispin (Tim Matthews); Donald (Gary Bakewell); Alphonse (Jean Luc Rebaliati); Alice (Hilary Lyon); Claire (Samantha Edmonds); Security Guard (Roger Frost); with Roy Hattersley as Himself

Janice manages to book Gareth as a guest on the popular Anita Lawrence television talk show, despite the host's penchant for grilling her guests alive.

Did you ever go on a vacation or outing that was so wonderful you decided to go back and visit the same places all over again? Apparently, the creators of *Chef!* had such a good time with the first season that they spent most of the second season dropping in on old familiar themes. As with outings and vacations, old themes are revisited with mixed results. "A Diploma of Miseries" returns to the arena of Gareth and fame explored in two episodes from the first go-round. Here, however, the now-familiar ground is only a pretext to create conflict between Gareth and Janice. This makes the episode, despite its funny moments, essentially a drama about relationships and Gareth's own self-centeredness. Once again we see that for all his pomposity in the kitchen, Gareth is totally inept outside its confines.

This is the first episode not written by Peter Tilbury; the scripting chores were handled by Geoff Deane. Labor party politician Roy Hattersley makes a brief cameo appearance as the abused talk show guest who appears before Gareth.

There is more than a touch of tension in "A Diploma of Miseries" between Gareth and Janice, and little of it is actually humorous. The conflict starts when Janice proudly announces that she has booked Gareth on a prestigious national television show. Rather than appreciating the coup this represents, Gareth replies that he would "rather be parboiled in a vat of wildebeest urine." Janice explodes in a verbal tirade that is all too convincing to be funny. Fortunately, the hard edge is taken off the scene when a cowed Gareth meekly agrees to go on the show.

As real as their conflict appears, fortunately their reconciliation is also genuine looking. Gareth arranges for a beautiful luxury picnic in the country for him and his wife. Before the meal can begin, however, Gareth produces a television and turns the set on to show Janice his on-air apology. After Janice accepts Gareth's televised apology, he removes the silver dome from the impeccably arranged table he has set up in the forest. Expecting a gourmet meal, Janice is surprised to find a lowly pizza on the tray to accompany the fine china and champagne. Gareth sheepishly explains that with all the other preparations involved in the event, he didn't have any time left to cook.

EPISODE 5: "MASTERCHEF" ★★★★

Air date: October 13, 1994. Cast: Gareth (Lenny Henry); Janice (Caroline Lee Johnson); Everton (Roger Griffiths); Gustave (Ian McNeice); Alphonse (Jean Luc Rebaliati); Donald (Gary Bakewell); Crispin (Tim Matthews); Debra (Pui Fan Lee); Policeman 1 (Jim McManus); Policeman 2 (Mark Williams)

Everton creates a signature dish that is so popular that soon he is being courted by TV cooking shows and having articles written about him in culinary magazines. Despite his urge to kill his assistant, Gareth is dissuaded when Janice suggests a more subtle approach to bringing Everton back to earth.

Heretofore one of the pillars of *Chef!* has been that while he is inept outside of his cooking realm, Gareth Blackstock is the undisputed czar of his culinary world. "Masterchef" invades and harpoons that one bastion of Gareth's massive ego in what is one of the most consistently funny entries in the entire run of the program. Writer Peter Tilbury, back after a one-show hiatus, performs this deflation of Gareth in degrees, each more devastating than the one before. The masterstroke in the entire premise is that Chef's undisputed sovereignty is toppled by none other than the previously incompetent Everton, whose cooking skill has grown immensely under Gareth's tutelage.

"Masterchef" has it all. Aside from the grade A script, there are wonderful performances by Lenny Henry and Roger Griffiths. Ian McNeice provides topnotch comic support, returning to the part of Gustave after a two-show absence. Unfortunately, this is his last appearance in the series.

"Masterchef" provides that rare blend of strong plotting and funny dialogue, which helps make it one of the best, fastest moving half hours of entertainment. Once Gareth learns that Everton has aspirations above his culinary station, he begins a long slow burn that would make Edgar Kennedy proud.

The heat on Gareth's boil is turned up with each level of recognition that his assistant receives. After a monumental internal combat, Gareth announces to Janice that he has risen above his jealousy. At this moment, of course, he finally blows his top when he opens his cooking magazine to see an article on Everton titled "Is This the Brain behind Le Chateau Anglais?" Janice urges her husband not to fire him immediately. Gareth agrees, pointing out that he will kill him first, then sack him.

When Gareth makes Everton "deputy chef," Everton is extremely pleased. The more experienced Gustave realizes the ridiculousness of the position and asks Everton if a six-gun and badge come with the promotion.

EPISODE 6: "PRIVATE LIVES" ★½

Air date: October 20, 1994. Cast: Gareth (Lenny Henry); Janice (Caroline Lee Johnson); Everton (Roger Griffiths); Gordon (Nick Brimble); Crispin (Tim Matthews); Debra (Pui Fan Lee); Donald (Gary Bakewell); Alphonse (Jean Luc Rebaliati); Cheryl (Kate McKenzie); Grant (David Cardy); William (Robin Ashenden); Lesley (Jenny Jay Williams); Tony (Andrew Francis)

Just as the Blackstocks are complaining that their work has erased any semblance of a private life, the personal problems of three of the staff spill over into the kitchen of Le Chateau Anglais.

A valiant experiment that doesn't quite pan out, "Private Lives" explores the personal problems of three lesser members of the kitchen staff. The primary reason that it doesn't work is that the plot leaves Lenny Henry very little to do, except to react to his supporting cast. Again, like too many of the shows in the second series, "Private Lives" tend towards the dramatic. Unfortunately, unlike "A Diploma of Miseries," in which the drama revolved around Gareth and Janice, we don't particularly care about the private lives of three fringe characters.

Ironically, for an episode that spotlights three members of the supporting cast, it is a guest cast member that has the few amusing moments. Nick Brimble, as Gordon, Donald's father, has some good turns playing the gloomy, cliché-spouting fugitive from justice.

EPISODE 7: "ENGLAND EXPECTS" ★★★★

Air date: October 27, 1994. Cast: Gareth (Lenny Henry); Janice (Caroline Lee Johnson); Everton (Roger Griffiths); Alphonse (Jean Luc Rebaliati); Donald (Gary Bakewell); Debra (Pui Fan Lee); Gaston (Guillaume Barriere); Marcel (Vincent Nemeth); Wine Merchant (Francois Domange); Wine Merchant's Wife (Patti Hannock); Chairman (Alain Debray); Passenger (Robin Driscoll); Air Hostess (Fiona Allen)

Invited to a prestigious international cooking competition in Lyon, France, Gareth decides to prepare English dishes made entirely with English ingredients — a move that brings him nothing but scorn from the French chefs.

The second season of *Chef!* ends on a triumphant note, both for the character of Gareth Blackstock and the show itself. Gareth wins a prestigious cooking competition, while the series provides a highly entertaining episode.

Writer (most notably for *Mr. Bean*), actor, and *Chef!* script editor Robin Driscoll makes a brief appearance as a passenger on the flight to France.

Perhaps the best scene in the episode occurs when Gareth and Everton enter a French wine merchant's cellar to buy a bottle of English wine. The entire exchange is in French but is easily understood. At first the merchant is incredulous that someone would be asking for English wine in France and tries to clarify his customer's request. When Gareth makes it clear that he does indeed want English wine, the man breaks into a gale of laughter. Gareth, realizing the futility of the effort, turns and walks out, leaving the merchant to explain the silly request of the "roast beef" customer.

Series Three 1996

EPISODE 1 ★★★

Air date: November 25, 1996. Cast: Gareth (Lenny Henry); Janice (Caroline Lee Johnson); Everton (Roger Griffiths); Cyril (Dave Hill); Gustave (Jeff Nutall); Savannah (Lorelei King); Vincenzo (Vincent Walsh); Relate Counselor (Adele Salem); Customer (Ray Armstrong)

Gareth must face Janice leaving him while he also copes with the sale of Le Chateau Anglais.

A radical shift in the format of *Chef!* from the show's first two series, this first episode of the third season (untitled, as are the rest of the entries in the season) manages to introduce the changes fairly well without overly relying on cumbersome exposition. While keeping the three core performers (although Caroline Lee Johnson's role would be severely trimmed by virtue of the plot line), this season presents three new faces and two new parts (Jeff Nutall replaces Ian McNeice in the role of Gustave). The main additions, Dave Hill's Cyril and Lorelei King's Savannah, take some getting used to, since they both are essentially on board as irritants, at least initially. Their function is not to provide laughs but to act as catalysts to good comebacks from those around them. Cyril, a loud, nouveau riche northerner is there to provide a foil for Lenny Henry's Gareth, and as such he does an admirable job. Savannah, on the other hand, is a name-dropping chef from southern California, whose best moments come as she provides fodder for Gustave's ego-deflating responses. These additions are both welcome as the standard Blackstock tirades so key to the humor of the first two seasons are gone, since the main character has become involved in more realistic, day-to-day events.

The episode begins as Janice finally leaves Gareth, no longer willing to compete with a restaurant for her husband's affections. Jarred by the loss of his wife, Gareth takes a reality check and promptly quits his job as chef at Le Chateau Anglais on the eve of the new owner's grand opening. Gareth almost manages to woo Janice back but ruins his opportunity when he returns to his kitchen to avert a disaster on the opening night. Although this ending — the kitchen being in a state of panic — fits well with the plot, it doesn't make sense given previous episodes of the show. In "Masterchef," for example, Everton proves that he can run the kitchen, as supposedly can Gustave when he is not drinking. Perhaps, we are led to believe, it is Savannah, who is given the job of chef, that is the weak link in the chain, although with two competent assistants beside her, this is a tad farfetched.

This episode was scripted by series creative consultant Geoff Deane, who previously wrote "A Diploma of Miseries" for the second season.

EPISODE 2 ★★

Air date: December 2, 1996. Cast: Gareth (Lenny Henry); Everton (Roger Griffiths); Cyril (Dave Hill); Savannah (Lorelei King); Gustave (Jeff Nutall); Renee (Sophie Walker); Vincenzo (Vincent Walsh)

Gareth is forced to hire Cyril's daughter, Renee, who not only disrupts the kitchen with her ineptitude but makes Everton fall in love with her.

This episode continues the linear story begun in the previous installment. Gareth is still without Janice (who, for the first time, is not seen) and is continuing his agony over the split. As such, most of the star's screen time is consumed with the comedy of anxiety, which, unfortunately, starts to wear thin. Even the promising antagonistic relationship between Gustave and Savannah, which seemed so promising in the first episode of the season, is barely seen. What remains for comedy is provided by the introduction of Cyril's daughter, Renee, nicely played by Sophie Walker. While this character, a paragon of professional artlessness (she was fired as a shepherd for losing a flock) and personal shallowness (she dumps the sweet Everton for someone else solely on the basis of automobile size), has her moments, she cannot sustain the entry. The script by Paul Makin does have some good construction and manages to refer to itself in a way that provides strong continuity, but it suffers from a lack of comic meat on a sturdy skeleton.

The story line, continuing as it does from the first episode, begins to take on something of the flavor of a soap opera, concerned as it is with the love lives of the two main characters (Gareth and Everton). This installment also introduces the plot twist involving Savannah's attraction to Gareth. Her infatuation with her boss, although little more than hinted at here, is presented in such a way that it almost certainly promises more to come in future episodes.

EPISODE 3 ★★★★

Air date: December 9, 1996. Cast: Gareth (Lenny Henry); Janice (Caroline Lee Johnson); Everton (Roger Griffiths); Cyril (Dave Hill); Savannah (Lorelei King); Gustave (Jeff Nutall); Renee (Sophie Walker); Vincenzo (Vincent Walsh); Pianist (John Altman); First Couple (Jan Goodman, Conor Mullen); American Couple (Kristen Marks, Stuart Fox); Businessmen (Sam McKenzie, Lawrence Elman)

Gareth is compelled by Cyril to mingle with the diners even while his marriage continues to disintegrate.

After two episodes of finding its way in the new format, the third entry of the third season of *Chef!* hits the mark solidly with a full portion of laughs and even a little poignancy. The primary reason for this success is the return of Lenny Henry to the fore as the show's primary funmaker. In the two previous installments, the character of Gareth was allowed to founder in his personal miseries, while the supporting cast was given a large measure of the comedy. Here, his marriage woes have not been soft-pedaled, but they have been attacked with a comic vengeance. Consequently, Henry is given much more to do comedically, which in turn enhances the funny business of his backup crew. Behind this strong lead, all the other characters — Cyril, Savannah, Everton, Gustave, and even Renee — turn in amusing, well-integrated performances and, most important, do so as an ensemble.

The story line itself is a well-conceived emotional roller coaster for Chef Blackstock by Paul Makin in his second offering of the series. Cyril orders Gareth to mingle with the patrons of the restaurant after seeing the practice done successfully in another establishment. The only problem is that the high strung Gareth doesn't "do mingle." In fact, he is terrified by the notion and hyperventilates at the mere mention of it. The first attempt to comply with Cyril's directive results in a hilarious bit in which Gareth stands like a zombie over a pair of diners, barely managing to squeak "hello" and frightening the couple. When he finally finds his voice, he only repeats topics suggested by the staff. Unfortunately, he blurts these all out in the same sentence by telling the guests his star sign, his shopping habits, and the fact that he likes sex.

At this juncture the writer cleverly introduces an outside influence on Gareth's mingling activities—Janice. Gareth's estranged wife returns, and each visit results in wild mood swings, which adversely affect the next meal's mingling. First Chef goes low—openly bawling as a pair of patrons lavishly praise his culinary offerings. At the next meal, coming after a session with Janice and her lawyer, he attacks some businessmen and drowns their cellular phone in the coffeepot. After a passionate reconcilement, Gareth turns into an ultrahip fifties version of a lounge singer (complete with a rendition of "The Lady Is a Tramp"). When the reunion proves to be short-lived, Gareth returns to the microphone but now sings a heart-wrenching version of "I Can't Live." All this provides wonderful comedy and, as stated above, even some tender moments. The scene between Gareth and Janice that leads to their brief reunion is warm and funny and reminds the viewers of the chemistry between them.

Episode 4 ★★★

Air date: December 16, 1996. Cast: Gareth (Lenny Henry); Everton (Roger Griffiths); Cyril (Dave Hill); Gustave (Jeff Nutall); Savannah (Lorelei King); Renee (Sophie Walker); Dad (Oliver Samuels); Minnie (Loretta Parnell); Florist (Lee Boswell)

Gareth's father returns to announce he is getting married again.

The fourth episode of the third series, scripted by Geoff Deane, plays more like a soap opera with jokes than a comedy episode. Most of the action darts back and forth between no fewer than four intertwined plot lines, all of which deal with serious emotions. Despite this format, the entry is consistently entertaining due partly to its quick pacing but primarily to its funny repartee. In any given scene, there is one character earnestly agonizing over one of the situations, while the other person(s) responds with clever comebacks.

All of the situations deal with romantic relationships. First, Cyril is upset because his daughter, Renee, is dating a man who is as old as he is. This is particularly hard on Everton, who is still not over his romance with Renee. Savannah is trying to manufacture a boyfriend to make Gareth jealous, while Gareth, in a reverse of Cyril's problem, is annoyed to learn that his father wants to marry a 28-year-old. The amount of story necessitates a fast pace so none of the scenes lasts more than a few minutes.

The character of Gustave manages to fare quite well despite (or perhaps because of) the fact that he is not directly involved in any of the story lines. In one nice little scene, Gustave confesses to the lovelorn Everton that he hasn't had a woman in over 14 years. He then recommends the same lifestyle choice to the young cook, noting that when one has a jar of pickled onions in one hand and the TV remote in the other, there is little need for a woman.

Episode 5 ★★★

Air date: December 23, 1996. Cast: Gareth (Lenny Henry); Janice (Caroline Lee Johnson); Everton (Roger Griffiths); Cyril (Dave Hill); Gustave (Jeff Nutall); Savannah (Lorelei King); Renee (Sophie Walker); Auntie Clarice (Mona Hammond); Rochelle (Jo Martin); Chantel (Yvette Rochester); DJ (Mistei)

Gareth agrees to cater Everton's cousin's wedding at the restaurant.

A continuation of the previous episode, this entry serves to heighten the level of romantic plotting. Like its predecessor, the primary focus is on the story line, with the jokes either given in response to the main action or by side characters. One of the latter is Everton's Auntie Clarice, whose daughter, Chantel, is getting married at Le Chateau Anglais. This character, brought to life by Mona Hammond, is a delightful Caribbean woman who enjoys taking a firm hand in the proceedings, especially when it comes to putting Gareth and her nephew in their places.

Romantically, the plots thicken, as many new players are added to the mix of episode four. First, Janice apparently has a new admirer, as Gareth witnesses her kissing another man in the opening scene. This incident emboldens Gareth later to shed any reluctance to pursue an old flame, Rochelle, who appears as the maid of honor for the wedding. Cyril also provides some amusement as he becomes enamored of Savannah, who of course is still infatuated with Gareth. Even old Gustave enters the fray when Auntie Clarice enlists him as a dancing partner at the reception.

Writer Geoff Deane manages to keep all the various threads of the plot moving along nicely and even frames the episode with brief appearances by Caroline Lee Johnson as Janice. The closing moments set up the series finale, as Janice returns, in the middle of a moment of passion between Gareth and Rochelle, to announce she is pregnant.

Episode 6 ★★★½

Air date: December 30, 1996. Cast: Gareth (Lenny Henry); Janice (Caroline Lee Johnson); Everton (Roger Griffiths); Cyril (Dave Hill); Savannah (Lorelei King); Gustave (Jeff Nutall); Renee (Sophie Walker); Rochelle (Jo Martin); Priest (Tony Rohr)

Gareth tries to decide whether to follow Rochelle to Paris or to try and reconcile with his wife, Janice.

The third season of *Chef!* wraps up with this last segment of the trilogy of episodes on relationships begun in episode four. Paul Makin returns to finish the tale begun by Geoff Deane, and he does an excellent job supplying a strong, witty script for the actors to follow. What could have been one of the best episodes of all three seasons is hampered, however, by one of the series' biggest flaws: the acting ability of its star. Unfortunately, while Lenny Henry is indeed a major comic talent, he is not quite the level of comic actor needed to successfully scale the heights required by this script. While this is not obvious in other offerings of *Chef!* it is quite evident here, especially in his scenes with Caroline Lee Johnson. One never gets the impression that Gareth is really all that upset about the tumultuous events transpiring in his life, as Henry substitutes manic behavior for the deep-seated emotional responses called for by the script. This is also obvious in the scenes in which Gareth and Everton are racing back and forth between the restaurant and the airport. Instead of being truly anxious about getting to his destination (and his destiny) in time, Gareth is easily distracted by a silly bit of business involving sunglasses. It would have been more believable if Everton had performed the sunglasses routine and Gareth reacted to it with frustration.

This criticism aside, the final episode manages some funny moments. The opening scene, in which Gareth tries to sort out his romantic entanglements by confessing them to a Priest, is priceless — especially when he holds up photos of the women in his life to the confessional screen for the Priest's opinion. There is also a humorous bit directly following this in which the staff surprises Gareth on his birthday. This scene allows each of the kitchen staff members to have a last individual moment in the limelight as they give him his presents one by one. Lorelei King as Savannah is particularly good as she presents Gareth with a book on overcoming anger, then turns violent on Gustave when he deems the work "American self-help, psychobabble cobblers." There is also an amusing, but ultimately overly repetitious routine, between Gareth and Everton, which takes place in the men's room.

Despite the previously mentioned flaws, the third season of *Chef!* must be considered an interesting, often successful experiment that expanded its original premise and explored new avenues of comedy. The creative staff and the star are to be commended.

Appendix: Popular and Recommended

One of the challenges in writing a book on the best of television comedy from a nation thousands of miles away is that of perceptions and opinions. For example, most Brits would certainly argue with the inclusion of some of the shows selected for analysis in this volume, while some of their country's best have been totally ignored. At the same time many American Brit-com fans will be mystified over the attention lavished on the relatively unknown (in America) *Dad's Army*, while the much more popular (again, over here) *Absolutely Fabulous* is not given the same spotlight in which to bask. As remedy, or at least as an apology for any favorites omitted in the bulk of this volume, there is this appendix. Something of an "honorable mention," the following are shows that are either popular in the United States or that have not been given a wide airing here, although they deserve one. In short, these 18 programs are the rest of the best of British television comedy, at least as viewed from the left edge of the Atlantic.

Absolutely Fabulous

BBC 1992–1996 by Jennifer Saunders (from an idea by Dawn French and Jennifer Saunders). Directed by Bob Spiers. Produced by Jon Plowman. 20 episodes

Basing this show on a sketch from the *French and Saunders* series, Jennifer Saunders adapted the concept of the relationship of a reprobate mother with her responsible teenage daughter into one of the biggest hits of the 1990s. Saunders played Edina Monsoon, a public relations agent who, along with her fashion editor friend (Joanna Lumley), delves into new behavioral lows for two middle-aged women. Balancing out the hard-smoking, hard-drinking, trend-chasing pair is Edina's daughter, Saffron (Julia Sawalha), a serious-minded, health-conscious student. While the dramatic tension between mother and daughter provided much of the interest in the stories, the absolutely outrageous ill behavior of Saunders and Lumley evoked most of the comedy. The fact that these two women were carrying on in the same way they had for more than 20 years became the primary situation of the series. Also providing support were Jane Horrock as Edina's incompetent secretary, Bubbles, and veteran comedic actress June Whitfield as Edina's mother. Unfortunately, aside from video, the main U.S. outlet for the series is commercial cable, where the flow of the scripts is constantly interrupted for advertisements.

'Allo, 'Allo

BBC 1982–1992 by Jeremy Lloyd and David Croft (with Paul Adam, John Chapman, Ian Davidson, Ronald Wolfe, and Ronald Chesney). Directed by David Croft, Mike Stephens, Susan Belbin, Martin Dennis, Richard Boden, Sue Longstaff, and John B. Hobbs. Produced by David Croft, John B. Hobbs, and Mike Stephens. 85 episodes

With *'Allo, 'Allo*, Jeremy Lloyd and David Croft did for World War II what they previously had for the retail trade with *Are You Being Served?* While poking fun at the Resistance in Nazi-occupied France may have been potentially dicey, the writers and actors played the spoof so broadly as to score a great international hit. The series was set in the cafe of Rene Artois (Gorden Kaye) and his wife, Edith (Carmen Silvera). Rene becomes involved with the Resistance when his café is used as a meeting place. The main plot of the series was the effort to return two downed British flyers (John D. Collins and Nicholas Frankau) to England. Of course this line usually took a back seat to the many subplots involving Rene's unrequited lust for his waitress, Yvette (Vicki Michelle); the constant interference of the occupying Germans; and the elaborate, often silly plans of Resistance operative Michelle (Kirsten Cooke). Probably the most inspired element of all involved Rene faking his own death to avoid arrest by the Gestapo, then continuing the series by pretending to be his own twin brother.

As Time Goes By

BBC 1992–1997 by Bob Larbey (from an idea by Colin Bostock-Smith). Directed and Produced by Sydney Lotterby. 47 episodes

This leisurely, genial comedy concentrated on the lives of two young lovers separated by the Korean War, who unexpectedly find each other 40 years later. Scripted by Bob Larbey from an idea by Colin Bostock-Smith, *As Time Goes By* recalls the warmth of Larbey's 1970s hit (with John Esmonde), *The Good Life*. Like *The Good Life*, the attraction of *As Time Goes By* was more in smiles than belly laughs and in likable, realistic characters than outrageous situations. Supporting the interesting, at times almost soap opera–like scripts were expert performances by Judi Dench (as Jean Pargetter) and Geoffrey Palmer (as Lionel Hardcastle) as the lovers. Moira Brookner, Philip Bretherton, and Jenny Funnell made up the remainder of the regulars in fine style. Most of the first series was taken up with the often uncomfortable situation of the two former lovers getting used to each other again. At first it seemed as if Lionel and Jean would not get back together, although the audience was always led to hope and suspect that this was ultimately a foregone conclusion. As is usually the case in real life, the relationship was brought along slowly and deliberately: the couple went through dating, then cohabitation, and eventually marriage. *As Time Goes By* also enjoyed success as a BBC Radio 2 adaptation, including scenes featuring the couple's earlier romance not disclosed in the television version.

Butterflies

BBC 1978–1983 by Carla Lane. Directed by John B. Hobbs, Sydney Lotterby, and Mandie Fletcher. Produced by Sydney Lotterby and Gareth Gwenlan. 29 episodes

Bittersweet is the best way to describe this popular series written and created by Carla Lane. Wendy Craig starred as Ria Parkinson, a married woman in her late thirties with two sons, who begins to feel her approaching middle-age with some reservations. Ria's husband, Ben (Geoffrey Palmer) is a good man although basically dull. Her sons (Nicholas Lyndhurst and Andrew Hall) are average teens, which of course creates tension between them and their staid father. The main focus of the series was Ria's ennui, which led to a sexless affair with a stimulating businessman (Bruce Montague). In ways a *Reggie Perrin* from the woman's point of view, *Butterflies* employed a variety of innovative devices to approach its subject matter. An American adaptation was attempted with Lane's involvement, but the property, which starred Jennifer Warren, never progressed past the pilot stage.

Father Ted

Channel 4 1995–1996 by Graham Linehan and Arthur Matthews. Directed by Declan Lowney. Produced by Geoffrey Perkins and Lissa Evans. 17 episodes

Channel 4 (C4), one of Britain's independent television outlets, scored heavily with this unorthodox comedy centered on the lives of three priests on Craggy Island off the coast of Ireland. Unlike more gentle ecclesiastical comedies, *Father Ted* was raucous, outrageous, usually irreverent, inventive, and purely hilarious. Written by Graham Linehan and Arthur Matthews, the scripts provided some of the most bizarre and, at times, surreal events to ever befall clergymen. Not that the three priests were average clergymen by any stretch of the imagination. All three had been banished to Craggy Island for different reasons; all were unsuitable in more mainstream parishes. The leader of the band was Father Ted Crilly (Dermot Morgan), who at first glance seems almost normal, but who had absconded with church funds in his previous assignment and gone on a Las Vegas spree. Under Father Ted is the young and wonderfully obtuse Father Dougal (Ardal O'Hanlon) and the older, constantly drunk, and permanently annoyed Father Jack (Frank Kelly).

Hancock's Half-Hour

BBC 1956–1960 by Ray Galton and Alan Simpson. Produced by Duncan Wood, Graeme Muir, and Francis Essex. 58 Episodes

Tony Hancock is British television's answer to Milton Berle, Jackie Gleason, and Sid Caesar wrapped into one. While this television comedy pioneer is all but unknown in the United States, one could not write a book on British TV comedy without at least a passing reference to the man who in many ways started it all. Born in 1924, Tony Hancock first appeared on television in 1948, although he wouldn't land his first regular series (a sketch program entitled *The Tony Hancock Show*) until 1956. This ITV series featured, among others, the exceptional writing of Ray Galton and Alan Simpson, who had written for the comedian on various radio programs. Hancock is probably best remembered for *Hancock's Half-Hour*, a BBC sitcom that also featured Sid James in comic support. In this series the comedian played a modified version of himself, much as Laurel and Hardy and Jack Benny had done previously. Like Laurel and Hardy, Anthony Aloysius St. John Hancock (his character's full name) stayed essentially the same person, although his profession and station changed from week to week. This afforded Galton and Simpson, the lone authors of the show, a wide range of situations in which to place Hancock's portrayal of the basic loser. The 58 episodes of *Hancock's Half-Hour* were followed in 1961 by another Galton and Simpson series entitled simply *Hancock*.

Following this series and a break with Galton and Simpson (see *Steptoe and Son*), Hancock's career and personal life went into a steady decline. The comedian took his own life in 1968 while in Australia working on a series for that country's television. There have been some NTSC–format tapes of *Hancock's Half-Hour* released in the United States, although not nearly as many as are available in the PAL format from Great Britain.

Jeeves and Wooster

ITV–Granada 1990–1993 Adapted by Clive Exton from the works of P. G. Wodehouse. Directed by Robert Young, Simon Langton, and Ferdinand Fairfax. Produced by Brian Eastman. 23 episodes.

Strong casting and good faithfulness to its source material made this Granada adaptation of P. G. Wodehouse's two most famous characters a joy to view both for aficionados of the original stories and for fans of Stephen Fry and Hugh Laurie. Although Laurie may have seemed perfect for the part, at first glance Fry perhaps was not due to his youthful appearance. Only a few moments of the premiere episode, however, dispelled most objections anyone may have had, as Fry's characterization more than fleshed out the sagely servant of the novels and short stories. In addition to its two stars, the entire production had a marvelous period feel thanks to the meticulous attention paid to all details. The fact that each hour-long episode was shot on film helped add to the series' production values.

Adapted by Clive Exton from the original Wodehouse, the scripts rarely strayed from their inspirations. Some *Jeeves and Wooster* episodes were shown in the United States on PBS's *Masterpiece Theater*, with Stephen Fry providing charming introductions to each installment, while others had their U.S. airing on the A&E cable network. All episodes are available on home video and are well worth viewing as either an introduction to Wodehouse or a faithful supplement to the written works.

Last of the Summer Wine

BBC 1973–1997 by Roy Clarke. Directed by Alan J W Bell, Sydney Lotterby, Ray Butt, and Martin Shardlow. Produced by Alan J W Bell, Sydney Lotterby, James Gilbert, Bernard Thompson, and Robin Nash. 162 episodes

Far and away the most prolific sit-com in British television history, this Roy Clarke creation began in 1972 as a pilot episode in the *Comedy Playhouse* series that spawned so many BBC comedies. *Last of the Summer Wine* centers on the exploits of a trio of older men whimsically wiling away their sunset years in Yorkshire. The first lineup was made up of Blamire (Michael Bates), who acted as titular leader; the more cautious Clegg (Peter Sallis); and Compo (Bill Owen), the most foolhardy of the bunch. Although it started slowly in the ratings, the BBC stuck with the show until it became a national institution (and, some complain, stayed with it far past its prime). Over the years the stars have changed. Bates left after the first two series and was replaced by Brian Wilde (*Porridge*) as Foggy Dewhurst, an ex-military man. Wilde himself left for seasons 9 through 11, during which time Michael Aldridge filled in as Seymour Utterthwaite.

Last of the Summer Wine is at times nostalgic and broad, reflective and outrageous. Unfortunately, as with many shows based on ensemble casts, it often takes a number of episodes to become familiar with the players. Due to the fact that only a handful of episodes are available in the States in the NTSC video format, this is not a luxury many Americans have been able to indulge.

Only Fools and Horses

BBC 1981–1997 by John Sullivan. Directed by Ray Butt, Tony Dow, Susan Belbin, Martin Shardlow, and Mandie Fletcher. Produced by Ray Butt, Gareth Gwenlan, and Bernard Thompson. 63 episodes

This John Sullivan series began as the story of three men without women, from three different generations stuck in a small flat in Peckham in South London. From these simple beginnings the series grew into a much-respected and much-enjoyed institution. Starting in 1981, the story centered on Del Trotter (David Jason of *Open All Hours*), a hustling entrepreneur who dreams of getting rich operating his seat-of-the-pants business from the back of his three-wheeled van. Reluctantly assisting Del in his endeavors is Rodney (Nicholas Lyndhurst), who although his brother, is younger enough than Del to be considered part of another generation. Rounding out the trio is Grandad (Lennard Pearce), whose main occupation seems to be watching two televisions simultaneously. Although the show started slowly with the viewers, it soon caught on to become a favorite. The death of Lennard Pearce necessitated the replacement of Grandad with Uncle Albert (Buster Merryfield), beginning in series four. In time the scope of the series expanded as the brothers developed more lasting relationships with women. To keep up with the increasing depth, the time of each episode was extended as well, first to 50 minutes and, ultimately, to 60 minutes for the final series in 1996. Unfortunately, *Only Fools and Horses* has never received a wide airing in the United States, although it is highly recommended for seasoned Brit-com fans with PAL format VCRs and Internet access to British video sales.

Open All Hours

BBC 1973–1985 by Roy Clarke. Produced by Sydney Lotterby and Robin Nash. 27 episodes.

As noted throughout this volume, many classic BBC comedies have been culled from anthology series, such as *Comedy Playhouse*. In 1973 it was remarkable not only that one series, *Seven of One*, produced two favorites series but that they starred the same actor. Of course, it is less remarkable when one considers that *Seven of One* was a showcase for the considerable comic talents of Ronnie Barker. Although it premiered on the *Seven of One* series, *Open All Hours* did not become a regular series until three years later, when its first group of six episodes was aired in February 1976. By then, the second show in *Seven of One* had already enjoyed most of its run as the prison comedy *Porridge*.

Open All Hours is a compact little character comedy built around northern shopkeeper Arkwright (Ronnie Barker) who, with his nephew Granville

(David Jason), runs a corner grocery store. Arkwright is a masterful creation as scripted by Roy Clarke and fleshed out by Barker. Cheaper than Jack Benny, Arkwright keeps his store open from early in the morning until late at night, although his customer base is small and his profit margin even smaller. Granville longs to experience the world outside the shop but must be content to dream of the existence passing him by while he toils under his uncle's watchful eye. His only moments of escape come on the store's delivery bicycle. Rounding out the regular cast was Lynda Baron as Nurse Gladys Emmanuel, the buxom neighbor who is the constant object of Arkwright's carnal lusting. Three episodes of this consistently humorous series were released by CBS-Fox video, although they were strung together as a continuous story.

Porridge

BBC 1973–1977 by Dick Clement and Ian La Frenais. Produced by Sydney Lotterby. 21 episodes.

The second entry from Ronnie Barker's *Seven of One* anthology was a story called *Prisoner and Escort,* which featured the rotund comedian as Norman Fletcher, a repeat criminal being taken to prison by a pair of guards. Although it was obviously series material, the writers of *Prisoner and Escort,* Dick Clement and Ian La Frenais, had to wait for over a year until the BBC decided that the situation warranted a full series. Thankfully, the powers that be at the BBC ultimately saw the potential since the ensuing series, *Porridge* (British slang for prison), is one of the finest situation comedies any nation has produced.

Porridge has all the elements of a classic: believable characters, clever scripts, comedy skimming just above the surface of drama, and that favorite BBC device — stasis.

Joining Barker's habitual criminal in the cell is Richard Beckinsale as Godber, a young, first-time offender who wants to go straight. The relationship between Fletcher and Godber soon develops into an avuncular one, as the older man helps acclimate the younger (as well as the viewer) to the realities of prison life. On the other side of the equation are two guards brought over from the pilot. The first, Mr. MacKay (Fulton Mackay) is a tough, no-nonsense Scot who gives his charges no quarter. The second, Mr. Barrowclough (Brian Wilde), is a much gentler soul who feels his mission is to rehabilitate the men through kinder means. The plots were as basic as the cast, usually focusing on the prisoners' attempts to make their plight slightly more bearable through the enjoyment of a pilfered tin of pineapple or a day's work on the outside. Although it came to an end after three series, the cast reunited in 1978 for a six-episode sequel, *Going Straight,* which showed Fletcher and Godber after prison. In addition, 1979 saw a feature film of *Porridge*, directed by coauthor Dick Clement.

Red Dwarf

BBC 1988–1997 by Rob Grant, Doug Naylor, Paul Alexander, Kim Fuller, Robert Llewellyn, and James Hendrie. Directed by Ed Bye, Juliet May, and Andy de Emmony. Produced by Ed Bye, Hilary Bevan Jones, and Justin Judd. 44 episodes.

An alternative comedy in the style of the *Blackadder* series, *Red Dwarf* is one of the BBC's biggest cult exports. Although it never achieved mainstream popularity in the United States (probably due to it being a space comedy), the fans of this series are legion. Created by Rob Grant and Doug Naylor, the series revolved around the adventures of a diverse group of misfits who staffed the twenty-first century mining ship *Red Dwarf*. A mishap wipes out the entire crew except for one, David Lister (Craig Charles), who is in suspended animation as a punishment. When Lister awakes, it is 3 million years later, and he finds a hologram of his former adversary, Rimmer (Chris Barrie). Also on board are Holly, the now aged computer, and a descendant of the ship's cat (Danny John-Jules), who over time has evolved into a near human. Like many of the best BBC comedies, *Red Dwarf* features antagonistic characters trapped in less-than-ideal situations (*Steptoe and Son*, *Porridge*). The series has been compared to *Dr. Who*, not only for its sci-fi bent, but also for its cheesy special effects. Its success during late-night PBS airings led to two abortive attempts to recreate the *Red Dwarf* formula for American production, but neither of these has reached a series commitment. Still, fans should take solace in the fact that all the originals are available on American format (NTSC) video.

Rising Damp

ITV–Yorkshire 1974–1978 by Eric Chappell. Directed and Produced by Ronnie Baxter, Vernon Lawrence, Len Lurcuck, and Ian McNaughton. 28 episodes.

Before bringing to life the title character of *The Fall and Rise of Reginald Perrin*, Leonard Rossiter starred in this ITV sitcom, which helped make him a household name. In *Rising Damp*, Rossiter played Rupert Rigsby, a bigoted and obnoxious boardinghouse landlord. Inhabiting Rigby's digs were a university administrator (Francis de la Tour), a medical student (Richard Beckinsale), and an African student (Don Warrington). While many of the plots were easily dismissed, the series succeeded on the strength of Rossiter's performance, running for four seasons. Especially remarkable is the fact that starting in 1976 Rossiter was also playing a totally different character on *Perrin*, although with no less acting skill and comic verve. *Rising Damp* has been shown in the United States on the A&E cable channel although often as predawn filler. Thankfully the series is available on easily ordered (although often overpriced) video in the NTSC format.

The Thin Blue Line

BBC 1995–1996 by Ben Elton. Directed by John Birkin. Produced by Geoffrey Perkins and Ben Elton. 14 episodes.

Author Ben Elton of *The Young Ones* and *Blackadder* fame is a self-avowed admirer of *Dad's Army*. As such in the mid-1990s Elton set out to create an ensemble comedy in the style of that earlier classic. The result was *The Thin Blue Line* starring Rowan Atkinson. While not set in a military venue, *The Thin Blue Line* is centered around a small police station where Inspector Raymond Fowler (Atkinson) presides over an odd crew of uniformed officers of various types. There are two women. One, Sgt. Dawkins (Serena Evans), is Fowler's frustrated lover, and the other, PC Habib (Mina Anwar), is probably the brightest of the cast. Together the women provide the Wilson character to Atkinson's Mainwaring imitation. Also there is a black officer, PC Gladstone (Rudolph Walker), who is something of a Godfrey type, while PC Goody is along as the most outrageously comical (à la Cpl. Jones, although he is more reminiscent of the fey Mr. Humphries from *Are You Being Served?*). Providing the friendly fire is Detective Grim (David Haig) in a role fashioned after Warden Hodges of *Dad's Army*. While the show had some fine moments of dialog and scored well in the ratings, one could not get past the notion that this was all painting-by-numbers and ultimately not worth the bother of such talents as Elton and Atkinson.

To the Manor Born

BBC 1979–1981 by Peter Spence (with Christopher Bond, one episode). Produced by Gareth Gwenlan. 21 episodes.

Riding high on her successful tenure on *The Good Life*, Penelope Keith launched into this genial sit-com, which proved equally, if not more, popular with the British public. Written by Peter Spence, *To the Manor Born* followed somewhat sequentially the life of Audrey fforbes-Hamilton (Keith), a recently widowed woman who is forced to sell her estate after discovering that her husband has left her flat broke. Audrey manages to hold onto the modest coach house on the estate while the manor is bought by a nouveau riche supermarket tycoon, Richard DeVere (Peter Bowles). As with many romantic comedies, the rest of the series (over three seasons) busied itself with the leisurely courtship of the two stars, taking them from initial antagonism to ultimate matrimony (the final episode attracted a then-record 24 million viewers in the U.K.). Providing capable support throughout this comfortably amusing series was Angela Thorne as Marjory, Audrey's best friend; John Rudling as the feeble but loyal butler, Brabinger; and Daphne Heard as Mrs. Polouvicka, DeVere's Czechoslovakian mother. As with other successful TV sit-coms, *To the Manor Born* was also adapted for BBC Radio 2 in ten episodes. Ironically, this was the property's originally intended format as conceived by Peter Spence in 1968.

The Vicar of Dibley

BBC 1994–1997 by Richard Curtis (with Paul Mayhew-Archer). Directed by Dewi Humphreys, John Howard Davies, and Gareth Carrivick. Produced by John Plowman and Sue Vertue. 10 episodes.

While her sketch series partner Jennifer Saunders was shaking up the conventional sitcom world with the outrageous *Absolutely Fabulous*, Dawn French was proving equally adept in the genre with this genial series. While *The Vicar of Dibley*, created by Richard Curtis (*Blackadder*, *Mr. Bean*), at first appeared somewhat controversial due to some of its subject matter (most obviously, the ordination of women), the series soon proved itself on the strength of its fine ensemble cast, which included not only French but Gary Waldhorn, James Fleet, and Emma Chambers.

Waiting for God

BBC 1990–1994 by Michael Aitkens. Directed by Gareth Gwenlan. Produced by Gareth Gwenlan and Sue Bysh. 47 episodes.

Most of the residents of the Bayview Retirement Home seemed quite happy to wile away their sunset years in peace; but this resignation drove one inhabitant, Diana Trent (Stephanie Cole), absolutely mad. Along with a new resident, the eccentric Tom Ballard (Graham Crowden), Diana's mission in this popular comedy was to shake up the establishment as she had done throughout her career as a journalist. Providing resistance for these two schemers was the manager of the home (Daniel Hill) and his mousy assistant (Janine Duvitski of *One Foot in the Grave*). While a popular entry on both sides of the Atlantic, *Waiting for God* was hampered by Diana's railings, which often veered too far into pessimism.

The Young Ones

BBC 1982–1984 by Ben Elton, Rik Mayall, and Lise Mayer (additional material by Alexei Sayle). Produced by Paul Jackson. 12 episodes.

Although only two series of six episodes each were produced of this sitcom, *The Young Ones* is significant as one of the first new wave, or alternative, comedies to break through into the public mainstream. Written by Ben Elton, Rik Mayall, and Lise Mayer, this program represented its genre well, being energetic, vital, childish, rude, and most important funny. *The Young Ones* starred Rik Mayall as Rik, a radical but stupid young man sharing an apartment with three other young people. Adrian Edmondson played the violent punk, Vyvyan, while Nigel Planer was the hippie Neil, and Christopher Ryan rounded out the quartet as the disturbingly normal Mike. Living in filth, the men for the most part didn't get along, serving as something of a dysfunctional *Monkees*, which after all was the societal point they were trying to make. The episodes are available on video in the United States.

Bibliography

Books

Cleese, John, and Connie Booth, *The Complete Fawlty Towers*, Pantheon, 1988.
Cornell, Paul, with Martin Day, and Keith Topping, *The Guinness Book of Classic British TV*, 2nd ed., Guinness, 1996.
Dunn, Clive, *Permission to Speak*, Century, 1986.
Galton, Ray, and Alan Simpson, *The Best of Hancock*, Robson, 1986.
_____, *The Best of Steptoe and Son*, Robson, 1988.
_____, *Hancock's Half-Hour*, Woburn, 1974.
Johnson, Kim, *The First 20 Years of Monty Python*, St. Martin's, 1989.
Kendal, Felicity, *White Cargo*, Michael Joseph, 1998.
Lewisohn, Mark, *Radio Times Guide to TV Comedy*, BBC Books, 1998.
Lowe, Stephen, *Arthur Lowe: A Life*, Nick Hern, 1996.
Lynn, Jonathan, and Antony Jay, *The Complete Yes, Minister*, BBC Books, 1984.
_____, *The Complete Yes, Prime Minister*, BBC Books, 1989.
Moss, Norman, *British/American Language Dictionary*, Passport, 1995.
Perry, Jimmy, and David Croft, *Dad's Army*, Elm Tree Book/Hamish Hamilton, 1975.
Pertwee, Bill, *Dad's Army: The Making of a Television Legend*, Pavilion, 1997.
_____, *A Funny Way to Make a Living*, Sunburst, 1996.
Rigelsford, Adrian, with Anthony Brown, and Geoff Tibballs, *Are You Being Served? The Inside Story*, KQED Books, 1995.
Roose-Evans, James, *One Foot on the Stage: The Biography of Richard Wilson*, Weidenfeld & Nicolson, 1996.
Tanitch, Robert, *Leonard Rossiter*, Robert Royce, 1985.
Taylor, Rod, *The Guinness Book of Sitcoms*, Guinness, 1994.
Webber, Richard, *The Life and Legacy of Reginald Perrin: A Celebration*, Virgin, 1996.
_____, with Jimmy Perry, and David Croft, *Dad's Army: A Celebration*, Virgin, 1997.

Newspapers and Periodicals

Abramson, Dan. "Looking for Mr. Lucas." *British Television* 6.
_____, "Que? Talking with Fawlty Towers' Manuel." *British Television* 10.
Baker, Nick. "Rise, Sir Humphrey." *Radio Times*, Jan. 8, 1986.
Bellamy, Guy. "The Traveller's Unrest." *Radio Times*, Feb. 17, 1979.

Berman, A. S. "Keeping Up Appearances' Richard: Liverpool Lothario?" *British Television* 9.

_____, "Penelope Keith: The Good Neighbour." *British Television* 8.

_____, "Yeah Chef!" *British Television* 6.

Billington, Michael. Review of *Dad's Army* premiere episode. *The Times* (London), Aug. 1, 1968.

"Carrying on the Good Life." *Radio Times*, Sept. 10, 1976.

Denslow, Anthony. "Rowan's Funny Turn." *Radio Times*, Jan. 4, 1986.

Devlin, Tim. "The Making of Dad's Army." *The Times* (London), Oct. 26, 1973.

Dunne, Colin. "Service with a Smile." *Radio Times*, Jan. 23, 1993.

"Expectant Father." *TV Times*, Sept. 23, 1978.

Greaves, William. "Act My Age?" *Radio Times*, Feb. 29, 1992.

Hobson, Louis B. "Atkinson Ready to Take on U.S." *Calgary Sun*, Sept. 26, 1997.

_____, "The Face that Launched a Thousand Laughs." *Calgary Sun*, Oct. 12, 1997.

Hunt, Albert, "One Dark Night." *Radio Times*, June 11, 1983.

Kemp, Gerard. "You Really Want to Know Where We Were When We Decided to Bring Them Back?" *Radio Times*, Feb. 26, 1970.

Khan, Naseem. "Men from the Ministry." *Radio Times*, Feb. 24, 1980.

Martin, Brendan. "The Etiquette of Being an Ex-priest." *Sunday Independent*, May 1, 1977.

McGill, Gordon. "The Laughter Lies in the Toil." *Radio Times*, Mar. 27, 1975.

McKay, John. "Bean's Back but on the Big Screen." *Canadian Press*, Oct. 2, 1997.

Okamoto, David. "Chef! Sugar, Spice and Nothing Nice." *Dallas Morning News*, Jan. 19, 1997.

"Over the Top Again..." *Radio Times*, Nov. 10, 1990.

Pearce, Garth. John Le Mesurier obituary. *Daily Express*, Nov. 16, 1983.

Reynolds, Stanley. "So Funny Because So Serious." *The Times* (London), Nov. 16, 1974.

Slotek, Jim. "No Laughing Matter — Making Mr. Bean Was 'Very Stressful and Taxing' for Rowan Atkinson." *Toronto Sun*, Mar. 16, 1996.

Stoddard, Patrick. "Blackadder Supreme as He Reaches the Final Frontier." *The Times* (London), Oct. 22, 1989.

Tatchell, Peter. "Steptoe and Son." *Laugh Magazine* (n.d.).

Thompson, Bob. "Mr. Bean, Unchained." *Toronto Sun*, Oct. 9, 1997.

Way, Peter. *Dad's Army: A Peter Way Magazine Special.* Peter Way, 1972.

White, Roland. "Oh, What an Ugly War!" *Radio Times*, Sept. 23, 1989.

Woodward, Ian. "Getting on Famously." *Radio Times*, Jan. 6, 1990.

Index